Revenue Statistics in Africa

1990-2015

Statistiques des recettes publiques en Afrique

1990-2015

This work is published under the responsibility of the Secretary-General of the OECD. The opinions expressed and arguments employed herein do not necessarily reflect the official views of the member countries of the OECD or its Development Centre, or of the member countries of the African Union or of ATAF.

Cet ouvrage est publié sous la responsabilité du Secrétaire général de l'OCDE. Les opinions et les arguments exprimés ici ne reflètent pas nécessairement les vues officielles des pays membres de l'OCDE ou de son Centre de développement, ou des pays membres de l'Union africaine ou de l'ATAF.

This document, as well as any data and map included herein, are without prejudice to the status of or sovereignty over any territory, to the delimitation of international frontiers and boundaries and to the name of any territory, city or area.

Ce document, ainsi que les données et cartes qu'il peut comprendre sont sans préjudice du statut de tout territoire, de la souveraineté s'exerçant sur ce dernier, du tracé des frontières et limites internationales, et du nom de tout territoire, ville ou region.

Please cite this publication as:
OECD/ATAF/AUC (2017), *Revenue Statistics in Africa 2017*, OECD Publishing, Paris.
http://dx.doi.org/10.1787/9789264280854-en-fr

Citer ce titre comme suit :
OCDE/ATAF/CUA (2017), *Statistiques des recettes publiques en Afrique 2017*, Éditions OCDE, Paris.
http://dx.doi.org/10.1787/9789264280854-en-fr

ISBN 978-92-64-28084-7 (print/imprimé)
ISBN 978-92-64-28085-4 (PDF)

Corrigenda to OECD publications may be found on line at: *www.oecd.org/about/publishing/corrigenda.htm*.
Les corrigenda des publications de l'OCDE sont disponibles sur : *www.oecd.org/about/publishing/corrigenda.htm*.

Foreword

Revenue Statistics in Africa *is a joint publication by the OECD Centre for Tax Policy and Administration, the OECD Development Centre, the African Tax Administration Forum and the African Union Commission, with the technical support of the African Development Bank, the World Customs Organisation and the Centre de rencontres et d'études des dirigeants des administrations fiscales and the financial support of the European Union.*

The report presents detailed, internationally comparable data on both tax and non-tax revenues for sixteen African countries. Its approach is based on the well-established methodology of the OECD Revenue Statistics *database, which has become an essential reference source for OECD member countries and many more. Comparisons are also made with the average for OECD economies and for the economies featured in* Revenue Statistics in Latin America and the Caribbean.

The term "taxes" in this publication is confined to "compulsory, unrequited payments to general government". As outlined in the Interpretative Guide to the Revenue Statistics, taxes are "unrequited" in the sense that benefits provided by government to taxpayers are not normally in proportion to their payments. The OECD methodology classifies a tax according to its base: income, profits and capital gains (classified under heading 1000), payroll (heading 3000), property (heading 4000), goods and services (heading 5000) and other taxes (heading 6000). Compulsory social security contributions paid to general government are treated as taxes, and classified under heading 2000. Much greater detail on the tax concept and the classification of taxes are set out in the OECD Interpretative Guide in Annex A.

The term "non-tax revenue" includes all general government revenue that does not meet the OECD definition of taxation. Revenues that do not constitute taxation include grants (e.g. foreign aid), returns on government market investments, rents on the extraction of resources from public lands, sales of government-produced goods and services, and the collection of fines and forfeits. More details on these types of revenues, as well as an explanation of the use of cash or accrual basis of reporting in the publication are available in Annex B.

The report provides an overview of the main revenue trends in the sixteen participating African countries. It examines changes in the level of both tax and non-tax revenues as a percentage of GDP and the structure of these revenue streams between 1990 and 2015.

Avant-propos

Les Statistiques des recettes publiques en Afrique *est une publication conjointe du Centre de politique et d'administration fiscales de l'OCDE, du Centre de développement de l'OCDE, du Forum sur l'administration fiscale africaine (ATAF), et de la Commission de l'Union africaine, avec l'assistance technique de la Banque africaine de développement, de l'Organisation mondiale des douanes et du Centre de rencontres et d'études des dirigeants des administrations fiscales et le soutien financier de l'Union européenne.*

Le rapport fournit des données détaillées et comparables à l'échelle internationale, sur les recettes fiscales et non fiscales de seize pays africains. Son approche repose sur la méthodologie bien établie des Statistiques des recettes publiques de l'OCDE, *devenue une source de référence essentielle pour les pays membres de l'Organisation et au-delà. Des comparaisons sont également effectuées avec la moyenne des économies de l'OCDE et avec celle des économies couvertes par les* Statistiques des recettes publiques en Amérique latine et dans les Caraïbes.

Dans cette publication, le terme « impôts » fait référence uniquement aux « versements obligatoires sans contrepartie aux administrations publiques ». Comme indiqué dans le Guide d'interprétation pour les Statistiques des recettes publiques, les impôts sont « sans contrepartie » en ce sens que les prestations fournies par les administrations aux contribuables ne sont pas normalement proportionnelles à leurs paiements. La méthodologie de l'OCDE consiste à classer les impôts en fonction de l'assiette : le revenu, les bénéfices et les gains en capital (rubrique 1000), les salaires et la main-d'œuvre (rubrique 3000), le patrimoine (rubrique 4000), les biens et les services (rubrique 5000) et autres impôts (rubrique 6000). Les cotisations obligatoires de sécurité sociale versées aux administrations publiques sont aussi traitées comme des impôts et classées dans la rubrique 2000. Des informations plus détaillées sur la notion d'impôt et sur la classification des impôts sont présentées dans le Guide d'interprétation de l'OCDE figurant à l'annexe A.

Le terme « recettes non fiscales » recouvre toutes les recettes des administrations publiques qui ne sont pas considérées comme des « impôts » selon la définition de l'OCDE. Les recettes non fiscales incluent les dons (comme l'aide extérieure), les rendements d'investissements publics, les rentes tirées de l'extraction de ressources du domaine public, la vente de biens et de services produits par le secteur public, et les amendes et confiscations. On trouvera, à l'annexe B, des informations plus détaillées sur ces catégories de recettes ainsi qu'une explication de l'utilisation de l'enregistrement sur la base des décaissements ou des droits constatés.

Le rapport offre une vue d'ensemble des grandes tendances des recettes dans les seize pays d'Afrique couverts par la publication. Il examine les variations des niveaux de recettes fiscales et non fiscales en pourcentage du PIB ainsi que leurs composantes entre 1990 et 2015.

Acknowledgements

Revenue Statistics in Africa has been jointly produced by the Organisation for Economic Co-operation and Development (OECD) Centre for Tax Policy and Administration (CTP), the OECD Development Centre (DEV), the African Tax Administration Forum (ATAF) and the African Union Commission (AUC), with the technical support of the African Development Bank (AfDB), the World Customs Organisation (WCO), the Centre de rencontres et d'études des dirigeants des administrations fiscales (CREDAF) and the European Commission. The staff from these organisations with responsibility for producing the publication were: Emmanuelle Modica, Michelle Harding, Michael Sharratt and Talita Yamashiro Fordelone of CTP under the supervision of the Director Pascal Saint-Amans, Deputy Director Grace Perez-Navarro and the Head of the Tax Policy and Tax Statistics Division David Bradbury; Sébastien Markley, Bakary Traoré, Ines Zebdi and Arthur Minsat of DEV under the supervision of the Director of the Development Centre and Special Advisor to the OECD Secretary-General on Development Mario Pezzini, and of the Senior Communications Manager Henri-Bernard Solignac-Lecomte; Director of Research at ATAF Nara Monkam; Dossina Yeo, Senior Statistician and Jose Awong Alene, Statistician at the AUC under the Director of Economic Affairs Dr. René N'guettia Kouassi; Statistician Koua Louis Kouakou at AfDB heading the Division of Economic and Social Statistics; Technical Officer Thomas Cantens at WCO under the direction of Head of Research and Strategies Unit Robert Ireland; Secretary General Didier Cornillet of CREDAF; Policy Officer Vincent Bigot, Head of Domestic Revenue Mobilisation Sector Hubert Perr and Head of Budget Support, Public Finance Management, Domestic Revenue Mobilisation Unit Erica Gerretsen at the European Commission. Elizabeth Nash, Elisabeth Turner and Delphine Grandrieux at DEV ensured the production of the publication in both paper and electronic forms.

The authors would like to thank their colleagues working in national entities with whom they have consulted regularly. These institutions include finance ministries, national tax agencies and national statistical institutes of Cabo Verde, Cameroon, Côte d'Ivoire, the Democratic Republic of the Congo, Ghana, Kenya, Mauritius, Morocco, Niger, Rwanda, Senegal, South Africa, Swaziland, Togo, Tunisia and Uganda. They also wish to give their appreciation to the Government of Morocco for the secondments of Fadoua Bouhassoune and Hakime Lakhal at CTP, and to DEV and CTP colleagues for commenting on drafts and providing technical assistance.

Finally, the partners would like to thank the European Commission, the AUC, the ATAF, GIZ and the South African Revenue authority (SARS) that hosted, organised and funded the technical workshops in Pretoria, South Africa (June 2016).

This document was produced with the financial assistance of the European Union. The views expressed herein can in no way be taken to reflect the official opinion of the European Union.

Remerciements

La publication des *Statistiques des recettes publiques en Afrique* a été produite conjointement par le Centre de politique et d'administration fiscales (CPAF) de l'Organisation de coopération et de développement économiques (OCDE), le Centre de développement de l'OCDE (DEV), le Forum sur l'administration fiscale africaine (ATAF), et la Commission de l'Union africaine (CUA), avec l'assistance technique de la Banque africaine de développement (BAfD), l'Organisation mondiale des douanes (OMD), le Centre de rencontres et d'études des dirigeants des administrations fiscales (CREDAF), et la Commission européenne. Les agents de ces organisations auxquels la responsabilité de la publication a été confiée sont : Emmanuelle Modica, Michelle Harding, Michael Sharratt et Talita Yamashiro Fordelone du CPAF sous la supervision du Directeur du Centre Pascal Saint-Amans, Grace Perez-Navarro, Directrice adjointe du CPAF et David Bradbury, Chef de la Division des politiques fiscales et statistiques ; Sébastien Markley, Bakary Traoré, Ines Zebdi et Arthur Minsat de DEV sous la supervision du Directeur du Centre de développement Mario Pezzini, et de Henri-Bernard Solignac-Lecomte, Chef de la communication ; Nara Monkam, Directrice de recherche à l'ATAF ; Dossina Yeo, Statisticien principal et Jose Awong Alene, Statisticien de la CUA, sous la supervision de René N'guettia Kouassi, Directeur des affaires économiques ; Koua Louis Kouakou, statisticien à la BAfD, à la tête de la Division des statistiques économiques et sociales ; Thomas Cantens, Administrateur technique à l'OMD, sous la direction de Robert Ireland, Chef de l'Unité Recherche et stratégies ; Didier Cornillet, Secrétaire général du CREDAF ; Vincent Bigot, chargé de mission, Hubert Perr, Chef du secteur de la mobilisation des ressources intérieures et Erica Gerretsen, Chef de l'unité de l'appui budgétaire, gestion des finances publiques, et mobilisation des ressources intérieures à la Commission européenne. Elizabeth Nash, Elisabeth Turner et Delphine Grandrieux à DEV ont assuré la production de la publication sous forme imprimée et électronique.

Les auteurs tiennent à remercier leurs collègues des institutions nationales avec lesquels des consultations ont eu lieu régulièrement. Ces institutions sont notamment les ministères des Finances, les administrations fiscales nationales et les instituts statistiques nationaux de l'Afrique du Sud, du Cabo Verde, du Cameroun, de la République démocratique du Congo, de la Côte d'Ivoire, du Ghana, du Kenya, du Maroc, de Maurice, du Niger, de l'Ouganda, du Rwanda, du Sénégal, du Swaziland, du Togo et de la Tunisie. Ils souhaitent également exprimer leur reconnaissance au gouvernement marocain pour l'envoi en détachement de Fadoua Bouhassoune et Hakime Lakhal auprès du CPAF, ainsi qu'aux agents de DEV et du CPAF pour leurs commentaires sur les projets de texte et leur assistance technique.

Enfin, les partenaires ont à cœur de remercier la Commission européenne, la CUA, l'ATAF, GIZ et l'administration fiscale sud-africaine (SARS) d'avoir accueilli, organisé et financé les ateliers techniques à Pretoria, Afrique du Sud (juin 2016).

Ce document a été produit avec le soutien financier de l'Union européenne. Les opinions exprimées dans ce rapport ne peuvent en aucun cas refléter l'opinion officielle de l'Union européenne.

Table of contents

Table des matières

LIST OF TABLES/LISTE DE TABLEAUX

Chapter 1/Chapitre 1
Tax and non-tax revenue trends, 1990-2015/Tendances des recettes fiscales et non fiscales, 1990-2015

Chapter 3/Chapitre 3
Tax levels and tax structures, 1990-2015/Niveaux et structures des impôts, 1990-2015

Chapter 4/Chapitre 4

Country tables, 1997-2015 – Tax revenues/Tableaux pays, 1997-2015 – Recettes fiscales

Chapter 5/Chapitre 5

Non-tax revenues, 1997-2015/Recettes non fiscales, 1997-2015

LIST OF FIGURES/LISTE DE GRAPHIQUES

Chapter 1/Chapitre 1
Tax and non-tax revenue trends, 1990-2015/Tendances des recettes fiscales et non fiscales, 1990-2015

Revenue Statistics in Africa 1990-2015/Statistiques des recettes publiques en Afrique 1990-2015

Executive summary

Revenue Statistics in Africa provides internationally comparable data on tax and non-tax revenues for 16 African countries: Cabo Verde, Cameroon, Côte d'Ivoire, the Democratic Republic of the Congo, Ghana, Kenya, Mauritius, Morocco, Niger, Rwanda, Senegal, South Africa, Swaziland, Togo, Tunisia and Uganda. It also includes a special chapter on domestic resource mobilisation and external financial flows in Africa.

In this publication, "taxes" are defined as compulsory, unrequited payments to general government. Taxes are "unrequited" in the sense that benefits provided by government to taxpayers are not normally in proportion to their payments. Compulsory social security contributions paid to general government are classified as taxes. Non-tax revenue are all other revenues received by general government, including foreign aid, property revenue (including rents and royalties), sales of goods and services, and fines and penalties. More information on the classifications is set out in the Interpretative Guide in Annexes A and B.

Tax revenues

The average tax-to-GDP ratio in the 16 African countries (the "Africa (16) average") was 19.1% in 2015. Tax-to-GDP ratios, which are defined as total tax revenue, including social security contributions, as a percentage of gross domestic product (GDP), ranged from 10.8% in the Democratic Republic of the Congo to 30.3% in Tunisia. Thirteen countries had a lower tax-to-GDP ratio than the Latin American and the Caribbean (LAC) average of 22.8% in 2015, with the exceptions being Morocco, South Africa and Tunisia. The average in OECD countries in 2015 was 34.3%.

Africa's GDP growth remained robust in 2015 despite significant drops in global commodity prices and the weakening of global demand due to the slow recovery of developed countries from the financial crisis. Between 2014 and 2015, the Africa (16) average tax-to-GDP ratio also increased by 0.4 percentage points, slightly less than the LAC average (0.6 percentage points) and more than the OECD average (less than 0.1 percentage points). All countries but Kenya, Tunisia and Morocco had increases in their tax-to-GDP ratio over this period. Cabo Verde recorded the highest increase between 2014 and 2015 of 1.8 percentage points followed by Uganda and South Africa (both 1.1 percentage points). The increases in Cabo Verde were driven by tax reforms and tax administration modernisation. In South Africa, the rise was driven by increases in personal income tax revenue following a tax reform. In Uganda the increases were across the main tax categories.

Since 2000, the Africa (16) average tax-to-GDP ratio has increased by 5.0 percentage points, a similar increase to the LAC average (4.9 percentage points). In contrast, the OECD average grew much more slowly (0.3 percentage points). All African countries in the publication had higher tax-to-GDP ratios in 2015 than in 2000. The predominant drivers of the growth in tax-to-GDP ratios on average were increases in revenues from VAT and taxes on incomes and profits (2.2 and 2.3 percentage points respectively), whereas changes in social security contributions, property tax revenues, and other consumption taxes were much smaller.

The principal share of total tax revenue in the Africa (16) average was revenue from taxes on goods and services (57.2%) and particularly VAT (31.5% of total tax revenue). The share of revenue from taxes on income and profits amounted to 32.4%. Excluding social security contributions, the tax structure of the Africa (16) average resembled that of the LAC average (both as a percentage of GDP and of total tax revenue). However, the LAC average for social security contributions was more than twice as high as the Africa (16) average as a percentage of GDP.

Tax structures vary widely across countries. Kenya, South Africa and Swaziland obtained about half of their tax revenues from taxes on income and profits whereas this category ranged from 18.6% in Togo to 37.6% in Rwanda. Tunisia and Morocco displayed a different breakdown of revenues between the categories of taxes compared to the other 14 African countries, with the highest share of social security contributions (17.0% and 29.5% respectively). The share of social security contributions remains small in the other African countries ranging from less than 1.5% in Cabo Verde, Ghana, Kenya and South Africa to 11.2% in Côte d'Ivoire.

Non-tax revenues

As a percentage of GDP, total non-tax revenues were lower than tax revenues in all 16 African countries. Total non-tax revenues ranged from 0.6% of GDP in South Africa to 15.1% of GDP in Swaziland, where non-tax revenue is mostly payments from the revenue-sharing pool under the Southern African Customs Union, and is nearly as high as tax revenues at 15.3% of GDP. Of the 14 countries for which non-tax data is available over the past ten years, eight have shown a decreasing trend in non-tax revenue to GDP ratios, and only six have shown an increasing trend.

Non-tax revenue as a percentage of GDP varied significantly more than tax revenues over time. At times, the annual variation of non-tax revenues exceeded 1% of GDP from one year to the next. The greater variation was mainly explained by the volatility of grants and property income revenues (principally rents and royalties), with the latter directly affected by swings in commodity prices.

Grants comprised 7.2% of Niger's GDP and 6.3% of Rwanda's GDP. Property income revenues made up 2.8% of Cameroon's GDP, mainly from rents and royalties.

Special feature on domestic resource mobilisation

Domestic resource mobilisation is a key priority for African countries recognised under the African Union's Agenda 2063, the Regional Economic Communities' strategic priorities, as well as the universal Sustainable Development Goals (SDGs). In particular, countries committed to "improve domestic capacity for tax and other revenue collection" (SDG target 17.1).

Strengthening domestic resource mobilisation can have development benefits beyond the collection of revenues. Stronger fiscal institutions can improve state resilience and governance and an efficient tax administration also may have a positive effect on firm productivity. A higher capacity to collect taxes may also help reduce dependence on foreign aid.

While African countries have made significant efforts to strengthen domestic revenue mobilisation through tax policy and better tax administration, they continue to face challenges. These include a large informal sector estimated at 38% of sub-Saharan African GDP and a narrow tax base in resource rich countries that makes them more vulnerable to unstable resource revenues.

Revenue Statistics in Africa 1990-2015/Statistiques des recettes publiques en Afrique 1990-2015

Résumé

Les *Statistiques des recettes publiques en Afrique* présentent des données comparables à l'échelle internationale relatives aux recettes fiscales et non fiscales de seize pays africains : Afrique du Sud, Cabo Verde, Cameroun, République démocratique du Congo, Côte d'Ivoire, Ghana, Kenya, Maroc, Maurice, Niger, Ouganda, Rwanda, Sénégal, Swaziland, Togo et Tunisie. La publication comprend également un chapitre spécial sur la mobilisation des ressources intérieures et les flux financiers externes en Afrique.

Dans cette publication, les « impôts » sont définis comme des versements, obligatoires et sans contrepartie, aux administrations publiques. Les impôts sont dits « sans contrepartie » au sens où les prestations fournies aux contribuables par les administrations publiques ne sont en règle générale pas proportionnelles aux montants acquittés. Les cotisations de sécurité sociale obligatoires versées aux administrations publiques sont considérées comme des impôts. Les recettes non fiscales sont toutes les autres recettes perçues par les administrations publiques, comprenant l'aide extérieure, les revenus de la propriété (y compris loyers et redevances), ventes de biens et de services, et amendes et confiscations. Des informations plus détaillées sur les classifications sont présentées dans le Guide d'interprétation en Annexes A et B.

Recettes fiscales

Le ratio moyen impôts-PIB dans les seize pays africains (la « Moyenne Afrique (16) ») était de 19.1 % en 2015. Les ratios impôts-PIB, définis comme le total des recettes fiscales, y compris les cotisations de sécurité sociale, exprimés en pourcentage du produit intérieur brut (PIB), vont de 10.8 % en République démocratique du Congo à 30.3 % en Tunisie. Dans treize pays à l'exception de l'Afrique du Sud, du Maroc et de la Tunisie, le ratio impôts-PIB était inférieur à la moyenne des pays d'Amérique latine et des Caraïbes qui s'élevait à 22.8 % en 2015. La moyenne dans les pays de l'OCDE en 2015 était de 34.3 %.

La croissance du PIB africain est restée solide en 2015, malgré des baisses importantes des prix des matières premières au niveau mondial et un fléchissement de la demande mondiale dû à la lente reprise des pays développés après la crise financière. Entre 2014 et 2015, le ratio moyen impôts-PIB des pays d'Afrique (16) a également augmenté de 0.4 point de pourcentage, une hausse légèrement inférieure à la moyenne des pays d'Amérique latine et des Caraïbes (0.6 point de pourcentage), mais supérieure à la moyenne des pays de l'OCDE (moins de 0.1 point de pourcentage). Tous les pays à l'exception du Kenya, de la Tunisie et du Maroc ont connu des hausses de leur ratio impôts-PIB sur la période. Le Cabo Verde a enregistré la hausse la plus importante entre 2014 et 2015, de 1.8 point de pourcentage, suivi de l'Afrique du Sud et de l'Ouganda (tous deux augmentant de 1.1 point de pourcentage). L'augmentation au Cabo Verde s'explique par des réformes fiscales et une modernisation de l'administration fiscale. En Afrique du Sud, cette augmentation s'explique par la hausse des recettes provenant de l'impôt sur le revenu, suite à une réforme fiscale. En Ouganda, les hausses ont été observées dans les principales catégories d'impôts.

Depuis 2000, le ratio moyen impôts-PIB des pays d'Afrique (16) a augmenté de 5.0 points de pourcentage, une hausse similaire à la moyenne des pays d'Amérique latine et Caraïbes (4.9 points de pourcentage). En revanche, la moyenne des pays de l'OCDE a augmenté beaucoup plus timidement (0.3 point de pourcentage). Tous les pays africains de la publication avaient des ratios impôt-PIB plus importants en 2015 qu'en 2000. Les moteurs principaux de la croissance du ratio moyen impôts-PIB ont été les hausses des recettes provenant de la TVA et des impôts sur le revenu et les bénéfices (à hauteur de 2.2 et 2.3 points de pourcentage respectivement). Les variations observées au niveau des cotisations de sécurité sociale, des recettes des impôts sur le patrimoine et des autres impôts sur la consommation ont été bien plus modestes.

La part principale du total des recettes fiscales dans la moyenne des pays d'Afrique (16) était attribuable aux recettes provenant des taxes sur les biens et les services (57.2 %) et particulièrement à la TVA (31.5 % des recettes fiscales totales). La part des recettes provenant des impôts sur le revenu et les bénéfices s'élevait à 32.4 %. Hors cotisations de sécurité sociale, la structure fiscale de la moyenne des pays d'Afrique (16) ressemble à celle de la moyenne des pays d'Amérique latine et Caraïbes (à la fois en pourcentage du PIB et des recettes fiscales totales). Cependant, pour les cotisations de sécurité sociale, la moyenne des pays d'Amérique latine et Caraïbes était deux fois supérieure à celle de la moyenne des pays d'Afrique (16) en pourcentage du PIB.

Les structures fiscales varient de façon importante entre les pays. En Afrique du Sud, au Kenya et au Swaziland, environ la moitié des recettes fiscales provenaient des impôts sur le revenu et les bénéfices, alors que cette catégorie allait de 18.6 % au Togo à 37.6 % au Rwanda. En Tunisie et au Maroc, la répartition des recettes entre les catégories d'impôts est différente de celle des 14 autres pays africains avec la part des cotisations de sécurité sociale la plus élevée (respectivement de 17.0 % et 29.5 %). La part des cotisations de sécurité sociale reste faible dans les autres pays d'Afrique, allant de moins de 1.5 % au Cabo Verde, Ghana, Kenya et Afrique du Sud à 11.2 % en Côte d'Ivoire.

Recettes non fiscales

En pourcentage du PIB, le total des recettes non fiscales est inférieur au total des recettes fiscales dans les seize pays d'Afrique. Le total des recettes non fiscales, qui va de 0.6 % du PIB en Afrique du Sud à 15.1 % du PIB au Swaziland (les recettes non fiscales étant essentiellement constituées de versements en provenance du fonds de partage des recettes institué en vertu de l'Union douanière d'Afrique australe), est presque aussi élevé que celui des recettes fiscales, qui ressort à 15.3 % du PIB. Sur les 14 pays pour lesquels les données relatives aux recettes non fiscales sont disponibles pour les dix dernières années, huit ont montré une tendance à la baisse des ratios recettes non fiscales-PIB, et seulement six ont montré une tendance croissante.

Les recettes non fiscales exprimées en pourcentage du PIB varient de façon plus importante que les recettes fiscales au fil du temps. Par moments, la variation annuelle des recettes non fiscales a pu dépasser 1 % du PIB d'une année à l'autre. La variation la plus importante s'explique principalement par la volatilité des dons et des recettes tirées des impôts sur la propriété (principalement les loyers et redevances), le dernier élément étant directement affecté par les variations des prix des matières premières.

Les dons ont représenté 7.2 % du PIB du Niger et 6.3 % du PIB du Rwanda. Les recettes tirées des impôts sur la propriété ont représenté 2.8 % du PIB du Cameroun, provenant principalement des loyers et redevances.

Étude spéciale sur la mobilisation des ressources intérieures

La mobilisation des ressources intérieures est une priorité cruciale pour les pays africains, reconnue à ce titre dans l'Agenda 2063 de l'Union africaine, dans les priorités stratégiques des communautés économiques régionales ainsi que dans les Objectifs de développement durable (ODD). En particulier, les pays se sont engagés « à améliorer les capacités nationales de collecte d'impôts et d'autres recettes » (ODD17.1).

Renforcer la mobilisation des ressources intérieures a des avantages au-delà de la perception des recettes. Des institutions budgétaires plus solides peuvent améliorer la résilience de l'État et la gouvernance, et une administration de l'impôt efficiente peut avoir des retombées positives en termes de productivité des entreprises. Une meilleure capacité à collecter l'impôt peut également réduire la dépendance à l'aide étrangère.

Les pays africains ont déployé des efforts considérables pour renforcer la mobilisation de leurs recettes intérieures en s'appuyant sur des politiques fiscales et sur une amélioration de l'administration de l'impôt, mais des difficultés subsistent. Parmi celles-ci, on peut citer l'importance du secteur informel, qui représenterait selon les estimations 38 % du PIB de l'Afrique sub-saharienne, et l'étroitesse de la base d'imposition dans les pays riches en ressources qui les rend plus vulnérables à l'instabilité des recettes tirées de ces ressources.

Chapter 1

Tax and non-tax revenue trends, 1990-2015

Chapitre 1

Tendances des recettes fiscales et non fiscales, 1990-2015

Revenue Statistics in Africa 1990-2015/Statistiques des recettes publiques en Afrique 1990-2015

Chapter 1

Tax and non-tax revenue trends, 1990-2015

Introduction

In light of the United Nations' 2030 Agenda for Sustainable Development, awareness of the need to mobilise government revenue in developing countries to fund public goods and services is increasing. Taxation provides a predictable and sustainable source of government revenue, in contrast with the volatility of development assistance and mineral royalties.

This report presents internationally comparable data on the tax and non-tax revenues of sixteen African countries: Cabo Verde, Cameroon, Côte d'Ivoire, the Democratic Republic of the Congo, Ghana, Kenya, Mauritius, Morocco, Niger, Rwanda, Senegal, South Africa, Swaziland, Togo, Tunisia and Uganda. This chapter discusses the trends in these countries of several key tax and non-tax indicators including the tax-to-GDP ratio, the tax structure, the share of tax revenue by level of government and the non-tax revenue-to-GDP ratio. The discussion supplements the detailed country information found in Chapters 4 and 5.

Cross-country comparisons of revenue data for the countries included in this publication are presented here, with the averages of the 16 African countries, of 24 Latin American and Caribbean (LAC) countries (see OECD/ECLAC/CIAT/IDB, 2017) and of the 35 OECD countries (see OECD, 2016). There are, however, no corresponding OECD or LAC figures for non-tax revenues.

TAX REVENUES

1.1. Tax ratios

The average tax-to-GDP ratio in the 16 African countries of this publication (referred to in this chapter as the "Africa (16) average") was 19.1% in 2015 (Figure 1.1). The tax-to-GDP ratio is measured as tax revenues (including social security contributions paid to the general government) as a proportion of gross domestic product (GDP). The Africa (16) average needs to be interpreted with caution due to the incompleteness or unavailability of social security contributions data in some African countries in this publication.[1] Tax-to-GDP ratios varied widely in countries included in this publication and ranged from 10.8% in the Democratic Republic of the Congo to 30.3% in Tunisia.

Tax-to-GDP ratios in 2015

The sixteen countries in this report fall into two distinct groups with respect to their tax-to-GDP ratios. The first group of three countries (Morocco, South Africa and Tunisia) had tax ratios ranging from 26.1% to 30.3% of GDP in 2015, well above the Latin America and the Caribbean average of 22.8%. Countries in the second group (Cabo Verde, Cameroon, Côte d'Ivoire, the Democratic Republic of the Congo, Ghana, Kenya, Mauritius, Niger, Rwanda, Senegal, Swaziland, Togo and Uganda) all have tax ratios below the LAC average.

In 2015, the Africa (16) average tax-to-GDP ratio of 19.1% was 0.4 percentage points higher than in 2014 (Figure 1.3). The latest rise in the Africa (16) average tax-to-GDP ratio occurred while the whole of Africa's economic performance remained robust in 2015 despite global challenges such as the weakening of global demand due to the slow recovery of developed countries from the financial crisis, the fall of commodity prices and regional shocks. Growth in real GDP in Africa was at 3.4% in 2015 which was the second fastest region after East Asia (AfDB/OECD/UNDP, 2017). The increase in the Africa (16) average between 2014 and 2015 was slightly lower than the LAC average increase of 0.6 percentage points but higher than that of the OECD average of less than 0.1 percentage points.

Figure 1.1. **Tax-to-GDP ratios (total tax revenue as % of GDP), 2015**

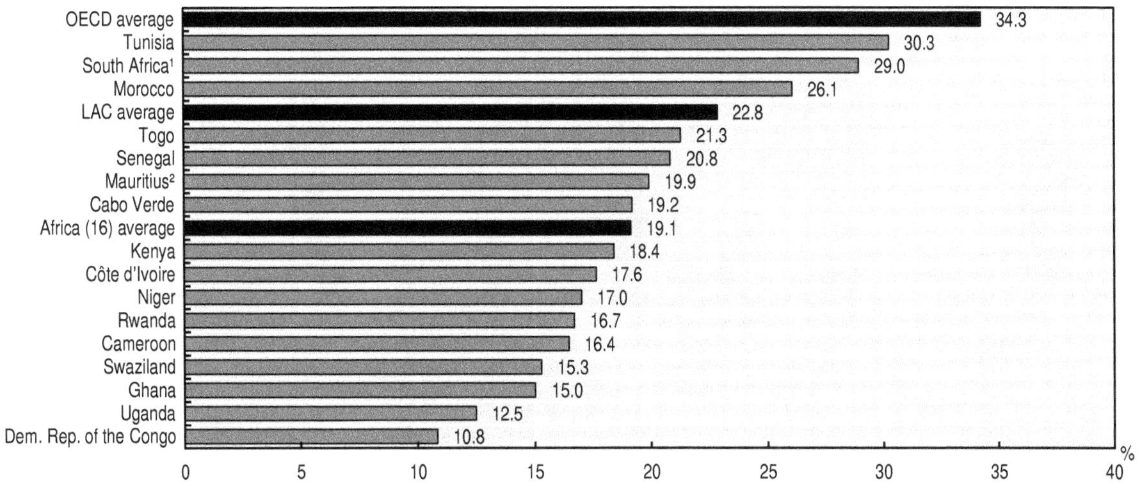

Notes: The figures include sub-national government tax revenues for Mauritius, Morocco, South Africa and Swaziland. The Africa (16) average, the averages for LAC (24 Latin American and Caribbean countries) and the OECD (35 countries) are unweighted.

The Africa (16) average should be interpreted with caution as data for social security contributions are not available or are partial in a few countries. Specifically, in The Democratic Republic of the Congo, Togo and Uganda social security contributions data are not available, and in Cameroon, Kenya and Senegal only partial information on social security contributions are available. See the country tables in Chapter 4 for further information.

1. The tax-to-GDP ratio should be interpreted with caution as it includes payments made by South Africa to the Southern African Customs Union (SACU) pool.
2. Data for 2015 are estimated.

Source: Table 3.1 in Chapter 3 and OECD/ATAF/AUC (2017), "Revenue Statistics in Africa: Comparative tables", *OECD Tax Statistics* (database), *http://dx.doi.org/10.1787/be755711-en*, for the LAC average.

StatLink *http://dx.doi.org/10.1787/888933568566*

Box 1.1. **Tax-to-GDP ratios in regional organisations**

Most African countries in this publication are member countries of regional African organisations whose members adopt common tax and external tariff rules and form a customs union.

Côte d'Ivoire, Niger, Senegal and Togo belong to the West African Economic and Monetary Union (WAEMU, also known by its French acronym, UEMOA), which also includes Benin, Burkina Faso, Guinea-Bissau and Mali. The objectives of the WAEMU are to reinforce the economic and financial competitiveness of the member states; assure the convergence of economic performance and economic policies; create a common market by having a common external tariff (CET); a common trade policy; free movement of persons, goods, and capital; and co-ordination of national sectors policies. In the WAEMU, Senegal and Togo had higher tax-to-GDP ratios than the Africa (16) average, and the tax-to-GDP ratios of the four WAEMU countries of this publication ranged from 17.0% in Niger to 21.3% in Togo (Figure 1.2).

Kenya, Rwanda and Uganda belong to the East Africa Community (EAC), which also includes Burundi, South Sudan and Tanzania. The EAC's aim is to reach greater regional economic integration, and so it has established a free trade area and a customs union, and is working toward a common market. In 2015, the three EAC countries in this publication had lower tax-to-GDP ratios than the Africa (16) average, ranging from 12.5% in Uganda to 18.4% in Kenya.

Box 1.1. **Tax-to-GDP ratios in regional organisations** *(cont.)*

Figure 1.2. **Tax-to-GDP ratios in EAC and WAEMU countries, 2015**

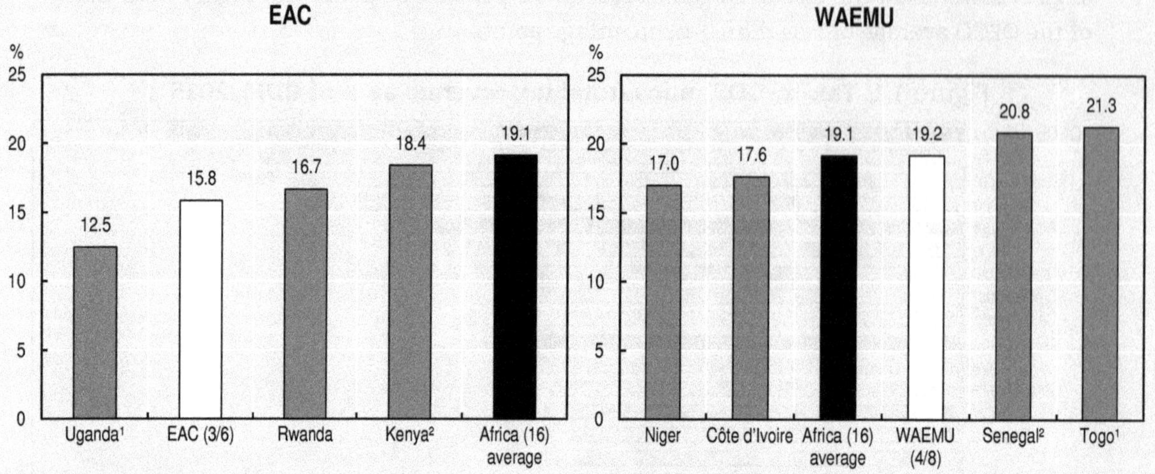

Notes: The Africa (16) average should be interpreted with caution as data for social security contributions are not available or are partial in a few countries.

1. The tax-to-GDP ratios exclude social security contributions revenues as these data are not available.
2. The tax-to-GDP ratios exclude some social security contributions data for Kenya (but these revenues are deemed to be negligible) and for Senegal (social security contributions figures include social security contributions from the Institution de Prévoyance Retraites du Sénégal (IPRES) and exclude the data from the Caisse de Sécurité Sociale (CSS) as they are not available).

Source: Table 3.1 in Chapter 3.

StatLink http://dx.doi.org/10.1787/888933568585

Figure 1.3. **Change in tax-to-GDP ratios between 2014 and 2015 (percentage points of GDP)**

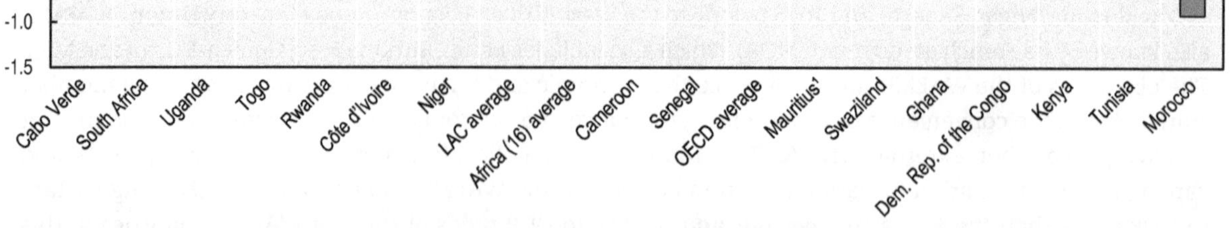

Notes: The figures include sub-national government tax revenues for Mauritius, Morocco, South Africa and Swaziland. The Africa (16) average, the averages for LAC (24 Latin American and Caribbean countries) and the OECD (35 countries) are unweighted.

The Africa (16) average should be interpreted with caution as data for social security contributions are not available or are partial in a few countries. Specifically, in the Democratic Republic of the Congo, Togo and Uganda social security contributions data are not available, and in Cameroon, Kenya, and Senegal only partial information on social security contributions are available. See the country tables in Chapter 4 for further information.

1. The change in tax-to-GDP ratio is calculated using estimated 2015 data.

Source: Authors' calculations based on data in Table 3.1 in Chapter 3 and OECD/ATAF/AUC (2017), "Revenue Statistics in Africa: Comparative tables", *OECD Tax Statistics* (database), *http://dx.doi.org/10.1787/be755711-en*, for the LAC average.

StatLink http://dx.doi.org/10.1787/888933568604

Thirteen countries recorded an increase in their tax-to-GDP ratio in 2015 whereas tax-to-GDP ratios decreased in Kenya, Morocco and Tunisia (Figure 1.3). Cabo Verde recorded the highest increase of 1.8 percentage points followed by South Africa and Uganda (both by 1.1 percentage points) whereas Morocco and Tunisia had the largest decreases, of 0.9 and 0.7 percentage points respectively.

The main drivers for the increase in the tax-to-GDP ratio for the Africa (16) average in 2015 were increases of 0.2 percentage points in revenue from taxes on specific consumption (mainly excises and customs duties) and of 0.1 percentage points in revenue from general consumption (mainly VAT[2]) and from personal income tax (Figure 1.4). However, there is great heterogeneity among countries with respect to the annual changes between 2014 and 2015. Changes as a percentage of GDP in revenue from corporate income tax revenues showed the largest variations among countries (Figure 1.4).

Figure 1.4. **Change in tax-to-GDP ratios by main tax heading between 2014 and 2015 (percentage points of GDP)**

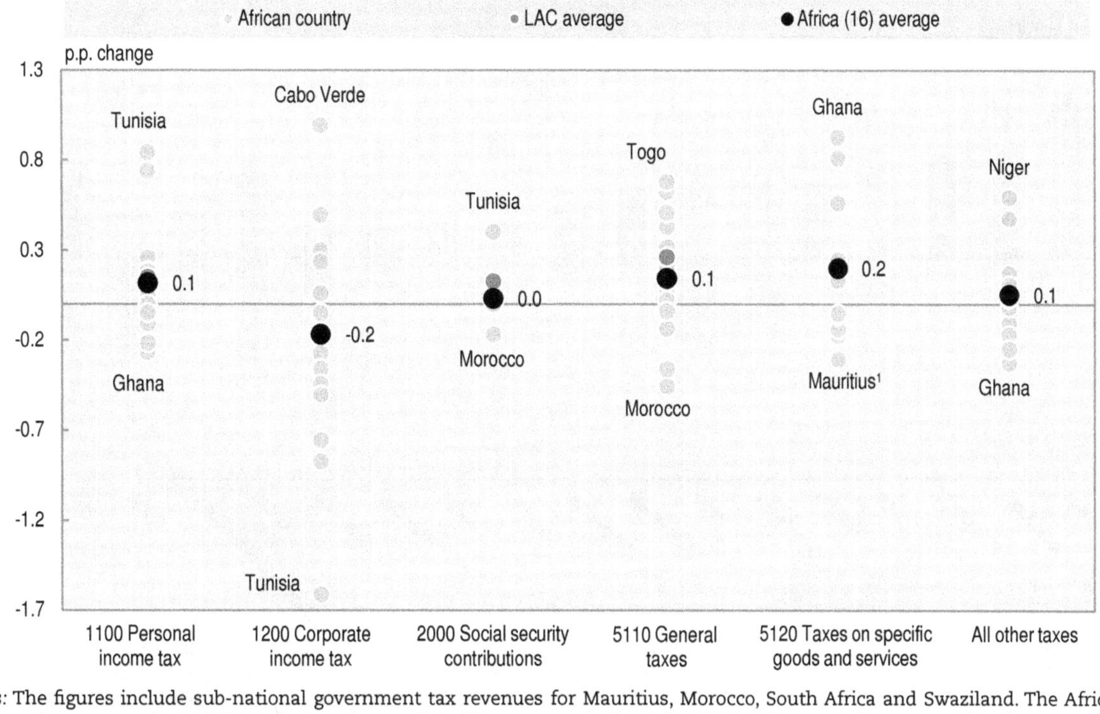

Notes: The figures include sub-national government tax revenues for Mauritius, Morocco, South Africa and Swaziland. The Africa (16) average, the averages for LAC (24 Latin American and Caribbean countries) and the OECD (35 countries) are unweighted.

The Africa (16) average should be interpreted with caution as data for social security contributions are not available or are partial in a few countries. Specifically, in the Democratic Republic of the Congo, in Togo and Uganda social security contributions data are not available, and in Cameroon, Kenya, and Senegal only partial information on social security contributions are available. See the country tables in Chapter 4 for further information.

1. The changes in each tax category are calculated using estimated 2015 data.

Source: Authors' calculations based on data in OECD/ATAF/AUC (2017), "Revenue Statistics in Africa: Comparative tables", *OECD Tax Statistics* (database), *http://dx.doi.org/10.1787/be755711-en*.

StatLink http://dx.doi.org/10.1787/888933568623

The biggest increases in tax-to-GDP ratios between 2014 and 2015 occurred in Cabo Verde, South Africa and Uganda. In Cabo Verde, the change was explained by increases as percentage of GDP in VAT revenues (0.6 percentage points) and corporate income tax revenue (1.0 percentage points). In South Africa the main driver was personal income taxes which increased by 0.7 percentage points. In Uganda the increases were across the main tax categories.

In Cabo Verde, the increases in VAT and corporate income tax revenue follow the improvement of the tax administration system through a restructuring of the revenue administration in late 2014, as well as increased efforts to collect tax arrears in these tax categories (IMF, 2016a). In South Africa, the 2015 budget reform of the personal income tax (PIT) contributed to the increase in PIT revenue. Personal income tax rates were raised by one percentage point for all taxpayers earning more than a certain threshold, and tax brackets and rebates were adjusted for inflation. This reform aimed to raise more tax revenues from individuals with higher incomes (National Treasury, 2015).

Figure 1.5. **Change in tax-to-GDP ratios by main tax heading between 2014 and 2015 and by country (percentage points of GDP)**

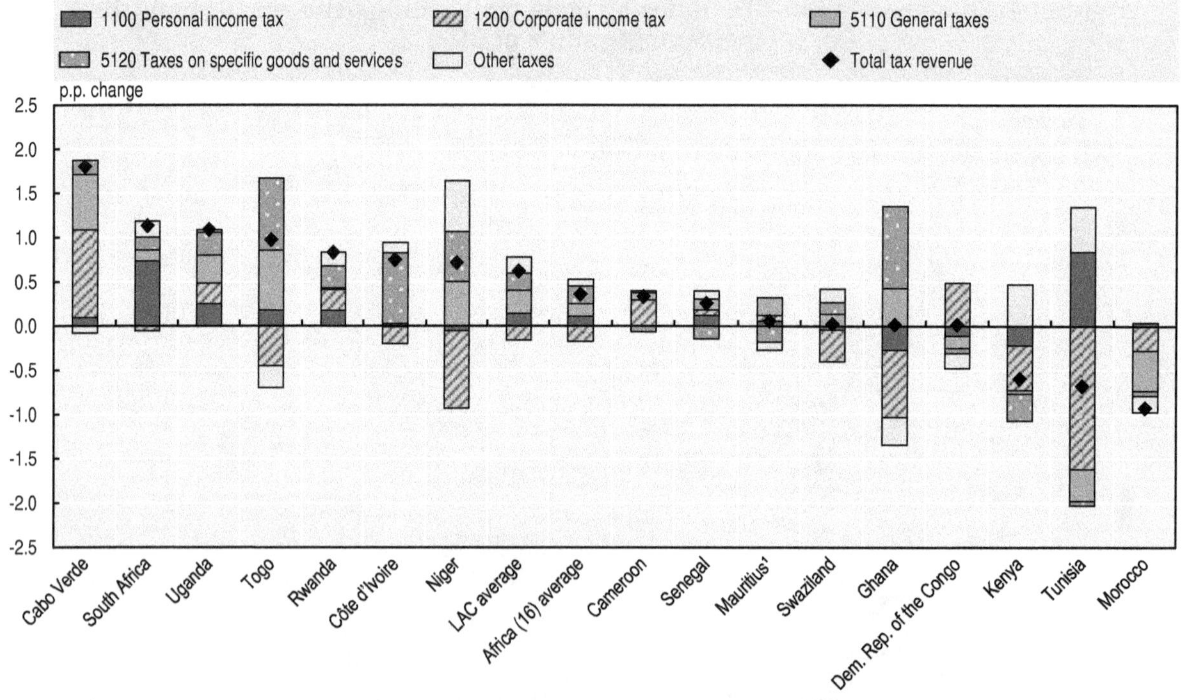

Note: The figures include sub-national government tax revenues for Mauritius, Morocco, South Africa and Swaziland.
The Africa (16) average, the averages for LAC (24 Latin American and Caribbean countries) and the OECD (35 countries) are unweighted.
The Africa (16) average should be interpreted with caution as data for social security contributions are not available or are partial in a few countries. Specifically, in the Democratic Republic of the Congo, Togo and Uganda social security contributions data are not available, and in Cameroon, Kenya, and Senegal only partial information on social security contributions are available. See the country tables in Chapter 4 for further information.
1. The changes in each tax category are calculated using estimated 2015 data.
Source: Authors' calculations based on data in OECD/ATAF/AUC (2017), "Revenue Statistics in Africa: Comparative tables", *OECD Tax Statistics* (database), *http://dx.doi.org/10.1787/be755711-en*.

StatLink *http://dx.doi.org/10.1787/888933568642*

Morocco had the largest decrease in tax-to-GDP ratio of 0.9 percentage points. Decreases in revenue as a percentage of GDP occurred across all the main categories, predominantly in VAT (by 0.5 percentage points) and corporate income tax (by 0.3 percentage points). In Tunisia a sharp decrease in corporate tax revenues of 1.6 percentage points of GDP was offset by increases in personal income tax revenue and revenue from other taxes (principally social security contributions). This followed the recent reform of the corporate income tax system in Tunisia, which reduced the corporate income tax rate from 30% to 25%.

Changes in corporate income tax revenue as a percentage of GDP between 2014 and 2015 varied significantly across African countries (Figure 1.6). In 2015, Ghana, Kenya, Niger and Tunisia recorded decreases of 0.5 percentage points and over. The decrease in Ghana is mainly due to the decrease of corporate income tax revenue from oil companies, which decreased from 0.7% of GDP to 0.03% of GDP due to the continued drop in oil prices; a major shock since Ghana has been exporting petroleum since 2011 (NGRI, 2015).

Figure 1.6. **Annual changes in revenue from taxes on income and profits, by sub-category and by country between 2014 and 2015 (percentage points of GDP)**

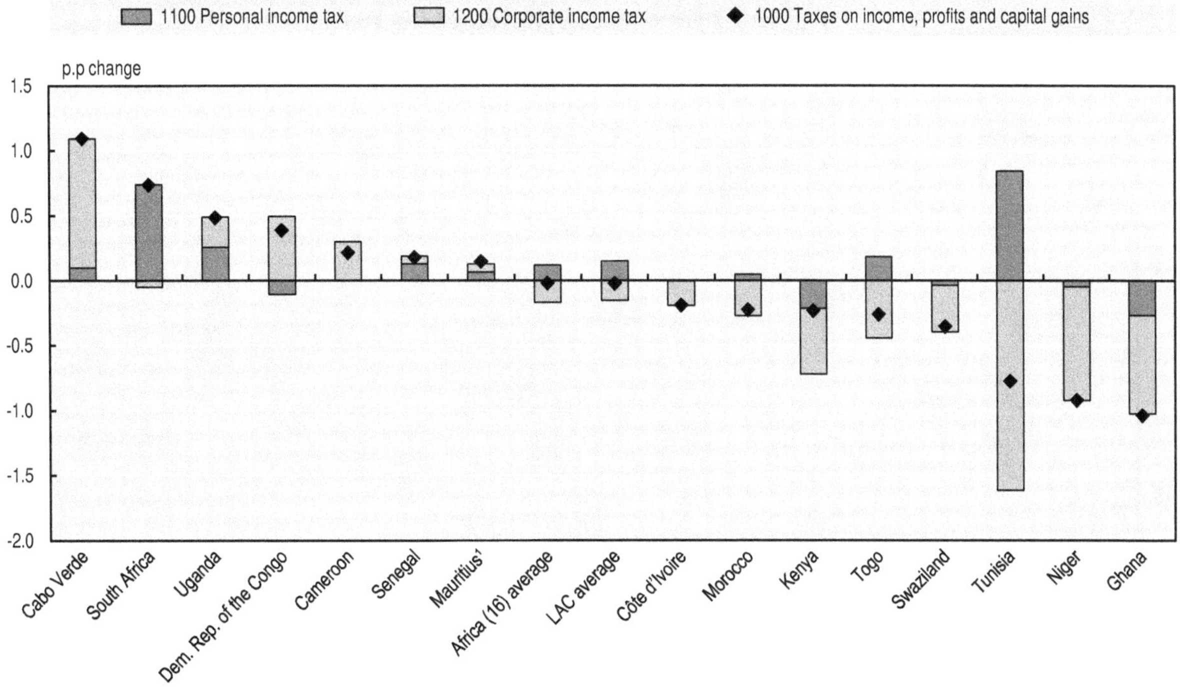

Note: The Africa (16) average, the averages for LAC (24 Latin American and Caribbean countries) and the OECD (35 countries) are unweighted.

1. The changes in each tax category are calculated using estimated 2015 data.

Source: Authors' calculations based on data in OECD/ATAF/AUC (2017), "Revenue Statistics in Africa: Comparative tables", *OECD Tax Statistics* (database), *http://dx.doi.org/10.1787/be755711-en*.

StatLink http://dx.doi.org/10.1787/888933568661

Evolution of tax-to-GDP ratios since 2000

The average tax-to-GDP ratio in the sixteen African countries has, with the exception of the 2008-10 period, risen continuously between 2000 and 2015 (Figure 1.7). It increased by 5.0 percentage points from 14.2% in 2000 to 19.1% in 2015. This growth reflects favourable macroeconomic conditions, changes in tax policy and strengthening of tax administrations. This trend is similar to the trend of the LAC countries which increased by 4.9 percentage points on average over the same period. It contrasts with the much slower growth in the OECD area where the ratio has been relatively stable, reaching 34.3% in 2015, 0.3 percentage points above its corresponding level in 2000.

The global financial crisis briefly interrupted the steady growth of the Africa (16) average tax-to-GDP ratio. The crisis resulted in a decrease of the Africa (16) average of 0.4 percentage points between 2008 and 2010. The fall in economic activity and commodity prices contributed to this decrease. Over the same period, some of the sixteen African countries implemented measures in an effort to stimulate the economy. For example, Morocco reduced the corporate income tax (CIT) rate by 5 percentage points in 2008 with a view to improving competitiveness and to help companies be more resilient during the financial crisis (see Box 1.2). The LAC average decreased by 0.5 percentage points over this same period. In contrast, the OECD average was mainly affected by the crisis between 2007 and 2009. Over this period, the OECD tax-to-GDP ratio was more significantly affected, registering a decrease of 1.3 percentage points. The OECD area also recovered more slowly, regaining its pre-crisis tax-to-GDP level of 33.8% in 2013, whereas the Africa (16) average recovered more quickly, exceeding its pre-crisis level (17.7% in 2008) in 2011.

Figure 1.7. **Tax-to-GDP ratios, 2000-15**

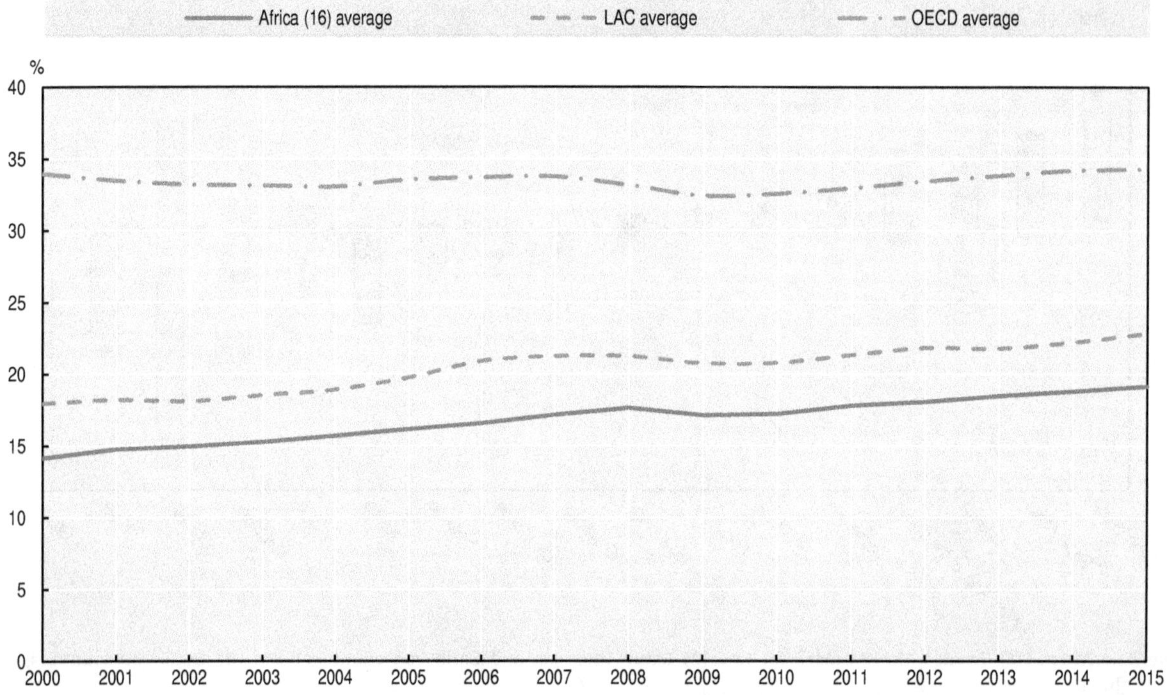

Notes: The figures include sub-national government tax revenues for Mauritius, Morocco, South Africa and Swaziland.
The Africa (16) average, the averages for LAC (24 Latin American and Caribbean countries) and the OECD (35 countries) are unweighted. The Africa (16) average should be interpreted with caution as data for social security contributions are not available or are partial in a few countries. Specifically, in the Democratic Republic of the Congo, Togo and Uganda social security contributions data are not available, and in Cameroon, Kenya, and Senegal only partial information on social security contributions are available. See the country tables in Chapter 4 for further information.

Source: Table 3.1 in Chapter 3 for the OECD and Africa (16) averages and OECD/ATAF/AUC (2017), "Revenue Statistics in Africa: Comparative tables", *OECD Tax Statistics* (database), *http://dx.doi.org/10.1787/be755711-en*, for the LAC average.

StatLink *http://dx.doi.org/10.1787/888933568680*

The growth in tax revenues occurred during a period in which African countries adopted major structural reforms in their tax administrations and undertook significant changes to their tax systems. For many countries, the reforms were aimed at strengthening and modernising tax administrations. Among the reform initiatives introduced were taxpayer offices specialising in large and/or medium-sized companies; self-assessment systems; taxpayer segmentation; and modern risk management (Kloeden, D, 2011; Fossat and Bua, 2013). Some countries undertook tax reforms to expand their tax base; eliminating certain exemptions; and simplifying tax legislation. As the (AfDB/OECD/ECA, 2010) explains, "...*many countries have successfully enlarged their tax bases. Tunisia's has increased its own at a yearly average of 3.5%, South Africa has more than doubled it, ..., while Côte d'Ivoire has rebuilt its tax base after civil war*". These changes were often accompanied by programmes to educate taxpayers about tax systems and to improve taxpayer services, such as the introduction of electronic tax service facilities.

Box 1.2. **Main tax and tax administration reforms in Morocco between 2004 and 2013**

Between 2004 and 2013, Morocco undertook a number of key tax policy reforms, accompanied by a reorganisation and strengthening of its tax administrations. These reforms contributed to an increase in total tax revenues from 23.1% of GDP in 2004 to 28.1% in 2013.

Over this period, Morocco reformed VAT, corporate income tax (*impôt sur les sociétés*) and personal income tax (*impôt sur le revenu*). The most substantial reforms concerned the VAT system. Changes to the VAT system occurred nearly every year and included measures to expand the tax base, simplify taxation rules for certain products and to reduce the number of products subject to exonerations and reduced rates. The number of VAT rates was also reduced. The Direction Générale des Impôts (DGI) estimated that these reforms resulted in a series of increases in VAT revenues: 18% (domestic nominal VAT revenue) between 2004 and 2005; 4.2% (domestic nominal VAT revenue) between 2006 and 2007 and 24% (domestic and customs nominal VAT revenue) between 2009 and 2010. Between 2004 and 2013, VAT revenue as percentage of GDP increased by 2.8 percentage points, accounting for 56% of the total increase in tax revenue over this period. In comparison, VAT revenue growth in all of the other countries included in this publication was lower than 1.0 percentage point, with the exception of Togo, where it increased by 3.2 percentage points.

Reforms were also made to the corporate tax system in 2008, 2011 and 2013, with a view to improving competitiveness and assisting companies during the financial crisis. The main measures included:

- reducing the CIT rate from 35% to 30% and the tax on profits on the financial sector from 39.6% to 37% in 2008
- the reduction of the CIT rate for small companies whose turnover did not exceed 3 million Dirhams in 2011
- further exonerations and reduced CIT rates for targeted small companies in 2013.

As a result of these reforms and the financial crisis, corporate income tax revenues decreased by 2 percentage points as a percentage of GDP between 2008 and 2013. However, across a longer time period (2004 to 2013), this category increased by 1.5 percentage points, due to exceptional corporate income tax revenue in some years following enforcement measures and strong economic performance prior to the financial crisis.

The personal tax system was reformed in 2007, 2009 and 2010 with the goal to improve the purchasing power of households. Over this period marginal personal income tax rates were reduced; tax scales were restructured; and the threshold for exempt income increased significantly. Due to these reforms, the Direction Générale des Impôts (DGI) estimated that these measures led to a total reduction in revenue of 11 billion Dirhams over the period. As a percentage of GDP, personal income tax revenues reduced by 0.7 percentage points between 2007 and 2010.

Significant improvements were made to tax administrations between 2004 and 2013. Targeted taxpayer services were created in 2005 (e.g. large taxpayers, small companies) to better address the affairs of these groups and to provide them with more tailored services. These efforts led to an increase to the number of registered VAT, CIT and PIT taxpayers of 8-13% in 2007. In addition, the collection of corporate income tax and VAT revenues was passed to the DGI, resulting in an estimated growth of 22% in corporate income tax revenue between 2004 and 2005. Finally, tax audits and inspections were reinforced, leading to an increase in compliance by companies.

Source: Lakhal, H, Moroccan Ministry of Finance (DGI), based on an analysis undertaken while on secondment at the OECD.

The introduction of VAT was the most important tax reform in Africa since the 1980s. Twelve countries introduced VAT before 2000. Cabo Verde and Rwanda introduced VAT in 2004 and 2001, respectively, and both the Democratic Republic of the Congo and Swaziland introduced VAT in 2012. In many countries the introduction of VAT was accompanied by major tax administration reforms that contributed to increases in VAT revenues over that period. Between 2000 and 2015, VAT revenue as a percentage of GDP for the sixteen African countries on average increased by 2.2 percentage points, from 3.7% of GDP in 2000 to 5.9% in 2015 (Figure 1.8). Over the same period, revenue from other taxes on goods and services (essentially excises, customs and import duties) as a percentage of GDP decreased on average. This decline was associated with the trade liberalisation that resulted in changes in the taxation of imported and exported goods, as well as of specific goods and services, in African countries. These changes included the reduction of import tariffs, the narrowing of the base of products, services subject to excises, and the elimination of taxes on exports.

Box 1.3. **Tax system and tax administration reforms in Rwanda**

Tax collection in Rwanda has become more effective since 2000; due to significant fiscal and administrative reforms together with other initiatives (AfDB, 2010). The objective of the government was to expand the tax base by registering informal businesses and simplifying compliance processes. Rwanda established the Small and Medium Taxpayers Office in 2006 and implemented the block management system (designed to manage the tax affairs of Small and Medium Taxpayers by segmenting the businesses into manageable blocks). These reforms have had a major impact in increasing tax revenues. The compliance rate of large taxpayers has improved significantly to reach 97%. This is an important development considering that these taxpayers contribute around 75% of total domestic tax revenues. Other reforms contributing to the increase of tax revenues included the introduction of a VAT in 2001, and new income tax laws and tax rates in 2005 and 2006. The compliance enforcement system was also strengthened, enabling better identification of risks and more systematic tax inspections and penalties. In addition, the tax authorities strengthened their internal processes, leading to efficiency improvements and a reduction in the cost of collection. Other non-fiscal measures also had an impact on tax revenues, such as the increase of expenditure on priority agriculture and infrastructure projects.

The trends observed for these different tax types in the 16 African countries are on average very similar to those recorded in the Latin America and the Caribbean region (Figures 1.8). Between 2000 and 2015, the African (16) average VAT revenue increased slightly faster than the LAC average, to reach almost the same level in 2015 (6.0% of GDP). Over the same period, the Africa (16) average revenue from taxes on income and profits increased by 2.3 percentage points from 3.9% to 6.2% of GDP, whereas the LAC average increased by 2.1 percentage points from 4.1% to 6.2% of GDP. Both the Africa (16) average and the LAC average have shown significant decreases in revenue from other taxes on goods and services. In contrast, revenues from taxes on income and profits, VAT and other taxes on goods and services as percentage of GDP were relatively flat over this period for the OECD region with a slight increase in VAT revenue by 0.3 percentage points.[3]

Figure 1.8. **Revenue from taxes on income and profits, VAT and other tax headings as a percentage of GDP, 2000-15**

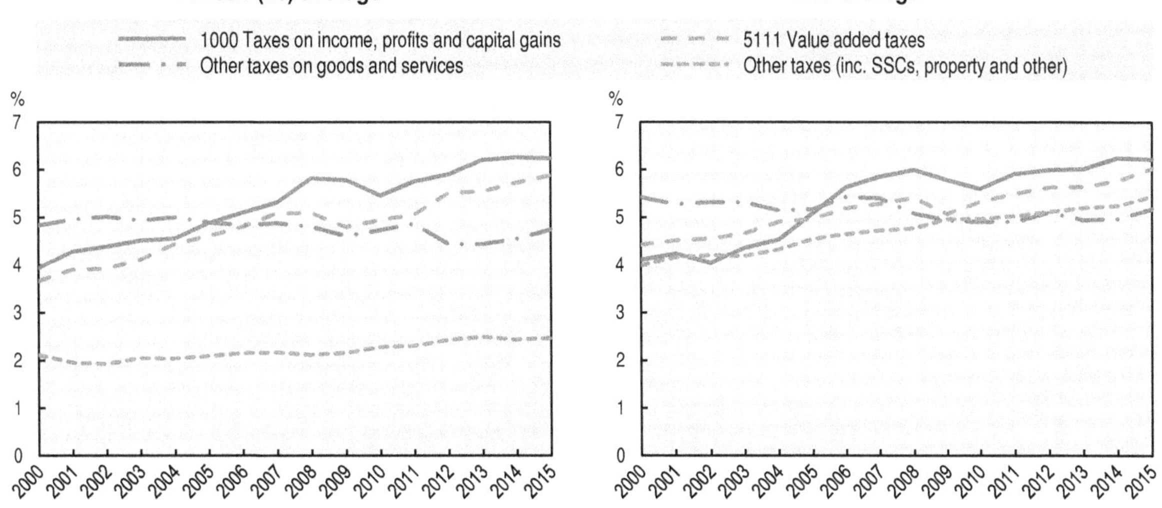

Notes: The figures include sub-national government tax revenues for Mauritius, Morocco, South Africa and Swaziland.
The Africa (16) average, the averages for LAC (24 Latin American and Caribbean countries) and the OECD (35 countries) are unweighted.
The Africa (16) average for the "Other taxes (incl. social security contributions, property taxes and other)" series should be interpreted with caution as data for social security contributions are not available or are partial in a few countries. Specifically, in the Democratic Republic of the Congo, Togo and Uganda social security contributions data are not available, and in Cameroon, Kenya and Senegal only partial information on social security contributions is available. See the country tables in Chapter 4 for further information.
The Africa (16) average excludes Kenya in 2000 as the data are not available.

Source: Authors' calculations based on OECD/ATAF/AUC (2017), "Revenue Statistics in Africa: Comparative tables", *OECD Tax Statistics* (database), *http://dx.doi.org/10.1787/be755711-en*.

StatLink http://dx.doi.org/10.1787/888933568699

While the trends in income taxes, value-added taxes and other goods and service taxes were very similar between the Africa (16) and the LAC average, revenue from social security contributions, property taxes and other taxes differed between 2000 and 2015, explaining the difference in the tax-to-GDP ratio. In 2015, the revenue from social security contributions, property taxes and other taxes amounted to 2.5% of GDP in Africa (16) compared to 5.4% of GDP in the LAC region. In 2015, social security contribution revenues as a percentage of GDP in the LAC area stood at 3.8% compared to the Africa (16) average of 1.7%.[4] Social security contribution revenues in the LAC region as a percentage of GDP increased by 1.1 percentage points between 2000 and 2015 whereas the Africa (16) average increased by 0.2 percentage points. From the 1980s onwards, many LAC countries have made substantial reforms to their social security systems that contributed to the increase of social security contributions revenues.

In Africa, revenue from taxes on income and profits increased from 3.9% of GDP in 2000 to 6.2% in 2015. This trend is mainly driven by corporate tax revenue, which increased by 1.3 percentage points from 1.5% to 2.8% of GDP (Figure 1.9). Between 2008 and 2010, corporate income tax revenue as a percentage of GDP dropped by 0.4 percentage points. It has increased steadily since 2010, although experiencing a slight decrease of 0.2 percentage points between 2014 and 2015. The latter decrease may be partly explained by a drop in commodities prices. In contrast, personal income tax revenue as a percentage of GDP has been increasing steadily since 2000 and reached its highest-ever level in 2015 (3.2%). From 2013, the growth rate of personal income tax revenue as a percentage of GDP was higher than that of corporate income tax revenue. The latter was partially affected by the slight slowdown of the African economic environment and lower commodity prices.

Figure 1.9. **Revenue from taxes on income and profits, by sub-category as a percentage of GDP for the Africa (16) average, 2000-15**

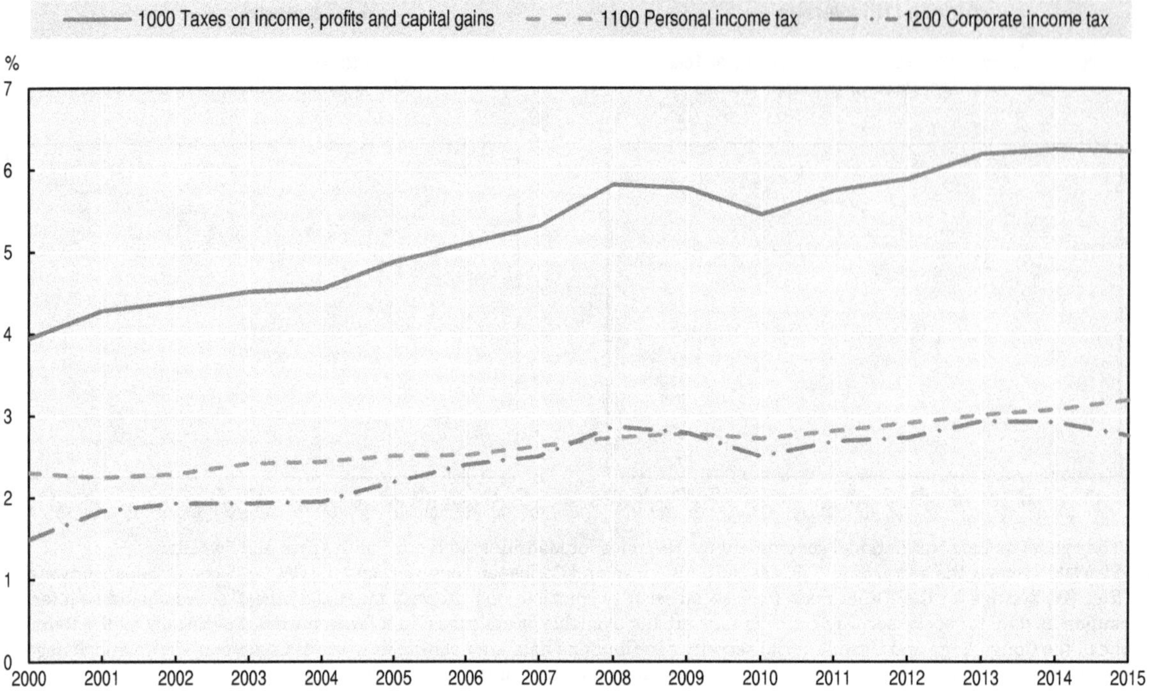

Notes: The Africa (16) averages exclude Kenya in 2000 as the data are not available.

A small proportion (4%) of revenue from taxes on incomes and profits could not be allocated to 1200 corporate income tax revenue and 1100 personal income tax revenue.

Source: Authors' calculations based on data on OECD/ATAF/AUC (2017), "Revenue Statistics in Africa: Comparative tables", *OECD Tax Statistics* (database), *http://dx.doi.org/10.1787/be755711-en.*

StatLink http://dx.doi.org/10.1787/888933568718

The evolution of tax-to-GDP ratios has been different for each country between 2000 and 2015 (Figure 1.10). The Democratic Republic of the Congo and Togo recorded the highest increases of more than 10 percentage points.

Over the same period, and in particular since 2006, Togo has made significant efforts to improve the structure, operations and processes of its administrations and establish stronger revenue authorities to collect revenues. Various programmes supported by development partners, such as the AfDB, the EU, IMF, and the World Bank, were implemented during this period. They included extensive structural reforms and modernisation of the three administrations: the DGI (*Direction générale des impôts*), the DGD (*Direction générale des douanes*) and the DGTCP (*Direction générale du trésor et de la comptabilité publique*). They aimed to improve the financial management of public finances and to mobilise domestic resources more efficiently. For example, in 2006 the African Development Bank financed the programme "The Institutional Support to Economic and Financial Governance Reform" (PARCI – *Projet d'appui au renforcement des capacités institutionnelles*). Another programme was to reform Togo's public finance management system (*Plan d'Actions de Mise en œuvre de la Réforme de Gestion des Finances Publiques*). The latter included initiatives to: increase the number of tax offices; tackle fraud and tax evasion; establish the monitoring of revenue systems; increase the number of registered taxpayers; modernise information systems; and reinforce staff capacity. These latter initiatives were implemented between 2010 and 2012 and may have contributed to the increase in tax revenues as percentage of GDP between

2012 and 2015. Tax-to-GDP ratio increased by 4.9 percentage points over this period, representing 50% of the total increase since 2000. Another reform was the establishment of the OTR (Office Togolais des Recettes) in 2014, which unified customs and tax services into a single administration.

Figure 1.10. **Change in tax-to-GDP ratios between 2000 and 2015 (percentage points of GDP)**

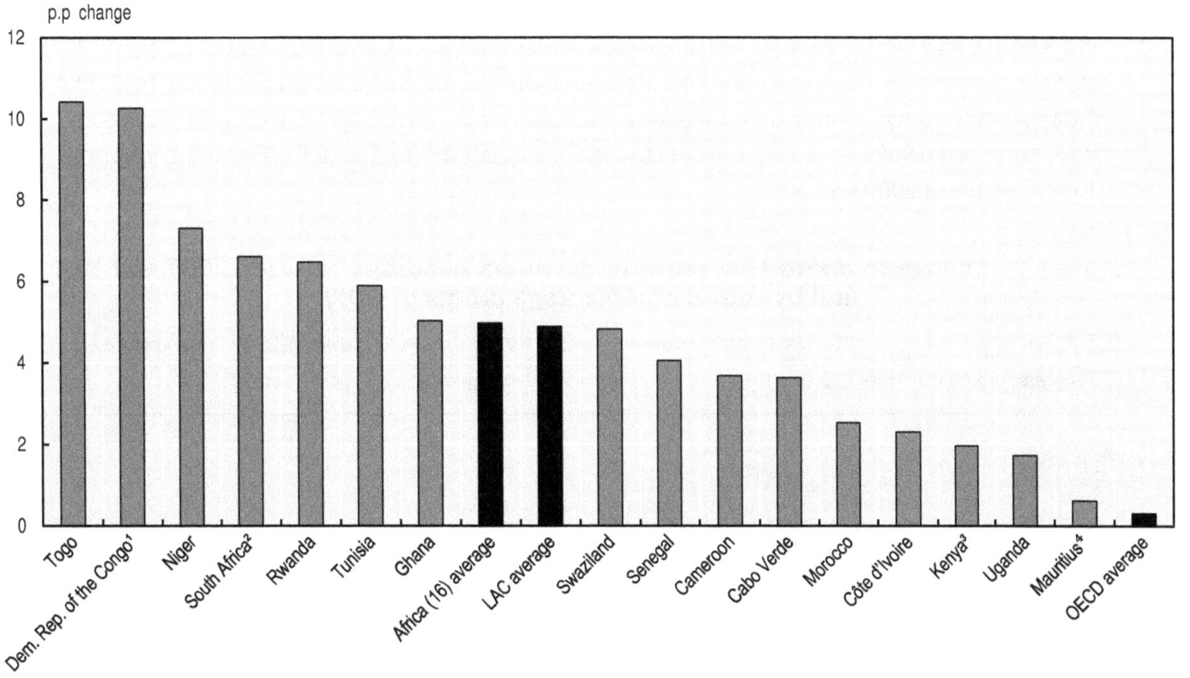

Notes: The figures include sub-national government tax revenues for Mauritius, Morocco, South Africa and Swaziland.
The Africa (16) average, the averages for LAC (24 Latin American and Caribbean countries) and the OECD (35 countries) are unweighted. The Africa (16) average should be interpreted with caution as data for social security contributions are not available or are partial in a few countries. Specifically, in the Democratic Republic of the Congo, Togo and Uganda social security contributions data are not available, and in Cameroon, Kenya, and Senegal only partial information on social security contributions are available. See the country tables in Chapter 4 for further information.
1. Some tax revenue data are not available in 2000 due to unavailability of data prior to 2010 from the "*Direction Générale des Recettes Administratives, Judiciaires, Domaniales et de Participations* (DGRAD)". However it is estimated to be negligible and lower than 1% of total tax revenue.
2. Local and provincial data prior to 2003 are not available for South Africa.
3. The increase for Kenya is between 2001 and 2015 given the data unavailability for years prior to 2001 (fiscal year 2000/01)
4. The change in tax-to-GDP ratio is calculated using estimated 2015 data.

Source: Authors' calculations based on data in Table 3.1 in Chapter 3 and OECD/ATAF/AUC (2017), "Revenue Statistics in Africa: Comparative tables", *OECD Tax Statistics* (database), *http://dx.doi.org/10.1787/be755711-en*, for the LAC average.

StatLink *http://dx.doi.org/10.1787/888933568737*

The introduction of VAT in the Democratic Republic of the Congo partly explained the increase over the 2000 to 2015 period, accounting for nearly 50% of the increase. Tax revenues in the Democratic Republic of the Congo were particularly low in 2000 (0.6% of GDP), partially due to weaker tax administration capacity during a period of internal conflict. In addition, the Democratic Republic of the Congo recorded negative annual GDP growth (in real terms) between 1998 and 2002 and experienced hyperinflation until 2003 (OPM, 2013). In periods of high inflation the lag between tax base valuation and tax collection in particular for corporate tax revenues can lead to a loss of revenue for the Government (IMF, 2001).

The main contributor to the increase in tax-to-GDP ratios between 2000 and 2015 was VAT revenue followed by corporate tax revenue (Figure 1.11). The biggest increases in VAT revenue as percentage of GDP (over 3 percentage points) occurred in the four countries that introduced VAT in the 2000s (Cabo Verde, the Democratic Republic of the Congo, Rwanda and Swaziland) and in Togo (by 5.5 percentage points). Morocco had an increase of 2.5 percentage points that has largely been attributed to important VAT reforms between 2004 and 2013 (see Box 1.2). Exceptions to these trends are Côte d'Ivoire, Kenya, Senegal, Tunisia and Uganda. Tunisia registered the biggest increase in social security contributions as percentage of GDP of 3.6 percentage points over the period. The widening of pension coverage in Tunisia since 2002 may have contributed to this increase (International Social Security Association, 2014). The second biggest increase in Tunisia, of 2.3 percentage points was registered in personal income tax revenue. This category was also the main driver in the increases in tax-to-GDP ratios seen in Kenya, Senegal and Uganda over the same period. In Côte d'Ivoire, revenue from taxes on specific consumption was the main contributor to the increase (mainly import duties) between 2000 and 2015.

Figure 1.11. **Change in tax-to-GDP ratios by main tax headings between 2000 and 2015 and by country (percentage points of GDP)**

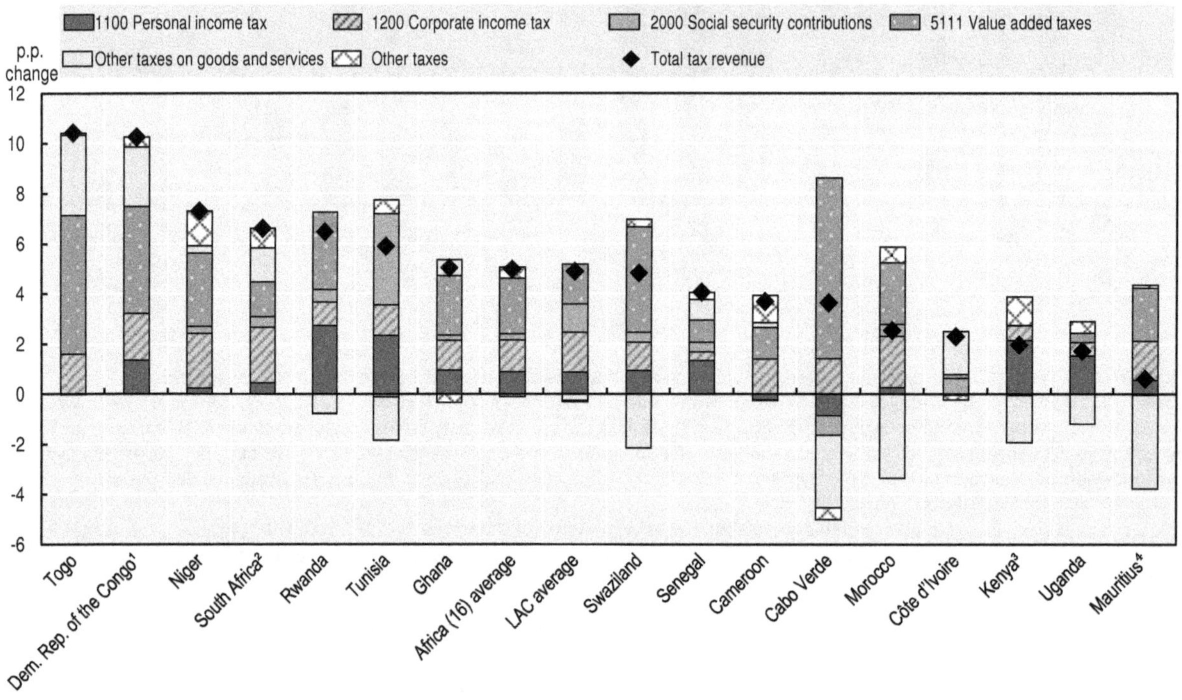

Notes: The figures include sub-national government tax revenues for Mauritius, Morocco, South Africa and Swaziland.

The Africa (16) average, the averages for LAC (24 Latin American and Caribbean countries) and the OECD (35 countries) are unweighted. The Africa (16) average series should be interpreted with caution as data for social security contributions is not available or are partial in a few countries. Specifically, in the Democratic Republic of the Congo, Togo, and Uganda, social security contributions data are not available, and in Cameroon, Kenya, and Senegal only partial information on social security contributions is available. See the country tables in Chapter 4 for further information.

1. Some tax revenue data are not available in 2000 due to unavailability of data prior to 2010 from the "*Direction Générale des Recettes Administratives, Judiciaires, Domaniales et de Participations* (DGRAD)". However it is estimated to be negligible and lower than 1% of total tax revenue.
2. Local and provincial data prior to 2003 are not available for South Africa.
3. The increase for Kenya is between 2001 and 2015 given the data unavailability for years prior to 2001 (fiscal year 2000/01)
4. The changes in each tax category are calculated using estimated 2015 data.

Source: Authors' calculations based on data on OECD/ATAF/AUC (2017), "Revenue Statistics in Africa: Comparative tables", *OECD Tax Statistics* (database), *http://dx.doi.org/10.1787/be755711-en.*

StatLink http://dx.doi.org/10.1787/888933568756

Factors influencing tax-to-GDP ratios

Tax-to-GDP ratios are influenced by a variety of domestic and international factors. Domestically, macroeconomic characteristics such as the importance of agriculture in the economy, resource endowments, openness to trade and the size of the informal economy can influence tax-to-GDP ratios. The power of tax administrations, the levels of corruption and tax morale (or willingness of people to pay taxes) are also strongly linked to the level of tax revenues (OECD, 2014). Geographic location is also relevant: landlocked countries are less able to impose taxes on goods and services entering the country than island countries. In addition, international factors, including the tax policies of other countries, can impact tax-to-GDP ratios.

Tax-to-GDP ratios tend to be higher in high-income countries: in general, OECD countries collect a higher amount of tax revenues than non-OECD countries, measured as a percentage of GDP. Several of the 16 African countries have lower income and development levels and lower tax-to-GDP ratios than the Latin American and Caribbean countries (Figure 1.12). African countries show a higher range of GDP per capita compared to Latin American and Caribbean countries and OECD countries.

Figure 1.12. **Tax-to-GDP ratios and GDP per capita (in PPP) in African countries, Latin American and Caribbean, OECD and selected Asian countries, 2015**

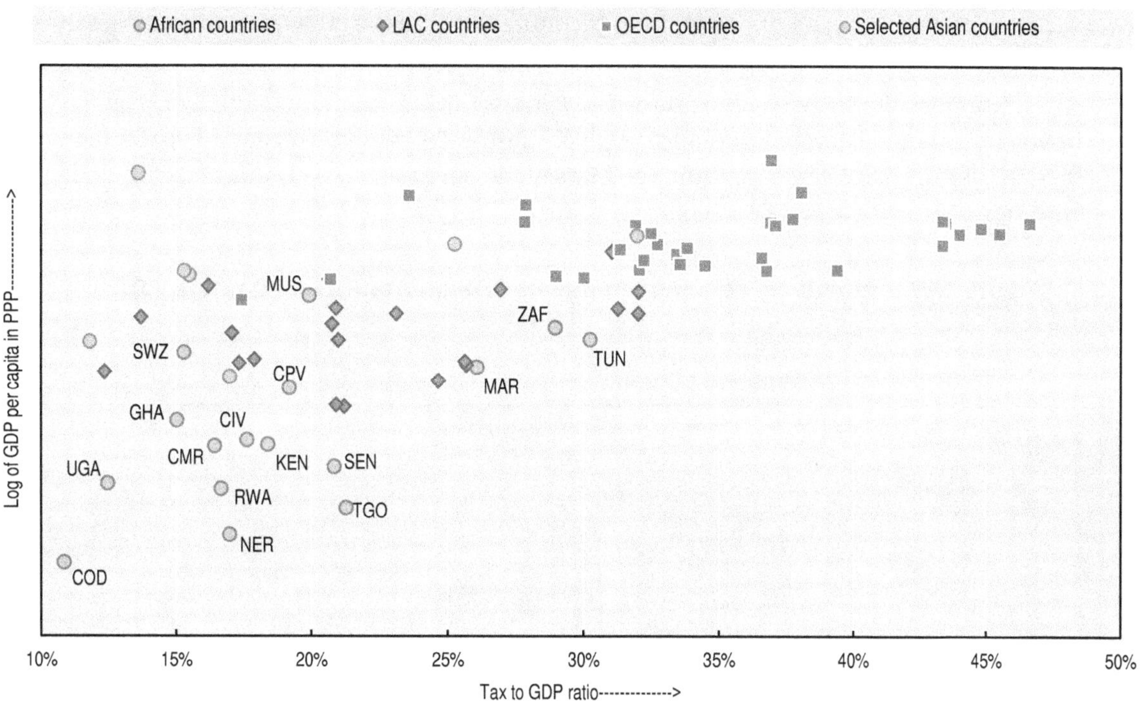

Notes: The y-axis is on a logarithmic scale. The purchasing-power-parity (PPP) between two countries is the rate at which the currency of one country needs to be converted into that of a second country to ensure that a given amount of the first country's currency will purchase the same volume of goods and services in the second country as it does in the first. The implied PPP conversion rate is expressed as national currency per current international dollar. An international dollar has the same purchasing power as the US dollar has in the United States. An international dollar is a hypothetical currency that is used as a means of translating and comparing costs from one country to the other using a common reference point, the US dollar (Definitions derived from IMF, 2017 and WHO, 2015).

Source: IMF (2017), *World Economic Outlook*, March 2017, International Monetary Fund for figures of GDP per capita. Tax-to-GDP ratios are sourced from the regional Revenue Statistics publications (*www.oecd.org/tax/tax-policy/revenue-statistics-comparable-tax-revenue-data.htm*).

StatLink http://dx.doi.org/10.1787/888933568775

The countries with the lowest tax to GDP ratios are among those with the highest share of agriculture (including forestry, hunting and fishing[5]) in their economies (Figure 1.13). Higher shares of agriculture in GDP are said to be associated with lower tax-to-GDP ratios in many studies (Addison and Levin, 2012; Profeta and Scabrosetti, 2010). This finding is partly mirrored in the revenue data for the African countries featured in this publication, where most countries with higher shares of agriculture in their economies display lower tax-to-GDP ratios. Cameroon, Côte d'Ivoire, the Democratic Republic of the Congo, Ghana, Kenya, Niger, Rwanda and Uganda have share of agriculture as percentage of GDP above 20% and a tax-to-GDP ratio below 19%. Togo is a notable exception: over 40% of its economy is devoted to agriculture and Togo's tax-to-GDP ratio is relatively high (21.3%). In many countries, agriculture is a challenging sector to tax:

- Most people in this sector in developing economies are on low incomes and many are not registered for tax purposes (EPS PEAKS, 2013).
- There is less taxation of the agricultural sector in Africa due to a high level of informality and a low level of monetisation. Payments are often made in cash or in kind by African farmers as opposed to through banks and almost none of them keep good business accounts (AfDB/OECD/ECA, 2010).
- The agriculture sector benefits from numerous tax exemptions. For example, in Rwanda, agricultural enterprises are exempt from paying VAT on agricultural inputs and products. There are also VAT exemptions for the agriculture sector in the other African countries in this publication, including in Côte d'Ivoire, Niger, Senegal and Togo.

In contrast, the share of agriculture in GDP in the OECD is no more than 2% on average. However, it should be noted that a low agriculture-to-GDP ratio is no guarantee of a high tax-to-GDP ratio. Cabo Verde, Mauritius and Swaziland have a small agricultural sector, along with relatively low tax-to-GDP ratio.

Figure 1.13. **Agriculture as a percentage of GDP and tax-to-GDP ratios, 2015**

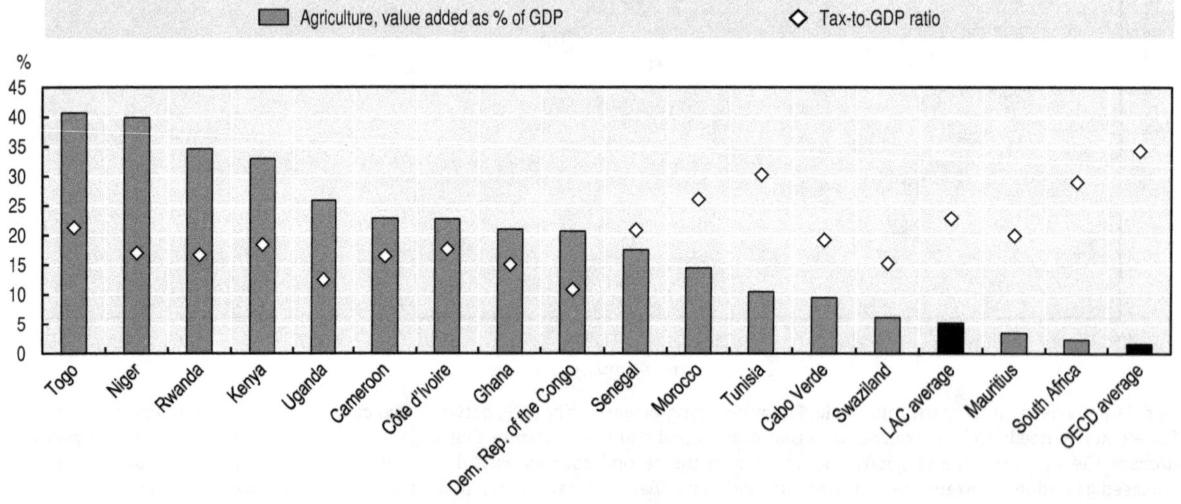

Note: This indicator includes forestry, hunting, and fishing, as well as cultivation of crops and livestock production. The agriculture, value added as percentage of GDP for the OECD average and Swaziland relate to 2014 as 2015 data are not available.

Source: Table 3.1 for tax-to-GDP ratios figures and OECD/ATAF/AUC (2017), "Revenue Statistics in Africa: Comparative tables", *OECD Tax Statistics* (database), *http://dx.doi.org/10.1787/be755711-en*, for the LAC average. World Bank for figures on agriculture, value added as percentage of GDP.

StatLink http://dx.doi.org/10.1787/888933568794

The relatively low tax-to-GDP ratio in Mauritius may be partly explained by the level of tax rates in this country. Mauritius has one of the lowest tax rate regimes in Africa (Sokeechand and Hussen, 2013), with a flat rate of 15% for corporate, income and value-added taxes and no taxation of capital gains or dividends. The tax-to-GDP ratio in Mauritius is comparatively low relative to countries with comparable income levels, at 19.9%. In contrast, the corporate tax rate is 30% or above in Cameroon, the Democratic Republic of the Congo, Morocco, Niger, Rwanda, Senegal and Uganda, and between 25% and 30% for the remaining eight African countries, which also typically tax capital income (Sokeechand and Hussen, 2013).

Resource-rich countries which receive substantial revenues from oil exports often exhibit low tax ratios due to narrow tax bases. Countries with more revenues from natural resources tend to resort less to more politically demanding forms of taxation such as income taxes (AfDB/OECD/UNECA, 2010) and have relatively narrow tax bases. Cameroon, Côte d'Ivoire, the Democratic Republic of the Congo, Ghana and South Africa have been classified by the International Monetary Fund (IMF) as "resource-rich".[6] In Cameroon and Côte d'Ivoire, the main exports of mineral resources are petroleum (AfDB/OECD/UNDP, 2015) and small pools of taxpayers bear the vast majority of the tax burden: in Cameroon, 55% of all corporate taxes in 2013 were paid by only ten companies (IMF, 2014a). The size of the informal sector in Côte d'Ivoire is estimated at 90% (UNDP, 2013). As a result the tax ratios of both countries are at the lower end of African countries. During the 2000's both these countries put in place various initiatives to address the over-exploitation of the available tax base (AfDB/OECD/ECA, 2010). Côte d'Ivoire has reduced preferential measures to priority sectors and others particularly affected by the 2002 crisis. Cameroon's government put in place programmes in 2009 and 2010 to bring in new taxpayers from the informal sector (AfDB/OECD/UNECA, 2010). In recent years both countries have continued to strengthen tax policy and administrations with a view to expanding their tax base (IMF, 2013; IMF, 2014a).

1.2. Tax structures

The tax structure measures the composition of tax revenues by different tax types. This is an important indicator since different taxes have different economic and social effects. Across the 16 countries in this publication, the composition of taxes varies widely, reflecting their different policy choices, economic structures and conditions, tax administration capabilities and historical factors.

Evolution of tax structures

The Africa (16) average tax structure (defined as the share of major tax types in total tax revenue) shifted towards greater revenue shares from VAT and from taxes on income and profits between 2000 and 2015. VAT revenue accounted for the highest share in 2015 at 31.5% of the total tax revenues, an increase of 7.2 percentage points between 2000 and 2015 (Figure 1.14). The revenue share of taxes on specific goods and services (excises, customs and import duties) was the second highest at 24.4% of total tax revenue, even though it has declined by 11.1 percentage points since 2000. The share of revenues from corporate and personal income taxes grew by 2.9 and 0.9 percentage points respectively to 14.6% and 16.3% of total tax revenues over the same period.

Figure 1.14. **Tax structure, Africa (16) average, 2000 and 2015**

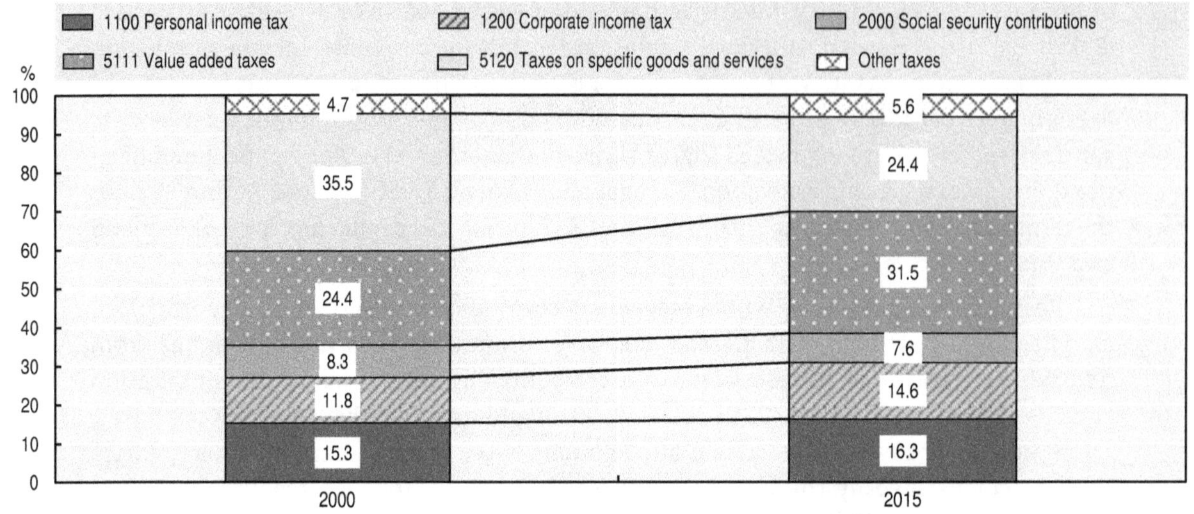

Notes: The Africa (16) average should be interpreted with caution as data for social security contributions are not available or are partial in a few countries. Specifically, in The Democratic Republic of the Congo, Togo and Uganda social security contributions data are not available, and in Cameroon, Kenya and Senegal only partial information on social security contributions are available. See the country tables in Chapter 4 for further information.

The Africa (16) average excludes Kenya in 2000 as the data are not available.

Source: Authors' calculations based on data on OECD/ATAF/AUC (2017), "Revenue Statistics in Africa: Comparative tables", *OECD Tax Statistics* (database), *http://dx.doi.org/10.1787/be755711-en*.

StatLink http://dx.doi.org/10.1787/888933568813

Among African countries, tax structures vary considerably. Figure 1.15 shows the decomposition of tax revenues between income taxes (both personal and corporate), social security contributions, and taxes on goods and services (including VAT and other goods and services taxes). While taxes on goods and services accounted for more than 50% of tax revenues in all countries, except in Morocco, South Africa, Swaziland and Tunisia, they ranged from 35.8% of revenues in Tunisia to just under 80% of tax revenues in Togo. Social security contributions were most significant in Côte d'Ivoire, Morocco and Tunisia.

Morocco and Tunisia displayed a relatively even breakdown of revenues between the categories of taxes compared to the other 14 African countries (Figure 1.15). This is explained by the higher share of social security contributions revenue as a percentage of total tax revenue in both countries and a lower share of revenue from taxes on goods and services. Morocco and Tunisia displayed the highest share of revenue from social security contributions (17.0% and 29.5% respectively) and the lowest levels from taxes on goods and services (43.6% and 35.8% respectively). The share of revenue from taxes on income and profits is around 30% in both countries.

Kenya, South Africa and Swaziland obtained about half of their tax revenues from taxes on income and profits, a greater share than that collected by other countries in this report, and also greater than the OECD and LAC averages. Among these countries, income tax revenues ranged from 47.1% of total tax revenue in Kenya to 51.8% in South Africa. While this share is higher than the revenue share from taxes on goods and services in South Africa and Swaziland, it is slightly lower in Kenya. In the remaining sub-Saharan African countries in this publication, revenue from taxes on income and profits was less than 20% of total tax revenue in Côte d'Ivoire and Togo; between 25% and 35% in Cabo Verde, Cameroon, the Democratic Republic of the Congo, Mauritius, Niger, Senegal and Uganda; and between 35% and 40% in Rwanda and Ghana.

Figure 1.15. **Tax structure, by country, 2015**

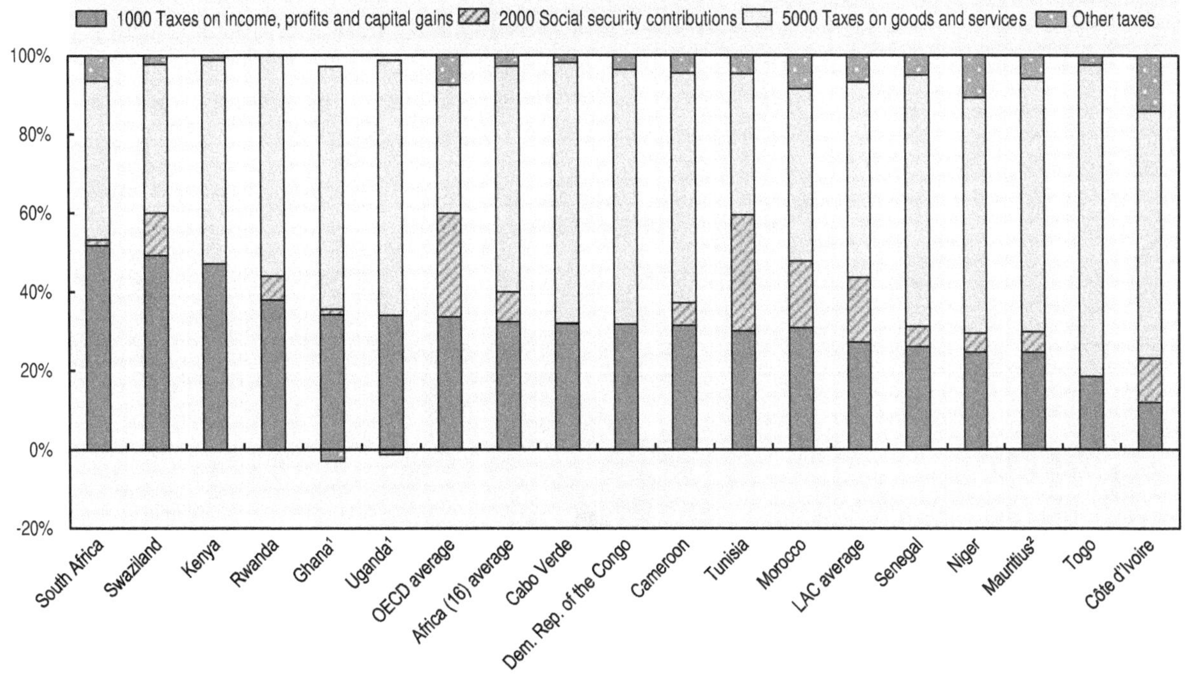

Notes: The figures include sub-national government tax revenues for Mauritius, Morocco, South Africa and Swaziland. The Africa (16) average, the averages for LAC (24 Latin American and Caribbean countries) and the OECD (35 countries) are unweighted.

The Africa (16) average should be interpreted with caution as data for social security contributions are not available or are partial in a few countries. Specifically, in the Democratic Republic of the Congo, Togo and Uganda social security contributions data are not available, and in Cameroon, Kenya, and Senegal only partial information on social security contributions are available. See the country tables in Chapter 4 for further information.

1. Revenue from other taxes is negative due to the allocation of tax refunds in this category. It was not possible to breakdown this revenue by the main type of tax category.

2. 2015 data are estimated.

Source: Authors' calculations based on data on OECD/ATAF/AUC (2017), "Revenue Statistics in Africa: Comparative tables", *OECD Tax Statistics* (database), *http://dx.doi.org/10.1787/be755711-en.*

StatLink *http://dx.doi.org/10.1787/888933568832*

The importance of social security contributions[7] varies greatly across the 16 countries in this publication. The share of social security contributions in total tax revenue is highest in Morocco and Tunisia as previously mentioned. Social security contributions are a far smaller proportion of total tax revenue in the remaining countries that reported social security contributions, ranging from less than 1.5% in Cabo Verde, Ghana, Kenya and South Africa to 11.2% in Côte d'Ivoire. This variation reflects the diversity of the social security programmes and contribution rates in African countries. For example, social security contributions in South Africa consist only of contributions to the Unemployment Insurance Fund (UIF). Other social risks, such as old age, sickness and maternity, are dealt with via social assistance programmes – which differ from social security programmes in that they are non-contributory. In contrast, social security schemes in Morocco and Tunisia are modelled on the French system and cover a wider range of risks including old-age, disability, sickness and maternity, work injury (Tunisia), unemployment (Morocco) and family benefits (SSA, 2015).

VAT is the main component of revenue from taxes on goods and services in most African countries. However there is wide heterogeneity within the 16 African countries with regard to the share of VAT in the total tax revenue (Figure 1.16). VAT revenue shares ranged from 19.8% in Tunisia to 44.2% in Togo. This is partially the result of differences in the design of the VAT: rates and tax bases vary widely across countries. For example, VAT standard rates ranged between 14% in South Africa and Swaziland to 20% in Morocco. The share of VAT revenue in the Africa (16) average at 31.5% is slightly higher than that of the LAC average (28.4%) and more than 10 percentage points higher than the OECD VAT revenue share of 20.1%. However as a percentage of GDP, the VAT revenue share for the Africa (16) average remains lower than the LAC average (6.0%) and OECD average (6.8%).

Figure 1.16. **Revenue from VAT as a percentage of total tax revenue by country and of GDP by country, 2015**

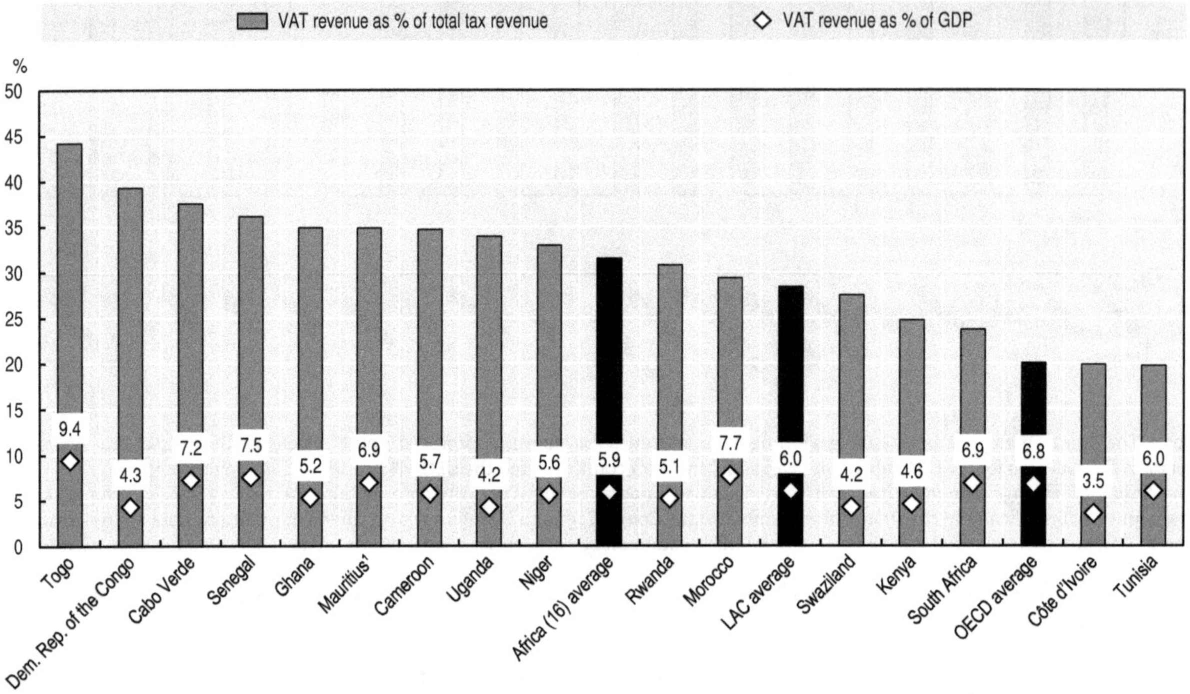

Note: The data for the OECD average are for 2014 as the data are not available for 2015.

1. Data for 2015 are estimated.

Source: Authors' calculations based on data on OECD/ATAF/AUC (2017), "Revenue Statistics in Africa: Comparative tables", *OECD Tax Statistics* (database), *http://dx.doi.org/10.1787/be755711-en*.

StatLink http://dx.doi.org/10.1787/888933568851

The Africa (16) average share of corporate income tax revenues to total tax revenue amounted to 14.6% and was higher than the OECD average of 8.8% (2014 figure) but lower than the LAC average of 15.8% (Table 1.1). Reported as a percentage of GDP, the Africa (16) average and the OECD average displayed a similar share of corporate income tax revenues at 2.9% and 2.8% of GDP respectively (Table 1.1). Within countries, the share of corporate income tax revenues to total tax revenue ranged from 7.4% in Uganda to 19.7% in Swaziland in 2015.

In contrast, the Africa (16) average share of personal income tax revenues to total tax revenue at 16.3% was much lower than the OECD average of 24.0% (2014 figure) but higher than the LAC average (9.1%). As a percentage of GDP, the share of personal income tax revenues of the OECD average at 8.4% was more than double the Africa (16) average at 3.1%. South Africa was the only country to have a higher share of personal income tax revenue in comparison to the OECD average, at 9.7% of GDP. In the remaining countries personal income tax revenue ranged from 0.0% of GDP in Côte d'Ivoire to 5.9 % in Tunisia.

Nine African countries collected a higher proportion of their revenue from corporate income taxes than from personal income taxes. In contrast, as a percentage of total tax revenues, the share of personal income tax revenue is more than double the share of corporate income tax revenue in Kenya, South Africa and Uganda.

Table 1.1. **Corporate income tax revenues and personal income tax revenues as a percentage of total tax revenues and of GDP**

	As percentage of total tax revenue		As percentage of GDP	
	Corporate income tax	Personal income tax	Corporate income tax	Personal income tax
Cabo Verde	14.4	17.4	2.8	3.3
Cameroon	19.5	6.7	3.2	1.1
Côte d'Ivoire	11.0	0.3	1.9	0.0
Dem. Rep. of the Congo	18.3	13.3	2.0	1.4
Ghana	18.4	17.1	2.8	2.6
Kenya	11.8	26.6	2.2	4.9
Mauritius	13.7	9.5	2.7	1.9
Morocco	16.3	14.5	4.2	3.8
Niger	18.3	6.3	3.1	1.1
Rwanda	15.6	22.3	2.6	3.7
Senegal	8.7	15.7	1.8	3.3
South Africa	16.4	33.4	4.7	9.7
Swaziland	19.7	28.7	3.0	4.4
Togo	14.0	4.6	3.0	1.0
Tunisia	10.4	19.5	3.2	5.9
Uganda	7.4	24.6	0.9	3.1
Africa (16) average	14.6	16.3	2.9	3.1
LAC average	15.8	9.1	3.7	2.2
OECD average	8.8	24.0	2.8	8.4

Notes: The Africa (16) average, the averages for LAC (24 Latin American and Caribbean countries) and the OECD (35 countries) are unweighted.
The data for the OECD average are for 2014 as the data are not available for 2015.
The figures for Cameroon, Kenya and LAC average should be interpreted with caution as 18%-20% of their revenue from taxes on income and profits cannot be allocated to corporate income tax revenue (1200) or personal income tax revenue (1100).

Source: Authors' calculations based on data on OECD/ATAF/AUC (2017), "Revenue Statistics in Africa: Comparative tables", *OECD Tax Statistics* (database), *http://dx.doi.org/10.1787/be755711-en.*

StatLink *http://dx.doi.org/10.1787/888933569896*

1.3. Taxes by level of government

The analysis of taxation by level of government in this publication is limited by a lack of data on sub-central government tax revenues. Data on sub-central tax revenues were only available in four countries: Mauritius,[8] Morocco, South Africa and Swaziland. Sub-national government finances are not always well tracked in Africa. In some countries, where financial statements exist, they have not been recorded electronically.

Revenues collected at sub-national levels are considered to be low in the 16 African countries. Where there is no existing data, officials believe that these revenues constitute only a marginal percentage of total tax revenues. AfDB/OECD/UNECA, 2010 states that "*local tax collection is estimated to be of the order of 1% of national income in Africa with a high concentration in large urban centres*". AfDB/OECD/UNDP, 2015 states that "*in Africa on average, the weight of local government revenue is 7% of the total revenue of local, regional and national governments combined*". Additional figures from the African Development Bank show that local tax revenue in Côte d'Ivoire and Senegal accounts for a small proportion of total tax revenue (around 3-4%[9] of total tax revenue).

Where data exist, reported sub-national tax revenues remain low. In 2015, sub-central government revenues as a percentage of all tax revenues were less than 1% in Mauritius, 1.4% in Swaziland, 3.4% in Morocco and 4.8% in South Africa.

Revenues from property taxes are the most important source of tax revenue for sub-central governments in Mauritius, Morocco, South Africa and Swaziland. They represent more than 80% of the total tax revenue in the four countries. Most of the remainder derives from taxes on goods and services. There are wide differences in local taxation in Africa and many countries do not levy any local taxes on buildings and landholdings, or on economic activities (AfDB/OECD/UNDP, 2015). Property taxes generally contribute more to local government revenues in Africa's English speaking countries than in its French-speaking ones (AfDB/OECD/UNDP, 2015).

Sub-central governments generally have limited tax collection responsibilities and most tax revenue collection remains principally at the central government level. AfDB/OECD/UNDP, 2015 observed that "*Many local governments receive a significant share of their total revenues from central government transfers*". This is partly because many local tax systems in Africa are a legacy from French and English administrations and have changed little since independence. This is particularly true in French-speaking countries, such as Cameroon, Côte d'Ivoire, Morocco and Senegal and, where local revenues are often collected by the central government on the local government's behalf whereas in South Africa, local revenues come from their own collection (89% in 2007) (Fjeldstad, Chambas and Brun, 2014). Local governments in Mauritius rely heavily on transfers from the central government (IMF, 2014b).

Local governments in most of sub-Saharan Africa have limited resources and their tax administrations' instruments are not appropriately equipped to collect taxes efficiently or to properly account for them. This results in high collection costs and an extensive number of low-yield taxes. Moreover the processing of data on revenues collections and the exchange of information with other public institutions is poor and there is usually little co-operation with the central government. This leads to the duplication of taxes or taxes that are contrary to national objectives (such as local taxes on export crops). Apart from South Africa, appropriate property registers are lacking, which is a real challenge for the collection of property taxes (Fjeldstad, Chambas and Brun, 2014). In Mauritius, for instance, property tax provides a low yield partly due to outdated cadastres and valuations of property (IMF, 2014b).

Although many African countries have undertaken major reforms of their central tax legislation and administrations over the last decades, less has been done at the local government level. Central government taxation has been a greater priority because of the need to reduce national fiscal deficits. It is also easier and less costly to reform central tax legislation and systems than those for local taxes and the potential benefits of tax reform in terms of higher revenue are greater. Morocco has been reforming local government tax systems and administrations since 2007 to strengthen local tax revenue (Boisard, de Freitas and Hidouci, 2014). Other countries in this publication, such as Cameroon, Côte d'Ivoire (AfDB/OECD/UNECA, 2010) and recently Tunisia (World Bank, 2015) have started processes of fiscal decentralisation that will empower local governments. South Africa, for example, has successfully decentralised urban property tax collection and has developed a modern system to collect property tax revenue. Municipal governments there benefit from appropriate expertise and resources (Monkam and Moore, 2015). Monkam and Moore, 2015 further explain that "In South Africa, provincial governments provide local authorities with additional administrative support and training to assist with valuation, issuing bills and collection".

NON-TAX REVENUES

Introduction

Non-tax revenues provide important context to analyses of public revenues. Two governments may have similar levels of taxes and spending, but their finances could be very different due to differences in their respective non-tax revenues. A clear picture of government finances therefore should take into account all of a government's revenues including both tax and non-tax, despite the added challenges of collecting non-tax revenue data (Box 1.4). This is particularly the case in African countries, many of which obtain a substantial portion of their public finances from resource rents or from grants.

The main categories of non-tax revenues[10] included here are:

- Grants from foreign governments or international organisations (budget aid, food aid, capital transfers, current transfers, project grants, programme grants, international debt relief, etc.);
- Property income (e.g. mining royalties and returns on government investment);
- Sales of goods and services (which includes some administrative fees);
- Fines and penalties;
- Miscellaneous and unidentified revenues (which includes revenues that would have been classified in another non-tax revenue category if the revenues were properly identified).

Among the special revenue streams that do not meet the definition of taxation is, notably, Swaziland's revenue from the Southern African Customs Union (SACU), a revenue sharing scheme funded from a common pool of excise and tariff revenues from Botswana, Lesotho, Namibia, South Africa and Swaziland (Box 1.5).

1.4. Non-tax revenues as percentage of GDP

There was a wide range of reported non-tax revenues as a percent of GDP for the 16 countries in *Revenue Statistics in Africa* in 2015. These ranged from 15.1% of GDP for Swaziland (mostly SACU revenues) down to 0.6% of GDP for South Africa. In every country, non-tax revenues were lower than tax revenues (Figure 1.17).

Although tax revenues as a percent of GDP are on a generally increasing trend in the 16 *Revenue Statistics in Africa* countries, this does not appear to be the case for non-tax revenues (see Table 1.2). Of the 14 countries for which non-tax data is available over the past ten years, eight have shown a decreasing trend in non-tax revenue to GDP ratios, and only six have shown an increasing trend.

Non-tax revenue collections show a great deal of annual variation. As can be seen in Figure 1.18, showing the coefficient of variation[11] of tax and non-tax revenues over the most recent ten years of data, there tends to be more variation in non-tax revenues than in tax revenues. In general, the volatility of non-tax revenue is due to the instability of grant and property revenues, which generally constitute the majority of non-tax revenues. The levels of grant revenues change according to the priorities of donors which can shift substantially over time. Property income can change sharply due to movements in mineral prices, or when a major new mine opens up, bringing about a surge of mineral production. This contrasts with the more stable level of variation in the reported tax revenues of the sixteen *Revenue Statistics in Africa* countries. On the other hand, the variability of non-tax revenues for Rwanda (mostly grants) was comparable to the variability of its tax revenue.

Figure 1.17. **Total tax and non-tax revenue by country as a percentage of GDP, 2015**

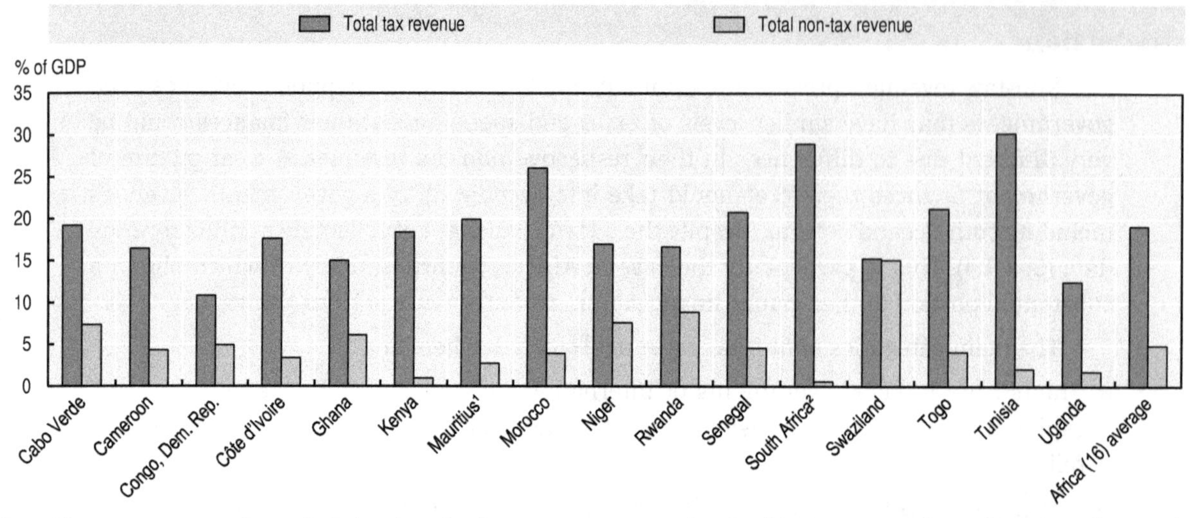

Notes: The non-tax revenue figures include sub-national government revenues for Mauritius, Morocco, and Swaziland, the only countries for which data on such revenues are reported. In 2015, these represented, respectively, 7.6%, 37%, and <1% of all non-tax revenue collected for each country. For these countries, sub-national tax revenues were, respectively, <1%, 3.4% and 1.4% of all tax revenues collected. South Africa reported 4.8% of its tax revenue as coming from state and local governments, but no sub-national non-tax revenue was reported.
1. Data for 2015 are estimated.
2. The tax-to-GDP ratio should be interpreted with caution as it includes payments made by South Africa to the Southern African Customs Union (SACU) pool, which do not meet the OECD definition of taxation.
The Africa (16) averages are unweighted for the 16 African countries included in this publication. The Africa (16) average tax-to-GDP ratio should be interpreted with caution because of missing values and incomplete data. Data on social security contributions are not available for the Democratic Republic of Congo, Togo and Uganda and are only partially available in Cameroon, Kenya, and Senegal. Data on property taxes are not available for Ghana and Uganda, and only partially available for the Democratic Republic of the Congo. See the country tables in Chapter 4 and Chapter 5 for further information.
Source: Table 3.1 in Chapter 3 and Table 5.1 in Chapter 5.

StatLink http://dx.doi.org/10.1787/888933568870

Table 1.2. **Total non-tax revenue as a percentage of GDP, 2015**

Country	2000	2005	2010	2011	2012	2013	2014	2015
Côte d'Ivoire	1.1	2.3	1.7	1.5	1.9	2.5	2.6	3.4
Cabo Verde	7.6	9.2	9.7	5.6	6.0	6.2	5.3	7.4
Cameroon	8.0	6.9	4.8	6.2	5.0	4.9	4.2	4.3
Congo, Dem. Rep.	..	..	9.9	3.9	5.7	3.6	5.3	4.9
Ghana[1]	2.2	4.3	5.0	5.3	6.1	6.2	5.6	6.1
Kenya[2]	..	2.9	0.9	..	..	1.3	0.9	1.0
Mauritius[3]	2.8	2.5	3.8	3.5	3.1	3.2	2.7	2.7
Morocco	2.2	3.0	3.6	3.9	3.7	4.1	3.8	3.9
Niger	..	8.2	6.3	4.9	8.0	9.5	8.0	7.6
Rwanda	11.8	12.7	12.3	12.3	8.8	11.2	9.4	8.9
Senegal	2.7	2.3	3.2	2.9	3.8	3.8	5.2	4.6
South Africa	0.5	0.5	0.6	0.7	0.7	0.7	0.6	0.6
Swaziland[4]	12.4	15.9	8.1	6.8	19.5	17.4	17.1	15.1
Togo	2.1	2.5	7.2	6.2	4.3	5.3	4.2	4.1
Tunisia	4.6	2.6	2.9	4.0	3.5	3.6	2.4	2.1
Uganda	..	6.7	2.9	2.1	2.2	1.2	1.3	1.8

Notes: ".." indicates that the data are incomplete for the country in the particular year.
The figures include sub-national government non-tax revenues for Mauritius, Morocco and Swaziland.
1. Data prior to 2010 excludes oil and mineral royalties that could not be distinguished from tax revenues.
2. The data are incomplete for 2011 and 2012.
3. Data for 2015 are estimated.
4. Figures exclude grants prior to 2012 as the data are not available.
Source: Table 5.1 in Chapter 5.

StatLink http://dx.doi.org/10.1787/888933569915

Figure 1.18. **Coefficients of variation (CV) for tax and non-tax revenue, 2006-15**

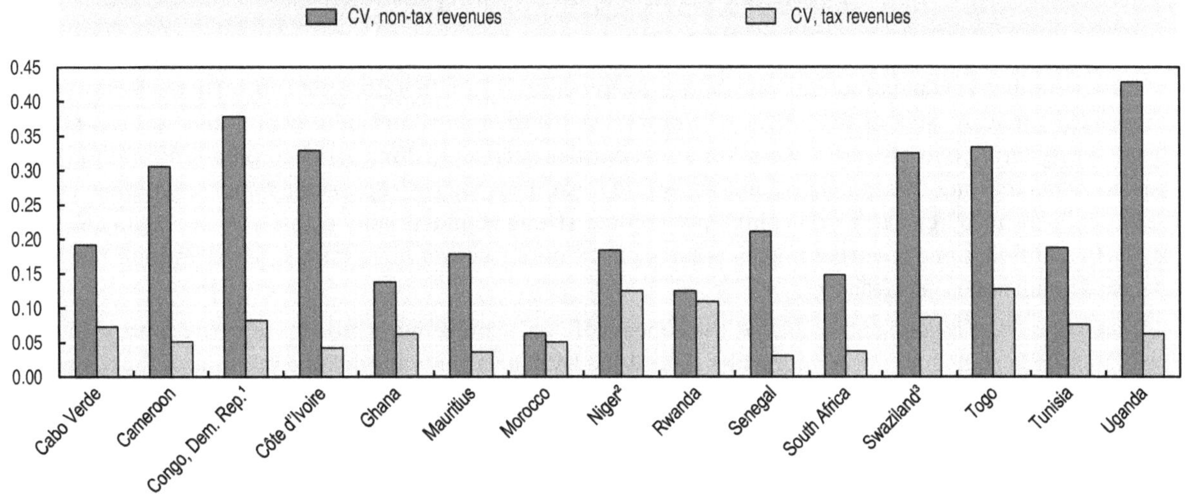

Notes: The figures include sub-national government non-tax revenues for Mauritius, Morocco and Swaziland.

1. Due to the incompleteness of data, the CV has not been calculated for Kenya and was calculated over the 2010-15 period for the Democratic Republic of the Congo.

2. The CV for Niger was calculated without using data from the year 2006 when there was a spike in grant revenue.

3. The CV for Swaziland was calculated without using data on grant revenue over the years 2006-11 when it was missing.

Source: Authors' calculations based on Table 3.1 in Chapter 3 and Table 5.1 in Chapter 5.

StatLink http://dx.doi.org/10.1787/888933568889

Non-tax revenues have been observed to change sharply from one year to the next. Over the most recent decade, twelve countries showed at least one year-over-year increase in non-tax revenue that was at least 1% of GDP and ten countries showed at least one year-over-year decrease in non-tax revenue that was at least 1% of GDP. By far the most dramatic spike in non-tax revenues occurred in 2006 for Niger, when non-tax revenues went from 8.2% of GDP in 2005 to 47.9% in 2017 and then back down to 8.0% the subsequent year. This spike was due to a large debt write-down in 2006 (see the section on grants, below).

Box 1.4. **Non-tax revenues, data quality issues**

Non-tax revenues are not always included within revenue statistics publications. Part of the reason for this is that it is often more difficult to obtain and vet non-tax revenue data than tax revenue data, and harder to integrate them into a harmonised dataset.

Data on non-tax revenues are not as readily available as tax revenue data, since they don't tend to appear on standard government budget documents or public datasets, and aren't always under the responsibility of the custodians of tax statistics.

When non-tax revenue data are found, they often lack the detail found in tax data and sometimes crucial information is missing. For example, some countries have values for total non-tax revenues in some years, with no breakdown beyond grants and other non-tax revenues categories. Not only does this reduce the quality of the statistical analysis, but it also makes data verification more difficult. Since data on non-tax revenues often come from several different sources, there can be years when some subcategories of non-tax revenues are reported and others are not. For example, there can be cases where grants are reported starting in the year 2000, but property income is only reported from 2010 onwards. Cases where total non-tax revenues are reported, but may reflect incomplete coverage will be indicated where appropriate in *Revenue Statistics in Africa*.

Box 1.4. **Non-tax revenues, data quality issues** *(cont.)*

It is possible that non-tax revenue data are not subject to the same level of scrutiny as tax revenues. Many of these revenues are not part of the main budgeting process and are therefore not subject to the same types of oversight mechanisms as tax revenues. Grants, legal settlements, and mining and oil contracts often involve very large payments by powerful external entities such as multinational corporations and foreign governments that lack transparency. Some aspects of these deals may be kept secret, for example when large contracts with resource extraction companies contain strong confidentiality clauses (AfDB/OECD/UNECA, 2010). In addition, some countries negotiate large payments that cover many categories of revenue, making detailed breakdowns less feasible.

Even when there is good data available, the concept of non-tax revenue is broader than the concept of tax revenue, which could make accounting less clear. A tax liability is generally defined in terms of the national currency either before or after payment. In contrast, this is not the case for non-tax revenues which can take the form of capital transfers, which are not necessarily valued in the national currency at the time of transaction. For example, a person might donate their historic home to the government in order for it to be made into a museum. This will be a form of government revenue, but the actual numeric monetary value of this gift may not be entirely clear for budgeting purposes

1.5. Structure of non-tax revenues

Tables 1.3 and 1.4 show the contribution of each sub-category of non-tax revenue to the total non-tax revenue as percentage of GDP in 2015 for each country included in this publication.

The data in Table 1.3 are shown in Figure 1.19 in terms of the proportion of total non-tax revenue attributed to each subcategory. In this figure, revenues from interest and dividends were combined with other property income to yield a value for all property income not explicitly identified as rents and royalties. When these non-tax revenue mixes for all the countries are shown side-by-side, five distinct groups of countries are apparent:

- The Democratic Republic of the Congo, Niger, Rwanda, Senegal, Togo and Uganda all receive a majority of their non-tax revenue in the form of grants;
- Cameroon receives a majority of its non-tax revenue from rents and royalties;
- South Africa receives a majority of its non-tax revenue from property income other than rents and royalties;
- Swaziland receives 92% of its non-tax revenue from miscellaneous and unclassified non-tax revenues, which consist almost entirely of SACU revenues;
- The remaining seven countries have a more balanced revenue profile: Côte d'Ivoire receives more revenue from grants than from any other non-tax revenue category whereas Kenya and Tunisia receive the most non-tax revenue from property income other than rents and royalties and Cabo Verde, Ghana, Mauritius, and Morocco receive more revenue from sales of goods and services.

Table 1.3. **Non-tax revenues by sub-category as a percentage of GDP, 2015**

Category	Cabo Verde	Cameroon	Congo, Dem. Rep.	Côte d'Ivoire	Ghana	Kenya	Mauritius[1]	Morocco
Total non-tax revenue	7.4	4.3	4.9	3.4	6.1	1.0	2.7	3.9
Grants	2.5	0.1	3.4	1.5	1.9	0.3	0.5	0.0
Property income	0.6	2.8	0.9	1.5	1.9	0.3	1.1	0.9
Rents and royalties	..	2.7	0.8	1.3	0.7	0.0	0.2	0.5
Interest and dividends	..	0.1	0.1	0.2	1.2	0.2	0.2	0.4
Other property income	..	0.0	0.0	0.0	0.0	0.1	0.7	0.0
Sales of good and services	2.9	1.1	0.5	0.2	2.3	0.2	1.0	1.6
Fines, penalties and forfeits	0.3	0.2	0.1	0.0	0.0	0.0	0.1	0.3
Miscellaneous and unidentified revenue[2]	1.1	0.1	0.0	0.3	0.0	0.2	0.1	1.1
Total tax revenue	*19.2*	*16.4*	*10.8*	*17.6*	*15.0*	*18.4*	*19.9*	*26.1*
Total sum of tax and non-tax revenue	*26.6*	*20.7*	*15.7*	*21.0*	*21.2*	*19.4*	*22.6*	*30.0*
Country	Niger	Rwanda[3]	Senegal	South Africa	Swaziland	Togo	Tunisia	Uganda[3]
Total non-tax revenue	7.6	8.9	4.6	0.6	15.1	4.1	2.1	1.8
Grants	5.5	6.3	2.9	0.0	0.2	2.3	0.3	1.4
Property income	1.0	..	1.1	0.4	0.8	1.0	1.0	..
Rents and royalties	0.8	..	0.4	0.1	0.0	0.2	0.4	..
Interest and dividends	0.2	..	0.6	0.2	0.7	0.9	0.6	..
Other property income	0.0	..	0.0	0.1	0.1	0.0	0.0	..
Sales of good and services	0.9	..	0.0	0.1	0.1	0.3	0.0	0.0
Fines, penalties and forfeits	0.2	..	0.3	0.0	0.1	0.0	0.4	..
Miscellaneous and unidentified revenue[2]	0.2	2.6	0.3	0.0	13.9	0.5	0.2	0.3
Total tax revenue	*17.0*	*16.7*	*20.8*	*29.0*	*15.3*	*21.3*	*30.3*	*12.5*
Total sum of tax and non-tax revenue	*24.6*	*25.6*	*25.4*	*29.6*	*30.4*	*25.4*	*32.3*	*14.2*

Notes: ".." indicates that the data are incomplete for the country in the particular year.

The figures include sub-national government non-tax revenues for Mauritius, Morocco, and Swaziland.

1. Data for 2015 are estimated.
2. Including capital transfers not elsewhere classified and voluntary transfers other than grants.
3. Non-tax revenues aside from grants were not disaggregated in the data, and are therefore classified as miscellaneous and unidentified revenues.

Source: Table 5.2 in Chapter 5.

StatLink http://dx.doi.org/10.1787/888933569934

Figure 1.19. **Non-tax revenue mix, 2015**

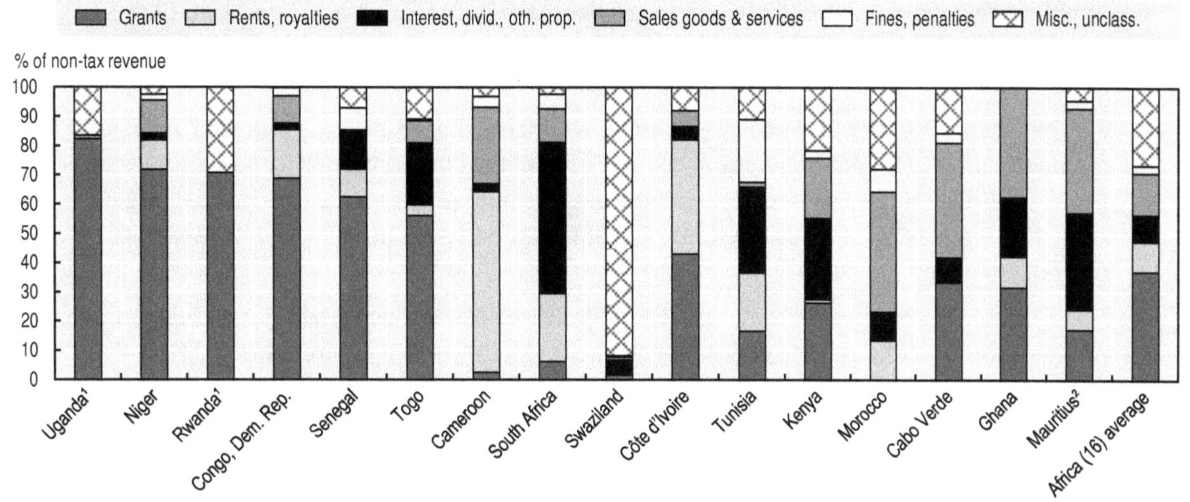

Notes: The figures include sub-national government non-tax revenues for Mauritius, Morocco and Swaziland.

1. Non-tax revenues aside from grants were not disaggregated in the data, and are therefore classified as miscellaneous and unidentified revenues.
2. Data for 2015 are estimated.

Source: Table 5.2 in Chapter 5.

StatLink http://dx.doi.org/10.1787/888933568908

Grants

There was enormous variation in the amount of grants received by countries in Africa in 2015 (Figure 1.20), ranging from negligible or none reported (Cameroon, Morocco and South Africa) to Niger and Rwanda, where grants made up over 5% of GDP.

Figure 1.20. **Grants as a percentage of GDP, 2015**

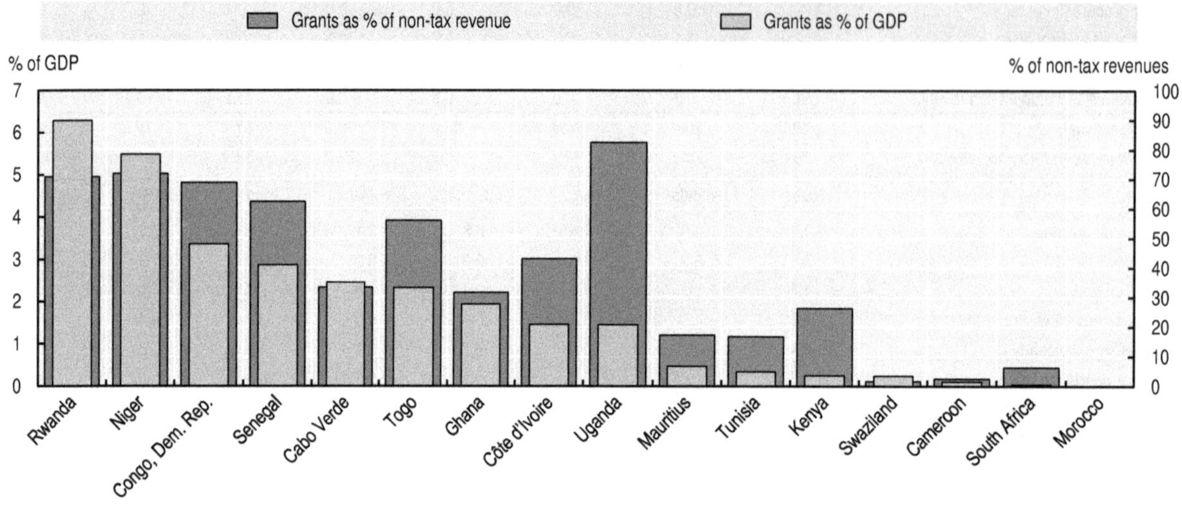

Source: Tables 5.2 and 5.3 in Chapter 5.

StatLink http://dx.doi.org/10.1787/888933568927

Countries in Africa with higher GDP per capita tended to receive less grants as a percentage of GDP than those with lower GDP per capita (Figure 1.21). This can be attributed both to the effect of a larger denominator in the non-tax revenue to GDP ratio for higher-income countries, but may also be because a country with a higher income does not tend to provide as strong a justification for international assistance. On the other hand, the converse is not necessarily true. Countries with low GDP per capita receive higher or lower amounts of grants depending on individual circumstances. Among the four countries with GDP per capita between 1 200 and 1 500 USD, for example, the reported grants as percentage of GDP in 2015 ranged from 0.1% of GDP for Cameroon to 1.9% of GDP for Ghana.

Between 2000 and 2015, there were five countries that in at least one year received grants in excess of 5% of GDP. A look at the variation in the grant revenues for these countries (Figure 1.22) shows the high variability of the grant revenues these countries faced. The 2006 debt write-off for Niger stands out in particular here, which was almost entirely responsible for the large grants in 2006.

One major source of international assistance to African governments is debt relief programmes such as the Heavily-Indebted Poor Countries (HIPC) programme. This was launched in 1996 by the IMF and the World Bank as a successor to the Multilateral Debt Relief Initiative (MDRI) and aimed to remove debt burdens from lower income countries facing significant debt distress. Of the 39 countries deemed eligible for this programme, 33 were sub-Saharan countries. There were nine *Revenue Statistics in Africa* countries (Cameroon, Côte d'Ivoire, the Democratic Republic of the Congo, Ghana, Niger, Rwanda, Senegal, Togo, and Uganda) that received debt relief for which they were eligible under HIPC and MDRI (IMF, 2016b). This has led to spikes in grant revenues in some cases.

Figure 1.21. **Grants as a percentage of GDP vs GDP per capita in USD, 2015**

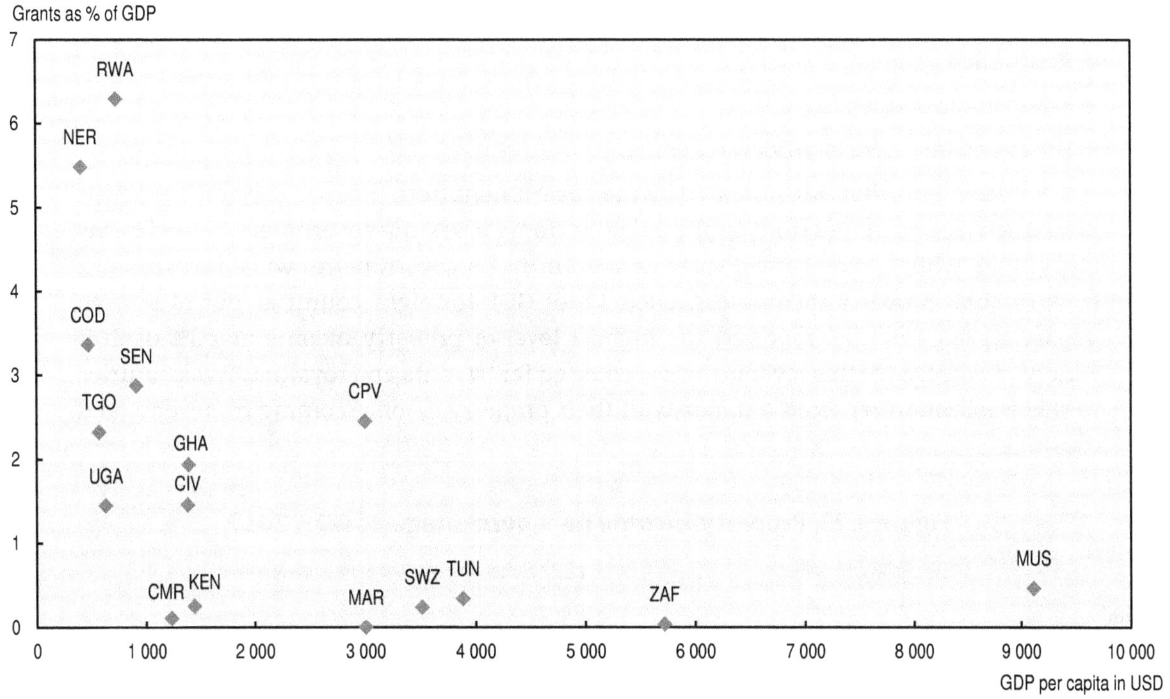

Source: Table 5.2 in Chapter 5 and IMF, *World Economic Outlook*, April 2017 for GDP per capita figures.

StatLink http://dx.doi.org/10.1787/888933568946

Figure 1.22. **Grants as a percentage of GDP, 2000-15**

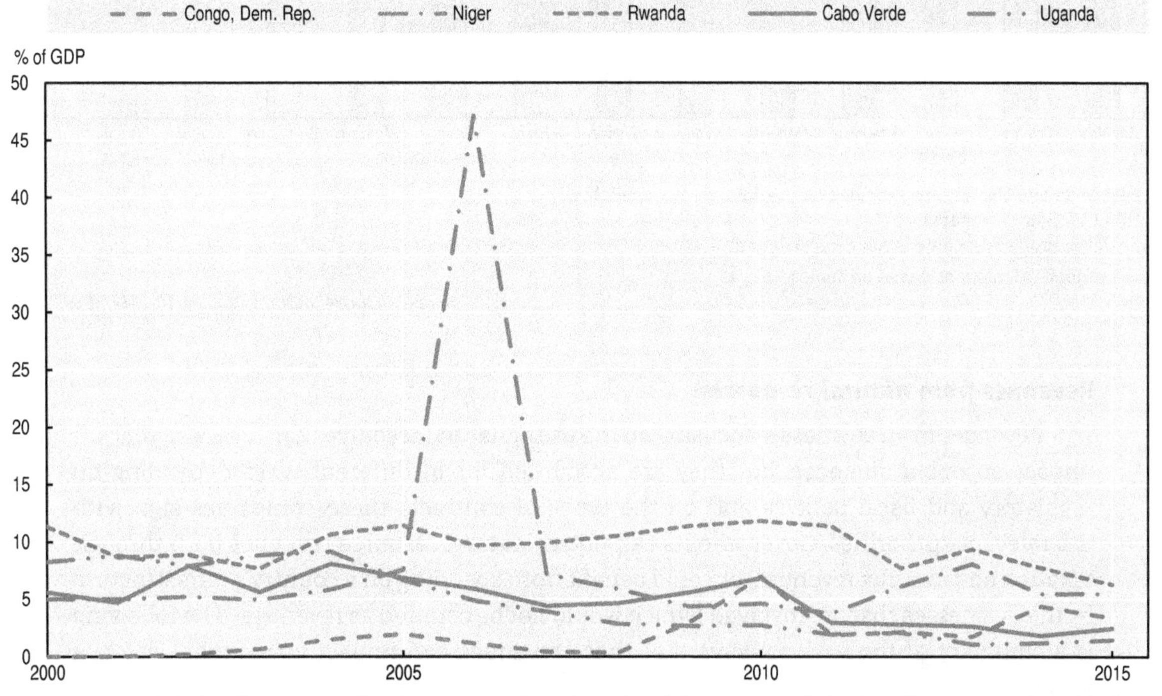

Source: Revenue Statistics in Africa comparative data on OECD/ATAF/AUC (2017), "Revenue Statistics in Africa: Comparative tables", *OECD Tax Statistics* (database), *http://dx.doi.org/10.1787/be755711-en.*

StatLink http://dx.doi.org/10.1787/888933568965

Property income revenue

Property income can be considered in three categories:

- Rents and royalties;
- Interest and dividends;
- Other and unallocable property income.

Rents and royalties are obtained by the government from prospecting and extracting non-renewable resources from public lands, or from harvesting government-owned farms and forests, while interest and dividends are returns on government-owned investments. In 2015, total property income exceeded 1% of GDP for eight countries out of sixteen (Figure 1.23). Cameroon reported the highest level of property income at 2.8% of GDP. Ninety-six percent of this revenue was accounted for by rents and royalties. Five countries in this publication reported a majority of their property income coming from rents and royalties.

Figure 1.23. **Property income as a percentage of GDP, 2015**

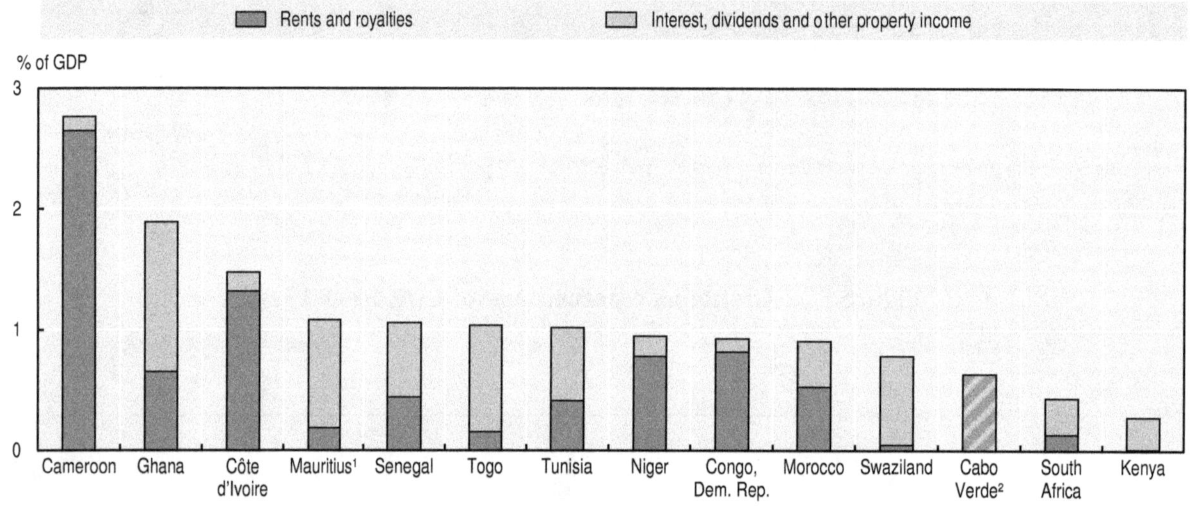

Notes: Rwanda and Uganda are excluded as the data are not available.

1. Data for 2015 are estimated.
2. Cabo Verde property income is not disaggregated.

Source: Authors' calculations based on Tables 5.5-5.12.

StatLink http://dx.doi.org/10.1787/888933568984

Revenues from natural resources

Revenues from businesses focusing on the use of natural resources can have a significant impact on public finances, but they are accounted for in different ways depending on regulatory and fiscal policies and on the types of contracts these companies sign with the relevant authorities. Governments can obtain natural resource revenues both through taxation and non-tax revenues, or could benefit from spending on a country's infrastructure by the businesses that are involved (which would not be counted as revenues). The following is a summary of the various ways that these revenues can impact government balance sheets:[12]

1. Rents and royalties are the most direct form of revenue relating to natural resource wealth. The government charges fees to companies and individuals in exchange for the

right to access government lands. It does this in its capacity as landowner, and these fees are generally decided through negotiation. These are recorded under property income.

2. Payment for services provided by the government is another source of non-tax revenue paid for by businesses in the primary sector. This can include, for example, payments for environmental inspections by government officials, or payments for the construction of infrastructure. These are recorded under sales of goods and services.
3. Ownership of a corporation, public or other, that exploits natural resources on the government's behalf results in government revenues in the form of profits and dividends. These are recorded under property income.
4. Taxes or levies can be designed to target companies or individuals who access natural resources. It may sometimes be difficult to make a distinction between a tax on companies operating on public lands, and a royalty charged to such companies.
5. Taxes targeting the activity of natural resource exploitation could be introduced such as an excise tax on the sale of materials extracted from public lands, or a tax on mining that targets the activity, rather than the individual or company exploiting natural resources. These, too, will be recorded as taxes.
6. Companies and individuals exploiting natural resources are generally subject to all the same taxes (e.g. income taxes, VATs) as the rest of the population. These general taxes will be included on government financial statements, but not necessarily attributed to sectors exploiting natural resources.
7. Companies and individuals may use some of the wealth they obtain from natural resource extraction to build infrastructure or provide services. Where this satisfies demand for public investment or services, it could result in a savings on government expenditure, but it would not be recorded as revenue. In some cases, as a condition for access to publically owned natural resources, governments may demand that companies and individuals provide certain services, for example paying for at least part of the cost of constructing and maintaining roads to mines.

The natural resource sector consists essentially of renewable resources (agriculture, forestry, fishing and hunting) and non-renewable resources (oil, natural gas, and other minerals). As seen in Figure 1.24, the natural resources available to African countries vary a great deal. On average, within the *Revenue Statistics in Africa* countries, renewable resources made up 20.8% of GDP, while mining (including gas and petroleum) amounted to 4.7% of GDP. Kenya, Niger, Rwanda, and Togo all had renewable resource industries exceeding 30% of GDP. Four countries had mining (including gas and petroleum) industries exceeding 5% of GDP (Côte d'Ivoire, the Democratic Republic of the Congo, South Africa and Tunisia) while Cameroon and Ghana had mining (including gas and petroleum) industries contributing just under 5% of GDP. Five of these countries are classified by the World Bank as "resource rich" for the purposes of their data analysis: Cameroon, Côte d'Ivoire, the Democratic Republic of the Congo, Ghana, and South Africa.

Although there are rents and royalties extracted from the renewable resource sector (timber royalties in Cameroon, for example) most rents and royalties collected by governments come from mining, especially oil royalties. Mineral resources such as oil are unequally distributed among countries. The Democratic Republic of Congo, for example, has 22% of GDP devoted to mineral extraction, making for a lucrative potential source of revenue.

Figure 1.24. **Primary industries as a percentage of GDP, most recent year**

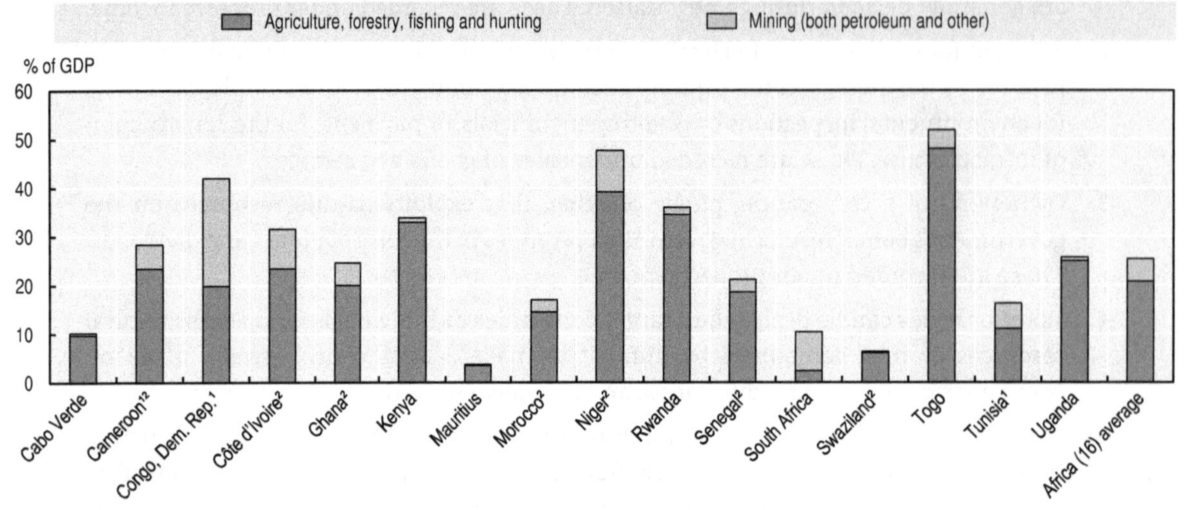

1. The only countries that reported mining broken down into petroleum and non-petroleum mining were Cameroon, the Democratic Republic of Congo, and Tunisia.

2. For Cameroon, Côte d'Ivoire, Ghana, Morocco, Niger and Senegal the reported year was 2016. For Swaziland, the reported year was 2014. For all other years, the reported year was 2015.

Source: AfDB/OECD/UNDP (2015), *African Economic Outlook*.

StatLink http://dx.doi.org/10.1787/888933569003

The World Bank has calculated estimates of the total resource rents extracted within each country.[13] Total natural resources rents are the sum of oil rents, natural gas rents, coal rents (hard and soft), mineral rents, and forest rents in both the private and public sectors. It is calculated by taking the difference between the total value of the natural resources extracted, and the cost of the extraction. Natural resources rents will be captured partly by the private companies involved in the extraction, and the governments that tax this activity or obtain royalty payments.

Figure 1.25 shows a comparison between World Bank estimates of natural resource rents and the rents and royalties reported in *Revenue Statistics in Africa*. The essential difference between the two figures is that the former includes both private and government revenue from natural resources, while the latter only reports government non-tax revenue. Necessarily, the World Bank estimate of natural resource rents will be much higher than the rents and royalties reported in the *Revenue Statistics in Africa* data. Governments of countries up and to the left of the graph are capturing a greater share of their country's natural resource wealth through rents and royalties than countries down and to the right of the graph although the amount of natural resource wealth captured by governments through ordinary taxation or other non-tax revenue is not reported on the vertical axis.

Natural resource revenues tend to be a highly volatile source of financing (Figure 1.26). Three of the Revenue Statistics in Africa countries managed to obtain rents and royalties valued at more than 1% of GDP over the past ten years, and all three of these countries saw substantial year-over-year drops in these funds. Côte d'Ivoire and the Democratic Republic of the Congo saw their rents and royalties drop to less than a quarter of their peak. Cameroon saw its rents and royalties drop to 39% of its peak value, a difference amounting to over 4% of GDP. These kinds of fluctuations can obviously have a massive impact on government financing.

Figure 1.25. **Total natural resources rents extracted vs revenue from rents and royalties collected by government as a percentage of GDP, 2015**

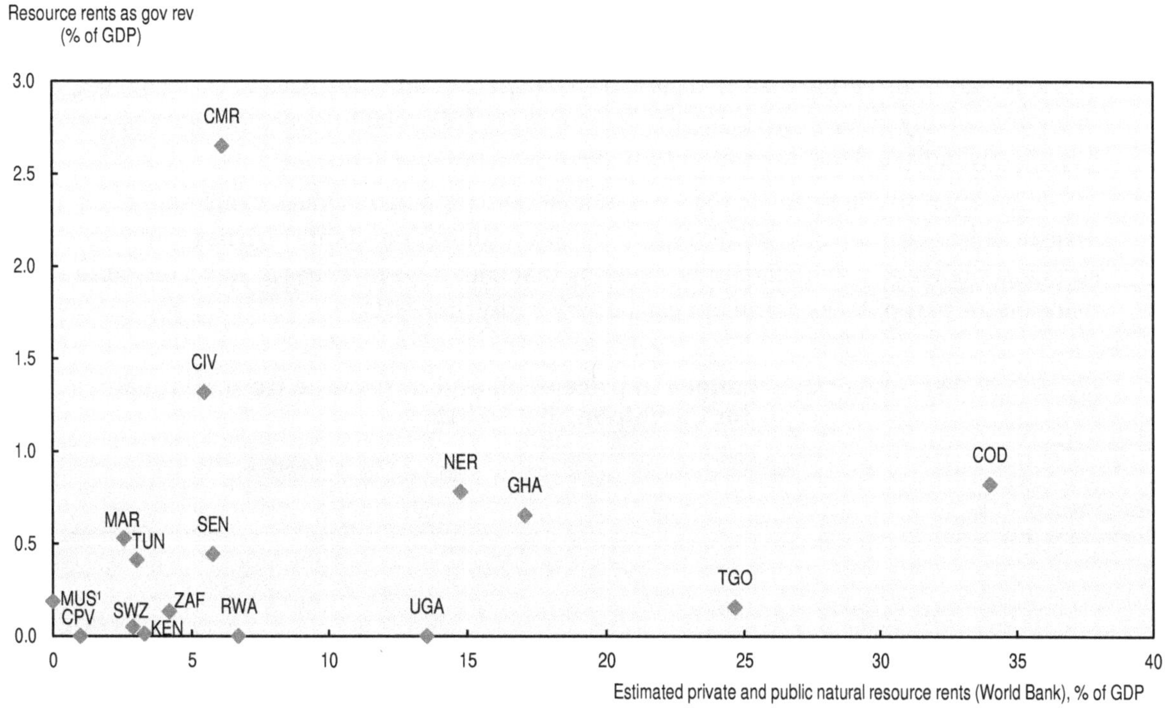

Notes: No data on rents and royalties were reported for Cabo Verde, Rwanda, and Uganda.

1. Data for 2015 are estimated.

Source: Table 5.1 in Chapter 5 for data on resource rents collected as government revenue and World Bank, *World Development Indicators* for natural resource rents (accessed 3 July 2017).

StatLink http://dx.doi.org/10.1787/888933569022

Figure 1.26. **Property income as a percentage of GDP, 2006-15**

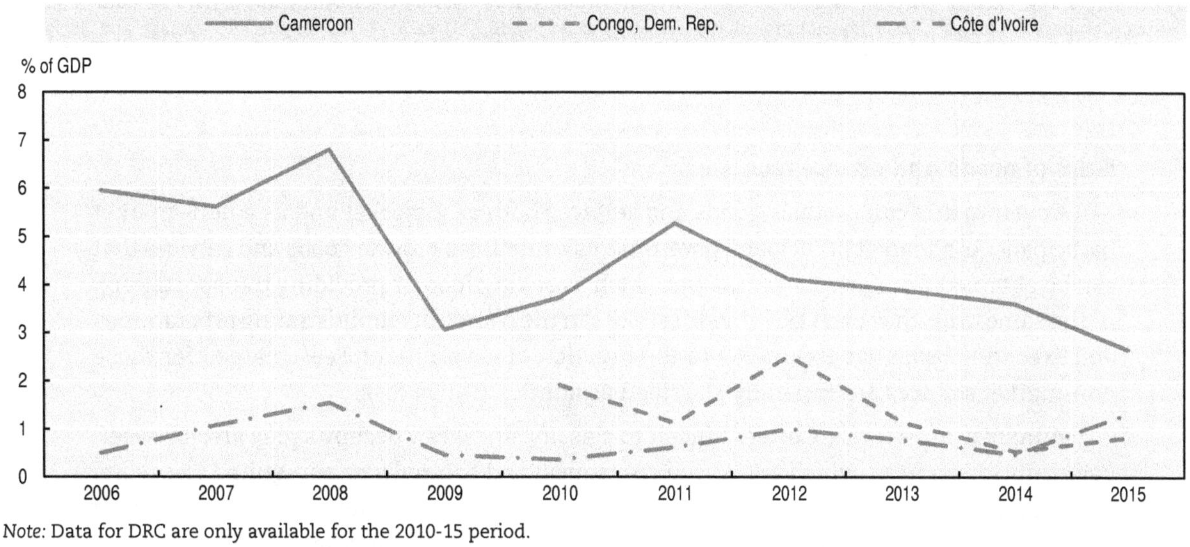

Note: Data for DRC are only available for the 2010-15 period.

Source: Revenue Statistics in Africa comparative data on OECD/ATAF/AUC (2017), "Revenue Statistics in Africa: Comparative tables", *OECD Tax Statistics* (database), *http://dx.doi.org/10.1787/be755711-en*.

StatLink http://dx.doi.org/10.1787/888933569041

A high dependence on the production of primary goods increases exposure to the impact of swings in commodity prices. For example, since 1990, the price of gold has risen as high as 35.8% over the previous year, and has plunged by as much as 15.4%. The price of oil was 57.1% higher in 2000 than it was a year earlier, while in 2009, it was 37.8% lower than the previous year. Considering that changes in oil royalties for Cameroon have tracked changes in oil prices fairly closely in recent years (Figure 1.27), this volatility in commodity prices has directly impacted the finances of the government of Cameroon.

In addition to the financial risks mentioned here, mining revenues can create other difficulties for governments. An IMF paper notes that mining projects are high risk, with high sunk costs, but high potential returns, meaning that with large revenues at stake, mistakes made on the part of the government can be very costly (IMF, 2011).

Figure 1.27. **Year-over-year changes in price of oil and in revenue from oil royalties for Cameroon, 1995-2015**

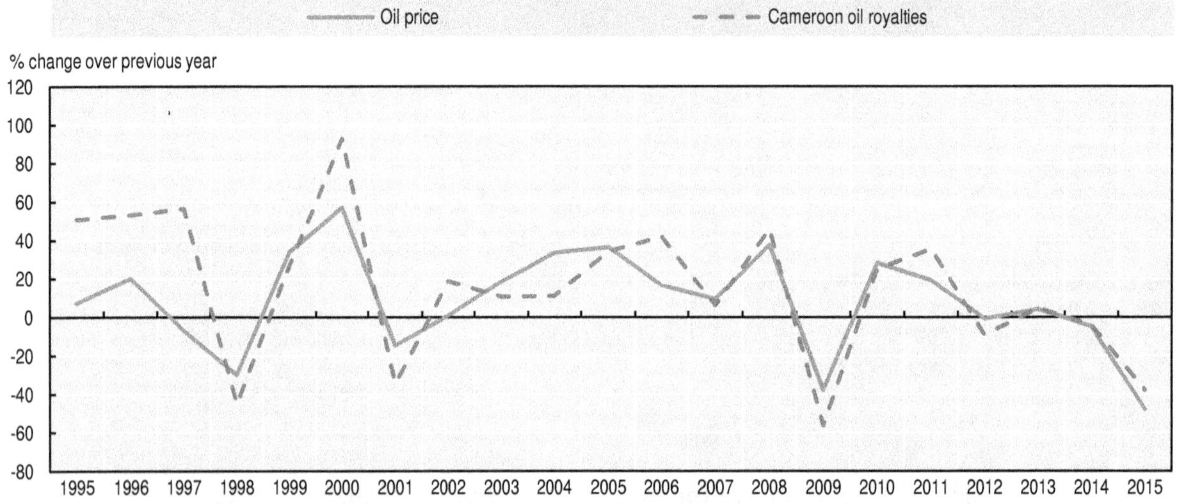

Source: Authors' calculations based on Revenue Statistics in Africa comparative data on OECD/ATAF/AUC (2017), "Revenue Statistics in Africa: Comparative tables", *OECD Tax Statistics* (database), *http://dx.doi.org/10.1787/be755711-en*, for the LAC average and Economic Research Division, Federal Reserve Bank of St. Louis for oil prices.

StatLink http://dx.doi.org/10.1787/888933569060

Sales of goods and service revenue

Governments can produce goods and services both as a market and as a non- market participant. As a market participant, governments sometimes provide goods and services that can be obtained from private companies (such as selling food or providing transportation). At the same time, they can also provide services in the course of administrating programmes and executing laws that are unique to the function of government. Fees charged for these non-market services are generally classified as administrative fees.

Administrative fees are often difficult to classify since they occupy a grey area between payments for services (which are non-tax revenues) and compulsory unrequited payments collected during government operations (which are taxes).[14] Court fees and fees for driver's licences, passports, patent registrations, and marriage certificates tend to be classified as non-tax revenues. When administrative fees are classified as taxes, they are typically assigned to one of the following categories:

- 4400 Taxes on financial and capital transactions (for example, taxes on sales of land);

- 5200 Taxes on use of goods and performing activities (for example hunting licences, vehicle registrations);
- 6000 Other taxes (for example, sales of fiscal stamps, where stamps are used to pay for taxes and administrative fees).

Five countries generated revenues from sales of goods and services and administrative fees amounting to at least 1% of GDP in 2015 (see Figure 1.28). The countries generating the most revenue were Cabo Verde (2.9% of GDP), Ghana (2.3% of GDP), and Morocco (1.6% of GDP).

Figure 1.28. **Sales of goods and services and administrative fees as a percentage of GDP and as a percentage of total revenue collected, 2015**

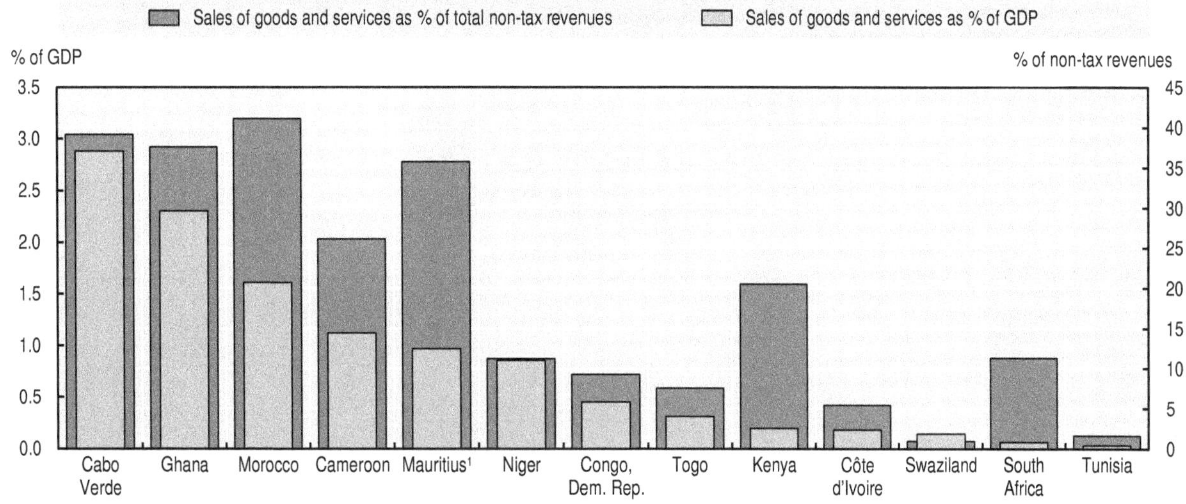

Notes: The figures include sub-national government non-tax revenues for Mauritius, Morocco and Swaziland.
Rwanda and Uganda are excluded as the data are not available for Rwanda and are incomplete for Uganda. Senegal reported no revenue from sales of goods and services.
1. Data for 2015 are estimated.
Source: Tables 5.2 and 5.3 in Chapter 5.

StatLink http://dx.doi.org/10.1787/888933569079

Morocco (41.1% of total non-tax revenues) Cabo Verde (39.1%), Ghana (37.5%), and Mauritius (35.7%) generate the largest percentage of their non-tax revenues through sales of goods and services and administrative fees. Of the other countries providing this data, the corresponding percentages range from 1.2% in Uganda to 26.1% in Cameroon.

Fifty-six percent of the revenue from government sales of goods and services are collected at the local level in Morocco. Fees made up 96% of revenues listed under sales of goods and services for Cabo Verde. In Ghana, most revenues listed as sales of goods and services were fees and charges collected by MDAs (Municipalities, Departments and Agencies) or MMDAs (Metropolitan, Municipal and District Assemblies). In Mauritius, 13% of sales of goods and services were collected at the local level and 9% by social security funds. It included a large number of different fees for various government services including route air navigation, police services, as well as receipts from the sale of a range of different products including ground water, animal feed and forest produce. Kenya did not generate high amounts of revenue through sales of goods and services, but this constituted over a fifth of their total non-tax revenue in 2015.

Fines and forfeits

Fines and forfeits can sometimes be an important source of revenue but they are subject to volatility. Some small fines, such as speeding tickets, are obtained on a regular and a predictable basis. In some countries, a percentage of these revenues are used to finance policing activities directly and are therefore not reported in the statistics.

In general, most countries in this publication had negligible revenues from fines, forfeits and penalties; however Cabo Verde, Morocco, Senegal, and Tunisia stood out as having larger revenues in this category, with a few years standing out in particular (Figure 1.29). In Tunisia, the percentage of fines and penalties to GDP rose from 0.15% to 0.97% between 2011 and 2013 and then fell back to 0.43% in 2014. In Senegal, this ratio was 0.37% of GDP in 2013 and 0.65% in 2014 compared with negligible values in the three previous years. Although fines, penalties and forfeits are not the most important source of government funding, this shows that there are occasions when actions or reforms within the civil service can have a serious impact on government finances.

Figure 1.29. **Fines, penalties and forfeits as a percentage of GDP, 2011-15**

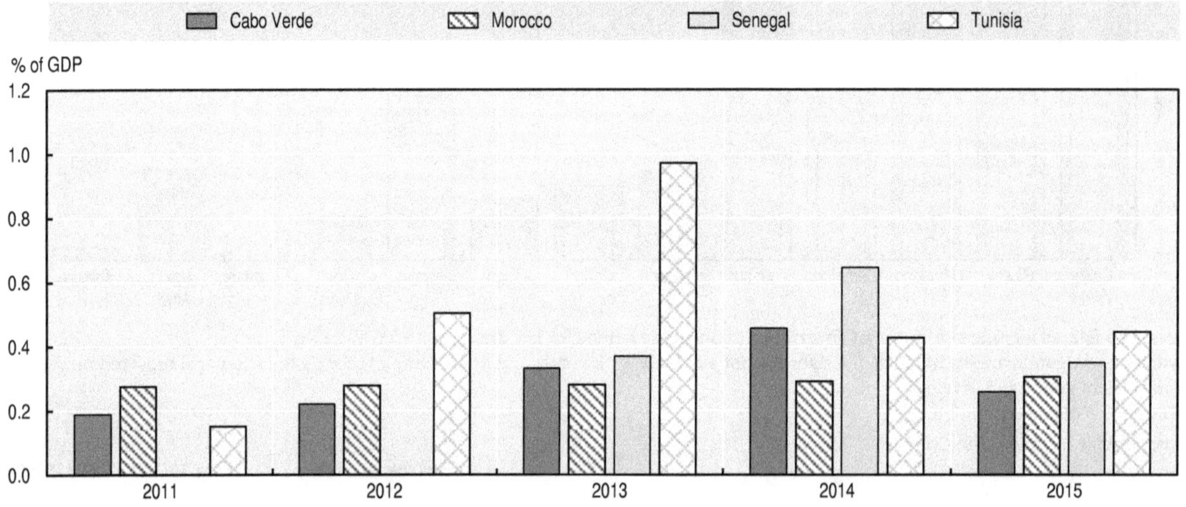

Note: The figures include sub-national government revenues for Morocco.

Source: Revenue Statistics in Africa comparative data OECD/ATAF/AUC (2017), "Revenue Statistics in Africa: Comparative tables", *OECD Tax Statistics* (database), *http://dx.doi.org/10.1787/be755711-en*.

StatLink *http://dx.doi.org/10.1787/888933569098*

Since the publication of the first edition of *Revenue Statistics in Africa*, an important change was made to the classification of fines and forfeits collected from the non-payment or late payment of taxes. In this edition, these are now classified as non-tax revenues. In previous editions, these were classified as tax revenues under the classification of the tax for which the penalty was incurred (see Annex A and Annex B for more explanations).

The effect of this change on the reported revenues between the first and second edition of *Revenue Statistics in Africa* has turned out to be negligible. This may partly be due to the fact that this classification change has no effect on penalties for late or non-payment of taxes that cannot be disaggregated from other tax revenues.

Miscellaneous or unidentified revenue

There are some notable categories of non-tax revenue that do not fit in with any of the categories listed above. These include:

1. Capital transfers not included elsewhere;
2. Voluntary donations to government agencies from individuals or corporations (not including donations from international organisations such as the IMF, which are classified as grants);
3. Insurance claims paid to government agencies;
4. Payments covering different categories in the classification list where a breakdown is not available;
5. Payments whose proper classification is unknown due to a lack of data. Rwanda and Uganda did not disaggregate non-tax revenue outside of grants, and so these were included in this category;
6. SACU revenues to Swaziland.

These revenues can be a significant component of non-tax revenues in specific years (Figure 1.30). In 2014, for example, 45% of the non-tax revenues in Côte d'Ivoire were classified in this category. Other revenues that were under this heading include exceptional voluntary contributions to government in Tunisia, capital transfers from special statutory funds in Mauritius, and, in Morocco, payments made to government in exchange for the right to compete with state institutions in the provision of services. SACU revenues, classified as "miscellaneous and unidentified" are over 90% of all Swazi revenues for most years.

Figure 1.30. **The year between 2011 and 2015 when miscellaneous and unidentified revenue was highest, as a percentage of total non-tax revenue**

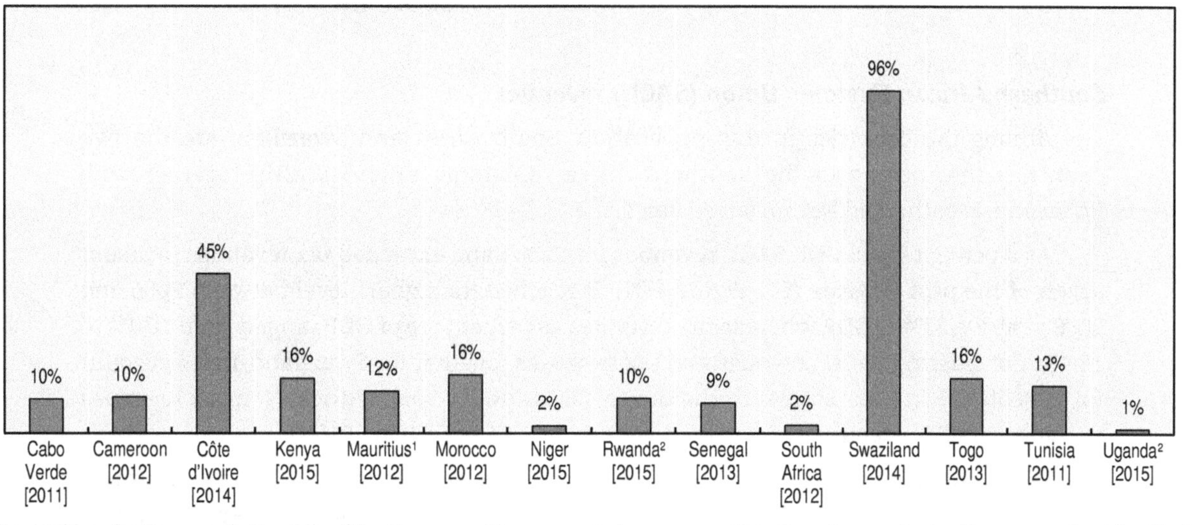

Note: Neither the Democratic Republic of the Congo nor Ghana reported revenues within the category of miscellaneous and unidentified revenues between 2011 and 2015.

1. Data for 2015 are estimated.

2. Data for property income, sales of goods and services and fines, penalties and forfeits are included in miscellaneous and unidentified revenue. These data could not be disaggregated to allocate revenue to the relevant non-tax revenue categories.

Sources: Revenue Statistics in Africa comparative data on OECD/ATAF/AUC (2017), "Revenue Statistics in Africa: Comparative tables", OECD *Tax Statistics* (database), *http://dx.doi.org/10.1787/be755711-en*; authors' calculations based on Tables 5.5 and 5.12.

StatLink http://dx.doi.org/10.1787/888933569117

Levels of miscellaneous and unidentified revenue are generally variable, with periodic spikes (Figure 1.31). This could be due to large capital transfers, revenue streams that are short-lived, or funds that are reclassified as unidentified due to lack of information. Insufficient data are available for a proper analysis of this category, but the incidence of higher values for this category could reflect a greater degree of uncertainty as to the true amount of revenue within the other non-tax revenue classifications.

Figure 1.31. **Miscellaneous and unidentified revenue as a percentage of total non-tax revenue, 2000-15**

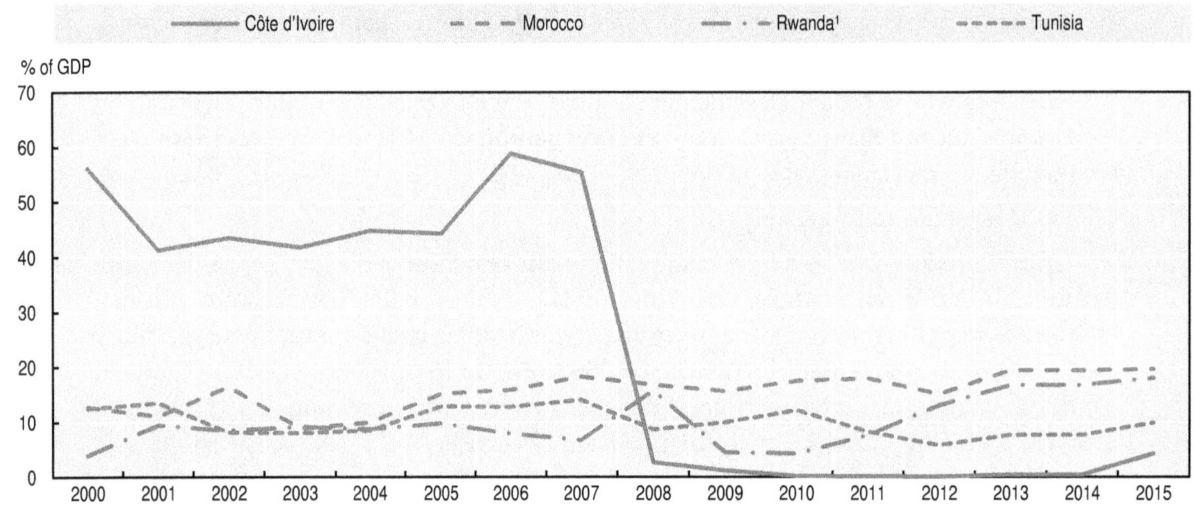

1. Data for property income, sales of goods and services and fines, penalties and forfeits are included in miscellaneous and unidentified revenue. These data could not be disaggregated to allocate revenue to the relevant non-tax revenue categories.

Source: Authors' calculations based on Tables 5.5-5.12.

StatLink http://dx.doi.org/10.1787/888933569136

Southern African Customs Union (SACU) revenues

Among the countries in this publication, South Africa and Swaziland are the two countries that belong to the Southern African Customs Union (SACU), together with Botswana, Lesotho and Namibia (see Box 1.5).

As a percentage of GDP, SACU revenues for Swaziland exceeded tax revenues in all but seven of the past 20 years (See Figure 1.32). It reached its highest level between 2006 and 2008 at above 20% of GDP, whereas tax revenues as percentage of GDP ranged from 10.4% to 15.4%. Considering SACU revenues and tax revenues together for Swaziland, these account for 29% of GDP in 2015, similar to the tax-to-GDP ratio for South Africa. Non-tax revenues excluding SACU revenues in Swaziland were only 1.3% of GDP in 2015.

When comparing South Africa and Swaziland, the treatment of SACU revenues must be considered with care. Both countries contribute to the SACU pool and receive a revenue share determined by the same funding formula. However Swaziland is a net recipient of the SACU pool and SACU revenues are accounted in the non-tax revenues whereas South Africa is the only country whose payments into the SACU pool exceed its level of receipts from the pool (see Box 1.5 for more details).

Figure 1.32. **Tax, non-tax revenues and SACU revenues in South Africa and Swaziland as a percentage of GDP, 2015**

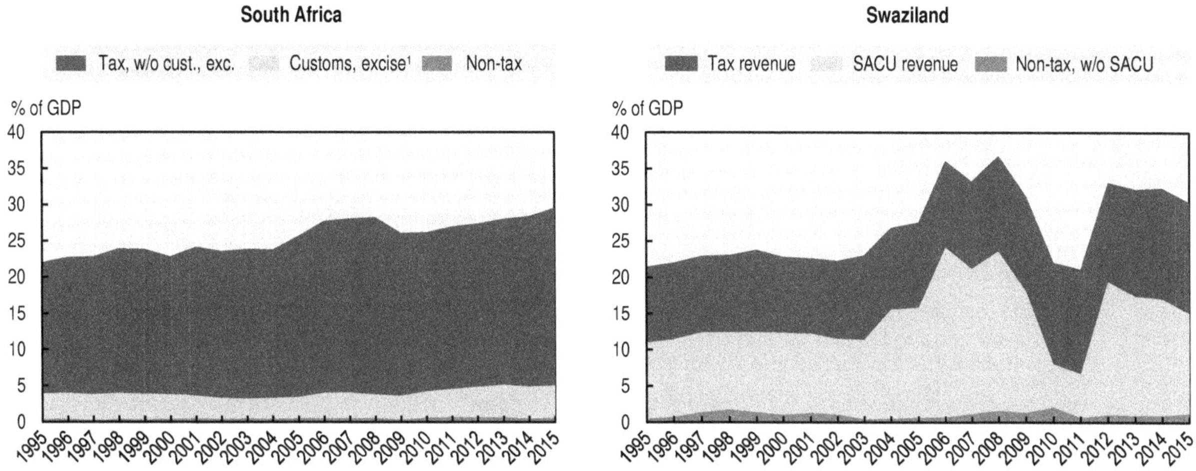

1. Customs and Excises as percentage of GDP includes Southern African Customs Union (SACU) payments made by South Africa to other SACU partner countries, which is not considered revenue under OECD definitions. Payments made to the SACU pool represent around 1% of GDP in South Africa.

Source: Revenue Statistics in Africa comparative data on OECD/ATAF/AUC (2017), "Revenue Statistics in Africa: Comparative tables", *OECD Tax Statistics* (database), *http://dx.doi.org/10.1787/be755711-en*.

StatLink http://dx.doi.org/10.1787/888933569155

Box 1.5. **SACU Revenue**

The Southern African Customs Union (SACU) encompasses Botswana, Lesotho, Namibia, South Africa and Swaziland, and is headquartered in Windhoek, Namibia. Its vision is "an economic community with equitable and sustainable development, dedicated to the welfare of its people for a common future".

SACU is the oldest customs union in the world, having been founded initially in 1899 between the British colony of Cape of Good Hope and the Orange Free State Boer Republic. Subsequent agreements in 1910 and 1969 included Botswana, Lesotho and Swaziland. Following Namibia's independence in 1990 and the end of apartheid in South Africa in 1994, new negotiations led to the current SACU agreement, which was signed in 2002.

The SACU agreement provides for free movement of SACU manufactured products within the union, without tariffs or duties being applicable. It also provides for common external tariffs and for the payment of customs and excise duties into a common pool to be shared between the SACU countries under the revenue sharing formula set out in the Annex to the agreement.

The revenue sharing agreement includes three components:

- The customs component, which divides the gross amount of customs duties according to the value of goods each country imports from other SACU countries in a given year (as a percentage of intra SACU imports);
- The excise component, which divides the gross amount of excise duties according to each country's GDP as percentage of total SACU GDP; and
- The development component, which is funded from 15% of the excise component and is weighted toward less developed SACU countries using a formula based on GDP per capita.

In this publication, revenue from excises, tariffs, and customs duties are included as tax revenues in the country that collected the revenue. They are included under headings 5121 (Excises) and 5123 (Customs and import duties) in the tax revenue tables. Revenues received from the SACU pool are included as miscellaneous revenue in the non-tax revenue tables, as seen in Table 5.17 for Swaziland. In the case of South Africa, where payments exceed the revenue share received from the SACU pool, the payments net of the share received are recorded as a memorandum item in the non-tax revenue table (Table 5.16).

Sources: SACU (2017), SACU (2014).

Notes

1. The data for social security contributions are not available for the Democratic Republic of the Congo, Ghana (prior to 2008), Togo and Uganda and are incomplete for Cameroon (social security contributions include only pensions contributions), Kenya (but are deemed to be negligible) and for Senegal (figures include social security contributions from the Institution de Prévoyance Retraites du Sénégal (IPRES) but exclude data from the Caisse de Sécurité Sociale (CSS) as they are not available).
2. Value-added tax.
3. Change between 2000 and 2014 as data for 2015 are not available.
4. The Africa (16) average for social security contributions as a percentage of GDP should be interpreted with caution due to the unavailability and incompleteness of social security contributions data in some African countries in this publication.
5. Agriculture here refers to the definition of Agriculture used in World Bank national accounts data, which corresponds to ISIC divisions 1-5. See documentation of World Bank online datasets for more details. *http://data.worldbank.org/indicator/NV.AGR.TOTL.ZS*
6. A country is considered rich in hydrocarbons and/or mineral resources if it meets either of the following criteria: (i) an average share of hydrocarbon and/or mineral fiscal revenues in total fiscal revenue of at least 25% during the period 2000-05 or (ii) an average share of hydrocarbon and/or mineral export proceeds in total export proceeds of at least 25% (IMF, 2007).
7. The data for social security contributions are unavailable for Ghana (prior to 2008), the Democratic Republic of the Congo, Togo and Uganda and are incomplete for Kenya (but are deemed to be negligible) and for Senegal (figures include social security contributions from the Institution de Prévoyance Retraites du Sénégal (IPRES) and exclude the data from the Caisse de Sécurité Sociale (CSS) as they are not available).
8. The data from Mauritius were derived from financial statements produced by Statistics Mauritius.
9. This figure probably includes other revenues such as fees for utilities services or for other public services such as road tolls that are not classified as tax revenue in this publication.
10. Please see the Interpretative Guide to non-tax revenue in Annex B of this report for the definitions of these revenue categories.
11. The coefficient of variation is a standard measure of dispersion representing the ratio of the standard deviation over the mean.
12. Mansour and Rota-Graziosi (2013) note that taxes on oil extraction can include corporate income tax, excise taxes on energy products, un-refunded sales taxes such as VATs and non-tax revenue can include royalties, profit sharing, dividends received from state enterprises, and dividends and other investment income received from government direct participation in extractive enterprises.
13. Data and methodology can be found at the World Bank World Development Indicators website at *http://data.worldbank.org/indicator/NY.GDP.TOTL.RT.ZS*. The calculation of natural resource rents is based on sources and methods described in "*The Changing Wealth of Nations: Measuring Sustainable Development in the New Millennium*" (World Bank, 2011).
14. See paragraphs 9-13 of the OECD Interpretive Guide in Annex A for an explanation of how administrative fees are classified in this publication.

References

Addison, T. and J. Levin (2012), *The Determinants of Tax Revenue in Sub-Saharan Africa*, Swedish Business School at Örebro University, Örebro, Sweden, *http://oru.diva-portal.org/smash/record.jsf?pid=diva2%3A570456&dswid=4207*.

AfDB (2010), *Domestic Resource Mobilization for Poverty Reduction in East Africa: Rwanda case study*, African Development Bank, Abidjan, *www.afdb.org/fileadmin/uploads/afdb/Documents/Project-and-Operations/Rwanda%20case%20study%20paper%20final.pdf*.

AfDB/OECD/UNDP (2017), *African Economic Outlook 2017: Entrepreneurship and Industrialisation*, OECD Publishing, Paris, *http://dx.doi.org/10.1787/aeo-2017-en*.

AfDB/OECD/UNDP (2015), *African Economic Outlook 2015: Regional Development and Spatial Inclusion*, OECD Publishing, Paris, *http://dx.doi.org/10.1787/aeo-2015-en*.

AfDB/OECD/UNECA (2010), *African Economic Outlook 2010: Domestic Resource Mobilisation and Aid*, OECD Publishing, Paris, *http://dx.doi.org/10.1787/aeo-2010-en*.

Boisard, S., C. de Freitas and G. Hidouci (2014), *Renforcer les recettes fiscales locales pour financer le développement urbain en Afrique*, Fonds Mondial pour le Développement des Villes (FMDV), Paris, *http://delog.org/web/wp-content/uploads/2016/03/Etude-FMDV-Fiscalite%CC%81-locale-Villes-Afrique-8-Cas.pdf*.

EPS PEAKS (2013), "Taxation and Developing Countries", Overseas Development Institute training notes, London, *www.odi.org/sites/odi.org.uk/files/odi-assets/events-documents/5045.pdf*.

Fjeldstad, O-H., G. Chambas and J-F. Brun (2014), "Local government taxation in Sub-Saharan Africa: a review and an agenda for research", *CMI Working Paper*, WP 2014: 2, Chr. Michelsen Institute, Bergen, *www.cmi.no/publications/file/5098-local-government-taxation-in-sub-saharan-africa.pdf*.

Fossat, P. and M. Bua (2013), "Tax administration reform in the francophone countries of sub-Saharan Africa", *IMF Working Paper*, WP/13/173, International Monetary Fund, Washington, DC, *www.imf.org/external/pubs/ft/wp/2013/wp13173.pdf*.

IMF (2017), *World Economic Outlook*, International Monetary Fund, Washington, DC. *www.imf.org/en/Publications/WEO/Issues/2017/04/04/world-economic-outlook-april-2017*.

IMF (2016a), "2016 article IV consultation—press release; staff report; and statement by the executive director for Cabo Verde", *IMF Country report*, No. 16/366, International Monetary Fund, Washington, DC, September, *www.imf.org/external/pubs/ft/scr/2016/cr16366.pdf*.

IMF (2016b), "Heavily indebted poor countries (HIPC) initiative and multilateral debt relief initiative (MDRI): Statistical update", *IMF Policy Papers*, International Monetary Fund, Washington, DC, *www.imf.org/en/Publications/Policy-Papers/Issues/2016/12/31/Heavily-Indebted-Poor-Countries-Initiative-and-Multilateral-Debt-Relief-Initiative-PP5024*.

IMF (2014a), "Cameroon: 2014 article IV consultation", *IMF Country Report*, No. 14/212, International Monetary Fund, Washington, DC, July, *www.imf.org/external/pubs/ft/scr/2014/cr14212.pdf*.

IMF (2014b), "Mauritius: 2014 article IV consultation-staff report", *IMF Country Report*, No. 14/107, International Monetary Fund, Washington, DC, May, *www.imf.org/external/pubs/ft/scr/2014/cr14107.pdf*.

IMF (2013), "Côte d'Ivoire: 2013 article IV consultation and fourth review under the extended credit facility arrangement," *IMF Country Report*, No. 13/367, International Monetary Fund, Washington, DC, December, *www.imf.org/external/pubs/ft/scr/2013/cr13367.pdf*.

IMF (2011), *Revenue Mobilization in Developing Countries*, International Monetary Fund, Washington, DC, *www.imf.org/external/np/pp/eng/2011/030811.pdf*.

IMF (2007), *Guide on Resource Revenue Transparency*, International Monetary Fund, Washington, DC, *www.imf.org/external/np/pp/2007/eng/051507g.pdf*.

IMF (2001), "Democratic Republic of Congo: Selected issues and statistical appendix", *IMF Country Report*, No. 01/123, International Monetary Fund, Washington, DC, July, *www.imf.org/external/pubs/ft/scr/2001/cr01123.pdf*.

Kloeden, D. (2011), "Revenue administration reforms in anglophone Africa since the early 1990s", *IMF Working Paper*, WP/11/162, International Monetary Fund, Washington, DC, *www.imf.org/external/pubs/ft/wp/2011/wp11162.pdf*.

Mansour M. and G. Rota-Graziosi (2013), "Tax coordination, tax competition, and revenue mobilization in the West African Economic and Monetary Union", *IMF Working Paper*, WP/13/163, International Monetary Fund, Washington, DC, *www.imf.org/external/pubs/ft/wp/2013/wp13163.pdf*.

Monkam, N. and M. Moore (2015), *How Property Tax Would Benefit Africa*, Africa Research Institute, London, UK, *www.africaresearchinstitute.org/publications/property-tax-benefit-africa*.

National Treasury (2015), *Budget Review 2015*, *Budget Review 2015*, Pretoria, South Africa *www.treasury.gov.za/documents/national%20budget/2015/review/FullReview.pdf*.

NGRI (2015), "An analysis of Ghana's 2015 oil revenue performance: Testing the model", Natural Resource Governance Institute, *https://resourcegovernance.org/blog/analysis-ghanas-2015-oil-revenue-performance-testing-model*.

OECD (2016), *Revenue Statistics 2016*, OECD Publishing, Paris, *http://dx.doi.org/10.1787/rev_stats-2016-en-fr*.

OECD (2014), *Development Co-operation Report 2014: Mobilising Resources for Sustainable Development*, OECD Publishing, Paris, *http://dx.doi.org/10.1787/dcr-2014-en*.

OECD/ATAF/AUC (2017), "Revenue Statistics in Africa: Comparative tables", *OECD Tax Statistics* (database), OECD Publishing, Paris, *http://dx.doi.org/10.1787/be755711-en.*

OECD/ECLAC/CIAT/IDB, (2017), *Revenue Statistics in Latin America and the Caribbean 2017*, OECD Publishing, Paris, *http://dx.doi.org/10.1787/rev_lat_car-2017-en-fr.*

OPM (2013), *The Impact of Mining in the Democratic Republic of Congo*, Oxford Policy Management, *www.opml.co.uk/sites/default/files/DRC%20mining%20report%20-%20OPM%20-%20Final%20Eng.pdf.*

Profeta, P. and S. Scabrosetti (2010), *The Political Economy of Taxation: Lessons from Developing Countries*, Edward Elgar Publishing, *https://books.google.fr/books?isbn=1849805490.*

SACU (2017), *Southern African Customs Union Agreement 2002 (As amended on 12 April 2013)*, downloaded from SACU website: *www.sacu.int/list.php?type=Agreements*

SACU (2014), *Implementing a Common Agenda Towards Regional Integration: 2014 Annual Report*, 2002 Southern African Customs Union, *www.sacu.int/docs/reports_annual/2014/annual_report.pdf.*

Sokeechand, K.R. and G. Hussen (2013), "The Mauritian experience", presentation prepared for regional workshop on "Effectiveness of and alternatives to tax incentives as instruments to generate employment and attract investments in Lusaka", 12-13 February, Zambia, International Tax Compact, *www.taxcompact.net/documents/workshop-lusaka/2013-02-13_itc_Rambaksh-Sokeechand_MRA-MoF-Mauritius.pdf.*

SSA (2015), *Social Security Through the World: Africa, 2015*, SSA Publication, No. 13-11802, Social Security Administration, Washington, DC, *www.ssa.gov/policy/docs/progdesc/ssptw/2014-2015/africa/ssptw15africa.pdf.*

UNDP (2013), *Rapport national sur le développement humain 2013: Emploi, changements structurels et développement humain en Côte d'Ivoire*, United Nations Development Programme, New York, *www.ci.undp.org/content/cote_divoire/fr/home/library/poverty/rndh_2013.html.*

WHO (2015), "Purchasing Power Parity 2005", World Health Organization, *www.who.int/choice/costs/ppp/en/.*

World Bank (2015), « Note d'orientation du financement des collectivités locales », World Bank, Washington, DC, *www-wds.worldbank.org/external/default/WDSContentServer/WDSP/IB/2015/10/13/090224b0831405d5/2_0/Rendered/PDF/Note0d0orienta0ollectivites0locales.pdf.*

Further reading

AfDB (2010), *Sénégal : Évaluation du potentiel de recettes publiques*, African Development Bank, *www.afdb.org/fileadmin/uploads/afdb/Documents/Project-and-Operations/Pages%20from%20SENEGAL_%20Evaluation%20du%20potentiel%20des%20recettes%20publiques%20Eng.pdf.*

AfDB/OECD/UNDP (2014), *African Economic Outlook 2014: Global Value Chains and Africa's Industrialisation*, OECD Publishing, Paris, *http://dx.doi.org/10.1787/aeo-2014-en.*

Besley, T. and T. Persson (2013), "Taxation and development", (Chapter prepared for *Handbook of Public Economics*, edited by Auerbach, A., R. Chetty,M. Feldstein and E. Saez), econ.lse.ac.uk/staff/tbesley/papers/TaxationAndDevelopment.pdf.

Bird, R. and E. Zolt (2003), *Introduction to Tax Policy Design and Development*, draft module prepared for a course on Practical Issues of Tax Policy in Developing Countries, World Bank, 28 April-1 May, *www1.worldbank.org/publicsector/LearningProgram/PracticalIssues/papers/introduction%20to%20tax%20policy/WBI%20Module%201(Bird&Zolt)April10.doc.*

Cruce, F. (2011), "Evaluating value added tax in Morocco," *Minor Field Study Series*, No. 209, Department of Economics at the University of Lund, Lund, *https://liveatlund.lu.se/intranets/LUSEM/NEK/mfs/MFS/209.pdf.*

IMF (2015a), *Current Challenges in Revenue Mobilization: Improving Tax Compliance*, International Monetary Fund, Washington, DC, *www.imf.org/external/np/pp/eng/2015/020215a.pdf.*

IMF (2015b), "Debt relief under the heavily indebted poor countries (HIPC) initiative", *International Monetary Fund Factsheet*, Washington, DC, September, *www.imf.org/external/np/exr/facts/hipc.htm.*

IMF (2014), *Government Finance Statistics Manual 2014*, International Monetary Fund, Washington, DC, *www.imf.org/external/Pubs/FT/GFS/Manual/2014/gfsfinal.pdf.*

IMF (2010), "Tunisia: Preliminary conclusions of the 2000 article IV mission", International Monetary Fund, Washington, DC, *www.imf.org/external/np/ms/2010/061510a.htm*, (accessed January 7, 2015).

ISSA (2014), *Africa: Strategic Approaches to Improve Social Security*, International Social Security Association, Geneva, *www.issa.int/details?uuid=3c1e0654-a158-48db-a5dc-892b36b78ae3*.

John, J.D. (2009), "Taxation, governance and resource mobilisation in Sub-Saharan Africa: A survey of key issues (WP)", *Sub-Saharan Africa Working Paper*, No. 49/2009, Real Instituto Elcano, Madrid,*www.realinstitutoelcano.org/wps/portal/web/rielcano_en/contenido?WCM_GLOBAL_CONTEXT=/elcano/elcano_in/zonas_in/dt49-2009*.

Keen, M. and M. Mansour (2009), "Revenue mobilization in Sub-Saharan Africa: Challenges from globalization", *IMF Working Paper*, WP/09/157, International Monetary Fund, Washington, DC, *www.imf.org/external/pubs/ft/wp/2009/wp09157.pdf*.

Lewis, C. and T. Alton (2015), "How can South Africa's tax system meet revenue raising challenges?", *OECD Economics Department Working Papers*, No. 1276, OECD Publishing, Paris, *dx.doi.org/10.1787/5jrp1g0xztbr-en*.

Mascagni, G., M. Moore and R. McCluskey (2014), *Tax Revenue Mobilisation in Developing Countries: Issues and Challenge*, European Union, Brussels, *www.ids.ac.uk/files/dmfile/TaxRevenueMobilisationinDevelopingCountries.pdf*.

Thomas, A. and J.P. Treviño (2013), "Resource dependence and fiscal effort in Sub-Saharan Africa", *IMF Working Paper*, WP/13/188, International Monetary Fund, Washington, DC, *www.imf.org/external/pubs/ft/wp/2013/wp13188.pdf*.

Prichard, W., A. Cobham and A. Goodall (2014), "The ICTD government revenue dataset", *ICTD Working Paper*, No. 19, Institute of Development Studies, Brighton, *https://assets.publishing.service.gov.uk/media/57a089be40f0b652dd0003b2/ICTD-WP19.pdf*.

Revenue Statistics in Africa 1990-2015/Statistiques des recettes publiques en Afrique 1990-2015

Chapitre 1

Tendances des recettes fiscales et non fiscales, 1990-2015

Introduction

Dans le contexte du Programme de développement durable des Nations unies à l'horizon 2030, la prise de conscience de la nécessité de mobiliser des recettes publiques dans les pays en développement pour financer des biens et des services publics va crescendo. L'impôt représente une source de recettes publiques prévisible et stable, contrairement à l'aide au développement et aux redevances minières, marquées par une forte volatilité.

Le présent rapport contient des données internationalement comparables sur les recettes fiscales et non fiscales de seize pays africains : l'Afrique du Sud, le Cabo Verde, le Cameroun, la République démocratique du Congo, la Côte d'Ivoire, le Ghana, le Kenya, le Maroc, Maurice, le Niger, l'Ouganda, le Rwanda, le Sénégal, le Swaziland, le Togo et la Tunisie. Ce chapitre est consacré à l'évolution, observée dans ces pays, de plusieurs indicateurs essentiels fiscaux et non fiscaux : le ratio impôts-PIB, la structure fiscale, la part des recettes fiscales représentée par chaque niveau d'administration et le ratio recettes non fiscales-PIB. L'analyse proposée vient compléter les informations détaillées par pays figurant aux chapitres 4 et 5.

Des comparaisons internationales entre les données relatives aux recettes des pays couverts par la publication sont présentées, de même que des comparaisons avec les moyennes des 16 pays d'Afrique, des 24 pays d'Amérique latine et Caraïbes (ALC) (consulter OCDE, et al., 2017) et des 35 pays de l'OCDE (consulter OCDE, 2016), destinées à servir de comparateurs. On ne dispose cependant pas de chiffres équivalents concernant les pays de l'OCDE et d'Amérique latine et Caraïbes pour les recettes non fiscales.

RECETTES FISCALES

1.1. Niveaux d'imposition

Le ratio moyen impôts-PIB dans les 16 pays d'Afrique couverts par la publication (visé au présent chapitre comme moyenne des pays d'Afrique (16)) s'est établi à 19.1 % en 2015 (graphique 1.1). Le ratio impôts-PIB correspond aux recettes fiscales (y compris les cotisations de sécurité sociale versées à l'administration générale) exprimées en pourcentage du produit intérieur brut (PIB). Il convient d'interpréter la moyenne des pays d'Afrique (16) avec prudence en raison du fait que les données relatives aux cotisations de sécurité sociale[1] sont incomplètes ou indisponibles pour certains pays africains considérés. Les ratios impôts-PIB varient considérablement selon les pays, de 10.8 % en République démocratique du Congo à 30.3 % en Tunisie.

Ratios impôts-PIB en 2015

Les seize pays sur lesquels porte le rapport se répartissent en deux groupes distincts si l'on considère les recettes fiscales rapportées au PIB. Le premier groupe réunit des pays, au nombre de trois (Afrique du Sud, Maroc et Tunisie), dont les recettes fiscales représentaient en 2015 entre environ 26.1 % et 30.3 % du PIB, soit nettement plus que la moyenne des pays d'Amérique latine et Caraïbes ressortant à 22.8 %. Le second groupe (Cabo Verde, Cameroun, Côte d'Ivoire, Ghana, Kenya, Maurice, Niger, Ouganda, République démocratique du Congo, Rwanda, Sénégal, Swaziland, Togo,) se compose de pays dont les ratios impôts-PIB sont tous inférieurs à la moyenne des pays d'Amérique latine et Caraïbes.

Graphique 1.1. **Ratios impôts-PIB (total des recettes fiscales en pourcentage du PIB), 2015**

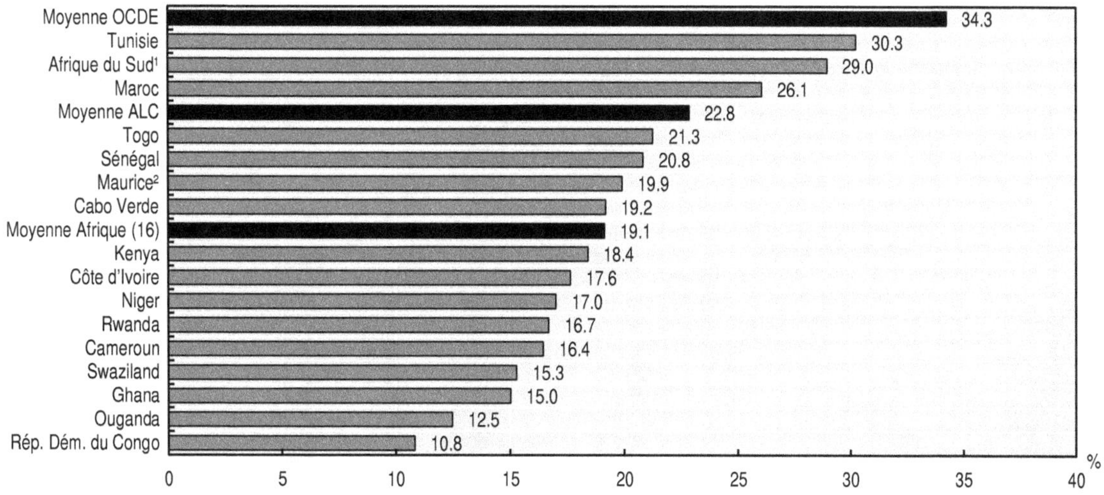

Notes : Les chiffres prennent en compte les recettes fiscales des administrations infranationales pour l'Afrique du Sud, Maurice, le Maroc et le Swaziland. La moyenne Afrique (16) et les moyennes ALC (24 pays d'Amérique latine et Caraïbes) et OCDE (35 pays) sont des moyennes non pondérées.

Il convient d'interpréter la moyenne des pays d'Afrique (16) avec précaution car des données relatives aux cotisations de sécurité sociale sont indisponibles ou incomplètes pour quelques pays. En particulier, les données relatives aux cotisations de sécurité sociale ne sont pas disponibles pour l'Ouganda, la République démocratique du Congo et le Togo, et elles sont incomplètes pour le Cameroun, le Kenya et le Sénégal. Voir les tableaux par pays au chapitre 4 pour plus de précisions.

1. Il convient d'interpréter le ratio impôt-PIB avec prudence car il prend en compte les sommes recouvrées au profit de l'Union douanière de l'Afrique australe (SACU) par l'Afrique du Sud.
2. Les données pour 2015 sont des estimations.

Source : Tableau 3.1 figurant au chapitre 3 et dans OCDE/ATAF/CUA (2017), « Statistiques des recettes publiques en Afrique: Tableaux comparatifs », *Statistiques fiscales de l'OCDE* (base de données), *http://dx.doi.org/10.1787/7f54581d-fr*, pour la moyenne des pays ALC.

StatLink http://dx.doi.org/10.1787/888933569174

Encadré 1.1. **Ratios impôts-PIB des membres d'organisations régionales**

La plupart des pays d'Afrique couverts par la publication font partie d'organisations régionales africaines dont les membres adoptent des règles communes en matière fiscale et douanière et forment une union douanière.

La Côte d'Ivoire, le Niger, le Sénégal et le Togo adhèrent à l'Union économique et monétaire ouest-africaine (UEMOA), dont font également partie le Bénin, le Burkina Faso, la Guinée-Bissau et le Mali. L'UEMOA a vocation à renforcer la compétitivité économique et financière des États membres, à assurer la convergence de leurs résultats et de leurs politiques économiques, à créer un marché commun, en mettant en place un Tarif extérieur commun (TEC), une politique commerciale commune ainsi que la liberté de circulation des personnes, des marchandises et des capitaux, et à coordonner les politiques sectorielles nationales. Au sein de l'UEMOA, le Sénégal et le Togo se situaient au-dessus de la moyenne des pays d'Afrique (16), et les ratios variaient de 17.0 % au Niger à 21.3 % au Togo (graphique 1.2).

Encadré 1.1. **Ratios impôts-PIB des membres d'organisations régionales** *(suite)*

Le Kenya, l'Ouganda et le Rwanda sont membres de la Communauté d'Afrique de l'Est (CAE), à laquelle adhèrent également le Burundi, le Sud-Soudan et la Tanzanie. La CAE a pour mission de favoriser une intégration économique régionale plus poussée ; elle a dans cette optique créée une zone de libre-échange et une union douanière. Elle œuvre aussi à l'ouverture d'un marché commun. En 2015, les trois pays de la CAE couverts par la publication affichaient des ratios impôts-PIB inférieurs à la moyenne des pays d'Afrique (16) qui allaient de 12.5 % en Ouganda à 18.4 % au Kenya.

Graphique 1.2. **Ratios impôts-PIB dans les pays de la CAE et de l'UEMOA, 2015**

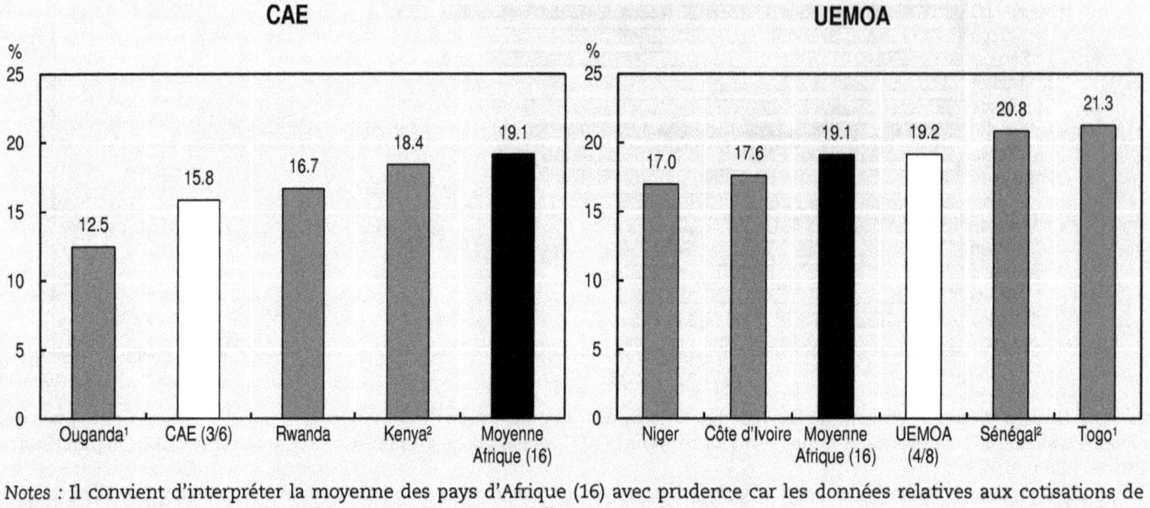

Notes : Il convient d'interpréter la moyenne des pays d'Afrique (16) avec prudence car les données relatives aux cotisations de sécurité sociale ne sont pas disponibles ou ne sont que partielles pour quelques pays.

1. Les ratios impôts-PIB ne prennent pas en compte les données relatives aux cotisations de sécurité sociale car elles ne sont pas disponibles.
2. Les ratios impôts-PIB ne prennent pas en compte certaines données relatives aux cotisations de sécurité sociale pour le Kenya (mais ces recettes sont considérées comme négligeables) et le Sénégal (les chiffres tiennent compte des données relatives aux cotisations de sécurité sociale communiquées par l'Institution de Prévoyance Retraites du Sénégal (IPRES), mais pas des données émanant de la Caisse de Sécurité Sociale (CSS) car elles ne sont pas disponibles).

Source : Tableau 3.1 figurant au chapitre 3.

StatLink http://dx.doi.org/10.1787/888933569193

En 2015, le ratio moyen impôts-PIB pour les pays d'Afrique (16), s'élevant à 19.1 %, était supérieur de 0.4 point de pourcentage à ce qu'il était en 2014 (graphique 1.3). Ce résultat est conforme à l'ensemble des résultats économiques de l'Afrique, qui sont restés solides en 2015 malgré les défis mondiaux auxquels le continent a dû faire face, notamment l'essoufflement de la demande mondiale due à la lenteur de la reprise dans les pays développés après la crise financière, le dévissage des prix des matières premières et les chocs régionaux. La croissance du PIB en volume réel en Afrique a été estimée à 3.4 % en 2015, ce qui place le continent à la deuxième place derrière l'Asie de l'Est (BAfD/OCDE/PNUD, 2017). La progression de la moyenne des pays d'Afrique (16) observée entre 2014 et 2015 a été légèrement plus timide que celle observée dans les pays d'Amérique latine et des Caraïbes, soit 0.6 point de pourcentage, mais supérieure à celle de la moyenne des pays de l'OCDE, inférieure à 0.1 point de pourcentage.

Treize pays ont enregistré une hausse des recettes fiscales rapportées au PIB en 2015 tandis qu'au Kenya, au Maroc et en Tunisie, la tendance a été inverse (graphique 1.3). Le Cabo Verde est le pays qui affiche la plus forte augmentation des recettes fiscales exprimées en pourcentage du PIB, soit 1.8 point de pourcentage, suivi de l'Afrique du Sud et de l'Ouganda (tous deux avec 1.1 point de pourcentage) ; le Maroc et la Tunisie sont les pays qui accusent le repli le plus marqué, soit 0.9 et 0.7 point de pourcentage respectivement.

Graphique 1.3. **Variation des ratios impôts-PIB entre 2014 et 2015 (en points de pourcentage du PIB)**

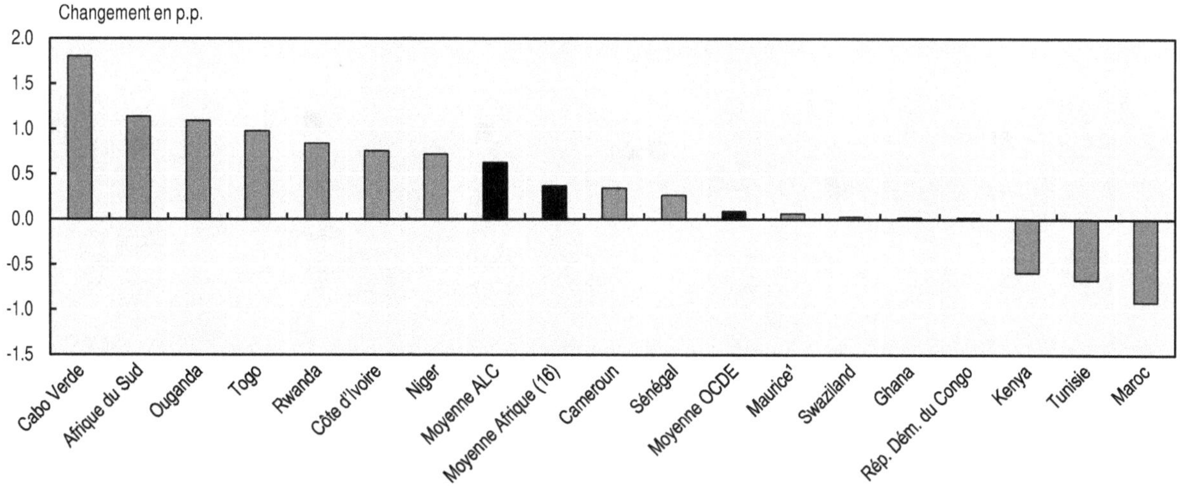

Notes : Les chiffres prennent en compte les recettes fiscales des administrations infranationales pour l'Afrique du Sud, le Maroc, Maurice et le Swaziland. La moyenne Afrique (16) et les moyennes ALC (24 pays d'Amérique latine et Caraïbes) et OCDE (35 pays) sont des moyennes non pondérées.

Il convient d'interpréter la moyenne des pays d'Afrique (16) avec prudence car les données relatives aux cotisations de sécurité sociale ne sont pas disponibles ou ne sont que partielles pour quelques pays. Plus précisément, les données relatives aux cotisations de sécurité sociale ne sont pas disponibles pour l'Ouganda, la République démocratique du Congo et le Togo et, dans le cas du Cameroun, du Kenya et du Sénégal, les données disponibles relatives aux cotisations de sécurité sociale ne sont que partielles. Pour plus de précisions, se reporter aux tableaux par pays présentés dans le chapitre 4.

1. La variation du ratio impôts-PIB est calculée à l'aide de données estimées pour 2015.

Source : Calculs de l'auteur à partir de données présentées dans le tableau 3.1 figurant au chapitre 3 et OCDE/ATAF/CUA (2017), « Statistiques des recettes publiques en Afrique: Tableaux comparatifs », *Statistiques fiscales de l'OCDE* (base de données), *http://dx.doi.org/10.1787/7f54581d-fr*, pour la moyenne des pays ALC.

StatLink *http://dx.doi.org/10.1787/888933569212*

Les principaux moteurs de la progression du ratio moyen impôts-PIB des pays d'Afrique (16) constatée en 2015 ont été la hausse de 0.2 point de pourcentage des recettes provenant des impôts spécifiques sur la consommation (droits d'accise et droits de douane essentiellement) et de 0.1 point de pourcentage des recettes provenant des impôts généraux sur la consommation (TVA[2] principalement) et des impôts sur le revenu (graphique 1.4). On observe cependant une grande hétérogénéité entre les pays dans les variations annuelles entre 2014 et 2015. Les différences les plus marquées transparaissent dans les variations, en pourcentage du PIB, des recettes tirées de l'impôt sur les bénéfices des sociétés (graphique 1.4).

C'est en Afrique du Sud, au Cabo Verde et en Ouganda que le ratio impôts-PIB a le plus fortement augmenté entre 2014 et 2015. Au Cabo Verde, cette augmentation s'explique par celle rapportée au PIB, des recettes de TVA (0.6 point de pourcentage) et des recettes tirées de l'impôt sur les bénéfices des sociétés (1.0 point de pourcentage). En Afrique du Sud, le principal moteur a été les recettes tirées de l'impôt sur le revenu des personnes physiques qui a augmenté de 0.7 point de pourcentage. En Ouganda, des hausses ont été observées dans les principales catégories d'impôts.

Graphique 1.4. **Variations des ratios impôts-PIB (en points de pourcentage du PIB) observées entre 2014 et 2015 par principales rubriques d'impôts**

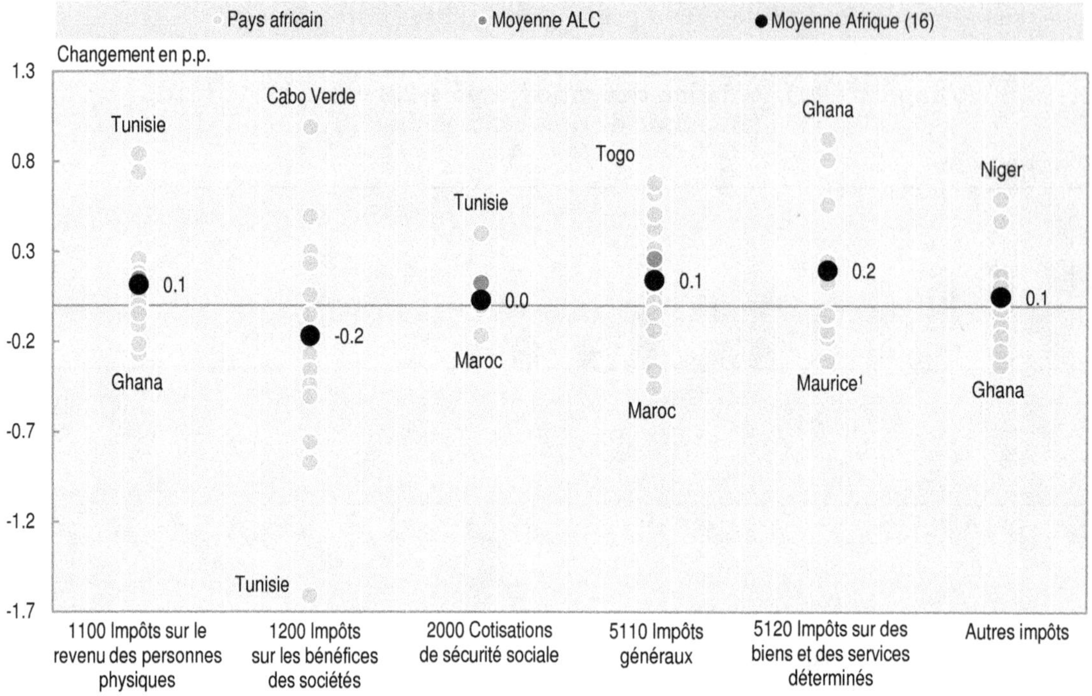

Notes : Les chiffres prennent en compte les recettes fiscales des administrations infranationales pour l'Afrique du Sud, le Maroc, Maurice et le Swaziland. La moyenne Afrique (16) et les moyennes ALC (24 pays d'Amérique latine et Caraïbes) et OCDE (35 pays) sont des moyennes non pondérées.

Il convient d'interpréter la moyenne des pays d'Afrique (16) avec prudence car les données relatives aux cotisations de sécurité sociale ne sont pas disponibles ou ne sont que partielles pour quelques pays. Plus précisément, les données relatives aux cotisations de sécurité sociale ne sont pas disponibles pour l'Ouganda, la République démocratique du Congo et le Togo et, dans le cas du Cameroun, du Kenya et du Sénégal, les données disponibles relatives aux cotisations de sécurité sociale ne sont que partielles. Pour plus de précisions, se reporter aux tableaux par pays présentés dans le chapitre 4.

1. La variation du ratio impôts-PIB est calculée à l'aide de données estimées pour 2015.

Source : Calculs de l'auteur à partir de données figurant dans OCDE/ATAF/CUA (2017), « Statistiques des recettes publiques en Afrique: Tableaux comparatifs », *Statistiques fiscales de l'OCDE* (base de données), *http://dx.doi.org/10.1787/7f54581d-fr.*

StatLink *http://dx.doi.org/10.1787/888933569231*

Au Cabo Verde, l'augmentation des recettes de TVA et des recettes tirées de l'impôt sur les bénéfices des sociétés apparaissent après une amélioration du système d'administration de l'impôt résultant d'une restructuration de l'administration fiscale conduite fin 2014 ainsi qu'à une intensification des efforts déployés pour recouvrer des arriérés d'impôts relevant de ces catégories d'impôts (FMI, 2016a). En Afrique du Sud, la réforme de l'impôt sur le revenu des personnes physiques prévue au budget 2015 a contribué à l'augmentation des recettes correspondantes. Les taux de l'impôt sur le revenu des personnes physiques ont été relevés d'un point de pourcentage pour l'ensemble des contribuables au-delà d'un certain seuil de revenu, et les tranches d'imposition et les abattements ont été revus compte tenu de l'inflation. Cette réforme avait pour objet d'accroître les recettes fiscales recouvrées auprès des catégories de contribuables les plus aisées (National Treasury, 2015).

Graphique 1.5. **Variations des ratios impôts-PIB (en points de pourcentage du PIB) observées entre 2014 et 2015 par principales rubriques d'impôts et par pays**

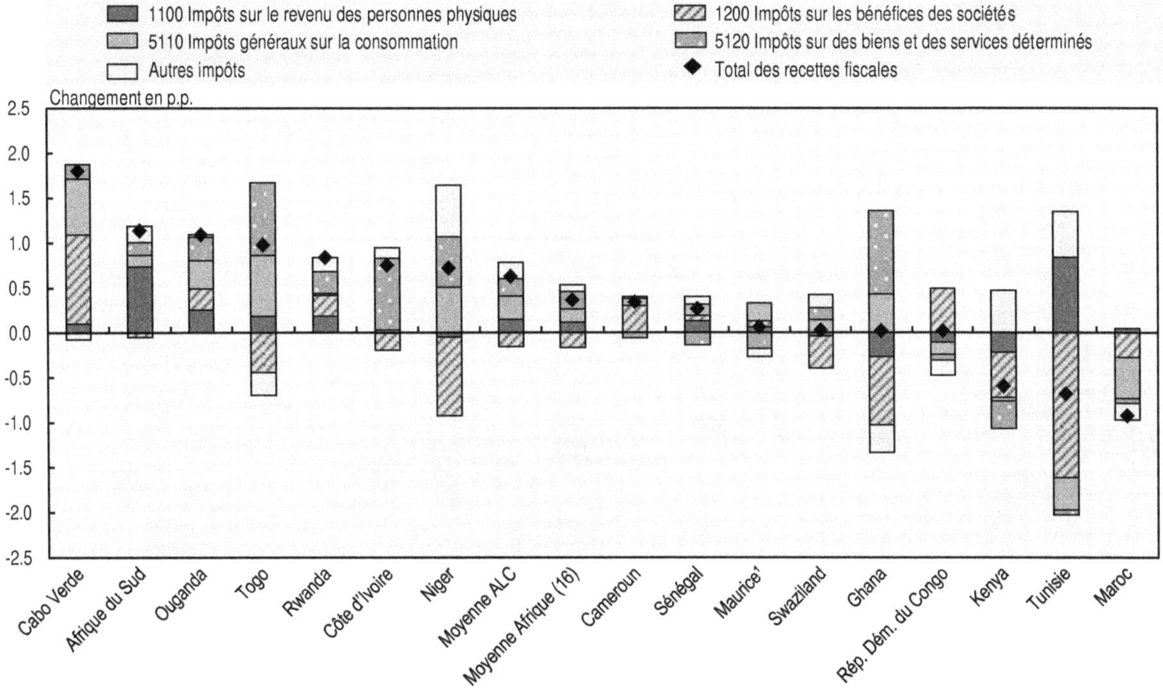

Notes : Les chiffres prennent en compte les recettes fiscales des administrations infranationales pour l'Afrique du Sud, le Maroc, Maurice et le Swaziland. La moyenne Afrique (16) et les moyennes ALC (24 pays d'Amérique latine et Caraïbes) et OCDE (35 pays) sont des moyennes non pondérées.

Il convient d'interpréter la moyenne des pays d'Afrique (16) avec prudence car les données relatives aux cotisations de sécurité sociale ne sont pas disponibles ou ne sont que partielles pour quelques pays. Plus précisément, les données relatives aux cotisations de sécurité sociale ne sont pas disponibles pour l'Ouganda, la République démocratique du Congo et le Togo et, dans le cas du Cameroun, du Kenya et du Sénégal, les données disponibles relatives aux cotisations de sécurité sociale ne sont que partielles. Pour plus de précisions, se reporter aux tableaux par pays présentés dans le chapitre 4.

1. La variation du ratio impôts-PIB est calculée à l'aide de données estimées pour 2015.

Source : Calculs de l'auteur à partir de données figurant dans OCDE/ATAF/CUA (2017), « Statistiques des recettes publiques en Afrique: Tableaux comparatifs », *Statistiques fiscales de l'OCDE* (base de données), *http://dx.doi.org/10.1787/7f54581d-fr*.

StatLink http://dx.doi.org/10.1787/888933569250

Le Maroc accuse le recul le plus marqué du ratio impôts-PIB, soit 0.9 point de pourcentage. Des mouvements de repli sont observés pour toutes les grandes catégories d'impôts, et principalement un fléchissement des recettes de TVA en pourcentage du PIB (de 0.5 point de pourcentage) et des recettes tirées de l'impôt sur les bénéfices des sociétés (de 0.3 point de pourcentage). En Tunisie, la forte baisse des recettes tirées de l'imposition des sociétés, de 1.6 point de pourcentage du PIB, a été contrebalancée par une hausse des recettes de l'imposition du revenu des personnes physiques et d'autres prélèvements (cotisations de sécurité sociale principalement). La baisse des recettes tirées de l'imposition des bénéfices des sociétés est consécutive à la réforme récente du système d'imposition des bénéfices des sociétés qui s'est concrétisée par un abaissement du taux de l'impôt sur les sociétés, lequel a été ramené de 30 % à 25 %.

Pour ce qui est des variations, entre 2014 et 2015, des recettes provenant de l'impôt sur les bénéfices des sociétés, exprimées en pourcentage du PIB, on observe des écarts notables entre les pays (graphique 1.6). En 2015, le Ghana, le Kenya, le Niger et la Tunisie ont enregistré des baisses de 0.5 point de pourcentage, voire plus. Au Ghana, la contraction est essentiellement due à l'effondrement des recettes tirées de l'impôt sur les bénéfices des sociétés pétrolières, passées de 0.7 % à 0.03 % du PIB à la suite du dévissage prolongé des prix du pétrole, une crise majeure dans ce pays exportateur de pétrole depuis 2011 (NGRI, 2015).

Graphique 1.6. **Variations annuelles, entre 2014 et 2015, des recettes tirées des impôts sur le revenu et les bénéfices, par sous-rubrique et par pays (points de pourcentage du PIB)**

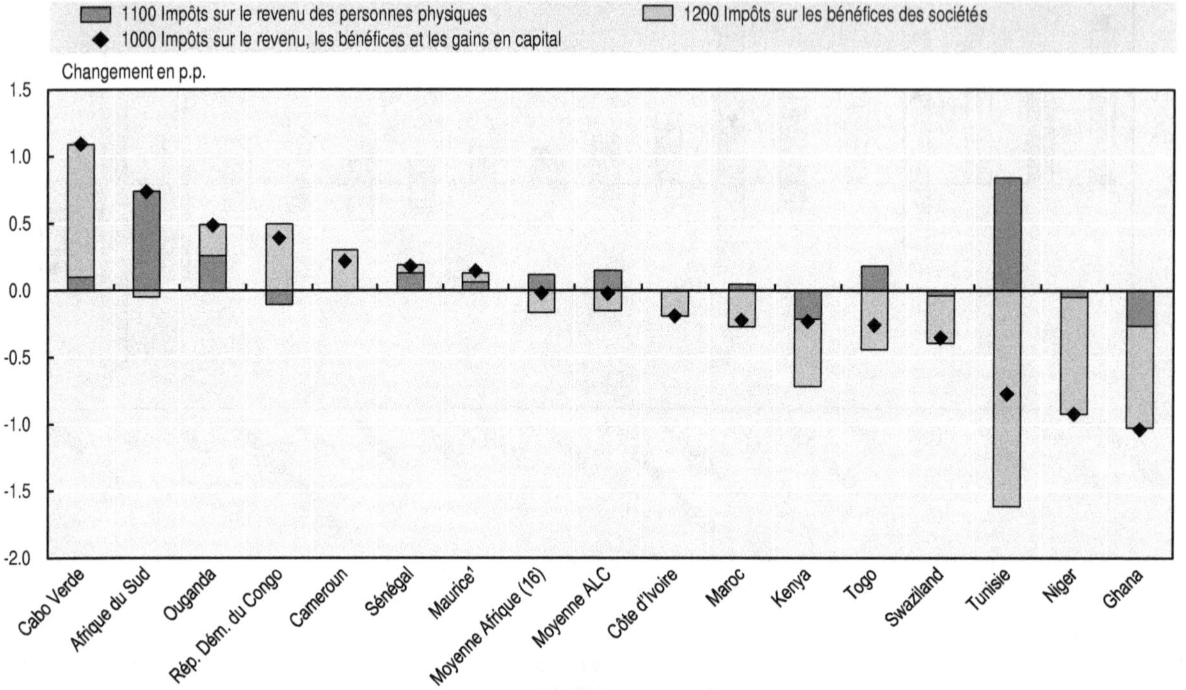

Note : La moyenne Afrique (16) et les moyennes ALC (24 pays d'Amérique latine et Caraïbes) et OCDE (35 pays) sont des moyennes non pondérées.

1. Les données pour 2015 sont des estimations.

Source : Calculs de l'auteur à partir de données figurant dans OCDE/ATAF/CUA (2017), « Statistiques des recettes publiques en Afrique: Tableaux comparatifs », *Statistiques fiscales de l'OCDE* (base de données), *http://dx.doi.org/10.1787/7f54581d-fr*.

StatLink *http://dx.doi.org/10.1787/888933569269*

Évolution des ratios impôts-PIB depuis 2000

Le ratio moyen impôts-PIB dans 16 pays d'Afrique n'a cessé de progresser entre 2000 et 2015 sauf pendant la période 2008-10 (graphique 1.7). Il a gagné cinq points de pourcentage, passant de 14.2 % en 2000 à 19.1 % en 2015, grâce à des conditions macroéconomiques favorables, à des évolutions dans l'orientation de la politique fiscale et la conception de la fiscalité, et au renforcement des administrations fiscales. Cette tendance fait écho à celle mise en évidence dans les pays d'Amérique latine et des Caraïbes, soit une augmentation de 4.9 points de pourcentage en moyenne du ratio impôts-PIB pendant la même période. Le mouvement ascendant a en revanche été beaucoup plus lent dans la zone OCDE où le ratio impôts-PIB moyen a été relativement stable, atteignant 34.3 % en 2015, soit 0.3 point de pourcentage de plus qu'en 2000.

La crise financière mondiale a brièvement interrompu l'ascension régulière du ratio moyen impôts-PIB dans les pays d'Afrique (16). Elle a fait baisser la moyenne des pays d'Afrique (16) de 0.4 point de pourcentage entre 2008 et 2010, le déclin de l'activité économique et des prix des matières premières expliquant en partie cette évolution. Pendant cette période, certains des 16 pays africains considérés ont mis en œuvre des mesures visant à stimuler l'activité économique. Le Maroc par exemple a réduit le taux de l'impôt sur les bénéfices des sociétés de 5 points de pourcentage en 2008 en vue d'améliorer la compétitivité de ses entreprises et de les aider à devenir plus résistantes pendant la crise financière (voir encadré 1.2). La moyenne des pays d'Amérique latine et des Caraïbes a reculé de 0.5 point de pourcentage. La moyenne de l'OCDE en revanche a surtout subi le contrecoup de la crise entre 2007 et 2009. C'est pendant cette phase que le ratio impôts-PIB a été le plus nettement altéré, avec une contraction se chiffrant à 1.3 point de pourcentage. La zone de l'OCDE s'est aussi remise plus lentement puisqu'elle n'a renoué qu'en 2013 avec le niveau d'avant la crise, soit 33.8 %, alors que les pays d'Afrique (16) sont parvenus dès 2011 à dépasser le ratio impôts-PIB de 17.7 % en 2008.

Graphique 1.7. **Ratios impôts-PIB, 2000-15**

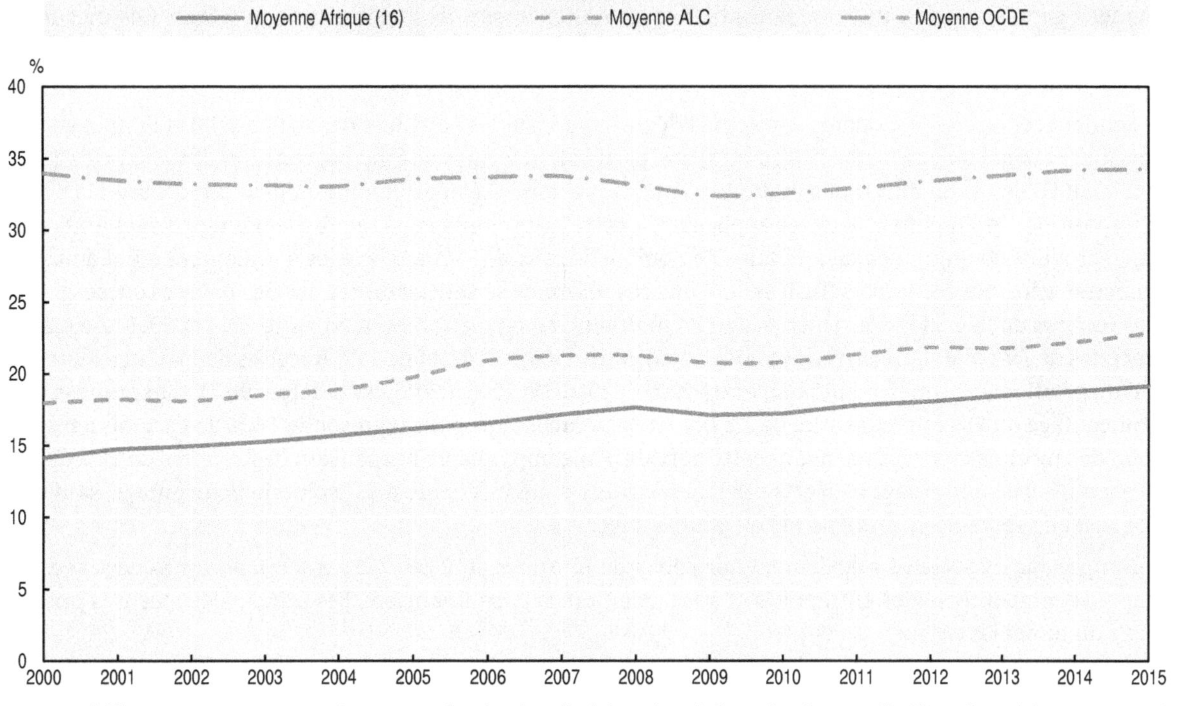

Notes : Les chiffres prennent en compte les recettes fiscales des administrations infranationales pour l'Afrique du Sud, le Maroc, Maurice et le Swaziland. La moyenne Afrique (16) et les moyennes ALC (24 pays d'Amérique latine et des Caraïbes) et OCDE (35 pays) sont des moyennes non pondérées. Il convient d'interpréter la moyenne des pays d'Afrique (16) avec prudence car les données relatives aux cotisations de sécurité sociale ne sont pas disponibles ou ne sont que partielles pour quelques pays. Plus précisément, les données relatives aux cotisations de sécurité sociale ne sont pas disponibles pour l'Ouganda, la République démocratique du Congo et le Togo et, dans le cas du Cameroun, du Kenya et du Sénégal, les données disponibles relatives aux cotisations de sécurité sociale ne sont que partielles. Pour plus de précisions, se reporter aux tableaux par pays présentés dans le chapitre 4.

Source : Tableau 3.1 du chapitre 3 pour la moyenne des pays de l'OCDE et d'Afrique (16) et OCDE/ATAF/CUA (2017), « Statistiques des recettes publiques en Afrique: Tableaux comparatifs », *Statistiques fiscales de l'OCDE* (base de données), *http://dx.doi.org/10.1787/7f54581d-fr*, pour la moyenne des pays ALC.

StatLink *http://dx.doi.org/10.1787/888933569288*

L'accroissement des recettes fiscales est survenu pendant la période au cours de laquelle les pays africains ont procédé à des réformes structurelles majeures au sein de leurs administrations fiscales et entrepris de modifier radicalement leurs systèmes fiscaux. Pour nombre de pays, les réformes ont eu pour but de renforcer et de moderniser les administrations fiscales. Parmi les réformes adoptées, on compte l'introduction de bureaux des gros contribuables et/ou des moyens contribuables, des systèmes tels que l'impôt déclaratif, le ciblage des contribuables et une gestion moderne des risques (Kloeden, D., 2011), (Fossat et Bua, 2013). Certains pays ont engagé des réformes fiscales en vue d'élargir la base imposable, d'éliminer certaines exonérations et de simplifier la législation fiscale. Comme l'explique la (BAfD/OCDE/CEA, 2010) « de nombreux pays sont parvenus à élargir leur assiette fiscale. La Tunisie, par exemple, accroît la sienne au rythme annuel de 3.5 % ; l'Afrique du Sud et l'Égypte ont doublé la leur au cours des cinq dernières années ; et la Côte d'Ivoire est parvenue à reconstituer la sienne après la guerre civile. » Ces changements se sont souvent accompagnés de programmes destinés à éduquer les contribuables et à améliorer les services aux contribuables (notamment grâce à l'informatisation des services fiscaux).

Encadré 1.2. **Principales réformes de la fiscalité et de l'administration fiscale conduites au Maroc entre 2004 et 2013**

Entre 2004 et 2013, le Maroc a entrepris un certain nombre de réformes fiscales essentielles qui ont été menées parallèlement à une réorganisation et un renforcement de l'administration fiscale. Ces mesures ont contribué à accroître le montant total des recettes fiscales qui ont été portées de 23.1 % du PIB en 2004 à 28.1 % en 2013.

Pendant cette période, le Maroc a réformé la TVA, l'impôt sur les bénéfices des sociétés (IS) et l'impôt sur le revenu des personnes physiques (IR). La majeure partie des réformes de fond ont concerné le système de TVA qui a fait l'objet de modifications pratiquement chaque année, ayant notamment pour but d'élargir la base d'imposition, de simplifier les règles applicables à certains produits et de réduire le nombre d'exonérations et de produits soumis à des taux réduits. Le nombre de taux de TVA applicables a également été réduit. La Direction générale des Impôts (DGI) estime que ces réformes se sont traduites par des hausses successives des recettes de TVA : de 18 % (recettes de TVA intérieure en termes nominaux) entre 2004 et 2005 ; de 4.2 % (recettes de TVA intérieure en termes nominaux) entre 2006 et 2007, et de 24 % (recettes de TVA intérieure et à l'importation en termes nominaux) entre 2009 et 2010. De 2004 à 2013, les recettes de TVA, exprimées en pourcentage du PIB, ont augmenté de 2.8 points de pourcentage, pour représenter 56 % de l'accroissement total des recettes observées pendant cette période. Par comparaison, l'expansion des recettes de TVA dans l'ensemble des autres pays couverts par la publication a été inférieure à 1.0 point de pourcentage, sauf au Togo où elle est ressortie à 3.2 points de pourcentage.

L'impôt sur les sociétés a également fait l'objet de réformes en 2008, 2011 et 2013, réformes destinées à doper la compétitivité des entreprises et à les aider lors la crise financière. Les principales mesures prises ont notamment consisté :

- en 2008, à ramener le taux de l'IS de 35 % à 30 % et de l'impôt sur les bénéfices dans le secteur financier de 39.6 % à 37 % ;
- en 2011, à abaisser le taux de l'IS applicable aux petites entreprises dont le chiffre d'affaires est inférieur à 3 millions MAD ;
- en 2013, à accorder de nouvelles exonérations et à appliquer des taux réduits d'IS à certaines petites entreprises ciblées.

À la suite de ces réformes et de la crise financière, les recettes tirées de l'impôt sur les bénéfices des sociétés, exprimées en pourcentage du PIB, ont reculé de 2 points de pourcentage entre 2008 et 2013. Sur un laps de temps plus long (2004 à 2013), elles ont cependant progressé d'1.5 point de pourcentage à cause des recettes exceptionnelles recouvrées pendant les années ayant suivi l'application des mesures de réforme des services répressifs et une phase de bons résultats économiques avant la crise financière.

Le système d'imposition des personnes physiques a été réformé en 2007, 2009 et 2010 afin d'améliorer le pouvoir d'achat des ménages. Pendant cette période, les taux d'imposition marginaux des revenus des personnes physiques ont été abaissés, les barèmes d'imposition réaménagés et le seuil d'exonération des revenus relevé sensiblement. La DGI estime que ces réformes sont à l'origine d'une diminution des recettes de 11 milliards MAD au total pendant la période considérée. En pourcentage du PIB, les recettes issues de l'impôt sur le revenu des personnes physiques ont diminué de 0.7 point de pourcentage entre 2007 et 2010.

Encadré 1.2. **Principales réformes de la fiscalité et de l'administration fiscale conduites au Maroc entre 2004 et 2013** *(suite)*

Les administrations fiscales ont été sensiblement améliorées entre 2004 et 2013. Des services au contribuable ciblés ont été créés en 2005 (à l'intention notamment des gros contribuables et des petites entreprises) afin que l'administration fiscale puisse mieux gérer les affaires de ces contribuables et qu'elle leur offre des services plus adaptés à leurs besoins. Ces efforts ont favorisé un accroissement de la proportion de contribuables immatriculés à la TVA et de contribuables payant l'IS et l'IR entre 8 % et 13 % en 2007. En outre, c'est la DGI qui a été chargée du recouvrement de l'impôt sur les bénéfices des sociétés et de la TVA : il en est résulté une hausse estimée à 22 % des recettes provenant de l'impôt sur les sociétés entre 2004 et 2005. Enfin, les vérifications et contrôles fiscaux ont été renforcés, ce qui a amélioré la discipline fiscale des entreprises.

Source : Lakhal, H, Direction Générale des Impôts (DGI), à partir d'une analyse entreprise pendant un détachement auprès de l'OCDE.

L'adoption de la TVA a été la réforme la plus importante conduite en Afrique en matière fiscale depuis les années 80. Douze pays ont institué cette taxe avant 2000. Le Cabo Verde et le Rwanda l'ont introduite respectivement en 2004 et en 2001, et la République démocratique du Congo et le Swaziland en 2012. Dans de nombreux pays, la mise en place de la TVA s'est accompagnée de réformes de grande ampleur des administrations fiscales qui ont contribué à l'accroissement des recettes de TVA pendant la période considérée. Entre 2000 et 2015, les recettes de TVA, rapportées au PIB, ont augmenté en moyenne de 2.2 points de pourcentage dans les seize pays d'Afrique couverts, passant de 3.7 % à 5.9 % (graphique 1.8). Les recettes provenant d'autres impôts sur les biens et services (droits d'accise, droits de douane et droits à l'importation essentiellement), toujours exprimées en pourcentage du PIB, se sont contractées en moyenne pendant la même période. Ce fléchissement est allé de pair avec la libéralisation des échanges qui a entraîné dans les pays africains des modifications de l'imposition des biens importés et exportés et de l'imposition de biens et services spécifiques, à savoir notamment un abaissement des droits à l'importation, une réduction de l'assiette pour les produits et services soumis à des droits d'accise et l'élimination des taxes sur les exportations.

Les tendances observées pour ces différents types d'impôt dans les 16 pays d'Afrique couverts sont en moyenne très similaires à celles qui se sont dessinées dans les pays d'Amérique latine et des Caraïbes (graphique 1.8). Entre 2000 et 2015, les recettes de TVA moyennes des pays d'Afrique couverts (16) ont progressé en moyenne à un rythme légèrement plus rapide que celles des pays d'Amérique latine et des Caraïbes, au point d'atteindre pratiquement le même niveau en 2015 (soit 6.0 % du PIB). Pendant cette période, les recettes moyennes tirées des impôts sur le revenu et les bénéfices ont crû de 2.3 points de pourcentage dans les pays d'Afrique (16), passant de 3.9 % à 6.2 % du PIB, alors que dans les pays d'Amérique latine et des Caraïbes, elles ont grimpé de 2.1 points de pourcentage de 4.1 % à 6.2 % du PIB. Tant en Afrique (16) qu'en d'Amérique latine et dans les Caraïbes, les recettes moyennes provenant d'autres impôts sur les biens et services ont essuyé de fortes contractions alors que les recettes tirées des impôts sur le revenu et les bénéfices, de la TVA et d'autres impôts sur les biens et services ont été relativement stables sur la période en pourcentage du PIB dans la zone OCDE, malgré une légère érosion des recettes de TVA, de 0.3 point de pourcentage[3].

Encadré 1.3. **Réformes du système fiscal et de l'administration fiscale au Rwanda**

La perception des impôts au Rwanda a gagné en efficacité depuis 2000 grâce à des réformes d'ordre fiscal et administratif notables couplées à d'autres initiatives (BAfD, 2010). L'objectif des pouvoirs publics était d'élargir la base d'imposition en obtenant l'immatriculation des entreprises du secteur informel et en simplifiant les procédures imposées aux contribuables pour l'exécution de leurs obligations fiscales. Le Rwanda a créé en 2006 le Bureau des moyens et petits contribuables et institué un système de gestion par bloc du fichier des contribuables (destiné à permettre de mieux traiter les dossiers des moyens et petits contribuables en regroupant les entreprises par blocs homogènes). Ces réformes ont eu des effets considérables en termes de hausse des recettes fiscales. Le taux de respect de leurs obligations fiscales par les contribuables s'est sensiblement amélioré pour les gros contribuables, jusqu'à atteindre 97 %. C'est une évolution importante si l'on considère que ces contribuables procurent environ 75 % du montant total des recettes fiscales du pays. D'autres réformes ont contribué à l'accroissement des recettes fiscales, notamment l'adoption de la TVA en 2001 et l'application d'une nouvelle législation sur l'imposition des revenus et de nouveaux taux d'imposition en 2005 et 2006. Le système en place pour faire respecter la législation fiscale a en outre été renforcé de façon à permettre un meilleur repérage des risques ainsi que des vérifications fiscales plus systématiques et la généralisation de l'application de pénalités. Par ailleurs, la consolidation des procédures internes de l'administration fiscale s'est traduite par une amélioration de son efficacité et par une réduction des coûts de recouvrement. D'autres mesures non fiscales ont également des effets sur les recettes fiscales, comme l'accroissement des dépenses consacrées à des projets prioritaires dans les domaines de l'agriculture et des infrastructures.

Graphique 1.8. **Recettes tirées des impôts sur le revenu et les bénéfices, de la TVA et d'autres rubriques d'impôt, en pourcentage du PIB, 2000-15**

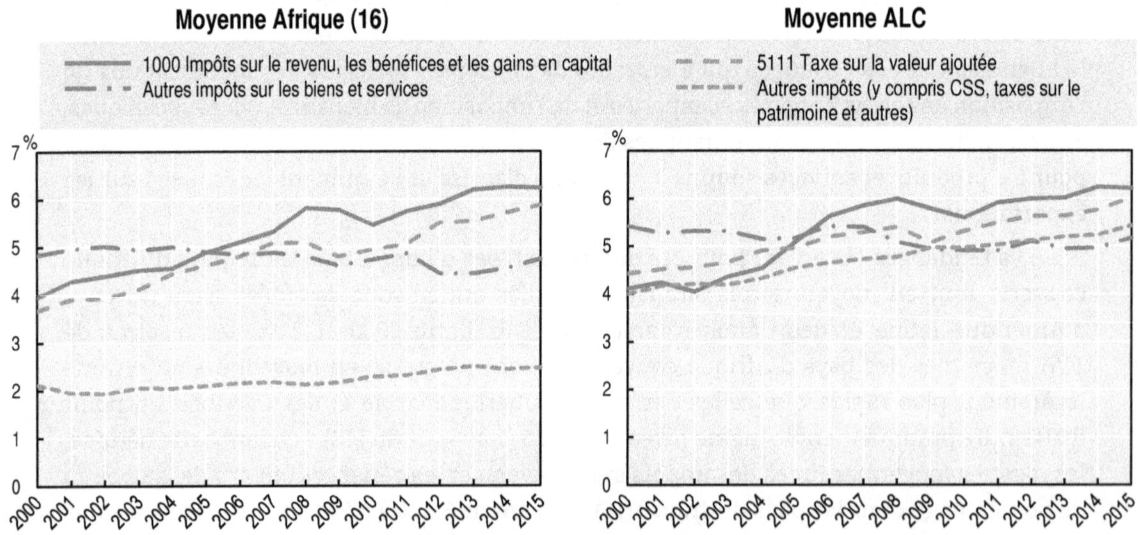

Notes : Les chiffres prennent en compte les recettes fiscales des administrations infranationales pour l'Afrique du Sud, le Maroc, Maurice et le Swaziland. La moyenne Afrique (16) et les moyennes ALC (24 pays d'Amérique latine et Caraïbes) et OCDE (35 pays) sont des moyennes non pondérées.

Il convient d'interpréter la moyenne des pays d'Afrique (16) avec prudence car les données relatives aux cotisations de sécurité sociale ne sont pas disponibles ou ne sont que partielles pour quelques pays. Plus précisément, les données relatives aux cotisations de sécurité sociale ne sont pas disponibles pour l'Ouganda, la République démocratique du Congo et le Togo et, dans le cas du Cameroun, du Kenya et du Sénégal, les données disponibles relatives aux cotisations de sécurité sociale ne sont que partielles. Pour plus de précisions, se reporter aux tableaux par pays présentés dans le chapitre 4.

La moyenne des pays d'Afrique (16) exclut le Kenya en 2000 faute de données disponibles.

Source : Calculs de l'auteur à partir de données figurant dans OCDE/ATAF/CUA (2017), « Statistiques des recettes publiques en Afrique: Tableaux comparatifs », *Statistiques fiscales de l'OCDE* (base de données), *http://dx.doi.org/10.1787/7f54581d-fr*.

StatLink http://dx.doi.org/10.1787/888933569307

Si les tendances observées concernent les impôts sur le revenu, les taxes sur la valeur ajoutée et d'autres impôts sur les biens et services ont été très similaires, au vu des moyennes, dans les pays d'Afrique (16) et de la région ALC, les évolutions entre 2000 et 2015 ont en revanche été différentes en ce qui concerne les recettes provenant des cotisations de sécurité sociale, des impôts sur le patrimoine et autres impôts, ce qui explique l'écart entre les ratios impôts-PIB. En 2015, ces recettes représentaient 2.5 % du PIB en Afrique (16) contre 5.4 % dans la région d'Amérique latine et des Caraïbes. La part des recettes provenant des cotisations de sécurité sociale, en pourcentage du PIB, s'est maintenue en 2015 à 3.8 % dans les pays ALC, contre 1.7 % en moyenne dans les pays d'Afrique (16)[4]. Les recettes tirées des cotisations de sécurité sociale, en pourcentage du PIB, ont augmenté de 1.1 point de pourcentage dans la région ALC entre 2000 et 2015 alors qu'en moyenne en Afrique (16), elle n'a progressé que de 0.2 point de pourcentage. À partir des années 80, un grand nombre de pays de la région ALC ont conduit de vastes réformes de leurs systèmes de sécurité sociale qui ont contribué à l'essor des recettes provenant des cotisations de sécurité sociale.

La moyenne Afrique (16) des recettes tirées des impôts sur le revenu et les bénéfices a été portée de 3.9 % du PIB en 2000 à 6.2 % en 2015. Cet essor résulte pour l'essentiel des recettes issues de l'impôt sur les bénéfices des sociétés, qui ont bondi d'1.3 point de pourcentage, de 1.5 % à 2.8 % du PIB (graphique 1.9). Entre 2008 et 2010, les recettes tirées de l'impôt sur les bénéfices des sociétés ont chuté, en pourcentage du PIB, de 0.4 point de pourcentage, avant de suivre une pente ascendante régulière à partir de 2010, si l'on excepte un léger recul de 0.2 point de pourcentage entre 2014 et 2015 qui peut s'expliquer en partie par la chute des prix des matières premières. En revanche, la part des recettes issues de l'impôt sur le revenu des personnes physiques n'a cessé de progresser, en pourcentage du PIB, depuis 2000 et atteint un niveau sans précédent en 2015 (3.2 %). Depuis 2013, le taux de croissance des recettes de l'impôt sur le revenu des personnes physiques, en pourcentage du PIB, est supérieur à celui des recettes de l'impôt sur les bénéfices des sociétés, lequel a subi les effets du léger ralentissement de l'activité économique en Afrique et de la baisse des prix des matières premières.

Les ratios impôts-PIB ont évolué différemment dans chaque pays entre 2000 et 2015 (graphique 1.10). La République démocratique du Congo et le Togo ont enregistré les plus fortes hausses, supérieures à 10 points de pourcentage.

Au cours de la période étudiée, et plus particulièrement depuis 2006, le Togo a déployé d'importants efforts pour améliorer l'organisation, le fonctionnement et les procédures de son administration et pour se doter d'une administration fiscale plus forte afin de mobiliser davantage de recettes publiques. Plusieurs initiatives ont alors été mises en œuvre, avec le soutien de partenaires du développement, tels que la BAfD, la Banque mondiale, le FMI et l'UE. Ces actions ont notamment permis de conduire des réformes structurelles majeures et de moderniser les trois grandes administrations des finances publiques : la Direction Générale des Impôts (DGI), la Direction Générale des Douanes (DGD) et la Direction Générale du Trésor et de la Comptabilité Publique (DGTCP). Ces initiatives visaient à améliorer la gestion des finances publiques et à mobiliser plus efficacement les ressources nationales. À titre d'exemple, la Banque africaine de développement a financé en 2006 le programme baptisé « Projet d'appui au renforcement des capacités institutionnelles en gouvernance économique et financière » (PARCI), et le Togo a mené à bien le Plan d'Actions de Mise en œuvre de la Réforme de Gestion des Finances Publiques. Ce dernier prévoyait des mesures visant à : densifier le réseau des centres des impôts ; lutter contre la fraude fiscale ; mettre en place un mécanisme de suivi des recettes ; augmenter le nombre de contribuables recensés ;

moderniser les systèmes d'information ; et renforcer les capacités des agents. Ces actions, mises en place entre 2010 et 2012, ont peut-être contribué à la hausse des recettes fiscales en pourcentage du PIB enregistrée entre 2012 et 2015. Au cours de ces trois années, le ratio impôts-PIB a en effet affiché une progression de 4.9 points de pourcentage, soit 50 % de sa progression cumulée depuis 2000. En 2014, le pays a par ailleurs regroupé ses services douaniers et fiscaux au sein d'une même administration, avec la création de l'Office togolais des recettes (OTR).

Graphique 1.9. **Recettes tirées des impôts sur le revenu et les bénéfices, par sous-rubrique en pourcentage du PIB, moyenne Afrique (16), 2000-15**

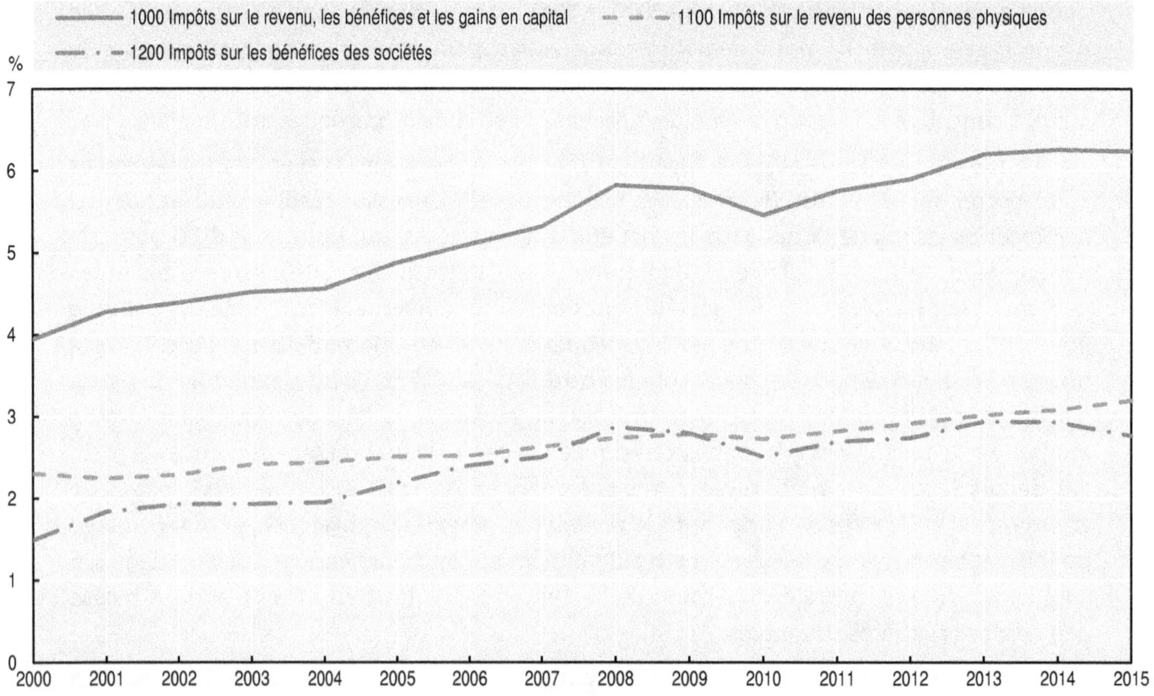

Notes : Les moyennes Afrique (16) excluent le Kenya en 2000 faute de données disponibles.

Une petite fraction (4 %) des recettes tirées des impôts sur le revenu et sur les bénéfices n'a pas pu être imputée à la rubrique 1200 Recettes de l'impôt sur les bénéfices des sociétés ou rubrique 1100 Recettes de l'impôt sur le revenu des personnes physiques.

Source : Calculs de l'auteur à partir de données présentées dans OCDE/ATAF/CUA (2017), « Statistiques des recettes publiques en Afrique: Tableaux comparatifs », *Statistiques fiscales de l'OCDE* (base de données), *http://dx.doi.org/10.1787/7f54581d-fr*.

StatLink http://dx.doi.org/10.1787/888933569326

La mise en place de la TVA en République démocratique du Congo explique en partie l'augmentation intervenue au cours de la période, puisqu'elle est à l'origine de 50 % de cette hausse. Les recettes fiscales en République démocratique du Congo étaient particulièrement faibles en 2000 (0.6 % du PIB), en partie à cause du manque de capacités de l'administration fiscale dans une période de conflits internes. En outre, la République démocratique du Congo a enregistré une croissance annuelle négative de son PIB (en termes réels) entre 1998 et 2002 et a connu une hyperinflation jusqu'en 2003 (OPM, 2013). Dans les périodes d'inflation élevée, le décalage entre la valorisation de la base d'imposition et les recettes effectivement recouvrées, notamment pour l'impôt sur les sociétés, peut entraîner un manque à gagner pour l'État (FMI, 2001).

Graphique 1.10. **Variation des ratios impôts-PIB entre 2000 et 2015 (points de pourcentage du PIB)**

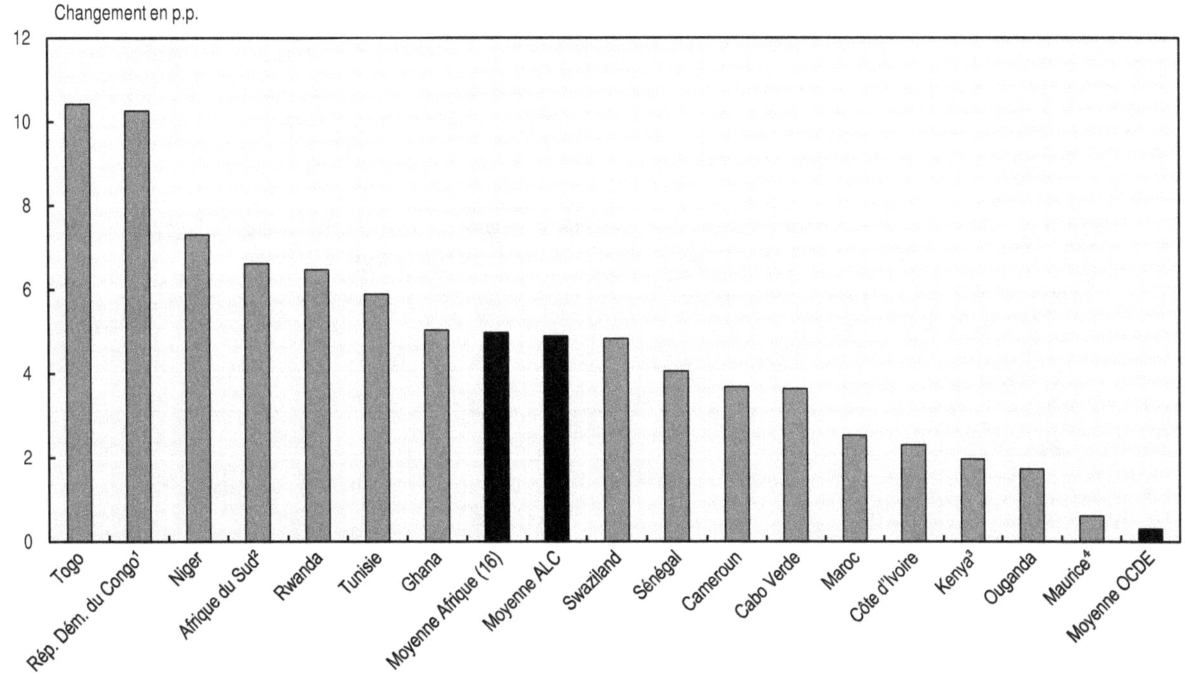

Notes : Les chiffres prennent en compte les recettes fiscales des administrations infranationales pour l'Afrique du Sud, le Maroc, Maurice et le Swaziland. La moyenne Afrique (16) et les moyennes ALC (24 pays d'Amérique latine et Caraïbes) et OCDE (35 pays) sont des moyennes non pondérées.

Il convient d'interpréter la moyenne des pays d'Afrique (16) avec prudence car les données relatives aux cotisations de sécurité sociale ne sont pas disponibles ou ne sont que partielles pour quelques pays. Plus précisément, les données relatives aux cotisations de sécurité sociale ne sont pas disponibles pour l'Ouganda, la République démocratique du Congo et le Togo et, dans le cas du Cameroun, du Kenya et du Sénégal, les données disponibles relatives aux cotisations de sécurité sociale ne sont que partielles. Pour plus de précisions, se reporter aux tableaux par pays présentés dans le chapitre 4.

1. Certaines données sur les recettes fiscales font défaut en 2000 parce que la *Direction Générale Des Recettes Administratives, Judiciaires, Domaniales et de Participations* (DGRAD) ne les a pas communiquées pour les années antérieures à 2010. Néanmoins, elles sont jugées négligeables et inférieures à 1 % du total des recettes fiscales.
2. La variation du ratio impôt-PIB est calculée à partir de données estimées pour 2015.
3. Les données des administrations locales et provinciales avant 2003 ne sont pas disponibles.
4. L'augmentation pour le Kenya concerne la période 2001 à 2015 faute de données disponibles pour les années antérieures à 2001 (exercice 2000/01).

Source : Calculs des auteurs à partir de données présentées dans le tableau 3.1 figurant au chapitre 3 et dans OCDE/ATAF/CUA (2017), « Statistiques des recettes publiques en Afrique: Tableaux comparatifs », *Statistiques fiscales de l'OCDE* (base de données), *http://dx.doi.org/10.1787/7f54581d-fr*, pour la moyenne des pays ALC.

StatLink *http://dx.doi.org/10.1787/888933569345*

La hausse des ratios impôts-PIB intervenue entre 2000 et 2015 est avant tout imputable à l'augmentation en pourcentage du PIB des recettes issues de la TVA, et en second lieu des recettes générées par l'impôt sur les bénéfices des sociétés (graphique 1.11). Les plus fortes hausses des recettes de la TVA en pourcentage du PIB (plus de 3 points de pourcentage) se sont produites dans les quatre pays qui ont mis en place une TVA dans les années 2000 (Cabo Verde, République démocratique du Congo, Rwanda et Swaziland) et au Togo (5.5 points de pourcentage). Au Maroc, l'augmentation de 2.5 points de pourcentage est principalement attribuable à une réforme de la TVA de grande ampleur menée entre 2004 et 2013 (voir l'encadré 1.2). La Côte d'Ivoire, le Kenya, l'Ouganda, le Sénégal et la Tunisie font exception à ces tendances. La Tunisie a enregistré la plus forte progression des recettes de cotisations de sécurité sociale en pourcentage du PIB, soit 3.6 points de pourcentage, au cours de la période. L'élargissement de la couverture du régime de retraite tunisien depuis 2002 peut avoir contribué à cette hausse (International Social Security Association, 2014). Toujours en Tunisie, la deuxième plus forte hausse, équivalente à 2.3 points de pourcentage, concernait les recettes de l'impôt sur le revenu des personnes physiques. Cette catégorie est également à l'origine des augmentations des ratios impôts-PIB observées au Kenya, en Ouganda et au Sénégal au cours de la même période. En Côte d'Ivoire, les recettes tirées des impôts spécifiques sur la consommation ont été le principal moteur de l'augmentation (surtout les droits de douanes) entre 2000 et 2015.

Graphique 1.11. **Variation des ratios impôts-PIB par principales rubriques d'impôt entre 2000 et 2015 et par pays (points de pourcentage du PIB)**

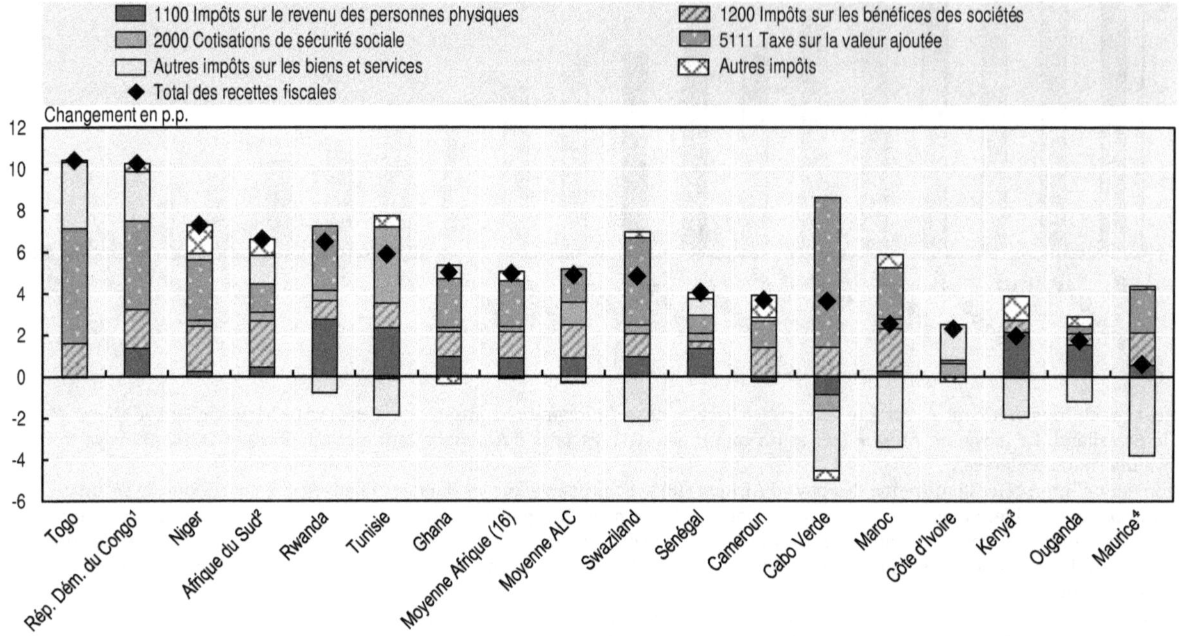

Notes : Les chiffres prennent en compte les recettes fiscales des administrations infranationales pour l'Afrique du Sud, le Maroc, Maurice et le Swaziland. La moyenne Afrique (16) et les moyennes ALC (24 pays d'Amérique latine et Caraïbes) et OCDE (35 pays) sont des moyennes non pondérées.

Il convient d'interpréter la moyenne des pays d'Afrique (16) avec prudence car les données relatives aux cotisations de sécurité sociale ne sont pas disponibles ou ne sont que partielles pour quelques pays. Plus précisément, les données relatives aux cotisations de sécurité sociale ne sont pas disponibles pour l'Ouganda, la République démocratique du Congo et le Togo et, dans le cas du Cameroun, du Kenya et du Sénégal, les données disponibles relatives aux cotisations de sécurité sociale ne sont que partielles. Pour plus de précisions, se reporter aux tableaux par pays présentés dans le chapitre 4.

1. Certaines données relatives aux recettes fiscales font défaut en 2000 parce que la *Direction Générale Des Recettes Administratives, Judiciaires, Domaniales Et De Participations* (DGRAD) ne les a pas communiquées pour les années antérieures à 2010. Néanmoins, elles sont jugées négligeables et inférieures à 1 % du total des recettes fiscales.
2. Afrique du Sud : les données des administrations locales et provinciales avant 2003 ne sont pas disponibles.
3. L'augmentation pour le Kenya concerne la période 2001 à 2015 faute de données disponibles pour les années antérieures à 2001 (exercice 2000/01).
4. Les variations par principales rubriques sont calculées à partir de données estimées pour 2015.

Source : Calculs des auteurs à partir de données présentées dans OCDE/ATAF/CUA (2017), « Statistiques des recettes publiques en Afrique: Tableaux comparatifs », *Statistiques fiscales de l'OCDE* (base de données), *http://dx.doi.org/10.1787/7f54581d-fr*.

StatLink http://dx.doi.org/10.1787/888933569364

Facteurs ayant un effet sur les ratios impôts-PIB

Les ratios impôts-PIB sont influencés par divers facteurs de portée nationale et internationale. Sur le plan national, des caractéristiques macroéconomiques telles que l'importance de l'agriculture dans l'économie, les dotations en ressources, l'ouverture aux échanges et la taille de l'économie informelle peuvent agir sur les ratios impôts-PIB. Le pouvoir de l'administration fiscale, le niveau de corruption et le civisme fiscal (le consentement à l'impôt) sont aussi étroitement liés au niveau des recettes fiscales (OCDE, 2014). En outre, l'emplacement géographique peut exercer une influence sur les ratios impôts-PIB : par exemple, les pays enclavés peuvent plus difficilement taxer les biens et services au port d'entrée que les pays ayant un accès à la mer. Enfin, des facteurs internationaux, y compris les politiques fiscales d'autres pays, peuvent se répercuter sur les ratios impôts-PIB.

Les ratios impôts-PIB sont généralement supérieurs dans les pays à haut revenu : en général, les pays de l'OCDE collectent des recettes fiscales plus importantes que les pays hors OCDE, en pourcentage du PIB. Plusieurs pays africains parmi les seize étudiés affichent des niveaux de revenu et de développement plus faibles et des ratios impôts-PIB plus bas que les pays d'Amérique latine et des Caraïbes (graphique 1.12). Les pays africains enregistrent un éventail de PIB par habitant plus important que les pays d'Amérique latine et des Caraïbes et ceux de l'OCDE.

Graphique 1.12. **Ratios impôts-PIB et PIB par habitant (en PPA) dans les pays d'Afrique, d'Amérique latine et des Caraïbes, dans les pays de l'OCDE et dans certains pays d'Asie, 2015**

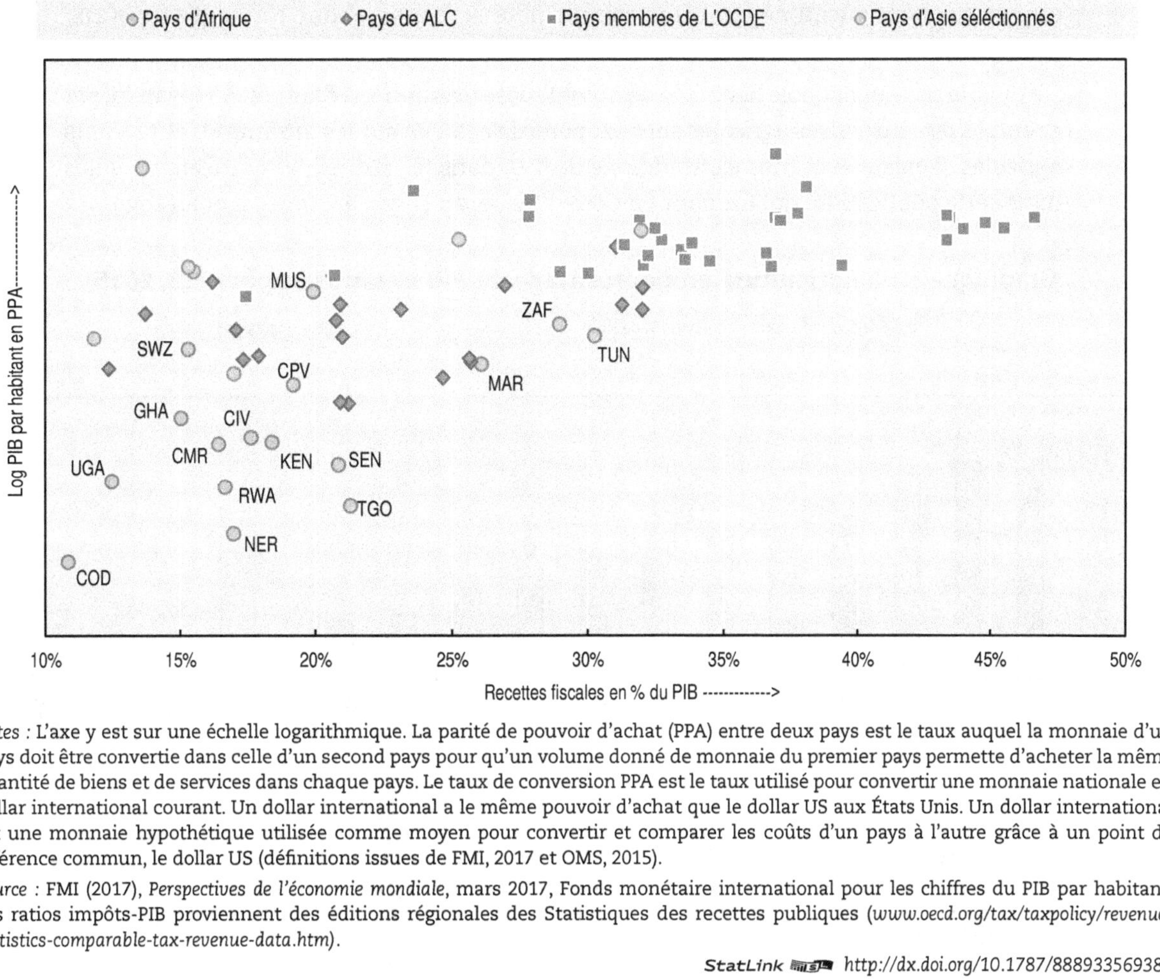

Notes : L'axe y est sur une échelle logarithmique. La parité de pouvoir d'achat (PPA) entre deux pays est le taux auquel la monnaie d'un pays doit être convertie dans celle d'un second pays pour qu'un volume donné de monnaie du premier pays permette d'acheter la même quantité de biens et de services dans chaque pays. Le taux de conversion PPA est le taux utilisé pour convertir une monnaie nationale en dollar international courant. Un dollar international a le même pouvoir d'achat que le dollar US aux États Unis. Un dollar international est une monnaie hypothétique utilisée comme moyen pour convertir et comparer les coûts d'un pays à l'autre grâce à un point de référence commun, le dollar US (définitions issues de FMI, 2017 et OMS, 2015).

Source : FMI (2017), *Perspectives de l'économie mondiale*, mars 2017, Fonds monétaire international pour les chiffres du PIB par habitant. Les ratios impôts-PIB proviennent des éditions régionales des Statistiques des recettes publiques (*www.oecd.org/tax/taxpolicy/revenue-statistics-comparable-tax-revenue-data.htm*).

StatLink http://dx.doi.org/10.1787/888933569383

Les pays qui enregistrent les ratios impôts-PIB les plus faibles sont également ceux dans lesquels la part de l'agriculture (y compris la sylviculture, la chasse et la pêche)[5] dans l'économie est la plus élevée (graphique 1.13). Un pourcentage plus élevé du PIB généré par l'agriculture est généralement associé à un ratio impôts-PIB plus faible (Addison et Levin, 2012 ; Profeta et Scabrosetti, 2010). Ce résultat est en partie cohérent avec les données disponibles pour les pays d'Afrique étudiés dans cette publication, puisque la plupart des pays où l'agriculture occupe une place importante dans l'économie affichent des ratios impôts-PIB plus faibles. Le Cameroun, la Côte d'Ivoire, le Ghana, le Kenya, le Niger, l'Ouganda, la République démocratique du Congo et le Rwanda enregistrent tous une part de l'agriculture dans le PIB supérieure à 20 % et un ratio impôts-PIB inférieur à 19 %. Le Togo fait notablement exception : alors que l'agriculture représente 40 % de son économie, son ratio impôts-PIB est relativement élevé (21.3 %). Dans de nombreux pays, l'agriculture est un secteur difficile à taxer :

- la plupart des personnes qui travaillent dans le secteur agricole dans les économies en développement perçoivent de faibles revenus et ne sont pas déclarées (EPS PEAKS, 2013).
- En outre, le secteur agricole en Afrique est moins taxé en raison de l'ampleur de l'activité informelle et du faible degré de monétisation. Les exploitants agricoles africains effectuent souvent leurs paiements en espèces ou en nature, sans passer par le système bancaire, et pratiquement aucun ne tient une comptabilité en bonne et due forme (BAfD/OCDE/CEA, 2010).
- De plus, le secteur agricole bénéficie de nombreuses exemptions d'impôt. Au Rwanda, par exemple, les entreprises agricoles sont exonérées de la TVA sur les intrants et les produits agricoles. Il existe aussi des exonérations de TVA dans les autres pays africains étudiés dans cette publication, notamment en Côte d'Ivoire, au Niger, au Sénégal et au Togo.

Graphique 1.13. **Agriculture en pourcentage du PIB et ratios impôts-PIB, 2015**

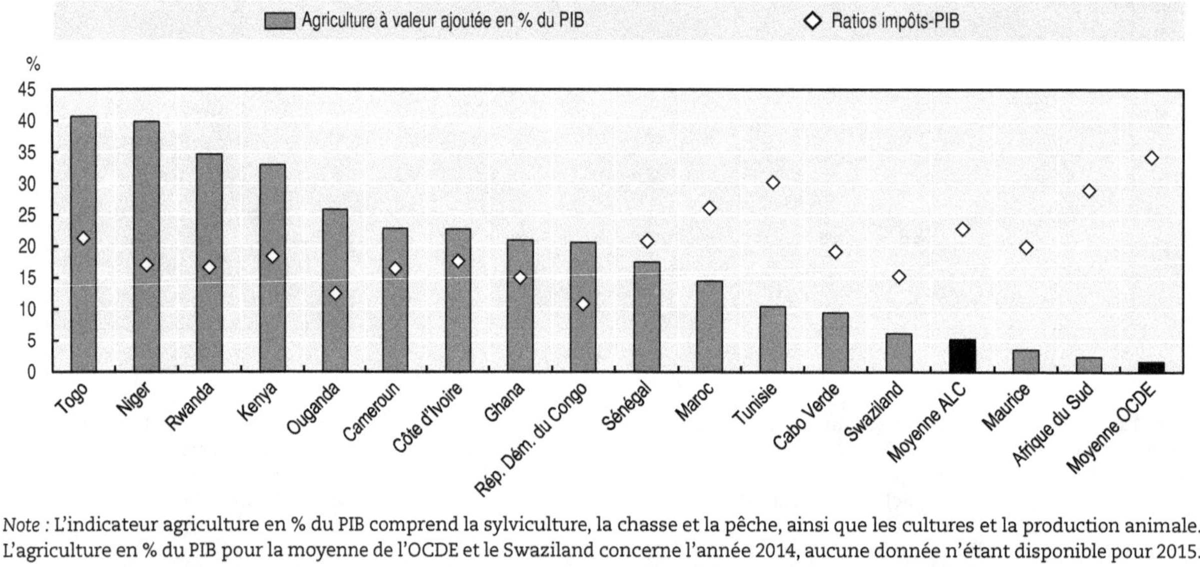

Note : L'indicateur agriculture en % du PIB comprend la sylviculture, la chasse et la pêche, ainsi que les cultures et la production animale. L'agriculture en % du PIB pour la moyenne de l'OCDE et le Swaziland concerne l'année 2014, aucune donnée n'étant disponible pour 2015.

Source : Tableau 3.1 pour les chiffres relatifs au ratio impôts-PIB et OCDE/ATAF/CUA (2017), « Statistiques des recettes publiques en Afrique: Tableaux comparatifs », *Statistiques fiscales de l'OCDE* (base de données), *http://dx.doi.org/10.1787/7f54581d-fr*, pour la moyenne des pays ALC. Banque mondiale pour les chiffres relatifs à l'agriculture en % du PIB.

StatLink http://dx.doi.org/10.1787/888933569402

Cependant, dans les pays de l'OCDE, l'agriculture ne représente guère plus de 2 % du PIB en moyenne. Il convient de noter qu'une faible part de l'agriculture dans le PIB n'assure pas un ratio impôt-PIB élevé. Le Cabo Verde, Maurice et le Swaziland comptent un secteur agricole de petite taille et enregistrent un ratio impôts-PIB relativement faible.

Le ratio impôts-PIB relativement faible à Maurice peut s'expliquer en partie par le niveau des taux d'imposition en vigueur dans ce pays. En effet, Maurice est l'un des pays d'Afrique qui offre le régime fiscal le plus attractif (Sokeechand et Hussen, 2013), avec des taux uniques de 15 % pour l'impôt sur les sociétés, l'impôt sur le revenu des personnes physiques et la TVA et l'exonération des plus-values et des dividendes. À 19.9 %, le ratio impôts-PIB à Maurice est relativement faible comparé à des pays ayant un niveau de revenu analogue. À l'inverse, le taux de l'impôt sur les sociétés est supérieur ou égal à 30 % au Cameroun, au Maroc, au Niger, en Ouganda, en République démocratique du Congo, au Rwanda et au Sénégal, tandis qu'il est compris entre 25 % et 30 % dans les huit pays africains restants, qui en général taxent les gains en capital (Sokeechand et Hussen, 2013).

Les pays riches en ressources qui tirent des recettes substantielles des exportations de pétrole affichent souvent un faible ratio impôts-PIB qui s'explique par l'étroitesse de leurs bases d'imposition. Les pays qui tirent d'importantes recettes de leurs ressources naturelles ont généralement moins recours à des formes d'imposition plus contraignantes politiquement, comme l'impôt sur le revenu (BAfD/OCDE/CEA, 2010), et leurs bases d'imposition sont relativement étroites. Par exemple, l'Afrique du Sud, le Cameroun, la Côte d'Ivoire, le Ghana et la République démocratique du Congo sont considérés par le Fonds monétaire international comme des pays « riches en ressources naturelles»[6]. Au Cameroun et en Côte d'Ivoire, les principales exportations de ressources minérales sont le pétrole (BAfD/OCDE/PNUD, 2015) et un groupe restreint de contribuables supporte l'essentiel de la charge fiscale : au Cameroun, par exemple, seulement dix entreprises ont payé 55 % du total des impôts sur les bénéfices des sociétés en 2013 (FMI, 2014a). On estime que le secteur informel en Côte d'Ivoire représente 90 % de l'économie (PNUD, 2013). Par conséquent, les ratios impôts-PIB de ces deux pays sont relativement bas. Au cours des années 2000, ces deux pays ont engagé diverses initiatives visant à remédier à la surexploitation de la base d'imposition disponible (BAfD/OCDE/CEA, 2010). La Côte d'Ivoire a décidé de limiter l'application des mesures préférentielles aux secteurs prioritaires et à ceux qui ont été particulièrement touchés par la crise de 2002. En 2009 et 2010, le gouvernement camerounais a mis en place des programmes destinés à mobiliser de nouveaux contribuables provenant du secteur informel (BAfD/OCDE/CEA, 2010). Ces dernières années, ces deux pays ont continué de renforcer leur politique et leur administration fiscales dans le but d'élargir leur base d'imposition (FMI, 2013 ; FMI, 2014a).

1.2. Structures fiscales

La structure fiscale mesure la composition des recettes fiscales en fonction des différents types d'impôts. Il s'agit là d'un indicateur important, car différents impôts ont différents effets économiques et sociaux. La composition des impôts varie beaucoup dans les seize pays étudiés, ce qui reflète des différences concernant leurs choix politiques, leurs structures et situations économiques, les capacités de leur administration fiscale et d'autres facteurs historiques.

Évolution des structures fiscales

En moyenne, la structure fiscale des seize pays d'Afrique étudiés (à savoir la part des principaux impôts dans les recettes fiscales totales) révèle une progression des recettes tirées de la TVA et des impôts sur le revenu et sur les bénéfices entre 2000 et 2015. La TVA représentait la plus grande part en 2015, avec 31.5 % du total des recettes fiscales, soit une augmentation de 7.2 points de pourcentage entre 2000 et 2015 (graphique 1.14). La part des impôts sur des biens et services spécifiques (droits d'accise, droits de douane et droits à l'importation) arrivait en deuxième position, soit 24.4 % des recettes fiscales totales, avec un recul de 11.1 points de pourcentage depuis 2000. La part des recettes tirées des impôts sur les bénéfices des sociétés et sur le revenu des personnes physiques a progressé respectivement de 2.9 et de 0.9 points de pourcentage, atteignant 14.6 % et 16.3 % du total des recettes fiscales au cours de la même période.

Graphique 1.14. **Structure fiscale, moyenne Afrique (16), 2000 et 2015**

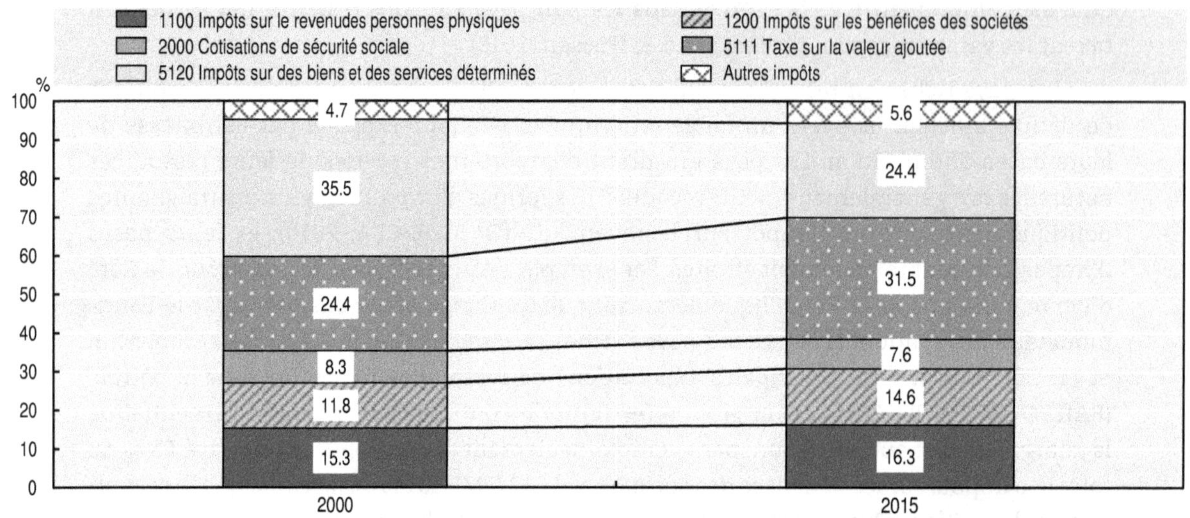

Notes : Il convient d'interpréter la moyenne des pays d'Afrique (16) avec prudence car les données relatives aux cotisations de sécurité sociale ne sont pas disponibles ou ne sont que partielles pour quelques pays. Plus précisément, les données relatives aux cotisations de sécurité sociale ne sont pas disponibles pour l'Ouganda, la République démocratique du Congo et le Togo et, dans le cas du Cameroun, du Kenya et du Sénégal, les données disponibles relatives aux cotisations de sécurité sociale ne sont que partielles. Pour plus de précisions, se reporter aux tableaux par pays présentés dans le chapitre 4.

La moyenne Afrique (16) exclut le Kenya en 2000 parce que les données ne sont pas disponibles.

Source : Calculs de l'auteur à partir de données présentées dans OCDE/ATAF/CUA (2017), « Statistiques des recettes publiques en Afrique: Tableaux comparatifs », *Statistiques fiscales de l'OCDE* (base de données), *http://dx.doi.org/10.1787/7f54581d-fr*.

StatLink *http://dx.doi.org/10.1787/888933569421*

Les structures fiscales sont très variables d'un pays africain à l'autre. Le graphique 1.15 illustre la ventilation des recettes fiscales entre impôts sur le revenu (personnes physiques et sociétés), cotisations de sécurité sociale et impôts sur les biens et services (y compris la TVA ainsi que d'autres impôts sur les biens et services). Bien que les impôts sur les biens et services génèrent plus de 50 % des recettes fiscales dans tous les pays sauf l'Afrique du Sud, le Maroc, le Swaziland et la Tunisie, ils vont de 35.8 % des recettes en Tunisie jusqu'à 80 % au Togo. C'est en Côte d'Ivoire, au Maroc et en Tunisie que la part des cotisations de sécurité sociale dans le total des recettes fiscales est la plus élevée.

Par comparaison avec les quatorze autres pays africains, le Maroc et la Tunisie affichent une répartition relativement homogène des recettes entre les principales catégories d'impôts (graphique 1.15). Cette situation s'explique par une part relativement plus élevée des recettes tirées des cotisations de sécurité sociale en pourcentage du total des recettes fiscales dans ces deux pays, et par une part plus faible des recettes issues des impôts sur les biens et services. Le Maroc et la Tunisie sont les pays où la part des recettes provenant des cotisations de sécurité sociale (respectivement 17.0 % et 29.5 %) est la plus élevée et celle issue des impôts sur les biens et services (respectivement 43.6 % et 35.8 %) la plus faible. La part des recettes tirées des impôts sur le revenu et sur les bénéfices avoisine 30 % dans ces deux pays.

Graphique 1.15. **Structure fiscale, par pays, 2015**

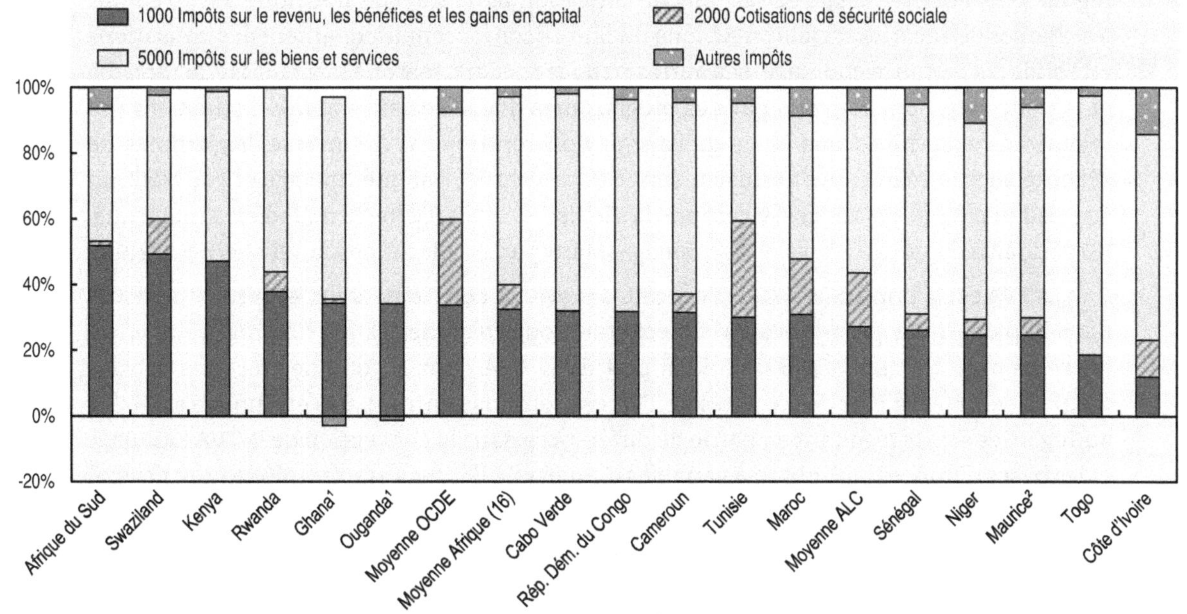

Notes : Les chiffres prennent en compte les recettes fiscales des administrations infranationales pour l'Afrique du Sud, le Maroc, Maurice et le Swaziland. La moyenne Afrique (16) et les moyennes ALC (24 pays d'Amérique latine et Caraïbes) et OCDE (35 pays) sont des moyennes non pondérées.

Il convient d'interpréter la moyenne des pays d'Afrique (16) avec prudence car les données relatives aux cotisations de sécurité sociale ne sont pas disponibles ou ne sont que partielles pour quelques pays. Plus précisément, les données relatives aux cotisations de sécurité sociale ne sont pas disponibles pour l'Ouganda, la République démocratique du Congo et le Togo et, dans le cas du Cameroun, du Kenya et du Sénégal, les données disponibles relatives aux cotisations de sécurité sociale ne sont que partielles. Pour plus de précisions, se reporter aux tableaux par pays présentés dans le chapitre 4.

1. Les recettes tirées d'autres impôts sont négatives en raison de l'imputation des remboursements d'impôt dans cette catégorie. Il n'a pas été possible de ventiler ces recettes par principal type d'impôt.
2. Les données pour 2015 sont des estimations.

Source : Calculs de l'auteur à partir de données présentées dans OCDE/ATAF/CUA (2017), « Statistiques des recettes publiques en Afrique: Tableaux comparatifs », *Statistiques fiscales de l'OCDE* (base de données), *http://dx.doi.org/10.1787/7f54581d-fr*.

StatLink *http://dx.doi.org/10.1787/888933569440*

L'Afrique du Sud, le Kenya et le Swaziland ont mobilisé près de la moitié de leurs recettes fiscales grâce aux impôts sur le revenu et les bénéfices, soit une fraction plus élevée que celle recouvrée par d'autres pays étudiés, mais également que la moyenne des pays de l'OCDE et ALC. Parmi ces pays, les recettes générées par l'impôt sur le revenu étaient comprises entre 47.1 % du total des recettes fiscales au Kenya et 51.8 % en Afrique du Sud. Bien que cette proportion soit supérieure à celle des recettes provenant des impôts sur les biens et services au Swaziland et en Afrique du Sud, elle est légèrement inférieure au Kenya. Dans les autres pays d'Afrique sub-saharienne étudiés dans cette publication, les recettes issues des impôts sur les revenus et les bénéfices étaient inférieures à 20 % du total des recettes fiscales en Côte d'Ivoire et au Togo, comprises entre 25 % et 35 % au Cabo Verde, au Cameroun, à Maurice, au Niger, en Ouganda, en République démocratique du Congo et au Sénégal, et comprises entre 35 % et 40 % au Ghana et au Rwanda.

L'importance des cotisations de sécurité sociale[7] est très variable entre les seize pays couverts par ce rapport. La part des cotisations de sécurité sociale dans le total des recettes fiscales est la plus élevée au Maroc et en Tunisie, comme indiqué précédemment. Elles occupent une place beaucoup plus modeste dans le total des recettes fiscales dans les autres pays qui en prélèvent, allant de moins de 1.5 % en Afrique du Sud, au Cabo Verde, au Ghana et au Kenya à 11.2 % en Côte d'Ivoire. Cette hétérogénéité reflète la diversité des régimes de sécurité sociale et des taux de cotisation dans les pays d'Afrique. Par exemple, les charges de sécurité sociale en Afrique du Sud se composent uniquement des cotisations au Fonds d'assurance chômage. Les autres risques sociaux, tels que la vieillesse, la maladie et la maternité, sont couverts par des programmes d'aide sociale – qui se distinguent des régimes de sécurité sociale en ce qu'ils sont non contributifs. À l'inverse, les régimes de sécurité sociale marocain et tunisien sont calqués sur le système français et couvrent un éventail plus large de risques, y compris la vieillesse, l'incapacité, la maladie, la maternité, les accidents du travail (Tunisie), le chômage (Maroc) et les allocations familiales (SSA, 2015).

La TVA est la principale source de recettes provenant des impôts sur les biens et services dans la plupart des pays africains. On constate toutefois une grande hétérogénéité entre les seize pays africains s'agissant de la part de la TVA dans le total des recettes fiscales (graphique 1.16). La part des recettes de TVA est comprise entre 19.8 % en Tunisie et 44.2 % au Togo. Ces écarts résultent en partie de différences dans la conception de la TVA : les taux et les bases d'imposition sont très variables d'un pays à l'autre. Par exemple, le taux normal de TVA va de 14 % en Afrique du Sud et au Swaziland à 20 % au Maroc. La part moyenne des recettes de la TVA pour les 16 pays d'Afrique étudiés, de 31.5 %, est légèrement supérieure à la moyenne des pays ALC (28.4 %) et dépasse de plus de 10 points de pourcentage celle de la zone OCDE (20.1 %). Toutefois, en pourcentage du PIB, la part des recettes de la TVA pour la moyenne des 16 pays africains reste inférieure aux moyennes de la zone OCDE (6.8 %) et des pays ALC (6.0 %).

Graphique 1.16. **Recettes de la TVA en pourcentage du total des recettes fiscales et du PIB par pays, 2015**

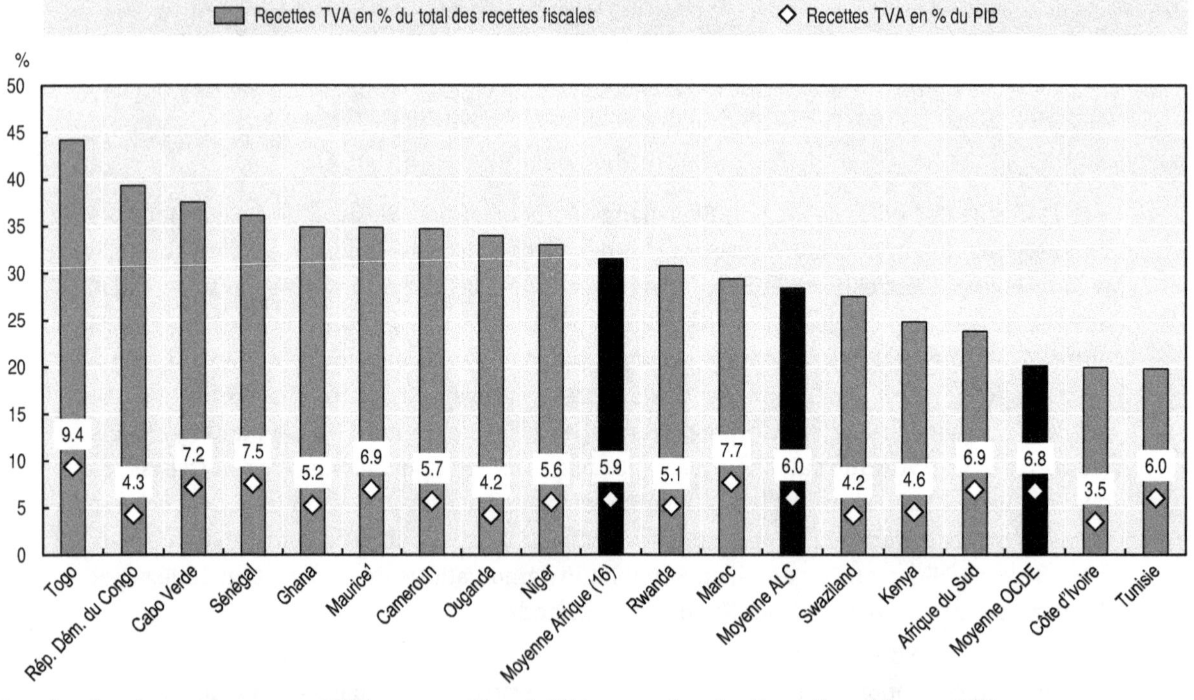

Note : Les données pour la moyenne OCDE concernent l'année 2014, aucune donnée n'étant disponible pour 2015.

1. Les données pour 2015 sont des estimations.

Source : Calculs de l'auteur à partir de données présentées dans OCDE/ATAF/CUA (2017), « Statistiques des recettes publiques en Afrique: Tableaux comparatifs », *Statistiques fiscales de l'OCDE* (base de données), *http://dx.doi.org/10.1787/7f54581d-fr*.

StatLink *http://dx.doi.org/10.1787/888933569459*

La part moyenne des recettes issues de l'impôt sur les bénéfices des sociétés dans le total des recettes fiscales en Afrique (14.6 %) est supérieure à la moyenne de l'OCDE de 8.8 % (chiffre de 2014) mais inférieure à la moyenne des pays ALC (15.8 %) (tableau 1.1). En pourcentage du PIB, la moyenne Afrique (16) et la moyenne OCDE révèlent une part similaire des recettes issues de l'impôt sur les bénéfices des sociétés, de respectivement 2.9 % et 2.8 % du PIB (tableau 1.1). Si l'on procède à une comparaison entre pays, la part des recettes tirées de l'impôt sur les bénéfices des sociétés dans le total des recettes fiscales en 2015 oscillait entre 7.4 % en Ouganda et 19.7 % au Swaziland.

Tableau 1.1. **Recettes de l'impôt sur les bénéfices et de l'impôt sur le revenu en pourcentage du total des recettes fiscales et du PIB, 2015**

	En % du total des recettes fiscales		En % du PIB	
	Impôts sur les bénéfices des sociétés	Impôts sur le revenu des personnes physiques	Impôts sur les bénéfices des sociétés	Impôts sur le revenu des personnes physiques
Afrique du Sud	16.4	33.4	4.7	9.7
Cabo Verde	14.4	17.4	2.8	3.3
Cameroun	19.5	6.7	3.2	1.1
Rép. Dém. du Congo	18.3	13.3	2.0	1.4
Côte d'Ivoire	11.0	0.3	1.9	0.0
Ghana	18.4	17.1	2.8	2.6
Kenya	11.8	26.6	2.2	4.9
Maroc	16.3	14.5	4.2	3.8
Maurice	13.7	9.5	2.7	1.9
Niger	18.3	6.3	3.1	1.1
Ouganda	7.4	24.6	0.9	3.1
Rwanda	15.6	22.3	2.6	3.7
Sénégal	8.7	15.7	1.8	3.3
Swaziland	19.7	28.7	3.0	4.4
Togo	14.0	4.6	3.0	1.0
Tunisie	10.4	19.5	3.2	5.9
Moyenne Afrique (16)	**14.6**	**16.3**	**2.9**	**3.1**
Moyenne ALC	**15.8**	**9.1**	**3.7**	**2.2**
Moyenne OCDE	**8.8**	**24.0**	**2.8**	**8.4**

Notes : Les chiffres prennent en compte les recettes fiscales des administrations infranationales pour l'Afrique du Sud, Maurice, le Maroc et le Swaziland. La moyenne Afrique (16) et les moyennes ALC (24 pays d'Amérique latine et Caraïbes) et OCDE (35 pays) sont des moyennes non pondérées.

Les données pour la moyenne OCDE concernent l'année 2014, aucune donnée n'étant disponible pour 2015.

Les chiffres concernant le Cameroun, le Kenya et les pays ALC doivent être interprétés avec précaution car 18 % à 20 % de leurs recettes issues des impôts sur le revenu et sur les bénéfices ne peuvent pas être attribuées à la catégorie Recettes de l'impôt sur les bénéfices des sociétés (1200) ou Recettes de l'impôt sur le revenu des personnes physiques (1100).

Sources : Calculs de l'auteur à partir de données présentées dans OCDE/ATAF/CUA (2017), « Statistiques des recettes publiques en Afrique: Tableaux comparatifs », *Statistiques fiscales de l'OCDE* (base de données), *http://dx.doi.org/10.1787/7f54581d-fr.*

StatLink *http://dx.doi.org/10.1787/888933569953*

En revanche, la part moyenne, dans les 16 pays d'Afrique, des recettes de l'impôt sur le revenu des personnes physiques dans le total des recettes fiscales, soit 16.3 %, était bien inférieure à la moyenne de l'OCDE de 24.0 % (chiffre de 2014) mais supérieure à la moyenne ALC (9.1 %). En pourcentage du PIB, la part des recettes de l'impôt sur le revenu des personnes physiques de la moyenne des pays de l'OCDE atteignait 8.4 %, soit plus du double de la moyenne Afrique (16) de 3.1 %. L'Afrique du Sud est l'unique pays où la part des recettes de l'impôt sur le revenu des personnes physiques, à 9.7 % du PIB, dépasse celle de la moyenne de l'OCDE. Dans les autres pays, les recettes générées par l'impôt sur le revenu des personnes physiques oscillaient entre 0.0 % du PIB en Côte d'Ivoire et 5.9 % en Tunisie.

Dans neuf pays africains, les recettes tirées des impôts sur les bénéfices des sociétés sont plus élevées que celles des impôts sur le revenu des personnes physiques. À l'inverse, en pourcentage du total des recettes fiscales, la part des recettes de l'impôt sur le revenu des personnes physiques est plus de deux fois supérieure à celle des impôts sur les bénéfices des sociétés en Afrique du Sud, au Kenya et en Ouganda.

1.3. Impôts par niveaux d'administration

L'analyse de la répartition des impôts par niveaux d'administration effectuée dans cette publication est limitée par le manque de données sur les recettes fiscales perçues par les administrations infranationales. Ces données n'étaient disponibles que pour quatre pays : l'Afrique du Sud, le Maroc, Maurice[8] et le Swaziland. Les finances des collectivités locales ne sont pas toujours bien suivies en Afrique. Dans certains pays, lorsque des états financiers existent, ils ne font pas l'objet d'un archivage électronique.

Les recettes fiscales des collectivités locales sont considérées comme faibles dans les seize pays africains. Lorsqu'il n'existe pas de données, les spécialistes estiment que ces recettes ne représentent qu'un pourcentage marginal du total des rentrées fiscales. Selon la (BAfD/OCDE/CEA, 2010), « les recettes mobilisées par les collectivités locales sont estimées à environ 1 % du revenu national en Afrique, et se concentrent dans les grands centres urbains ». D'après la (BAfD/OCDE/PNUD, 2015), « en Afrique, en moyenne, le poids des recettes des administrations locales équivaut à 7 % des recettes totales perçues par les collectivités locales et régionales et l'administration centrale combinées ». Des chiffres supplémentaires émanant de la Banque africaine de développement montrent que les recettes des collectivités locales en Côte d'Ivoire et au Sénégal représentent une faible proportion du total des rentrées fiscales (de l'ordre de 3-4 %[9]).

Lorsque des données sont disponibles, elles montrent que les recettes des administrations infranationales déclarées restent minimes. En 2015, les recettes des administrations infranationales en pourcentage du total des recettes fiscales étaient de moins de 1 % à Maurice, 1.4 % au Swaziland, 3.4 % au Maroc et 4.8 % en Afrique du Sud.

Les impôts sur le patrimoine constituent la plus importante source de revenu pour les administrations infranationales en Afrique du Sud, au Maroc, à Maurice et au Swaziland. Ils représentent environ plus de 80 % du total des recettes fiscales dans les quatre pays. Le solde se compose principalement des impôts sur les biens et services. On observe de grandes disparités en la matière, et de nombreux pays ne lèvent aucune taxe locale sur les bâtiments et la propriété foncière, voire même sur les activités économiques (BAfD/OCDE/PNUD, 2015). Les impôts sur le patrimoine contribuent généralement plus aux recettes des collectivités locales dans les pays anglophones d'Afrique que dans les pays francophones (BAfD/OCDE/PNUD, 2015).

Les compétences fiscales dévolues aux administrations infranationales sont généralement limitées, et la responsabilité du recouvrement de l'impôt incombe avant tout à l'administration centrale. BAfD/OCDE/PNUD, 2015 observent que « de nombreuses administrations locales perçoivent une fraction importante de leurs recettes totales grâce aux transferts opérés par l'administration centrale ». Cette situation tient en partie au fait que les systèmes fiscaux au niveau local ont été hérités des administrations française et anglaise et n'ont pratiquement pas été modifiés depuis l'indépendance. C'est notamment vrai en Afrique francophone. Dans les pays francophones comme le Maroc, le Sénégal, la Côte d'Ivoire et le Cameroun, les recettes locales sont souvent collectées par l'administration centrale pour le compte des administrations locales, tandis qu'en Afrique du Sud, elles le sont directement par les collectivités locales (89 % en 2007) (Fjeldstad, Chambas et Brun, 2014). Les administrations locales mauriciennes sont largement tributaires des transferts de l'administration centrale (FMI, 2014b).

Les collectivités locales dans la plupart des pays d'Afrique sub-saharienne se heurtent à des contraintes de ressources et les outils dont disposent leurs administrations fiscales sont inadaptés pour procéder à un recouvrement efficient des impôts et les imputer correctement en comptabilité. Cette situation entraîne des coûts de recouvrement élevés et un grand nombre d'impôts peu productifs. En outre, le traitement des données relatives aux recettes collectées et l'échange de renseignements avec d'autres institutions publiques sont peu développés, et les administrations locales coopèrent généralement peu avec l'administration centrale. Cela se traduit par des impôts en double ou qui vont à l'encontre des objectifs nationaux (comme des taxes locales sur les cultures d'exportation). À l'exception de l'Afrique du Sud, les registres fonciers en bonne et due forme font défaut, ce qui entrave la collecte des impôts fonciers (Fjeldstad, Chambas et Brun, 2014). À Maurice, par exemple, la taxe foncière est peu productive en partie à cause de cadastres périmés et de valeurs de biens qui ne sont plus à jour (FMI, 2014b).

Bien que de nombreux pays africains aient entrepris de vastes réformes de leur administration fiscale centrale et de la législation correspondante au cours des dernières décennies, il n'y a guère eu d'initiatives de ce genre au niveau des administrations locales. On a donné la priorité aux recettes perçues par l'administration centrale parce que c'est à cet échelon que la nécessité de réduire les déficits budgétaires s'est fait sentir le plus. Par ailleurs, il est plus simple et moins coûteux de réformer la législation et les systèmes fiscaux au niveau national qu'au niveau local, et les avantages potentiels de la réforme fiscale en termes d'accroissement des recettes sont plus importants. En 2007, le Maroc a lancé une réforme du système fiscal et des administrations fiscales locales en vue d'augmenter les recettes générées par les impôts locaux (Boisard, de Freitas et Hidouci, 2014). D'autres pays étudiés dans cette publication, comme le Cameroun, la Côte d'Ivoire (BAfD/OCDE/CEA, 2010) et récemment la Tunisie (Banque mondiale, 2015), ont engagé des processus de décentralisation budgétaire qui donneront des pouvoirs accrus aux administrations locales et devraient améliorer la collecte des recettes. L'Afrique du Sud est un exemple de pays qui a décentralisé avec succès le processus de recouvrement de la taxe foncière urbaine. Elle a mis en place un système moderne de collecte des recettes de la taxe foncière et les autorités municipales reçoivent un appui approprié en termes d'expertise et de moyens (Monkam et Moore, 2015). Monkam et Moore, 2015 précisent qu'« en Afrique du Sud, les autorités provinciales apportent aux autorités locales un soutien administratif et une formation pour faciliter le calcul de l'impôt, l'émission des avis de recouvrement et la collecte ».

RECETTES NON FISCALES

Introduction

Les recettes non fiscales représentent une toile de fond importante pour l'interprétation des recettes publiques. En effet, deux pays qui présentent des niveaux de recettes fiscales et de dépenses publiques comparables peuvent néanmoins se trouver dans des situations financières très éloignées en raison de différences dans les recettes non fiscales qu'ils perçoivent. Par conséquent, pour obtenir une vision précise de la situation financière d'une administration, il convient de tenir compte de l'ensemble des recettes publiques, fiscales et non fiscales, malgré les défis particuliers qui entourent la collecte des données relatives aux recettes non fiscales (encadré 1.4). C'est particulièrement le cas pour un grand nombre de pays africains pour lesquels les rentes tirées de ressources naturelles ou les dons peuvent représenter une fraction significative des recettes publiques.

Les principales catégories[10] de recettes non fiscales examinées ici sont les suivantes :

- dons émanant de pays étrangers ou d'organisations internationales (aide budgétaire, aide alimentaire, transferts de capitaux, transferts courants, subventions de projets, bourses de programme, allégement de la dette internationale, etc) ;
- revenus de la propriété (par exemple : redevances minières, rémunération d'investissements publics) ;
- ventes de biens et de services par l'état (ce qui inclut certains frais administratifs) ;
- amendes et pénalités ;
- recettes diverses et non identifiées (ce qui englobe des recettes qui auraient pu être classées dans l'une des catégories précédentes si elles avaient été identifiées plus précisément).

Parmi les sources particulières de recettes diverses qui ne répondent pas à la définition d'une recette fiscale figurent les recettes issues de l'Union douanière d'Afrique australe (SACU), dispositif qui regroupe d'abord, puis répartit entre les pays concernés, des recettes tirées de droits d'accise et de droits de douane revenant à l'Afrique du Sud, au Botswana, au Lesotho, à la Namibie et au Swaziland (encadré 1.5).

1.4. Recettes non fiscales exprimées en pourcentage du PIB

Dans les 16 pays couverts par cette publication, les recettes non fiscales exprimées en pourcentage du PIB varient dans une large fourchette, en partant de 0.6 % en Afrique du Sud à 15.1 % du PIB au Swaziland (recettes de la SACU, pour l'essentiel) . Dans tous les pays étudiés, les recettes non fiscales étaient inférieures aux recettes fiscales (graphique 1.17).

Alors que les recettes fiscales exprimées en pourcentage du PIB suivent pour la plupart une tendance à la hausse dans les 16 pays africains étudiés, il semble qu'il en aille autrement des recettes non fiscales (voir tableau 1.2). Sur les 14 pays pour lesquels les données relatives aux recettes non fiscales sont disponibles pour les dix dernières années, huit ont montré une tendance à la baisse des ratios recettes non fiscales-PIB, et seulement six ont montré une tendance croissante.

Graphique 1.17. **Recettes fiscales et non fiscales totales par pays, en pourcentage du PIB, 2015**

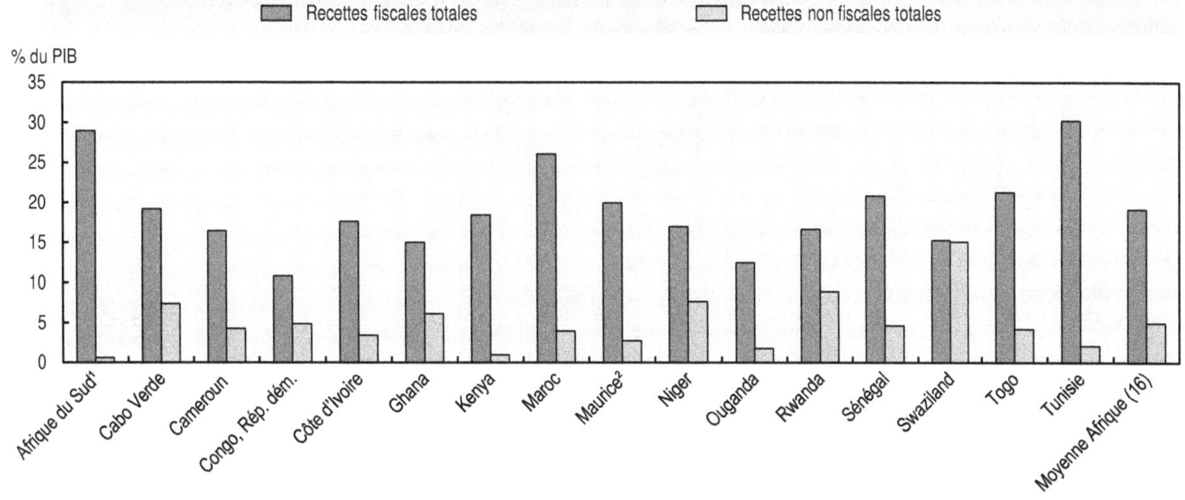

Notes : Les données relatives aux recettes non fiscales incluent des recettes perçues par les administrations infranationales pour le Maroc, Maurice et le Swaziland, les seuls pays pour lesquels ces données sont disponibles. En 2015, les recettes non fiscales perçues par les administrations infranationales pour ces pays représentaient respectivement 7.6 %, 37 % et plus de 1 % des recettes non fiscales totales de chaque pays. Les recettes fiscales perçues par les administrations infranationales pour ces pays étaient respectivement de moins de 1 %, 3.4 % et 1.4 % du total des recettes fiscales. L'Afrique du Sud rapportait 4.8 % de ces recettes fiscales provenant des administrations au niveau provincial et local, cependant aucune recette non fiscale n'a été rapportée.

1. Il convient d'interpréter le ratio impôt-PIB avec prudence car il prend en compte les sommes recouvrées au profit de l'Union douanière de l'Afrique australe (SACU) par l'Afrique du Sud, qui ne correspondent pas à la définition des recettes fiscales de l'OCDE. Les moyennes Afrique (16) représentent des moyennes non pondérées pour les 16 pays africains inclus dans cette publication. Il convient d'interpréter la moyenne pour le ratio impôts-PIB avec prudence car des données relatives aux cotisations de sécurité sociale sont indisponibles ou incomplètes pour quelques pays. En particulier, les données relatives aux cotisations de sécurité sociale ne sont pas disponibles pour l'Ouganda, la République démocratique du Congo et le Togo, et elles sont incomplètes pour le Cameroun, le Kenya et le Sénégal. Les données sur les taxes foncières ne sont pas disponibles pour le Ghana et l'Ouganda, et ne sont que partiellement disponibles pour la République démocratique du Congo. Voir les tableaux par pays au chapitre 4 pour plus de précisions.

2. Les données pour 2015 sont des estimations.

Source : Tableau 3.1 du chapitre 3 et tableau 5.1 du chapitre 5.

StatLink http://dx.doi.org/10.1787/888933569478

Encadré 1.4. **Les problèmes de qualité propres aux données relatives aux recettes non fiscales**

Les recettes non fiscales ne sont pas systématiquement incluses dans les publications consacrées aux statistiques des recettes publiques. Cela s'explique notamment par le fait que les données relatives aux recettes non fiscales sont souvent plus difficiles à collecter et à valider que les données fiscales, et requièrent plus de travail avant de pouvoir les intégrer au sein d'une base de données harmonisée.

Les données relatives aux recettes non fiscales sont moins faciles à utiliser que celles portant sur les recettes fiscales, dans la mesure où elles sont fréquemment absentes des documents budgétaires de référence et des bases de données publiques, et où elles ne relèvent pas toujours de la responsabilité des services chargés d'établir les statistiques fiscales.

En outre, lorsque ces données existent, elles sont souvent dépourvues du niveau de détail que présentent les données fiscales et les précisions nécessaires font parfois défaut. Certains pays, par exemple, fournissent pour certaines années un total agrégé de leurs recettes non fiscales, sans autre détail à part la répartition entre les aides sous formes de dons et les autres catégories de recettes non fiscales. Non seulement cet état de fait abaisse la qualité des analyses statistiques, mais il complique également la vérification des données. Dans la mesure où les données relatives aux recettes non fiscales proviennent fréquemment de plusieurs sources différentes, il arrive que, pour une année donnée, les statistiques soient disponibles pour certaines sous-catégories de recettes, et manquantes pour d'autres. On peut ainsi être confronté à des bases

Encadré 1.4. **Les problèmes de qualité propres aux données relatives aux recettes non fiscales** *(suite)*

de données contenant, par exemple les détails sur les dons à compter de l'année 2000, mais les revenus de la propriété ne sont disponibles seulement qu'à partir de 2010. Dans la présente publication, une note est insérée chaque fois que nécessaire pour mentionner quelles bases de données relatives aux recettes non fiscales peuvent être le résultat d'une couverture incomplète.

Il est par ailleurs possible que les données sur les recettes non fiscales ne fassent pas l'objet de vérifications aussi strictes que celles relatives aux recettes fiscales. Nombre de ces recettes ne sont pas incluses dans le processus budgétaire principal et les données correspondantes ne sont pas soumises aux mêmes mécanismes de contrôle que dans le cas de recettes fiscales. Les dons, les règlements de différends juridiques, les contrats d'exploitation minière ou pétrolière donnent souvent lieu à des versements très importants de la part de grandes entités extérieures telles que des entreprises multinationales ou des administrations qui n'offrent pas le degré de transparence approprié. Ces accords peuvent inclure des dispositions tenues secrètes, par exemple lorsqu'un contrat important signé avec une entreprise exploitant des ressources naturelles est assorti de clauses de confidentialité très strictes (BAfD/OCDE/CEA, 2010). De plus, il est plus difficile d'établir des ventilations détaillées dès lors qu'un pays négocie un versement élevé qui recouvre plusieurs catégories de recettes.

Même lorsque des données de qualité sont disponibles, leur comptabilisation n'est pas exempte de difficultés, la notion de recettes non fiscales étant plus large que celle de recettes fiscales. De plus, les créances fiscales détenues par l'État sont le plus souvent comptabilisées en monnaie nationale, que ce soit avant ou après leur paiement. Cela n'est pas le cas des recettes non fiscales, puisqu'elles peuvent prendre la forme de transferts de capital qui ne sont pas systématiquement valorisés en monnaie nationale lors de la transaction. À titre d'exemple, une personne peut faire don à l'État d'un édifice historique afin qu'il soit transformé en musée. Ce don représente une recette publique dont la valeur monétaire réelle peut ne pas être connue avec précision aux fins de sa comptabilisation.

Tableau 1.2. **Total des recettes non fiscales en pourcentage du PIB**

Pays	2000	2005	2010	2011	2012	2013	2014	2015
Afrique du Sud	0.5	0.5	0.6	0.7	0.7	0.7	0.6	0.6
Cabo Verde	7.6	9.2	9.7	5.6	6.0	6.2	5.3	7.4
Cameroun	8.0	6.9	4.8	6.2	5.0	4.9	4.2	4.3
Congo, Rép. dém.	..	..	9.9	3.9	5.7	3.6	5.3	4.9
Côte d'Ivoire	1.1	2.3	1.7	1.5	1.9	2.5	2.6	3.4
Ghana[1]	2.2	4.3	5.0	5.3	6.1	6.2	5.6	6.1
Kenya[2]	..	2.9	0.9	..	..	1.3	0.9	1.0
Maroc	2.2	3.0	3.6	3.9	3.7	4.1	3.8	3.9
Maurice[3]	2.8	2.5	3.8	3.5	3.1	3.2	2.7	2.7
Niger	..	8.2	6.3	4.9	8.0	9.5	8.0	7.6
Ouganda	..	6.7	2.9	2.1	2.2	1.2	1.3	1.8
Rwanda	11.8	12.7	12.3	12.3	8.8	11.2	9.4	8.9
Sénégal	2.7	2.3	3.2	2.9	3.8	3.8	5.2	4.6
Swaziland[4]	12.4	15.9	8.1	6.8	19.5	17.4	17.1	15.1
Togo	2.1	2.5	7.2	6.2	4.3	5.3	4.2	4.1
Tunisie	4.6	2.6	2.9	4.0	3.5	3.6	2.4	2.1

Notes : Le symbole « .. » signale des données incomplètes pour l'année considérée.
Les chiffres prennent en compte les recettes non fiscales des administrations infranationales pour le Maroc, Maurice et le Swaziland.
1. Les données antérieures à 2010 n'incluent pas les redevances pétrolières ou minières qui n'ont pu être distinguées des recettes fiscales.
2. Les données sont incomplètes pour 2011 et 2012.
3. Les données pour 2015 sont des estimations.
4. Les chiffres antérieurs à 2012 n'incluent pas les dons, pour lesquels les données ne sont pas disponibles.
Source : Tableau 5.1 du chapitre 5.

StatLink http://dx.doi.org/10.1787/888933569972

Le montant des recettes non fiscales recouvrées affiche de fortes variations annuelles. Le graphique 1.18, qui présente le coefficient de variation[11] des recettes fiscales et non fiscales au cours des dix dernières années de données disponibles, met en évidence les variations plus marquées des recettes non fiscales. Cette volatilité découle en grande partie de la forte instabilité des deux catégories qui représentent en règle générale l'essentiel des recettes non fiscales, à savoir les aides sous forme de dons et les revenus de la propriété. Le montant des dons perçus évolue en fonction des priorités des donateurs, qui peuvent être fortement modifiées au fil des ans. Quant aux revenus de la propriété, ils peuvent varier brutalement selon les cours des minéraux, ou sous l'effet de l'ouverture d'un nouveau site d'extraction minière qui entraîne une forte hausse de la production. Cette volatilité contraste avec l'évolution plus stable des recettes dans les 16 pays étudiés. On notera cependant que le Rwanda enregistre des niveaux de variation comparables des recettes fiscales et non fiscales (lesquelles sont, pour l'essentiel, des dons).

Graphique 1.18. **Coefficients de variation (CV) des recettes fiscales et non fiscales, 2006-15**

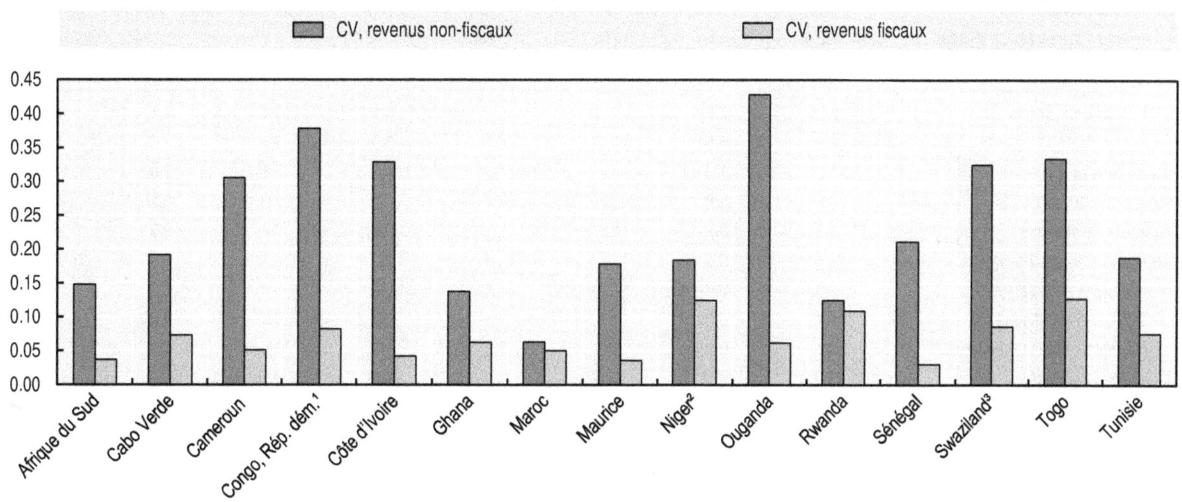

Notes : Les chiffres prennent en compte les recettes non fiscales des administrations infranationales pour le Maroc, Maurice et le Swaziland.

1. En raison de la nature incomplète des données, le CV n'a pas été calculé pour le Kenya, et l'a été sur la période 2010-15 seulement pour la République démocratique du Congo.
2. Le CV pour le Niger a été calculé sans utiliser les données de l'année 2006, alors qu'il y avait un pic des recettes provenant des dons.
3. Le CV pour le Swaziland a été calculé sans utiliser de données sur les recettes provenant des dons au cours des années 2006-11, alors qu'il manquait.

Source : Calculs des auteurs à partir de données présentées dans les tableaux 3.1 du chapitre 3 et 5.1 du chapitre 5.

StatLink http://dx.doi.org/10.1787/888933569497

Les recettes non fiscales montrent de fortes fluctuations au fil des ans. Au cours de la dernière décennie écoulée, douze des pays étudiés ont enregistré au moins une fois une hausse annuelle de leurs recettes non fiscales représentant 1 % du PIB voire plus, et dix ont affiché au moins une fois une baisse annuelle de ces recettes de la même ampleur. L'augmentation la plus spectaculaire s'est produite en 2006 au Niger, dont les recettes non fiscales sont passées de 8.2 % du PIB en 2005 à 47.9 % en 2017, avant de retomber à 8.0 % l'année suivante. Cette fluctuation s'explique par une importante opération d'annulation de la dette en 2006 (voir la section consacrée aux dons ci-après).

1.5. Structure des recettes non fiscales

Les tableaux 1.3 et 1.4 montrent quelle était, en 2015, la contribution des différentes sous-catégories dans le total des recettes non fiscales, en pourcentage du PIB dans chaque pays couvert par la présente publication.

Tableau 1.3. **Recettes non fiscales par sous-rubrique en pourcentage du PIB, 2015**

Pays	Afrique du Sud	Cabo Verde	Cameroun	Congo, Rép. dém.	Côte d'Ivoire	Ghana	Kenya	Maroc
Total des recettes non fiscales	0.6	7.4	4.3	4.9	3.4	6.1	1.0	3.9
Dons	0.0	2.5	0.1	3.4	1.5	1.9	0.3	0.0
Revenus de la propriété	0.4	0.6	2.8	0.9	1.5	1.9	0.3	0.9
Loyers et redevances	0.1	..	2.7	0.8	1.3	0.7	0.0	0.5
Intérêts et dividendes	0.2	..	0.1	0.1	0.2	1.2	0.2	0.4
Autres revenus de la propriété	0.1	..	0.0	0.0	0.0	0.0	0.1	0.0
Ventes de biens et de services	0.1	2.9	1.1	0.5	0.2	2.3	0.2	1.6
Amendes, pénalités et confiscations	0.0	0.3	0.2	0.1	0.0	0.0	0.0	0.3
Recettes diverses et non identifiées[1]	0.0	1.1	0.1	0.0	0.3	0.0	0.2	1.1
Total recettes fiscales	*29.0*	*19.2*	*16.4*	*10.8*	*17.6*	*15.0*	*18.4*	*26.1*
Total recettes fiscales et non fiscales	*29.6*	*26.6*	*20.7*	*15.7*	*21.0*	*21.2*	*19.4*	*30.0*
Pays	**Maurice[2]**	**Niger**	**Ouganda[3]**	**Rwanda[3]**	**Sénégal**	**Swaziland**	**Togo**	**Tunisie**
Total recettes non fiscales	2.7	7.6	1.8	8.9	4.6	15.1	4.1	2.1
Dons	0.5	5.5	1.4	6.3	2.9	0.2	2.3	0.3
Revenus de la propriété	1.1	1.0	..	..	1.1	0.8	1.0	1.0
Loyers et redevances	0.2	0.8	..	..	0.4	0.0	0.2	0.4
Intérêts et dividendes	0.2	0.2	..	..	0.6	0.7	0.9	0.6
Autres revenus de la propriété	0.7	0.0	..	..	0.0	0.1	0.0	0.0
Ventes de biens et de services	1.0	0.9	..	..	0.0	0.1	0.3	0.0
Amendes, pénalités et confiscations	0.1	0.2	..	..	0.3	0.1	0.0	0.4
Recettes diverses et non identifiées[1]	0.1	0.2	0.3	2.6	0.3	13.9	0.5	0.2
Total recettes fiscales	*19.9*	*17.0*	*12.5*	*16.7*	*20.8*	*15.3*	*21.3*	*30.3*
Total recettes fiscales et non fiscales	*22.6*	*24.6*	*14.2*	*25.6*	*25.4*	*30.4*	*25.4*	*32.3*

Notes : Le symbole « .. » signale des données manquantes ou incomplètes pour la catégorie de recettes considérée.

Les chiffres prennent en compte les recettes non fiscales des administrations infranationales pour le Maroc, Maurice et le Swaziland.

1. Y compris les transferts de capitaux non classés ailleurs et les transferts autres que les dons.
2. Les données pour 2015 sont des estimations.
3. Les recettes non fiscales autres que les dons ne sont pas ventilées par sous-catégories et sont donc classées dans la rubrique « recettes diverses et non identifiées ».

Source : Tableau 5.2 du chapitre 5.

StatLink http://dx.doi.org/10.1787/888933569991

Le graphique 1.19 reprend les données du tableau 1.3 et montre la part relative de chaque sous-catégorie dans le total des recettes non fiscales des pays étudiés. Dans ce graphique, les recettes correspondant aux intérêts et dividendes ont été associées aux autres revenus de la propriété pour obtenir le montant des revenus de la propriété qui ne sont pas explicitement identifiés comme des loyers et des redevances. L'analyse comparative de la structure des recettes non fiscales dans les différents pays étudiés permet de distinguer cinq profils de pays :

- l'Ouganda, le Niger, la République démocratique du Congo, le Rwanda, le Sénégal et le Togo perçoivent la majorité de leurs recettes non fiscales sous forme de dons ;
- au Cameroun, ce sont les loyers et redevances qui prédominent ;
- en Afrique du Sud, les revenus de la propriété autres que les loyers et les redevances représentent l'essentiel des recettes non fiscales ;

- au Swaziland, 92 % des recettes non fiscales relèvent de la sous-catégorie des recettes diverses et non identifiées, qui correspondent quasi exclusivement à des recettes de la SACU ;
- dans les sept autres pays, la répartition est plus équilibrée et aucune sous-catégorie ne représente plus de la moitié du total : parmi ces pays, en Côte d'Ivoire, le premier poste est celui des dons ; au Kenya et en Tunisie, la principale sous-catégorie est celle des revenus de la propriété autres que les loyers et redevances ; enfin, au Cabo Verde, au Ghana, au Maroc et à Maurice, la première place revient aux ventes de biens et de services.

Graphique 1.19. **Structure des recettes non fiscales, 2015**

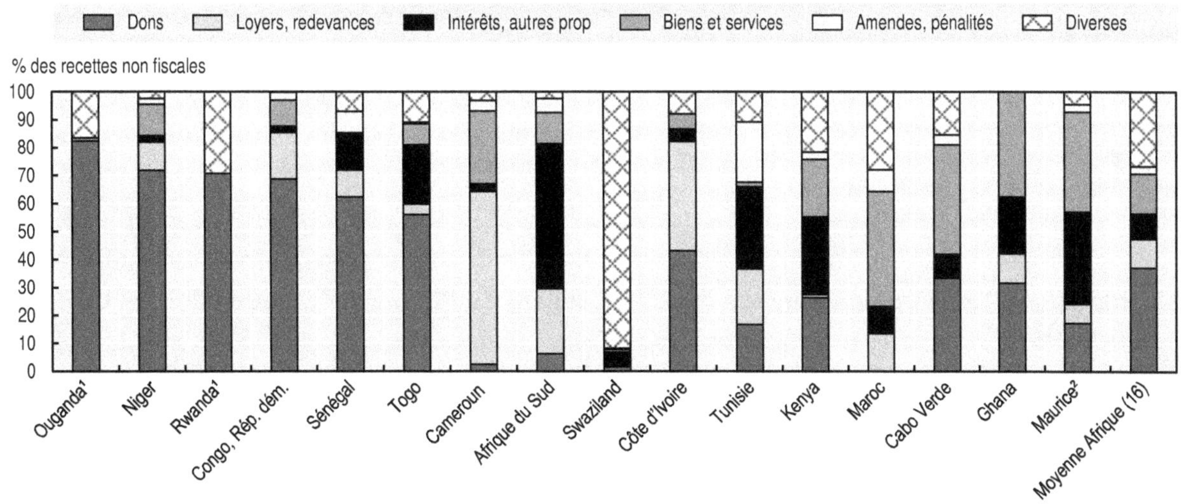

Notes : Les chiffres prennent en compte les recettes non fiscales des administrations infranationales pour le Maroc, Maurice et le Swaziland.

1. Les recettes non fiscales autres que les dons ne sont pas ventilées par sous-catégories et sont donc classées comme des recettes diverses et non identifiées.
2. Les données pour 2015 sont des estimations

Source : Tableau 5.2 figurant dans le chapitre 5.

StatLink http://dx.doi.org/10.1787/888933569516

Les dons

En 2015, le montant des dons reçus variait considérablement selon les pays étudiés (graphique 1.20), et s'échelonnait de montants négligeables ou non rapportés (Afrique du Sud, Cameroun et Maroc) jusqu'à des niveaux supérieurs à 5 % du PIB (Niger et Rwanda).

Dans les pays africains dont le PIB par habitant est plus élevé, les dons perçus tendent à représenter un moindre pourcentage du PIB que dans les pays disposant d'un PIB par habitant moins important (graphique 1.21). Une double explication peut être avancée : d'une part, pour les pays à revenu plus élevé, le ratio recettes non fiscales – PIB est calculé avec un plus grand dénominateur, et, d'autre part, ces pays peuvent être considérés comme moins prioritaires lors de l'attribution de l'aide internationale. Néanmoins, la proposition réciproque n'est pas toujours vérifiée. Dans les pays dont le PIB par habitant est peu élevé, on observe ainsi que le niveau des dons reçus varie au cas par cas. Ainsi en 2015, parmi les quatre pays dont le PIB par habitant est compris entre 1 200 et 1 500 USD, les dons répertoriés exprimés en pourcentage du PIB variaient de 0.1 % pour le Cameroun à 1.9 % pour le Ghana.

Graphique 1.20. **Dons en pourcentage du PIB, 2015**

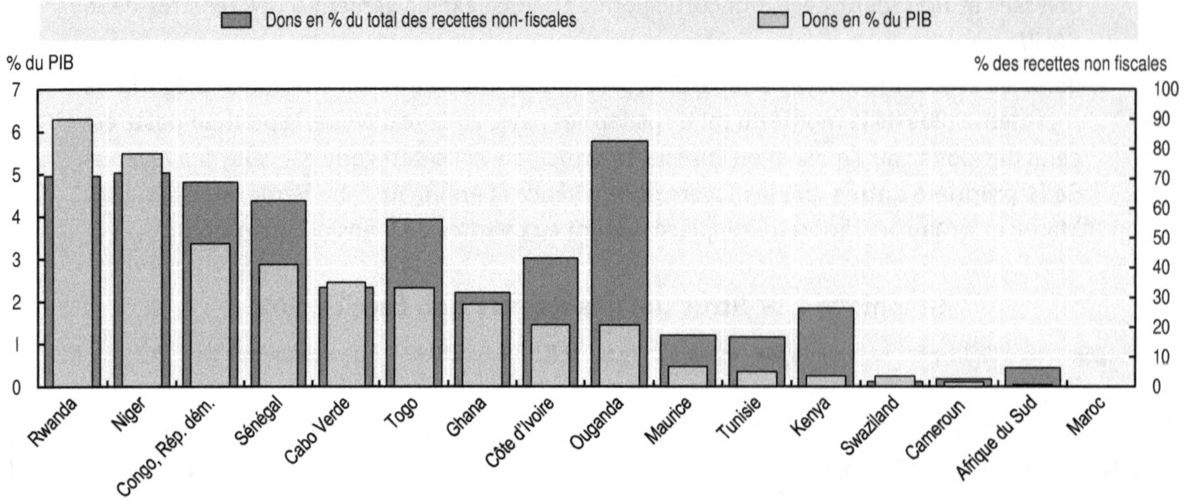

Source : Tableaux 5.2 et 5.3 figurant dans le chapitre 5.

StatLink http://dx.doi.org/10.1787/888933569535

Graphique 1.21. **Dons en pourcentage du PIB au regard du PIB par habitant en dollars US, 2015**

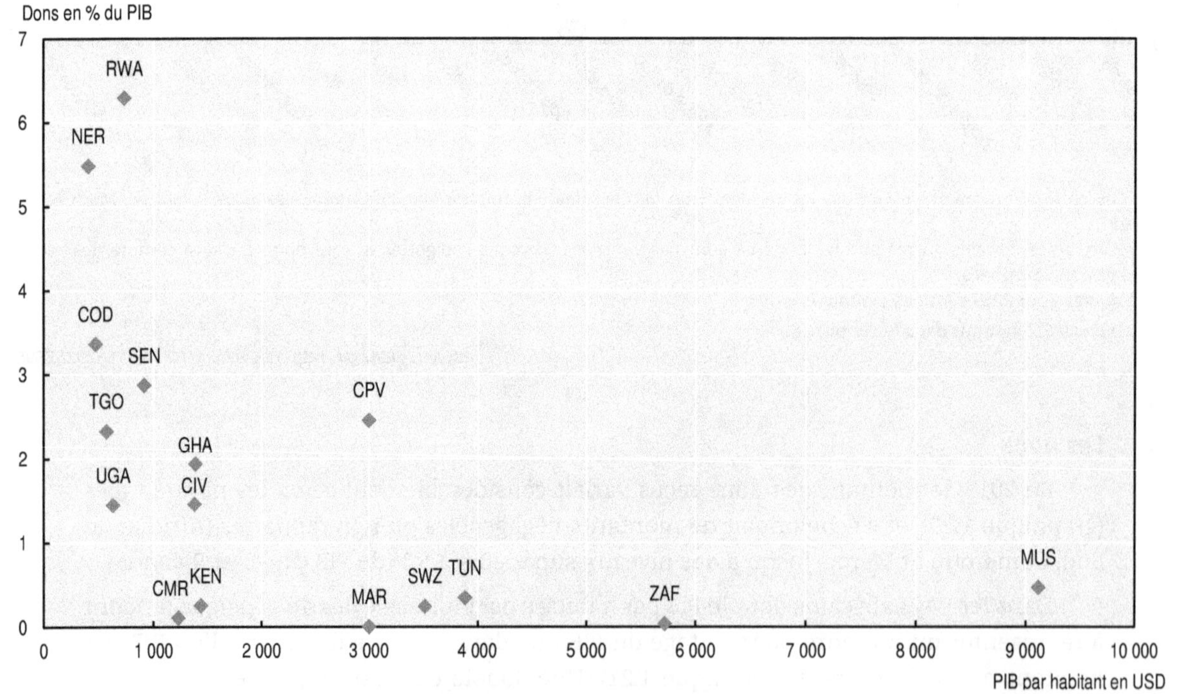

Source : Tableau 5.2 figurant dans le chapitre 5 et FMI, *Perspectives de l'économie mondiale*, avril 2017, pour les valeurs du PIB par habitant.

StatLink http://dx.doi.org/10.1787/888933569554

Entre 2000 et 2015, cinq pays ont enregistré au moins une fois des recettes annuelles liées aux dons qui représentaient plus de 5 % du PIB. L'analyse de l'évolution des recettes perçues sous formes de dons (graphique 1.22) montre qu'ils sont confrontés à la volatilité marquée de cette catégorie de recettes. Un exemple frappant est l'opération d'annulation de la dette dont le Niger a bénéficié en 2006, qui a représenté la quasi-totalité de l'important volume de dons enregistré la même année.

Graphique 1.22. **Dons en pourcentage du PIB, 2000-15**

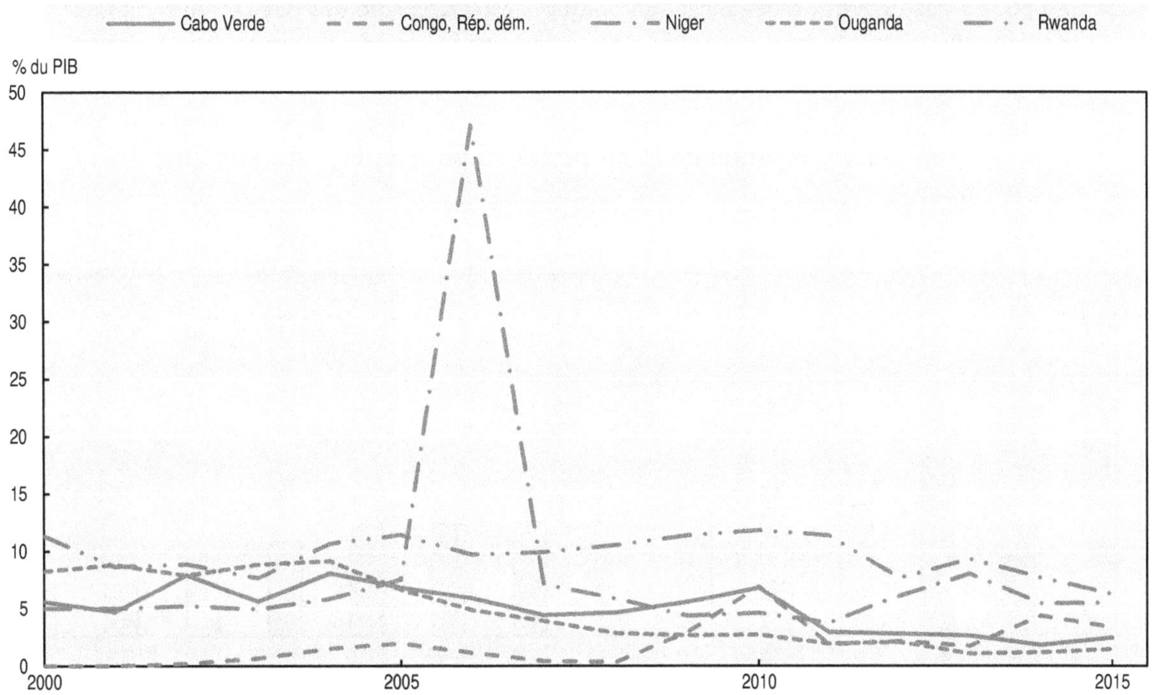

Source : Données comparatives des Statistiques des recettes publiques en Afrique disponibles à l'adresse OCDE/ATAF/CUA (2017), « Statistiques des recettes publiques en Afrique: Tableaux comparatifs », *Statistiques fiscales de l'OCDE* (base de données), *http://dx.doi.org/10.1787/7f54581d-fr*.

StatLink http://dx.doi.org/10.1787/888933569573

Les programmes d'allégement de la dette, comme l'Initiative en faveur des pays pauvres très endettés (PPTE), représentent l'une des principales sources d'aide internationale pour les gouvernements africains. L'initiative PPTE a été lancée en 1996 par le FMI et la Banque mondiale dans la lignée de l'Initiative d'allégement de la dette multilatérale (IADM), avec pour objectif de réduire le fardeau de la dette des pays à faible revenu surendettés. Parmi les 39 pays retenus comme éligibles à cette initiative, 33 étaient des pays d'Afrique subsaharienne. Neuf des pays étudiés dans la présente publication (Cameroun, Côte d'Ivoire, Ghana, Niger, République démocratique du Congo, Rwanda, Sénégal et Togo) ont ainsi bénéficié d'allégements au titre de l'Initiative PPTE et de l'IADM (FMI, 2016b). Dans certains cas, cela s'est traduit par des variations brutales des recettes perçues sous formes de dons.

Revenus de la propriété

On distingue ici trois grandes sous-catégories de recettes :

- les loyers et redevances ;
- les intérêts et dividendes ;
- les autres revenus de la propriété non attribuables.

L'État perçoit des loyers et des redevances en contrepartie d'activités de prospection et d'exploitation de ressources naturelles non renouvelables sur des terres appartenant au domaine public, ou de l'exploitation de fermes et de forêts détenues par l'État, tandis que les intérêts et dividendes sont une rémunération d'investissements réalisés par l'État. En 2015, le montant total des recettes perçues sous forme de revenu de la propriété a dépassé 1 % du PIB dans huit des seize pays étudiés. C'est au Cameroun que le montant des revenus de la propriété était le plus élevé, avec 2.8 % du PIB. Ce montant correspondait pour 96 % à des loyers et redevances (graphique 1.23). Dans cinq des pays étudiés dans la présente publication, la majeure partie des revenus de la propriété proviennent de loyers et de redevances.

Graphique 1.23. **Revenus de la propriété en pourcentage du PIB, 2015**

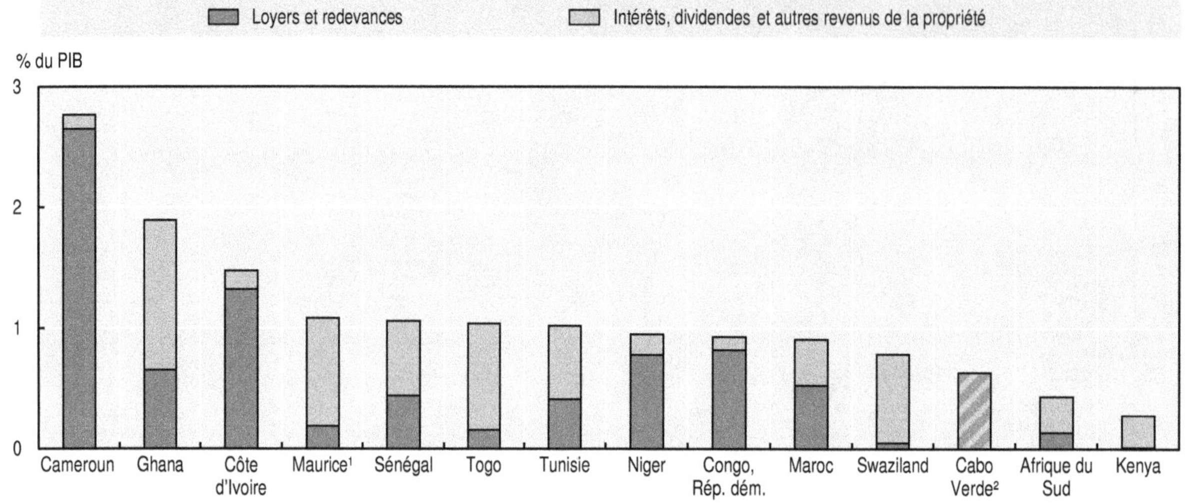

Notes : L'Ouganda et le Rwanda ne figurent pas dans ce graphique car les données requises ne sont pas disponibles.
1. Les données pour 2015 sont en partie des estimations.
2. Le revenu de la propriété du Cabo Verde n'est pas ventilé.

Source : Calculs des auteurs basés sur les tableaux 5.5-5.12.

StatLink http://dx.doi.org/10.1787/888933569592

Recettes issues de ressources naturelles

Les recettes provenant des entreprises qui ont pour principale activité l'exploitation de ressources naturelles peuvent avoir des retombées importantes sur les finances publiques, cependant, les pays suivent plusieurs méthodes de comptabilisation selon leur cadre budgétaire et réglementaire et selon le type de contrat conclu avec les entreprises concernées. Les pays peuvent percevoir des recettes issues de ressources naturelles sous la forme de recettes fiscales ou non fiscales, ou bénéficier de dépenses d'investissement dans leurs infrastructures engagées par des entreprises de ce secteur (ce qui n'est alors pas comptabilisé comme une recette publique). Ces revenus peuvent produire des effets dans les comptes de l'État de diverses manières, que l'on peut résumer comme suit[12] :

1. Les recettes au titre de loyers et redevances présentent le lien le plus direct avec la richesse en ressources naturelles d'un pays. L'État perçoit des rémunérations acquittées par des entreprises et des particuliers en contrepartie d'un droit d'accès à des terres appartenant au domaine public. Il agit en sa qualité de propriétaire des terrains concernés, et les montants versés sont en règle générale fixés à l'issue d'une négociation. Ces recettes sont ensuite rattachées aux revenus de la propriété.
2. Les paiements pour services fournis par les administrations publiques constituent une autre source de recettes non fiscales émanant d'entreprises du secteur primaire. Cela peut notamment inclure la rémunération de contrôles environnementaux réalisés par des

agents de l'administration, ou des paiements au titre de la construction d'infrastructures. Ces recettes sont incluses dans la catégorie des ventes des biens et services.

3. Les participations au capital de sociétés, publiques ou non, qui exploitent des ressources naturelles au nom de l'État, génèrent des recettes sous forme de bénéfices et dividendes. Ces recettes sont ensuite rattachées aux revenus de la propriété.
4. Il est possible d'instituer des taxes ou des droits conçus de manière à cibler les sociétés ou les particuliers qui ont accès à des ressources naturelles. Il peut s'avérer difficile de différencier une taxe appliquée aux entreprises qui exploitent des terres appartenant l'État d'une redevance acquittée par ces mêmes entreprises.
5. Des taxes et des droits ciblant l'exploitation de ressources naturelles peuvent être mise en place, notamment un droit d'accise sur les matières premières extraites de terres appartenant au domaine public, ou une taxe minière ciblant l'activité d'exploitation des ressources naturelles plutôt que le particulier ou la société qui réalise cette activité. Les revenus correspondants sont alors classés parmi les recettes fiscales.
6. Les sociétés et les particuliers qui exploitent des ressources naturelles acquittent le plus souvent les mêmes impôts et taxes que les autres contribuables (par exemple : imposition sur le revenu, TVA). Ces impôts et taxes de nature générale sont bien enregistrés dans les comptes publics, mais pas nécessairement dans la catégorie spécifique des recettes issues de ressources naturelles.
7. Par ailleurs, des sociétés et des particuliers sont susceptibles de consacrer une partie de la richesse qu'ils retirent de l'extraction de ressources naturelles à la construction d'infrastructures ou à la fourniture de services. Dès lors que ces infrastructures ou services répondent à une demande d'investissements ou de services publics, il peut en résulter une économie de dépenses publiques, qui toutefois ne sera pas comptabilisée comme une recette pour l'État. Dans certains cas, l'État impose, comme condition à l'accès aux ressources naturelles dont il est propriétaire, que les entreprises et particuliers concernés fournissent certains services, par exemple en prenant à leur charge une partie au moins du coût de construction et d'entretien des routes desservant les mines.

Le secteur des ressources naturelles correspond pour l'essentiel aux ressources naturelles renouvelables (agriculture, sylviculture, pêche et chasse) et aux ressources non renouvelables (pétrole, gaz naturel et autres minéraux). Comme le montre le graphique 1.24, les ressources naturelles dont disposent les pays africains varient considérablement. En moyenne, dans les 16 pays étudiés, les activités liées aux ressources renouvelables représentaient 20.8 % du PIB et celles liées à l'exploitation minière (gaz et pétrole inclus) s'établissaient à 4.7% % du PIB. Au Kenya, au Niger, au Rwanda et au Togo, l'activité liée aux ressources renouvelables dépassait 30 % du PIB. Les industries minières (gaz et pétrole inclus) représentent plus de 5 % du PIB dans quatre pays (Afrique du Sud, Côte d'Ivoire, République démocratique du Congo, et Tunisie), et légèrement moins de 5 % du PIB au Cameroun et au Ghana. Cinq de ces pays sont classés par la Banque mondiale parmi les pays « riches en ressources » aux fins de ses analyses de données : l'Afrique du Sud, le Cameroun, la Côte d'Ivoire, le Ghana, et la République démocratique du Congo.

Si certains loyers et redevances peuvent être perçus en lien avec des ressources renouvelables (redevances forestières au Cameroun, par exemple), la plupart des loyers et des redevances proviennent d'activités d'extraction minière, et notamment de redevances pétrolières. Les ressources minérales, telles que le pétrole, sont réparties inégalement entre les pays. En République démocratique du Congo, par exemple, l'exploitation minière représente 22 % du PIB, soit une importante source de recettes publiques potentielles.

Graphique 1.24. **Industries primaires en pourcentage du PIB, année la plus récente**

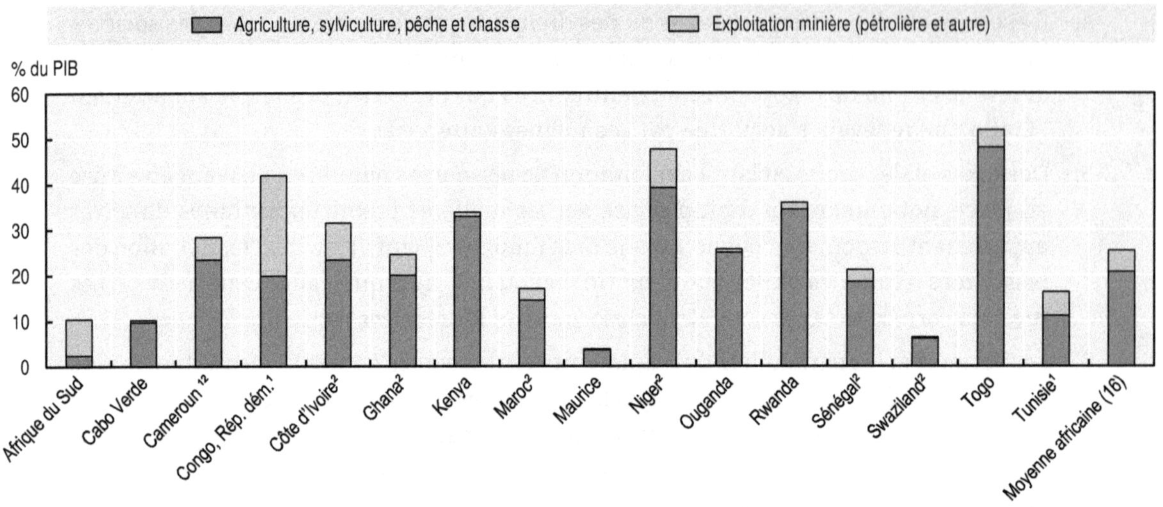

1. Les seuls pays qui ont ont ventilé le secteur minier entre l'exploitation minière pétrolière et non pétrolière sont le Cameroun, la République démocratique du Congo et la Tunisie.
2. Pour le Cameroun, la Côte d'Ivoire, le Ghana, le Maroc, le Niger et le Sénégal l'année rapportée est l'année 2016. Pour le Swaziland, l'année rapportée est l'année 2014. Pour tous les autres pays, les données sont relatives à l'année 2015.

Source: BAfD/OCDE/PNUD (2015), *Perspectives Économiques en Afrique 2015*.

StatLink http://dx.doi.org/10.1787/888933569611

La Banque mondiale a établi des estimations du montant total des rentes tirées de ressources naturelles extraites dans chaque pays[13], en calculant la somme des loyers et redevances perçus sur l'extraction de pétrole, de gaz naturel, de charbon (anthracite et houille), de minéraux et sur les activités d'exploitation forestière à la fois dans les domaines publics et privés. Ces estimations sont fondées sur le calcul de la différence entre la valeur totale des ressources naturelles extraites et le coût de l'extraction. Cet écart de valeur, ou rente tirée des ressources naturelles, revient pour partie aux entreprises privées qui réalisent l'extraction, et pour partie à l'administration qui impose leur activité et perçoit des redevances.

Le graphique 1.25 présente une comparaison entre les estimations de la Banque mondiale concernant les rentes tirées des ressources naturelles et les montants déclarés à ce titre dans les *Statistiques des recettes publiques en Afrique*. La différence essentielle entre les deux chiffres est que le premier comprend les recettes totales (privées et publiques) tirées des ressources naturelles, tandis que le dernier ne fait que reporter les recettes publiques. Nécessairement, l'estimation de la Banque mondiale sur les recettes issues des ressources naturelles sera beaucoup plus élevée que les recettes rapportées dans la présente publication. Les gouvernements des pays un haut et à gauche du graphique reçoivent une plus grande part de la richesse des ressources naturelles à travers des loyers et des redevances que les pays en bas et à droite du graphique, bien que la richesse en ressources naturelles obtenue par les gouvernements provenant des recettes fiscales ou autres recettes non fiscales ne sont pas représentés sur l'axe vertical.

Graphique 1.25. **Total des bénéfices tirés des ressources naturelles au regard des recettes publiques provenant des loyers et redevances en pourcentage du PIB, 2015**

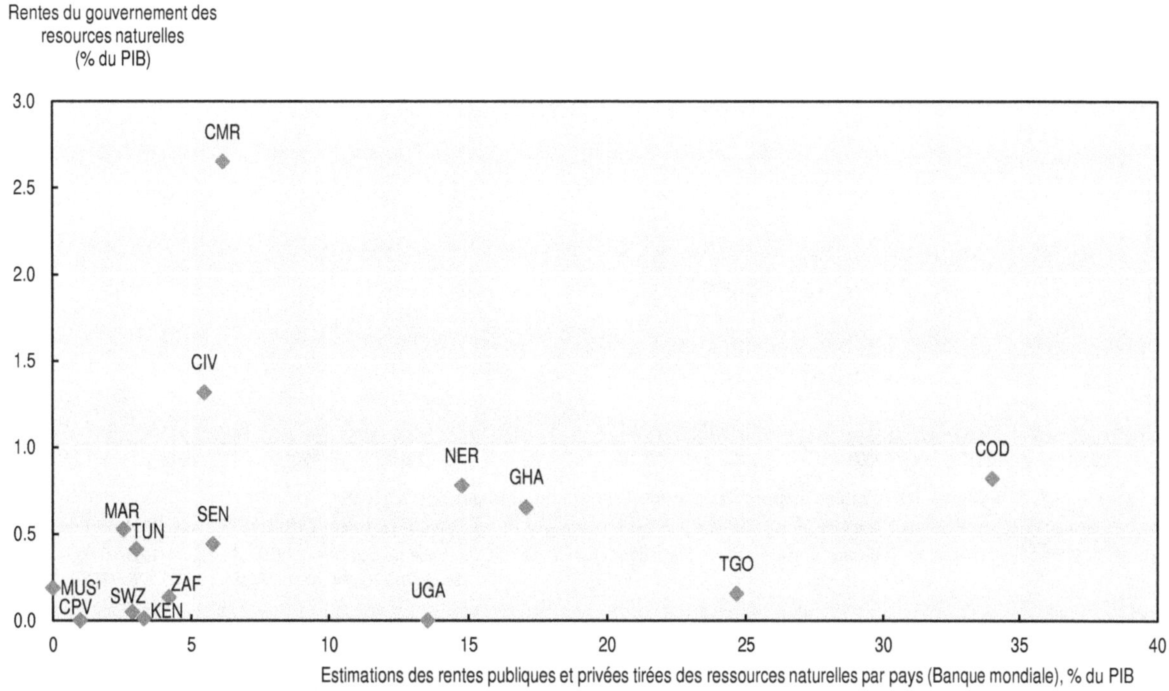

Note : Le Cabo Verde, l'Ouganda et le Rwanda n'ont transmis aucune donnée concernant les loyers et redevances.
1. Les données pour 2015 sont des estimations.

Source : Tableau 5.1 du chapitre 5 pour les rentes tirées des ressources naturelles comptabilisées en tant que recettes publiques, et Banque mondiale, *Indicateurs du développement dans le monde*, pour les rentes tirées des ressources naturelles (site consulté le 3 juillet 2017).

StatLink http://dx.doi.org/10.1787/888933569630

Les recettes issues de ressources naturelles constituent une source de financement souvent marquée par une forte volatilité (graphique 1.26). Trois des seize pays africains ont réussi à collecter des recettes provenant des loyers et redevances évaluées à plus de 1 % du PIB sur les dix dernières années. Par contre, la République démocratique du Congo et la Côte d'Ivoire ont vu ces recettes baisser pour se situer à moins d'un quart de leurs valeurs maximales respectives. Au Cameroun aussi les recettes provenant des loyers et redevances se situent à 39 % de sa valeur maximale, soit une baisse équivalente à plus de 4 % du PIB. Cela représente évidemment un impact massif sur le financement du gouvernement.

Par ailleurs, une forte dépendance à l'égard de la production de biens primaires accroît la vulnérabilité face aux fluctuations des prix des matières premières. À titre d'exemple, depuis 1990, les plus fortes variations interannuelles du cours de l'or ont atteint 35.8 % à la hausse et 15.4 % à la baisse. De plus, les prix du pétrole ont pu connaître une flambée de 57.1 % en 2000 par rapport à l'année antérieure, mais également une chute brutale de 37.8 % entre 2008 et 2009. Étant donné ses liens forts avec les variations interannuelles des redevances pétrolières (graphique 1.27), les récentes chutes des cours du pétrole ont eu des répercussions directes sur le budget du gouvernement au Cameroun.

En plus des risques financiers mentionnés ici, les revenus miniers peuvent créer d'autres difficultés pour les gouvernements. Selon un document du FMI, les risques entourant les projets miniers sont élevés, avec non seulement des coûts irrécupérables importants, mais aussi des rendements potentiellement hauts. En d'autres termes, le montant des recettes en jeu est considérable, et toute erreur de la part de l'administration peut se révéler très coûteuse (FMI, 2011).

Graphique 1.26. **Revenus de la propriété en pourcentage du PIB, 2006-15**

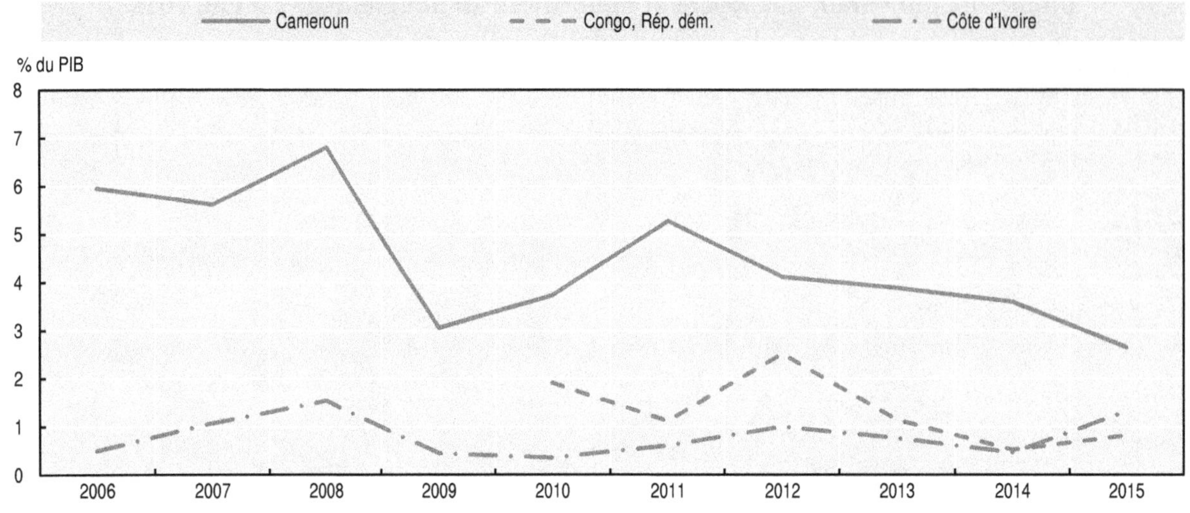

Note : Pour la RDC et le Ghana, les données disponibles couvrent uniquement la période 2010-15.

Source : Données comparatives des *Statistiques des recettes publiques en Afrique* disponibles à l'adresse OCDE/ATAF/CUA (2017), « Statistiques des recettes publiques en Afrique: Tableaux comparatifs », *Statistiques fiscales de l'OCDE* (base de données), *http://dx.doi.org/10.1787/7f54581d-fr*.

StatLink *http://dx.doi.org/10.1787/888933569649*

Graphique 1.27. **Variations interannuelles des prix du pétrole et des recettes issues des redevances pétrolières au Cameroun, 1995-2015**

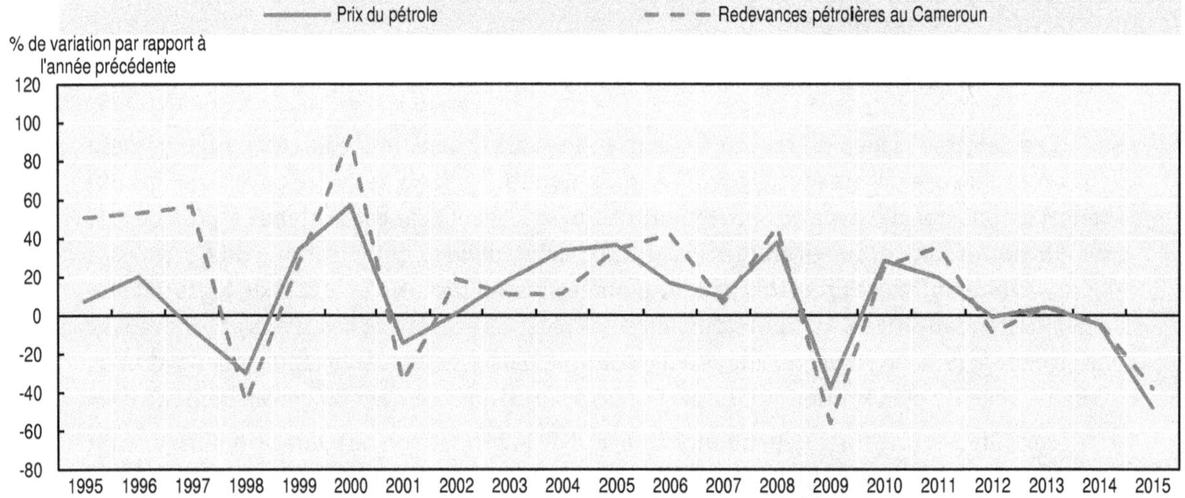

Source : Calculs des auteurs à partir de données comparatives des Statistiques des recettes publiques en Afrique, disponibles à l'adresse OCDE/ATAF/CUA (2017), « Statistiques des recettes publiques en Afrique: Tableaux comparatifs », *Statistiques fiscales de l'OCDE* (base de données), *http://dx.doi.org/10.1787/7f54581d-fr* et Service de recherche économique, Federal Reserve Bank of St. Louis pour les prix du pétrole.

StatLink *http://dx.doi.org/10.1787/888933569668*

Ventes de biens et de services

Les administrations peuvent produire des biens et des services aussi bien dans le secteur marchand que non marchand. Dans le secteur marchand, les administrations publiques fournissent parfois des biens et services pouvant être aussi fournis auprès d'entreprises privées (tels que la vente d'aliments ou la prestation de services de transport). En parallèle, elles peuvent assurer, au titre de la gestion de programmes ou de l'application du droit, différents services qui sont du seul ressort d'un État. Les frais correspondant à ces services non marchands sont le plus souvent classés en tant que frais administratifs.

Les frais administratifs sont souvent difficiles à classer, car ils se situent dans une zone grise, à mi-chemin entre les rémunérations de services (qui sont des recettes non fiscales) et les prélèvements obligatoires effectués sans contrepartie versés aux administrations publiques (qui sont des recettes fiscales)[14]. Les frais de justice, ainsi que les frais relatifs aux permis de conduire, passeports, enregistrements de brevets et certificats de mariage sont très souvent classés dans les recettes non fiscales. Lorsqu'ils sont classés comme des recettes fiscales, ces frais sont traditionnellement rattachés à l'une des catégories suivantes :

- 4400 – Impôts sur les transactions mobilières et immobilières (par exemple, les taxes sur les transactions foncières) ;
- 5200 – Impôts sur l'utilisation des biens et l'autorisation d'exercer des activités (par exemple, les permis de chasse, l'enregistrement des véhicules) ;
- 6000 – Autres impôts (par exemple, la vente de timbres fiscaux, dans les cas où ces timbres sont utilisés pour le paiement des taxes et frais administratifs).

Dans cinq des pays étudiés, les revenus provenant de ventes de biens et de services et de frais administratifs étaient égaux ou supérieurs à 1 % du PIB en 2015 (graphique 1.28). Lorsque ces recettes sont exprimées en pourcentage du PIB, on observe que les pays qui en perçoivent le plus sont le Cabo Verde (2.9 % du PIB), le Ghana (2.3 % du PIB) et le Maroc (1.6 % du PIB).

Graphique 1.28. **Ventes de biens et de services et frais administratifs, en pourcentage du PIB et en pourcentage du total des recettes non fiscales, 2015**

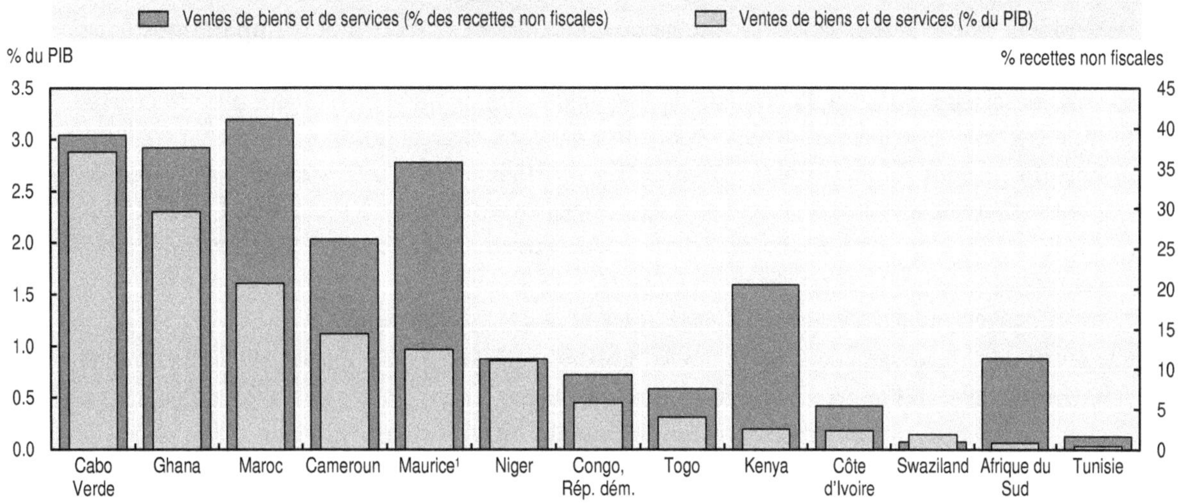

Notes : Les chiffres prennent en compte les recettes non fiscales des administrations infranationales pour le Maroc, Maurice et le Swaziland.

L'Ouganda et le Rwanda ne figurent pas dans ce graphique car les données étaient incomplètes concernant l'Ouganda et non disponibles concernant le Rwanda. Le Sénégal n'a déclaré aucune recette provenant de ventes de biens et de services.

1. Les données pour 2015 sont des estimations.

Source : Tableaux 5.2 et 5.3 figurant dans le chapitre 5.

StatLink http://dx.doi.org/10.1787/888933569687

Au Maroc (41.1 % du total des recettes non fiscales), au Cabo Verde (39.1 %), au Ghana (37.5 %) et à Maurice (36.1 %), les ventes de biens et services et les frais administratifs représentent la principale source de recettes non fiscales. Dans les autres pays qui ont transmis les données concernées, les pourcentages varient de 1.2 % en Ouganda à 26.1 % au Cameroun.

Au Maroc, 56 % des recettes issues des ventes de biens et de services sont collectées majoritairement au niveau local. Au Cabo Verde, les frais représentaient 96 % des recettes enregistrées dans cette même catégorie. Au Ghana, l'essentiel des recettes tirées des ventes de biens et de services étaient des frais et charges perçus soit au niveau des communes, départements et agences administratives, soit au niveau des districts, assemblées municipales et métropolitaines. À Maurice, 13 % des recettes liées aux ventes de biens et de services ont été collectées au niveau local, et 9 % par l'intermédiaire de fonds de sécurité sociale. Ces recettes sont générées par un ensemble de frais perçus au titre de différents services assurés par l'État, allant du contrôle de la navigation aérienne en route aux services de police, ainsi que par la vente d'une gamme de produits tels que les eaux souterraines, des aliments pour animaux et des produits forestiers. Le Kenya n'a pas tiré de recettes importantes de la vente de biens et de services, qui ont tout de même représenté plus d'un cinquième de ses recettes non fiscales totales en 2015.

Amendes et confiscations

Si les amendes et confiscations peuvent représenter une source importante de revenus, elles restent très volatiles. Certaines amendes de faibles montants, comme celles liées aux contraventions pour excès de vitesse, constituent des recettes régulières et prévisibles. Dans certains pays, une fraction de ces recettes est directement affectée au financement de missions de la police, et ne sont pas comptabilisées dans les statistiques. Ces petites amendes représentent une fraction négligeable du total des recettes non fiscales comptabilisées dans les statistiques officielles.

Les revenus perçus par les pays étudiés au titre d'amendes, confiscations et pénalités représentent, sauf exception, des montants négligeables ; on notera ainsi que le Cabo Verde, le Maroc le Sénégal et la Tunisie ont recouvré des recettes plus importantes sous cette catégorie, notamment de manière ponctuelle, certaines années affichant des valeurs élevées (graphique 1.29). En Tunisie, la valeur des amendes et pénalités en pourcentage du PIB a progressé, passant de 0.15 % en 2011 à 0.97 % en 2013, avant de retomber à 0.43 % en 2014. Au Sénégal, cette part a atteint 0.37 % du PIB en 2013 et 0.65 % en 2014 alors qu'elle était restée négligeable au cours des trois années antérieures. Si les amendes, pénalités et confiscations apportent une contribution modeste au financement de l'État, il est indéniable que certaines initiatives ou réformes en la matière au sein de la fonction publique peuvent avoir des retombées non négligeables sur les finances publiques.

Depuis la parution de la première édition des *Statistiques des recettes publiques en Afrique*, une modification importante a été apportée au classement des amendes et confiscations perçues au titre du non-paiement ou du paiement tardif d'impôts et de taxes. Dans la présente édition, les sommes ainsi recouvrées sont classées comme des recettes non fiscales. Dans les éditions précédentes, elles étaient comptabilisées parmi les recettes fiscales, dans la catégorie dont relevait l'impôt ayant justifié l'application de la pénalité (voir les annexes A et B pour plus de précisions).

Les effets de cette modification sur les recettes déclarées entre la première et la deuxième édition de cette publication se sont révélés négligeables. Cela peut s'expliquer en partie par le fait que les changements effectués dans la classification n'ont pas d'effet sur les pénalités au titre du non-paiement ou paiement en retard des impôts et taxes qui ne peuvent être distinguées des autres recettes fiscales.

Graphique 1.29. **Amendes, pénalités et confiscations en pourcentage du PIB, 2011-15**

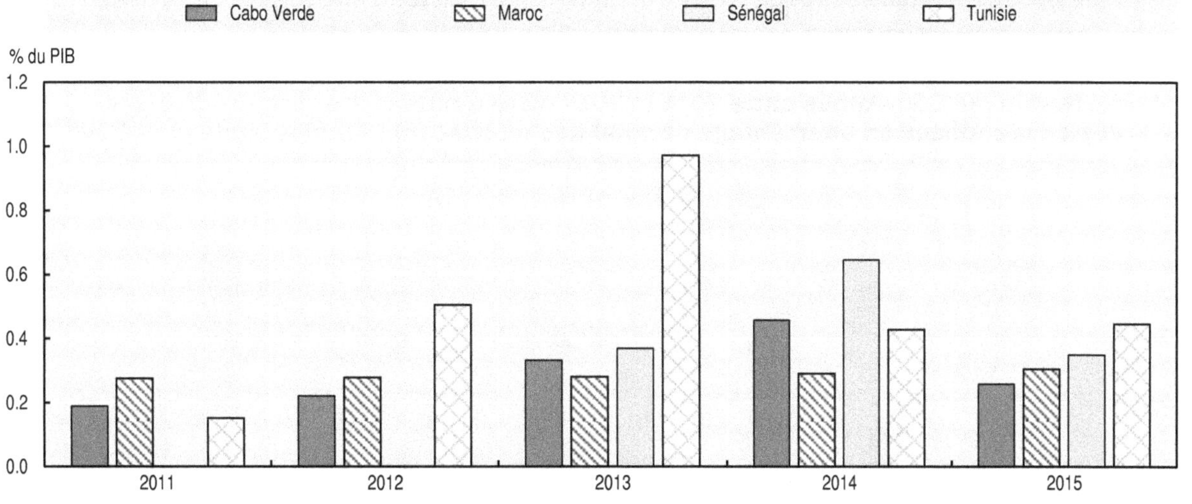

Note : Les chiffres prennent en compte les recettes non fiscales des administrations infranationales pour le Maroc.

Source : OCDE/ATAF/CUA (2017), « Statistiques des recettes publiques en Afrique: Tableaux comparatifs », *Statistiques fiscales de l'OCDE* (base de données), *http://dx.doi.org/10.1787/7f54581d-fr*.

StatLink http://dx.doi.org/10.1787/888933569706

Recettes diverses ou non identifiées

Certaines recettes non fiscales représentent des montants significatifs mais ne s'inscrivent dans aucune des catégories citées ci-dessus. Il s'agit notamment :

1. des transferts en capital non inclus par ailleurs ;
2. les dons volontaires à des organismes publics de la part de particuliers ou de sociétés (à l'exception des dons émanant d'organisations internationales comme le FMI, qui relèvent de la catégorie des dons).
3. des indemnités d'assurance versées aux administrations publiques ;
4. des versements couvrant différentes catégories de la classification et pour lesquels aucune ventilation n'est disponible ;
5. des paiements dont la classification appropriée n'est pas identifiable faute de données pertinentes ;
6. des recettes de la SACU dans le cas du Swaziland.

Certaines années, ces revenus peuvent représenter une fraction importante des recettes non fiscales (graphique 1.30). En 2014, par exemple, 45 % des recettes non fiscales de la Côte d'Ivoire relevaient de cette catégorie. Parmi les autres recettes susceptibles d'entrer dans cette rubrique figurent les contributions volontaires versées à l'administration en Tunisie, les transferts en capital depuis des fonds statutaires spéciaux à Maurice et, au Maroc, des montants versés à l'administration en contrepartie du droit à entrer en concurrence avec des institutions publiques pour la fourniture de services. Au Swaziland, les revenus reversés par la SACU, qui sont classés parmi les recettes diverses et non identifiées, représentent plus de 90 % du total des recettes pendant la plupart des années considérées.

Le niveau des recettes non identifiées est le plus souvent fluctuant, et peut afficher des pointes ponctuelles (graphique 1.31). Dans certains cas, ces variations sont liées à des transferts en capital importants, à des entrées de recettes éphémères, ou à des reclassifications de fonds dans la catégorie des recettes non identifiées en raison de l'absence de données. Les données disponibles sont insuffisantes pour mener une analyse concluante de cette catégorie, mais la présence de montants élevés dans cette rubrique peut conduire à s'interroger sur la précision des montants inscrits dans les autres catégories de recettes non fiscales.

Graphique 1.30. **Année entre 2011 et 2015 où le montant des recettes diverses et non identifiées en pourcentage du total des recettes non fiscales est le plus élevé**

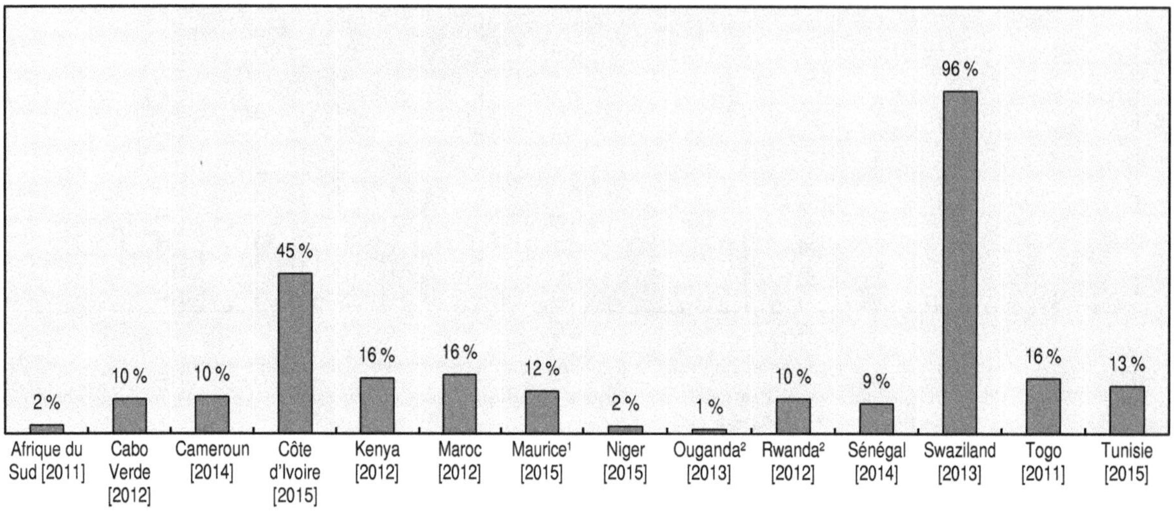

Notes : La République démocratique du Congo et le Ghana n'ont déclaré aucun revenu dans la catégorie des recettes diverses et non identifiées entre 2011 et 2015.

1. Les données pour 2015 sont des estimations.
2. Les données relatives aux revenus de la propriété, des ventes de biens et de services et des amendes, pénalités et confiscations sont incluses dans les recettes diverses et non identifiées. Ces données n'ont pu être désagrégées afin de les affecter aux catégories de recettes non fiscales concernées.

Sources : OCDE/ATAF/CUA (2017), « Statistiques des recettes publiques en Afrique: Tableaux comparatifs », *Statistiques fiscales de l'OCDE* (base de données), *http://dx.doi.org/10.1787/7f54581d-fr* et calculs des auteurs à partir de données présentées dans les tableaux 5.5-5.12.

StatLink *http://dx.doi.org/10.1787/888933569725*

Graphique 1.31. **Recettes diverses et non identifiées en pourcentage du total des recettes non fiscales, 2000-15**

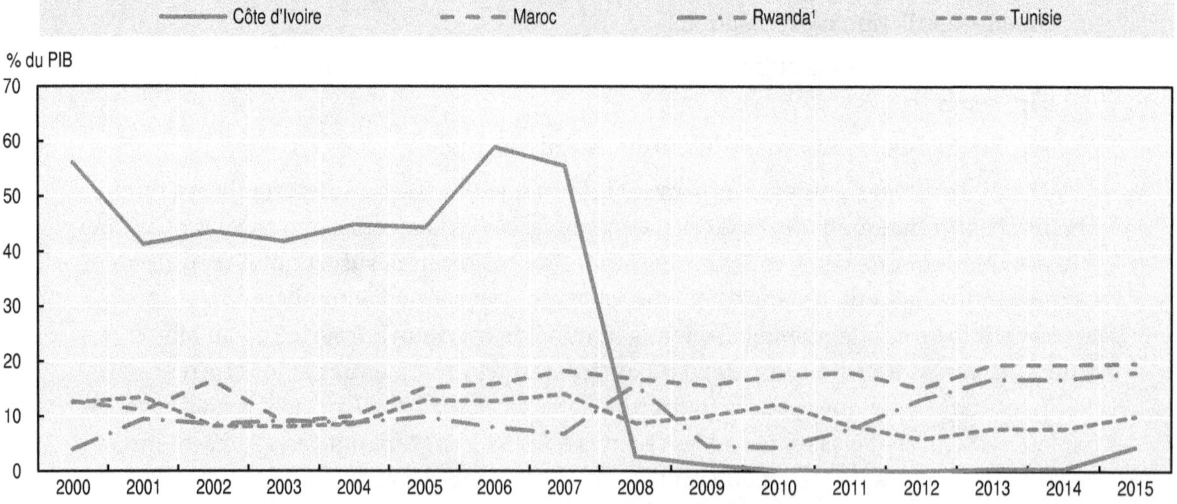

1. Les données relatives aux revenus de la propriété, des ventes de biens et de services et des amendes, pénalités et confiscations sont incluses dans les recettes diverses et non identifiées. Ces données n'ont pu être désagrégées afin de les affecter aux catégories de recettes non fiscales concernées.

Source : Calculs des auteurs à partir de données présentées dans les tableaux 5.5-5.12.

StatLink *http://dx.doi.org/10.1787/888933569744*

Recettes liées à l'Union douanière d'Afrique australe (SACU)

Parmi les pays qui font l'objet de cette étude, le Swaziland et l'Afrique du Sud appartiennent à l'Union douanière d'Afrique australe (*Southern African Customs Union*, SACU), aux côtés du Botswana, du Lesotho et de la Namibie (voir encadré 1.5).

En pourcentage du PIB, les revenus de la SACU pour le Swaziland dépassaient les recettes fiscales pour toutes les années sauf pour sept des 20 dernières années (voir graphique 1.32). Elles ont atteint leur niveau le plus élevé entre 2006 et 2008, avec plus de 20 % du PIB, alors que les recettes fiscales du pays étaient comprises entre 10.4 % et 15.4% du PIB sur la même période. On observe que, pour le Swaziland, la somme des recettes liées à la SACU et des recettes fiscales a représenté 29 % du PIB en 2015, ce qui est similaire au ratio impôts-PIB de l'Afrique du Sud. Si l'on exclut les montants reversés par la SACU, les recettes non fiscales du Swaziland n'ont représenté que 1.3 % du PIB en 2015.

Il convient de traiter avec une attention particulière les revenus liés à la SACU lorsque l'on souhaite comparer la situation du Swaziland et celle de l'Afrique du Sud. En effet, les deux pays participent au système de regroupement et de redistribution des recettes de la SACU, et la fraction de ces recettes qu'ils perçoivent est calculée en appliquant la même formule. Néanmoins, le Swaziland est un bénéficiaire net de ces opérations de mise en commun et de redistribution, et les montants ainsi perçus sont classées comme des recettes non fiscales, tandis que l'Afrique du Sud est le seul pays contributeur net du système (voir encadré 1.5 pour plus de précisions).

Graphique 1.32. **Recettes fiscales, non fiscales, et recettes provenant du fonds SACU pour le Swaziland et l'Afrique du Sud (en % du PIB), 2015**

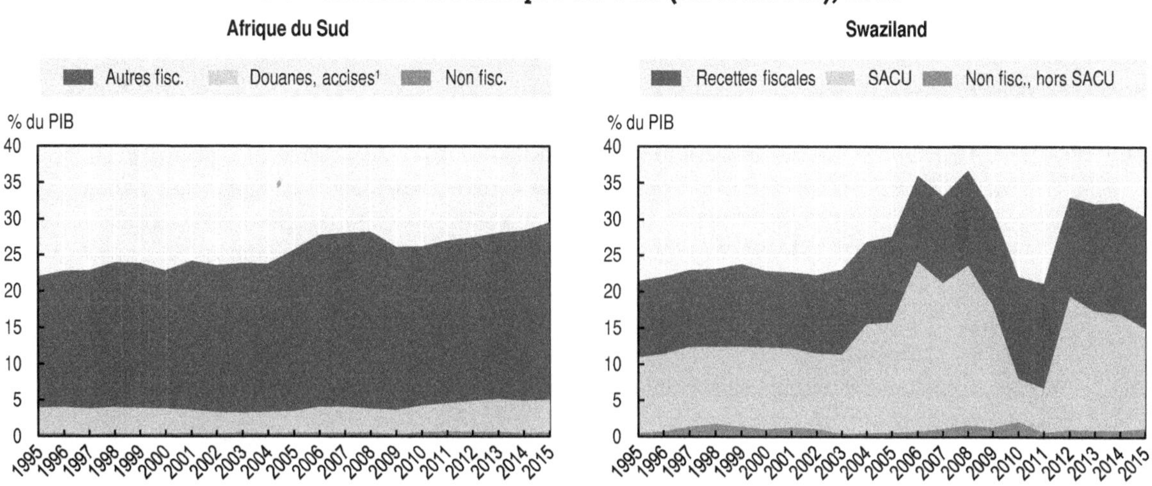

1. Il convient d'interpréter avec prudence les recettes des droits de douane et d'accise exprimé en pourcentage du PIB, car elles tiennent compte des paiements effectués par l'Afrique du Sud en faveur des autres pays membres de la SACU, paiements qui ne sont pas considérés comme des recettes dans la classification OCDE. Ces paiements versés à l'Union douanière d'Afrique australe représentent environ 1 % du PIB de l'Afrique du Sud.

Source : OCDE/ATAF/CUA (2017), « Statistiques des recettes publiques en Afrique: Tableaux comparatifs », *Statistiques fiscales de l'OCDE* (base de données), *http://dx.doi.org/10.1787/7f54581d-fr*.

StatLink http://dx.doi.org/10.1787/888933569763

Encadré 1.5. **Recettes issues de l'Union douanière d'Afrique australe**

L'Union douanière d'Afrique australe (*South African Customs Union*, SACU) compte cinq membres (Afrique du Sud, Botswana, Lesotho, Namibie et Swaziland) et son siège est établi à Windhoek, en Namibie. Cette union douanière vise à établir « une communauté économique qui favorise un développement équitable et durable, au service du bien-être des peuples, pour construire un avenir commun ».

La SACU, qui est la plus ancienne union douanière au monde, a été créée en 1899 entre la colonie britannique du Cap de Bonne-Espérance et la République boer de l'État libre d'Orange. Des accords conclus par la suite, en 1910 puis en 1969, ont marqué l'adhésion du Botswana, du Lesotho et du Swaziland. À la suite de l'accession à l'indépendance de la Namibie, en 1990, et à la fin de l'apartheid en Afrique du Sud, en 1994, de nouvelles négociations ont été ouvertes et pour aboutir à la conclusion, en 2002, de l'accord en vigueur à ce jour.

Cet accord prévoit la libre circulation entre les pays membres de la SACU de tous les produits manufacturés fabriqués dans ces pays, en franchise de droits. Il définit également des droits de douanes extérieures communes et la mise en commun des droits de douane et d'accise, en vue de leur partage entre les pays membres de la SACU suivant la formule de répartition des recettes qui figure en annexe à l'Accord.

Les règles de partage des recettes comprennent trois composantes :

- une composante douanière, qui divise le montant brut des droits de douane en fonction de la valeur des marchandises importées par chaque pays depuis les autres pays membres de la SACU au cours de l'année considérée (en pourcentage des importations totales intra-SACU) ;
- une composante portant sur les droits d'accise, qui divise le montant brut de ces droits selon le ratio correspondant au PIB de chaque pays rapporté au PIB total de la SACU ; et
- une composante de développement, financée par 15 % de la composante liée aux droits d'accise, et pondérée en faveur des pays moins développés de la SACU selon une formule fondée sur le PIB par habitant.

Dans la présente publication, les recettes issues des droits de douane et d'accise sont incluses dans les recettes fiscales du pays qui les a collectées. Elles sont rapportées dans les rubriques 5121 (accises) et 5123 (droits de douane et droits à l'importation) des tableaux des recettes fiscales. Les montants redistribués par la SACU sont classés dans les tableaux des recettes non fiscales, sous la rubrique des recettes diverses et non identifiées, comme le montre le tableau 5.17 dans le cas du Swaziland. Pour l'Afrique du Sud, qui est un contributeur net au mécanisme de la SACU, les contributions, nettes des reversements perçus, sont mentionnées pour mémoire dans le tableau des recettes non fiscales (tableau 5.16).

Sources : SACU (2017), SACU (2014).

Notes

1. Les données relatives aux cotisations de sécurité sociale ne sont pas disponibles pour le Ghana (avant 2008), l'Ouganda, la République démocratique du Congo, et le Togo et elles sont incomplètes pour le Cameroun (où elles n'englobent que les cotisations de retraite), le Kenya (où elles sont considérées comme négligeables) et le Sénégal (où les chiffres tiennent compte des données relatives aux cotisations de sécurité sociale communiquées par l'Institution de Prévoyance Retraites du Sénégal (IPRES), mais pas des données émanant de la Caisse de Sécurité Sociale (CSS) car elles ne sont pas disponibles).
2. Taxe sur la valeur ajoutée.
3. La variation est calculée sur la période 2000-14 car les données de 2015 ne sont pas disponibles.

4. La moyenne des pays d'Afrique (16), pour les cotisations de sécurité sociale rapportées au PIB, doit être interprétée avec précaution compte tenu du fait que les données relatives aux cotisations de sécurité sociale sont incomplètes ou inexistantes pour certains pays africains couverts par cette publication.
5. Le terme agriculture se réfère à la définition relative aux données des comptes nationaux de la Banque mondiale et correspond aux divisions CITI 01-05. Pour plus de précisions, consulter la documentation des bases de données de la Banque Mondiale *https://donnees.banquemondiale.org/indicateur/NV.AGR.TOTL.ZS*.
6. Un pays est considéré comme riche en hydrocarbures et/ou en ressources minérales s'il remplit un ou plusieurs des critères suivants : (i) la part moyenne des recettes tirées des hydrocarbures et/ou des ressources minérales dans le total des recettes fiscales est d'au moins 25 % au cours de la période 2000-05 ou (ii) la part moyenne des recettes d'exportations d'hydrocarbures et/ou de ressources minérales dans le total des recettes d'exportation est d'au moins 25 % (FMI, 2007).
7. Les données relatives aux cotisations de sécurité sociale ne sont pas disponibles pour le Ghana (avant 2008), le Togo, la République démocratique du Congo et l'Ouganda et sont incomplètes pour le Kenya (mais réputées négligeables) et pour le Sénégal (où les chiffres tiennent compte des cotisations de sécurité sociale versées par l'Institution de Prévoyance Retraites du Sénégal (IPRES), mais pas des données de la Caisse de Sécurité Sociale (CSS) car elles ne sont pas disponibles).
8. Les données concernant Maurice proviennent des états financiers établis par le Bureau des statistiques de Maurice.
9. Ce chiffre inclut probablement d'autres recettes, telles que les charges de services publics et d'autres services d'utilité publique tels que les péages routiers qui ne sont pas assimilés à la catégorie des recettes fiscales dans cette publication.
10. Voir le Guide d'interprétation sur les recettes non fiscales dans l'annexe B du présent rapport pour la définition de ces catégories de revenus.
11. Le coefficient de variation est un indicateur de dispersion obtenu en divisant l'écart-type par la moyenne arithmétique.
12. Mansour et Rota-Graziosi (2013) indiquent que les recettes fiscales liées à l'extraction pétrolière peuvent englober l'impôt sur les bénéfices des sociétés, les droits indirects sur des produits énergétiques ainsi que des montants non remboursés de taxes sur les ventes comme la TVA, tandis que les recettes non fiscales peuvent correspondre à des redevances, des participations aux bénéfices, des dividendes et d'autres revenus d'investissements perçus au titre de participations directes de l'administration au capital des entreprises qui réalisent des activités d'extraction.
13. Les données et les informations sur la méthodologie sont consultables sur le site des Indicateurs du développement dans le monde de la Banque mondiale, à l'adresse : data.worldbank.org/indicator/NY.GDP.TOTL.RT.ZS. Le calcul des rentes tirées des ressources naturelles s'appuie sur des sources et méthodes décrites dans le rapport « *The Changing Wealth of Nations: Measuring Sustainable Development in the New Millennium* » (Banque mondiale, 2011).
14. Pour plus de précisions sur la classification des redevances administratives, consulter, en annexe A, les paragraphes 9 à 13 du Guide d'interprétation de l'OCDE.

Références

Addison, T. et J. Levin (2012), *The Determinants of Tax Revenue in Sub-Saharan Africa*, Swedish Business School at Örebro University, Örebro, Suède, *http://oru.diva-portal.org/smash/record.jsf?pid=diva2%3A570456&dswid=4207*.

BAfD (2010), *Domestic Resource Mobilization for Poverty Reduction in East Africa: Rwanda case study*, Banque africaine de développement, Abidjan, *www.afdb.org/fileadmin/uploads/afdb/Documents/Project-and-Operations/Rwanda%20case%20study%20paper%20final.pdf*.

BAfD/OCDE/CEA (2010), *Perspectives économiques en Afrique 2010 : La mobilisation des ressources publiques et l'aide*, Éditions OCDE, Paris, *http://dx.doi.org/10.1787/aeo-2010-fr*.

BAfD/OCDE/PNUD (2017), *Perspectives économiques en Afrique 2017 : Entrepreneuriat et industrialisation*, Éditions OCDE, Paris, *http://dx.doi.org/10.1787/aeo-2017-fr*.

BAfD/OCDE/PNUD (2015), *Perspectives économiques en Afrique 2015 : Développement territorial et inclusion spatiale*, Éditions OCDE, Paris, *http://dx.doi.org/10.1787/aeo-2015-fr*.

Banque mondiale (2015), *Note d'orientation du financement des collectivités locales*, Banque mondiale, Washington, DC, *www-wds.worldbank.org/external/default/WDSContentServer/WDSP/IB/2015/10/13/090224b0831405d5/2_0/Rendered/PDF/Note0d0orienta0ollectivites0locales.pdf.*

Boisard, S., C. de Freitas et G. Hidouci (2014), *Renforcer les recettes fiscales locales pour financer le développement urbain en Afrique*, Fonds Mondial pour le Développement des Villes (FMDV), Paris, *http://delog.org/web/wp-content/uploads/2016/03/Etude-FMDV-Fiscalite%CC%81-locale-Villes-Afrique-8-Cas.pdf.*

EPS PEAKS (2013), « Taxation and Developing Countries », Overseas Development Institute training notes, Londres, *www.odi.org/sites/odi.org.uk/files/odi-assets/events-documents/5045.pdf.*

Fjeldstad, O-H., G. Chambas et J-F. Brun (2014), « Local government taxation in Sub-Saharan Africa: a review and an agenda for research », *CMI Working Paper*, WP 2014: 2, Chr. Michelsen Institute, Bergen, *www.cmi.no/publications/file/5098-local-government-taxation-in-sub-saharan-africa.pdf.*

FMI (2017), *Perspectives de l'économie mondiale*, Fonds monétaire international, Washington, DC. *www.imf.org/fr/Publications/WEO/Issues/2017/04/04/world-economic-outlook-april-2017*

FMI (2016a), « 2016 article IV consultation—press release; staff report; and statement by the executive director for Cabo Verde », *IMF Country report*, No. 16/366, Fonds monétaire international, Washington, DC, septembre, *www.imf.org/external/pubs/ft/scr/2016/cr16366.pdf.*

FMI (2016b), « Initiative en faveur des pays pauvres très endettés (PPTE) et Initiative d'allégement de la dette multilatérale (IADM) - Mise à jour statistique », *Documents de politique générale du FMI*, Fonds monétaire international, Washington, DC, *www.imf.org/en/Publications/Policy-Papers/Issues/2016/12/31/Heavily-Indebted-Poor-Countries-Initiative-and-Multilateral-Debt-Relief-Initiative-PP5024.*

FMI (2014a), « Cameroun : Consultations de 2014 au titre de l'article IV », *Rapport du FMI*, No. 14/212, Fonds monétaire international, Washington, DC, *www.imf.org/external/french/pubs/ft/scr/2014/cr14212f.pdf.*

FMI (2014b), « Mauritius: article IV Consultation-staff report, press release and statement by the executive director for Mauritius », *IMF Country Report*, No. 14/107, Fonds monétaire international, Washington, DC, *www.imf.org/external/pubs/ft* /scr/2014/cr14107.pdf.

FMI (2013), « Côte d'Ivoire : Consultations de 2013 au titre de l'article IV et quatrième revue de l'accord au titre de la facilité élargie de crédit », *Rapport du FMI*, No. 13/367, Fonds monétaire international, Washington, DC, *www.imf.org/external/french/pubs/ft/scr/2013/cr13367f.pdf.*

FMI (2011), *Mobilisation des recettes dans les pays en développement*, Fonds monétaire international, Washington, DC, *www.imf.org/external/french/np/pp/2011/030811f.pdf.*

FMI (2007), *Guide sur la transparence des recettes des ressources naturelles*, Fonds monétaire international, Washington, DC, *www.imf.org/external/np/fad/trans/fre/guidef.pdf.*

FMI (2001), « Democratic Republic of Congo: Selected issues and statistical appendix », *IMF Country Report*, No. 01/123, Fonds monétaire international, Washington, DC, juillet, *www.imf.org/external/pubs/ft/scr/2001/cr01123.pdf.*

Fossat, P. et M. Bua (2013), « Tax administration reform in the francophone countries of sub-Saharan Africa », *IMF Working Paper*, WP/13/173, Fonds monétaire international, Washington, DC, *www.imf.org/external/pubs/ft/wp/2013/wp13173.pdf.*

Kloeden, D. (2011), « Revenue administration reforms in anglophone Africa since the early 1990s », *IMF Working Paper*, WP/11/162, Fonds monétaire international, Washington, DC, *www.imf.org/external/pubs/ft/wp/2011/wp11162.pdf.*

Mansour M. et G. Rota-Graziosi (2013), « Tax coordination, tax competition, and revenue mobilization in the west african economic and monetary union », *IMF Working Paper*, WP/13/163, Fonds monétaire international, Washington, DC, *www.imf.org/external/pubs/ft/wp/2013/wp13163.pdf.*

Monkam, N. et M. Moore (2015), *How Property Tax Would Benefit Africa*, Africa Research Institute, London, *www.africaresearchinstitute.org/publications/property-tax-benefit-africa.*

National Treasury (2015), « Budget Review 2015 », Pretoria, South Africa, *www.treasury.gov.za/documents/national%20budget/2015/review/FullReview.pdf.*

NGRI (2015), « An analysis of Ghana's 2015 oil revenue performance: Testing the model », Natural Resource Governance Institute, *https://resourcegovernance.org/blog/analysis-ghanas-2015-oil-revenue-performance-testing-model.*

OCDE (2016), *Statistiques des recettes publiques 2016*, Éditions OCDE, Paris, *http://dx.doi.org/10.1787/rev_stats-2016-en-fr*

OCDE (2014), *Coopération pour le développement 2015 : Mobiliser les ressources au service du développement durable*, Éditions OCDE, Paris, *http://dx.doi.org/10.1787/dcr-2014-fr*.

OCDE/ATAF/CUA (2017), « Statistiques des recettes publiques en Afrique: Tableaux comparatifs », *Statistiques fiscales de l'OCDE* (base de données), *http://dx.doi.org/10.1787/7f54581d-fr*.

OCDE/CEPAL/CIAT/BID (2017), *Revenue Statistics in Latin America and the Caribbean 2017*, Éditions OCDE, Paris, *http://dx.doi.org/10.1787/rev_lat_car-2017-en-fr*.

OMS (2015), « Purchasing power parity 2005 », Organisation mondiale de la Santé, *www.who.int/choice/costs/ppp/en/*.

OPM (2013), *The Impact of Mining in the Democratic Republic of Congo*, Oxford Policy Management, *www.opml.co.uk/sites/default/files/DRC%20mining%20report%20-%20OPM%20-%20Final%20Eng.pdf*.

PNUD (2013), *Rapport national sur le développement humain 2013 : Emploi, changements structurels et développement humain en Côte d'Ivoire*, Programme des Nations Unies pour le développement, New York, *www.ci.undp.org/content/cote_divoire/fr/home/library/poverty/rndh_2013.html*.

Profeta, P. et S. Scabrosetti (2010), *The Political Economy of Taxation: Lessons from Developing Countries*, Edward Elgar Publishing, *https://books.google.fr/books?isbn=1849805490*.

SACU (2017), Southern African Customs Union Agreement 2002 (amendé le 12 April 2013), *www.sacu.int/list.php?type=Agreements*

SACU (2014), Implementing a Common Agenda Towards Regional Integration: 2014 Annual Report, 2002 Southern African Customs Union, *www.sacu.int/docs/reports_annual/2014/annual_report.pdf*.

Sokeechand, K.R. et G. Hussen (2013), « The Mauritian experience », presentation prepared for regional workshop on "Effectiveness of and alternatives to tax incentives as instruments to generate employment and attract investments in Lusaka", 12-13 February, Zambia, International Tax Compact, *www.taxcompact.net/documents/workshop-lusaka/2013-02-13_itc_Rambaksh-Sokeechand_MRA-MoF-Mauritius.pdf*.

SSA (2015), *Social Security Through the World: Africa 2015*, SSA Publication, No. 13-11802, Social Security Administration, Washington, DC, *www.ssa.gov/policy/docs/progdesc/ssptw/2014-2015/africa/ssptw15africa.pdf*.

Pour en savoir plus

AISS (2014), *Afrique : Approches stratégiques pour renforcer la sécurité sociale*, Association internationale de la sécurité sociale, Genève, *www.issa.int/details?uuid=3c1e0654-a158-48db-a5dc-892b36b78ae3*.

BAfD (2010), *Sénégal – Évaluation du potentiel de recettes publiques*, Banque africaine de développement, *www.afdb.org/fileadmin/uploads/afdb/Documents/Project-and-Operations/Pages%20from%20SENEGAL_%20Evaluation%20du%20potentiel%20des%20recettes%20publiques%20Eng.pdf*.

BAfD/OCDE/PNUD (2014), *Perspectives économiques en Afrique 2014 : Les chaînes de valeur mondiales et l'industrialisation de l'Afrique*, Éditions OCDE, Paris, *http://dx.doi.org/10.1787/aeo-2014-fr*.

Besley, T. et T. Persson (2013), *Taxation and Development*, (chapitre préparé pour le *Handbook of Public Economics*, édité par Auerbach, A., R. Chetty, M. Feldstein et E. Saez), *http://econ.lse.ac.uk/staff/tbesley/papers/TaxationAndDevelopment.pdf*.

Bird R. et E. Zolt (2003), « Introduction to tax policy design and development », module brouillon préparé pour un cours sur les questions pratiques de la politique fiscale dans les pays en développement, Banque Mondiale, 28 avril-1 mai, *www1.worldbank.org/publicsector/LearningProgram/PracticalIssues/papers/introduction%20to%20tax%20policy/WBI%20Module%201(Bird&Zolt)April10.doc*.

Cruce, F. (2011), "Evaluating value added tax in morocco," *Minor Field Study Series*, No. 209, Department of Economics at the University of Lund, Lund, *https://liveatlund.lu.se/intranets/LUSEM/NEK/mfs/MFS/209.pdf*

FMI (2015a), *Current Challenges in Revenue Mobilization: Improving Tax Compliance*, Fonds monétaire international, Washington, DC, *www.imf.org/external/np/pp/eng/2015/020215a.pdf*.

FMI (2015b), « Allégement de la dette au titre de l'initiative en faveur des pays pauvres très endettés (PPTE) », *International Monetary Fund Factsheet*, mars, Fonds monétaire international, Washington, DC, *www.imf.org/external/np/exr/facts/fre/pdf/hipcf.pdf*.

FMI (2014), *Government Finance Statistics Manual*, Fonds monétaire international, Washington, DC, *www.imf.org/external/Pubs/FT/GFS/Manual/2014/gfsfinal.pdf*.

FMI (2010), « Tunisie : Conclusions préliminaires de la mission de consultation au titre de l'article IV », Fonds monétaire international, Washington, DC, *www.imf.org/external/french/np/ms/2010/061510af.htm* (accessed 7 January 2015).

John, J.D. (2009), « Taxation, governance and resource mobilisation in Sub-Saharan Africa: A survey of key issues (WP) », *Sub-Saharan Africa Working Paper*, No. 49/2009, Real Instituto Elcano, Madrid, *www.realinstitutoelcano.org/wps/portal/web/rielcano_en/contenido?WCM_GLOBAL_CONTEXT=/elcano/elcano_in/zonas_in/dt49-2009*.

Keen, M. et M. Mansour (2009), « Revenue mobilization in Sub-Saharan Africa: Challenges from globalization », *IMF Working Paper*, WP/09/157, Fonds monétaire international, Washington, DC, *www.imf.org/external/pubs/ft/wp/2009/wp09157.pdf*.

Lewis, C. et T. Alton (2015), « How can South Africa's tax system meet revenue raising challenges? », *Documents de travail du Département des affaires économiques*, No. 1276, Éditions OCDE, Paris, *http://dx.doi.org/10.1787/5jrp1g0xztbr-en*.

Mascagni, G., M. Moore et R. McCluskey (2014), *Tax Revenue Mobilisation in Developing Countries Issues and Challenge*, Union européenne, Bruxelles, *www.ids.ac.uk/files/dmfile/TaxRevenueMobilisationinDevelopingCountries.pdf*.

Thomas, A. et J.P. Treviño (2013), « Resource dependence and fiscal effort in Sub-Saharan Africa », *IMF Working Paper*, WP/13/188, Fonds monétaire international, Washington, DC, *www.imf.org/external/pubs/ft/wp/2013/wp13188.pdf*.

Prichard, W., A. Cobham et A. Goodall (2014), « The ICTD government revenue dataset », *ICTD Working Paper*, No. 19, Institute of Development Studies, Brighton, *https://assets.publishing.service.gov.uk/media/57a089be40f0b652dd0003b2/ICTD-WP19.pdf*.

Chapter 2

SPECIAL FEATURE

Domestic resource mobilisation in Africa: Progress made, and long-term challenges

Chapitre 2

ÉTUDE SPÉCIALE

Mobilisation des ressources intérieures en Afrique : progrès réalisés, et défis à long terme

Revenue Statistics in Africa 1990-2015/Statistiques des recettes publiques en Afrique 1990-2015

Chapter 2

SPECIAL FEATURE

Domestic resource mobilisation in Africa: Progress made, and long-term challenges

Introduction

A key rationale behind the *Revenue Statistics in Africa* project is the desire to meet the need for better and more comparable datasets on government revenues in African countries. The aim is to support an improved understanding of the progress that African countries are making in mobilising domestic resources for development. The generation of savings by a government internally, especially through taxation, instead of through external sources such as loans, grants, aid or remittances, provides a more stable source of revenue over time.

International organisations and policy makers have made policies for domestic resource mobilisation area a priority. The Sustainable Development Goals (SDGs) ratified in 2015 included the target 17.1, to "improve domestic capacity for tax and other revenue collection". The *Revenue Statistics in Africa* project supports these international priorities by providing national governments and international organisations with the information and tools they can use to evaluate the capacity of countries to raise tax revenues from their own economies.

This chapter will explain why domestic resource mobilisation is important to policy makers, and examine African financial resources in the context of development priorities and evolving internal and external challenges. It draws on the data in this publication and also on the *African Economic Outlook 2017* (AfDB/OECD/UNDP, 2017) which examines this question in more detail.

Domestic revenue mobilisation goes beyond government financing

Domestic resource mobilisation is studied not only for its relationship to government finances, but also because it remains a vital area of study within the topic of public governance. It is a key part of the Sustainable Development Goals, and therefore an important area of international co-operation. It is also cited as a way to improve governance in fragile states, and even as a way to improve the business environment, thereby improving productivity.

Domestic resource mobilisation will help meet the Sustainable Development Goals

The Sustainable Development Goals, which replaced the Millennium Development Goals, have established a set of ambitious international development targets for the year 2030 that demand additional resources to be put forward. Already, many African countries are ramping up investments in public infrastructure projects. According to the latest *African Economic Outlook*, "public investments rose by about 3% of GDP in 2014 and are expected to remain at this level for the next five years" (AfDB/OECD/UNDP, 2017: 29). However, meeting the objectives of the SDGs will require an increase in annual public spending by up to 30%, according to some estimates (Baum et al., 2017). For example, sub-Saharan Africa will need to spend USD 93 billion per year to close its infrastructure gap (AfDB/OECD/UNDP, 2017). The Addis Ababa Action agenda in July 2015 advocated for countries to raise more funds by strengthening domestic revenue mobilisation through tax policy and better tax administration as a key means of achieving the Sustainable Development Goals.

African countries are attempting to increase domestic revenue mobilisation, but it is not always easy. Over the last decade, the 16 countries in *Revenue Statistics* have sustained their tax revenues (excluding the social security contributions SSCs), on a weighted average basis, as a percentage of GDP (Figure 2.1). The performance is even better when the social security contributions are included. This encouraging trend shows that their capacity to mobilise taxes is robust and less dependent on the volatility of international commodity prices. The tax revenues of the other African countries, however, have suffered more from the recent drop in commodity prices (see AfDB/OECD/UNDP, 2017, Chapter 1).

Figure 2.1. **Ratio of total tax to total GDP in *Revenue Statistics in Africa* (RSIA) countries compared with the rest of Africa**

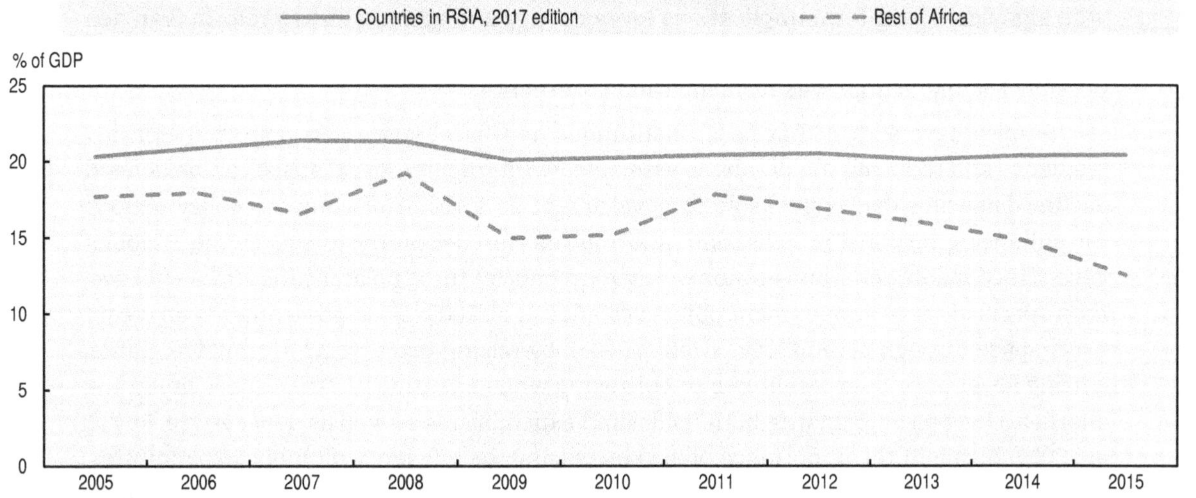

Note: For each country-group, the figures are the weighted averages using the sum of the total tax revenues in US dollars collected by all the countries in question divided by the sum of their GDP in US dollars. For comparability, the data reported in the figure do not include the social security contributions that are available only for the 16 countries in the *Revenue Statistics in Africa* project.

Source: IMF (2017a), *World Economic Outlook* (database).

StatLink http://dx.doi.org/10.1787/888933569782

International aid can play an important role by better encouraging domestic resources mobilisation. Aid for public sector policy and administrative management account for less than 2% of the total aid allocated to Africa (Figure 2.2).

Figure 2.2. **Aid for domestic resource mobilisation, as % of all ODA, by country**

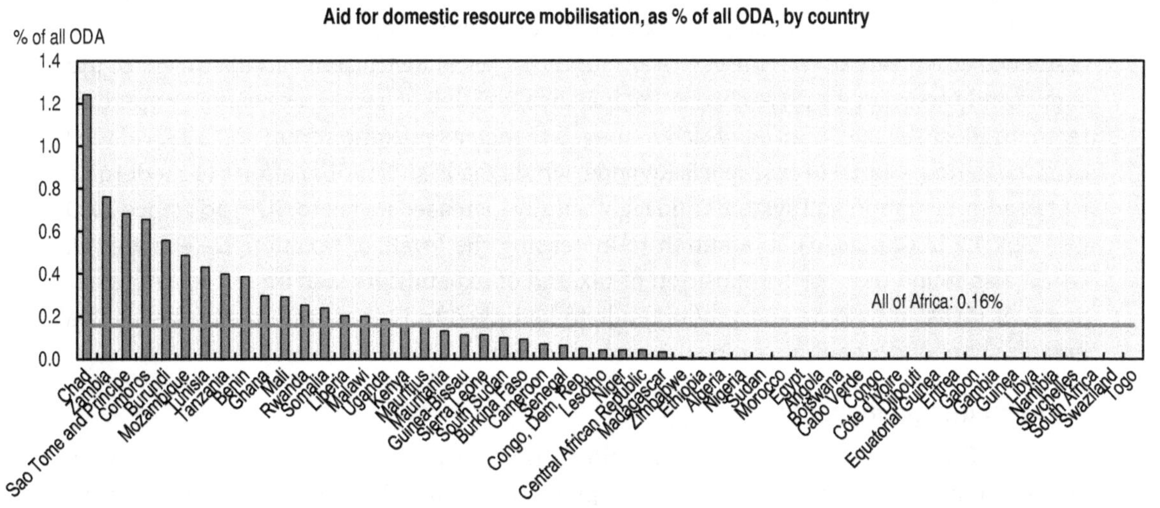

Source: OECD (2017), *QUIDS Dataset* (database), *https://stats.oecd.org/qwids/*.

StatLink http://dx.doi.org/10.1787/888933569801

Targeted foreign aid can help build the capacity of the state to mobilise tax revenue by supporting reforms of tax administration and building technical capacity (Ndikumana, 2015). Over time, if the state is able to deliver public services, it should be able to minimise its dependence on foreign aid (OECD, 2014).

Domestic resource mobilisation can build more resilient states

In 2016, out of 56 states in the world classified as fragile, 37 were located in Africa (OECD, 2016).[1] State fragility is often related to the existence of conflicts or post-conflict situations. Political conflict has been shown to have a negative effect on domestic resource mobilisation, with significant long-term implications for tax policy and administration reform (Van den Boogaard et al., 2016). However, the causality also goes the other way, with higher taxation possibly leading to improved resilience and governance.

Studies have shown that fiscal institutions and fiscal space can help in increasing resilience and reducing the problems associated with fragility. Fiscal space can be defined as "the financing that is available to government as a result of concrete policy actions for enhancing resource mobilisation, and the reforms necessary to secure the enabling governance, institutional and economic environments for these policy actions to be effective, for a specified set of development objectives" (Roy et al. 2009: 33). A government can create fiscal space through several ways (Heller, 2005): by raising taxes, securing outside grants, cutting lower priority expenditures or borrowing while ensuring it has the capacity in the short and long term to finance both its desired expenditures as well as debt service. Roy et al. (2009) highlight the importance of also increasing the efficiency of public expenditures, notably by lowering the unit cost of providing public services without reducing their quality and quantity.

Fiscal legitimacy is essential for building resilience in fragile states. Taxation often reveals interplay between state competence and government accountability in carrying out successful institutional reforms that strengthen domestic revenue mobilisation. Taydas and Peksen (2012) argue that higher spending shows a commitment from the government to its citizens' well-being. Di John (2010) showed that taxation is a way to legitimise state authority, and increase state resilience.

After studying the role of fiscal policies in 26 African countries over the period 1990-2013, Deléchat et al. (2015) conclude that high-quality fiscal institutions are associated with better fiscal outcomes. Analysing the experience of seven[2] countries that managed to build resilience after years of civil unrest, they found that fiscal institutions and fiscal space are significantly associated with resilience. For instance, creation of fiscal space was an important factor in these seven countries, which managed to increase taxation from 5% to 13% of GDP over the period. A notable example is Rwanda, which made substantial efforts to modernise its tax administration and systems and significantly increased its tax to GDP ratio since 2000 (see Box 1.2 in Chapter 1). In addition to increasing the levels of taxation, Déléchat et al. (2015) also found that the composition of tax and of expenditure was important. A higher share of taxes on income and profits tends to be linked to higher state resilience, as is a greater share of expenditure on health and education.

Taxation and productivity

An efficient tax system may have a positive effect on firm productivity. A 2017 IMF study showed that countries can reap substantial productivity gains by reducing resource (labour and capital) misallocation across firms resulting from a number of government policies or poorly functioning markets (IMF, 2017b). Such misallocations constitute an important source of total factor productivity (TFP) differences across countries and over time. When there is a high degree of resource dispersion, reallocating resources from firms with low productivity to firms with high productivity increases output, using the same resources in a more efficient way.

Removing tax distortions can also affect GDP growth positively. According to the same IMF study cited above, on a transition path of 20 years, reducing resource misallocation translates into a higher annual real GDP growth rate of 1.3% for emerging market economies and 0.9% for low income developing countries. Both tax policy and tax administration are important factors in tackling the productivity challenge. Adapting the tax system can ensure that firms will take decisions for business reasons, rather than for tax reasons.

Governments can enable total factor productivity gains by addressing tax treatments that are non-neutral or (at least) minimising differentiated tax treatments for businesses depending on their asset type, sources of financing, or firm characteristics such as formality and size. Lower compliance burdens can also reduce costs for business and free up productive resources, particularly for smaller firms. Effective enforcement is also important in maintaining and building trust in the tax system which ultimately depends on voluntary compliance. In addition, new technologies are enabling many tax administrations to decrease burdens by enhancing registration and identification procedures, use of the internet and mobile applications, e-filing and providing taxpayer services, including for enhanced guidance. Increasingly tax administration can follow a risk-based approach that includes strong audit capacity and taxpayer segmentation, reducing burdens on compliant taxpayers (IMF, 2017b).

There are many important challenges to improving domestic resource mobilisation

Although the 16 countries included in this publication have increased their tax-to-GDP ratios since 2000, domestic resource mobilisation in the continent in general is not keeping up with Africa's growth in GDP and the general economic and political progress on the continent. Consequently, taxation as a percentage of GDP has gone down almost four percentage points in the period from 2005 to 2015 (AfDB/OECD/UNDP, 2017). This shows that despite some genuine efforts and some progress, the challenges to domestic resource mobilisation in Africa have not gone away. Moreover, tax-to-GDP ratios remain comparatively low in most African countries, compared to those in other regions, even when countries have increased their tax-to-GDP ratios in recent years.

Correlation between natural resource revenues and public revenues

As mentioned in the first chapter of this publication, resource-rich countries often exhibit low tax-to-GDP ratios. Analysing the data on 35 resource-rich countries in the world over the period 1992-2009, Crivelli and Gupta (2014) found that for each additional percentage point of GDP in resource revenue, there is a corresponding reduction in domestic (non-resource) revenues of about 0.3 percentage points of GDP. However, the resource revenues can be very volatile while stronger fiscal institutions could help strengthen state resilience (Baum et al., 2017).

The African continent has been affected by the instability of resource revenues. It experienced a slowdown in domestic revenue mobilisation after a peak at USD 561.5 billion in 2012, mainly due to a fall in commodity and especially oil prices. The *African Economic*

Outlook reported "between 2012 and 2015, domestic revenue decreased by 22.2%. This drop in domestic revenue is mainly explained by the huge slump in resource revenue (43.7%) over the same period" (AfDB/OECD/UNDP, 2017: 64). These patterns are confirmed in this publication, with high volatility of non-tax revenues observed for the resource-rich countries in this publication, especially the Democratic Republic of the Congo and Niger.

Resource-rich countries, even though they have made efforts to improve tax revenue collection, were most affected by the fall in domestic revenue mobilisation. "Their overall revenue-GDP ratio decreased from 25% in 2012 to 19% in 2015" (AfDB/OECD/UNDP, 2017: 65). Between 2012 and 2015, resource revenue fell by more than 50% in Algeria, Angola, Chad and Gabon, mainly due to the narrow tax base in resource-rich countries. Cameroon and Côte d'Ivoire also showed narrow tax bases and relatively low tax-to-GDP ratios at less than 18% of GDP in 2015, which is lower than the average (unweighted) of the 16 countries featured in this publication at 19.1% (see Chapter 1). In contrast, non-resource-rich countries have increased their revenue mobilisation by 9.6% between 2012 and 2016, mainly due to the increase in direct taxes (12%) and indirect taxes (8%). The best performers in domestic revenue mobilisation among non-resource-rich countries were Ethiopia, Malawi, Rwanda, Seychelles, Swaziland and Togo. Rwanda and Togo have implemented significant tax and tax administration reforms that have strengthened their tax-to-GDP ratios (see Chapter 1).

Fragile, yet resource-rich countries pose an additional challenge to policy makers. Countries with natural resource revenues can expand their fiscal space quickly in order to address pressing social or infrastructural needs. However, if they do not put in place efficient tax systems, their situation could be harmful in the long term, especially if resource revenues eventually fall due to commodity price fluctuations.

Taxing the informal economy

A major obstacle to collecting tax revenues in Africa is the size of the informal economy, that is, workers and companies not reporting taxable income and often not engaging with public administration more generally. Efforts to broaden the tax base are undermined by the size of this informal sector, estimated at 38% of the GDP in sub-Saharan Africa in 2010-14 (IMF, 2017c: 51). The *African Economic Outlook 2010* focused on informality as a challenge for policy makers in terms of domestic revenue mobilisation. Informality hinders companies in their development. Informal firms tend to be less productive than formal firms. Research by Kanbur and Keen (2015) suggests that firms that engage in undeclared sales have lower total factor productivity than tax compliant firms. Furthermore, they also create unfair competition with compliant businesses.

There are a number of factors responsible for the informal economy. Informality will tend to be higher in countries where the cost of tax and other regulatory requirements is higher. Weak enforcement as well as difficulties in registering for tax and/or complying with tax requirements can also be significant drivers of informal activity. Complex tax codes and high compliance burdens, together with ineffective tax administration, are powerful incentives for small enterprises to remain informal (AfDB/OECD/UNECA, 2010). According to the World Bank's Informal Enterprise Survey, avoidance of taxes is the main reason for informal firms to not join the formal economy (AfDB/OECD/UNDP, 2017). This can have wider impacts on the economy, undermining taxpayer morale more generally, which ultimately reduces government's revenues (IMF/OECD/UN/World Bank, 2011).

Tax policies and better tax administrations in both emerging market economies and low-income countries can help reducing the prevalence of informality, but this requires a multifaceted approach. For example, by reducing opportunities for non-compliance at the same time as increasing understanding of tax requirements and simplifying administrative processes. In tackling the informal sector, care needs to be taken to facilitate firms in their transition from the formal economy toward legal activities, rather than simply closing them down and depressing overall economic activity. Part of the way to do this is helping firms to better access finance and markets. Research suggests that lower tax rates and reduced compliance costs can help Africa to boost the transition to formal business. A decrease in the size of the informal sector can help in broadening the current tax base, thus improving domestic revenue mobilisation in the continent (IMF, 2017b), and making it easier for firms to grow (AfDB/OECD/UNDP, 2017).

Taxation and external financial flows

The 2010 edition of the *African Economic Outlook* raised the possibility of foreign aid reducing incentives for governments to raise domestic revenue. Large foreign aid flows may reduce the urgency with which revenue collection is pursued, for example. When it comes to Official Development Assistance (ODA) there has been an important academic debate over whether this has a negative impact on domestic revenue mobilisation or not (AfDB/OECD/UNECA, 2010).

A higher capacity to collect taxes helps reduce dependence on ODA. Indeed, studies have found ODA and tax collection to be negatively correlated (Crivelli and Gupta, 2014; Gupta et al., 2004). At the same time, according to a study on 118 countries over the period 1980-2009 (Benedek et al., 2012), the negative association between ODA and domestic tax revenue has weakened over the years due to greater efforts at mobilising domestic revenues in many countries.

Beyond the general trends, the manner in which aid is delivered to countries and the way it is allocated (targeted activities and supported sectors) is crucial. The composition of aid matters, for example (e.g. whether dealing with grants or loans). The negative correlation between ODA and capacity to collect taxes is stronger in low-income countries and in countries with relatively weak institutions. This impact of grants on tax revenue can be mitigated by policy makers and donors if the capacity to mobilise revenue is strengthened.

ODA sent to countries in post conflict situations is often necessary for governments to be able to address their structural challenges and minimise the risk of a new conflict. For a certain period of time, these countries may need to rely on foreign aid to face the urgent needs of economic reconstruction. It is difficult for post-conflict countries to mobilise their own resources because of the often destructed economic activity, state capacity and national institutions (Di John, 2010).

There are ways for tax policy makers to increase the efficiency of tax collection

Several measures and practices have been adopted by African governments in recent years in order to make the duty of paying taxes simpler, increasing efficiency and compliance at the same time. This has borne fruit in terms of the amount of time it takes to file taxes in Africa. Although Africa is the continent with the second longest time to comply after South

America (PwC, 2017), it is clearly making progress. Paying taxes took 307 hours for a small to medium-sized manufacturer or retailer[3] on average in Africa in the year 2015, compared to 313 hours in 2014 and 316 in 2014.

Between 2005 and 2015, several African countries have reduced significantly the time needed each year to pay taxes. The best examples include Algeria, Kenya, Morocco, South Africa, and Tunisia; among others (see Figure 2.3). The data show a great diversity across the whole continent. For instance, in 2015, paying taxes took less than 125 hours in the top five countries in Africa with the easiest system for paying taxes, while it needed more than 700 hours in the bottom five countries.

Figure 2.3. **Number of hours per year to pay taxes, by country**

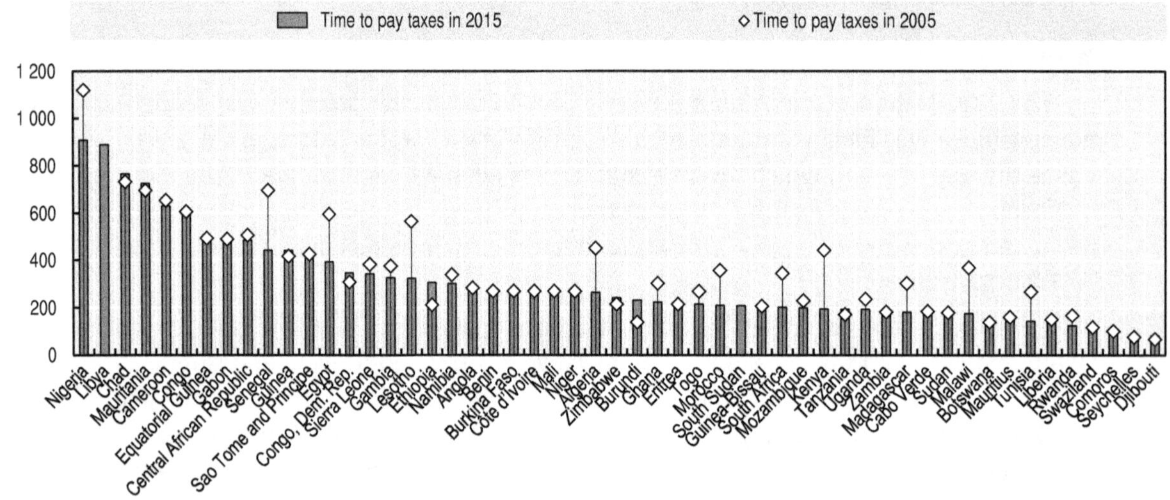

Source: World Bank (2017), "Paying Taxes", *Doing Business*, *www.doingbusiness.org/data/exploretopics/paying-taxes/good-practices.*

StatLink http://dx.doi.org/10.1787/888933569820

A number of countries are also expanding their domestic revenue by boosting the revenue from taxes through various measures. For example, Ethiopia is taking action to boost tax compliance. The Ethiopian Revenue Authority conducted an experiment showing that businesses receiving letters threatening them of an audit, or complementing them on paying their taxes increased their tax returns, respectively by 38% and 32%. It demonstrated that strengthening revenue authorities' capacity to collect taxes, analyse taxpayer data, and using behavioural techniques to influence taxpayers can increase compliance (AfDB/OECD/UNDP, 2017).

An example of an improvement to tax administrations that many countries have already adopted is e-filing tax systems (Che Azmi and Kamarulzaman, 2010). Through an e-government platform, authorities can deliver information to its citizens, businesses and public administration electronically (see Chapter 5 of AfDB/OECD/UNDP, 2017). An electronic system to pay taxes can benefit the taxpayers, the firms and the tax authorities as well. For tax authorities, it reduces the workload and operational costs. It also increases tax compliance and saves time. For tax payers and firms, it is a time-saving method, reduces calculation errors and makes the paperwork easier to fill out. Both sides can benefit from a reduction of potential corruption or informal treatment. Such a system requires an awareness of e-filing options and benefits by people, and training by authorities if necessary (Coolidge and Yilmaz, 2014).

Success depends also on the presence of an enabling environment that allows digital government to flourish (Ledjou and Randrianasolo-Rakotobe, 2012). The e-filing system in South Africa is one of the good examples over the continent (see Box 2.1).

More generally the development of new technologies, including the growing use of mobile phones, offers the prospect for further improvements in the cost-effectiveness of tax administration for both the government and taxpayers. Applications already exist which allow small businesses to keep tax records as they conduct their business, thus reducing the time needed to be spent.

Box 2.1. **Electronic tax system in South Africa**

The South African government adopted the system of e-government in 2000, reshaping the tax collection system as well. In 2001, the South African Revenue Services (SARS) introduced the eFiling platform. The launch of this online tax management tool made it easier for citizens to complete paying taxes and also made it harder to evade taxes. As a result, SARS reported significant increases in the numbers of taxpayers filing, and filing on time, for instance in their 2011-12 annual report (SARS, 2012). SARS e-filing system is collecting taxes and trends indicate major improvements in tax revenue collections over time. This free service allows taxpayers, tax practitioners and businesses to register and submit returns and declarations, make payments and perform a number of other interactions with SARS in a secure online environment. Users can submit tax returns using their mobile phones as well. The website also contains information on how to proceed for users, with online videos, live online help facilities and calendar of deadlines (Ledjou, Randrianasolo-Rakotobe, 2012).

The perceived usefulness and the compatibility of this new technology with a taxpayer's occupation and day-to-day activities led people in South Africa to adopt the eFiling system (Jankeeparsad, Jankeeparsad and Nienaber, 2016). Another quantitative study on the perceived effect of eFiling on tax compliance was conducted in five municipal areas of a district of the North West Province. The study concludes that the majority of tax payers have positive experiences about eFiling and recognise its benefits, like cost saving, quicker turn-around times on refund and ease of transacting with SARS (Mongwakeste, 2015). eFiling fully replaces paper filing, leading to a reduction in compliance costs. It also allows for better monitoring of fiscal performance. On average, eFiling usage in South Africa is associated with a 22.4% reduction in tax compliance costs (Coolidge and Yilmaz, 2014).

For the 2015/16 fiscal year, more than three-quarters of the payments were made through the eFiling channel (75.9%), compared to 64.2% for the 2011/12 fiscal year and 30.8% for the 2007/08 fiscal year. In contrast, the payments made at branch offices decreased from 22% in 2007/08 to 0.3% in 2015/16. The third possible channel to pay taxes is through banks, representing 23.8% of the payments in 2015/16 (SARS, 2016).

Notes

1. To define fragility, the OECD international network on conflict and fragility (see OECD, 2016, p. 73) developed a framework that considers five dimensions: economic, environmental, political, security and societal.
2. Cameroon, Ethiopia, Mozambique, Niger, Nigeria, Rwanda and Uganda.
3. The figures for time to comply are based on estimates of the tax experiences of a fictional reference company, referred to as the "case study company". The case study company is a small to medium-size manufacturer and retailer with specific assumptions, deliberately chosen to ensure that its business can be compared worldwide on a like for like basis (see PwC, 2016 for more explanations).

References

AfDB/OECD/UNDP (2017), *African Economic Outlook 2017: Entrepreneurship and Industrialisation*, OECD Publishing, Paris, *http://dx.doi.org/10.1787/aeo-2017-en*.

AfDB/OECD/UNECA (2010), *African Economic Outlook 2010: Domestic Resource Mobilisation and Aid*, OECD Publishing, Paris, *http://dx.doi.org/10.1787/aeo-2010-en*.

Baum, A. et al. (2017), "Can they do it all? Fiscal space in low-income countries", *IMF Working Paper*, International Monetary Fund, Washington, DC,*www.imf.org/en/Publications/WP/Issues/2017/05/05/Can-They-Do-It-All-Fiscal-Space-in-Low-Income-Countries-44889*.

Benedek, D. et al. (2012), "Foreign aid and revenue: Still a crowding out effect?", *Working Paper*, No. 12/186, International Monetary Fund, Washington, DC.

Che Azmi, A.A. and Y. Kamarulzaman (2010), "Adoption of tax e-filing: A conceptual paper", *African Journal of Business Management*, Vol. 4(5), pp. 599-603, *www.academicjournals.org/article/article1380712917_Azmi%20and%20Kamarulzaman.pdf*.

Coolidge, J. and F. Yilmaz (2014), "Does e-filing reduce tax compliance costs in developing countries?", *Investment Climate in Practice*, No. 21, *https://openknowledge.worldbank.org/bitstream/handle/10986/20428/911910BRI0Box30D0VC0KNOWLEDGE0NOTES.pdf;sequence=1*.

Crivelli, E. and S. Gupta (2014), "Resource blessing, revenue curse? Domestic revenue effort in resource-rich countries", *European Journal of Political Economy*, Vol. 35, pp. 563-595, *https://doi.org/10.1016/j.ejpoleco.2014.04.001*.

Deléchat, C. et al. (2015), "Exiting from fragility in sub-Saharan Africa: The role of fiscal policies and fiscal institutions", *Working Paper*, No. 15/268, International Monetary Fund, Washington, DC, *www.imf.org/external/pubs/ft/wp/2015/wp15268.pdf*.

Di John, J. (2010), "Taxation, resource mobilisation and state performance", *Working paper*, No. 84, Crisis States Research Centre, London, *www.lse.ac.uk/internationalDevelopment/research/crisisStates/download/wp/wpSeries2/WP842.pdf*.

Gupta, S. et al. (2004), "Foreign aid and revenue response: Does the composition of aid matter?", *Working Paper*, No. 03/176, Washington, DC, *www.imf.org/external/pubs/ft/wp/2003/wp03176.pdf*.

Heller, P.S. (2005), "Understanding fiscal space", *IMF Policy Discussion Paper*, No. 05/4, International Monetary Fund, Washington, DC, *www.imf.org/external/pubs/ft/pdp/2005/pdp04.pdf*.

IMF (2017a), *World Economic Outlook* (database), International Monetary Fund, Washington, DC.

IMF (2017b), "Upgrading the tax system to boost productivity", in *Fiscal monitor: Achieving more with less*, IMF Publishing, Washington, DC, *www.imf.org/en/Publications/FM/Issues/2017/04/06/fiscal-monitor-april-2017*.

IMF (2017c), "The informal economy in Sub-Saharan Africa", in *Regional Economic Outlook: Sub-Saharan Africa*, April, IMF Publishing, Washington, DC, *www.imf.org/en/Publications/REO/SSA/Issues/2017/05/03/sreo0517*.

IMF/OECD/UN/World Bank (2011), "Supporting the development of more effective tax systems", A Report to the G20 Development Working Group, *www.oecd.org/ctp/48993634.pdf*

Jankeeparsad, R.W., T.R. Jankeeparsad and G. Nienaber (2016), "Acceptance of the electronic method of filing tax returns by South African taxpayers: An exploratory study", *Journal of Economic and Financial Sciences*; pp. 120-136, Johannesburg, *http://repository.up.ac.za/bitstream/handle/2263/53252/Jankeeparsad_Acceptance_2016.pdf?sequence=1&isAllowed=y*.

Kanbur, R. and M. Keen (2015), "Reducing informality", *Finance & Development*, Vol. 52, No. 1, International Monetary Fund, Washington, DC, *www.imf.org/external/pubs/ft/fandd/2015/03/kanbur.htm* (accessed June 2017).

Ledjou, J-M. and H. Randrianasolo-Rakotobe (2012), *Des Réseaux et des Hommes : Les Suds à l'Heure des Technologies de l'Information et de la Communication*, Karthala, Paris.

Mongwakeste, P.B. (2015), "Perceived effects of an electronic filing system on tax compliance in a district municipality, South Africa", North-West University, South Africa, *https://dspace.nwu.ac.za/bitstream/handle/10394/17381/Mongwaketse_PB.pdf?sequence=1*.

Ndikumana, L. (2015), "The role of foreign aid in post-conflict countries", *Working paper*, No. 30, Centre for Research on Peace and Development, KU Leuven, Belgium, *https://soc.kuleuven.be/crpd/files/working-papers/working-paper-ndikumana.pdf*.

OECD (2017), QUIDS Dataset (database), *https://stats.oecd.org/qwids/*.

OECD (2016), *States of Fragility 2016: Understanding Violence*, OECD Publishing, Paris, *http://dx.doi.org/10.1787/9789264267213-en*.

OECD (2014), *Fragile States 2014 : Domestic Revenue Mobilisation in Fragile States*, OECD, Paris, *http://reliefweb.int/sites/reliefweb.int/files/resources/FSR_2014.pdf*.

PwC (2017), *Paying Taxes 2017*, World Bank Group, *www.pwc.com/gx/en/paying-taxes/pdf/pwc-paying-taxes-2017-chapter4.pdf*.

SARS (2016), *Tax Statistics: Highlights*, National Treasury and the South African Revenue Service, Pretoria, *www.sars.gov.za/AllDocs/Documents/Tax%20Stats/Tax%20Stats%202016/Tax%20Stats%202016%20Highlights%20web.pdf*.

SARS (2012), *South African Revenue Service: Annual Report 2011-2012*, National Treasury and the South African Revenue Service, Pretoria, *www.sars.gov.za/AllDocs/SARSEntDoclib/AnnualReports/SARS-AR-16%20-%20Annual%20Report%202011-2012.pdf*.

Roy, R. et al. (2009), "Fiscal space for what? Analytical issues from a human development perspective", in Roy, R. and A. Heuty (eds.), *Policy Options for Financing Human Development: Fiscal Space*, Earthscan, London, *www.undp.org/content/dam/aplaws/publication/en/publications/poverty-reduction/poverty-website/fiscal-space-for-what/FiscalSpaceforWhat.pdf*.

Taydas, Z. and D. Peksen (2012), "Can states buy peace? Social welfare spending and civil conflicts", *Journal of Peace Research*, Vol. 49, No. 2, pp. 273-287, *http://journals.sagepub.com/doi/pdf/10.1177/0022343311431286*.

Van den Boogaard, V. et al. (2016), "Tax revenue mobilization in conflict-affected developing countries", *Wider Working Paper*, No. 2016/155, United Nations University UNU-WIDER, Helsinki, *www.wider.unu.edu/sites/default/files/wp2016-155.pdf*.

World Bank (2017), "Paying Taxes", *Doing Business*, World Bank, Washington, DC, *www.doingbusiness.org/data/exploretopics/paying-taxes/good-practices*, (accessed 11 July 2017).

Chapitre 2

ÉTUDE SPÉCIALE

Mobilisation des ressources intérieures en Afrique : progrès réalisés, et défis à long terme

Introduction

Une des motivations principales à l'origine de ce projet *Statistiques des recettes publiques en Afrique* est la volonté d'établir les statistiques des recettes publiques sur une base comparable et accessible. Le but est d'aider à mieux comprendre les progrès réalisés par les pays africains dans la mobilisation des ressources intérieures pour le développement. Les recettes intérieures que le gouvernement génère à travers la fiscalité permettent de garantir une source de revenus relativement plus stable au fil du temps, comparées aux apports financiers d'origine extérieurs issus des emprunts, dons, aide internationale et transferts de la diaspora.

Les organisations internationales et les décideurs politiques font de ce domaine une priorité d'action. Dans les Objectifs de développement durable ratifiés en 2015, il est notamment spécifié dans l'objectif 17.1 qu'il convient « d'améliorer les capacités nationales de collecte d'impôts et d'autres recettes ». Le présent projet d'harmonisation des *Statistiques des recettes publiques en Afrique* a pour ambition d'offrir aux gouvernements nationaux et aux organisations internationales des informations et des outils qu'ils pourront utiliser pour évaluer la capacité des différents pays à lever des recettes dans leurs propres économies.

Ce chapitre expliquera en quoi la mobilisation des ressources intérieures est importante pour les responsables de l'action publique, et examinera les ressources financières africaines dans le contexte des priorités pour le développement, et des défis internes et externes à surmonter. Il s'appuie sur les données de cette publication et celles du rapport *Perspectives économiques en Afrique 2017* (BAfD/OCDE/PNUD, 2017).

La mobilisation des ressources intérieures ne se limite pas au financement public

La mobilisation des ressources intérieures n'est pas étudiée uniquement en raison de sa relation par rapport aux finances publiques, mais aussi parce qu'elle reste un objet d'étude essentiel dans le domaine de la gouvernance publique. Elle représente de fait un élément clé des Objectifs de développement durable, et par conséquent une dimension importante de la coopération internationale. La mobilisation des ressources intérieures est également considérée comme une façon d'améliorer la gouvernance dans les États fragiles, et même comme un moyen d'améliorer l'environnement des affaires, et par conséquent la productivité.

La mobilisation des ressources intérieures aidera à financer les Objectifs de développement durable

Les nouveaux Objectifs de développement durable (ODD), qui remplacent les Objectifs du millénaire pour le développement, ont établi un agenda ambitieux pour le développement d'ici l'année 2030 qui nécessite une plus grande mobilisation des ressources financières à la fois à l'échelle internationale et nationale. Plusieurs pays africains intensifient leurs investissements dans des projets publics d'infrastructure. « En 2014, la part des investissements publics dans le PIB a augmenté de près de 3 % et devrait rester à ce niveau au cours des cinq prochaines années » (BAfD/OCDE/PNUD, 2017 : 31). Toutefois, selon certaines estimations, atteindre les ODD exigera un accroissement des contributions publiques annuelles dans des proportions pouvant atteindre 30 % (Baum et al., 2017). Par exemple, l'Afrique sub-saharienne aura besoin de 93 milliards USD par an pour combler son déficit infrastructurel (BAfD/OCDE/PNUD, 2017). Le Programme d'action d'Addis-Abeba en juillet 2015 recommande que les pays renforcent les systèmes de mobilisation des ressources intérieures en matière de politiques et d'administration fiscales.

Les pays africains tentent d'accroître la mobilisation des revenus intérieurs, mais ce n'est pas toujours facile. Au cours de la dernière décennie, les 16 pays inclus dans cette deuxième édition de publication des *Statistiques des recettes publiques* ont réussi à maintenir une certaine stabilité des recettes fiscales exprimées en pourcentage du PIB (graphique 2.1) sur une base moyenne pondérée. Ces pays font encore mieux si l'on tient compte des contributions à la sécurité sociale (chapitre 1). Cette tendance est encourageante et montre que leur capacité à mobiliser les recettes publiques est robuste et moins dépendante de la volatilité des cours mondiaux des matières premières. Les recettes des autres pays africains, en revanche, ont davantage pâti de la récente chute des prix des matières premières (voir BAfD/OCDE/PNUD, 2017, chapitre 1).

Graphique 2.1. **Ratio des recettes fiscales en pourcentage du PIB dans les pays inclus dans le projet *Statistiques des recettes publiques* en Afrique (SRPA) : comparaison par rapport au reste de l'Afrique**

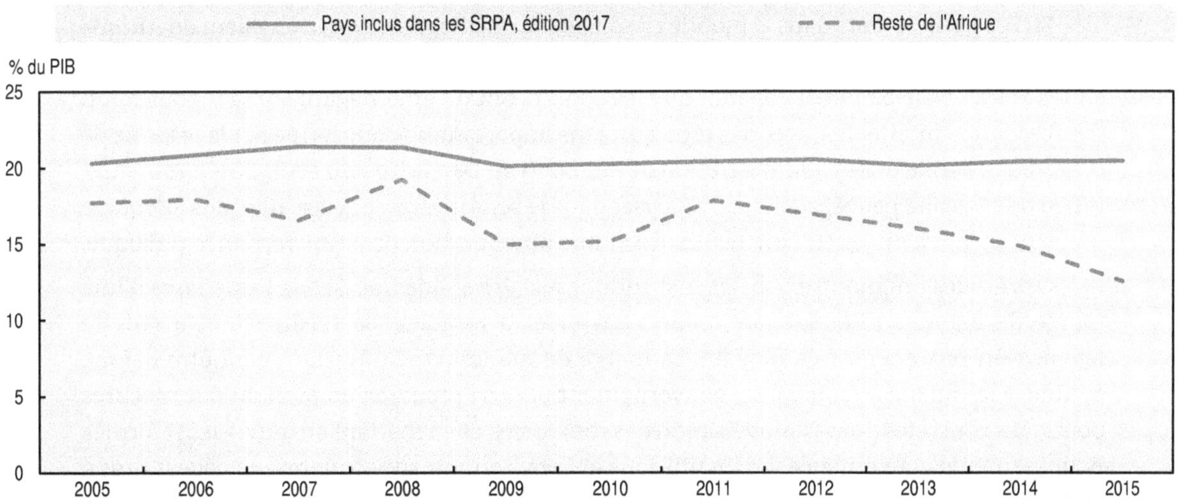

Note : Pour chaque groupe de pays, il s'agit des moyennes pondérées par la taille relative du produit intérieur brut de chaque pays, c'est-à-dire : la somme des recettes fiscales en dollars américains divisée par la somme des PIB de tous les pays. Pour des soucis de comparabilité avec les autres pays d'Afrique, les chiffres de ce graphique ne tiennent pas compte des contributions à la sécurité sociale.

Source : (FMI, 2017a), *World Economic Outlook* (database).

StatLink http://dx.doi.org/10.1787/888933569839

L'aide internationale peut jouer un rôle important en encourageant davantage la mobilisation des ressources intérieures. L'aide à destination des politiques dans le secteur public et la gestion administrative représente moins de 2 % de l'aide totale allouée à l'Afrique (graphique 2.2)

Une aide étrangère ciblée peut aider un état à se forger la capacité de mobiliser des recettes fiscales en appuyant la mise en œuvre de réformes de l'administration fiscale et la constitution de capacités techniques (Ndikumana, 2015). Au fil du temps, si un état est capable de fournir des services publics, il devrait pouvoir réduire sa dépendance par rapport à l'aide étrangère (OCDE, 2014).

Graphique 2.2. **Aide à la mobilisation des ressources intérieures, en % de toute l'APD, par pays**

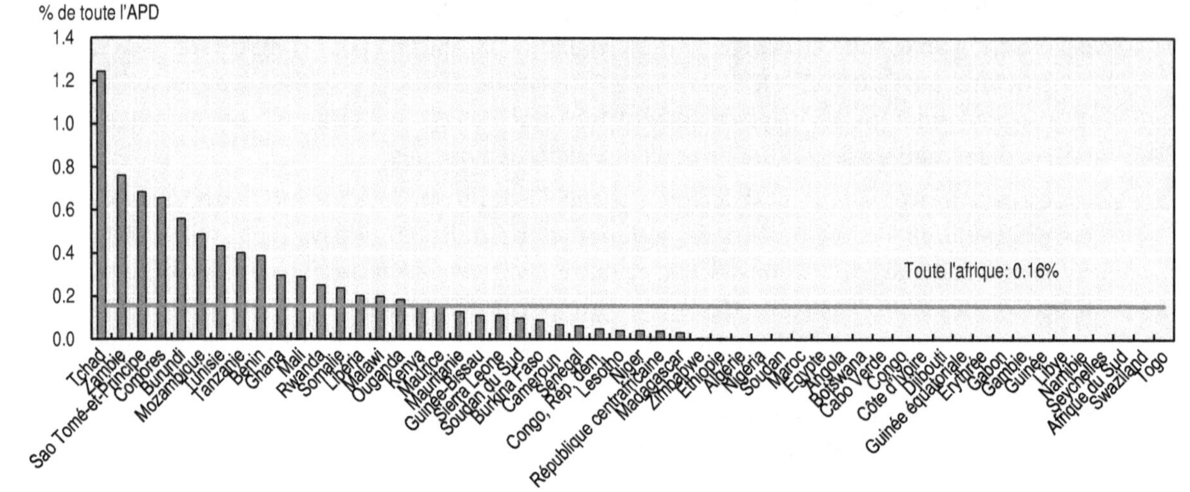

Source : OCDE (2017), *QUIDS Dataset, https://stats.oecd.org/qwids/.*

StatLink http://dx.doi.org/10.1787/888933569858

La mobilisation des ressources intérieures peut permettre de construire des États plus résilients

En 2016, sur 56 États dans le monde classifiés comme fragiles, 37 se trouvaient en Afrique (OCDE, 2016)[1]. La fragilité des états est souvent liée à l'existence de conflits politiques ou de situations de post-conflit. Il apparaît que les conflits ont un effet négatif sur la mobilisation des ressources intérieures, avec des répercussions importantes à long terme sur la réforme de la politique fiscale et de l'administration de l'impôt (Van Den Boogaard et al., 2016). Toutefois, le lien de causalité peut également s'analyser dans le sens inverse, une fiscalité plus adéquate pouvant mener à une meilleure résilience et une amélioration de la gouvernance publique.

Des études ont montré que des institutions fiscales solides, ainsi que l'existence d'une marge de manœuvre budgétaire, pourraient aider à renforcer la résilience et à réduire les problèmes associés à la fragilité. La marge de manœuvre budgétaire peut être définie comme « les financements qu'un gouvernement peut se procurer, en prenant des mesures politiques concrètes pour la mobilisation des ressources et en mettant en œuvre les réformes pour assurer la gouvernance, les institutions et l'environnement économique nécessaires à l'efficacité de ces politiques, pour un ensemble défini d'objectifs de développement » (Roy et al., 2009 : 33). Un gouvernement peut se créer une marge de manœuvre budgétaire par plusieurs moyens (Heller, 2005) : en augmentant les impôts, en cherchant des dons extérieurs, en limitant les dépenses faiblement prioritaires, ou en empruntant des ressources tout en vérifiant qu'il a la capacité non seulement de financer les programmes de dépenses voulus, mais aussi de payer le service de sa dette à court comme à plus long terme. Par ailleurs, Roy et al. (2009) soulignent également l'importance d'augmenter l'efficacité des dépenses publiques, à travers notamment la diminution du coût unitaire de la prestation qui préserve aussi bien la qualité que la quantité des services publics.

La légitimité fiscale est essentielle pour atteindre une bonne résilience dans les états fragiles. La fiscalité révèle d'une bonne interaction entre les compétences régaliennes et la responsabilisation du gouvernement dans la réalisation de réformes institutionnelles qui renforcent la mobilisation intérieures. Renforcer la mobilisation des ressources intérieures peut contribuer à la réussite de réformes institutionnelles. Taydas et Peksen

(2012) soutiennent que des dépenses plus importantes sont le signe d'un fort engagement de la part du gouvernement envers le bien-être de ses citoyens. Di John (2010) montre que la fiscalité est une manière de signaler l'autorité et la légitimité d'un état, et d'augmenter sa possibilité de résilience.

Après une série d'analyses économétriques sur le rôle joué par les politiques fiscales dans 26 pays d'Afrique sur la période 1990-2013, Deléchat et al. (2015) arrivent à la conclusion que des institutions fiscales de qualité sont associées à de meilleurs résultats budgétaires. En examinant le cas de sept pays[2] qui ont réussi à parvenir à un bon état de résilience à l'issue de plusieurs années de troubles civils, les auteurs ont trouvé que l'amélioration de la qualité des institutions fiscales et l'accroissement de la marge de manœuvre budgétaire ont joué un rôle significatif dans le processus de résilience. Ainsi par exemple, ces sept pays ont réussi à augmenter les recettes fiscales, passées de 5 % à 13 % du PIB sur la période. Un exemple notable est le Rwanda, qui a fait des efforts importants pour moderniser son administration et ses systèmes fiscaux et a sensiblement augmenté son ratio impôts-PIB depuis 2000 (voir encadré 1.2 au chapitre 1). Le changement opéré dans la composition des impôts semble avoir également participé à la résilience ; à travers notamment une contribution plus grande des impôts sur le revenu et les bénéfices. Ce constat vaut également pour la hausse de la part des dépenses consacrées aux secteurs de la santé et de l'éducation.

Imposition et productivité

Un système fiscal efficace peut avoir un effet positif sur la productivité des entreprises. Une étude du FMI de 2017 montre que des gains de productivité non négligeables sont possibles en remédiant à la mauvaise allocation des facteurs de production (travail et capital) entre les entreprises. Ces erreurs d'affectation sont très souvent le résultat d'un certain nombre de politiques gouvernementales ou de dysfonctionnements des marchés (FMI, 2017b). Elles constituent une source importante de divergence des niveaux de productivité totale des facteurs (PTF) entre les pays et à travers le temps. Quand le degré de dispersion est important, réallouer les ressources des entreprises dont les ressources sont faiblement productives vers les entreprises utilisant leurs ressources de manière fortement productive permet d'augmenter les rendements, puisque des ressources identiques sont utilisées de façon plus efficace.

Éliminer les distorsions peut également agir positivement sur la croissance du PIB. Selon la même étude du FMI, réduire la mauvaise allocation des ressources peut entraîner un taux de croissance annuel du PIB réel de 1.3 % sur une période de transition de 20 ans dans le cas des pays émergents, et de 0.9 % dans le cas des pays en développement à faible revenu. La politique fiscale et l'administration de l'impôt sont deux facteurs importants pour relever le défi de la productivité. En adaptant le système fiscal, on s'assure que les entreprises fondent leurs décisions sur les fondamentaux économiques du pays, et non sur des motivations uniquement fiscales.

Les gouvernements peuvent substantiellement augmenter la productivité totale des facteurs : en fournissant un traitement non neutre ou (au moins) en réduisant le recours à des régimes fiscaux qui modulent les impôts en fonction des types d'actifs, des sources de financement ou d'autres caractéristiques des entreprises telles que la formalité et la taille. Réduire la complexité des procédures fiscales tout en veillant à l'application rigoureuse des lois fiscales peut également aider à réduire les coûts et à libérer des ressources productives, notamment pour les petites entreprises. L'application rigoureuse des lois fiscales permet de créer des conditions de concurrence équitables tout en consolidant la confiance dans le système fiscal ce qui, au final, favorise le respect volontaire des règles fiscales. En outre, les nouvelles technologies permettent désormais à de nombreuses administrations fiscales d'alléger les procédures d'enregistrement et d'identification, et de diminuer les coûts de gestions à travers l'utilisation d'Internet et d'applications mobiles pour les déclarations électroniques, les conseils aux contribuables, etc. Les administrations fiscales gagneraient à suivre une approche axée sur le risque-personnalisée, et à recourir à une plus forte capacité de contrôle et une segmentation des contribuables (FMI, 2017b).

Mobilisation des ressources intérieures : les défis

Bien que les 16 pays inclus dans cette publication aient augmenté leurs ratios impôts-PIB depuis 2000, la mobilisation des ressources intérieures ne suit pas la croissance du PIB africain et le progrès économique et politique général sur le continent. En effet, les recettes fiscales en pourcentage du PIB a diminué de presque quatre points de pourcentage entre 2005 et 2015 (BAfD/OCDE/PNUD, 2017). Cela montre que malgré de véritables efforts et progrès, la mobilisation des ressources intérieures en Afrique fait toujours face à des difficultés. En outre, les ratios impôts-PIB restent relativement faibles dans la plupart des pays africains, comparée à d'autres régions du monde, même lorsque les pays ont augmenté leurs ratios impôts-PIB.

Lien entre les recettes provenant des ressources naturelles et autres recettes publiques

Comme déjà mentionné dans le chapitre 1 de cette publication, les pays riches en ressources affichent souvent de taux de recettes plus faibles en pourcentage du PIB. En analysant les données de 35 pays riches en ressources dans le monde sur la période 1992-2009, Crivelli et Gupta (2014) montrent que chaque point supplémentaire de pourcentage de PIB de recettes provenant des ressources naturelles correspond à une diminution des autres recettes intérieures (non liées aux ressources) d'environ 0.3 point de pourcentage du PIB. Cependant, les recettes provenant des ressources naturelles peuvent être sources de volatilité, alors que des institutions fiscales plus solides pourraient aider à renforcer la résilience (Baum et al., 2017).

Le continent africain a été touché par la volatilité des recettes provenant des ressources naturelles. Un ralentissement de la mobilisation des ressources intérieures a été observé après un pic à 561.5 milliards USD en 2012, principalement dû à une chute des prix des matières premières, et tout particulièrement du pétrole. Le rapport *Perspectives économiques en Afrique 2017* rapporte par exemple que « entre 2012 et 2015, les recettes publiques ont reculé de 22.2 %, une chute qui s'explique en grande partie par l'effondrement concomitant des recettes tirées des ressources naturelles (43.7 %) » (BAfD/OCDE/PNUD, 2017 : 70). Cela se voit dans la volatilité des recettes non fiscales pour les pays riches en ressources dans cette publication, notamment pour la République Democratic du Congo et le Niger.

Les pays riches en ressources naturelles, même s'ils ont fait des efforts pour améliorer la collecte des recettes fiscales, sont ceux qui ont été le plus affectés par la chute de la mobilisation des ressources intérieures. « Le ratio recettes totales/PIB a diminué, passant de 25 % en 2012 à 19 % en 2015 » (BAfD/OCDE/PNUD, 2017 : 71). Entre 2012 et 2015, les recettes provenant des ressources ont ainsi diminué de plus de 50 % en Algérie, en Angola, au Gabon et au Tchad, ce qui s'explique principalement par l'étroitesse de la base d'imposition dans les pays riches en ressources. Le Cameroun et la Côte d'Ivoire montrent également des bases fiscales étroites et des ratios impôts-PIB relativement faibles à moins de 18% du PIB en 2015, ce qui est inférieur à la moyenne non pondérée des 16 pays inclus dans cette publication s'élevant à 19.1% (voir chapitre 1).

En revanche, les pays pauvres en ressources ont vu la mobilisation de leurs ressources augmenter de 9.6 % entre 2012 et 2016, ce qui tient principalement à la hausse de l'imposition directe (12 %) et indirecte (8 %). Les pays les plus performants sur le front de la mobilisation des ressources intérieures sont l'Éthiopie, le Malawi, le Rwanda, les Seychelles, le Swaziland et le Togo. En matière de fiscalité et d'administration fiscale, le Rwanda et le Togo ont mis en place des réformes importantes qui ont renforcé leurs ratios de recettes/PIB (voir chapitre 1).

Les états fragiles mais riches en ressources représentent un défi supplémentaire pour les décideurs politiques. Les pays avec des recettes provenant des ressources naturelles peuvent étendre rapidement leur marge de manœuvre budgétaire afin de répondre à des besoins sociaux ou infrastructurels urgents. Toutefois, s'ils ne mettent pas en place des systèmes fiscaux efficaces, cela pourrait être nuisible sur le long terme, particulièrement si les revenus provenant des ressources venaient à chuter à cause des fluctuations du prix des matières premières.

Taxer l'économie informelle

L'importance de l'économie informelle en Afrique demeure un obstacle majeur à la collecte des recettes fiscales. Il s'agit notamment des travailleurs et entreprises exerçant en dehors des lois fiscales et des registres de l'administration publique. Les efforts pour élargir la base d'imposition sont compromis par la taille de ce secteur informel, estimé à 38 % du PIB en Afrique sub-saharienne en 2010-14 (FMI, 2017c : 55). L'édition 2010 des *Perspectives économiques en Afrique* avait déjà mis l'accent sur l'informalité comme un défi pour les décideurs politiques en termes de capacité de mobilisation des ressources intérieures. L'informalité handicape les entreprises dans leur développement. Les entreprises informelles tendent à être moins productives que les entreprises formelles. La recherche de Kanbur et Keen (2015) suggère que les entreprises qui ne déclarent pas leurs ventes ont une productivité totale des facteurs plus faible que les entreprises s'acquittant de leurs impôts. En outre elles génèrent une concurrence déloyale pour les entreprises respectueuses des lois fiscales.

Il existe un certain nombre de facteurs favorables à la prolifération de l'économie informelle. L'informalité a tendance à être plus élevée dans les pays où les taux de taxations et d'autres exigences réglementaires sont trop élevés. La complexité des procédures d'enregistrement à l'impôt ou encore la faible application de la discipline fiscale peuvent également constituer des facteurs incitatifs à l'informalité. Une législation fiscale complexe et des coûts de discipline fiscale élevés mis en place par une administration inefficace sont des incitations assez fortes pour que les petites entreprises restent dans le secteur informel (BAfD/OCDE/CEA, 2010). Selon les enquêtes *Entreprise Survey* de la Banque mondiale sur le secteur informel, l'évasion fiscale est la principale raison pour les entreprises informelles de ne pas rejoindre l'économie formelle (BAfD/OCDE/PNUD, 2017). Cela peut avoir des répercussions plus larges sur l'économie ; en sapant le moral des contribuables de manière plus générale, ce qui en fin de compte réduit les revenus du gouvernement (FMI/OCDE/ONU/Banque mondiale, 2011).

Les politiques fiscales et une administration fiscale renforcée peuvent contribuer à réduire la prévalence de l'économie informelle dans les pays émergents et les pays à faible revenu. Mais cela exige une approche à multiples facettes : réduire les possibilités de non-respect de la discipline fiscale, promouvoir une plus grande connaissance des obligations fiscales, simplifier les procédures de déclarations, etc. Par exemple, faciliter la transition vers l'économie formelle d'entreprises non enregistrées requiert, entre autres, à aider ces dernières à accéder plus facilement au financement et aux marchés. Les travaux de recherche montrent que des taux d'imposition plus faibles et des coûts de discipline fiscale plus bas peuvent aider le continent africain à favoriser la transition vers l'économie formelle. Une diminution de la taille du secteur informel peut aider à élargir l'actuelle base d'imposition, et ainsi améliorer la mobilisation des ressources intérieures sur le continent (FMI, 2017b), et faciliter l'épanouissement des entreprises (BAfD/OCDE/PNUD, 2017).

Fiscalité et apports financiers extérieurs

Dans l'édition 2010 des *Perspectives économiques en Afrique*, la question de la possibilité que l'aide étrangère réduise les incitations faites aux gouvernements de lever des recettes intérieures a été posée. Des flux importants d'aide étrangère peuvent en effet réduire l'urgence avec laquelle la perception des recettes est opérée. L'impact négatif de l'Aide Publique au Développement (APD) sur la mobilisation des ressources intérieures fait l'objet d'un débat entre les chercheurs (BAfD/OCDE/CEA, 2010).

Une capacité plus grande à collecter les impôts réduit la dépendance par rapport à l'APD. En effet, des études ont montré qu'il y avait une corrélation négative entre l'APD et la collecte des taxes (Crivelli et Gupta, 2014 ; Gupta et al., 2004). Selon une étude portant sur 118 pays pendant la période 1980-2009 (Benedek et al., 2012), l'association négative entre l'APD et les recettes fiscales intérieures s'est affaiblie au fil du temps. Ceci est dû aux efforts plus importants qui ont été déployés pour mobiliser des ressources intérieures dans plusieurs pays.

Au-delà de cette tendance générale, la façon dont l'aide est fournie au pays et la façon dont elle est allouée (activités ciblées et secteurs soutenus) est importante. La composition de l'aide joue un rôle (par exemple : selon qu'il s'agisse de dons ou d'emprunts). La corrélation négative entre l'APD et la capacité de mobilisation des ressources est plus importante dans les pays à faible revenu et dans les pays dotés d'institutions relativement faibles. L'impact des dons sur les recettes fiscales peut être atténué par les décideurs politiques et les donneurs si la capacité de mobilisation des ressources est renforcée.

L'APD à destination des pays en situation de post-conflit est souvent nécessaire pour que les gouvernements soient en mesure de faire face aux défis structurels et de minimiser les risques de nouveau conflit. Pendant une certaine durée, ces pays sont souvent contraints de dépendre de l'aide étrangère pour faire face à des besoins urgents de reconstruction économique. Il peut être difficile pour ces pays en situation de post-conflit de mobiliser leurs propres ressources car l'activité économique, la capacité de l'État et les institutions nationales sont souvent réduites (Di John, 2010).

Perspectives pour les décideurs en matière de politique fiscale : il existe des possibilités d'accroître l'efficacité de la collecte des impôts

Plusieurs mesures et pratiques ont été adoptées par les gouvernements africains ces dernières années pour simplifier les procédures de paiement des impôts, tout en augmentant parallèlement l'efficacité du système et la discipline fiscale. Une telle approche a porté ses fruits en termes de délais requis pour se conformer à ses obligations fiscales en Afrique. Bien que l'Afrique soit encore le continent avec le temps le plus long pour les procédures de paiement d'impôts après l'Amérique du Sud (PwC, 2017), elle progresse clairement. Le délai nécessaire pour payer les impôts était de 307 heures en moyenne pour un fabricant ou revendeur de taille petite à moyenne[3] en Afrique pour l'année 2015, au lieu de 313 heures en 2014 et 316 en 2014.

Entre 2005 et 2015, plusieurs pays africains ont significativement diminué le temps requis chaque année pour payer ses impôts. Les meilleurs exemples comprennent entre autres l'Afrique du Sud, l'Algérie, le Kenya, le Maroc et la Tunisie (voir graphique 2.3). Les données montrent cependant une grande diversité à travers le continent. Par exemple, en 2015, payer ses impôts nécessitait moins de 125 heures dans les cinq meilleurs pays d'Afrique aux systèmes les plus simples, alors que 700 heures étaient nécessaires dans les cinq derniers pays.

Graphique 2.3. **Nombre d'heures par an pour payer ses impôts, par pays**

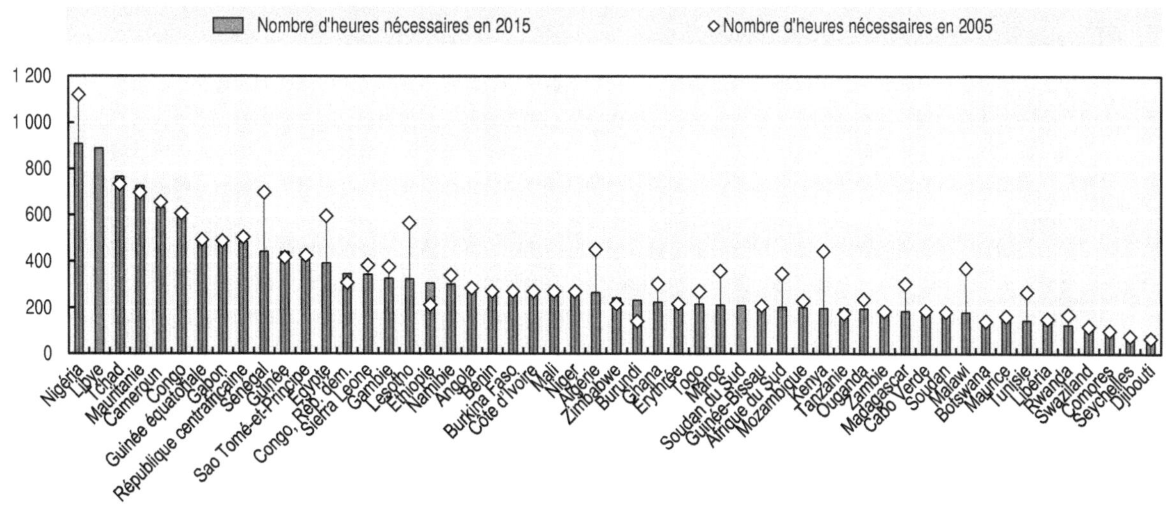

Source : Banque Mondiale (2017), « Paying Taxes » in *Doing Business*, Banque Mondiale, Washington, DC, *www.doingbusiness.org/data/exploretopics/paying-taxes/good-practices.*

StatLink http://dx.doi.org/10.1787/888933569877

Plusieurs pays accroissent également leurs ressources intérieures en favorisant la perception des taxes au moyen de diverses mesures. Par exemple, l'Éthiopie agit pour renforcer la discipline fiscale. L'administration fiscale éthiopienne a mené une expérience qui montre que les entreprises qui reçoivent des lettres de rappel sur les risques d'un contrôle ou au contraire les félicitant de s'être acquittés de leurs obligations fiscales déclaraient davantage leurs revenus, respectivement de 38 % et 32 %. Cela démontre que renforcer la capacité des autorités fiscales à collecter des taxes, à analyser les données des contribuables et à utiliser des techniques comportementales pour inciter les contribuables à payer leurs impôts, peut aider à accroître discipline fiscale (BAfD/OCDE/PNUD, 2017).

Le système fiscal en ligne est un exemple d'amélioration d'administration fiscale déjà en œuvre dans un nombre important de pays (Che Azmi et Kamarulazman, 2010). Grâce à une plateforme d'administration en ligne, les autorités peuvent fournir des informations sous forme électronique à leurs citoyens, aux entreprises et des renseignements concernant l'administration publique (voir chapitre 5, BAfD/OCDE/PNUD, 2017). Un système électronique de paiement des impôts peut bénéficier à la fois aux contribuables, aux entreprises et aux autorités fiscales. Pour les administrations fiscales, le système permet de réduire la charge de travail et les coûts de fonctionnement. Il augmente également le respect des obligations fiscales et représente un gain de temps. Pour les contribuables et les entreprises, c'est un moyen de gagner du temps, cela réduit également les erreurs de calcul et facilite le processus. Les deux parties bénéficient d'une réduction potentielle des risques de corruption ou de traitement informel. Un tel système nécessite néanmoins de sensibiliser les particuliers aux différentes options et bénéfices de déclaration en ligne, ainsi que des formations par les autorités si nécessaire (Coolidge et Yilmaz, 2014).

Le succès dépend également d'un environnement favorable permettant le développement d'une administration électronique (Ledjou et Randrianasolo-Rakotobe, 2012). Le cas du système eFiling en Afrique du Sud constitue l'un des bons exemples sur le continent (voir encadré 2.1).

Encadré 2.1. **Système fiscal électronique en Afrique du Sud**

Le gouvernement sud-africain a adopté le système d'administration électronique en 2000, réorganisant en même temps le système de collecte des impôts. En 2001, le Service Sud-Africain des Revenus (SARS) a introduit la plateforme eFiling. Pour les contribuables, le lancement de cet outil de gestion des taxes en ligne a rendu facile le paiement de leurs impôts et a réduit les possibilités de fraude fiscale. Résultat : les services SARS, dans leur rapport annuel 2011-12 par exemple, ont fait état d'une augmentation importante du nombre de contribuables payant leurs impôts, et à temps (SARS, 2012). Le système en ligne de SARS collecte les taxes et les tendances montrent des améliorations importantes de la perception des recettes fiscales au fil du temps. Ce service gratuit permet aux contribuables, aux fiscalistes et aux entreprises de s'enregistrer et de soumettre leur déclaration, de procéder à des paiements et de pratiquer diverses autres opérations avec SARS dans un environnement en ligne sécurisé. Les utilisateurs peuvent également soumettre leur déclaration via leur téléphone mobile. Le site internet contient également des informations à l'intention des utilisateurs, avec des vidéos, des services d'aide en ligne et un calendrier des dates à respecter (Ledjou et Randrianasolo-Rakotobe, 2012).

L'utilité perçue et la compatibilité de cette nouvelle technologie avec les activités quotidiennes et professionnelles des contribuables ont mené la population d'Afrique du Sud à adopter le système eFiling (Jankeeparsad, Jankeeparsad et Nienaber, 2016). Une autre étude quantitative sur l'effet perçu du système eFiling sur le respect de la discipline fiscale a été menée dans cinq municipalités d'un district de la province du Nord-Ouest. L'étude arrive à la conclusion qu'une majorité des contribuables ont eu des expériences positives avec le système eFiling et reconnaissent les avantages qu'il présente en termes de gain de temps, de rapidité des délais de remboursement et de facilité des interactions avec SARS (Mongwakeste, 2015). Le système eFiling remplace totalement les déclarations papier, ce qui a permis de réduire les coûts de discipline. En moyenne, l'utilisation d'eFiling en Afrique du Sud est associée à une réduction de 22.4 % des coûts du respect des obligations fiscales (Coolidge et Yilmaz, 2014).

Pour l'année fiscale 2015/16, plus de trois quarts des paiements ont été effectués via le système eFiling (75.9 %), contre 64.2 % pour l'année fiscale 2011/12 et 30.8 % pour l'année fiscale 2007/08. À l'inverse, les paiements effectués dans des centres des impôts ont diminué, passant de 22 % en 2007/08 à 0.3 % en 2015/16. La troisième possibilité de s'acquitter de ses impôts consiste à passer par les banques, qui ont représenté 23.8 % des paiements en 2015/16 (SARS, 2016).

Plus généralement, le développement de nouvelles technologies, y compris l'utilisation croissante des téléphones mobiles, offre la possibilité d'améliorer davantage le rendement de l'administration fiscale à la fois pour le gouvernement et pour les contribuables. Des applications permettent déjà aux petites entreprises d'archiver leurs registres d'impôts au fils et à mesure de leurs activités, ce qui réduit le temps nécessaire pour le paiement fiscal.

Notes

1. Pour définir la fragilité, le réseau international sur les situations de conflit et de fragilité de l'OCDE (voir OCDE, 2016, p. 73) a développé un cadre d'analyse qui prend en compte cinq dimensions : économique, environnementale, politique, sécuritaire et sociétale.
2. Cameroun, Éthiopie, Mozambique, Niger, Nigéria, Rwanda et Ouganda.
3. Les statistiques sur le nombre d'heures que nécessite le paiement de l'impôt sont basés sur des estimations d'expériences fiscales d'une entreprise de référence, mentionnée en tant que « entreprise d'étude de cas ». L'entreprise étude de cas est un fabricant ou revendeur de taille petite à moyenne avec des hypothèses spécifiques, choisies délibérément pour assurer la comparabilité à l'échelle mondiale et à structure d'entreprise comparable (voir PwC, 2016 pour plus d'explications).

Références

BAfD/OCDE/CEA (2010), *Perspectives économiques en Afrique 2010 : La mobilisation des ressources publiques et l'aide*, Éditions OCDE, Paris, *http://dx.doi.org/10.1787/aeo-2010-fr*.

BAfD/OCDE/PNUD (2017), *Perspectives économiques en Afrique 2017 : Entrepreneuriat et industrialisation*, Éditions OCDE, Paris, *http://dx.doi.org/10.1787/aeo-2017-fr*.

Banque Mondiale (2017), « Paying Taxes », in *Doing Business*, Banque Mondiale, Washington, DC, *www.doingbusiness.org/data/exploretopics/paying-taxes/good-practices*, (consulté le 11 juillet 2017).

Baum, A. et al. (2017), « Can they do it all? Fiscal space in low-income countries », *Working Paper*, Fonds monétaire international, Washington, DC, *www.imf.org/en/Publications/WP/Issues/2017/05/05/Can-They-Do-It-All-Fiscal-Space-in-Low-Income-Countries-44889*.

Benedek, D. et al. (2012), « Foreign aid and revenue: Still a crowding out effect? », *Working Paper*, No. 12/186, Fonds monétaire international, Washington, DC.

Che Azmi, A.A. and Y. Kamarulzaman (2010), « Adoption of tax e-filing: A conceptual paper », *African Journal of Business Management*, Vol. 4(5), pp. 599-603, *www.academicjournals.org/article/article1380712917_Azmi%20and%20Kamarulzaman.pdf*.

Coolidge, J. and F. Yilmaz (2014), « Does e-filing reduce tax compliance costs in developing countries? », *Investment Climate in Practice*, No. 21, *https://openknowledge.worldbank.org/bitstream/handle/10986/20428/911910BRI0Box30D0VC0KNOWLEDGE0NOTES.pdf;sequence=1*.

Crivelli, E. and S. Gupta (2014), « Resource blessing, revenue curse? Domestic revenue effort in resource-rich countries », *European Journal of Political Economy*, Vol. 35, pp. 563-595, *https://doi.org/10.1016/j.ejpoleco.2014.04.001*.

Deléchat, C. et al. (2015), « Exiting from fragility in sub-Saharan Africa: The role of fiscal policies and fiscal institutions », *Working Paper*, No. 15/268, Fonds monétaire international, Washington, DC, *www.imf.org/external/pubs/ft/wp/2015/wp15268.pdf*.

Di John, J. (2010), « Taxation, resource mobilisation and state performance », *Working paper*, No. 84, Crisis States Research Centre, Londres, *www.lse.ac.uk/internationalDevelopment/research/crisisStates/download/wp/wpSeries2/WP842.pdf*.

FMI (2017a), *World Economic Outlook* (database), Fonds monétaire international, Washington, DC.

FMI (2017b), « Upgrading the tax system to boost productivity », in *Fiscal monitor: Achieving more with less*, Fonds monétaire international, Washington, DC, *www.imf.org/en/Publications/FM/Issues/2017/04/06/fiscal-monitor-april-2017*.

FMI (2017c), « L'économie informelle en Afrique subsaharienne », in *Perspectives économiques régionales : Afrique subsaharienne*, avril 2017, Fonds monétaire international, Washington, DC, *www.imf.org/fr/Publications/REO/SSA/Issues/2017/05/03/sreo0517*.

FMI/OCDE/ONU/Banque mondiale, (2011), « Supporting the development of more effective tax systems », A Report to the G20 Development Working Group, *www.oecd.org/ctp/48993634.pdf.*

Gupta, S. et al. (2004), « Foreign aid and revenue response: Does the composition of aid matter? », *Working Paper*, No. 03/176, Washington, DC, *www.imf.org/external/pubs/ft/wp/2003/wp03176.pdf.*

Heller, P.S. (2005), « Understanding fiscal space », *IMF Policy Discussion Paper*, No. 05/4, Fonds monétaire international, Washington, DC, *www.imf.org/external/pubs/ft/pdp/2005/pdp04.pdf.*

Jankeeparsad, R.W., T.R. Jankeeparsad and G. Nienaber (2016), « Acceptance of the electronic method of filing tax returns by South African taxpayers: An exploratory study », *Journal of Economic and Financial Sciences;* pp. 120-136, Johannesburg, *http://repository.up.ac.za/bitstream/handle/2263/53252/Jankeeparsad_Acceptance_2016.pdf?sequence=1&isAllowed=y.*

Kanbur, R. and M. Keen (2015), « Reducing informality », *Finance & Development*, Vol. 52, No. 1, Fonds monétaire international, Washington, DC, *www.imf.org/external/pubs/ft/fandd/2015/03/kanbur.htm* (accessed June 2017).

Ledjou, J-M. and H. Randrianasolo-Rakotobe (2012), *Des Réseaux et des Hommes : Les Suds à l'Heure des Technologies de l'Information et de la Communication*, Karthala, Paris.

Mongwakeste, P.B. (2015), « Perceived effects of an electronic filing system on tax compliance in a district municipality, South Africa », North-West University, South Africa, *https://dspace.nwu.ac.za/bitstream/handle/10394/17381/Mongwaketse_PB.pdf?sequence=1.*

Ndikumana, L. (2015), « The role of foreign aid in post-conflict countries », *Working paper*, No. 30, Centre for Research on Peace and Development, KU Leuven, Belgium, *https://soc.kuleuven.be/crpd/files/working-papers/working-paper-ndikumana.pdf.*

OCDE (2017), *QUIDS Dataset, https://stats.oecd.org/qwids/.*

OCDE (2016), *Etats de fragilité 2016 : Comprendre la violence*, Éditions OCDE, Paris, *http://dx.doi.org/10.1787/9789264269996-fr.*

OCDE (2014), *Fragile States 2014 : Domestic Revenue Mobilisation in Fragile States*, OCDE, Paris, *http://reliefweb.int/sites/reliefweb.int/files/resources/FSR_2014.pdf.*

PwC (2017), *Paying Taxes 2017*, World Bank Group, *www.pwc.com/gx/en/paying-taxes/pdf/pwc-paying-taxes-2017-chapter4.pdf.*

SARS (2016), *Tax Statistics: Highlights*, National Treasury and the South African Revenue Service, Pretoria, *www.sars.gov.za/AllDocs/Documents/Tax%20Stats/Tax%20Stats%202016/Tax%20Stats%202016%20Highlights%20web.pdf.*

SARS (2012), *South African Revenue Service: Annual Report 2011-2012*, National Treasury and the South African Revenue Service, Pretoria, *www.gov.za/sites/www.gov.za/files/SARS-AR-16_Annual_Report_2011-2012a.pdf.*

Roy, R. et al. (2009), « Fiscal space for what? Analytical issues from a human development perspective », in Rathin Roy and Antoine Heuty(eds.), *Policy Options for Financing Human Development: Fiscal Space*, Earthscan, Londres, *www.undp.org/content/dam/aplaws/publication/en/publications/poverty-reduction/poverty-website/fiscal-space-for-what/FiscalSpaceforWhat.pdf.*

Taydas, Z. and D. Peksen (2012), « Can states buy peace? Social welfare spending and civil conflicts », *Journal of Peace Research*, Vol. 49, No. 2, pp. 273-287, *http://journals.sagepub.com/doi/pdf/10.1177/0022343311431286.*

Van den Boogaard, V. et al. (2016), « Tax revenue mobilization in conflict-affected developing countries », *Wider Working Paper*, No. 2016/155, United Nations University UNU-WIDER, Helsinki, *www.wider.unu.edu/sites/default/files/wp2016-155.pdf.*

Chapter 3

Tax levels and tax structures, 1990-2015

Chapitre 3

Niveaux et structures des impôts, 1990-2015

Chapter 3 / Chapitre 3

Comparative tables, 1990-2015

In all of the following tables a ("..") indicates not available. The main series in this volume cover the years 1990 to 2015.

Figures referring to 1991-96 in Table 3.1 and figures relating to 1998-99, 2001-04 and 2006-08 in Tables 3.4 to 3.19 have been omitted because of lack of space. Complete series are, however, available on line at OECD/ATAF/AUC (2017), "Revenue Statistics in Africa: Comparative tables", *OECD Tax Statistics* (database), *http://dx.doi.org/10.1787/be755711-en*.

Tableaux comparatifs, 1990-2015

Dans tous les tableaux suivants le symbole (« .. ») signifie que l'information n'est pas disponible. Les principales séries dans ce volume couvrent les années 1990 à 2015.

Les années 1991 à 1996 dans le tableau 3.1 et les années 1998-99, 2001-04 et 2006-08 dans les tableaux 3.4 à 3.19 ont été omis en raison du manque d'espace. Les séries complètes sont cependant disponibles en ligne sur OCDE/ATAF/CUA (2017), « Statistiques des recettes publiques en Afrique : Tableaux comparatifs », *Statistiques fiscales de l'OCDE* (base de données), *http://dx.doi.org/10.1787/7f54581d-fr*.

Table 3.1. Total tax revenue as percentage of GDP, 1990-2015
Tableau 3.1. Total des recettes fiscales en pourcentage du PIB, 1990-2015

	1990	1997	1998	1999	2000	2001	2002	2003	2004	2005
Cabo Verde	10.5	14.6	14.9	15.3	15.6	16.9	19.3	17.7	18.7	19.6
Cameroon / Cameroun	..	10.9	11.7	11.9	12.8	14.0	13.2	13.7	13.1	13.5
Congo, Dem. Rep. / Congo, Rép. dém.[1]	..	..	..	..	0.6	2.3	3.0	3.4	4.7	5.2
Côte d'Ivoire	21.6	17.1	15.9	15.9	15.3	15.6	15.9	14.6	15.8	15.6
Ghana	..	..	..	..	10.0	10.5	10.7	11.8	13.7	13.4
Kenya	..	..	..	..	..	16.4	15.9	16.5	16.9	18.2
Mauritius / Maurice[2]	23.3	18.8	18.9	19.0	19.3	17.2	16.7	18.0	18.1	18.7
Morocco / Maroc[3]	..	..	..	..	23.5	23.4	23.1	22.8	23.1	24.7
Niger	..	..	..	..	9.7	10.4	10.9	10.4	11.3	10.7
Rwanda[4]	..	10.3	10.8	10.8	10.2	11.3	12.4	12.2	12.1	12.1
Senegal / Sénégal[5]	..	15.3	15.4	16.1	16.8	16.8	17.7	17.7	18.2	19.3
South Africa / Afrique du Sud[6]	23.9	22.6	23.5	23.5	22.4	23.7	23.1	23.3	23.4	25.2
Swaziland	..	10.5	10.7	11.3	10.5	10.4	10.8	11.6	11.2	11.7
Togo	..	..	..	..	10.9	12.1	11.1	15.0	15.4	14.3
Tunisia / Tunisie[4]	..	..	..	..	24.4	24.7	24.8	24.2	24.1	24.2
Uganda / Ouganda	..	11.1	10.8	11.4	10.7	10.7	11.0	11.4	11.7	12.1
Africa (16) average / Moyenne Afrique (16)[7]	**..**	**..**	**..**	**..**	**14.2**	**14.8**	**15.0**	**15.3**	**15.7**	**16.2**
LAC Average / Moyenne ALC[8]	**15.8**	**17.5**	**17.4**	**17.7**	**18.0**	**18.2**	**18.1**	**18.5**	**18.9**	**19.8**
OECD Average / Moyenne OCDE[9]	**32.0**	**33.6**	**33.7**	**33.9**	**34.0**	**33.5**	**33.2**	**33.2**	**33.1**	**33.6**

	2006	2007	2008	2009	2010	2011	2012	2013	2014	2015
Cabo Verde	21.1	21.3	21.7	18.7	18.8	19.8	18.2	18.1	17.4	19.2
Cameroon / Cameroun	14.0	14.8	14.8	15.0	14.0	14.8	15.3	15.8	16.1	16.4
Congo, Dem. Rep. / Congo, Rép. dém.[1]	5.9	7.1	8.8	8.0	8.9	9.3	10.8	11.1	10.8	10.8
Côte d'Ivoire	16.2	17.1	16.9	16.8	16.5	15.3	17.7	17.6	16.9	17.6
Ghana	13.1	13.2	12.7	13.1	13.2	14.5	14.8	13.6	15.0	15.0
Kenya	17.2	17.9	18.7	18.0	17.7	18.4	17.7	17.8	19.0	18.4
Mauritius / Maurice[2]	18.7	17.8	19.5	20.1	19.8	19.6	20.1	19.8	19.9	19.9
Morocco / Maroc[3]	25.4	27.7	30.2	26.9	27.7	28.5	29.5	28.1	27.0	26.1
Niger	11.2	12.0	12.1	14.0	13.2	13.9	14.4	16.9	16.3	17.0
Rwanda[4]	11.9	12.2	13.3	12.8	13.1	13.8	14.4	15.4	15.8	16.7
Senegal / Sénégal[5]	19.7	20.1	19.0	18.9	19.8	19.9	19.5	19.3	20.6	20.8
South Africa / Afrique du Sud[6]	27.1	27.5	27.7	25.7	25.6	26.3	26.7	27.3	27.8	29.0
Swaziland	11.8	12.0	13.1	13.0	14.0	14.3	13.6	14.7	15.3	15.3
Togo	15.4	16.1	14.8	15.3	15.7	16.4	16.4	19.2	20.3	21.3
Tunisia / Tunisie[4]	24.3	25.2	26.8	26.6	27.2	29.1	29.1	29.8	30.9	30.3
Uganda / Ouganda	12.3	12.6	12.4	11.3	10.6	10.8	10.9	11.1	11.4	12.5
Africa (16) average / Moyenne Afrique (16)[7]	**16.6**	**17.2**	**17.7**	**17.1**	**17.2**	**17.8**	**18.1**	**18.5**	**18.8**	**19.1**
LAC Average / Moyenne ALC[8]	**20.9**	**21.3**	**21.3**	**20.8**	**20.8**	**21.3**	**21.8**	**21.8**	**22.2**	**22.8**
OECD Average / Moyenne OCDE[9]	**33.7**	**33.8**	**33.2**	**32.4**	**32.6**	**33.0**	**33.4**	**33.8**	**34.2**	**34.3**

Note: The figures include sub-national government tax revenues for Mauritius, Morocco, South Africa and Swaziland. Sub-national government tax revenues are not available in other countries or in South Africa prior to 2003.

Data on social security contributions are not available for the Democratic Republic of the Congo, Togo and Uganda and are only partially available in Cameroon, Kenya, and Senegal. Data on property taxes are not available for Ghana and Uganda, and only partially available for the Democratic Republic of the Congo. See the country tables in Chapter 4 for further information on data issues for individual countries.

1. The figures should be interpreted with caution as they are affected by macroeconomic instability in the early 2000s. For the years prior to 2010, the figures exclude some revenues collected by the *Direction Générale des Recettes Administratives, Judiciaires, Domaniales et de Participation* (DGRAD) which are estimated to be less than 1 % of total tax revenue. See Table 4.3 in Chapter 4 for further information.
2. Estimated figures for 2015.
3. Social security contributions in Morocco are estimated for years prior to 2002.
4. Rwanda and Tunisia do not include social security contributions in the tax-to-GDP ratio in their official publications as neither country considers them as taxes. They are included as tax revenue in this publication.
5. Social security contributions in Senegal are estimated for years prior to 2006. These figures include contributions to the Senegalese pension institute (IPRES) but do not include contributions to the social security fund (CSS) for which data is not available.
6. Includes payments made by South Africa to the Southern African Customs Union (SACU) pool, which do not meet the OECD definition of taxation.
7. Represents an unweighted average for the 16 African countries included in this publication. This average should be interpreted with caution due to missing and incomplete data for heading 2000 social security contributions and heading 4000 property taxes. The Africa (16) averages for these two sub-categories exclude countries where these data were not available. This average was not calculated for years prior to 2000 because for those years, data for some countries were not available.
8. Represents an unweighted average for the 24 Latin American and Caribbean (LAC) countries included in the publication *Revenue Statistics in Latin America and the Caribbean 2017*.
9. Represents an unweighted average for the 35 OECD countries.

Note : Les chiffres incluent les recettes fiscales collectées par les administrations infranationales pour l'Afrique du Sud, le Maroc, Maurice et le Swaziland. Les données des recettes fiscales collectées par les administrations infranationales ne sont pas disponibles pour les autres pays ou pour l'Afrique du Sud avant 2003.

Les données des cotisations de sécurité sociale ne sont pas disponibles pour la République démocratique du Congo, l'Ouganda et le Togo et ne sont que partiellement disponibles au Cameroun, au Kenya et au Sénégal. Voir les tableaux des pays au chapitre 4 pour plus d'informations sur les problèmes de données pour les pays individuels.

1. Les chiffres devraient être interprétés avec prudence car ils sont affectés par une instabilité macroéconomique au début des années 2000. Pour les années antérieures à 2010, les chiffres excluent certaines recettes perçues par la *Direction Générale des Recettes Administratives, Judiciaires, Domaniales et de Participation* (DGRAD) et sont estimées être inférieures à 1 % du total des recettes fiscales. Voir le tableau 4.3 du chapitre 4 pour plus d'informations.
2. Les chiffres sont estimés pour 2015.
3. Les cotisations de sécurité sociale au Maroc antérieures à 2002 sont estimées.
4. Le Rwanda et la Tunisie n'incluent pas les cotisations de sécurité sociale dans le ratio impôts-PIB dans leurs publications officielles car ces deux pays ne les considèrent pas comme des impôts. Elles sont incluses dans les recettes fiscales de cette publication.
5. Les cotisations de sécurité sociale au Sénégal antérieures à 2006 sont estimées. Les chiffres comprennent les cotisations de sécurité sociale de l'Institution de prévoyance retraite du Sénégal (IPRES) mais excluent les cotisations de sécurité sociale de la Caisse de Sécurité Sociale (CSS) qui ne sont pas disponibles.
6. Comprend les paiements effectués par l'Afrique du Sud au fond collectif de l'Union douanière d'Afrique australe (SACU), paiements qui ne répondent pas à la définition des recettes fiscales de la classification OCDE.
7. Représente la moyenne non pondérée des 16 pays Africains inclus dans cette publication. Il convient d'interpréter cette moyenne avec prudence à cause de valeurs manquantes ou incomplètes pour la rubrique 2000 cotisations de sécurité sociale et la rubrique 4000 taxes sur le patrimoine. Les moyennes Afrique (16) de ces deux sous-rubriques excluent les pays pour lesquels ces données ne sont pas disponibles. Cette moyenne n'a pas été calculée pour les années antérieures à 2000 car les données n'étaient pas disponibles pour certains pays.
8. Représente la moyenne non pondérée pour les 24 pays d'Amérique latine et des Caraïbes (ALC) inclus dans la publication *Revenue Statistics in Latin America and the Caribbean 2017*.
9. Représente la moyenne non pondérée des 35 pays de l'OCDE.

StatLink http://dx.doi.org/10.1787/888933570010

Table 3.2. Tax revenue of main headings as percentage of GDP, 2015
Tableau 3.2. Recettes fiscales sous les principales rubriques en pourcentage du PIB, 2015

	1000 Income & profits / Impôts & profits	2000 Social security / Sécurité sociale	3000 Payroll / Salaires	4000 Property / Patrimoine	5000 Goods and services / Biens et services	6000 Other taxes / Autres impôts
Cabo Verde	6.1	0.0	0.0	0.4	12.7	0.0
Cameroon / Cameroun	5.2	1.0	0.3	0.2	9.6	0.3
Congo, Dem. Rep. / Congo, Rép. dém.	3.4	..	0.1	0.0	7.0	0.2
Côte d'Ivoire	2.1	2.0	1.9	0.5	11.0	0.1
Ghana[1]	5.5	0.2	0.0	..	9.8	-0.5
Kenya	8.7	0.0	0.0	0.2	9.5	0.0
Mauritius / Maurice[2]	4.9	1.0	0.1	1.0	12.8	0.0
Morocco / Maroc	8.0	4.4	0.0	2.0	11.4	0.2
Niger	4.2	0.8	0.1	0.1	10.2	1.7
Rwanda[3]	6.3	1.0	0.0	0.0	9.3	0.0
Senegal / Sénégal	5.4	1.1	0.2	0.5	13.3	0.3
South Africa / Afrique du Sud[4]	15.0	0.4	0.4	1.5	11.7	0.0
Swaziland	7.5	1.6	0.0	0.4	5.8	0.0
Togo	4.0	..	0.1	0.1	16.8	0.3
Tunisia / Tunisie[3]	9.1	8.9	0.4	0.3	10.8	0.7
Uganda / Ouganda[1]	4.4	..	0.0	..	8.3	-0.2
Africa (16) average / Moyenne Afrique (16)[5]	**6.2**	**1.7**	**0.2**	**0.5**	**10.6**	**0.2**
LAC Average / Moyenne ALC[6]	**6.2**	**3.8**	**0.2**	**0.8**	**11.2**	**0.6**
OECD Average / Moyenne OCDE[7]	**11.6**	**9.1**	**0.4**	**1.9**	**11.0**	**0.2**

Note: The figures include sub-national government tax revenues for Mauritius, Morocco, South Africa and Swaziland. Sub-national government tax revenues are not available in other countries.

Heading 2000: data for social security contributions are not available for the Democratic Republic of the Congo, Togo and Uganda and are only partially available in Cameroon, Kenya, and Senegal.

Heading 4000: In the Democratic Republic of the Congo, Ghana and Uganda, revenues from property taxes are mainly levied by local governments for which data on revenue are not available. In the Democratic Republic of the Congo only data for property tax revenues levied by the *Direction Générale des Recettes Administratives, Judiciaires, Domaniales et de Participation* (DGRAD) are available for 2010-15.

See the country tables in Chapter 4 for further information on missing or incomplete data in individual countries.

1. The figures in the heading 6000 other taxes are negative due to the inclusion of tax refunds that could not be allocated to the main tax categories.
2. Estimated figures for 2015.
3. Rwanda and Tunisia do not include social security contributions in their tax-to-GDP ratio in their official publications as neither country considers them as taxes. They are included as tax revenue in this publication.
4. The figures for heading 5000 goods and services should be interpreted with caution as they include payments made by South Africa to the Southern African Customs Union (SACU) pool, which do not meet the OECD definition of taxation.
5. Represents an unweighted average for the 16 African countries included in this publication. The Africa (16) average should be interpreted with caution due to missing and incomplete data. The averages for heading 2000 social security contributions and heading 4000 property taxes exclude countries where these data were not available. This means that the Africa (16) average for the total tax revenues differs from the sum of average values for the subcategories. For example, in 2015, the average total tax revenue for Africa (16) as a percentage of GDP was 19.1%, but the sum of the average tax-to-GDP ratios for headings 1000, 2000, 3000, 4000, 5000, and 6000 was 19.5%.
6. Represents an unweighted average for the 24 Latin American and Caribbean (LAC) countries included in the publication *Revenue Statistics in Latin America and the Caribbean 2017*.
7. Represents an unweighted average for the 35 OECD countries. Data are for 2014 as data for 2015 are not available for headings 2000-6000.

Note : Les chiffres incluent les recettes fiscales collectées par les administrations infranationales pour l'Afrique du Sud, le Maroc, Maurice et le Swaziland. Les données des recettes fiscales collectées par les administrations infranationales ne sont pas disponibles pour les autres pays ou pour l'Afrique du Sud avant 2003.

Rubrique 2000 : les données des cotisations de sécurité sociale ne sont pas disponibles pour l'Ouganda, la République démocratique du Congo, et le Togo et sont partiellement disponibles au Cameroun, au Kenya et au Sénégal.

Rubrique 4000 : en République démocratique du Congo, au Ghana et en Ouganda, les recettes tirées des taxes foncières sont principalement perçues par les administrations locales dont les recettes ne sont pas disponibles. En République démocratique du Congo, seules les données relatives aux recettes fiscales foncières prélevées par la *Direction Générale des Recettes Administratives, Judiciaires, Domaniales et de Participation* (DGRAD) sont disponibles pour la période 2010-15.

Voir les tableaux des pays au chapitre 4 pour plus d'informations sur les données manquantes ou incomplètes dans chaque pays.

1. Les chiffres sont négatifs pour la rubrique 6000 « Autres impôts », ceci est attribuable à l'inclusion de remboursements d'impôts qui ne peuveut pas être ventilés entre les principales rubriques d'impôts.
2. Les chiffres sont estimés pour 2015.
3. Le Rwanda et la Tunisie n'incluent pas les cotisations de sécurité sociale dans le ratio impôts-PIB dans leurs publications officielles car aucun des deux pays ne les considère comme des impôts. Elles sont incluses comme recettes fiscales dans cette publication.
4. Les chiffres relatifs à la rubrique 5000 produits et services doivent être interprétés avec prudence car ils incluent les paiements effectués par l'Afrique du Sud à l'Union douanière d'Afrique australe (SACU), paiements qui ne répondent pas à la définition des recettes fiscales de la classification OCDE.
5. Représente la moyenne non pondérée pour les 16 pays africains inclus dans cette publication. Il convient d'interpréter la moyenne Afrique (16) avec prudence à cause de valeurs manquantes ou incomplètes. Les moyennes pour la rubrique « 2000 cotisations de sécurité sociale » et la rubrique « 4000 taxes sur le patrimoine » excluent les pays pour lesquels ces données ne sont pas disponibles. Cela signifie que la moyenne Afrique (16) pour le total des recettes fiscales diffère de la somme des moyennes des sous-rubriques. Par exemple en 2015, la moyenne des recettes fiscales pour l'Afrique (16) en pourcentage du PIB s'élevait à 19.1% alors que la somme des moyennes des recettes fiscales relatives aux catégories 1000, 2000, 3000, 4000, 5000 et 6000 était de 19.5%.
6. Représente la moyenne non pondérée pour les 24 pays d'Amérique latine et des Caraïbes (ALC) inclus dans la publication *Revenue Statistics in Latin America and the Caribbean 2017*.
7. Représente la moyenne non pondérée pour les 35 pays de l'OCDE. Les données sont pour 2014 car les données pour 2015 ne sont pas disponibles pour les rubriques 2000-6000.

StatLink http://dx.doi.org/10.1787/888933570029

Table 3.3. Tax revenue of main headings as percentage of total taxation, 2015
Tableau 3.3. Recettes fiscales sous les principales rubriques en pourcentage du total des recettes fiscales, 2015

	1000 Income & profits / Impôts & profits	2000 Social security / Sécurité sociale	3000 Payroll / Salaires	4000 Property / Patrimoine	5000 Goods and services / Biens et services	6000 Other taxes / Autres impôts
Cabo Verde	31.8	0.2	0.0	1.9	66.1	0.0
Cameroon / Cameroun	31.4	5.8	1.9	0.9	58.2	1.7
Congo, Dem. Rep. / Congo, Rép. dém.	31.7	..	1.3	0.3	64.7	2.0
Côte d'Ivoire	12.0	11.2	10.9	2.6	62.7	0.6
Ghana[1]	36.3	1.4	0.0	..	65.3	-3.0
Kenya	47.1	0.0	0.0	1.2	51.7	0.0
Mauritius / Maurice[2]	24.6	5.2	0.6	5.2	64.2	0.2
Morocco / Maroc	30.8	17.0	0.0	7.6	43.6	0.9
Niger	24.7	4.7	0.6	0.4	59.8	9.8
Rwanda[3]	37.9	6.0	0.0	0.1	56.0	0.0
Senegal / Sénégal	26.1	5.0	1.1	2.6	63.9	1.3
South Africa / Afrique du Sud[4]	51.8	1.4	1.3	5.2	40.3	0.0
Swaziland	49.2	10.7	0.0	2.3	37.7	0.0
Togo	18.6	..	0.6	0.3	78.9	1.6
Tunisia / Tunisie[3]	30.0	29.5	1.2	1.1	35.8	2.4
Uganda / Ouganda[1]	34.9	..	0.0	..	66.4	-1.3
Africa (16) average / Moyenne Afrique (16)[5]	**32.4**	**7.6**	**1.2**	**2.3**	**57.2**	**1.0**
LAC Average / Moyenne ALC[6]	**27.2**	**16.4**	**0.9**	**3.4**	**49.6**	**2.5**
OECD Average / Moyenne OCDE[7]	**33.7**	**26.2**	**1.1**	**5.6**	**32.6**	**0.7**

Note: The figures include sub-national government tax revenues for Mauritius, Morocco, South Africa and Swaziland. Sub-national government tax revenues are not available in other countries.

Heading 2000: data for social security contributions are not available for the Democratic Republic of the Congo, Togo and Uganda and are only partially available in Cameroon, Kenya, and Senegal.

Heading 4000: In the Democratic Republic of the Congo, Ghana and Uganda, revenues from property taxes are mainly levied by local governments for which data on revenue are not available. In the Democratic Republic of the Congo only data for property tax revenues levied by the *Direction Générale des Recettes Administratives, Judiciaires, Domaniales et de Participation* (DGRAD) are available for 2010-15.

See the country tables in Chapter 4 for further information on missing or incomplete data in individual countries.

1. The figures in the heading 6000 other taxes are negative due to the inclusion of tax refunds that could not be allocated to the main tax categories.
2. Estimated figures for 2015.
3. Rwanda and Tunisia do not include social security contributions in their tax-to-GDP ratio in their official publications as neither country considers them as taxes. They are included as tax revenue in this publication.
4. The figures for heading 5000 goods and services should be interpreted with caution as they include payments made by South Africa to the Southern African Customs Union (SACU) pool, which do not meet the OECD definition of taxation.
5. Represents an unweighted average for the 16 African countries included in this publication. The Africa (16) average should be interpreted with caution due to missing and incomplete data. The average tax revenues as percentage of total tax revenue for headings 1000, 2000, 3000, 4000, 5000, and 6000 do not add up to 100% as the averages for heading 2000 social security contributions and heading 4000 property taxes exclude countries where these data were not available.
6. Represents an unweighted average for the 24 Latin American and Caribbean (LAC) countries included in the publication *Revenue Statistics in Latin America and the Caribbean 2017*.
7. Represents an unweighted average for the 35 OECD countries. Data are for 2014 as data for 2015 were not available at the date of publication.

Note : Les chiffres incluent les recettes fiscales collectées par les administrations infranationales pour l'Afrique du Sud, le Maroc, Maurice et le Swaziland. Les données des recettes fiscales collectées par les administrations infranationales ne sont pas disponibles pour les autres pays ou pour l'Afrique du Sud avant 2003.

Rubrique 2000 : les données des cotisations de sécurité sociale ne sont pas disponibles pour l'Ouganda, la République démocratique du Congo, et le Togo et sont partiellement disponibles au Cameroun, au Kenya et au Sénégal.

Rubrique 4000 : en République démocratique du Congo, au Ghana et en Ouganda, les recettes tirées des taxes foncières sont principalement perçues par les administrations locales dont les recettes ne sont pas disponibles. En République démocratique du Congo, seules les données relatives aux recettes fiscales foncières prélevées par la *Direction Générale des Recettes Administratives, Judiciaires, Domaniales et de Participation* (DGRAD) sont disponibles pour la période 2010-15.

Voir les tableaux des pays au chapitre 4 pour plus d'informations sur les données manquantes ou incomplètes dans chaque pays.

1. Les chiffres sont négatifs pour la rubrique 6000 « Autres impôts », ceci est attribuable à l'inclusion de remboursements d'impôts qui ne peuveut pas être ventilés entre les principales rubriques d'impôts.
2. Les chiffres sont estimés pour 2015.
3. Le Rwanda et la Tunisie n'incluent pas les cotisations de sécurité sociale dans le ratio impôts-PIB dans leurs publications officielles car aucun des deux pays ne les considère comme des impôts. Elles sont incluses comme recettes fiscales dans cette publication.
4. Les chiffres relatifs à la rubrique 5000 produits et services doivent être interprétés avec prudence car ils incluent les paiements effectués par l'Afrique du Sud à l'Union douanière d'Afrique australe (SACU), paiements qui ne répondent pas à la définition des recettes fiscales de la classification OCDE.
5. Représente la moyenne non pondérée pour les 16 pays africains inclus dans cette publication. Il convient d'interpréter la moyenne Afrique (16) avec prudence à cause de valeurs manquantes ou incomplètes. La somme des moyennes des recettes fiscales pour les rubriques 1000, 2000, 3000, 4000 ,5000 et 6000 en pourcentage du total des recettes fiscales ne s'élève pas à 100% car les moyennes pour la rubrique « 2000 cotisations de sécurité sociale » et la rubrique « 4000 taxes sur le patrimoine » excluent les pays pour lesquels ces données ne sont pas disponibles.
6. Représente la moyenne non pondérée pour les 24 pays d'Amérique latine et des Caraïbes (ALC) inclus dans la publication *Revenue Statistics in Latin America and the Caribbean 2017*.
7. Représente la moyenne non pondérée pour les 35 pays de l'OCDE. Les données sont pour 2014 car les données pour 2015 n'étaient pas disponibles à la date de la publication.

StatLink http://dx.doi.org/10.1787/888933570048

Table 3.4. Taxes on income and profits (1000) as percentage of GDP
Tableau 3.4. Impôts sur le revenu et les bénéfices (1000) en pourcentage du PIB

	1997	2000	2005	2009	2010	2011	2012	2013	2014	2015
Cabo Verde	5.1	5.5	6.0	5.9	5.7	5.9	5.7	5.6	5.0	6.1
Cameroon / Cameroun	2.6	3.4	3.7	4.7	3.6	4.0	4.7	4.7	4.9	5.2
Congo, Dem. Rep. / Congo, Rép. dém.	..	0.2	1.0	2.1	2.4	2.3	2.5	2.6	3.0	3.4
Côte d'Ivoire	3.2	2.5	2.1	2.4	2.1	2.7	3.2	2.8	2.3	2.1
Ghana	..	3.2	4.2	5.6	5.3	5.9	6.5	5.9	6.5	5.5
Kenya	..	..	6.6	7.2	7.3	7.9	8.2	8.7	8.9	8.7
Mauritius / Maurice[1]	2.8	2.5	3.1	5.6	5.0	4.5	4.5	4.6	4.8	4.9
Morocco / Maroc	..	5.7	7.7	9.3	8.0	8.4	9.1	8.4	8.3	8.0
Niger	..	1.8	2.0	4.5	3.3	3.7	4.7	6.6	5.1	4.2
Rwanda	2.6	2.7	3.5	4.4	4.7	5.0	5.5	6.3	5.9	6.3
Senegal / Sénégal	3.2	3.7	4.5	4.6	5.1	4.9	5.3	5.1	5.3	5.4
South Africa / Afrique du Sud	12.8	12.7	13.4	14.3	13.4	13.6	13.7	13.9	14.3	15.0
Swaziland	5.8	5.4	6.2	7.1	7.2	7.5	5.9	7.2	7.9	7.5
Togo	..	2.3	3.5	3.4	2.8	2.9	2.7	3.7	4.2	4.0
Tunisia / Tunisie	..	5.5	7.0	8.0	8.1	9.2	8.4	9.2	9.8	9.1
Uganda / Ouganda	1.5	2.0	3.5	3.2	3.3	3.5	3.6	4.0	3.9	4.4
Africa (16) average / Moyenne Afrique (16)[2]	**..**	**3.9**	**4.9**	**5.8**	**5.5**	**5.8**	**5.9**	**6.2**	**6.3**	**6.2**
LAC Average / Moyenne ALC[3]	**4.0**	**4.1**	**5.1**	**5.8**	**5.6**	**5.9**	**6.0**	**6.0**	**6.2**	**6.2**
OECD Average / Moyenne OCDE[4]	**11.6**	**12.0**	**11.7**	**10.9**	**10.8**	**11.0**	**11.2**	**11.4**	**11.5**	**11.6**

Note: The figures include sub-national government tax revenues for Mauritius, Morocco, South Africa and Swaziland. Sub-national government tax revenues are not available in other countries or in South Africa prior to 2003.

1. Estimated figures for 2015.
2. Represents an unweighted average for the 16 African countries included in this publication. This average was not calculated for years prior to 2000 because for those years, data for some countries were not available.
3. Represents an unweighted average for the 24 Latin American and Caribbean (LAC) countries included in the publication *Revenue Statistics in Latin America and the Caribbean 2017*.
4. Represents an unweighted average for the 35 OECD countries.

Note : Les chiffres incluent les recettes fiscales collectées par les administrations infranationales pour l'Afrique du Sud, le Maroc, Maurice et le Swaziland. Les données des recettes fiscales collectées par les administrations infranationales ne sont pas disponibles pour les autres pays ou pour l'Afrique du Sud avant 2003.

1. Les chiffres sont estimés pour 2015.
2. Représente la moyenne non pondérée pour les 16 pays africains inclus dans cette publication. Cette moyenne n'a pas été calculée pour les années antérieures à 2000 car les données n'étaient pas disponibles pour certains pays.
3. Représente la moyenne non pondérée pour les 24 pays d'Amérique latine et des Caraïbes (ALC) inclus dans la publication *Revenue Statistics in Latin America and the Caribbean 2017*.
4. Représente la moyenne non pondérée pour les 35 pays de l'OCDE.

StatLink http://dx.doi.org/10.1787/888933570067

Table 3.5. Taxes on income and profits (1000) as percentage of total taxation
Tableau 3.5. Impôts sur le revenu et les bénéfices (1000) en pourcentage du total des recettes fiscales

	1997	2000	2005	2009	2010	2011	2012	2013	2014	2015
Cabo Verde	35.1	35.7	30.7	31.8	30.3	29.6	31.5	30.8	28.8	31.8
Cameroon / Cameroun	24.0	27.0	27.5	31.6	26.0	27.3	30.8	30.1	30.7	31.4
Congo, Dem. Rep. / Congo, Rép. dém.	..	34.0	18.6	25.9	26.8	25.2	23.2	23.4	28.2	31.7
Côte d'Ivoire	18.8	16.4	13.7	14.5	12.8	17.4	18.1	16.0	13.6	12.0
Ghana	..	31.9	31.2	42.8	39.8	40.8	43.9	43.1	43.3	36.3
Kenya	..	..	36.3	40.3	41.0	42.8	46.4	49.1	46.9	47.1
Mauritius / Maurice[1]	14.9	12.9	16.7	27.9	25.4	22.9	22.6	23.4	24.0	24.6
Morocco / Maroc	..	24.3	31.2	34.6	28.9	29.6	30.9	30.0	30.6	30.8
Niger	..	18.2	18.3	31.9	25.4	26.9	32.4	38.9	31.4	24.7
Rwanda	25.3	26.0	28.6	34.7	36.2	36.4	38.2	40.5	37.3	37.9
Senegal / Sénégal	21.0	22.1	23.1	24.2	25.9	24.7	27.1	26.4	25.5	26.1
South Africa / Afrique du Sud	56.6	56.7	53.4	55.5	52.4	51.9	51.4	50.7	51.2	51.8
Swaziland	55.0	52.0	53.3	55.0	51.6	52.1	43.2	48.8	51.7	49.2
Togo	..	21.6	24.6	22.1	17.8	17.9	16.6	19.4	20.8	18.6
Tunisia / Tunisie	..	22.7	28.9	30.0	29.7	31.7	29.0	30.7	31.8	30.0
Uganda / Ouganda	14.0	18.2	29.0	28.7	31.0	32.1	33.4	35.7	34.0	34.9
Africa (16) average / Moyenne Afrique (16)[2]	**..**	**28.0**	**29.1**	**33.2**	**31.3**	**31.8**	**32.4**	**33.6**	**33.1**	**32.4**
LAC Average / Moyenne ALC[3]	**22.4**	**22.5**	**25.3**	**28.0**	**26.7**	**27.8**	**27.8**	**27.9**	**28.1**	**27.2**
OECD Average / Moyenne OCDE[4]	**34.2**	**34.9**	**34.5**	**33.5**	**33.2**	**33.5**	**33.7**	**33.8**	**33.7**	**..**

Note: The figures include sub-national government tax revenues for Mauritius, Morocco, South Africa and Swaziland. Sub-national government tax revenues are not available in other countries or in South Africa prior to 2003.

1. Estimated figures for 2015.
2. Represents an unweighted average for the 16 African countries included in this publication. This average was not calculated for years prior to 2000 because for those years, data for some countries were not available.
3. Represents an unweighted average for the 24 Latin American and Caribbean (LAC) countries included in the publication *Revenue Statistics in Latin America and the Caribbean 2017.*
4. Represents an unweighted average for the 35 OECD countries.

Note : Les chiffres incluent les recettes fiscales collectées par les administrations infranationales pour l'Afrique du Sud, le Maroc, Maurice et le Swaziland. Les données des recettes fiscales collectées par les administrations infranationales ne sont pas disponibles pour les autres pays ou pour l'Afrique du Sud avant 2003.

1. Les chiffres sont estimés pour 2015.
2. Représente la moyenne non pondérée pour les 16 pays africains inclus dans cette publication. Cette moyenne n'a pas été calculée pour les années antérieures à 2000 car les données n'étaient pas disponibles pour certains pays.
3. Représente la moyenne non pondérée pour les 24 pays d'Amérique latine et des Caraïbes (ALC) inclus dans la publication *Revenue Statistics in Latin America and the Caribbean 2017.*
4. Représente la moyenne non pondérée pour les 35 pays de l'OCDE.

StatLink http://dx.doi.org/10.1787/888933570086

Table 3.6. Social security contributions (2000) as percentage of GDP
Tableau 3.6. Cotisations de sécurité sociale (2000) en pourcentage du PIB

	1997	2000	2005	2009	2010	2011	2012	2013	2014	2015
Cabo Verde	0.0	0.8	0.6	0.0	0.0	0.0	0.0	0.0	0.0	0.0
Cameroon / Cameroun	0.9	1.0	1.0	1.0	1.2	1.1	1.1	1.1	1.0	1.0
Congo, Dem. Rep. / Congo, Rép. dém.	..	..	..	..	..	..	..	..	..	..
Côte d'Ivoire	1.2	1.3	1.3	1.3	1.3	1.1	1.7	2.0	2.0	2.0
Ghana	..	..	..	0.2	0.2	0.1	0.2	0.2	0.2	0.2
Kenya	..	..	0.0	0.0	0.0	0.0	0.0	0.0	0.0	0.0
Mauritius / Maurice[1]	1.2	1.1	0.7	0.9	1.0	1.0	1.0	1.0	1.0	1.0
Morocco / Maroc[2]	..	3.9	4.0	4.0	4.9	5.3	5.4	5.3	4.6	4.4
Niger	..	0.5	0.4	0.6	0.7	0.7	0.7	0.8	0.8	0.8
Rwanda[3]	0.4	0.5	0.8	0.8	0.8	0.9	1.0	1.1	1.0	1.0
Senegal / Sénégal[4]	0.6	0.7	0.8	0.9	1.1	0.9	0.9	1.0	1.0	1.1
South Africa / Afrique du Sud	0.0	0.0	0.4	0.4	0.4	0.4	0.4	0.4	0.4	0.4
Swaziland	1.2	1.2	1.4	1.7	1.9	1.8	1.6	1.5	1.5	1.6
Togo	..	..	..	..	..	..	..	..	..	..
Tunisia / Tunisie[3]	..	5.3	5.5	7.0	7.3	8.1	8.3	8.7	8.5	8.9
Uganda / Ouganda	..	..	..	..	..	..	..	..	..	..
Africa (16) average / Moyenne Afrique (16)[5]	**..**	**1.5**	**1.4**	**1.5**	**1.6**	**1.6**	**1.7**	**1.8**	**1.7**	**1.7**
LAC Average / Moyenne ALC[6]	**2.5**	**2.6**	**2.8**	**3.2**	**3.3**	**3.3**	**3.5**	**3.6**	**3.6**	**3.8**
OECD Average / Moyenne OCDE[7]	**8.7**	**8.6**	**8.5**	**8.9**	**8.8**	**8.9**	**9.0**	**9.1**	**9.1**	**..**

Note: The figures include sub-national government tax revenues for Mauritius, Morocco, South Africa and Swaziland. Sub-national government tax revenues are not available in other countries or in South Africa prior to 2003.

Data on social security contributions are not available for the Democratic Republic of the Congo, Togo and Uganda and are only partially available in Cameroon, Kenya, and Senegal. See the country tables in Chapter 4 for further information on data issues for individual countries.

1. Estimated figures for 2015.
2. Estimated figures for years prior to 2002.
3. Rwanda and Tunisia do not include social security contributions in their tax-to-GDP ratio in their official publications as neither country considers them as taxes. They are included as tax revenue in this publication.
4. Estimated figures for years prior to 2006. These figures include contributions to the Senegalese pension institute (IPRES) but do not include contributions to the social security fund (CSS) for which data are not available.
5. Represents an unweighted average for the 16 African countries included in this publication. The Africa (16) average should be interpreted with caution as data for social security contributions are not available or partially available in a few countries. This average was not calculated for years prior to 2000 because for those years, data for some countries were not available.
6. Represents an unweighted average for the 24 Latin American and Caribbean (LAC) countries included in the publication *Revenue Statistics in Latin America and the Caribbean 2017*.
7. Represents an unweighted average for the 35 OECD countries.

Note : Les chiffres incluent les recettes fiscales collectées par les administrations infranationales pour l'Afrique du Sud, le Maroc, Maurice et le Swaziland. Les données des recettes fiscales collectées par les administrations infranationales ne sont pas disponibles pour les autres pays ou pour l'Afrique du Sud avant 2003.

Les données des cotisations de sécurité sociale ne sont pas disponibles pour l'Ouganda, la République démocratique du Congo, et le Togo et ne sont que partiellement disponibles au Cameroun, au Kenya et au Sénégal. Voir les tableaux des pays au chapitre 4 pour plus d'informations sur les problèmes des données pour chaque pays.

1. Les chiffres sont estimés pour 2015.
2. Les chiffres sont estimés pour les années antérieures à 2002.
3. Le Rwanda et la Tunisie n'incluent pas les cotisations de sécurité sociale dans le ratio impôts-PIB dans leurs publications officielles car aucun des deux pays ne les considère comme des impôts. Elles sont incluses comme recettes fiscales dans cette publication.
4. Les chiffres sont estimés pour les années antérieures à 2006. Ces chiffres comprennent les cotisations de sécurité sociale de l'Institution de prévoyance retraite du Sénégal (IPRES) et excluent les cotisations de sécurité sociale de la Caisse de Sécurité Sociale (CSS) qui ne sont pas disponibles.
5. Représente la moyenne non pondérée pour les 16 pays africains inclus dans cette publication. Il convient d'interpréter la moyenne Afrique (16) avec prudence car les données pour les cotisations de sécurité sociale ne sont pas disponibles ou partiellement disponibles dans quelques pays. Cette moyenne n'a pas été calculée pour les années antérieures à 2000 car les données n'étaient pas disponibles pour certains pays.
6. Représente la moyenne non pondérée pour les 24 pays d'Amérique latine et des Caraïbes (ALC) inclus dans la publication *Revenue Statistics in Latin America and the Caribbean 2017*.
7. Représente la moyenne non pondérée pour les 35 pays de l'OCDE.

StatLink http://dx.doi.org/10.1787/888933570105

Table 3.7. Social security contributions (2000) as percentage of total taxation
Tableau 3.7. Cotisations de sécurité sociale (2000) en pourcentage du total des recettes fiscales

	1997	2000	2005	2009	2010	2011	2012	2013	2014	2015
Cabo Verde	0.0	5.2	2.8	0.2	0.2	0.1	0.2	0.2	0.2	0.2
Cameroon / Cameroun	7.8	7.8	7.1	6.6	8.3	7.7	7.1	6.9	6.0	5.8
Congo, Dem. Rep. / Congo, Rép. dém.	..	..	..	..	..	..	..	..	..	..
Côte d'Ivoire	7.1	8.8	8.3	7.8	8.0	7.1	9.7	11.3	11.6	11.2
Ghana	..	..	..	1.2	1.2	0.9	1.2	1.3	1.3	1.4
Kenya	..	..	0.2	0.0	0.0	0.0	0.0	0.0	0.0	0.0
Mauritius / Maurice[1]	6.2	5.5	4.0	4.7	4.9	4.9	4.8	5.0	5.2	5.2
Morocco / Maroc[2]	..	16.8	16.2	14.8	17.6	18.5	18.2	19.0	17.0	17.0
Niger	..	5.4	3.8	4.4	5.3	5.3	4.8	4.7	5.1	4.7
Rwanda[3]	3.4	5.0	6.9	6.6	6.4	6.6	6.6	7.0	6.4	6.0
Senegal / Sénégal[4]	3.9	4.0	4.1	4.7	5.8	4.4	4.8	5.1	5.0	5.0
South Africa / Afrique du Sud	0.0	0.0	1.6	1.6	1.5	1.5	1.6	1.4	1.5	1.4
Swaziland	11.9	11.8	11.9	13.3	13.6	12.2	12.0	10.4	10.0	10.7
Togo	..	..	..	..	..	..	..	..	..	..
Tunisia / Tunisie[3]	..	21.6	22.8	26.1	27.0	27.7	28.6	29.0	27.5	29.5
Uganda / Ouganda	..	..	..	..	..	..	..	..	..	..
Africa (16) average / Moyenne Afrique (16)[5]	**..**	**8.3**	**7.5**	**7.1**	**7.7**	**7.5**	**7.7**	**7.8**	**7.4**	**7.6**
LAC Average / Moyenne ALC[6]	**13.9**	**14.7**	**14.3**	**15.4**	**15.5**	**15.4**	**15.7**	**16.2**	**16.3**	**16.4**
OECD Average / Moyenne OCDE[7]	**25.1**	**24.8**	**25.3**	**26.8**	**26.6**	**26.4**	**26.4**	**26.3**	**26.2**	**..**

Note: The figures include sub-national government tax revenues for Mauritius, Morocco, South Africa and Swaziland. Sub-national government tax revenues are not available in other countries or in South Africa prior to 2003.

Data on social security contributions are not available for the Democratic Republic of the Congo, Togo and Uganda and are only partially available in Cameroon, Kenya, and Senegal. See the country tables in Chapter 4 for further information on data issues for individual countries.

1. Estimated figures for 2015.
2. Estimated figures for years prior to 2002.
3. Rwanda and Tunisia do not include social security contributions in their tax-to-GDP ratio in their official publications as neither country considers them as taxes. They are included as tax revenue in this publication.
4. Estimated figures for years prior to 2006. These figures include contributions to the Senegalese pension institute (IPRES) but do not include contributions to the social security fund (CSS) for which data are not available.
5. Represents an unweighted average for the 16 African countries included in this publication. The Africa (16) average should be interpreted with caution as data for social security contributions are not available or partially available in a few countries. This average was not calculated for years prior to 2000 because for those years, data for some countries were not available.
6. Represents an unweighted average for the 24 Latin American and Caribbean (LAC) countries included in the publication *Revenue Statistics in Latin America and the Caribbean 2017.*
7. Represents an unweighted average for the 35 OECD countries.

Note : Les chiffres incluent les recettes fiscales collectées par les administrations infranationales pour l'Afrique du Sud, le Maroc, Maurice et le Swaziland. Les données des recettes fiscales collectées par les administrations infranationales ne sont pas disponibles pour les autres pays ou pour l'Afrique du Sud avant 2003.

Les données des cotisations de sécurité sociale ne sont pas disponibles pour l'Ouganda, la République démocratique du Congo, et le Togo et ne sont que partiellement disponibles au Cameroun, au Kenya et au Sénégal. Voir les tableaux des pays au chapitre 4 pour plus d'informations sur les problèmes des données pour chaque pays.

1. Les chiffres sont estimés pour 2015.
2. Les chiffres sont estimés pour les années antérieures à 2002.
3. Le Rwanda et la Tunisie n'incluent pas les cotisations de sécurité sociale dans le ratio impôts-PIB dans leurs publications officielles car aucun des deux pays ne les considère comme des impôts. Elles sont incluses comme recettes fiscales dans cette publication.
4. Les chiffres sont estimés pour les années antérieures à 2006. Ces chiffres comprennent les cotisations de sécurité sociale de l'Institution de prévoyance retraite du Sénégal (IPRES) et excluent les cotisations de sécurité sociale de la Caisse de Sécurité Sociale (CSS) qui ne sont pas disponibles.
5. Représente la moyenne non pondérée pour les 16 pays africains inclus dans cette publication. Il convient d'interpréter la moyenne Afrique (16) avec prudence car les données pour les cotisations de sécurité sociale ne sont pas disponibles ou partiellement disponibles dans quelques pays. Cette moyenne n'a pas été calculée pour les années antérieures à 2000 car les données n'étaient pas disponibles pour certains pays.
6. Représente la moyenne non pondérée pour les 24 pays d'Amérique latine et des Caraïbes (ALC) inclus dans la publication *Revenue Statistics in Latin America and the Caribbean 2017.*
7. Représente la moyenne non pondérée pour les 35 pays de l'OCDE.

StatLink http://dx.doi.org/10.1787/888933570124

Table 3.8. Taxes on property (4000) as percentage of GDP
Tableau 3.8. Impôts sur le patrimoine (4000) en pourcentage du PIB

	1997	2000	2005	2009	2010	2011	2012	2013	2014	2015
Cabo Verde	0.8	0.8	0.8	0.7	0.5	0.6	0.4	0.4	0.4	0.4
Cameroon / Cameroun	0.1	0.2	0.2	0.2	0.2	0.1	0.1	0.1	0.1	0.2
Congo, Dem. Rep. / Congo, Rép. dém.[1]	..	..	..	..	0.1	0.0	0.0	0.0	0.0	0.0
Côte d'Ivoire	0.4	0.4	0.5	0.4	0.4	0.3	0.4	0.5	0.5	0.5
Ghana[1]	..	..	..	..	..	..	..	..	..	..
Kenya	..	..	0.1	0.2	0.2	0.2	0.2	0.2	0.2	0.2
Mauritius / Maurice[2]	1.4	1.2	1.0	1.2	1.1	1.0	1.1	1.0	1.1	1.0
Morocco / Maroc	..	1.3	1.5	1.5	1.6	1.6	1.8	1.9	1.9	2.0
Niger	..	0.1	0.1	0.1	0.1	0.1	0.1	0.0	0.0	0.1
Rwanda	0.0	0.0	0.0	0.0	0.0	0.0	0.0	0.0	0.0	0.0
Senegal / Sénégal	0.4	0.3	0.5	0.6	0.6	0.6	0.5	0.5	0.5	0.5
South Africa / Afrique du Sud	0.4	0.4	1.2	1.3	1.3	1.3	1.3	1.4	1.4	1.5
Swaziland	0.1	0.1	0.3	0.3	0.3	0.4	0.3	0.4	0.3	0.4
Togo	..	0.0	0.0	0.1	0.0	0.0	0.0	0.0	0.1	0.1
Tunisia / Tunisie	..	0.3	0.2	0.3	0.3	0.3	0.3	0.3	0.3	0.3
Uganda / Ouganda[1]	..	..	..	..	..	..	..	..	..	..
Africa (16) average / Moyenne Afrique (16)[3]	**..**	**0.4**	**0.5**	**0.5**	**0.5**	**0.5**	**0.5**	**0.5**	**0.5**	**0.5**
LAC Average / Moyenne ALC[4]	**0.5**	**0.6**	**0.8**	**0.7**	**0.7**	**0.7**	**0.7**	**0.8**	**0.8**	**0.8**
OECD Average / Moyenne OCDE[5]	**1.7**	**1.8**	**1.8**	**1.7**	**1.7**	**1.8**	**1.8**	**1.9**	**1.9**	**..**

Note: The figures include sub-national government tax revenues for Mauritius, Morocco, South Africa and Swaziland. Sub-national government tax revenues are not available in other countries or in South Africa prior to 2003.

1. In the Democratic Republic of the Congo, Ghana and Uganda, revenues from property taxes are mainly levied by local governments whose revenues are not available. In the Democratic Republic of the Congo, only data for property tax revenues levied by the *Direction Générale des Recettes Administratives, Judiciaires, Domaniales et de Participation* (DGRAD) are available for 2010-15. See the country tables in Chapter 4 for further information.
2. Estimated figures for 2015.
3. Represents an unweighted average for the 16 African countries included in this publication. The Africa (16) average should be interpreted with caution as several countries collect property taxes at the local level, for which data is missing. This average was not calculated for years prior to 2000 because for those years, data for some countries were not available.
4. Represents an unweighted average for the 24 Latin American and Caribbean (LAC) countries included in the publication *Revenue Statistics in Latin America and the Caribbean 2017*.
5. Represents an unweighted average for the 35 OECD countries.

Note : Les chiffres incluent les recettes fiscales collectées par les administrations infranationales pour l'Afrique du Sud, le Maroc, Maurice et le Swaziland. Les données des recettes fiscales collectées par les administrations infranationales ne sont pas disponibles pour les autres pays ou pour l'Afrique du Sud avant 2003.

1. En République démocratique du Congo, au Ghana et en Ouganda, les revenus tirés des taxes foncières sont principalement perçus par les administrations locales dont les revenus ne sont pas disponibles. En République démocratique du Congo, seules les données relatives aux recettes fiscales foncières prélevées par la *Direction Générale des Recettes Administratives, Judiciaires, Domaniales et de Participation* (DGRAD) sont disponibles pour la période 2010-15. Voir les tableaux des pays au chapitre 4 pour plus d'informations.
2. Les chiffres sont estimés pour 2015.
3. Représente la moyenne non pondérée pour les 16 pays africains inclus dans cette publication. Il convient d'interpréter la moyenne Afrique (16) avec prudence car les données provenant des taxes foncières ne sont pas disponibles ou partiellement disponibles dans quelques pays. Cette moyenne n'a pas été calculée pour les années antérieures à 2000 car les données n'étaient pas disponibles pour certains pays.
4. Représente la moyenne non pondérée pour les 24 pays d'Amérique latine et des Caraïbes (ALC) inclus dans la publication *Revenue Statistics in Latin America and the Caribbean 2017*.
5. Représente la moyenne non pondérée pour les 35 pays de l'OCDE.

StatLink http://dx.doi.org/10.1787/888933570143

Table 3.9. Taxes on property (4000) as percentage of total taxation
Tableau 3.9. Impôts sur le patrimoine (4000) en pourcentage du total des recettes fiscales

	1997	2000	2005	2009	2010	2011	2012	2013	2014	2015
Cabo Verde	5.4	5.3	4.3	3.7	2.7	2.8	2.4	2.4	2.5	1.9
Cameroon / Cameroun	0.8	1.6	1.1	1.1	1.1	0.7	0.7	0.9	0.8	0.9
Congo, Dem. Rep. / Congo, Rép. dém.[1]	..	..	..	..	0.6	0.3	0.3	0.1	0.1	0.3
Côte d'Ivoire	2.6	2.8	3.1	2.5	2.4	2.1	2.5	3.0	2.7	2.6
Ghana[1]	..	..	..	..	..	..	..	..	..	..
Kenya	..	..	0.5	1.2	1.2	1.2	1.3	1.2	1.2	1.2
Mauritius / Maurice[2]	7.5	6.3	5.5	5.8	5.6	5.0	5.4	4.9	5.6	5.2
Morocco / Maroc	..	5.6	6.2	5.4	5.9	5.6	6.2	6.7	7.2	7.6
Niger	..	1.1	0.8	0.5	0.8	0.7	0.6	0.3	0.2	0.4
Rwanda	0.1	0.2	0.0	0.0	0.0	0.0	0.0	0.0	0.0	0.1
Senegal / Sénégal	2.4	2.0	2.6	2.9	3.1	2.8	2.6	2.6	2.5	2.6
South Africa / Afrique du Sud	1.6	1.8	4.6	4.9	5.2	4.9	4.8	5.0	5.1	5.2
Swaziland	0.8	0.8	2.7	2.3	2.3	2.5	2.5	2.5	2.3	2.3
Togo	..	0.3	0.3	0.3	0.3	0.3	0.3	0.2	0.3	0.3
Tunisia / Tunisie	..	1.1	1.0	1.1	1.0	1.2	1.1	1.1	1.0	1.1
Uganda / Ouganda[1]	..	..	..	..	..	..	..	..	..	..
Africa (16) average / Moyenne Afrique (16)[3]	**..**	**2.4**	**2.5**	**2.5**	**2.3**	**2.2**	**2.2**	**2.2**	**2.2**	**2.3**
LAC Average / Moyenne ALC[4]	**2.5**	**2.9**	**3.9**	**3.3**	**3.2**	**3.2**	**3.2**	**3.4**	**3.3**	**3.4**
OECD Average / Moyenne OCDE[5]	**5.3**	**5.5**	**5.5**	**5.5**	**5.5**	**5.5**	**5.5**	**5.6**	**5.6**	**..**

Note: The figures include sub-national government tax revenues for Mauritius, Morocco, South Africa and Swaziland. Sub-national government tax revenues are not available in other countries or in South Africa prior to 2003.

1. In the Democratic Republic of the Congo, Ghana and Uganda, revenues from property taxes are mainly levied by local governments whose revenues are not available. In the Democratic Republic of the Congo, only data for property tax revenues levied by the *Direction Générale des Recettes Administratives, Judiciaires, Domaniales et de Participation* (DGRAD) are available for 2010-15. See the country tables in Chapter 4 for further information.
2. Estimated figures for 2015.
3. Represents an unweighted average for the 16 African countries included in this publication. The Africa (16) average should be interpreted with caution as several countries collect property taxes at the local level, for which data is missing. This average was not calculated for years prior to 2000 because for those years, data for some countries were not available.
4. Represents an unweighted average for the 24 Latin American and Caribbean (LAC) countries included in the publication *Revenue Statistics in Latin America and the Caribbean 2017*.
5. Represents an unweighted average for the 35 OECD countries.

Note : Les chiffres incluent les recettes fiscales collectées par les administrations infranationales pour l'Afrique du Sud, le Maroc, Maurice et le Swaziland. Les données des recettes fiscales collectées par les administrations infranationales ne sont pas disponibles pour les autres pays ou pour l'Afrique du Sud avant 2003.

1. En République démocratique du Congo, au Ghana et en Ouganda, les revenus tirés des taxes foncières sont principalement perçus par les administrations locales dont les revenus ne sont pas disponibles. En République démocratique du Congo, seules les données relatives aux recettes fiscales foncières prélevées par la *Direction Générale des Recettes Administratives, Judiciaires, Domaniales et de Participation* (DGRAD) sont disponibles pour la période 2010-15. Voir les tableaux des pays au chapitre 4 pour plus d'informations.
2. Les chiffres sont estimés pour 2015.
3. Représente la moyenne non pondérée pour les 16 pays africains inclus dans cette publication. Il convient d'interpréter la moyenne Afrique (16) avec prudence car les données provenant des taxes foncières ne sont pas disponibles ou partiellement disponibles dans quelques pays. Cette moyenne n'a pas été calculée pour les années antérieures à 2000 car les données n'étaient pas disponibles pour certains pays.
4. Représente la moyenne non pondérée pour les 24 pays d'Amérique latine et des Caraïbes (ALC) inclus dans la publication *Revenue Statistics in Latin America and the Caribbean 2017*.
5. Représente la moyenne non pondérée pour les 35 pays de l'OCDE.

StatLink http://dx.doi.org/10.1787/888933570162

Table 3.10. Taxes on goods and services (5000) as percentage of GDP
Tableau 3.10. Impôts sur les biens et services (5000) en pourcentage du PIB

	1997	2000	2005	2009	2010	2011	2012	2013	2014	2015
Cabo Verde	8.7	8.4	12.2	12.0	12.6	13.4	12.0	12.1	11.9	12.7
Cameroon / Cameroun	7.4	8.1	8.4	8.7	8.7	9.0	8.9	9.2	9.6	9.6
Congo, Dem. Rep. / Congo, Rép. dém.	..	0.4	3.5	5.4	5.9	6.2	7.4	7.8	7.2	7.0
Côte d'Ivoire	10.6	9.2	10.0	10.8	10.9	9.5	10.3	10.2	10.2	11.0
Ghana	..	6.8	9.3	7.4	7.9	8.6	8.3	7.8	8.5	9.8
Kenya	..	..	11.5	10.5	10.2	10.3	9.3	8.8	9.9	9.5
Mauritius / Maurice[1]	13.3	14.4	13.7	12.3	12.6	13.1	13.4	13.1	12.8	12.8
Morocco / Maroc	..	12.3	11.2	11.9	12.9	12.9	12.9	12.2	11.9	11.4
Niger	..	6.9	7.8	8.2	8.3	8.5	8.0	8.4	9.1	10.2
Rwanda	7.3	7.0	7.8	7.5	7.5	7.9	7.9	8.1	8.9	9.3
Senegal / Sénégal	10.7	11.6	13.1	12.5	12.6	13.1	12.4	12.3	13.3	13.3
South Africa / Afrique du Sud	9.2	8.9	9.8	9.5	10.2	10.6	10.9	11.4	11.4	11.7
Swaziland	3.4	3.7	3.8	3.8	4.5	4.8	5.7	5.6	5.5	5.8
Togo	..	8.1	10.3	11.3	12.2	12.8	13.0	14.8	15.3	16.8
Tunisia / Tunisie	..	12.7	10.9	10.6	10.7	10.6	11.2	10.8	11.3	10.8
Uganda / Ouganda	9.6	9.1	8.8	8.1	7.2	7.2	7.3	7.4	7.7	8.3
Africa (16) average / Moyenne Afrique (16)[2]	**..**	**8.5**	**9.5**	**9.4**	**9.7**	**9.9**	**9.9**	**10.0**	**10.3**	**10.6**
LAC Average / Moyenne ALC[3]	**9.9**	**9.8**	**10.1**	**10.0**	**10.2**	**10.4**	**10.7**	**10.6**	**10.7**	**11.2**
OECD Average / Moyenne OCDE[4]	**10.9**	**10.9**	**10.8**	**10.3**	**10.6**	**10.6**	**10.8**	**10.8**	**11.0**	**..**

Note: The figures include sub-national government tax revenues for Mauritius, Morocco, South Africa and Swaziland. Sub-national government tax revenues are not available in other countries or in South Africa prior to 2003.

1. Estimated figures for 2015.
2. Represents an unweighted average for the 16 African countries included in this publication. This average was not calculated for years prior to 2000 because for those years, data for some countries were not available.
3. Represents an unweighted average for the 24 Latin American and Caribbean (LAC) countries included in the publication *Revenue Statistics in Latin America and the Caribbean 2017*.
4. Represents an unweighted average for the 35 OECD countries.

Note : Les chiffres incluent les recettes fiscales collectées par les administrations infranationales pour l'Afrique du Sud, le Maroc, Maurice et le Swaziland. Les données des recettes fiscales collectées par les administrations infranationales ne sont pas disponibles pour les autres pays ou pour l'Afrique du Sud avant 2003.

1. Les chiffres sont estimés pour 2015.
2. Représente la moyenne non pondérée pour les 16 pays africains inclus dans cette publication. Cette moyenne n'a pas été calculée pour les années antérieures à 2000 car les données n'étaient pas disponibles pour certains pays.
3. Représente la moyenne non pondérée pour les 24 pays d'Amérique latine et des Caraïbes (ALC) inclus dans la publication *Revenue Statistics in Latin America and the Caribbean 2017*.
4. Représente la moyenne non pondérée pour les 35 pays de l'OCDE.

StatLink http://dx.doi.org/10.1787/888933570181

Table 3.11. Taxes on goods and services (5000) as percentage of total taxation
Tableau 3.11. Impôts sur les biens et services (5000) en pourcentage du total des recettes fiscales

	1997	2000	2005	2009	2010	2011	2012	2013	2014	2015
Cabo Verde	59.5	53.8	62.3	64.3	66.8	67.4	65.9	66.6	68.5	66.1
Cameroon / Cameroun	67.4	63.6	62.1	57.9	61.8	61.1	57.9	58.2	59.3	58.2
Congo, Dem. Rep. / Congo, Rép. dém.	..	65.3	67.7	66.9	65.7	66.5	69.1	70.1	66.4	64.7
Côte d'Ivoire	62.3	59.8	63.9	64.5	66.0	62.4	58.1	57.6	60.6	62.7
Ghana	..	68.1	69.3	56.6	59.8	59.3	56.3	57.1	56.3	65.3
Kenya	..	..	63.0	58.4	57.7	55.9	52.3	49.7	51.9	51.7
Mauritius / Maurice[1]	70.8	74.7	73.2	60.9	63.6	66.6	66.7	66.1	64.4	64.2
Morocco / Maroc	..	52.1	45.5	44.3	46.7	45.4	43.8	43.3	44.1	43.6
Niger	..	71.7	72.7	58.3	62.9	61.2	55.7	49.4	55.9	59.8
Rwanda	71.3	68.8	64.5	58.7	57.4	57.0	55.2	52.5	56.3	56.0
Senegal / Sénégal	69.9	69.2	67.8	66.3	63.4	66.1	63.6	63.7	64.8	63.9
South Africa / Afrique du Sud	40.7	39.9	39.1	36.9	39.7	40.4	40.9	41.6	41.0	40.3
Swaziland	32.3	35.4	32.1	29.4	32.5	33.2	42.3	38.2	36.1	37.7
Togo	..	74.2	72.2	73.7	77.7	77.9	79.4	77.1	75.3	78.9
Tunisia / Tunisie	..	52.0	45.1	40.0	39.5	36.6	38.6	36.2	36.4	35.8
Uganda / Ouganda	86.5	84.6	73.1	71.7	68.4	67.1	67.0	66.2	67.8	66.4
Africa (16) average / Moyenne Afrique (16)[2]	**..**	**62.2**	**60.9**	**56.8**	**58.1**	**57.8**	**57.1**	**55.8**	**56.6**	**57.2**
LAC Average / Moyenne ALC[3]	**57.2**	**56.0**	**52.2**	**49.0**	**50.3**	**49.6**	**49.6**	**49.1**	**48.9**	**49.6**
OECD Average / Moyenne OCDE[4]	**33.4**	**33.0**	**32.9**	**32.3**	**32.9**	**32.7**	**32.6**	**32.4**	**32.6**	**..**

Note: The figures include sub-national government tax revenues for Mauritius, Morocco, South Africa and Swaziland. Sub-national government tax revenues are not available in other countries or in South Africa prior to 2003.

1. Estimated figures for 2015.
2. Represents an unweighted average for the 16 African countries included in this publication. This average was not calculated for years prior to 2000 because for those years, data for some countries were not available.
3. Represents an unweighted average for the 24 Latin American and Caribbean (LAC) countries included in the publication *Revenue Statistics in Latin America and the Caribbean 2017*.
4. Represents an unweighted average for the 35 OECD countries.

Note : Les chiffres incluent les recettes fiscales collectées par les administrations infranationales pour l'Afrique du Sud, le Maroc, Maurice et le Swaziland. Les données des recettes fiscales collectées par les administrations infranationales ne sont pas disponibles pour les autres pays ou pour l'Afrique du Sud avant 2003.

1. Les chiffres sont estimés pour 2015.
2. Représente la moyenne non pondérée pour les 16 pays africains inclus dans cette publication. Cette moyenne n'a pas été calculée pour les années antérieures à 2000 car les données n'étaient pas disponibles pour certains pays.
3. Représente la moyenne non pondérée pour les 24 pays d'Amérique latine et des Caraïbes (ALC) inclus dans la publication *Revenue Statistics in Latin America and the Caribbean 2017*.
4. Représente la moyenne non pondérée pour les 35 pays de l'OCDE.

StatLink http://dx.doi.org/10.1787/888933570200

Table 3.12. Taxes on general consumption (5110) as percentage of GDP
Tableau 3.12. Impôts généraux sur la consommation (5110) en pourcentage du PIB

	1997	2000	2005	2009	2010	2011	2012	2013	2014	2015
Cabo Verde	0.0	0.0	6.8	7.2	7.6	7.8	6.9	6.8	6.6	7.2
Cameroon / Cameroun	3.4	4.4	4.7	4.9	4.8	5.2	5.1	5.4	5.6	5.7
Congo, Dem. Rep. / Congo, Rép. dém.	..	0.1	1.9	3.1	3.2	3.5	4.5	4.8	4.4	4.3
Côte d'Ivoire	3.7	3.3	3.2	3.7	4.0	3.1	3.8	3.7	3.5	3.6
Ghana	..	2.9	3.9	4.2	4.2	4.8	4.5	4.2	4.8	5.2
Kenya	..	..	4.8	4.8	4.7	5.0	4.4	4.1	4.6	4.6
Mauritius / Maurice[1]	3.0	4.8	6.7	6.8	7.1	7.1	7.3	7.1	6.8	7.0
Morocco / Maroc	..	5.2	5.9	7.4	8.3	8.7	8.8	8.4	8.1	7.7
Niger	..	2.7	4.5	4.9	4.8	4.4	4.6	4.8	5.5	6.0
Rwanda	1.4	2.0	4.0	4.1	3.9	4.0	4.1	4.5	5.1	5.1
Senegal / Sénégal	5.4	6.6	7.7	7.2	7.5	7.7	7.2	7.0	7.4	7.5
South Africa / Afrique du Sud	5.6	5.5	6.6	5.9	6.2	6.4	6.4	6.6	6.8	6.9
Swaziland	2.8	3.0	3.2	3.2	3.8	3.8	4.5	4.1	4.1	4.2
Togo	..	4.0	5.7	6.3	6.8	7.4	7.6	8.4	9.0	9.7
Tunisia / Tunisie	..	6.2	5.6	5.9	6.1	6.1	6.3	6.1	6.5	6.2
Uganda / Ouganda	3.3	3.9	4.2	4.0	3.6	3.6	3.7	4.0	3.9	4.2
Africa (16) average / Moyenne Afrique (16)[2]	**..**	**3.6**	**5.0**	**5.2**	**5.4**	**5.5**	**5.6**	**5.6**	**5.8**	**5.9**
LAC Average / Moyenne ALC[3]	**5.2**	**5.6**	**6.2**	**6.3**	**6.5**	**6.6**	**6.9**	**6.9**	**7.0**	**7.2**
OECD Average / Moyenne OCDE[4]	**6.6**	**6.7**	**6.8**	**6.4**	**6.7**	**6.7**	**6.8**	**6.8**	**7.0**	..

Note: The figures include sub-national government tax revenues for Mauritius, Morocco, South Africa and Swaziland. Sub-national government tax revenues are not available in other countries or in South Africa prior to 2003.

1. Estimated figures for 2015.
2. Represents an unweighted average for the 16 African countries included in this publication. This average was not calculated for years prior to 2000 because for those years, data for some countries were not available.
3. Represents an unweighted average for the 24 Latin American and Caribbean (LAC) countries included in the publication *Revenue Statistics in Latin America and the Caribbean 2017.*
4. Represents an unweighted average for the 35 OECD countries.

Note : Les chiffres incluent les recettes fiscales collectées par les administrations infranationales pour l'Afrique du Sud, le Maroc, Maurice et le Swaziland. Les données des recettes fiscales collectées par les administrations infranationales ne sont pas disponibles pour les autres pays ou pour l'Afrique du Sud avant 2003.

1. Les chiffres sont estimés pour 2015.
2. Représente la moyenne non pondérée pour les 16 pays africains inclus dans cette publication. Cette moyenne n'a pas été calculée pour les années antérieures à 2000 car les données n'étaient pas disponibles pour certains pays.
3. Représente la moyenne non pondérée pour les 24 pays d'Amérique latine et des Caraïbes (ALC) inclus dans la publication *Revenue Statistics in Latin America and the Caribbean 2017.*
4. Représente la moyenne non pondérée pour les 35 pays de l'OCDE.

StatLink http://dx.doi.org/10.1787/888933570219

Table 3.13. Taxes on general consumption (5110) as percentage of total taxation
Tableau 3.13. Impôts généraux sur la consommation (5110) en pourcentage du total des recettes fiscales

	1997	2000	2005	2009	2010	2011	2012	2013	2014	2015
Cabo Verde	0.0	0.0	34.5	38.4	40.4	39.6	38.0	37.7	37.9	37.6
Cameroon / Cameroun	30.8	34.8	34.5	32.5	34.1	35.2	33.1	34.2	34.9	34.7
Congo, Dem. Rep. / Congo, Rép. dém.	..	18.4	37.3	38.1	35.5	37.7	42.1	43.6	40.6	39.3
Côte d'Ivoire	21.5	21.8	20.5	22.0	24.1	20.4	21.7	21.3	21.0	20.3
Ghana	..	28.8	29.0	31.9	31.8	32.8	30.1	31.2	32.1	34.9
Kenya	..	..	26.5	26.4	26.4	27.1	24.7	22.9	24.3	24.8
Mauritius / Maurice[1]	15.9	25.0	35.9	33.9	35.6	36.1	36.4	36.1	34.2	35.1
Morocco / Maroc	..	22.1	23.9	27.3	30.1	30.5	29.9	29.8	30.1	29.4
Niger	..	27.7	42.0	35.0	36.7	31.7	31.7	28.4	34.1	35.6
Rwanda	13.3	20.0	33.1	32.1	29.9	29.0	28.8	28.9	32.3	30.8
Senegal / Sénégal	35.0	39.6	40.0	38.0	37.7	38.5	36.8	36.2	36.0	36.1
South Africa / Afrique du Sud	24.9	24.6	26.1	23.1	24.3	24.5	23.8	24.0	24.3	23.8
Swaziland	26.5	28.5	27.4	25.0	27.3	26.5	33.1	27.6	26.6	27.5
Togo	..	36.5	39.4	41.2	43.4	44.8	46.4	43.7	44.3	45.4
Tunisia / Tunisie	..	25.3	23.2	22.1	22.3	20.9	21.8	20.5	21.1	20.3
Uganda / Ouganda	30.2	36.0	34.9	35.4	34.0	33.1	33.6	35.6	34.5	34.0
Africa (16) average / Moyenne Afrique (16)[2]	**..**	**25.9**	**31.8**	**31.4**	**32.1**	**31.8**	**32.0**	**31.4**	**31.8**	**31.8**
LAC Average / Moyenne ALC[3]	**29.3**	**30.1**	**30.7**	**30.2**	**31.2**	**31.0**	**31.2**	**31.2**	**31.2**	**31.8**
OECD Average / Moyenne OCDE[4]	**20.1**	**19.9**	**20.6**	**20.1**	**20.7**	**20.6**	**20.5**	**20.5**	**20.7**	**..**

Note: The figures include sub-national government tax revenues for Mauritius, Morocco, South Africa and Swaziland. Sub-national government tax revenues are not available in other countries or in South Africa prior to 2003.

1. Estimated figures for 2015.
2. Represents an unweighted average for the 16 African countries included in this publication. This average was not calculated for years prior to 2000 because for those years, data for some countries were not available.
3. Represents an unweighted average for the 24 Latin American and Caribbean (LAC) countries included in the publication *Revenue Statistics in Latin America and the Caribbean 2017*.
4. Represents an unweighted average for the 35 OECD countries.

Note : Les chiffres incluent les recettes fiscales collectées par les administrations infranationales pour l'Afrique du Sud, le Maroc, Maurice et le Swaziland. Les données des recettes fiscales collectées par les administrations infranationales ne sont pas disponibles pour les autres pays ou pour l'Afrique du Sud avant 2003.

1. Les chiffres sont estimés pour 2015.
2. Représente la moyenne non pondérée pour les 16 pays africains inclus dans cette publication. Cette moyenne n'a pas été calculée pour les années antérieures à 2000 car les données n'étaient pas disponibles pour certains pays.
3. Représente la moyenne non pondérée pour les 24 pays d'Amérique latine et des Caraïbes (ALC) inclus dans la publication *Revenue Statistics in Latin America and the Caribbean 2017*.
4. Représente la moyenne non pondérée pour les 35 pays de l'OCDE.

StatLink http://dx.doi.org/10.1787/888933570238

Table 3.14. Taxes on specific goods and services (5120) as percentage of GDP
Tableau 3.14. Impôts sur les biens et services déterminés (5120) en pourcentage du PIB

	1997	2000	2005	2009	2010	2011	2012	2013	2014	2015
Cabo Verde	8.7	8.4	5.4	4.8	5.0	5.5	5.1	5.2	5.3	5.5
Cameroon / Cameroun	4.0	3.6	3.6	3.7	3.8	3.8	3.8	3.7	3.9	3.8
Congo, Dem. Rep. / Congo, Rép. dém.	..	0.3	1.6	2.3	2.6	2.6	2.8	2.9	2.8	2.7
Côte d'Ivoire	6.7	5.5	6.5	6.7	6.5	6.3	6.1	6.0	6.2	7.1
Ghana	..	3.9	5.4	3.2	3.7	3.9	3.9	3.5	3.6	4.6
Kenya	..	..	6.4	5.6	5.4	5.2	4.8	4.6	5.1	4.8
Mauritius / Maurice[1]	10.1	9.4	6.3	4.4	4.6	5.0	5.2	5.0	4.9	4.8
Morocco / Maroc	..	6.8	5.1	4.2	4.3	4.0	3.8	3.5	3.5	3.4
Niger	..	4.2	3.2	3.2	3.4	4.1	3.4	3.5	3.5	4.1
Rwanda	5.9	4.9	3.8	3.4	3.5	3.8	3.7	3.6	3.8	4.0
Senegal / Sénégal	5.3	4.9	5.3	5.3	5.0	5.4	5.2	5.2	5.8	5.7
South Africa / Afrique du Sud	3.6	3.4	3.1	3.4	3.8	4.0	4.4	4.6	4.5	4.6
Swaziland	0.5	0.6	0.5	0.4	0.6	0.8	1.1	1.4	1.3	1.4
Togo	..	4.1	4.7	5.0	5.4	5.4	5.4	6.4	6.3	7.1
Tunisia / Tunisie	..	6.3	5.0	4.5	4.4	4.4	4.6	4.5	4.5	4.4
Uganda / Ouganda	6.0	5.0	4.2	3.9	3.4	3.4	3.5	3.2	3.6	3.9
Africa (16) average / Moyenne Afrique (16)[2]	**..**	**4.8**	**4.4**	**4.0**	**4.1**	**4.2**	**4.2**	**4.2**	**4.3**	**4.5**
LAC Average / Moyenne ALC[3]	**4.4**	**4.0**	**3.6**	**3.4**	**3.5**	**3.5**	**3.5**	**3.4**	**3.4**	**3.6**
OECD Average / Moyenne OCDE[4]	**3.7**	**3.6**	**3.4**	**3.2**	**3.3**	**3.3**	**3.3**	**3.3**	**3.3**	**..**

Note: The figures include sub-national government tax revenues for Mauritius, Morocco, South Africa and Swaziland. Sub-national government tax revenues are not available in other countries or in South Africa prior to 2003.

1. Estimated figures for 2015.
2. Represents an unweighted average for the 16 African countries included in this publication. This average was not calculated for years prior to 2000 because for those years, data for some countries were not available.
3. Represents an unweighted average for the 24 Latin American and Caribbean (LAC) countries included in the publication *Revenue Statistics in Latin America and the Caribbean 2017.*
4. Represents an unweighted average for the 35 OECD countries.

Note : Les chiffres incluent les recettes fiscales collectées par les administrations infranationales pour l'Afrique du Sud, le Maroc, Maurice et le Swaziland. Les données des recettes fiscales collectées par les administrations infranationales ne sont pas disponibles pour les autres pays ou pour l'Afrique du Sud avant 2003.

1. Les chiffres sont estimés pour 2015.
2. Représente la moyenne non pondérée pour les 16 pays africains inclus dans cette publication. Cette moyenne n'a pas été calculée pour les années antérieures à 2000 car les données n'étaient pas disponibles pour certains pays.
3. Représente la moyenne non pondérée pour les 24 pays d'Amérique latine et des Caraïbes (ALC) inclus dans la publication *Revenue Statistics in Latin America and the Caribbean 2017.*
4. Représente la moyenne non pondérée pour les 35 pays de l'OCDE.

StatLink http://dx.doi.org/10.1787/888933570257

Table 3.15. Taxes on specific goods and services (5120) as percentage of total taxation
Tableau 3.15. Impôts sur les biens et services déterminés (5120) en pourcentage du total des recettes fiscales

	1997	2000	2005	2009	2010	2011	2012	2013	2014	2015
Cabo Verde	59.5	53.8	27.7	25.8	26.4	27.9	27.9	28.9	30.6	28.6
Cameroon / Cameroun	36.3	28.5	27.0	24.9	27.2	25.5	24.5	23.6	24.0	23.1
Congo, Dem. Rep. / Congo, Rép. dém.	..	45.6	30.2	28.7	28.7	28.3	26.3	26.3	25.6	25.0
Côte d'Ivoire	39.5	35.8	41.3	40.0	39.5	40.9	34.3	33.9	37.0	40.0
Ghana	..	39.3	40.3	24.7	27.9	26.6	26.2	25.9	24.3	30.4
Kenya	..	..	35.2	31.2	30.6	28.3	27.0	26.2	27.0	26.2
Mauritius / Maurice[1]	53.9	48.7	33.6	21.9	23.1	25.2	25.6	25.2	24.9	23.9
Morocco / Maroc	..	28.9	20.6	15.8	15.6	13.9	12.9	12.3	12.9	13.1
Niger	..	43.3	30.4	22.9	25.8	29.2	23.7	20.7	21.5	23.9
Rwanda	57.2	47.9	31.0	26.3	26.9	27.5	25.8	23.4	23.9	24.1
Senegal / Sénégal	34.4	29.2	27.4	27.8	25.4	27.1	26.4	27.0	28.3	27.3
South Africa / Afrique du Sud	15.8	15.3	12.2	13.1	14.7	15.2	16.4	16.9	16.0	15.9
Swaziland	4.7	6.0	4.0	2.9	4.1	5.5	8.0	9.6	8.5	9.3
Togo	..	37.6	32.6	32.4	34.3	32.9	32.8	33.3	30.9	33.3
Tunisia / Tunisie	..	25.8	20.8	17.0	16.3	14.9	16.0	15.0	14.5	14.7
Uganda / Ouganda	53.7	46.4	34.9	34.4	32.4	31.9	31.7	29.0	31.6	30.9
Africa (16) average / Moyenne Afrique (16)[2]	**..**	**35.5**	**28.1**	**24.4**	**24.9**	**25.1**	**24.1**	**23.6**	**23.8**	**24.4**
LAC Average / Moyenne ALC[3]	**26.3**	**24.2**	**20.0**	**17.3**	**17.6**	**17.1**	**16.8**	**16.2**	**16.0**	**16.1**
OECD Average / Moyenne OCDE[4]	**11.5**	**11.1**	**10.4**	**10.1**	**10.2**	**10.0**	**10.0**	**9.8**	**9.6**	**..**

Note: The figures include sub-national government tax revenues for Mauritius, Morocco, South Africa and Swaziland. Sub-national government tax revenues are not available in other countries or in South Africa prior to 2003.

1. Estimated figures for 2015.
2. Represents an unweighted average for the 16 African countries included in this publication. This average was not calculated for years prior to 2000 because for those years, data for some countries were not available.
3. Represents an unweighted average for the 24 Latin American and Caribbean (LAC) countries included in the publication *Revenue Statistics in Latin America and the Caribbean 2017.*
4. Represents an unweighted average for the 35 OECD countries.

Note : Les chiffres incluent les recettes fiscales collectées par les administrations infranationales pour l'Afrique du Sud, le Maroc, Maurice et le Swaziland. Les données des recettes fiscales collectées par les administrations infranationales ne sont pas disponibles pour les autres pays ou pour l'Afrique du Sud avant 2003.

1. Les chiffres sont estimés pour 2015.
2. Représente la moyenne non pondérée pour les 16 pays africains inclus dans cette publication. Cette moyenne n'a pas été calculée pour les années antérieures à 2000 car les données n'étaient pas disponibles pour certains pays.
3. Représente la moyenne non pondérée pour les 24 pays d'Amérique latine et des Caraïbes (ALC) inclus dans la publication *Revenue Statistics in Latin America and the Caribbean 2017.*
4. Représente la moyenne non pondérée pour les 35 pays de l'OCDE.

StatLink http://dx.doi.org/10.1787/888933570276

Table 3.16. Gross domestic product for tax reporting years at market prices, in national currency units
Tableau 3.16. Produit intérieur brut pour les années de déclaration fiscale au prix du marché, en monnaie nationale

	1997	2000	2005	2009	2010	2011	2012	2013	2014	2015
Cabo Verde	50 292	70 536	96 690	135 879	138 569	147 924	150 351	153 723	154 436	156 525
Cameroon / Cameroun	5 324 762	6 612 385	8 749 600	11 040 329	11 699 685	12 545 700	13 514 687	14 607 000	15 845 868	16 807 044
Congo, Dem. Rep. / Congo, Rép. dém.	34 582	1 317 075	5 670 065	14 788 935	18 698 925	22 598 145	25 343 516	30 051 179	33 224 018	35 679 048
Côte d'Ivoire	6 841 856	7 630 266	9 011 755	11 463 500	12 324 723	12 112 687	13 673 079	15 449 272	17 461 003	19 368 482
Ghana	2 298	4 420	15 833	36 598	46 042	59 816	75 315	93 416	113 343	138 748
Kenya[1]	820 633	1 043 127	1 508 466	2 673 373	3 016 495	3 447 609	3 993 534	4 503 295	5 071 730	5 811 195
Mauritius / Maurice[1]	81 804	115 905	186 151	278 335	299 171	323 310	343 942	366 325	386 229	403 536
Morocco / Maroc	372 962	412 897	552 671	748 483	784 624	820 077	847 881	897 923	923 696	982 223
Niger	1 010 315	1 186 278	1 776 953	2 548 447	2 832 286	3 024 270	3 544 186	3 788 275	4 076 604	4 241 524
Rwanda	546 535	676 000	1 440 000	3 057 000	3 367 000	3 897 000	4 494 000	4 929 000	5 466 000	5 956 000
Senegal / Sénégal	2 727 198	3 331 768	4 592 673	6 030 586	6 400 738	6 783 016	7 263 157	7 338 232	7 583 165	8 078 113
South Africa / Afrique du Sud	703 117	946 324	1 639 254	2 507 677	2 748 008	3 024 951	3 262 545	3 534 327	3 796 460	4 032 796
Swaziland[2]	9 150 754	12 464 896	20 642 335	30 775 140	32 935 064	35 379 111	39 035 176	42 659 123	46 646 479	50 109 161
Togo	939 567	921 475	1 115 676	1 493 526	1 571 487	1 772 342	1 999 109	2 134 500	2 276 600	2 461 986
Tunisia / Tunisie	22 944	29 433	41 871	58 890	63 055	64 492	70 354	75 152	80 816	84 656
Uganda / Ouganda[1]	6 617 801	9 300 795	16 049 113	33 726 102	40 868 624	48 630 513	57 668 897	64 848 278	70 879 585	77 763 730

Note: All figures are in millions, except for Swaziland figures, which are in thousands.

1. The GDP for Kenya and Uganda in all years and for Mauritius in the years preceding 2010 are adjusted using the formula GDP(n)/2+GDP(n-1)/2. This is done in order to make the value of the GDP correspond more closely to a July(n-1)-to-June(n) fiscal year. The GDP for Mauritius is not adjusted from 2010 to 2015 because public finance data is reported on a calendar year for those years.
2. The GDP for Swaziland is adjusted using the following formula: GDP(n)*3/4+GDP(n+1))/4 in order to make it correspond more closely to an April(n)-to-March(n+1) fiscal year.

Source: IMF, *World Economic Outlook*, April 2017, OECD National Accounts data for South Africa.

Note : Tous les chiffres sont en millions, à l'exception des chiffres du Swaziland qui sont en milliers.

1. Le PIB pour le Kenya et l'Ouganda pour toutes les années et pour Maurice dans les années antérieures à 2010 est ajusté selon la formule PIB(n)/2+PIB(n-1)/2 afin de le faire correspondre le mieux possible à une année fiscale de juillet (n-1) à juin (n). Le PIB pour Maurice n'est pas ajusté de 2010 à 2015 car les données relatives aux finances publiques sont rapportées sur une année civile pour ces années.
2. Le PIB pour le Swaziland est ajusté selon la formule suivante : PIB(n)*3/4+PIB(n+1))/4 afin de les faire correspondre le mieux possible à un année fiscale de avril (n) à mars (n +1).

Source : FMI, *Perspectives de l'économie mondiale*, avril 2017, données des comptes nationaux de l'OCDE pour l'Afrique du Sud.

StatLink http://dx.doi.org/10.1787/888933570295

Table 3.17. Gross domestic product for tax reporting years at market prices, in millions of US Dollars at market exchange rates
Tableau 3.17. Produit intérieur brut pour les années de déclaration fiscale au prix du marché, en millions de dollars US aux taux de change du marché

	1997	2000	2005	2009	2010	2011	2012	2013	2014	2015
Cabo Verde	540	589	1 090	1 712	1 664	1 865	1 752	1 851	1 861	1 575
Cameroon / Cameroun	9 841	9 027	16 617	23 442	23 667	26 612	26 487	29 576	32 101	28 431
Congo, Dem. Rep. / Congo, Rép. dém.	28 819	19 077	11 951	18 315	20 641	24 575	27 566	32 676	35 918	38 496
Côte d'Ivoire	11 735	10 748	17 115	24 341	24 931	25 693	26 797	31 281	35 373	32 764
Ghana	11 195	8 107	17 461	25 590	32 174	39 565	41 939	47 806	38 616	37 375
Kenya[1]	13 654	14 245	19 533	36 458	38 511	40 836	46 046	52 775	58 312	62 559
Mauritius / Maurice[1]	4 205	4 504	6 534	9 238	9 718	11 263	11 446	11 932	12 613	11 511
Morocco / Maroc	39 147	38 859	62 343	92 897	93 217	101 371	98 266	106 826	109 881	100 593
Niger	1 733	1 671	3 375	5 411	5 729	6 415	6 946	7 670	8 258	7 175
Rwanda	1 808	1 718	2 584	5 380	5 774	6 492	7 316	7 623	8 010	8 277
Senegal / Sénégal	4 672	4 693	8 722	12 805	12 948	14 388	14 235	14 858	15 362	13 665
South Africa / Afrique du Sud	152 587	136 361	257 772	295 937	375 348	416 595	397 388	366 060	349 819	316 076
Swaziland[2]	1 948	1 748	3 271	3 860	4 593	4 847	4 671	4 391	4 208	2 947
Togo	1 610	1 299	2 117	3 171	3 179	3 759	3 918	4 322	4 612	4 165
Tunisia / Tunisie	20 747	21 473	32 272	43 624	44 054	45 810	45 044	46 253	47 605	43 156
Uganda / Ouganda[1]	6 212	6 003	8 944	17 929	19 396	20 660	22 949	25 463	27 328	26 817

1. The GDP for Kenya and Uganda in all years and for Mauritius in the years preceding 2010 are adjusted using the formula GDP(n)/2+GDP(n-1)/2. This is done in order to make the value of the GDP correspond more closely to a July(n-1)-to-June(n) fiscal year. The GDP for Mauritius is not adjusted from 2010 to 2015 because public finance data is reported on a calendar year for those years.
2. The GDP for Swaziland is adjusted using the following formula: GDP(n)*3/4+GDP(n+1))/4 in order to make it correspond more closely to an April(n)-to-March(n+1) fiscal year.

Source: IMF, *World Economic Outlook*, April 2017, OECD National Accounts data for South Africa.

1. Le PIB pour le Kenya et l'Ouganda pour toutes les années et pour Maurice dans les années antérieures à 2010 est ajusté selon la formule PIB(n)/2+PIB(n-1)/2 afin de le faire correspondre le mieux possible à une année fiscale de juillet (n-1) à juin (n). Le PIB pour Maurice n'est pas ajusté de 2010 à 2015 car les données relatives aux finances publiques sont rapportées sur une année civile pour ces années.
2. Le PIB pour le Swaziland est ajusté selon la formule suivante : PIB(n)*3/4+PIB(n+1))/4 afin de les faire correspondre le mieux possible à un année fiscale de avril (n) à mars (n +1).

Source : FMI, *Perspectives de l'économie mondiale*, avril 2017, données des comptes nationaux de l'OCDE pour l'Afrique du Sud.

StatLink http://dx.doi.org/10.1787/888933570314

Table 3.18. Exchange rates used, national currency per US dollar
Tableau 3.18. Taux de change utilisés, unités de monnaie nationale par dollar des ÉU

	1997	2000	2005	2009	2010	2011	2012	2013	2014	2015
Cabo Verde	0.0107	0.0084	0.0113	0.0126	0.0120	0.0126	0.0117	0.0120	0.0121	0.0101
Cameroon / Cameroun	0.0018	0.0014	0.0019	0.0021	0.0020	0.0021	0.0020	0.0020	0.0020	0.0017
Congo, Dem. Rep. / Congo, Rép. dém.	0.8333	0.0145	0.0021	0.0012	0.0011	0.0011	0.0011	0.0011	0.0011	0.0011
Côte d'Ivoire	0.0017	0.0014	0.0019	0.0021	0.0020	0.0021	0.0020	0.0020	0.0020	0.0017
Ghana	4.8726	1.8341	1.1028	0.6992	0.6988	0.6614	0.5568	0.5118	0.3407	0.2694
Kenya	0.0166	0.0137	0.0129	0.0136	0.0128	0.0118	0.0115	0.0117	0.0115	0.0108
Mauritius / Maurice	0.0514	0.0389	0.0351	0.0332	0.0325	0.0348	0.0333	0.0326	0.0327	0.0285
Morocco / Maroc	0.1050	0.0941	0.1128	0.1241	0.1188	0.1236	0.1159	0.1190	0.1190	0.1024
Niger	0.0017	0.0014	0.0019	0.0021	0.0020	0.0021	0.0020	0.0020	0.0020	0.0017
Rwanda	0.0033	0.0025	0.0018	0.0018	0.0017	0.0017	0.0016	0.0015	0.0015	0.0014
Senegal / Sénégal	0.0017	0.0014	0.0019	0.0021	0.0020	0.0021	0.0020	0.0020	0.0020	0.0017
South Africa / Afrique du Sud	0.2170	0.1441	0.1572	0.1180	0.1366	0.1377	0.1218	0.1036	0.0921	0.0784
Swaziland[1]	0.0002	0.0001	0.0002	0.0001	0.0001	0.0001	0.0001	0.0001	0.0001	0.0001
Togo	0.0017	0.0014	0.0019	0.0021	0.0020	0.0021	0.0020	0.0020	0.0020	0.0017
Tunisia / Tunisie	0.9042	0.7296	0.7708	0.7408	0.6987	0.7103	0.6402	0.6155	0.5891	0.5098
Uganda / Ouganda	0.0009	0.0006	0.0006	0.0005	0.0005	0.0004	0.0004	0.0004	0.0004	0.0003

Note: The exchange rate is calculated by taking the ratio of the estimated fiscal year GDP in national currency for Table 3.16 by the estimated fiscal year GDP in US dollars in Table 3.17.

1. For Swaziland, the ratio reported is Swaziland's GDP in thousands of Lilangeni divided by the same GDP in millions of US dollars.

Note : Le taux de change est calculé en faisnt le ratio du PIB de l'année budgétaire estimée en monnaie nationale du tableau 3.16 par rapport à l'année budgétaire estimée en dollars américains du tableau 3.17.

1. Pour le Swaziland, le ratio rapporté est le PIB du Swaziland en milliers de Lilangeni divisé par le même PIB en millions de dollars américains.

StatLink http://dx.doi.org/10.1787/888933570333

Table 3.19. Total tax revenue in millions of US Dollars at market exchange rates
Tableau 3.19. Total des recettes fiscales en millions de dollars US aux taux de change du marché

	1997	2000	2005	2009	2010	2011	2012	2013	2014	2015
Cabo Verde	79	92	214	319	313	370	319	336	324	302
Cameroon / Cameroun	1 076	1 151	2 248	3 508	3 318	3 934	4 061	4 666	5 168	4 674
Congo, Dem. Rep. / Congo, Rép. dém.	..	109	620	1 469	1 839	2 286	2 969	3 619	3 884	4 170
Côte d'Ivoire	2 002	1 648	2 673	4 093	4 117	3 931	4 745	5 511	5 968	5 775
Ghana	..	810	2 336	3 349	4 244	5 745	6 198	6 498	5 793	5 614
Kenya	..	..	3 549	6 551	6 819	7 518	8 154	9 373	11 075	11 512
Mauritius / Maurice	790	870	1 225	1 860	1 922	2 211	2 306	2 360	2 505	2 294
Morocco / Maroc	..	9 150	15 407	25 035	25 779	28 883	28 976	30 039	29 671	26 236
Niger	..	162	361	759	755	890	1 001	1 299	1 343	1 219
Rwanda	186	175	313	686	756	895	1 051	1 176	1 268	1 380
Senegal / Sénégal	715	788	1 685	2 417	2 565	2 856	2 782	2 864	3 161	2 848
South Africa / Afrique du Sud	34 409	30 486	64 859	76 017	95 929	109 397	106 233	100 109	97 383	91 584
Swaziland	205	183	383	501	642	695	634	645	642	450
Togo	..	141	303	485	498	617	641	829	936	886
Tunisia / Tunisie	..	5 230	7 808	11 614	11 965	13 343	13 086	13 780	14 725	13 057
Uganda / Ouganda	689	645	1 078	2 022	2 055	2 230	2 508	2 835	3 110	3 344

Note: The figures are derived by multiplying the total tax revenue data in the tables from Chapter 4 by the exchange rate data in Table 3.18.

Note : Les chiffres sont calculés en multipliant les données des recettes fiscales totales des tableaux du chapitre 4 par les données des taux de change du tableau 3.18.

StatLink http://dx.doi.org/10.1787/888933570352

Chapter 4

Country tables, 1997-2015 – Tax revenues

Chapitre 4

Tableaux pays, 1997-2015 – Recettes fiscales

Chapter 4 / Chapitre 4

Country tables, 1990-2015

In all of the following tables a ("..") indicates not available or not applicable. The main series in this volume cover the years 1990 to 2015.

Figures referring to 1998-99, 2001-04 and 2006-08 in Tables 4.1 to 4.16 have been omitted because of lack of space. Complete series are, however, available on line at *http://dx.doi.org/10.1787/93add7a4-en*.

Tableaux pays, 1990-2015

Dans tous les tableaux suivants le symbole (« .. ») signifie que l'information n'est pas disponible ou qu'elle n'est pas applicable. Les principales séries dans ce volume couvrent les années 1990 à 2015.

Les années 1998-99, 2001-04 et 2006-08 dans les tableaux 4.1 à 4.16 ont été omis en raison du manque d'espace. Les séries complètes sont cependant disponibles en ligne sur *http://dx.doi.org/10.1787/ef1bbbc4-fr*.

Table 4.1. Cabo Verde
Details of tax revenue / Recettes fiscales détaillées

Million CVE

	1997	2000	2005	2009	2010	2011	2012	2013	2014	2015
Recettes fiscales totales	**7 326**	**10 974**	**18 972**	**25 357**	**26 038**	**29 327**	**27 352**	**27 877**	**26 859**	**30 044**
1000 Impôts sur revenu, bénéfices et gains en capital	**2 571**	**3 913**	**5 815**	**8 061**	**7 892**	**8 678**	**8 616**	**8 596**	**7 747**	**9 561**
1100 Des personnes physiques	1 928	2 958	3 516	4 453	4 645	4 877	4 994	4 793	4 998	5 222
1110 Sur le revenu et les bénéfices	..	..	..	..	..	..	..	..	..	..
1120 Sur les gains en capital	..	..	..	..	..	..	..	..	..	..
1200 Des sociétés	643	955	2 299	3 607	3 247	3 801	3 622	3 802	2 749	4 339
1210 Sur les bénéfices	..	..	..	..	..	..	..	..	..	..
1220 Sur les gains en capital	..	..	..	..	..	..	..	..	..	..
1300 Non ventilables entre 1100 et 1200	0	0	0	0	0	0	0	0	0	0
2000 Cotisations de sécurité sociale	**0**	**569**	**533**	**46**	**42**	**37**	**41**	**43**	**56**	**46**
2100 A la charge des salariés	..	..	..	..	..	..	..	..	..	..
2110 Sur la base du salaire	..	..	..	..	..	..	..	..	..	..
2120 Sur la base de l'impôt sur les revenus	..	..	..	..	..	..	..	..	..	..
2200 A la charge des employeurs	..	..	..	..	..	..	..	..	..	..
2210 Sur la base du salaire	..	..	..	..	..	..	..	..	..	..
2220 Sur la base de l'impôt sur le revenu	..	..	..	..	..	..	..	..	..	..
2300 A charge des travailleurs indép. ou sans emploi	..	..	..	..	..	..	..	..	..	..
2310 Sur la base du salaire	..	..	..	..	..	..	..	..	..	..
2320 Sur la base de l'impôt sur le revenu	..	..	..	..	..	..	..	..	..	..
2400 Non ventilables entre 2100, 2200 et 2300	..	569	533	46	42	37	41	43	56	46
2410 Sur la base du salaire	..	569	533	46	42	37	41	43	56	46
Contributions pour la sécurité sociale	..	11	1	27	28	26	34	38	49	40
Taxe sociale unique	..	558	532	19	14	11	8	5	7	6
2420 Sur la base de l'impôt sur le revenu	..	0	0	0	0	0	0	0	0	0
3000 Sur salaires ou main d'oeuvre	**0**	**0**	**0**	**0**	**0**	**0**	**0**	**0**	**0**	**0**
4000 Impôts sur le patrimoine	**394**	**584**	**810**	**951**	**701**	**835**	**668**	**668**	**668**	**572**
4100 Impôts périodiques sur la propriété immobilière	0	0	0	0	0	0	0	0	0	0
4110 Ménages	..	..	..	..	..	..	..	..	..	..
4120 Autres agents	..	..	..	..	..	..	..	..	..	..
4200 Impôts périodiques sur l'actif net	0	0	0	0	0	0	0	0	0	0
4210 Personnes physiques	..	..	..	..	..	..	..	..	..	..
4220 Sociétés	..	..	..	..	..	..	..	..	..	..
4300 Impôts sur mut. par décès, succ. et donations	0	0	0	0	0	0	0	0	0	0
4310 Impôts sur mut. par décès et successions	..	..	..	..	..	..	..	..	..	..
4320 Impôts sur les donations	..	..	..	..	..	..	..	..	..	..
4400 Impôts sur transact. mobilières et immob.	394	584	810	951	701	835	668	668	668	572
4500 Impôts non-périodiques	0	0	0	0	0	0	0	0	0	0
4510 Sur l'actif net	..	..	..	..	..	..	..	..	..	..
4520 Autres non-périodiques	..	..	..	..	..	..	..	..	..	..
4600 Autres impôts périodiques sur patrimoine	0	0	0	0	0	0	0	0	0	0
5000 Impôts sur les biens et services	**4 361**	**5 908**	**11 813**	**16 300**	**17 403**	**19 777**	**18 028**	**18 570**	**18 388**	**19 866**
5100 Impôts sur production, vente, transfert, etc.	4 361	5 908	11 813	16 300	17 403	19 777	18 028	18 570	18 388	19 866
5110 Impôts généraux	0	0	6 552	9 747	10 521	11 603	10 405	10 523	10 170	11 283
5111 Taxes sur la valeur ajoutée	..	..	6 552	9 747	10 521	11 603	10 405	10 523	10 170	11 283
TVA sur les importations (DGA)	..	..	4 193	5 900	6 180	7 544	6 515	6 602	6 253	6 358
TVA domestique (DGCI)	..	..	2 359	3 847	4 341	4 060	3 890	3 921	3 917	4 925
5112 Impôts sur les ventes	..	..	0	0	0	0	0	0	0	0
5113 Autres impôts	..	..	0	0	0	0	0	0	0	0
5120 Impôts sur biens et services déterminés	4 361	5 908	5 261	6 553	6 882	8 174	7 623	8 047	8 219	8 582
5121 Accises	1 518	1 938	1 030	1 334	1 494	2 236	2 041	2 235	2 065	2 073
Taxe spéciale sur la consommation	1 518	1 812	838	1 147	1 227	1 706	1 499	1 664	1 507	1 478
Taxe écologique	0	126	192	187	267	531	543	571	558	595
5122 Bénéfices des monopoles fiscaux	0	0	0	0	0	0	0	0	0	0
5123 Droits de douane et droits à l'importation	2 843	3 971	4 231	5 219	5 389	5 938	5 516	5 434	5 497	5 828
5124 Taxes à l'exportation	0	0	0	0	0	0	0	0	0	0
5125 Impôts sur biens d'équipement	0	0	0	0	0	0	0	0	0	0
5126 Impôts sur services déterminés	0	0	0	0	0	0	66	378	657	681
Contribution touristique	..	..	..	..	..	..	0	329	598	646
Autres (taxe incendie, taxe touristique)	..	..	..	..	..	..	66	49	59	35
5127 Autres impôts sur commerce et transact. internat.	0	0	0	0	0	0	0	0	0	0
5128 Autres impôts	0	0	0	0	0	0	0	0	0	0
5130 Non ventilables entre 5110 et 5120	0	0	0	0	0	0	0	0	0	0
5200 Impôts sur utilisation des biens et exerc. activites	0	0	0	0	0	0	0	0	0	0
5210 Impôts périodiques	..	..	..	..	..	..	..	..	..	..
5211 A la charge des ménages: véhicules à moteur	..	..	..	..	..	..	..	..	..	..
5212 A la charge autres agents: véhicules à moteur	..	..	..	..	..	..	..	..	..	..
5213 Autres impôts périodiques	..	..	..	..	..	..	..	..	..	..
5220 Impôts non-périodiques	..	..	..	..	..	..	..	..	..	..

Table 4.1. Cabo Verde *(cont.)*
Details of tax revenue / Recettes fiscales détaillées

Million CVE

	1997	2000	2005	2009	2010	2011	2012	2013	2014	2015
5300 Non ventilables entre 5100 et 5200	0	0	0	0	0	0	0	0	0	0
6000 Autres impôts	**0**	**0**	**0**	**0**	**0**	**0**	**0**	**0**	**0**	**0**
6100 A la charge exclusive des entreprises	..	..	..	..	..	..	..	..	..	..
6200 A la charge d'autres agents	..	..	..	..	..	..	..	..	..	..

Note: Année civile se terminant le 31 décembre.

Les données sont sur la base des encaissements.

Les chiffres n'incluent pas les données recettes fiscales collectées par les collectivités locales car elles ne sont pas disponibles.

Le prélèvement communautaire de la CEDEAO (Communauté économique des États de l'Afrique de l'Ouest) n'est pas compris parmi les impôts selon le guide d'interprétation de l'OCDE (voir § 4). La classification nationale du Cabo Verde le compte comme une recette fiscale. Cette recette qui n'est pas comprise dans le total des recettes fiscales ou des recettes non fiscales est présentée à titre de rubrique « Pour mémoire » dans le tableau 5.5 du chapitre 5.

Rubrique 4400: Cette rubrique comprend les droits de timbre, classifiés au Cabo Verde dans la rubrique « autres impôts ».

Rubrique 5126 : La taxe incendie et le taxe touristique sont classifiés dans la rubrique « autres impôts » au Cabo Verde.

Source: Ministère de Finance et du Plan du Cabo Verde.

StatLink http://dx.doi.org/10.1787/888933570371

Table 4.2. Cameroon / Cameroun
Details of tax revenue / Recettes fiscales détaillées

Million XAF

	1997	2000	2005	2009	2010	2011	2012	2013	2014	2015
Recettes fiscales totales	**582 398**	**843 400**	**1 183 857**	**1 652 112**	**1 640 028**	**1 854 735**	**2 072 275**	**2 304 490**	**2 550 983**	**2 763 093**
1000 Impôts sur revenu, bénéfices et gains en capital	**140 000**	**228 100**	**325 764**	**522 719**	**425 741**	**505 594**	**637 416**	**693 317**	**784 122**	**867 834**
1100 Des personnes physiques	66 400	87 100	66 598	97 774	102 793	116 950	130 516	158 622	175 021	185 512
1110 Sur le revenu et les bénéfices	66 400	87 100	66 548	97 743	102 728	116 928	130 483	158 338	174 190	184 213
Traitements, salaires, pensions et rentes viagères	40 100	60 800	17 722	80 469	86 440	96 097	101 245	120 908	127 331	135 738
Revenus fonciers	0	0	2 225	2 715	2 402	4 487	5 346	6 135	13 247	12 405
Bénéfices artisanaux, industriels et commerciaux	0	0	3 904	6 116	5 342	6 609	11 648	16 267	13 648	21 010
Bénéfices agricoles	0	0	77	29	47	7	14	22	27	56
Bénéfices des professions non commerciales	0	0	249	462	295	397	577	612	592	2 875
Autres impôts sur le revenu	26 300	26 300	42 372	7 952	8 202	9 331	11 653	14 394	19 345	12 130
1120 Sur les gains en capital	0	0	50	31	65	22	33	284	831	1 299
Impôts sur plus-values sur cession immobilière	..	..	46	29	46	8	17	263	830	1 297
Impôts sur les autres gains en capital	..	..	3	2	19	14	16	21	1	2
1200 Des sociétés	57 100	119 400	217 495	362 677	256 404	311 102	421 796	428 360	460 571	538 969
1210 Sur les bénéfices	57 100	119 400	217 495	362 677	256 404	311 102	421 796	428 360	460 571	538 969
Bénéfices des sociétés pétrolières	19 000	39 000	76 523	188 766	83 764	96 729	160 589	169 689	161 724	171 891
Bénéfices des sociétés non pétrolières	38 100	80 400	140 972	173 911	172 639	214 373	261 207	258 671	298 847	367 078
1220 Sur les gains en capital	..	..	..	..	..	..	..	..	..	..
1300 Non ventilables entre 1100 et 1200	16 500	21 600	41 671	62 268	66 544	77 542	85 105	106 335	148 530	143 353
Taxe spéciale sur les revenus payés à l'étranger	11 000	12 400	19 198	34 250	38 877	42 626	43 572	61 708	97 511	84 412
Impôts sur les revenus des capitaux mobiliers	5 500	9 200	21 619	27 218	27 629	32 441	38 313	40 177	44 489	48 774
Centimes additionnels communaux sur l'impôt sur le revenu	0	0	854	800	39	2 475	3 219	4 450	6 530	10 166
2000 Cotisations de sécurité sociale	**45 598**	**65 500**	**83 903**	**109 161**	**135 747**	**143 734**	**147 543**	**160 134**	**153 707**	**160 992**
2100 A la charge des salariés	11 998	19 747	24 123	31 477	33 297	34 741	34 414	42 212	40 917	44 669
2110 Sur la base du salaire	11 998	19 747	24 123	31 477	33 297	34 741	34 414	42 212	40 917	44 669
2120 Sur la base de l'impôt sur le revenu	0	0	0	0	0	0	0	0	0	0
2200 A la charge des employeurs	..	..	..	..	..	..	..	..	..	..
2210 Sur la base du salaire	..	..	..	..	..	..	..	..	..	..
2220 Sur la base de l'impôt sur le revenu	..	..	..	..	..	..	..	..	..	..
2300 A charge des travailleurs indép. ou sans emploi	..	..	..	..	..	..	..	..	..	..
2310 Sur la base du salaire	..	..	..	..	..	..	..	..	..	..
2320 Sur la base de l'impôt sur le revenu	..	..	..	..	..	..	..	..	..	..
2400 Non ventilables entre 2100, 2200 et 2300	33 600	45 753	59 780	77 684	102 450	108 993	113 129	117 922	112 790	116 323
2410 Sur la base du salaire	33 600	45 753	59 780	77 684	102 450	108 993	113 129	117 922	112 790	116 323
2420 Sur la base de l'impôt sur le revenu	0	0	0	0	0	0	0	0	0	0
3000 Sur salaires ou main d'oeuvre	**0**	**0**	**8 644**	**18 063**	**17 860**	**30 792**	**40 427**	**39 817**	**46 902**	**53 572**
4000 Impôts sur le patrimoine	**4 500**	**13 100**	**13 361**	**17 897**	**18 003**	**12 973**	**15 087**	**20 816**	**21 024**	**25 437**
4100 Impôts périodiques sur la propriété immobilière	100	500	1 318	1 716	1 552	386	59	1 714	1 692	1 743
4110 Ménages	..	..	..	..	..	..	..	..	..	..
4120 Autres agents	..	..	..	..	..	..	..	..	..	..
4200 Impôts périodiques sur l'actif net	0	0	0	0	0	0	0	0	0	0
4210 Personnes physiques	..	..	..	..	..	..	..	..	..	..
4220 Sociétés	..	..	..	..	..	..	..	..	..	..
4300 Impôts sur mut. par décès, succ. et donations	0	0	33	25	39	176	176	157	214	62
4310 Impôts sur mut. par décès et successions	..	..	33	25	39	176	176	157	214	62
4320 Impôts sur les donations	..	..	0	0	0	0	0	0	0	0
4400 Impôts sur transact. mobilières et immob.	4 400	12 600	12 010	16 156	16 412	12 411	14 853	18 945	19 117	23 632
Droits d'enregistrement sur les mutations entre vifs	..	..	82	50	32	96	96	287	586	391
Droits d'enregistrement sur les mutations immobilières	..	..	1 909	2 052	2 747	411	3 650	3 343	3 250	3 080
Droits de bail	..	..	3 976	4 147	4 602	3 373	2 575	2 337	2 725	2 364
Droits autres mutations et transactions	..	..	6 043	9 907	9 031	8 532	8 532	12 978	12 556	17 797
4500 Impôts non-périodiques	0	0	0	0	0	0	0	0	0	0
4510 Sur l'actif net	..	..	..	..	..	..	..	..	..	..
4520 Autres non-périodiques	..	..	..	..	..	..	..	..	..	..
4600 Autres impôts périodiques sur patrimoine	0	0	0	0	0	0	0	0	0	0
5000 Impôts sur les biens et services	**392 300**	**536 700**	**735 016**	**956 328**	**1 012 746**	**1 132 350**	**1 199 972**	**1 341 989**	**1 513 344**	**1 607 836**
5100 Impôts sur production, vente, transfert, etc.	390 600	534 000	727 979	948 886	1 004 898	1 124 800	1 192 226	1 333 576	1 503 461	1 598 001
5110 Impôts généraux	179 100	293 800	408 818	537 431	558 854	652 187	684 934	788 850	891 189	958 786
5111 Taxes sur la valeur ajoutée	179 100	293 800	408 818	537 428	558 847	652 164	684 924	788 830	891 164	958 747
Valeur ajoutée intérieure	87 000	186 500	251 019	303 271	299 504	373 531	373 917	472 885	532 980	604 046
Valeur ajoutée à la porte	92 100	107 300	157 799	234 157	259 343	278 633	311 008	315 945	358 184	354 701
5112 Impôts sur les ventes	0	0	0	0	0	0	0	0	0	0
5113 Autres impôts	0	0	0	4	8	23	10	21	25	39
5120 Impôts sur biens et services déterminés	211 500	240 200	319 161	411 455	446 043	472 613	507 292	544 726	612 272	639 216

Table 4.2. Cameroon / Cameroun (*cont.*)
Details of tax revenue / Recettes fiscales détaillées

Million XAF

	1997	2000	2005	2009	2010	2011	2012	2013	2014	2015
5121 Accises	77 400	84 000	114 306	158 910	164 943	182 730	198 030	220 643	240 269	289 280
Droits d'accises intérieure	19 300	26 500	42 755	80 572	68 414	81 616	84 068	95 553	98 327	170 164
Droits d'accises à la porte	1 100	1 900	2 198	317	12 936	15 861	15 867	14 817	14 762	14 608
Taxe spéciale sur les produits pétroliers	57 000	55 600	69 345	78 019	82 962	84 580	97 423	109 598	118 515	103 773
Vignette sur tabac et produits manufacturés	0	0	8	2	632	672	672	675	8 665	736
5122 Bénéfices des monopoles fiscaux	0	0	0	0	0	0	0	0	0	0
5123 Droits de douane et droits à l'importation	85 700	119 900	189 364	240 690	261 731	268 898	289 838	299 976	345 511	320 314
5124 Taxes à l'exportation	45 900	24 300	1 725	6 174	8 793	8 082	7 482	13 054	15 089	17 133
5125 Impôts sur biens d'équipement	0	0	0	0	0	0	0	0	0	0
5126 Impôts sur services déterminés	1 200	1 100	3 108	107	3 600	4 392	4 603	4 930	5 238	5 035
5127 Autres impôts sur commerce et transact. internat.	0	0	0	0	0	0	0	0	0	0
5128 Autres impôts	1 300	10 900	10 658	5 574	6 977	8 512	7 340	6 123	6 165	7 454
5130 Non ventilables entre 5110 et 5120	0	0	0	0	0	0	0	0	0	0
5200 Impôts sur utilisation des biens et exerc. activités	1 700	2 700	7 037	7 442	7 848	7 550	7 746	8 413	9 883	9 835
5210 Impôts périodiques	1 700	2 700	7 037	7 442	7 848	7 550	7 746	8 413	9 883	9 835
5211 A la charge des ménages: véhicules à moteur	1 300	1 600	4 987	5 622	6 111	5 803	6 138	6 640	7 819	7 539
5212 A la charge autres agents: véhicules à moteur	400	1 100	1 902	1 669	1 663	1 676	1 530	1 707	1 985	2 213
5213 Autres impôts périodiques	0	0	149	151	74	71	78	67	79	83
5220 Impôts non-périodiques	0	0	0	0	0	0	0	0	0	0
5300 Non ventilables entre 5100 et 5200	0	0	0	0	0	0	0	0	0	0
6000 Autres impôts	**0**	**0**	**17 169**	**27 946**	**29 932**	**29 292**	**31 829**	**48 416**	**31 885**	**47 424**
6100 A la charge exclusive des entreprises	..	..	..	..	..	..	..	..	..	..
6200 A la charge d'autres agents	..	..	..	..	..	..	..	..	..	..

Note: Année civile se terminant le 31 décembre.

Les données sont sur la base des encaissements.

Les chiffres n'incluent pas les données des recettes fiscales collectées par les collectivités locales car elles ne sont pas disponibles.

Rubrique 2000 : Les cotisations de sécurité sociale incluent uniquement les cotisations pour les retraites et ne couvrent pas les cotisations pour les autres risques comme le chômage, invalidité, etc.

Les recettes fiscales incluent les amendes de l'enregistrement, les pénalités sur impôts et taxes et les amendes douanières qui sont désormais considérées comme des recettes non fiscales suite à un changement de la classification OCDE depuis la publication de la première édition. Cependant, il n'a pas été possible pour cette édition de séparer le versement des amendes et pénalités des recettes correspondant aux impôts auxquels ces amendes et pénalités se rattachent. La classification nationale du Cameroun les compte comme des recettes fiscales.

Les taxes domaniales, la taxe à l'extraction des carrières et la redevance à la production des eaux sont incluses dans les recettes non fiscales dans la rubrique « loyers et redevances » comme le préconise la classification OCDE (voir le guide d'interprétation en Annexe A). La classification nationale du Cameroun les compte comme des recettes fiscales.

Source: Ministère des Finances du Cameroun.

StatLink http://dx.doi.org/10.1787/888933570390

Table 4.3. Congo, Dem. Rep./Congo, Rép. dém.
Details of tax revenue / Recettes fiscales détaillées

Million CDF

	1997	2000	2005	2009	2010	2011	2012	2013	2014	2015
Recettes fiscales totales	..	**7 551**	**293 945**	**1 185 788**	**1 665 702**	**2 101 842**	**2 729 797**	**3 328 329**	**3 592 407**	**3 865 236**
1000 Impôts sur revenu, bénéfices et gains en capital	..	**2 565**	**54 761**	**307 575**	**447 039**	**529 008**	**633 044**	**778 242**	**1 011 930**	**1 225 021**
1100 Des personnes physiques	..	996	24 243	154 403	208 715	275 091	398 726	480 564	516 140	515 851
1110 Sur le revenu et les bénéfices	..	996	24 243	154 403	208 715	275 091	398 726	480 564	516 140	515 851
Impôt sur les revenus des nationaux	..	899	15 444	121 919	162 931	228 883	332 907	394 400	421 427	417 443
Impôt sur les revenus/ Institutions Politiques	..	0	0	3 336	1 842	13 376	17 583	16 089	20 027	16 698
Impôt sur les revenus/ Fonctionnaire et Agents publics	..	0	0	0	0	0	0	4 900	9 298	12 825
Impôt sur les revenus/ Régies financières	..	0	0	0	0	0	0	7 237	9 727	8 186
Impôt sur les revenus/ Expatriés	..	81	7 514	29 024	43 779	31 371	45 402	55 787	55 507	59 921
Impôt sur les revenus/ proféssions libérales	..	15	1 286	124	44	1 319	2 612	1 653	0	0
Taxe ad valorem sur les gains des parieurs (DGRAD)	..	0	0	0	119	142	222	498	152	779
1120 Sur les gains en capital	..	..	..	..	..	..	..	..	..	..
1200 Des sociétés	..	1 569	30 518	153 172	237 938	253 838	234 286	297 669	495 784	709 095
Impôts sur les revenus des capitaux mobiliers	..	30	2 065	15 501	23 356	27 053	37 918	45 672	49 931	53 212
1210 Sur les bénéfices	..	1 540	28 453	137 671	214 582	226 785	196 367	251 998	445 853	655 884
Impôt sur les bénéfices des sociétés non pétrolières	..	1 061	22 942	120 382	194 758	203 431	171 735	220 318	390 544	607 004
Impôt sur les bénéfices/non résidents	..	0	0	0	0	0	0	23 360	42 882	46 124
Impôt sur les bénéfices/ entreprises individuelles	..	410	3 523	17 289	19 823	23 354	24 633	8 320	12 426	2 756
Impôts sur les revenus locatifs	..	69	1 988	0	0	0	0	0	0	0
1220 Sur les gains en capital	..	..	..	..	..	..	..	..	..	..
1300 Non ventilables entre 1100 et 1200	..	0	0	0	386	80	33	9	6	75
2000 Cotisations de sécurité sociale	..	..	..	..	..	..	..	..	..	..
2100 A la charge des salariés	..	..	..	..	..	..	..	..	..	..
2110 Sur la base du salaire	..	..	..	..	..	..	..	..	..	..
2120 Sur la base de l'impôt sur les revenus	..	..	..	..	..	..	..	..	..	..
2200 A la charge des employeurs	..	..	..	..	..	..	..	..	..	..
2210 Sur la base du salaire	..	..	..	..	..	..	..	..	..	..
2220 Sur la base de l'impôt sur le revenu	..	..	..	..	..	..	..	..	..	..
2300 A charge des travailleurs indép. ou sans emploi	..	..	..	..	..	..	..	..	..	..
2310 Sur la base du salaire	..	..	..	..	..	..	..	..	..	..
2320 Sur la base de l'impôt sur le revenu	..	..	..	..	..	..	..	..	..	..
2400 Non ventilables entre 2100, 2200 et 2300	..	..	..	..	..	..	..	..	..	..
2410 Sur la base du salaire	..	..	..	..	..	..	..	..	..	..
2420 Sur la base de l'impôt sur le revenu	..	..	..	..	..	..	..	..	..	..
3000 Sur salaires ou main d'oeuvre	..	**56**	**2 630**	**13 576**	**15 370**	**18 107**	**37 328**	**49 092**	**49 047**	**48 503**
Impôt sur les rémunérations des expatriés (IERE)	..	56	2 630	13 576	15 370	18 107	37 328	49 092	49 047	48 503
4000 Impôts sur le patrimoine	..	..	..	..	**9 644**	**5 363**	**9 431**	**4 918**	**1 940**	**12 983**
4100 Impôts périodiques sur la propriété immobilière	..	..	..	..	3 695	2 828	6 288	3 113	1 192	8 817
4110 Ménages	..	..	..	..	..	..	..	..	..	..
4120 Autres agents	..	..	..	..	..	..	..	..	..	..
4200 Impôts périodiques sur l'actif net	..	..	..	..	0	0	0	0	0	0
4210 Personnes physiques	..	..	..	..	..	..	..	..	..	..
4220 Sociétés	..	..	..	..	..	..	..	..	..	..
4300 Impôts sur mut. par décès, succ. et donations	..	..	..	..	0	0	0	0	0	0
4310 Impôts sur mut. par décès et successions	..	..	..	..	..	..	..	..	..	..
4320 Impôts sur les donations	..	..	..	..	..	..	..	..	..	..
4400 Impôts sur transact. mobilières et immob.	..	..	..	..	5 949	2 535	3 143	1 805	748	4 166
4500 Impôts non-périodiques	..	..	..	..	0	0	0	0	0	0
4510 Sur l'actif net	..	..	..	..	..	..	..	..	..	..
4520 Autres non-périodiques	..	..	..	..	..	..	..	..	..	..
4600 Autres impôts périodiques sur patrimoine	..	..	..	..	0	0	0	0	0	0
5000 Impôts sur les biens et services	..	**4 931**	**199 076**	**793 401**	**1 094 565**	**1 398 438**	**1 885 978**	**2 334 733**	**2 384 546**	**2 499 915**
5100 Impôts sur production, vente, transfert, etc.	..	4 833	198 497	791 107	1 068 789	1 387 159	1 865 845	2 326 713	2 379 811	2 485 416
5110 Impôts généraux	..	1 390	109 602	451 325	590 594	792 547	1 148 278	1 452 156	1 460 277	1 519 687
5111 Taxes sur la valeur ajoutée	..	0	0	0	0	0	1 086 347	1 424 386	1 458 376	1 519 544
TVA intérieure	..	0	0	0	0	0	475 159	583 798	585 321	639 995
TVA à l'importation	..	0	0	0	0	0	611 188	840 588	873 055	879 549
5112 Impôts sur les ventes	..	0	0	0	110	0	0	0	0	0

Table 4.3. Congo, Dem. Rep./Congo, Rép. dém. (cont.)
Details of tax revenue / Recettes fiscales détaillées

Million CDF

	1997	2000	2005	2009	2010	2011	2012	2013	2014	2015
5113 Autres impôts	..	1 390	109 602	451 325	590 484	792 547	61 930	27 770	1 901	143
Impôt sur le chiffre d'affaires (ICA)/ ventes locales	..	195	20 440	90 125	110 004	119 016	15 250	7 912	405	143
Impôt sur le chiffre d'affaires (ICA)/ prestations de services	..	409	28 534	135 850	181 338	261 441	45 428	16 411	1 310	0
Impôt sur le chiffre d'affaires (ICA)/ travaux immobiliers	..	14	3 971	5 897	5 969	7 297	1 173	3 426	186	0
Impôt sur le chiffre d'affaires (ICA)/ exportation produits miniers	..	0	2	0	0	0	0	0	0	0
Impôt sur le chiffre d'affaires (ICA)/ exportation hors produits miniers	..	6	0	0	0	0	0	0	0	0
Impôt sur le chiffre d'affaires (ICA) à l'importation	..	768	56 654	219 453	291 557	403 323	0	0	0	0
Autres impôts généraux sur les biens et services (DGRAD)	..	0	0	0	1 616	1 470	79	21	0	0
5120 Impôts sur biens et services déterminés	..	3 442	88 896	339 782	478 194	594 613	717 568	874 558	919 533	965 729
5121 Accises	..	1 417	26 357	122 581	195 838	210 455	242 066	331 946	330 661	396 426
Droits d'accises perçus en régime intérieur	..	1 380	19 891	85 692	153 005	180 379	200 454	259 581	243 462	239 329
Droits d'accises perçus à l'importation	..	37	6 466	36 888	30 573	29 288	40 113	71 940	87 134	153 841
Redevances sur produits spécifiques (DGRAD)	..	0	0	0	12 259	788	1 500	425	65	3 256
5122 Bénéfices des monopoles fiscaux	..	0	0	0	0	0	0	0	0	0
5123 Droits de douane et droits à l'importation	..	1 942	56 349	209 159	270 089	370 539	463 492	533 071	580 820	560 340
5124 Taxes à l'exportation	..	83	6 190	8 042	7 725	10 799	8 182	7 311	7 171	5 446
Droits de sortie sur les minerais	..	82	5 623	5 731	3 850	4 940	3 245	2 551	2 791	3 238
Droits de sortie sur les produits agricoles	..	1	567	2 007	3 046	5 845	4 937	4 760	4 380	2 208
Droits de sortie sur les autres produits	..	0	0	304	829	15	0	0	0	0
5125 Impôts sur biens d'équipement	..	0	0	0	0	0	0	0	0	0
5126 Impôts sur services déterminés	..	0	0	0	4 543	2 820	3 827	2 231	882	3 518
5127 Autres impôts sur commerce et transact. internat.	..	0	0	0	0	0	0	0	0	0
5128 Autres impôts	..	0	0	0	0	0	0	0	0	0
5130 Non ventilables entre 5110 et 5120	..	0	0	0	0	0	0	0	0	0
5200 Impôts sur utilisation des biens et exerc. activites	..	98	579	2 294	25 776	11 279	20 132	8 019	4 735	14 499
5210 Impôts périodiques	..	0	0	0	1 564	1 979	1 637	450	201	881
5211 A la charge des ménages: véhicules à moteur	..	0	0	0	0	0	0	0	0	0
5212 A la charge autres agents: véhicules à moteur	..	0	0	0	3	9	63	2	27	7
5213 Autres impôts périodiques	..	0	0	0	1 561	1 970	1 574	448	174	874
5220 Impôts non-périodiques	..	98	579	2 294	24 212	9 301	18 496	7 570	4 534	13 617
Immatriculation des véhicules routiers (plaques)	..	98	579	2 294	2 681	3 623	2 513	2 353	2 507	1 366
Autorisations d'exportation et d'importation	..	0	0	0	2 910	901	5 172	688	205	3 567
Taxe d'implementation établisssements dangereux, insalubres et incommodes	..	0	0	0	1 203	437	2 428	525	658	2 849
Autres autorisations	..	0	0	0	17 419	4 340	8 382	4 004	1 164	5 836
5300 Non ventilables entre 5100 et 5200	..	0	0	0	0	0	0	0	0	0
6000 Autres impôts	**..**	**0**	**37 477**	**71 236**	**99 085**	**150 926**	**164 016**	**161 344**	**144 945**	**78 815**
Recettes des produits pétroliers	..	..	37 477	71 236	98 431	150 622	163 425	161 220	144 910	78 417
Droits proportionnels sur les S.A.R.L. (DGRAD)	..	..	0	0	654	304	591	123	35	398
6100 A la charge exclusive des entreprises	..	..	..	..	..	..	..	..	..	..
6200 A la charge d'autres agents	..	..	..	..	..	..	..	..	..	..

Note: Année civile se terminant le 31 décembre.

Les données sont sur la base des encaissements.

Les chiffres n'incluent pas les données des recettes fiscales collectées par les collectivités locales car elles ne sont pas disponibles.

Les données entre 2000 à 2003 doivent être interprétées avec prudence car elles sont largement affectées par des taux d'inflation élevés.

Rubrique 2000 : Les données de cotisations de sécurité sociales ne sont pas disponibles.

Les recettes provenant de la vente des imprimés sont incluses dans les recettes non fiscales (Ventes de biens et services) comme le préconise la classification OCDE (voir le guide d'interprétation en Annexe A). Elles sont considérées comme des recettes fiscales en République Démocratique du Congo.

Rubriques 1110, 5113, 5121, 5220, 6000 : Pour la période 2010-15, ces rubriques contiennent des recettes provenant de la *Direction Générale des Recettes Administratives, Judiciaires, Domaniales et de Participation* (DGRAD) et sont annotées comme telles. Elles sont incluses dans les recettes fiscales comme le préconise la classification OCDE (voir le guide d'interprétation en Annexe A) mais considérées comme des recettes non fiscales en République Démocratique du Congo.

Rubriques 1300, 4100, 4400, 5112, 5126, 5128, 5212, 5213: Pour la période 2010-15, ces rubriques contiennent des recettes provenant exclusivement de la DGRAD. Elles sont incluses dans les recettes fiscales comme le préconise la classification OCDE (voir le guide d'interprétation en Annexe A) mais considérées comme des recettes non fiscales en République Démocratique du Congo. Le total des recettes provenant de la DGRAD considérées comme recettes fiscales représentent en moyenne 1 % du total des recettes fiscales.

Source: Ministère des Finances de la République Démocratique du Congo.

StatLink http://dx.doi.org/10.1787/888933570409

Table 4.4. Côte d'Ivoire
Details of tax revenue / Recettes fiscales détaillées

Million XOF

	1997	2000	2005	2009	2010	2011	2012	2013	2014	2015
Recettes fiscales totales	**1 167 169**	**1 169 607**	**1 407 276**	**1 927 828**	**2 035 467**	**1 853 339**	**2 420 964**	**2 721 780**	**2 946 103**	**3 413 748**
1000 Impôts sur revenu, bénéfices et gains en capital	**218 938**	**192 282**	**192 895**	**278 665**	**260 799**	**322 305**	**437 625**	**436 606**	**401 740**	**408 237**
1100 Des personnes physiques	5 455	5 108	6 184	6 189	6 970	5 736	7 339	9 202	9 430	9 411
1110 Sur le revenu et les bénéfices	5 433	5 093	6 164	6 164	6 937	5 709	7 301	9 166	9 388	9 368
Impôt général sur le revenu	0	0	323	336	1 420	115	761	995	635	174
Impôt BIC hors pétrole-gaz (personnes physiques)	5 392	5 045	5 770	5 738	5 431	5 504	6 424	8 017	8 610	9 008
impôt sur le revenu des valeurs mobilières (personnes pysiques)	41	48	71	90	86	90	115	154	143	186
1120 Sur les gains en capital	22	16	20	25	33	27	39	36	42	43
Impôt sur le revenu des capitaux (personnes physiques)	22	16	20	25	33	27	39	36	42	43
1200 Des sociétés	157 299	148 900	176 272	260 252	240 768	306 584	415 300	407 968	371 821	375 893
1210 Sur les bénéfices	149 971	143 603	169 683	251 941	229 732	297 735	402 448	395 918	357 867	361 782
Impôt BIC pétrole-gaz	0	0	0	76 872	63 649	128 537	201 519	141 732	92 389	71 985
Impôt BIC hors pétrole-gaz (personnes morales)	136 507	127 710	146 074	145 264	137 500	139 347	162 629	202 949	217 980	228 043
Impôt sur le revenu des valeurs mobilières (personnes morales)	13 464	15 892	23 609	29 805	28 583	29 851	38 300	51 237	47 499	61 753
1220 Sur les gains en capital	7 328	5 297	6 589	8 311	11 036	8 849	12 852	12 050	13 954	14 111
Impôt sur le revenu des capitaux (personnes morales)	7 328	5 297	6 589	8 311	11 036	8 849	12 852	12 050	13 954	14 111
1300 Non ventilables entre 1100 et 1200	56 185	38 274	10 439	12 225	13 061	9 985	14 986	19 436	20 489	22 934
Acompte d'impôt sur le revenu du secteur informel	52 369	33 983	5 882	6 713	7 624	6 850	9 128	12 286	12 509	14 637
Impôt synthétique	3 816	4 291	4 557	5 512	5 437	3 136	5 858	7 150	7 980	8 296
2000 Cotisations de sécurité sociale	**83 054**	**102 700**	**116 818**	**151 180**	**162 754**	**131 021**	**235 903**	**307 259**	**340 667**	**383 540**
2100 A la charge des salariés	..	..	..	..	64 364	51 191	93 605	121 401	135 406	151 728
2110 Sur la base du salaire	..	..	..	..	..	..	..	..	..	..
2120 Sur la base de l'impôt sur les revenus	..	..	..	..	..	..	..	..	..	..
2200 A la charge des employeurs	..	..	..	..	98 390	79 830	142 299	185 858	205 261	231 812
2210 Sur la base du salaire	..	..	..	..	..	..	..	..	..	..
2220 Sur la base de l'impôt sur le revenu	..	..	..	..	..	..	..	..	..	..
2300 A charge des travailleurs indép. ou sans emploi	..	..	..	..	0	0	0	0	0	0
2310 Sur la base du salaire	..	..	..	..	..	..	..	..	..	..
2320 Sur la base de l'impôt sur le revenu	..	..	..	..	..	..	..	..	..	..
2400 Non ventilables entre 2100, 2200 et 2300	83 054	102 700	116 818	151 180	0	0	0	0	0	0
2410 Sur la base du salaire	..	..	..	..	..	..	..	..	..	..
2420 Sur la base de l'impôt sur le revenu	..	..	..	..	..	..	..	..	..	..
3000 Sur salaires ou main d'oeuvre	**104 982**	**138 023**	**148 912**	**196 175**	**207 243**	**198 849**	**269 501**	**313 695**	**322 884**	**372 524**
Fonds de formation professionnelle	6 089	6 990	7 473	8 702	9 776	8 012	10 754	12 783	12 484	11 805
Impôt sur traitements et salaires (ITS), solde	98 893	131 033	141 439	187 473	197 467	190 837	258 748	300 912	310 400	360 719
4000 Impôts sur le patrimoine	**30 581**	**32 732**	**43 879**	**48 123**	**49 706**	**38 442**	**61 144**	**82 326**	**79 839**	**89 025**
4100 Impôts périodiques sur la propriété immobilière	21 824	24 664	34 032	37 316	38 009	30 278	49 013	61 322	64 645	72 284
4110 Ménages	..	..	..	..	..	..	..	..	..	..
4120 Autres agents	..	..	..	..	..	..	..	..	..	..
4200 Impôts périodiques sur l'actif net	0	0	0	0	0	0	0	0	0	0
4210 Personnes physiques	..	..	..	..	..	..	..	..	..	..
4220 Sociétés	..	..	..	..	..	..	..	..	..	..
4300 Impôts sur mut. par décès, succ. et donations	0	0	0	0	0	0	0	0	0	0
4310 Impôts sur mut. par décès et successions	..	..	..	..	..	..	..	..	..	..
4320 Impôts sur les donations	..	..	..	..	..	..	..	..	..	..
4400 Impôts sur transact. mobilières et immob.	8 757	8 068	9 847	10 807	11 697	8 164	12 131	21 004	15 194	16 741
4500 Impôts non-périodiques	0	0	0	0	0	0	0	0	0	0
4510 Sur l'actif net	..	..	..	..	..	..	..	..	..	..
4520 Autres non-périodiques	..	..	..	..	..	..	..	..	..	..
4600 Autres impôts périodiques sur patrimoine	0	0	0	0	0	0	0	0	0	0
5000 Impôts sur les biens et services	**727 054**	**699 518**	**899 719**	**1 242 966**	**1 344 200**	**1 156 614**	**1 405 960**	**1 568 130**	**1 783 891**	**2 139 367**
5100 Impôts sur production, vente, transfert, etc.	712 481	674 206	870 744	1 195 901	1 294 834	1 136 339	1 353 779	1 502 963	1 710 241	2 057 979
5110 Impôts généraux	251 446	255 297	288 885	424 587	490 521	378 695	524 503	579 050	619 100	692 416
5111 Taxes sur la valeur ajoutée	251 446	255 297	267 106	401 132	473 711	369 742	514 898	570 444	610 020	680 080
Taxes sur la valeur ajoutée (DGI)	82 346	106 797	104 204	173 249	178 761	145 883	195 936	228 450	255 464	286 171
Taxes sur la valeur ajoutée (DGD)	169 100	148 500	162 902	227 883	294 950	223 860	318 962	341 994	354 556	393 909
5112 Impôts sur les ventes	0	0	0	0	0	0	0	0	0	0
5113 Autres impôts	0	0	21 779	23 455	16 810	8 953	9 605	8 606	9 080	12 336
Taxe ad-valorem (taxe domaniale)	..	..	0	0	0	0	8 917	7 972	8 760	12 185
Contribution à la reconstitution nationale	..	..	21 779	23 455	1 567	296	436	123	63	71
Taxe de solidarité pour la sortie de crise	..	..	0	0	15 243	8 656	251	511	257	80
5120 Impôts sur biens et services déterminés	461 035	418 909	581 859	771 314	804 314	757 644	829 277	923 913	1 091 140	1 365 563

Table 4.4. Côte d'Ivoire *(cont.)*
Details of tax revenue / Recettes fiscales détaillées

Million XOF

	1997	2000	2005	2009	2010	2011	2012	2013	2014	2015
5121 Accises	75 919	74 908	59 977	120 478	128 698	73 865	97 017	122 689	130 450	243 162
Taxe SIDA	0	0	0	385	740	767	845	832	908	821
Taxe sur le caoutchouc	0	0	0	0	0	0	16 828	17 780	3 124	78
Taxe sur le tabac pour le dévelopment du sport	0	0	0	1 505	1 708	1 568	1 954	1 946	2 158	2 029
Taxe sur les sacs et sachets en matière plastique	0	0	0	0	0	0	4	179	172	113
Taxe sur les boissons '	1 779	3 642	2 986	4 014	5 050	4 885	6 100	7 609	14 563	18 213
Taxes sur le carburant	242	290	122	91	81	61	80	81	95	105
Taxes sur le tabac	12 898	15 518	10 933	10 877	12 040	12 096	13 307	13 191	19 817	14 771
Diverses taxes spécifiques à la DGD	61 000	50 300	38 391	95 347	96 560	43 842	44 381	64 166	72 567	183 719
Diverses accises spécifiques à la DGD	0	5 158	7 545	8 258	12 520	10 646	13 519	16 904	17 046	23 314
5122 Bénéfices des monopoles fiscaux	0	0	0	0	0	0	0	0	0	0
5123 Droits de douane et droits à l'importation	178 700	126 512	167 701	213 444	288 039	256 698	344 173	383 583	459 675	486 850
5124 Taxes à l'exportation	173 200	185 114	320 201	377 133	331 261	374 771	304 216	326 539	363 222	473 333
Droits d'enregistrement du café et cacao	0	21 114	58 039	150 610	103 669	95 775	74 308	27 389	38 033	86 244
Taxe sur le cacao et café (DGD)	165 900	156 700	253 148	217 587	221 180	273 686	222 760	291 819	316 371	377 418
Taxe sur le bois et autres produits (DGD)	7 300	7 300	9 014	8 936	6 412	5 310	7 149	7 331	8 819	9 671
5125 Impôts sur biens d'équipement	0	0	0	0	0	0	0	0	0	0
5126 Impôts sur services déterminés	33 217	32 375	33 980	60 259	56 315	52 310	83 871	91 102	137 793	162 218
Contribution de solidarité sur les billets d'avion	0	0	0	234	216	249	279	709	1 274	3 088
Taxe d'embarquement sur les titres de transport aérien affecté à l'Office ivoirien du tourisme et de l'hôtellerie (OITH)	0	0	0	718	799	608	1 332	1 680	2 054	2 569
Taxe pour la promotion de la culture	0	0	0	1 613	1 598	1 172	1 610	1 874	2 279	1 884
Taxe pour le développement des nouvelles technologies de l'information et de la communication (NTIC) en zone rurale	0	0	0	17 538	11 486	10 088	14 150	14 938	16 528	16 977
Taxe sur les télécommunications	0	0	0	0	0	0	17 925	22 177	43 080	50 618
Taxes sur les transports urbains	0	0	0	868	1 019	412	613	394	174	3
Prélèvement aux jeux de casino	449	168	339	286	378	13	230	245	273	163
Taxe d'abattage	2 522	2 434	1 810	937	1 125	716	1 349	1 335	1 280	1 299
Taxe sur la publicité	19	137	93	251	300	328	408	508	411	437
Taxe pour le développement touristique	0	0	0	0	0	0	1 085	972	1 001	1 298
Taxe spécifique sur les communications téléphoniques	0	0	0	0	0	0	0	0	16 667	20 425
Taxe sur les assurances	8 238	6 942	8 666	8 757	7 739	7 500	11 512	11 466	12 214	14 435
Taxe sur les encours bancaires	1 966	2 002	2 030	2 992	3 627	3 739	1 106	2	3	0
Taxe sur les opérations bancaires	20 023	20 692	21 042	26 066	28 028	27 487	32 273	34 805	40 554	49 023
5127 Autres impôts sur commerce et transact. internat.	0	0	0	0	0	0	0	0	0	0
5128 Autres impôts	0	0	0	0	0	0	0	0	0	0
5130 Non ventilables entre 5110 et 5120	0	0	0	0	0	0	0	0	0	0
5200 Impôts sur utilisation des biens et exerc. activites	14 573	25 312	28 975	47 065	49 366	20 275	52 180	65 167	73 651	81 388
5210 Impôts périodiques	14 573	25 312	28 975	47 065	49 366	20 275	52 180	65 167	73 651	81 388
5211 A la charge des ménages: véhicules à moteur	2 354	4 176	5 942	7 928	9 171	283	10 197	12 183	13 403	14 926
5212 A la charge autres agents: véhicules à moteur	0	0	0	0	0	0	0	0	0	0
5213 Autres impôts périodiques	12 219	21 136	23 033	39 137	40 195	19 991	41 983	52 984	60 248	66 462
5220 Impôts non-périodiques	0	0	0	0	0	0	0	0	0	0
5300 Non ventilables entre 5100 et 5200	0	0	0	0	0	0	0	0	0	0
6000 Autres impôts	**2 560**	**4 352**	**5 053**	**10 719**	**10 765**	**6 109**	**10 831**	**13 764**	**17 082**	**21 055**
6100 A la charge exclusive des entreprises	0	0	0	3 823	3 732	4 005	5 822	5 428	5 622	6 979
Fonds de soutien à l'habitat	..	..	..	266	45	0	0	0	0	0
Fonds interprofessionnel pour la recherche et le conseil agricole	..	..	..	3 557	3 687	4 005	5 822	5 428	5 622	6 979
6200 A la charge d'autres agents	2 560	4 352	5 053	6 896	7 033	2 104	5 008	8 336	11 460	14 076

Note: Année civile se terminant le 31 décembre.

Les données sont sur la base des encaissements.

Les chiffres n'incluent pas les données des recettes fiscales collectées par les collectivités locales car elles ne sont pas disponibles.

Rubriques 1110 et 1210 : Les recettes provenant de l'impôt général sur le revenu, l'impôt BIC hors pétrole-gaz et l'impôt sur le revenu des valeurs mobilières ont pu être ventilées entre personnes physiques et personnes morales dans cette édition. Ces recettes étaient rapportées dans la rubrique 1300 (non ventilables entre 1100 et 1200) dans la première édition des *Statistiques des recettes publiques en Afrique*.

Rubriques 1210 et 1220 : Les recettes provenant de l'impôt sur le revenu des capitaux ont pu être ventilées entre personnes physiques et personnes morales dans cette édition. Ces recettes étaient rapportées dans la rubrique 1300 (non ventilables entre 1100 et 1200) dans la première édition des *Statistiques des recettes publiques en Afrique*.

Rubrique 3000 : les recettes provenant de l'impôt sur traitements et salaires (ITS), solde étaient rapportées dans la rubrique 1300 (non ventilables entre 1100 et 1200) dans la première édition des *Statistiques des recettes publiques en Afrique*. Elles ont été reclassifiées dans la rubrique 3000 (sur salaires ou main d'œuvre) car ces recettes sont levées sur la masse salariale et non sur le revenu.

La rubrique 5113 comprend la taxe ad-valorem, une taxe domaniale. Les recettes de cette taxe ainsi que des autres taxes domaniales et de la taxe d'exploitation pétrolière étaient rapportées comme des recettes fiscales dans la rubrique 5128 (autres impôts) dans la première édition des *Statistiques des recettes publiques en Afrique*. Les recettes autres que celles de la taxe ad-valorem sont considérées comme des recettes non fiscales selon la classification OCDE (voir le guide d'interprétation en Annexe A) et ont été classifiées comme telles dans cette édition dans la rubrique « Loyers et redevances ». La classification nationale de la Côte d'Ivoire les compte comme des recettes fiscales.

La rubrique 5113 comprend la Contribution à la reconstruction nationale (CRN) instituée en 2004 pour cinq ans et arrivée à expiration en 2009. Elle a été remplacée par la Contribution pour la sortie de crise. Celle-ci était basée sur les charges d'exploitation des entreprises réalisant un chiffre d'affaire annuel supérieur ou égal à 1 milliard de francs, au titre de l'exercice clos au 31 décembre 2009.

La rubrique 6100 comprend le Fonds de soutien à l'habitat alimenté par des recettes fiscales affectées (contribution patronale sur la masse salariale, taxes sur services déterminés et taxe sur le carburant). Il n'est pas possible de distinguer ces différents éléments d'où sa classification dans la rubrique 6100. Cette taxe a été supprimée en 2010.

Les recettes de la taxe audiovisuelle et la redevance radiodiffusion télévision ivoirienne (RTI) étaient rapportées dans la rubrique 5126 (Impôts sur services déterminés) dans la première édition des *Statistiques des recettes publiques en Afrique*. Elles sont considérées comme des recettes non fiscales selon la classification OCDE (voir le guide d'interprétation en Annexe A) et ont été classifiées comme telles dans cette édition dans la rubrique « vente de biens et services ». La classification nationale de la Côte d'Ivoire les compte comme des recettes fiscales.

Source: Ministère de l'Économie et des Finances.

StatLink http://dx.doi.org/10.1787/888933570428

Table 4.5. Ghana
Details of tax revenue / Recettes fiscales détaillées

Million GHS

	1997	2000	2005	2009	2010	2011	2012	2013	2014	2015
Total tax revenue	..	**442**	**2 119**	**4 789**	**6 073**	**8 686**	**11 130**	**12 697**	**17 003**	**20 842**
1000 Taxes on income, profits and capital gains	..	**141**	**662**	**2 052**	**2 417**	**3 542**	**4 885**	**5 470**	**7 360**	**7 570**
1100 Of individuals	..	71	351	1 390	1 115	1 493	2 368	2 549	3 219	3 570
1110 On income and profits	..	71	351	1 390	1 115	1 493	2 368	2 549	3 219	3 570
Employees income tax	..	..	..	..	1 015	1 361	2 204	2 368	3 000	3 310
Self employers income/profit tax	..	..	..	..	100	132	164	182	219	260
1120 On capital gains	..	..	..	..	..	..	..	..	..	..
1200 Corporate	..	70	311	662	1 080	1 699	2 385	2 785	3 992	3 837
1210 On profits	..	70	311	662	1 080	1 699	2 385	2 785	3 992	3 837
Income/profit tax on companies not including taxes on oil companies	..	70	311	662	988	1 568	2 362	2 316	3 034	3 620
Income/profit tax on oil companies	..	0	0	0	0	0	0	419	797	45
National fiscal stabilisation levy	..	0	0	0	85	129	23	50	162	172
National reconstruction levy	..	0	0	0	7	3	0	0	0	0
1220 On capital gains	..	..	..	..	..	..	..	..	..	..
1300 Unallocable between 1100 and 1200	..	0	0	0	222	349	132	136	149	163
Other direct taxes aside from oil and mineral royalties	..	..	..	..	222	349	132	136	149	163
2000 Social security contributions	..	..	..	**58**	**73**	**79**	**138**	**159**	**218**	**289**
2100 Employees	..	..	..	..	..	..	..	..	..	..
2110 On a payroll basis	..	..	..	..	..	..	..	..	..	..
2120 On an income tax basis	..	..	..	..	..	..	..	..	..	..
2200 Employers	..	..	..	..	..	..	..	..	..	..
2210 On a payroll basis	..	..	..	..	..	..	..	..	..	..
2220 On an income tax basis	..	..	..	..	..	..	..	..	..	..
2300 Self-employed or non-employed	..	..	..	..	..	..	..	..	..	..
2310 On a payroll basis	..	..	..	..	..	..	..	..	..	..
2320 On an income tax basis	..	..	..	..	..	..	..	..	..	..
2400 Unallocable between 2100, 2200 and 2300	..	..	..	58	73	79	138	159	218	289
2410 On a payroll basis	..	..	..	58	73	79	138	159	218	289
Social Security and National Insurance Trust (SSNIT) contributions to the National Health Insurance Scheme (NHIS)	..	..	..	58	73	79	138	159	218	289
2420 On an income tax basis	..	..	..	0	0	0	0	0	0	0
3000 Taxes on payroll and workforce	..	**0**	**0**	**0**	**0**	**0**	**0**	**0**	**0**	**0**
4000 Taxes on property	..	..	..	..	..	..	..	..	..	..
4100 Recurrent taxes on immovable property	..	..	..	..	..	..	..	..	..	..
4110 Households	..	..	..	..	..	..	..	..	..	..
4120 Others	..	..	..	..	..	..	..	..	..	..
4200 Recurrent taxes on net wealth	..	..	..	..	..	..	..	..	..	..
4210 Individual	..	..	..	..	..	..	..	..	..	..
4220 Corporate	..	..	..	..	..	..	..	..	..	..
4300 Estate, inheritance and gift taxes	..	..	..	..	..	..	..	..	..	..
4310 Estate and inheritance taxes	..	..	..	..	..	..	..	..	..	..
4320 Gift taxes	..	..	..	..	..	..	..	..	..	..
4400 Taxes on financial and capital transactions	..	..	..	..	..	..	..	..	..	..
4500 Non-recurrent taxes	..	..	..	..	..	..	..	..	..	..
4510 On net wealth	..	..	..	..	..	..	..	..	..	..
4520 Other non-recurrent taxes	..	..	..	..	..	..	..	..	..	..
4600 Other recurrent taxes on property	..	..	..	..	..	..	..	..	..	..
5000 Taxes on goods and services	..	**301**	**1 469**	**2 710**	**3 628**	**5 154**	**6 271**	**7 250**	**9 581**	**13 610**
5100 Taxes on production, sale, transfer, etc	..	301	1 469	2 710	3 628	5 154	6 271	7 250	9 581	13 610
5110 General taxes	..	127	614	1 529	1 934	2 848	3 353	3 965	5 453	7 273
5111 Value added taxes	..	127	614	1 529	1 934	2 848	3 353	3 965	5 453	7 273
Value added taxes	..	127	499	1 268	1 618	2 376	2 777	3 317	4 672	6 254
VAT (external collection)	..	..	..	..	970	1 389	1 716	1 983	2 757	3 489
VAT (domestic collection)	..	..	..	..	649	987	1 061	1 334	1 915	2 766
National Health Insurance Levy (NHIL)	..	0	116	261	316	472	576	648	782	1 019
National Health Insurance Levy (customs collection)	..	..	..	..	183	285	364	405	463	558
National Health Insurance Levy (domestic collection)	..	..	..	..	133	186	212	243	319	461
5112 Sales tax	..	0	0	0	0	0	0	0	0	0
5113 Other	..	0	0	0	0	0	0	0	0	0
5120 Taxes on specific goods and services	..	173	854	1 181	1 695	2 306	2 918	3 285	4 127	6 337

Table 4.5. Ghana (*cont.*)
Details of tax revenue / Recettes fiscales détaillées

Million GHS

	1997	2000	2005	2009	2010	2011	2012	2013	2014	2015
5121 Excises	..	75	443	330	374	606	730	694	764	2 402
Petroleum taxes aside from energy fund levy and road fund levy	..	..	..	..	221	407	545	525	618	2 163
Energy fund levy	..	..	..	..	36	32	0	0	0	0
Other excise duties	..	..	..	..	118	168	186	169	147	239
5122 Profits of fiscal monopolies	..	0	0	0	0	0	0	0	0	0
5123 Customs and import duties	..	81	348	746	1 052	1 511	1 887	2 231	2 773	3 078
5124 Taxes on exports	..	18	63	17	95	5	103	100	319	371
Levies on cocoa exports	..	..	..	..	95	5	103	100	319	371
5125 Taxes on investment goods	..	0	0	0	0	0	0	0	0	0
5126 Taxes on specific services	..	0	0	88	174	184	197	260	272	486
Communication service tax	..	..	..	88	137	135	128	174	217	252
Airport tax	..	..	..	0	37	49	69	86	55	235
5127 Other taxes on internat. trade and transactions	..	0	0	0	0	0	0	0	0	0
5128 Other taxes	..	0	0	0	0	0	0	0	0	0
5130 Unallocable between 5110 and 5120	..	0	0	0	0	0	0	0	0	0
5200 Taxes on use of goods and perform activities	..	0	0	0	0	0	0	0	0	0
5210 Recurrent taxes	..	..	..	..	..	..	..	..	..	..
5211 Paid by households: motor vehicles	..	..	..	..	..	..	..	..	..	..
5212 Paid by others: motor vehicles	..	..	..	..	..	..	..	..	..	..
5213 Paid in respect of other goods	..	..	..	..	..	..	..	..	..	..
5220 Non-recurrent taxes	..	..	..	..	..	..	..	..	..	..
5300 Unallocable between 5100 and 5200	..	0	0	0	0	0	0	0	0	0
6000 Other taxes	**..**	**0**	**-12**	**-31**	**-45**	**-89**	**-164**	**-182**	**-157**	**-627**
6100 Paid solely by business	..	..	0	0	0	0	0	0	0	0
6200 Other	..	..	-12	-31	-45	-89	-164	-182	-157	-627
Tax refunds	..	..	-12	-31	-45	-89	-164	-182	-157	-627

Note: Year ending 31st December. The data are on a cash basis.

Figures exclude tax revenues collected by sub-national governments as the data are not available.

Heading 1110: Between 2000 and 2009, this heading includes revenue from the national fiscal stabilisation levy, the national reconstruction levy, the airport tax, and other direct taxes aside from oil and mineral royalties, which could only be disaggregated over the period 2010-15.

Heading 1210: Between 2000 and 2009, this heading does not include revenue from the national fiscal stabilisation levy, and the national reconstruction levy.

Heading 1300: Between 2000 and 2009, these funds are included within the totals under heading 1110.

Heading 5126: Between 2000 and 2009, these funds do not include the airport tax.

Heading 4000: Property tax is levied annually by local authorities. Revenue from property tax is not available.

Heading 2000: The data are not available from 2000 to 2007.

Heading 5111: The national health insurance levy is a tax on goods and services whose funds are allocated to the National Health Insurance Scheme (NHIS).

Royalties from oil and mineral royalties are reported as taxes on income and property in Ghana's budget documents. For the period 2010-15, the only period for which the detailed breakdown is available, these revenues are classified as non-tax revenue (Heading "Rents and royalties") in accordance with the OECD classification, as set out in the Interpretative Guide in Annex A.

Source: Ghana Statistical Service.

StatLink http://dx.doi.org/10.1787/888933570447

Table 4.6. Kenya
Details of tax revenue / Recettes fiscales détaillées

Million KES

	1997	2000	2005	2009	2010	2011	2012	2013	2014	2015
Total tax revenue	..	..	**274 084**	**480 363**	**534 138**	**634 703**	**707 171**	**799 842**	**963 284**	**1 069 393**
1000 Taxes on income, profits and capital gains	..	..	**99 557**	**193 745**	**219 227**	**271 603**	**327 903**	**392 395**	**451 793**	**504 077**
1100 Of individuals	..	..	55 818	106 856	124 392	148 483	180 716	216 416	259 007	284 222
1110 On income and profits	..	..	55 818	106 856	124 392	148 483	180 716	216 416	259 007	284 222
Paye As You Earn (PAYE)	..	..	52 767	103 413	120 593	143 785	175 141	211 061	252 974	277 068
Individual income tax	..	..	3 051	3 443	3 799	4 698	5 575	5 355	6 033	7 154
1120 On capital gains	..	..	..	..	..	..	..	..	..	..
1200 Corporate	..	..	31 947	62 633	67 661	86 352	94 643	110 626	135 971	126 541
1210 On profits	..	..	31 947	62 633	67 661	86 352	94 643	110 626	135 971	126 541
Corporation tax	..	..	31 947	62 633	67 661	86 352	94 643	110 626	135 971	126 541
1220 On capital gains	..	..	..	..	..	..	..	..	..	..
1300 Unallocable between 1100 and 1200	..	..	11 792	24 256	27 174	36 768	52 544	65 354	56 816	93 313
Withholding tax	..	..	11 792	24 256	27 174	36 768	52 544	65 354	56 816	92 678
Capital gains tax	..	..	0	0	0	0	0	0	0	636
2000 Social security contributions	..	..	**558**	**0**	**0**	**0**	**0**	**0**	**0**	**0**
2100 Employees	..	..	558	..	..	..	..	..	..	..
Women and children's pension	..	..	558	..	..	..	..	..	..	..
2110 On a payroll basis	..	..	..	..	..	..	..	..	..	..
2120 On an income tax basis	..	..	..	..	..	..	..	..	..	..
2200 Employers	..	..	0	..	..	..	..	..	..	..
2210 On a payroll basis	..	..	..	..	..	..	..	..	..	..
2220 On an income tax basis	..	..	..	..	..	..	..	..	..	..
2300 Self-employed or non-employed	..	..	0	..	..	..	..	..	..	..
2310 On a payroll basis	..	..	..	..	..	..	..	..	..	..
2320 On an income tax basis	..	..	..	..	..	..	..	..	..	..
2400 Unallocable between 2100, 2200 and 2300	..	..	0	..	..	..	..	..	..	..
2410 On a payroll basis	..	..	..	..	..	..	..	..	..	..
2420 On an income tax basis	..	..	..	..	..	..	..	..	..	..
3000 Taxes on payroll and workforce	..	..	**0**	**0**	**0**	**0**	**0**	**0**	**0**	**0**
4000 Taxes on property	..	..	**1 244**	**5 909**	**6 465**	**7 851**	**9 097**	**9 670**	**11 203**	**12 630**
4100 Recurrent taxes on immovable property	..	..	185	1 149	1 133	1 045	1 206	1 076	1 133	1 051
Immovable property (Stand premia on town plots)	..	..	7	63	86	133	83	0	63	6
Land rent	..	..	0	1 086	1 047	913	1 123	1 076	1 071	1 045
4110 Households	..	..	..	..	..	..	..	..	..	..
4120 Others	..	..	..	..	..	..	..	..	..	..
4200 Recurrent taxes on net wealth	..	..	0	0	0	0	0	0	0	0
4210 Individual	..	..	..	..	..	..	..	..	..	..
4220 Corporate	..	..	..	..	..	..	..	..	..	..
4300 Estate, inheritance and gift taxes	..	..	0	0	0	0	0	0	0	0
4310 Estate and inheritance taxes	..	..	..	..	..	..	..	..	..	..
4320 Gift taxes	..	..	..	..	..	..	..	..	..	..
4400 Taxes on financial and capital transactions	..	..	1 059	4 761	5 332	6 805	7 891	8 594	10 069	11 579
Stamp duty-domestic taxes	..	..	940	4 761	5 332	6 805	7 891	8 594	10 069	11 579
4500 Non-recurrent taxes	..	..	0	0	0	0	0	0	0	0
4510 On net wealth	..	..	..	..	..	..	..	..	..	..
4520 Other non-recurrent taxes	..	..	..	..	..	..	..	..	..	..
4600 Other recurrent taxes on property	..	..	0	0	0	0	0	0	0	0
5000 Taxes on goods and services	..	..	**172 726**	**280 445**	**308 283**	**355 050**	**369 975**	**397 570**	**500 039**	**552 536**
5100 Taxes on production, sale, transfer, etc	..	..	169 176	276 847	304 497	351 121	365 723	392 619	494 128	546 051
5110 General taxes	..	..	72 656	127 008	141 152	171 809	174 933	183 404	233 724	265 501
5111 Value added taxes	..	..	72 656	126 878	141 041	171 679	174 788	183 219	233 558	264 872
VAT-Ordinary imports	..	..	28 287	55 557	57 594	74 535	85 744	88 024	114 556	127 744
VAT-Oil imports	..	..	4 186	4 851	5 353	6 860	8 608	6 661	10 621	7 894
VAT-Net	..	..	40 183	66 470	78 095	90 284	80 436	88 534	108 380	129 234
5112 Sales tax	..	..	0	0	0	0	0	0	0	0
5113 Other	..	..	0	131	111	130	145	185	167	630
Turnover tax	..	..	0	131	111	130	145	185	167	630
5120 Taxes on specific goods and services	..	..	96 520	149 839	163 345	179 312	190 791	209 215	260 404	280 550
5121 Excises	..	..	57 314	87 914	93 803	99 712	98 291	105 288	119 122	130 910
Excise duty-Oil	..	..	24 876	32 675	35 780	35 459	30 759	33 148	38 416	42 687
Excise duty-Domestic	..	..	15 744	23 785	23 755	28 573	30 879	33 261	35 855	38 246
Road maintenance levy[1]	..	..	9 645	21 570	23 781	24 102	24 184	25 002	28 163	30 890
Excise duty-Imports	..	..	4 235	6 814	6 994	8 016	8 584	10 307	13 151	15 175
Sugar levy[1]	..	..	1 587	1 270	1 590	1 638	1 748	1 726	1 585	1 329
Petroleum development levy[1]	..	..	1 041	1 415	1 586	1 570	1 595	1 702	1 794	1 817
Petroleum regulatory levy[1]	..	..	0	122	134	135	136	143	158	301
Second hand motor vehicles purchase tax	..	..	186	265	183	220	407	0	0	466
5122 Profits of fiscal monopolies	..	..	0	0	0	0	0	0	0	0

Table 4.6. Kenya *(cont.)*
Details of tax revenue / Recettes fiscales détaillées

Million KES

	1997	2000	2005	2009	2010	2011	2012	2013	2014	2015
5123 Customs and import duties	..	..	32 873	51 184	57 047	66 349	76 878	82 743	113 701	120 612
Import duty-Ordinary	..	..	22 722	35 325	40 382	44 860	50 944	56 734	65 580	72 347
Import declaration fees	..	..	9 724	14 970	15 836	20 467	24 846	24 270	26 627	27 119
Railway development levy[1]	..	..	0	0	0	0	0	0	19 721	18 940
Import duty-Oil	..	..	427	889	797	923	969	1 163	1 016	1 387
Merchant superintendent shipping levy[1]	..	..	0	0	32	100	118	576	757	820
5124 Taxes on exports	..	..	0	0	0	0	0	0	0	0
5125 Taxes on investment goods	..	..	0	0	0	0	0	0	0	0
5126 Taxes on specific services	..	..	6 333	10 741	12 495	13 250	15 622	21 184	27 581	29 028
Excise on air time	..	..	2 982	6 630	7 893	7 796	8 985	11 315	12 302	13 122
Airport revenue[1]	..	..	1 846	2 144	2 464	3 026	3 460	6 281	6 837	6 619
Aviation revenue[1]	..	..	1 505	1 967	2 138	2 428	3 178	3 589	3 468	3 565
Excise on financial services	..	..	0	0	0	0	0	0	4 973	5 722
5127 Other taxes on internat. trade and transactions	..	..	0	0	0	0	0	0	0	0
5128 Other taxes	..	..	0	0	0	0	0	0	0	0
5130 Unallocable between 5110 and 5120	..	..	0	0	0	0	0	0	0	0
5200 Taxes on use of goods and perform activities	..	..	3 550	3 598	3 786	3 929	4 252	4 952	5 911	6 485
5210 Recurrent taxes	..	..	3 550	3 598	3 786	3 929	4 252	4 952	5 911	6 485
5211 Paid by households: motor vehicles	..	..	3 266	3 209	3 367	3 499	3 840	4 488	5 415	6 010
Road transport fees	..	..	2 793	2 409	2 499	2 648	2 767	3 027	3 691	3 947
Advance and other taxes	..	..	473	800	868	851	1 073	1 461	1 725	2 064
5212 Paid by others: motor vehicles	..	..	0	0	0	0	0	0	0	0
5213 Paid in respect of other goods	..	..	284	389	419	430	412	464	496	475
Kenya Bureau of Standards (KEBS) tax[1]	..	..	284	389	419	430	412	464	496	475
5220 Non-recurrent taxes	..	..	0	0	0	0	0	0	0	0
5300 Unallocable between 5100 and 5200	..	..	0	0	0	0	0	0	0	0
6000 Other taxes	**..**	**..**	**0**	**264**	**164**	**199**	**196**	**206**	**250**	**150**
Other taxes[1]	..	..	0	264	164	199	196	206	250	150
6100 Paid solely by business	..	..	..	..	..	..	..	..	..	..
6200 Other taxes not solely paid by business	..	..	..	..	..	..	..	..	..	..

Note: Data are reported on a fiscal year basis beginning 1st July. For example, the data for 2015 represent July 2014 to June 2015.
The data are on a cash basis.
Figures exclude tax revenues collected by sub-national governments as the data are not available.
Heading 2000: Data on social security contributions are not readily available but are deemed to be minimal.
Heading 4100: The data for the immovable property (Stand premia on town plots) tax are not readily available for the years 2001-04 and 2006. No estimation was undertaken given the magnitude of the figures.
Heading 5121: Data for the second hand motor vehicles purchase tax are not readily available for the years 2001-04, 2006, 2013 and 2014. No estimation was undertaken given the magnitude of the figures.

1. These revenues are collected by the Kenya Revenue Authority (KRA) on behalf of other agencies. The national classification of Kenya classifies all agency revenues as non-tax revenues.

Source: Kenya Revenue Authority (KRA).

StatLink http://dx.doi.org/10.1787/888933570466

Table 4.7. Mauritius / Maurice

Details of tax revenue / Recettes fiscales détaillées

Million MUR

	1997	2000	2005	2009	2010	2011	2012	2013	2014	2015
Total tax revenue	**15 367**	**22 390**	**34 901**	**56 048**	**59 172**	**63 458**	**69 300**	**72 447**	**76 718**	**80 409**
1000 Taxes on income, profits and capital gains	**2 287**	**2 881**	**5 829**	**15 629**	**15 005**	**14 560**	**15 642**	**16 956**	**18 385**	**19 793**
1100 Of individuals	1 220	1 540	2 553	4 175	4 583	4 913	5 331	6 214	7 049	7 614
1110 On income and profits	..	..	..	..	..	..	..	..	..	..
1120 On capital gains	..	..	..	..	..	..	..	..	..	..
1200 Corporate	1 067	1 341	3 276	10 592	9 457	8 788	9 380	9 763	10 268	10 993
1210 On profits	1 067	1 341	3 276	10 592	9 457	8 788	9 380	9 763	10 268	10 993
Income Tax - companies & bodies corporate	..	..	..	10 259	8 428	7 847	8 372	8 727	8 972	9 788
Special levy on banks	..	..	..	333	455	448	482	473	772	748
Solidarity levy on telecommunication companies	..	..	..	0	424	376	397	438	358	331
Corporate social responsibility	..	..	..	0	150	116	130	125	167	127
Special contribution from hotels	..	..	..	0	0	0	0	0	0	0
1220 On capital gains	..	..	..	..	..	..	..	..	..	..
1300 Unallocable between 1100 and 1200	0	0	0	862	965	859	931	979	1 068	1 186
Tax deduction at source	0	0	0	862	965	859	931	979	1 068	1 186
2000 Social security contributions	**948**	**1 230**	**1 387**	**2 616**	**2 880**	**3 100**	**3 302**	**3 658**	**3 959**	**4 210**
2100 Employees	..	..	462	640	713	782	840	904	1 004	1 065
2110 On a payroll basis	..	..	..	..	..	..	..	..	..	..
2120 On an income tax basis	..	..	..	..	..	..	..	..	..	..
2200 Employers	..	..	925	1 280	1 426	1 564	1 680	1 807	2 009	2 130
2210 On a payroll basis	..	..	..	..	..	..	..	..	..	..
2220 On an income tax basis	..	..	..	..	..	..	..	..	..	..
2300 Self-employed or non-employed	..	..	0	0	1	1	1	1	1	1
2310 On a payroll basis	..	..	..	..	..	..	..	..	..	..
2320 On an income tax basis	..	..	..	..	..	..	..	..	..	..
2400 Unallocable between 2100, 2200 and 2300[1]	948	1 230	0	696	741	753	782	947	945	1 014
2410 On a payroll basis	..	..	..	..	..	..	..	..	..	..
2420 On an income tax basis	..	..	..	..	..	..	..	..	..	..
3000 Taxes on payroll and workforce	**101**	**140**	**204**	**263**	**176**	**187**	**201**	**235**	**507**	**474**
Extra-budgetary taxes on payroll and workforce[1]	101	140	204	263	176	187	201	235	507	474
4000 Taxes on property	**1 147**	**1 411**	**1 920**	**3 245**	**3 328**	**3 184**	**3 719**	**3 568**	**4 299**	**4 145**
4100 Recurrent taxes on immovable property	171	205	240	347	417	417	238	267	279	196
Local government recurrent taxes on immovable property[1]	171	205	240	337	410	410	235	261	275	193
Campement taxes	0	0	0	10	6	6	4	6	4	3
4110 Households	..	..	..	..	..	..	..	..	..	..
4120 Others	..	..	..	..	..	..	..	..	..	..
4200 Recurrent taxes on net wealth	0	0	0	0	0	0	0	0	0	0
4210 Individual	..	..	..	..	..	..	..	..	..	..
4220 Corporate	..	..	..	..	..	..	..	..	..	..
4300 Estate, inheritance and gift taxes	0	0	0	0	0	0	0	0	0	0
4310 Estate and inheritance taxes	..	..	..	..	..	..	..	..	..	..
4320 Gift taxes	..	..	..	..	..	..	..	..	..	..
4400 Taxes on financial and capital transactions	976	1 206	1 680	2 891	2 902	2 747	3 471	3 277	4 000	3 907
Land transfer tax	..	..	409	1 348	1 190	1 243	1 618	1 496	1 652	1 650
Registration duty on transfer of immovable property	..	..	562	1 053	1 180	959	1 382	1 239	1 522	1 708
Tax on transfer of leasehold rights in state lands	..	..	0	161	175	119	187	272	374	157
Registration duty on transfer of shares	..	..	0	79	84	121	32	24	182	122
Registration duty on fixed and floating charges	..	..	116	161	180	213	168	169	162	157
Stamp duties	..	..	14	71	75	81	85	78	109	112
Registration duty on loans	..	..	0	7	9	4	0	0	0	0
Mortgages, inscriptions and transcriptions	..	..	10	12	11	8	0	0	0	0
Other taxes on financial and capital transactions	..	..	568	0	0	0	0	0	0	0
4500 Non-recurrent taxes	0	0	0	6	10	20	9	24	20	43
4510 On net wealth	..	..	..	0	0	0	0	0	0	0
4520 Other non-recurrent taxes	..	..	..	6	10	20	9	24	20	43
4600 Other recurrent taxes on property	0	0	0	0	0	0	0	0	0	0
5000 Taxes on goods and services	**10 873**	**16 717**	**25 546**	**34 145**	**37 618**	**42 244**	**46 247**	**47 864**	**49 379**	**51 599**
5100 Taxes on production, sale, transfer, etc	10 727	16 514	24 259	31 396	34 853	38 949	42 934	44 450	45 300	47 430
5110 General taxes	2 442	5 604	12 529	18 980	21 095	22 921	25 204	26 158	26 225	28 212
5111 Value added taxes	0	5 604	12 529	18 980	21 095	22 714	24 958	26 000	26 060	28 036
5112 Sales tax	2 442	0	0	0	0	0	0	0	0	0
5113 Other	0	0	0	0	0	207	245	158	165	176
Extra-budgetary general taxes on goods and services[1]	..	..	..	0	0	136	148	158	165	176
Local government general taxes on goods and services[2]	..	..	..	0	0	72	97	0	0	0

Table 4.7. Mauritius / Maurice (*cont.*)
Details of tax revenue / Recettes fiscales détaillées

Million MUR

	1997	2000	2005	2009	2010	2011	2012	2013	2014	2015
5120 Taxes on specific goods and services	8 285	10 910	11 730	12 282	13 660	16 014	17 716	18 293	19 075	19 218
Unallocated taxes on goods and services	..	..	4 094	..	..	..	..	0	0	0
5121 Excises	..	..	2 840	8 506	9 331	11 502	13 052	13 570	14 423	14 834
Spirits, liquors and alcoholic beverages	..	..	1 220	2 124	2 351	3 097	3 705	4 122	4 170	4 448
Tobacco products	..	..	1 617	2 098	2 371	3 039	3 420	3 697	3 823	3 851
Motor vehicles and motor cycle	..	..	0	1 852	1 928	1 942	2 340	2 054	2 400	2 471
Petroleum products (including MID levy)	..	..	0	2 213	2 421	3 018	3 099	3 069	3 219	3 292
PET bottles and other plastic products	..	..	0	124	159	205	255	223	242	250
Sugar content of soft drinks	..	..	0	0	0	0	0	177	330	344
Energy inefficient products	..	..	0	0	0	0	0	1	5	4
Extra-budgetary excise taxes[2]	..	..	0	0	0	15	13	13	0	0
Other excises	..	..	1	96	101	186	220	214	233	175
5122 Profits of fiscal monopolies	..	..	0	0	0	0	0	0	0	0
5123 Customs and import duties	..	..	3 899	1 501	1 525	1 560	1 506	1 389	1 239	1 302
5124 Taxes on exports	..	..	0	0	0	0	0	0	0	0
5125 Taxes on investment goods	..	..	0	0	0	0	0	0	0	0
5126 Taxes on specific services	..	..	898	2 137	2 731	2 945	3 152	3 334	3 413	3 083
Taxes on the national lottery and other lotteries	..	..	14	16	694	623	588	682	652	436
Betting taxes on horse racing, football, etc.	..	..	269	569	658	786	773	793	934	837
Gaming taxes on casinos and gaming houses	..	..	614	962	818	744	495	541	529	591
Passenger fee on air tickets	..	..	0	591	561	793	1 204	1 219	1 213	1 173
Levy on messaging services	..	..	0	0	0	0	92	99	85	46
Hotel and restaurant tax	..	..	0	0	0	0	0	0	0	0
5127 Other taxes on internat. trade and transactions	..	..	0	0	0	0	0	0	0	0
5128 Other taxes	..	..	0	138	73	7	7	0	0	0
Temporary solidarity tax on hotels	..	..	0	102	0	0	0	0	0	0
Local government taxes on goods and services[2]	..	..	0	37	73	7	7	0	0	0
5130 Unallocable between 5110 and 5120	0	0	..	134	98	14	15	0	0	0
Extra-budgetary taxes on goods and services[2]	..	..	..	134	98	14	15	0	0	0
5200 Taxes on use of goods and perform activities	146	203	1 287	2 749	2 765	3 295	3 313	3 414	4 080	4 169
5210 Recurrent taxes	146	203	1 287	1 861	1 934	2 292	2 368	2 343	2 364	2 703
5211 Paid by households: motor vehicles	0	0	652	1 023	1 117	1 155	1 211	1 291	1 345	1 362
5212 Paid by others: motor vehicles	0	0	0	0	0	0	0	0	0	0
5213 Paid in respect of other goods	146	203	635	838	816	1 137	1 157	1 052	1 019	1 342
Company licences	..	..	103	154	148	156	160	236	235	306
Incorporation & lodging fees, search duty, etc.	..	..	5	9	9	10	9	18	18	18
Tourist enterprise licences	..	..	33	69	74	81	81	85	85	91
Gambling licences	..	..	48	89	100	224	349	352	317	368
Liquor licences	..	..	10	11	10	25	21	24	23	25
Freeport licences	..	..	0	5	0	0	2	8	7	6
Pharmacy licences	..	..	1	5	1	1	1	1	1	2
Fishing vessel licences	..	..	38	33	52	39	43	64	54	43
Registration of factories	..	..	2	2	2	3	3	3	3	3
Registration of associations	..	..	1	2	2	2	2	1	1	1
Recruitment licences	..	..	0	0	2	0	0	0	0	0
Environment protection fee	..	..	132	159	141	302	145	130	160	391
Advertising structure fee	..	..	0	0	0	0	62	68	67	63
Regional government taxes on use of goods and permission to use goods[1]	0	0	2	2	2	3	2	2	3	3
Local government taxes on use of goods and permission to use goods[2]	146	203	244	281	255	271	251	0	0	0
Other recurrent taxes on goods and activities	..	..	16	19	20	21	27	62	45	23
5220 Non-recurrent taxes	..	..	0	888	832	1 003	944	1 071	1 716	1 466
Processing fee on application for acquisition of Integrated Resort Scheme (IRS), Real Estate Scheme (RES) and Invest-Hotel Scheme (IHS)	..	..	..	0	0	0	0	2	3	4
Registration duty on transfer of motor vehicles	..	..	..	792	794	818	895	972	1 196	1 277
Land conversion tax	..	..	..	96	38	185	49	96	518	185
5300 Unallocable between 5100 and 5200	..	..	0	0	0	0	0	0	0	0
6000 Other taxes	**11**	**12**	**14**	**150**	**164**	**183**	**189**	**165**	**189**	**188**
Mauritius Revenue Authority penalties	0	0	0	0	0	0	34	34	59	74
Unidentified local government taxes[2]	0	0	0	0	0	0	18	0	0	0
Unidentified taxes	11	12	14	150	164	183	137	131	130	114
6100 Paid solely by business	..	..	..	..	..	..	..	..	..	..
6200 Other	..	..	..	..	..	..	..	..	..	..

Note: Data are on a fiscal year basis beginning 1st July for years prior to 2010 (for example the data for 2009 represent July 2008 to June 2009) and are on a calendar year basis from 2010 onwards.

Data for the central government budgetary tax prior to 2007 and all extra-budgetary, regional and local data were classified according to the IMF Government Finance Statistics Manual. The 1986 manual was used for data up to 2009 and the 2001 manual for data up to 2009 onwards. Data from 2007 onwards are classified under the OECD classification, as set out in the Interpretative Guide in Annex A.

Mauritius went back to a July-June fiscal year in 2015 and figures are not available for all revenue categories for the 2015 calendar year. Where data were missing among budgetary central government revenues, quarterly revenue figures at the aggregate level were used along with fiscal year revenue data to produce estimates for the calendar year 2015. For 2015 revenues aside from central government revenues, linear interpolation was used in some cases to estimate revenues. These cases are flagged with footnotes.

Heading 1210: the solidarity levy on telecommunications companies, the corporate social responsibility tax and the special contribution from hotels are classified as "other taxes" by the Mauritius Revenue Authority.

Heading 2000: Social security contributions collected by the central government are taken from the IMF GFS 2001 dataset.

Heading 5213: the Environment protection fee and advertising structure fee are classified as other taxes by the Mauritius Revenue Authority.

Heading 5220: includes the registration duty on transfer of motor vehicles and the land conversion tax that are classified as taxes on property by the Mauritius Revenue Authority.

1. Values for 2015 are estimated using linear trends.
2. Missing values for 2015 are set to zero.

Source: Mauritius Revenue Authority for the central government budgetary tax data from 2007 to 2015; Statistics Mauritius for extra-budgetary, local and regional government tax revenues from 1990 to 2015, as well as for budgetary central government tax revenues up to 2006; Ministry of Finance budget estimates for detailed revenue figures for the period July 2005-June 2008 and for the figures used to estimate calendar year 2015 revenues.

StatLink http://dx.doi.org/10.1787/888933570485

Table 4.8. Morocco / Maroc
Details of tax revenue / Recettes fiscales détaillées

Million MAD

	1997	2000	2005	2009	2010	2011	2012	2013	2014	2015
Recettes fiscales totales	..	**97 226**	**136 587**	**201 710**	**216 987**	**233 661**	**250 022**	**252 490**	**249 422**	**256 179**
1000 Impôts sur revenu, bénéfices et gains en capital	..	**23 656**	**42 613**	**69 769**	**62 646**	**69 071**	**77 317**	**75 636**	**76 342**	**78 952**
1100 Des personnes physiques	..	14 540	23 661	27 117	26 598	29 405	33 717	34 846	34 573	37 214
1110 Sur le revenu et les bénéfices	..	12 473	21 009	23 324	22 391	24 727	28 492	30 047	30 651	32 797
Salaires	..	10 829	18 830	19 396	19 409	21 769	25 052	25 815	26 452	28 277
Revenus professionnels	..	1 645	2 179	3 928	2 982	2 958	3 440	4 232	4 199	4 520
1120 Sur les gains en capital	..	2 067	2 653	3 793	4 207	4 678	5 225	4 799	3 922	4 417
1200 Des sociétés	..	9 116	18 952	42 653	36 049	39 667	43 600	40 790	41 769	41 738
1210 Sur les bénéfices	..	8 330	16 962	38 808	31 164	34 277	37 936	33 579	34 327	32 693
Bénéfices	..	8 084	16 494	36 943	29 381	32 409	34 896	31 581	31 017	30 553
Produits bruts versés aux sociétés étrangères	..	246	468	1 865	1 783	1 868	3 040	1 999	3 310	2 140
1220 Sur les gains en capital	..	787	1 990	3 845	4 884	5 390	5 665	7 211	7 442	9 045
1300 Non ventilables entre 1100 et 1200	..	0	0	0	0	0	0	0	0	0
2000 Cotisations de sécurité sociale	..	**16 309**	**22 130**	**29 768**	**38 142**	**43 330**	**45 568**	**47 979**	**42 476**	**43 511**
2100 A la charge des salariés	..	0	0	0	0	0	0	0	0	0
2110 Sur la base du salaire	..	..	..	..	..	..	..	..	..	..
2120 Sur la base de l'impôt sur les revenus	..	..	..	..	..	..	..	..	..	..
2200 A la charge des employeurs	..	0	0	0	0	0	0	0	0	0
2210 Sur la base du salaire	..	..	..	..	..	..	..	..	..	..
2220 Sur la base de l'impôt sur le revenu	..	..	..	..	..	..	..	..	..	..
2300 A charge des travailleurs indép. ou sans emploi	..	0	0	0	0	0	0	0	0	0
2310 Sur la base du salaire	..	..	..	..	..	..	..	..	..	..
2320 Sur la base de l'impôt sur le revenu	..	..	..	..	..	..	..	..	..	..
2400 Non ventilables entre 2100, 2200 et 2300	..	16 309	22 130	29 768	38 142	43 330	45 568	47 979	42 476	43 511
2410 Sur la base du salaire	..	..	..	..	..	..	..	..	..	..
2420 Sur la base de l'impôt sur le revenu	..	..	..	..	..	..	..	..	..	..
3000 Sur salaires ou main d'oeuvre	..	**0**	**0**	**0**	**0**	**0**	**0**	**0**	**0**	**0**
4000 Impôts sur le patrimoine	..	**5 405**	**8 403**	**10 988**	**12 703**	**13 137**	**15 456**	**17 002**	**17 926**	**19 555**
4100 Impôts périodiques sur la propriété immobilière	..	3 340	4 415	4 983	5 741	5 485	5 770	7 397	6 101	6 878
4110 Ménages	..	1 989	2 866	3 282	3 899	3 564	3 770	4 878	3 888	4 449
Taxe d'habitation	..	517	696	295	382	298	290	430	301	399
Taxe sur les terrains non bâtis	..	135	236	717	840	627	831	1 121	901	1 113
Taxe sur les services communaux	..	1 337	1 934	2 270	2 677	2 640	2 649	3 327	2 685	2 937
4120 Autres agents	..	1 351	1 549	1 701	1 842	1 920	2 000	2 519	2 213	2 429
4200 Impôts périodiques sur l'actif net	..	0	0	0	0	0	0	0	0	0
4210 Personnes physiques	..	..	..	..	..	..	..	..	..	..
4220 Sociétés	..	..	..	..	..	..	..	..	..	..
4300 Impôts sur mut. par décès, succ. et donations	..	0	0	0	0	0	0	0	0	0
4310 Impôts sur mut. par décès et successions	..	..	..	..	..	..	..	..	..	..
4320 Impôts sur les donations	..	..	..	..	..	..	..	..	..	..
4400 Impôts sur transact. mobilières et immob.	..	2 065	3 988	6 005	6 962	7 652	9 686	9 605	11 825	12 677
4500 Impôts non-périodiques	..	0	0	0	0	0	0	0	0	0
4510 Sur l'actif net	..	..	..	..	..	..	..	..	..	..
4520 Autres non-périodiques	..	..	..	..	..	..	..	..	..	..
4600 Autres impôts périodiques sur patrimoine	..	0	0	0	0	0	0	0	0	0
5000 Impôts sur les biens et services	..	**50 655**	**62 100**	**89 282**	**101 384**	**106 168**	**109 460**	**109 215**	**110 024**	**111 763**
5100 Impôts sur production, vente, transfert, etc.	..	49 539	60 701	86 882	99 056	103 842	106 929	106 303	107 068	108 846
5110 Impôts généraux	..	21 476	32 607	55 077	65 247	71 321	74 772	75 260	74 995	75 271
5111 Taxes sur la valeur ajoutée	..	21 476	32 607	55 077	65 247	71 321	74 772	75 260	74 995	75 271
5112 Impôts sur les ventes	..	0	0	0	0	0	0	0	0	0
5113 Autres impôts	..	0	0	0	0	0	0	0	0	0
5120 Impôts sur biens et services déterminés	..	28 063	28 094	31 805	33 809	32 521	32 157	31 043	32 073	33 575
5121 Accises	..	15 223	15 631	19 843	21 382	22 086	22 983	23 150	24 119	25 661
Taxes intérieures de consommation	..	15 183	15 544	19 629	21 132	21 861	22 731	22 873	23 849	25 366
Taxe sur la vente de produits forestiers	..	4	18	22	26	24	24	31	20	29
Taxe sur les débits de boissons	..	23	37	122	143	131	138	161	156	162
Taxe sur les eaux minerales et de table	..	13	31	70	81	70	90	85	94	104
5122 Bénéfices des monopoles fiscaux	..	0	0	0	0	0	0	0	0	0
5123 Droits de douane et droits à l'importation	..	12 810	12 386	11 805	12 242	10 262	9 003	7 681	7 738	7 715
5124 Taxes à l'exportation	..	0	0	0	0	0	0	0	0	0
5125 Impôts sur biens d'équipement	..	0	0	0	0	0	0	0	0	0
5126 Impôts sur services déterminés	..	30	78	157	184	174	170	212	216	199
Taxe de séjour	..	26	68	137	160	155	149	178	191	172
Taxe sur le transport public de voyageurs	..	4	10	20	24	19	21	34	25	27
5127 Autres impôts sur commerce et transact. internat.	..	0	0	0	0	0	0	0	0	0
5128 Autres impôts	..	0	0	0	0	0	0	0	0	0
5130 Non ventilables entre 5110 et 5120	..	0	0	0	0	0	0	0	0	0
5200 Impôts sur utilisation des biens et exerc. activites	..	1 116	1 398	2 400	2 328	2 326	2 531	2 913	2 956	2 918

Table 4.8. Morocco / Maroc (cont.)
Details of tax revenue / Recettes fiscales détaillées

Million MAD

	1997	2000	2005	2009	2010	2011	2012	2013	2014	2015
5210 Impôts périodiques	..	964	1 134	1 594	1 385	1 448	1 560	1 933	1 973	1 955
5211 A la charge des ménages: véhicules à moteur	..	959	1 119	1 566	1 352	1 418	1 525	1 898	1 937	1 920
5212 A la charge autres agents: véhicules à moteur	..	0	0	0	0	0	0	0	0	0
5213 Autres impôts périodiques	..	5	15	28	33	30	35	35	36	35
Taxe sur les permis de chasse	..	5	15	28	33	30	35	35	36	35
5220 Impôts non-périodiques	..	152	265	805	943	878	971	980	983	962
Taxe sur les opérations de construction	..	113	230	600	703	664	722	720	718	708
Taxe sur les opérations de lotissement	..	39	35	205	240	214	249	260	265	254
5300 Non ventilables entre 5100 et 5200	..	0	0	0	0	0	0	0	0	0
6000 Autres impôts	**..**	**1 201**	**1 341**	**1 903**	**2 112**	**1 955**	**2 221**	**2 657**	**2 654**	**2 398**
Droits de timbres	..	1 132	1 260	1 537	1 683	1 601	1 853	2 061	2 010	2 092
Taxes locales	..	69	81	366	429	354	368	596	644	306
6100 A la charge exclusive des entreprises	..	..	..	..	..	..	..	..	..	..
6200 A la charge d'autres agents	..	..	..	..	..	..	..	..	..	..

Note: Année civile se terminant le 31 décembre.

Les données sont sur la base des encaissements.

Les impôts affectés aux Fonds Spéciaux du Trésor sont compris dans les données.

Rubrique 2000 : Les données de cotisations de sécurité sociales sont estimées pour les années 2000 et 2001.

Les recettes des majorations et pénalités relatives aux impôts sont désormais considérées comme des recettes non fiscales suite à un changement de la classification OCDE depuis la publication de la première édition. La classification nationale du Maroc les compte comme des recettes fiscales.

Source: Ministère de l'Économie et des Finances.

StatLink http://dx.doi.org/10.1787/888933570504

Table 4.9. Niger
Details of tax revenue / Recettes fiscales détaillées

Million XOF

	1997	2000	2005	2009	2010	2011	2012	2013	2014	2015
Recettes fiscales totales	..	**114 819**	**190 218**	**357 448**	**373 461**	**419 410**	**510 995**	**641 408**	**663 171**	**720 540**
1000 Impôts sur revenu, bénéfices et gains en capital	..	**20 891**	**34 848**	**114 008**	**94 839**	**112 674**	**165 625**	**249 555**	**208 403**	**177 695**
1100 Des personnes physiques	..	9 634	12 268	21 910	19 756	23 876	33 695	43 022	45 698	45 502
1110 Sur le revenu et les bénéfices	..	9 634	12 217	21 857	19 623	23 658	33 494	42 693	45 468	45 294
Impôt sur les traitements et salaires	..	8 000	11 207	20 905	18 575	22 551	32 633	41 663	44 638	44 198
Impôt synthétique	..	1 530	803	879	974	1 023	785	881	762	1 030
Impôt général sur le revenu (IGR)	..	104	207	74	74	84	77	150	68	66
1120 Sur les gains en capital	..	0	51	53	133	218	202	328	229	208
Impôts sur les plus-values de cessions immobilières (IPVCI)	..	0	51	53	133	218	202	328	229	208
1200 Des sociétés	..	11 257	22 580	92 098	75 083	88 797	131 930	206 534	162 705	132 194
1210 Sur les bénéfices	..	11 257	22 580	92 098	75 083	88 797	131 930	206 534	162 705	132 194
Impôt sur les bénéfices (ISB)	..	10 933	21 605	82 554	67 863	76 340	117 388	192 631	146 385	121 448
Bénéfices non commerciaux (BNC) (arriérés)	..	126	239	0	0	0	0	0	0	0
Impôt sur le revenu des valeurs mobilières (IRVM)	..	198	736	6 590	5 695	7 665	12 767	10 428	11 484	7 900
Recettes portuaires	..	0	0	2 954	1 525	4 792	1 775	3 475	4 836	2 846
1220 Sur les gains en capital	..	..	..	..	..	..	..	..	..	..
1300 Non ventilables entre 1100 et 1200	..	0	0	0	0	0	0	0	0	0
2000 Cotisations de sécurité sociale	..	**6 216**	**7 305**	**15 851**	**19 950**	**22 243**	**24 740**	**29 972**	**33 610**	**34 117**
2100 A la charge des salariés	..	..	..	..	..	..	..	..	..	..
2110 Sur la base du salaire	..	..	..	..	..	..	..	..	..	..
2120 Sur la base de l'impôt sur les revenus	..	..	..	..	..	..	..	..	..	..
2200 A la charge des employeurs	..	..	..	..	..	..	..	..	..	..
2210 Sur la base du salaire	..	..	..	..	..	..	..	..	..	..
2220 Sur la base de l'impôt sur le revenu	..	..	..	..	..	..	..	..	..	..
2300 A charge des travailleurs indép. ou sans emploi	..	..	..	..	..	..	..	..	..	..
2310 Sur la base du salaire	..	..	..	..	..	..	..	..	..	..
2320 Sur la base de l'impôt sur le revenu	..	..	..	..	..	..	..	..	..	..
2400 Non ventilables entre 2100, 2200 et 2300	..	6 216	7 305	15 851	19 950	22 243	24 740	29 972	33 610	34 117
2410 Sur la base du salaire	..	..	..	..	..	..	..	..	..	..
2420 Sur la base de l'impôt sur le revenu	..	..	..	..	..	..	..	..	..	..
3000 Sur salaires ou main d'oeuvre	..	**401**	**533**	**762**	**1 121**	**1 513**	**1 732**	**2 816**	**3 478**	**3 978**
Taxe d'apprentissage (TAP)	..	401	533	762	1 121	1 513	1 732	2 816	3 478	3 978
4000 Impôts sur le patrimoine	..	**1 253**	**1 590**	**1 866**	**2 906**	**2 899**	**3 297**	**1 729**	**1 612**	**2 742**
4100 Impôts périodiques sur la propriété immobilière	..	1 253	1 590	1 866	2 906	2 899	3 297	1 729	1 612	2 742
Taxe immobilière	..	1 015	1 150	1 860	2 904	2 898	3 297	1 729	1 612	2 742
Taxe foncière	..	238	440	0	0	0	0	0	0	0
Impôt forfaitaire de droit de propriétés immobilière et foncière	..	0	0	6	2	1	0	0	0	0
4110 Ménages	..	..	..	..	..	..	..	..	..	..
4120 Autres agents	..	..	..	..	..	..	..	..	..	..
4200 Impôts périodiques sur l'actif net	..	0	0	0	0	0	0	0	0	0
4210 Personnes physiques	..	..	..	..	..	..	..	..	..	..
4220 Sociétés	..	..	..	..	..	..	..	..	..	..
4300 Impôts sur mut. par décès, succ. et donations	..	0	0	0	0	0	0	0	0	0
4310 Impôts sur mut. par décès et successions	..	..	..	..	..	..	..	..	..	..
4320 Impôts sur les donations	..	..	..	..	..	..	..	..	..	..
4400 Impôts sur transact. mobilières et immob.	..	0	0	0	0	0	0	0	0	0
4500 Impôts non-périodiques	..	0	0	0	0	0	0	0	0	0
4510 Sur l'actif net	..	..	..	..	..	..	..	..	..	..
4520 Autres non-périodiques	..	..	..	..	..	..	..	..	..	..
4600 Autres impôts périodiques sur patrimoine	..	0	0	0	0	0	0	0	0	0
5000 Impôts sur les biens et services	..	**82 383**	**138 312**	**208 312**	**234 839**	**256 826**	**284 525**	**316 594**	**370 745**	**431 233**
5100 Impôts sur production, vente, transfert, etc.	..	81 489	137 675	207 154	233 477	255 507	282 855	314 669	368 641	428 892
5110 Impôts généraux	..	31 766	79 938	125 164	136 966	132 886	161 766	181 930	225 855	256 546
5111 Taxes sur la valeur ajoutée	..	31 766	79 938	125 164	136 966	132 886	139 400	154 469	197 683	237 621
TVA intérieure	..	12 375	31 686	71 387	76 999	64 184	86 318	91 790	130 060	145 529
TVA à la douane (DGD)	..	19 391	48 252	53 777	59 967	68 702	53 082	62 679	67 623	92 092
5112 Impôts sur les ventes	..	0	0	0	0	0	0	0	0	0
5113 Autres impôts	..	0	0	0	0	0	22 366	27 461	28 171	18 925
Redevance ad valorem	..	0	0	0	0	0	22 366	27 461	28 171	18 925
5120 Impôts sur biens et services déterminés	..	49 722	57 737	81 990	96 511	122 621	121 089	132 739	142 787	172 345
5121 Accises	..	13 754	17 716	25 936	28 505	34 374	45 255	43 727	39 124	51 081
Taxe intérieure sur les produits pétroliers (TIPP) (y compris DGD)	..	4 313	6 654	9 552	11 694	12 860	19 146	14 195	11 913	19 375
Taxe sur les tabacs et les cigarettes	..	4 600	4 862	10 224	11 279	14 736	13 520	17 085	14 001	17 926
Taxe sur les boissons alcoolisés (TBA)	..	882	1 033	1 132	1 263	1 437	3 579	2 619	1 817	2 684
Taxe d'exploitation artisanale (TEA)	..	0	0	0	0	0	0	0	2	22
Autres droits d'accises	..	3 959	5 166	5 029	4 269	5 341	9 011	9 829	11 391	11 074

Table 4.9. Niger (*cont.*)

Details of tax revenue / Recettes fiscales détaillées

Million XOF

	1997	2000	2005	2009	2010	2011	2012	2013	2014	2015
5122 Bénéfices des monopoles fiscaux	..	0	0	0	0	0	0	0	0	0
5123 Droits de douane et droits à l'importation	..	22 930	26 854	28 635	36 286	42 371	36 126	45 430	46 536	59 517
Droits de douane	..	14 722	24 354	23 925	28 141	35 982	32 329	40 171	40 976	53 226
Redevance statistique à l'importation	..	1 652	2 493	4 688	8 144	6 389	3 790	5 260	5 558	6 283
Droits divers (y compris T.C.I.)	..	6 556	7	23	0	0	7	0	1	8
5124 Taxes à l'exportation	..	11 671	12 012	24 645	27 567	38 613	32 817	36 352	37 377	31 025
Taxes sur les réexportations	..	9 997	11 069	23 197	25 405	35 396	26 880	28 647	30 923	25 657
Redevance statistique à l'exportation	..	1 673	943	1 213	1 465	2 408	5 904	7 682	6 340	5 342
Taxe forfaitaire sur l'exercise des activités de réexportation et/ou transit de tabacs et cigarettes (TFEAR)	..	0	0	235	697	809	33	23	113	25
5125 Impôts sur biens d'équipement	..	0	0	0	0	0	0	0	0	0
5126 Impôts sur services déterminés	..	1 238	902	2 601	3 080	6 157	5 772	6 614	19 074	30 399
Taxe sur la terminaison du trafic international entrant (TATTIE)	..	0	0	0	0	0	0	0	12 184	18 666
Taxe sur l'utilisation du réseau de télécommunication (TURTEL)	..	0	0	0	0	2 672	1 929	2 133	2 332	5 349
Taxe sur les recettes des loteries	..	877	104	1 276	1 303	1 517	1 835	2 040	2 238	3 377
Taxe unique sur les assurances (TUA)	..	361	792	1 263	1 490	1 607	1 725	2 114	2 008	2 310
Impôt sur les gains des loteries	..	0	5	0	0	26	30	29	25	550
Taxe sur les jeux de hasard (TJH)	..	0	0	38	246	301	219	294	284	140
Taxe sur la publicité commerciale extérieure (TPCE)	..	0	0	23	41	33	34	4	3	8
5127 Autres impôts sur commerce et transact. internat.	..	0	0	0	0	0	0	0	0	0
5128 Autres impôts	..	130	254	172	1 074	1 107	1 120	616	677	324
Droits miniers	..	130	254	172	1 074	1 107	1 120	616	667	295
Droit fixe mine	..	0	0	0	0	0	0	0	9	28
Droit fixe pétrole	..	0	0	0	0	0	0	0	0	1
5130 Non ventilables entre 5110 et 5120	..	0	0	0	0	0	0	0	0	0
5200 Impôts sur utilisation des biens et exerc. activites	..	894	637	1 158	1 362	1 319	1 671	1 925	2 104	2 341
5210 Impôts périodiques	..	529	637	1 158	1 362	1 319	1 671	1 914	2 073	2 316
Vignette	..	520	625	1 149	1 354	1 311	1 664	1 903	2 055	2 310
5211 A la charge des ménages: véhicules à moteur	..	0	0	0	0	0	0	0	0	0
5212 A la charge autres agents: véhicules à moteur	..	0	0	0	0	0	0	0	0	0
5213 Autres impôts périodiques	..	9	12	10	8	8	7	11	18	6
Permis de chasse et visite	..	0	1	0	0	3	2	3	9	2
Taxe sur les armes à feu (TAF)	..	9	11	10	8	5	5	8	9	4
5220 Impôts non-périodiques	..	365	0	0	0	0	0	11	31	25
Péage routier	..	365	..	..	..	..	..	0	0	0
Redevance plaque d'immatriculation	..	0	..	..	..	..	..	11	31	25
5300 Non ventilables entre 5100 et 5200	..	0	0	0	0	0	0	0	0	0
6000 Autres impôts	**..**	**3 676**	**7 630**	**16 649**	**19 807**	**23 255**	**31 076**	**40 743**	**45 324**	**70 775**
Droits d'enregistrement	..	2 166	4 835	8 474	8 048	10 981	18 026	27 711	29 642	51 113
Prélèvement pour compte des collectivités locales	..	0	0	4 021	6 512	6 731	7 671	6 463	8 161	11 727
Taxe sur certains frais généraux des entreprises (TCFGE)	..	310	776	1 729	1 963	2 266	2 323	3 211	4 060	4 132
Droits de timbre	..	1 201	2 019	2 427	3 283	3 277	3 056	3 358	3 460	3 803
6100 A la charge exclusive des entreprises	..	..	..	..	..	..	..	..	..	..
6200 A la charge d'autres agents	..	..	..	..	..	..	..	..	..	..

Note: Année civile se terminant le 31 décembre.

Les données sont sur la base des encaissements.

Les chiffres n'incluent pas les données des recettes fiscales collectées par les collectivités locales car elles ne sont pas disponibles.

Les recettes provenant du domaine public, des redevances minières, des redevances superficiaires des mines et du pétrole et des amendes et pénalités relatives aux impôts sont incluses dans les recettes non fiscales dans cette publication comme le préconise la classification OCDE (voir le guide d'interprétation en Annexe A). La classification du Niger compte ces recettes comme des recettes fiscales.

Rubriques 5111 et 5121 : Ces rubriques contiennent des recettes provenant de la *Direction Générale des Douanes* (DGD) et sont annotées comme telles.

Rubrique 5220 : Cette rubrique comprend les recettes de la redevance plaques d'immatriculation collectées par la *Direction Générale du Trésor et de la Comptabilité Publique* (DGTCP) entre 2005 et 2015 comme le préconise la classification OCDE (voir le guide d'interprétation en Annexe A). La classification du Niger compte ces recettes comme des recettes non fiscales.

Source: Institut National de la Statistique.

StatLink http://dx.doi.org/10.1787/888933570523

Table 4.10. Rwanda
Details of tax revenue / Recettes fiscales détaillées

Million RWF

	1997	2000	2005	2009	2010	2011	2012	2013	2014	2015
Total tax revenue	**56 249**	**68 909**	**174 606**	**389 940**	**440 724**	**537 439**	**645 448**	**760 158**	**865 554**	**993 048**
1000 Taxes on income, profits and capital gains	**14 205**	**17 943**	**49 911**	**135 218**	**159 567**	**195 395**	**246 467**	**308 107**	**322 827**	**376 582**
1100 Of individuals	4 313	6 622	24 587	81 595	102 037	124 133	157 814	182 996	193 212	221 459
1110 On income and profits	4 313	6 622	24 587	81 595	102 037	124 133	157 814	182 996	193 212	221 459
Pay As You Earn	..	..	..	..	..	..	..	..	..	216 750
Rental income tax	..	..	..	..	..	..	..	..	..	4 709
1120 On capital gains	..	..	..	..	..	..	..	..	..	..
1200 Corporate	9 893	11 322	25 324	53 623	57 530	71 262	88 653	125 111	129 615	155 123
1210 On profits	9 893	11 322	25 324	53 623	57 530	71 262	88 653	125 111	129 615	155 123
Corporate income tax	7 245	3 603	11 606	27 881	26 459	30 756	32 815	48 962	39 157	..
Withholding tax	545	59	605	6 932	10 764	16 227	32 383	42 363	49 948	..
Personal income tax	1 045	868	2 210	6 558	7 316	7 264	7 530	7 828	6 950	..
Other taxes on profits	1 058	6 792	10 903	12 253	12 991	17 015	15 926	25 958	33 561	..
1220 On capital gains	..	..	..	..	..	..	..	..	..	..
1300 Unallocable between 1100 and 1200	0	0	0	0	0	0	0	0	0	0
2000 Social security contributions	**1 915**	**3 423**	**11 988**	**25 741**	**28 235**	**35 636**	**42 890**	**53 123**	**55 530**	**59 687**
2100 Employees	717	1 283	4 493	9 652	10 586	13 361	16 081	19 918	20 821	22 379
2110 On a payroll basis	717	1 283	4 493	9 652	10 586	13 361	16 081	19 918	20 821	22 379
2120 On an income tax basis	0	0	0	0	0	0	0	0	0	0
2200 Employers	1 196	2 138	7 488	16 086	17 644	22 269	26 802	33 197	34 701	37 299
2210 On a payroll basis	1 196	2 138	7 488	16 086	17 644	22 269	26 802	33 197	34 701	37 299
2220 On an income tax basis	0	0	0	0	0	0	0	0	0	0
2300 Self-employed or non-employed	2	3	6	4	4	6	7	8	9	9
2310 On a payroll basis	2	3	6	4	4	6	7	8	9	9
2320 On an income tax basis	0	0	0	0	0	0	0	0	0	0
2400 Unallocable between 2100, 2200 and 2300	0	0	0	0	0	0	0	0	0	0
2410 On a payroll basis	..	..	..	..	..	..	..	..	..	..
2420 On an income tax basis	..	..	..	..	..	..	..	..	..	..
3000 Taxes on payroll and workforce	**0**	**0**	**0**	**0**	**0**	**0**	**0**	**0**	**0**	**0**
4000 Taxes on property	**48**	**130**	**43**	**79**	**97**	**69**	**28**	**18**	**19**	**632**
4100 Recurrent taxes on immovable property	48	130	42	78	96	69	28	18	19	632
4110 Households	48	130	42	78	96	69	28	18	19	632
4120 Others	0	0	0	0	0	0	0	0	0	0
4200 Recurrent taxes on net wealth	0	0	0	0	0	0	0	0	0	0
4210 Individual	..	..	..	..	..	..	..	..	..	..
4220 Corporate	..	..	..	..	..	..	..	..	..	..
4300 Estate, inheritance and gift taxes	0	0	0	0	0	0	0	0	0	0
4310 Estate and inheritance taxes	..	..	..	..	..	..	..	..	..	..
4320 Gift taxes	..	..	..	..	..	..	..	..	..	..
4400 Taxes on financial and capital transactions	0	0	0	0	0	0	0	0	0	0
4500 Non-recurrent taxes	0	0	0	0	0	0	0	0	0	0
4510 On net wealth	..	..	..	..	..	..	..	..	..	..
4520 Other non-recurrent taxes	..	..	..	..	..	..	..	..	..	..
4600 Other recurrent taxes on property	0	0	1	1	0	0	0	0	0	0
5000 Taxes on goods and services	**40 081**	**47 413**	**112 664**	**228 901**	**252 826**	**306 339**	**356 062**	**398 910**	**487 178**	**556 147**
5100 Taxes on production, sale, transfer, etc	39 683	46 777	111 848	227 785	250 214	304 131	352 857	397 084	485 735	545 092
5110 General taxes	7 485	13 777	57 747	125 055	131 665	156 082	186 016	219 501	279 275	305 544
5111 Value added taxes	7 485	13 777	57 747	125 055	131 665	156 082	186 016	219 501	279 275	305 544
5112 Sales tax	0	0	0	0	0	0	0	0	0	0
5113 Other	0	0	0	0	0	0	0	0	0	0
5120 Taxes on specific goods and services	32 198	32 999	54 101	102 730	118 548	148 049	166 842	177 583	206 461	239 548
5121 Excises	11 637	18 849	22 614	55 078	75 236	98 005	99 071	105 304	121 220	134 076
Beers	8 109	7 146	9 371	19 311	22 548	28 760	33 372	34 319	36 872	45 950
Petroleum	540	7 857	6 515	16 605	30 941	40 346	33 489	35 982	37 283	47 043
Stragic reserves levy	0	0	0	0	0	0	0	0	0	4 185
Other Excises	2 988	3 846	6 728	19 162	21 746	28 900	32 210	35 003	47 065	36 899
5122 Profits of fiscal monopolies	0	0	0	0	0	0	0	0	0	0
5123 Customs and import duties	16 299	14 151	31 488	47 620	43 313	50 044	67 770	72 280	85 241	105 472
Import duties	12 447	9 260	22 071	35 303	26 215	31 413	45 891	46 448	55 106	69 731
Road Maintenance Fund	2 077	2 531	3 644	9 833	14 843	17 219	20 588	23 865	25 167	29 620
Infrastructure development levy	0	0	0	0	0	0	0	0	0	3 837
Other customs and import duties	1 776	2 360	5 773	2 484	2 254	1 412	1 292	1 967	4 968	2 284
5124 Taxes on exports	4 262	0	0	33	0	0	0	0	0	0
5125 Taxes on investment goods	0	0	0	0	0	0	0	0	0	0
5126 Taxes on specific services	0	0	0	0	0	0	0	0	0	0
5127 Other taxes on internat. trade and transactions	0	0	0	0	0	0	0	0	0	0
5128 Other taxes	0	0	0	0	0	0	0	0	0	0
5130 Unallocable between 5110 and 5120	0	0	0	0	0	0	0	0	0	0

Table 4.10. Rwanda (cont.)
Details of tax revenue / Recettes fiscales détaillées

Million RWF

	1997	2000	2005	2009	2010	2011	2012	2013	2014	2015
5200 Taxes on use of goods and perform activities	398	636	816	1 116	2 612	2 208	3 205	1 825	1 442	11 055
5210 Recurrent taxes	398	636	816	1 116	2 612	2 208	3 205	1 825	1 442	11 055
5211 Paid by households: motor vehicles	398	636	816	1 116	2 612	2 208	3 205	1 825	1 442	3 252
5212 Paid by others: motor vehicles	0	0	0	0	0	0	0	0	0	0
5213 Paid in respect of other goods	0	0	0	0	0	0	0	0	0	7 803
5220 Non-recurrent taxes	0	0	0	0	0	0	0	0	0	0
5300 Unallocable between 5100 and 5200	0	0	0	0	0	0	0	0	0	0
6000 Other taxes	**0**	**0**	**0**	**0**	**0**	**0**	**0**	**0**	**0**	**0**
6100 Paid solely by business	..	..	..	..	..	..	..	..	..	..
6200 Other	..	..	..	..	..	..	..	..	..	..

Note: Year ending 31st December. From 2008, the figures for social security contributions are on a fiscal year basis beginning 1st July. For example, data for 2015 represent July 2014 to June 2015.

The data are on a cash basis.

Figures exclude tax revenues collected by sub-national governments as the data are not available.

Figures include fines related to tax revenues as it is not possible to split these out from tax revenues. These revenues are now classified as non-tax revenues following a change in the OECD classification. Rwanda considers these revenues as tax revenues.

Heading 2000: Rwanda does not include social security contributions in their tax revenue data as the Rwandan authorities do not consider them as taxes.

Source: Rwanda Revenue Authority.

StatLink http://dx.doi.org/10.1787/888933570542

Table 4.11. Senegal / Sénégal
Details of tax revenue / Recettes fiscales détaillées

Million XOF

	1997	2000	2005	2009	2010	2011	2012	2013	2014	2015
Recettes fiscales totales	**417 544**	**559 295**	**887 248**	**1 138 498**	**1 267 799**	**1 346 487**	**1 419 281**	**1 414 720**	**1 560 432**	**1 683 628**
1000 Impôts sur revenu, bénéfices et gains en capital	**87 500**	**123 771**	**204 800**	**275 078**	**328 200**	**333 200**	**384 040**	**373 800**	**398 500**	**438 800**
1100 Des personnes physiques	53 600	64 021	102 600	175 378	192 900	213 700	240 640	217 300	238 200	264 200
1110 Sur le revenu et les bénéfices	53 000	63 370	101 100	173 578	191 000	211 400	238 140	214 400	234 700	261 100
1120 Sur les gains en capital	600	651	1 500	1 800	1 900	2 300	2 500	2 900	3 500	3 100
1200 Des sociétés	29 000	49 418	83 900	78 000	106 100	98 000	113 900	135 700	133 800	147 300
1210 Sur les bénéfices	29 000	49 418	83 900	78 000	106 100	98 000	113 900	135 700	133 800	147 300
1220 Sur les gains en capital	..	..	..	..	..	..	..	..	..	..
1300 Non ventilables entre 1100 et 1200	4 900	10 332	18 300	21 700	29 200	21 500	29 500	20 800	26 500	27 300
2000 Cotisations de sécurité sociale	**16 474**	**22 215**	**36 568**	**53 889**	**72 999**	**59 627**	**67 611**	**72 000**	**77 932**	**84 850**
2100 A la charge des salariés	..	..	..	..	..	..	..	..	77 932	84 850
2110 Sur la base du salaire	..	..	..	..	..	..	..	..	31 173	33 940
2120 Sur la base de l'impôt sur les revenus	..	..	..	..	..	..	..	..	46 759	50 910
2200 A la charge des employeurs	..	..	..	..	..	..	..	..	0	0
2210 Sur la base du salaire	..	..	..	..	..	..	..	..	..	..
2220 Sur la base de l'impôt sur le revenu	..	..	..	..	..	..	..	..	..	..
2300 A charge des travailleurs indép. ou sans emploi	..	..	..	..	..	..	..	..	0	0
2310 Sur la base du salaire	..	..	..	..	..	..	..	..	..	..
2320 Sur la base de l'impôt sur le revenu	..	..	..	..	..	..	..	..	..	..
2400 Non ventilables entre 2100, 2200 et 2300	16 474	22 215	36 568	53 889	72 999	59 627	67 611	72 000	0	0
2410 Sur la base du salaire	..	..	..	..	..	..	..	..	..	..
2420 Sur la base de l'impôt sur le revenu	..	..	..	..	..	..	..	..	..	..
3000 Sur salaires ou main d'oeuvre	**5 650**	**6 668**	**9 440**	**10 000**	**10 800**	**12 400**	**15 100**	**16 100**	**16 900**	**18 100**
4000 Impôts sur le patrimoine	**9 900**	**11 200**	**23 200**	**33 200**	**39 100**	**38 200**	**37 200**	**36 600**	**39 600**	**44 149**
4100 Impôts périodiques sur la propriété immobilière	0	0	0	0	0	0	0	0	0	0
4110 Ménages	..	..	..	..	..	..	..	..	..	..
4120 Autres agents	..	..	..	..	..	..	..	..	..	..
4200 Impôts périodiques sur l'actif net	0	0	0	0	0	0	0	0	0	0
4210 Personnes physiques	..	..	..	..	..	..	..	..	..	..
4220 Sociétés	..	..	..	..	..	..	..	..	..	..
4300 Impôts sur mut. par décès, succ. et donations	2 178	2 464	5 104	5 481	12 445	9 669	7 651	7 809	8 086	471
4310 Impôts sur mut. par décès et successions	..	..	..	..	..	..	..	..	..	..
4320 Impôts sur les donations	..	..	..	..	..	..	..	..	..	..
4400 Impôts sur transact. mobilières et immob.	7 722	8 736	18 096	27 719	26 655	28 531	29 549	28 791	31 514	43 678
Droits de mutation sur vente ou échanges d'immeubles	..	..	..	16 388	15 418	15 710	19 398	15 713	18 352	15 863
Droits d'enregistrement autre que patrimoine	..	..	..	11 331	11 237	12 821	10 151	13 078	13 162	27 815
4500 Impôts non-périodiques	0	0	0	0	0	0	0	0	0	0
4510 Sur l'actif net	..	..	..	..	..	..	..	..	..	..
4520 Autres non-périodiques	..	..	..	..	..	..	..	..	..	..
4600 Autres impôts périodiques sur patrimoine	0	0	0	0	0	0	0	0	0	0
5000 Impôts sur les biens et services	**291 820**	**386 940**	**601 700**	**754 431**	**804 400**	**890 060**	**902 830**	**900 820**	**1 010 700**	**1 075 029**
5100 Impôts sur production, vente, transfert, etc.	289 920	384 590	597 700	749 731	799 400	884 060	896 830	894 420	1 002 700	1 066 929
5110 Impôts généraux	146 240	221 410	354 800	432 821	478 000	518 930	522 090	512 200	561 400	608 140
5111 Taxes sur la valeur ajoutée	146 240	221 410	354 800	432 821	478 000	518 930	522 090	512 200	561 400	608 140
5112 Impôts sur les ventes	0	0	0	0	0	0	0	0	0	0
5113 Autres impôts	0	0	0	0	0	0	0	0	0	0
5120 Impôts sur biens et services déterminés	143 680	163 180	242 900	316 910	321 400	365 130	374 740	382 220	441 300	458 789
5121 Accises	6 140	61 100	82 700	83 600	82 600	77 800	79 800	76 095	84 100	88 821
Taxe spécifique sur les prod. pétroliers	..	..	62 600	59 300	63 900	55 600	53 800	53 740	59 600	61 520
Taxes sur les tabacs	..	..	8 483	9 016	9 647	9 931	13 116	13 205	13 289	14 566
Taxes sur les corps gras	..	..	4 148	1 745	978	993	1 375	2 648	1 447	1 965
Taxes sur les alcools	..	..	3 535	5 987	5 297	5 278	4 975	5 498	5 382	5 516
Taxe sur la cola	..	..	278	439	273	203	183	48	26	19
Taxe sur les thés	..	..	121	334	154	95	102	125	124	153
Taxe sur le café	..	..	140	502	175	216	153	285	367	428
Taxe sur les produits comestiques	..	..	0	0	0	0	0	500	1 400	1 465
Autres accises non classées ailleurs	..	..	3 395	6 277	2 176	5 484	6 096	46	2 466	3 189
5122 Bénéfices des monopoles fiscaux	0	0	0	0	0	0	0	0	0	0
5123 Droits de douane et droits à l'importation	129 500	90 340	138 900	163 810	181 600	203 800	195 200	218 000	221 100	226 100
5124 Taxes à l'exportation	0	0	0	0	0	0	0	0	0	0
5125 Impôts sur biens d'équipement	0	0	0	0	0	0	0	0	0	0
5126 Impôts sur services déterminés	8 040	11 740	21 300	37 600	45 000	55 900	62 500	63 825	69 500	71 200
Taxe sur les activités financières (TAF)	6 400	9 340	17 600	28 500	30 600	34 300	39 100	40 340	45 800	47 700
Redevance d'utilisation des télécommunications	0	0	0	5 100	10 000	16 700	18 600	18 645	18 700	19 500
Taxe sur les contrats d'assurances	1 640	2 400	3 700	4 000	4 400	4 900	4 800	4 840	5 000	4 000
5127 Autres impôts sur commerce et transact. internat.	0	0	0	0	0	0	0	0	0	0

Table 4.11. Senegal / Sénégal (*cont.*)
Details of tax revenue / Recettes fiscales détaillées

Million XOF

	1997	2000	2005	2009	2010	2011	2012	2013	2014	2015
5128 Autres impôts	0	0	0	31 900	12 200	27 630	37 240	24 300	66 600	72 668
Fonds de sécurisation des importations de produits pétroliers	..	..	..	31 900	12 200	27 630	32 240	19 400	62 600	69 451
Contribution spéciale des produits des mines et carrières	..	..	..	0	0	0	5 000	4 900	4 000	3 218
5130 Non ventilables entre 5110 et 5120	0	0	0	0	0	0	0	0	0	0
5200 Impôts sur utilisation des biens et exerc. activites	1 900	2 350	4 000	4 700	5 000	6 000	6 000	6 400	8 000	8 100
5210 Impôts périodiques	1 900	2 350	4 000	4 700	5 000	6 000	6 000	6 400	8 000	8 100
5211 A la charge des ménages: véhicules à moteur	..	..	..	..	..	..	..	..	..	..
5212 A la charge autres agents: véhicules à moteur	..	..	..	..	..	..	..	..	..	..
5213 Autres impôts périodiques	..	..	..	..	..	..	..	..	..	..
5220 Impôts non-périodiques	0	0	0	0	0	0	0	0	0	0
5300 Non ventilables entre 5100 et 5200	0	0	0	0	0	0	0	0	0	0
6000 Autres impôts	**6 200**	**8 500**	**11 540**	**11 900**	**12 300**	**13 000**	**12 500**	**15 400**	**16 800**	**22 700**
6100 A la charge exclusive des entreprises	..	..	..	..	..	..	..	..	..	..
6200 A la charge d'autres agents	..	..	..	..	..	..	..	..	..	..

Note: Année civile se terminant le 31 décembre.

Les données sont sur la base des encaissements.

Les chiffres n'incluent pas les données des recettes fiscales collectées par les collectivités locales car elles ne sont pas disponibles.

Les chiffres ne comprennent pas les taxes parafiscales car elles ne sont pas disponibles. Les taxes parafiscales pourraient s'élever à un montant d'environ 70 milliards, objectif programmé du gouvernement dans la loi de finances 2015.

La rubrique 2000 comprend les cotisations de sécurité sociale de l'Institution de prévoyance retraite du Sénégal (IPRES) et exclut les cotisations de sécurité sociale de la Caisse de Sécurité Sociale (CSS) qui ne sont pas disponibles. Les cotisations de sécurité sociale au Sénégal antérieures à 2006 sont estimées.

La rubrique 5126 comprend la redevance sur l'accès ou l'utilisation du réseau des télécommunications publiques (RUTEL) classifiée comme accise au Sénégal.

Les recettes fiscales incluent les amendes et pénalités sur impôts et taxes désormais considérées comme des recettes non fiscales suite à un changement de la classification OCDE depuis la publication de la première édition. Il n'a pas été possible pour cette édition de séparer le versement des amendes et pénalités des recettes correspondant aux impôts auxquels ces amendes et pénalités se rattachent. La classification nationale du Sénégal les compte comme des recettes fiscales.

Source: Ministère de l'Économie, des Finances et du Plan.

StatLink http://dx.doi.org/10.1787/888933570561

Table 4.12. South Africa / Afrique du Sud
Details of tax revenue / Recettes fiscales détaillées

Million ZAR

	1997	2000	2005	2009	2010	2011	2012	2013	2014	2015
Total tax revenue	**158 556**	**211 566**	**412 457**	**644 142**	**702 316**	**794 345**	**872 171**	**966 559**	**1 056 866**	**1 168 516**
1000 Taxes on income, profits and capital gains	**89 772**	**119 979**	**220 197**	**357 740**	**368 118**	**412 135**	**447 924**	**490 305**	**541 543**	**604 879**
1100 Of individuals	65 681	87 105	122 279	198 117	219 886	243 056	267 952	300 559	338 974	389 883
1110 On income and profits	65 681	87 105	122 279	198 117	219 886	243 056	267 952	300 559	338 974	389 883
1120 On capital gains	..	..	..	..	..	..	..	..	..	..
1200 Corporate	19 409	23 987	82 628	142 319	132 275	149 777	155 751	173 738	182 083	191 348
1210 On profits	19 409	23 987	82 628	142 319	132 275	149 777	155 751	173 738	182 083	191 348
1220 On capital gains	..	..	..	..	..	..	..	..	..	..
1300 Unallocable between 1100 and 1200	4 682	8 887	15 290	17 303	15 957	19 303	24 220	16 008	20 486	23 647
2000 Social security contributions	**0**	**0**	**6 446**	**10 455**	**10 754**	**11 947**	**13 788**	**13 909**	**15 337**	**16 828**
2100 Employees	..	..	3 223	5 227	5 377	5 974	6 894	6 955	7 669	8 414
2110 On a payroll basis	..	..	0	0	0	0	0	0	0	0
2120 On an income tax basis	..	..	3 223	5 227	5 377	5 974	6 894	6 955	7 669	8 414
2200 Employers	..	..	3 223	5 227	5 377	5 974	6 894	6 955	7 669	8 414
2210 On a payroll basis	..	..	0	0	0	0	0	0	0	0
2220 On an income tax basis	..	..	3 223	5 227	5 377	5 974	6 894	6 955	7 669	8 414
2300 Self-employed or non-employed	..	..	0	0	0	0	0	0	0	0
2310 On a payroll basis	..	..	..	..	..	..	..	..	..	..
2320 On an income tax basis	..	..	..	..	..	..	..	..	..	..
2400 Unallocable between 2100, 2200 and 2300	..	..	0	0	0	0	0	0	0	0
2410 On a payroll basis	..	..	..	..	..	..	..	..	..	..
2420 On an income tax basis	..	..	..	..	..	..	..	..	..	..
3000 Taxes on payroll and workforce	**0**	**870**	**4 839**	**7 737**	**8 240**	**9 885**	**11 334**	**11 900**	**13 264**	**15 111**
4000 Taxes on property	**2 592**	**3 829**	**18 916**	**31 700**	**36 257**	**39 296**	**42 129**	**48 182**	**53 513**	**60 783**
4100 Recurrent taxes on immovable property	0	0	8 292	23 159	27 190	31 041	33 984	38 150	41 502	46 291
4110 Households	..	..	7 954	22 566	26 694	30 533	33 502	37 659	40 950	45 807
4120 Others	..	..	338	593	496	509	482	491	551	484
4200 Recurrent taxes on net wealth	0	0	0	0	0	0	0	0	0	0
4210 Individual	..	..	..	..	..	..	..	..	..	..
4220 Corporate	..	..	..	..	..	..	..	..	..	..
4300 Estate, inheritance and gift taxes	304	436	626	888	855	1 065	887	1 266	1 519	2 065
4310 Estate and inheritance taxes	287	417	598	815	794	1 013	820	1 163	1 349	1 918
4320 Gift taxes	17	19	28	73	61	53	67	103	170	147
4400 Taxes on financial and capital transactions	439	1 094	1 718	3 294	2 912	2 919	3 147	3 617	4 098	5 069
4500 Non-recurrent taxes	1 850	2 299	8 280	4 359	5 300	4 270	4 112	5 149	6 394	7 358
4510 On net wealth	0	0	0	0	0	0	0	0	0	0
4520 Other non-recurrent taxes	1 850	2 299	8 280	4 359	5 300	4 270	4 112	5 149	6 394	7 358
4600 Other recurrent taxes on property	0	0	0	0	0	0	0	0	0	0
5000 Taxes on goods and services	**64 471**	**84 467**	**161 196**	**237 451**	**278 924**	**321 102**	**356 967**	**402 257**	**433 237**	**470 916**
5100 Taxes on production, sale, transfer, etc	64 471	84 467	157 868	233 027	273 602	315 028	350 226	394 896	425 654	463 058
5110 General taxes	39 461	52 059	107 553	148 721	170 548	194 296	207 480	231 545	256 482	277 532
5111 Value added taxes	39 461	52 059	107 553	148 708	170 552	194 295	207 472	231 528	256 464	277 530
5112 Sales tax	0	0	0	14	-5	1	9	16	17	2
5113 Other	0	0	0	0	0	0	0	0	0	0
5120 Taxes on specific goods and services	25 010	32 408	50 315	84 306	103 054	120 732	142 746	163 352	169 172	185 526
5121 Excises	19 091	24 341	35 490	63 158	76 240	87 407	96 044	103 156	112 446	137 512
5122 Profits of fiscal monopolies	0	0	0	0	0	0	0	0	0	0
5123 Customs and import duties	6 273	7 714	13 294	19 134	25 196	30 930	43 584	54 881	54 631	43 965
Import duties	..	..	13 294	19 134	25 196	30 930	37 470	42 794	44 390	32 130
Ad valorem Imported	..	..	0	0	0	0	4 251	8 011	7 573	3 340
Excise Imported	..	..	0	0	0	0	1 862	4 076	2 668	8 495
5124 Taxes on exports	0	0	0	19	61	65	60	72	118	121
5125 Taxes on investment goods	0	0	0	0	0	0	0	0	0	0
5126 Taxes on specific services	0	0	1 320	1 922	2 252	2 405	2 792	2 967	2 992	3 224
5127 Other taxes on internat. trade and transactions	-353	353	211	73	-695	-74	266	2 276	-1 015	703
5128 Other taxes	0	0	0	0	0	0	0	0	0	0
5130 Unallocable between 5110 and 5120	0	0	0	0	0	0	0	0	0	0
5200 Taxes on use of goods and perform activities	0	0	3 328	4 424	5 322	6 073	6 741	7 361	7 583	7 858
5210 Recurrent taxes	..	..	3 328	4 424	5 322	6 073	6 741	7 361	7 583	7 858
5211 Paid by households: motor vehicles	..	..	2 644	3 321	4 046	4 762	5 224	5 742	5 879	6 234
5212 Paid by others: motor vehicles	..	..	661	830	1 012	1 191	1 306	1 436	1 470	1 558
5213 Paid in respect of other goods	..	..	23	273	264	120	210	184	234	66
5220 Non-recurrent taxes	..	..	0	0	0	0	0	0	0	0
5300 Unallocable between 5100 and 5200	0	0	0	0	0	0	0	0	0	0
6000 Other taxes	**1 721**	**2 421**	**863**	**-941**	**23**	**-20**	**29**	**5**	**-29**	**-1**
6100 Paid solely by business	0	0	0	0	0	0	0	0	0	0
6200 Other	1 721	2 421	863	-941	23	-20	29	5	-29	-1

Note: Year ending 31st December. Some fiscal year data have been adjusted to align to calendar years. Social security contributions and taxes at provincial and local level are reported on a fiscal year basis beginning 1st April. For example, the data for 2015 represent April 2015 to March 2016.

Data prior to 1995/96 were restated retrospectively to aggregate the revenues from TBVC States and Self-Governing Territories.

With the adoption of the interim Constitution in 1994, these were abolished.

-TBVC States: Transkei, Bophuthatswana, Venda and Ciskei.

- Self-Governing Territories: Gazankulu, Kangwane, Kwandebele, Kwazulu, Lebowa and Qwaqwa.

Tax revenues on national and provincial government level in South Africa are on a cash basis, while local authorities and public entities are on an accrual basis.

Tax revenues at the local and provincial levels are only available from 2003 (representing fiscal year 2003/04).

Headings 1110 and 1120: The figures include Capital Gains Tax (CGT). CGT cannot been listed separately under 1120 and 1220 because the data that South African Revenue Service (SARS) collated for CGT are for liability raised and not actual CGT collections received. The figures exclude interest and fines from 1994 onwards.

Heading 1300: includes revenue from the small business tax amnesty, the tax on retirement funds, the SDC/dividends tax and other small revenues.

Heading 2000: the social security contributions in South Africa consist of contributions to the Unemployment Insurance Fund (UIF). Standard practice in South Africa is to classify UIF under non-tax revenue. The methodology applied in the compilation of the data was to allocate 50% of the total social security contributions (UIF) to each of employees and employers.

Heading 4120: the figures refer to penalties and collection charges on property rates.

Heading 5111: includes interests and fines.

Heading 5121: following the OECD classification, the Road accident fund (RAF) is classified as an excise. The national classification of South Africa classifies this revenue as a social security contribution.

Headings 5121 and 5123: The data for customs duties and excise include revenue on import duties plus specific and ad valorem excise duties that will be paid to Botswana, Lesotho, Namibia and Swaziland (BLNS) through the revenue sharing agreement.

Heading 5123: SARS only started separately reporting ordinary custom duties on imported goods, specific excise duties on imported goods and ad valorem duties on imported goods from April 2012. From April 2014 onwards, the Customs Duty amounts for the specific tariff headings under chapter 27 (Mineral Fuels) were treated as fuel levies (5121 Excises).

Headings 5127 and 6200: include negative figures due to refund accounting adjustments.

Heading 5211: an 80:20 ratio was used to split provincial recurrent motor vehicle taxes based on research about South Africa's commercial and private household motor vehicle fleet.

Heading 6200: includes stamp duties and fees plus unallocated tax revenue.

Taxes that were discontinued and introduced (causing breaks in the data) include the following:

a. Ordinary levy discontinued in March 2003 (heading 5127).

b. Demutualisation charge has been included in heading 4400. There were two collections in March 1999 and August 1999.

c. Secondary Tax on Companies (STC) in heading 1300 effective from July 1993 and changed to Dividends Tax (DT) in April 2012.

d. Small business tax amnesty (heading 1300) effective from March 2007.

e. VAT (heading 5111) effective from September 1991 at a rate of 10% and increased to 14% in 1993. Prior to that, sales tax data was restated to VAT.

f. Levy on financial services (heading 4400) effective from January 1992.

g. Skills development levy (heading 3000) effective from May 2000.

h. Excises (5121)

- Plastic bags effective from June 2005.
- Electricity levy effective from August 2009.
- Incandescent light bulbs effective from March 2010.
- CO2 tax effective from September 2010.

i. Air departure tax (heading 5126) effective from December 2000.

j. Universal services fund (heading 5213) effective from March 2006.

Source: Data on national government taxation from the South African Revenue Service (SARS); data on social security contributions, and taxes levied at the provincial and local level from the National Treasury of South Africa.

StatLink http://dx.doi.org/10.1787/888933570580

Table 4.13. Swaziland
Details of tax revenue / Recettes fiscales détaillées

Thousand SZL

	1997	2000	2005	2009	2010	2011	2012	2013	2014	2015
Total tax revenue	**961 137**	**1 302 977**	**2 416 969**	**3 993 069**	**4 601 770**	**5 071 268**	**5 299 107**	**6 269 671**	**7 116 193**	**7 658 721**
1000 Taxes on income, profits and capital gains	**528 572**	**677 241**	**1 288 611**	**2 195 887**	**2 373 042**	**2 640 775**	**2 288 944**	**3 061 856**	**3 676 053**	**3 770 878**
1100 Of individuals	255 703	427 518	804 247	1 367 681	1 448 624	1 604 825	1 363 901	1 772 230	2 061 795	2 195 492
1110 On income and profits	255 703	427 518	804 247	1 367 681	1 448 624	1 604 825	1 363 901	1 772 230	2 061 795	2 195 492
Pay-as-you-earn tax (PAYE)	248 877	421 201	733 178	1 253 507	1 321 331	1 510 134	1 326 807	1 751 679	2 048 527	2 175 815
Provisional income tax (farmers, directors, individuals)	1 568	1 821	16 061	11 817	75 393	69 384	15 907	128	77	119
Taxes on interest, dividends and trust income	0	0	8 087	15 712	35 459	8 184	12 572	652	388	606
Personal income tax on non-residents	133	119	406	72 915	2 886	2 631	5 002	1 253	747	1 165
Tax on benefits	0	0	5 215	11 071	11 254	12 032	61	16 553	9 864	15 385
Withholding tax on resident suppliers of goods and services	0	0	40 063	30	114	12	258	85	51	79
Personal income tax on the self employed	4 636	3 656	229	1 001	621	213	1 719	3	4	4
Lottery levy	489	721	1 009	1 628	1 566	2 234	1 576	1 878	2 139	2 320
1120 On capital gains	..	..	..	..	..	..	..	..	..	..
1200 Corporate	250 929	235 974	461 179	808 561	904 652	968 390	872 683	1 215 768	1 569 882	1 506 964
1210 On profits	250 929	235 974	461 179	808 561	904 652	968 390	872 683	1 215 768	1 569 882	1 506 964
Corporate income tax on resident companies	249 704	233 074	393 997	674 252	738 681	814 531	736 640	1 059 687	1 468 423	1 358 128
Taxes on royalties	0	0	53 694	110 221	144 171	132 004	124 316	45 027	26 832	41 850
Corporate income tax on non-resident companies	1 225	2 900	13 488	24 088	21 800	21 856	11 728	111 054	74 627	106 986
1220 On capital gains	..	..	..	..	..	..	..	..	..	..
1300 Unallocable between 1100 and 1200	21 941	13 749	23 185	19 645	19 766	67 560	52 361	73 857	44 376	68 422
Income taxes on non-residents	19 567	11 139	20 293	15 231	15 404	62 753	50 160	71 963	42 883	66 886
Other taxes on income	2 374	2 610	2 891	4 414	4 362	4 807	2 201	1 894	1 493	1 537
2000 Social security contributions	**114 087**	**153 871**	**286 847**	**532 165**	**626 150**	**620 313**	**637 227**	**654 474**	**710 456**	**822 564**
2100 Employees	28 525	38 488	71 806	127 461	156 719	159 456	159 602	164 092	177 678	205 848
2110 On a payroll basis	..	..	..	..	..	..	..	..	..	..
2120 On an income tax basis	..	..	..	..	..	..	..	..	..	..
2200 Employers	85 562	115 383	215 041	404 704	469 430	460 858	477 626	490 382	532 779	616 716
2210 On a payroll basis	..	..	..	..	..	..	..	..	..	..
2220 On an income tax basis	..	..	..	..	..	..	..	..	..	..
2300 Self-employed or non-employed	0	0	0	0	0	0	0	0	0	0
2310 On a payroll basis	..	..	..	..	..	..	..	..	..	..
2320 On an income tax basis	..	..	..	..	..	..	..	..	..	..
2400 Unallocable between 2100, 2200 and 2300	0	0	0	0	0	0	0	0	0	0
2410 On a payroll basis	..	..	..	..	..	..	..	..	..	..
2420 On an income tax basis	..	..	..	..	..	..	..	..	..	..
3000 Taxes on payroll and workforce	**0**	**0**	**0**	**0**	**0**	**0**	**0**	**0**	**0**	**0**
4000 Taxes on property	**7 734**	**10 349**	**65 650**	**92 268**	**106 435**	**125 485**	**130 824**	**158 277**	**162 522**	**175 827**
4100 Recurrent taxes on immovable property	..	..	40 730	62 165	67 637	79 104	85 449	91 221	96 184	105 514
Local property taxes	..	..	40 730	62 165	67 637	79 104	85 449	91 221	96 184	105 514
4110 Households	..	..	..	..	..	..	..	..	..	..
4120 Others	..	..	..	..	..	..	..	..	..	..
4200 Recurrent taxes on net wealth	..	..	0	0	0	0	0	0	0	0
4210 Individual	..	..	..	..	..	..	..	..	..	..
4220 Corporate	..	..	..	..	..	..	..	..	..	..
4300 Estate, inheritance and gift taxes	..	..	1	17	0	0	0	15 897	9 473	14 776
4310 Estate and inheritance taxes	..	..	1	17	0	0	0	15 897	9 473	14 776
Tax on trust beneficiaries	..	..	1	17	0	0	0	15 897	9 473	14 776
4320 Gift taxes	..	..	0	0	0	0	0	0	0	0
4400 Taxes on financial and capital transactions	7 734	10 349	24 918	30 087	38 798	46 381	45 375	51 158	56 865	55 538
Transfer duties	2 627	5 377	13 333	18 186	26 371	24 035	27 434	34 301	33 379	30 101
Stamp duties	5 107	4 972	11 585	11 901	12 427	22 346	17 941	16 857	23 486	25 437
4500 Non-recurrent taxes	0	0	0	0	0	0	0	0	0	0
4510 On net wealth	..	..	..	..	..	..	..	..	..	..
4520 Other non-recurrent taxes	..	..	..	..	..	..	..	..	..	..
4600 Other recurrent taxes on property	0	0	0	0	0	0	0	0	0	0
5000 Taxes on goods and services	**310 744**	**461 517**	**775 861**	**1 172 750**	**1 496 143**	**1 684 695**	**2 242 111**	**2 395 065**	**2 567 161**	**2 889 452**
5100 Taxes on production, sale, transfer, etc	299 904	449 319	758 289	1 114 987	1 441 793	1 623 679	2 182 110	2 330 458	2 498 758	2 821 029
5110 General taxes	254 784	371 664	661 491	997 644	1 255 389	1 342 238	1 756 482	1 731 031	1 894 950	2 107 173
5111 Value added taxes	0	0	0	0	0	0	1 623 295	1 695 188	1 883 319	2 107 173
5112 Sales tax	254 784	371 664	661 491	997 644	1 255 389	1 342 238	133 188	35 843	11 631	0
5113 Other	0	0	0	0	0	0	0	0	0	0
5120 Taxes on specific goods and services	45 120	77 655	96 799	117 343	186 404	281 441	425 628	599 427	603 809	713 856
5121 Excises	42 270	75 416	73 379	91 300	147 560	206 034	381 457	549 427	572 993	666 808
Fuel taxes	42 270	75 416	73 379	91 300	147 560	206 034	381 457	549 427	572 993	666 808
5122 Profits of fiscal monopolies	0	0	0	0	0	0	0	0	0	0
5123 Customs and import duties	0	0	0	0	0	0	0	0	0	0

Table 4.13. Swaziland (cont.)
Details of tax revenue / Recettes fiscales détaillées

Thousand SZL

	1997	2000	2005	2009	2010	2011	2012	2013	2014	2015
5124 Taxes on exports	5	0	7	5	2	3	3	1	0	2
Cattle export tax	5	0	7	5	2	3	3	1	0	2
5125 Taxes on investment goods	0	0	0	0	0	0	0	0	0	0
5126 Taxes on specific services	2 845	2 239	23 413	26 038	38 843	75 404	44 168	49 999	30 816	47 046
Tax on management fees	0	0	16 592	24 405	37 276	73 167	42 590	44 763	26 675	41 605
Taxes on lotteries, gaming and betting	2 845	2 239	6 820	1 632	1 567	2 235	1 576	5 235	4 141	5 441
Other taxes on services and hospitality	1	0	2	1	1	2	2	1	0	0
5127 Other taxes on internat. trade and transactions	0	0	0	0	0	0	0	0	0	0
5128 Other taxes	0	0	0	0	0	0	0	0	0	0
5130 Unallocable between 5110 and 5120	0	0	0	0	0	0	0	0	0	0
5200 Taxes on use of goods and perform activities	10 841	12 198	17 572	57 763	54 350	61 015	60 001	64 607	68 403	68 423
5210 Recurrent taxes	7 070	7 677	12 832	30 308	29 575	32 291	31 900	35 347	37 889	37 711
5211 Paid by households: motor vehicles	4 132	4 399	1 486	11 042	10 689	12 087	12 054	13 778	14 963	15 834
5212 Paid by others: motor vehicles	0	0	0	0	0	0	0	0	0	0
5213 Paid in respect of other goods	2 938	3 278	11 346	19 266	18 886	20 203	19 846	21 569	22 927	21 877
Trading licences	1 131	1 270	8 246	12 582	10 824	12 627	12 139	13 304	14 369	14 109
Company licences	1 333	1 425	2 316	5 827	7 128	6 567	6 688	7 255	7 513	6 593
Special activities licences (gaming, casino, labor agents, cattle slaughter)	475	583	784	858	934	1 009	1 020	1 009	1 044	1 176
5220 Non-recurrent taxes	3 771	4 521	4 740	27 455	24 776	28 725	28 101	29 260	30 513	30 712
Road tolls	3 319	4 064	3 938	26 771	24 121	28 090	27 431	28 589	29 829	30 180
Firearm registration fees	452	457	802	684	655	634	670	672	684	532
5300 Unallocable between 5100 and 5200	0	0	0	0	0	0	0	0	0	0
6000 Other taxes	**0**	**0**	**0**	**0**	**0**	**0**	**0**	**0**	**0**	**0**
6100 Paid solely by business	..	..	..	..	..	..	..	..	..	..
6200 Other	..	..	..	..	..	..	..	..	..	..

Note: Data are reported on a fiscal year basis beginning 1st April. For example, the data for 2014 represent April 2014 to March 2015.

The data are on a cash basis.

Heading 5211: This heading includes revenue from motor vehicle licences, the change of ownership fees and the registration of new motor vehicles. These revenues are considered as tax revenue according to the OECD classification, described in the interpretative guide in Annex A. The national classification of Swaziland classifies these revenues as non-tax revenues.

Heading 5213: This heading includes revenue from business and sundry licences. These revenues are considered as tax revenues according to the OECD classification, described in the interpretative guide in Annex A. The national classification of Swaziland classifies them as non-tax revenues.

Heading 5220: This heading includes revenue from the registrations of specific goods (e.g firearms). These revenues are considered as tax revenues under the OECD classification, as set out in the Interpretative Guide in Annex A. The national classification of Swaziland classifies these revenues as non-tax revenues.

Revenue from PAYE Penalties, tax interest and penalties on taxes are considered as non-tax revenue under the OECD classification, as set out in the Interpretative Guide in Annex A. The national classification of Swaziland classifies these revenues as tax revenues.

Source: Swaziland Revenue Authority.

StatLink http://dx.doi.org/10.1787/888933570599

Table 4.14. Togo
Details of tax revenue / Recettes fiscales détaillées

Million XOF

	1997	2000	2005	2009	2010	2011	2012	2013	2014	2015
Recettes fiscales totales	..	**100 017**	**159 896**	**228 427**	**246 280**	**291 003**	**327 180**	**409 242**	**461 990**	**523 697**
1000 Impôts sur revenu, bénéfices et gains en capital	..	**21 640**	**39 315**	**50 416**	**43 947**	**52 088**	**54 447**	**79 420**	**96 010**	**97 374**
1100 Des personnes physiques	..	8 962	16 158	15 145	15 676	17 294	19 054	24 684	17 934	23 848
1110 Sur le revenu et les bénéfices	..	8 962	16 158	15 145	15 676	17 294	19 054	24 684	17 934	23 848
Impôt sur le revenu des transporteurs routiers	..	452	514	481	393	186	265	204	266	374
Retenue sur les revenus des capitaux mobiliers	..	912	1 582	1 551	5 071	4 040	3 131	4 457	3 454	3 456
Impôt sur le revenu des personnes physiques (non ventilé)	..	7 598	14 062	13 113	10 212	13 069	15 658	20 023	14 215	20 018
1120 Sur les gains en capital	..	..	..	..	..	..	..	..	..	..
1200 Des sociétés	..	12 678	23 157	35 271	28 271	34 794	35 392	54 736	78 076	73 526
1210 Sur les bénéfices	..	12 678	23 157	35 271	28 271	34 794	35 392	54 736	78 076	73 526
Impôt sur les sociétés	..	7 672	13 440	16 474	13 435	19 363	19 139	28 622	31 195	35 840
Recouvrement des exercices antérieurs	..	2 525	5 878	13 611	9 919	12 644	13 776	23 247	41 104	30 996
Prélèvement bénéfices industriels et commerciaux (BIC)	..	2 481	3 839	5 186	4 917	2 787	2 477	2 867	5 777	6 691
1220 Sur les gains en capital	..	..	..	..	..	..	..	..	..	..
1300 Non ventilables entre 1100 et 1200	..	0	0	0	0	0	0	0	0	0
2000 Cotisations de sécurité sociale	..	..	..	..	..	..	..	..	..	..
2100 A la charge des salariés	..	..	..	..	..	..	..	..	..	..
2110 Sur la base du salaire	..	..	..	..	..	..	..	..	..	..
2120 Sur la base de l'impôt sur les revenus	..	..	..	..	..	..	..	..	..	..
2200 A la charge des employeurs	..	..	..	..	..	..	..	..	..	..
2210 Sur la base du salaire	..	..	..	..	..	..	..	..	..	..
2220 Sur la base de l'impôt sur le revenu	..	..	..	..	..	..	..	..	..	..
2300 A charge des travailleurs indép. ou sans emploi	..	..	..	..	..	..	..	..	..	..
2310 Sur la base du salaire	..	..	..	..	..	..	..	..	..	..
2320 Sur la base de l'impôt sur le revenu	..	..	..	..	..	..	..	..	..	..
2400 Non ventilables entre 2100, 2200 et 2300	..	..	..	..	..	..	..	..	..	..
2410 Sur la base du salaire	..	..	..	..	..	..	..	..	..	..
2420 Sur la base de l'impôt sur le revenu	..	..	..	..	..	..	..	..	..	..
3000 Sur salaires ou main d'oeuvre	..	**1 865**	**2 213**	**3 899**	**4 746**	**4 389**	**5 396**	**4 636**	**7 599**	**3 328**
Taxe complémentaire à l'impôt sur le revenu	..	36	70	397	1 044	538	1 015	1 220	5 159	630
Taxes/salaires	..	1 829	2 144	3 502	3 702	3 851	4 380	3 415	2 440	2 698
4000 Impôts sur le patrimoine	..	**340**	**519**	**781**	**760**	**834**	**992**	**971**	**1 220**	**1 475**
4100 Impôts périodiques sur la propriété immobilière	..	340	519	781	760	834	992	971	1 220	1 475
Taxe foncière sur les propriétés bâties	..	243	355	461	425	480	504	469	699	861
Droits d'immatriculation des propriétés foncières	..	96	164	320	335	355	487	502	521	613
4110 Ménages	..	..	..	..	..	..	..	..	..	..
4120 Autres agents	..	..	..	..	..	..	..	..	..	..
4200 Impôts périodiques sur l'actif net	..	0	0	0	0	0	0	0	0	0
4210 Personnes physiques	..	..	..	..	..	..	..	..	..	..
4220 Sociétés	..	..	..	..	..	..	..	..	..	..
4300 Impôts sur mut. par décès, succ. et donations	..	0	0	0	0	0	0	0	0	0
4310 Impôts sur mut. par décès et successions	..	..	..	..	..	..	..	..	..	..
4320 Impôts sur les donations	..	..	..	..	..	..	..	..	..	..
4400 Impôts sur transact. mobilières et immob.	..	0	0	0	0	0	0	0	0	0
4500 Impôts non-périodiques	..	0	0	0	0	0	0	0	0	0
4510 Sur l'actif net	..	..	..	..	..	..	..	..	..	..
4520 Autres non-périodiques	..	..	..	..	..	..	..	..	..	..
4600 Autres impôts périodiques sur patrimoine	..	0	0	0	0	0	0	0	0	0
5000 Impôts sur les biens et services	..	**74 249**	**115 428**	**168 356**	**191 432**	**226 548**	**259 691**	**315 475**	**348 068**	**413 303**
5100 Impôts sur production, vente, transfert, etc.	..	74 148	115 286	168 165	191 301	226 291	259 361	315 097	347 245	412 214
5110 Impôts généraux	..	36 489	63 068	94 183	106 811	130 426	151 891	178 990	204 468	237 865
5111 Taxes sur la valeur ajoutée	..	35 655	62 014	92 535	105 043	128 411	149 584	175 635	200 493	231 388
Taxe sur la valeur ajoutée (Douanes)	..	25 101	44 182	63 106	69 840	89 433	98 240	97 847	128 864	161 480
Taxe sur la valeur ajoutée (Intérieure)	..	10 553	17 832	27 365	35 203	38 978	51 344	39 114	57 653	64 160
Soutien à la politique pétrolière	..	0	0	2 064	0	0	0	38 675	13 976	5 748
5112 Impôts sur les ventes	..	0	0	0	0	0	0	0	0	0
5113 Autres impôts	..	834	1 054	1 648	1 768	2 015	2 307	3 355	3 975	6 477
Taxe professionnelle unique	..	143	148	327	317	365	357	312	346	471
Taxe professionnelle	..	691	906	1 321	1 451	1 650	1 950	3 042	3 629	6 006
5120 Impôts sur biens et services déterminés	..	37 634	52 191	73 951	84 457	95 831	107 461	136 107	142 776	174 349
5121 Accises	..	12 751	14 721	15 253	16 090	15 862	20 206	30 270	29 358	35 126
Droits d'accises/produits pétroliers	..	11 738	11 771	10 368	11 468	12 748	13 947	19 722	16 850	17 954
Autres droits d'accises	..	1 012	2 951	4 885	4 622	3 114	6 259	3 847	7 033	8 240
Prélèvement dette secteur pétrolier	..	0	0	0	0	0	0	6 701	5 475	8 932
5122 Bénéfices des monopoles fiscaux	..	0	0	0	0	0	0	0	0	0

Table 4.14. Togo (cont.)
Details of tax revenue / Recettes fiscales détaillées

Million XOF

	1997	2000	2005	2009	2010	2011	2012	2013	2014	2015
5123 Droits de douane et droits à l'importation	..	22 559	35 143	56 751	61 676	71 528	76 984	93 471	99 201	122 750
Droits de douane	..	18 519	30 023	48 761	52 941	60 999	65 744	80 115	83 234	101 730
Redevance statistique	..	2 717	3 720	6 096	6 763	7 968	8 379	10 104	12 740	13 578
Timbre douanier	..	94	138	228	297	321	336	424	359	424
Cartes et vignettes	..	186	209	246	238	372	441	406	385	369
Taxe de protection et d'entretien des infrastructures	..	1 039	1 050	1 418	1 434	1 863	2 078	2 418	2 476	2 958
Produits des crédits en douane	..	2	2	1	2	1	1	4	6	5
Prélèvement national de solidarité	..	0	0	0	0	0	0	0	0	3 686
Remises	..	1	0	0	0	0	0	0	0	0
Entrepôts fictifs	..	1	2	1	3	3	4	0	1	0
5124 Taxes à l'exportation	..	302	314	1 041	1 430	1 756	1 506	1 881	2 544	2 728
Taxe spéciale de réexportation	..	302	314	1 041	1 430	1 756	1 506	1 235	1 947	2 260
Redevance minière (66,67%)	..	0	0	0	0	0	0	646	597	468
5125 Impôts sur biens d'équipement	..	0	0	0	0	0	0	0	0	0
5126 Impôts sur services déterminés	..	2 022	2 012	905	5 261	6 685	8 765	10 485	11 674	13 746
Taxe sur les produits des jeux de hasard	..	149	201	216	343	280	736	882	643	899
Taxe/convention d'assurance	..	207	332	690	747	811	1 158	1 227	1 275	1 812
Taxe sur les activités financières	..	1 666	1 480	0	4 171	5 594	6 871	8 377	9 756	11 035
5127 Autres impôts sur commerce et transact. internat.	..	0	0	0	0	0	0	0	0	0
5128 Autres impôts	..	0	0	0	0	0	0	0	0	0
5130 Non ventilables entre 5110 et 5120	..	25	28	32	33	34	10	0	0	0
5200 Impôts sur utilisation des biens et exerc. activites	..	101	141	191	132	258	330	378	823	1 088
5210 Impôts périodiques	..	101	141	191	132	258	330	378	823	1 088
5211 A la charge des ménages: véhicules à moteur	..	0	0	0	0	0	0	0	0	0
5212 A la charge autres agents: véhicules à moteur	..	0	0	0	0	0	0	3	26	62
5213 Autres impôts périodiques	..	101	141	191	132	258	330	375	797	1 027
5220 Impôts non-périodiques	..	0	0	0	0	0	0	0	0	0
5300 Non ventilables entre 5100 et 5200	..	0	0	0	0	0	0	0	0	0
6000 Autres impôts	**..**	**1 923**	**2 422**	**4 975**	**5 396**	**7 143**	**6 655**	**8 741**	**9 093**	**8 218**
Droits de timbres	..	1 457	1 637	2 373	3 078	2 655	3 250	2 849	2 760	3 418
Droits d'enregistrement	..	465	784	2 602	2 318	4 488	3 405	5 891	6 333	4 801
6100 A la charge exclusive des entreprises	..	..	..	..	..	..	..	..	..	..
6200 A la charge d'autres agents	..	..	..	..	..	..	..	..	..	..

Note: Année civile se terminant le 31 décembre.

Les données sont sur la base des encaissements.

Les chiffres n'incluent pas les données des recettes fiscales collectées par les collectivités locales car elles ne sont pas disponibles.

Rubrique 2000 : Les données de cotisations de sécurité sociales ne sont pas disponibles.

Rubrique 5111 : les recettes relatives à l'impôt de soutien à la politique pétrolière sont levées à partir des recettes douanières de TVA.

Rubrique 5121 : le prélèvement pour apurement de la dette du secteur pétrolier (PADSP) est considéré comme une recette fiscale dans cette publication comme le préconise (voir le guide d'interprétation en Annexe A). La classification nationale du Togo compte ces recettes comme des recettes non fiscales.

La classification nationale du Togo compte les amendes et pénalités relatives aux impôts, les confiscations et ventes en douane et les remboursements du prélèvement communautaire de solidarité comme des recettes fiscales. Ces recettes sont classifiées comme des recettes non fiscales dans cette publication comme le préconise la classification OCDE (voir le guide d'interprétation en Annexe A).

Source: Office Togolais des Recettes.

StatLink http://dx.doi.org/10.1787/888933570618

Table 4.15. Tunisia / Tunisie
Details of tax revenue / Recettes fiscales détaillées

Million TND

	1997	2000	2005	2009	2010	2011	2012	2013	2014	2015
Recettes fiscales totales	..	**7 169**	**10 130**	**15 679**	**17 126**	**18 784**	**20 439**	**22 390**	**24 998**	**25 613**
1000 Impôts sur revenu, bénéfices et gains en capital	..	**1 624**	**2 927**	**4 701**	**5 091**	**5 959**	**5 921**	**6 879**	**7 955**	**7 678**
1100 Des personnes physiques	..	1 049	1 565	2 435	2 658	2 918	3 188	3 711	4 096	5 003
1110 Sur le revenu et les bénéfices	..	1 037	1 560	2 423	2 644	2 905	3 173	3 686	4 058	4 965
Traitements et salaires	..	743	1 160	1 843	2 006	2 326	2 640	3 068	3 260	3 549
Honoraires, commissions, courtage et loyers	..	20	93	158	184	177	180	205	236	364
Intérêts des dépôts des comptes spéciaux d'épargne	..	65	43	61	68	90	82	102	125	159
Revenus des capitaux mobiliers	..	32	63	79	75	62	57	69	87	212
Avances sur les marchés	..	27	24	48	50	45	41	46	56	313
Bénéfices industriels et commerciaux	..	43	56	90	94	78	76	95	98	119
Bénéfices non commerciaux	..	17	24	39	49	44	41	46	71	76
Impôt forfaitaire	..	14	16	23	25	13	23	22	31	36
Revenus agricoles	..	5	4	8	8	5	9	11	15	19
Revenus fonciers et autres	..	6	4	6	8	7	9	10	12	14
Autres impôts sur le revenu et bénéfices	..	66	73	69	78	59	15	13	67	105
1120 Sur les gains en capital	..	12	5	12	14	12	15	25	38	39
1200 Des sociétés	..	575	1 360	2 264	2 432	3 041	2 730	3 165	3 855	2 673
1210 Sur les bénéfices	..	575	1 359	2 253	2 424	3 035	2 722	3 159	3 848	2 659
Sociétés pétrolières	..	96	459	647	813	999	1 117	1 439	1 575	950
Sociétés non-pétrolières	..	359	644	926	864	1 258	822	779	1 138	1 088
Avances sur les marchés	..	33	97	309	356	346	331	389	478	222
Avance au titre des importations	..	7	28	97	111	124	156	166	184	198
Revenus des capitaux mobiliers	..	58	68	114	113	144	141	174	215	72
Honoraires, commissions, courtage et loyers	..	16	52	128	125	125	127	169	183	86
Redevances servies aux non résidents	..	3	8	30	39	35	26	36	53	18
Autres impôts sur les bénéfices	..	3	3	2	3	3	2	8	22	25
1220 Sur les gains en capital	..	0	1	12	8	6	7	6	7	14
1300 Non ventilables entre 1100 et 1200	..	0	2	2	2	1	3	3	4	2
2000 Cotisations de sécurité sociale	..	**1 551**	**2 307**	**4 098**	**4 629**	**5 210**	**5 839**	**6 504**	**6 882**	**7 549**
2100 A la charge des salariés	..	..	..	..	..	..	..	..	..	..
2110 Sur la base du salaire	..	..	..	..	..	..	..	..	..	..
2120 Sur la base de l'impôt sur les revenus	..	..	..	..	..	..	..	..	..	..
2200 A la charge des employeurs	..	..	..	..	..	..	..	..	..	..
2210 Sur la base du salaire	..	..	..	..	..	..	..	..	..	..
2220 Sur la base de l'impôt sur le revenu	..	..	..	..	..	..	..	..	..	..
2300 A charge des travailleurs indép. ou sans emploi	..	..	..	..	..	..	..	..	..	..
2310 Sur la base du salaire	..	..	..	..	..	..	..	..	..	..
2320 Sur la base de l'impôt sur le revenu	..	..	..	..	..	..	..	..	..	..
2400 Non ventilables entre 2100, 2200 et 2300	..	1 551	2 307	4 098	4 629	5 210	5 839	6 504	6 882	7 549
2410 Sur la base du salaire	..	..	..	..	..	..	..	..	..	..
2420 Sur la base de l'impôt sur le revenu	..	..	..	..	..	..	..	..	..	..
3000 Sur salaires ou main d'oeuvre	..	**107**	**114**	**171**	**199**	**212**	**224**	**242**	**285**	**315**
Fonds de promotion des logements	..	72	74	115	124	136	143	147	177	191
Taxe de formation professionnelle	..	35	40	56	75	76	81	96	107	124
4000 Impôts sur le patrimoine	..	**81**	**104**	**172**	**177**	**218**	**228**	**244**	**257**	**282**
4100 Impôts périodiques sur la propriété immobilière	..	7	7	9	10	4	8	8	8	11
4110 Ménages	..	7	7	9	10	4	8	8	8	11
4120 Autres agents	..	0	0	0	0	0	0	0	0	0
4200 Impôts périodiques sur l'actif net	..	0	0	0	0	0	0	0	0	0
4210 Personnes physiques	..	..	..	..	..	..	..	..	..	..
4220 Sociétés	..	..	..	..	..	..	..	..	..	..
4300 Impôts sur mut. par décès, succ. et donations	..	0	0	0	0	0	0	0	0	0
4310 Impôts sur mut. par décès et successions	..	..	..	..	..	..	..	..	..	..
4320 Impôts sur les donations	..	..	..	..	..	..	..	..	..	..
4400 Impôts sur transact. mobilières et immob.	..	74	97	164	168	213	220	236	248	271
4500 Impôts non-périodiques	..	0	0	0	0	0	0	0	0	0
4510 Sur l'actif net	..	..	..	..	..	..	..	..	..	..
4520 Autres non-périodiques	..	..	..	..	..	..	..	..	..	..
4600 Autres impôts périodiques sur patrimoine	..	0	0	0	0	0	0	0	0	0
5000 Impôts sur les biens et services	..	**3 729**	**4 567**	**6 266**	**6 768**	**6 866**	**7 892**	**8 116**	**9 099**	**9 168**
5100 Impôts sur production, vente, transfert, etc.	..	3 665	4 458	6 131	6 612	6 724	7 726	7 948	8 903	8 977
5110 Impôts généraux	..	1 814	2 347	3 468	3 819	3 918	4 465	4 581	5 267	5 211
5111 Taxes sur la valeur ajoutée	..	1 792	2 301	3 400	3 750	3 850	4 383	4 460	5 117	5 068
5112 Impôts sur les ventes	..	0	0	0	0	0	0	0	0	0
5113 Autres impôts	..	21	46	69	69	69	82	121	150	144
5120 Impôts sur biens et services déterminés	..	1 851	2 111	2 663	2 793	2 806	3 261	3 367	3 637	3 765

Table 4.15. Tunisia / Tunisie (*cont.*)
Details of tax revenue / Recettes fiscales détaillées

Million TND

	1997	2000	2005	2009	2010	2011	2012	2013	2014	2015
5121 Accises	..	1 023	1 340	1 781	1 814	1 801	2 109	2 143	2 315	2 397
Tabac	..	371	602	826	799	893	1 033	1 014	1 085	1 087
Boissons alcoolisées	..	147	146	154	174	164	218	267	303	290
Essences et huiles	..	260	269	257	268	266	263	258	279	305
Voitures	..	86	91	180	242	167	241	251	251	289
Produits alimentaires	..	19	28	34	31	31	32	35	45	42
Ciment	..	11	13	15	17	17	16	18	20	17
Autres accises	..	131	192	314	282	262	306	299	332	369
5122 Bénéfices des monopoles fiscaux	..	0	0	0	0	0	0	0	0	0
5123 Droits de douane et droits à l'importation	..	654	524	578	620	617	763	796	882	918
Hors tabac	..	566	424	401	428	432	562	570	603	639
Redevances sur prestations douanières à l'importation	..	68	82	115	142	139	157	166	182	155
Taxe conjoncturelle sur ventes du ciment importé	..	0	0	0	0	0	0	18	41	61
Tabac	..	9	12	21	23	22	28	27	31	27
Autres droits de douane	..	0	4	3	4	3	2	2	2	1
Prèlevements à l'importation	..	12	3	34	20	19	11	11	18	29
Autres taxes et prélèvements à l'importation	..	1	1	4	3	4	3	3	5	7
5124 Taxes à l'exportation	..	11	9	19	27	36	43	38	38	41
5125 Impôts sur biens d'équipement	..	0	0	0	0	0	0	0	0	0
5126 Impôts sur services déterminés	..	162	237	283	330	352	346	389	401	409
Taxe sur les télécommunications	..	72	91	103	136	150	139	160	151	147
Taxe de compensation sur les transports	..	55	84	97	105	102	113	119	123	126
Taxe sur les assurances	..	33	59	79	86	97	92	109	120	129
Autres impôts sur services déterminés	..	2	2	3	3	3	2	2	8	7
5127 Autres impôts sur commerce et transact. internat.	..	0	0	0	0	0	0	0	0	0
5128 Autres impôts	..	0	1	2	2	1	1	1	1	1
5130 Non ventilables entre 5110 et 5120	..	0	0	0	0	0	0	0	0	0
5200 Impôts sur utilisation des biens et exerc. activites	..	64	109	135	156	142	167	168	196	191
5210 Impôts périodiques	..	55	77	94	103	98	111	116	124	134
5211 A la charge des ménages: véhicules à moteur	..	36	44	55	60	56	64	69	74	81
5212 A la charge autres agents: véhicules à moteur	..	18	28	39	43	41	47	46	49	53
5213 Autres impôts périodiques	..	1	6	0	0	0	0	0	0	0
5220 Impôts non-périodiques	..	9	32	41	53	44	56	53	72	57
5300 Non ventilables entre 5100 et 5200	..	0	0	0	0	0	0	0	0	0
6000 Autres impôts	**..**	**77**	**111**	**270**	**262**	**320**	**335**	**406**	**520**	**622**
Droits de timbres	..	25	32	157	133	215	208	256	288	334
Droits d'enregistrements	..	40	67	95	107	85	103	124	145	181
Droits sur les voyages à l'étranger	..	0	0	0	0	0	0	0	30	33
Divers	..	12	12	18	22	19	24	26	58	76
6100 A la charge exclusive des entreprises	..	..	..	..	..	..	..	..	..	..
6200 A la charge d'autres agents	..	..	..	..	..	..	..	..	..	..

Note: Année civile se terminant le 31 décembre.

Les données sont sur la base des encaissements.

Les chiffres n'incluent pas les données des recettes fiscales collectées par les collectivités locales car elles ne sont pas disponibles.

Les impôts affectés aux Fonds spéciaux du Trésor et aux Fonds de concours sont compris dans les données pour la période 2000-15.

La rubrique 1210 exclut les redevances des compagnies pétrolières. En Tunisie, elles sont considérées comme un complément de l'impôt sur les sociétés depuis avril 2012.

Les cotisations de sécurité sociale sous la rubrique 2000 ne sont pas considérées comme des recettes fiscales en Tunisie.

Source: Ministère des Finances pour toutes les données des recettes fiscales. Ministère des Affaires Sociales pour les données de cotisations de sécurité sociale.

StatLink http://dx.doi.org/10.1787/888933570637

Table 4.16. Uganda / Ouganda
Details of tax revenue / Recettes fiscales détaillées

Million UGX

	1997	2000	2005	2009	2010	2011	2012	2013	2014	2015
Total tax revenue	**733 544**	**999 659**	**1 935 003**	**3 803 052**	**4 329 610**	**5 250 150**	**6 303 346**	**7 220 538**	**8 065 048**	**9 697 884**
1000 Taxes on income, profits and capital gains	**102 453**	**181 905**	**560 351**	**1 092 461**	**1 340 327**	**1 686 313**	**2 104 213**	**2 578 064**	**2 744 735**	**3 387 654**
1100 Of individuals	79 577	142 306	400 329	811 643	968 399	1 208 508	1 448 015	1 757 795	1 989 167	2 382 480
1110 On income and profits	79 577	142 306	400 329	811 643	968 399	1 208 508	1 448 015	1 757 795	1 989 167	2 382 480
PAYE	38 332	83 471	245 325	555 710	657 920	825 644	996 933	1 196 504	1 397 556	1 612 994
Rental income tax	2 800	5 500	8 292	10 961	10 105	15 350	0	0	0	27 649
Other income tax	9 319	11 220	13 899	21 626	19 001	8 014	1 685	17 898	53 616	42 189
Withholding taxes	29 125	42 115	132 813	223 347	281 373	359 500	449 398	543 392	537 995	699 648
WHT on imports	15 499	23 349	47 399	64 606	68 581	84 766	120 477	154 012	131 294	152 787
WHT on general supplies	0	0	85 414	78 082	120 061	218 314	234 302	223 256	232 028	282 825
WHT on government payments	0	0	0	19 914	44 446	55 672	94 159	154 236	60 016	89 368
WHT on management and professional fees	0	0	0	44 510	24 886	84	0	1 982	35 883	45 447
WHT on dividends	0	0	0	9 259	11 237	70	28	5 455	33 926	61 823
WHT non-residents	0	0	0	4 510	1 356	14	296	4 451	44 832	57 106
Other WHT or unidentified	13 627	18 766	0	2 466	10 806	581	135	1	17	10 293
1120 On capital gains	..	..	..	..	..	..	..	..	..	..
1200 Corporate	22 849	35 391	151 738	218 998	305 274	404 237	553 927	597 635	486 636	714 772
1210 On profits	22 849	35 391	151 738	218 998	305 274	404 237	553 927	597 635	486 636	714 772
1220 On capital gains	..	..	..	..	..	..	..	..	..	..
1300 Unallocable between 1100 and 1200	27	4 207	8 284	61 819	66 654	73 568	102 271	222 635	268 932	290 401
2000 Social security contributions	**..**	**..**	**..**	**..**	**..**	**..**	**..**	**..**	**..**	**..**
2100 Employees	..	..	..	..	..	..	..	..	..	..
2110 On a payroll basis	..	..	..	..	..	..	..	..	..	..
2120 On an income tax basis	..	..	..	..	..	..	..	..	..	..
2200 Employers	..	..	..	..	..	..	..	..	..	..
2210 On a payroll basis	..	..	..	..	..	..	..	..	..	..
2220 On an income tax basis	..	..	..	..	..	..	..	..	..	..
2300 Self-employed or non-employed	..	..	..	..	..	..	..	..	..	..
2310 On a payroll basis	..	..	..	..	..	..	..	..	..	..
2320 On an income tax basis	..	..	..	..	..	..	..	..	..	..
2400 Unallocable between 2100, 2200 and 2300	..	..	..	..	..	..	..	..	..	..
2410 On a payroll basis	..	..	..	..	..	..	..	..	..	..
2420 On an income tax basis	..	..	..	..	..	..	..	..	..	..
3000 Taxes on payroll and workforce	**0**	**0**	**0**	**0**	**0**	**0**	**0**	**0**	**0**	**0**
4000 Taxes on property	**..**	**..**	**..**	**..**	**..**	**..**	**..**	**..**	**..**	**..**
4100 Recurrent taxes on immovable property	..	..	..	..	..	..	..	..	..	..
4110 Households	..	..	..	..	..	..	..	..	..	..
4120 Others	..	..	..	..	..	..	..	..	..	..
4200 Recurrent taxes on net wealth	..	..	..	..	..	..	..	..	..	..
4210 Individual	..	..	..	..	..	..	..	..	..	..
4220 Corporate	..	..	..	..	..	..	..	..	..	..
4300 Estate, inheritance and gift taxes	..	..	..	..	..	..	..	..	..	..
4310 Estate and inheritance taxes	..	..	..	..	..	..	..	..	..	..
4320 Gift taxes	..	..	..	..	..	..	..	..	..	..
4400 Taxes on financial and capital transactions	..	..	..	..	..	..	..	..	..	..
4500 Non-recurrent taxes	..	..	..	..	..	..	..	..	..	..
4510 On net wealth	..	..	..	..	..	..	..	..	..	..
4520 Other non-recurrent taxes	..	..	..	..	..	..	..	..	..	..
4600 Other recurrent taxes on property	..	..	..	..	..	..	..	..	..	..
5000 Taxes on goods and services	**634 359**	**845 835**	**1 414 113**	**2 725 439**	**2 961 165**	**3 524 324**	**4 226 226**	**4 779 448**	**5 468 931**	**6 438 279**
5100 Taxes on production, sale, transfer, etc	615 074	823 285	1 350 040	2 654 052	2 871 634	3 411 758	4 119 915	4 660 669	5 325 586	6 288 808
5110 General taxes	221 285	359 755	674 981	1 345 327	1 470 584	1 735 249	2 118 763	2 567 489	2 778 653	3 293 693
5111 Value added taxes	221 285	359 755	674 981	1 345 327	1 470 584	1 735 249	2 118 763	2 567 489	2 778 653	3 293 693
VAT on imports	133 454	195 496	375 862	819 377	799 173	1 011 007	1 195 517	1 288 318	1 424 759	1 783 518
VAT on phone talk time	0	0	0	54 628	93 277	68 244	98 331	142 033	141 352	151 747
VAT on beer	11 542	11 586	16 771	24 542	37 034	52 441	75 167	97 365	96 412	108 831
VAT on electricity	0	0	0	54 520	74 584	45 062	60 668	135 306	162 673	112 812
VAT on sugar	0	0	0	46 346	64 276	72 225	62 439	109 802	71 294	110 801
VAT on soft drinks	5 018	5 139	12 028	16 665	15 846	25 845	28 283	34 901	30 268	32 385
VAT on cement	0	0	0	21 712	25 161	21 017	24 228	30 237	37 356	53 086
VAT on cigarettes	8 074	6 905	6 641	1 382	1 411	1 406	1 223	2 538	6 767	16 760
Other VAT	63 196	140 630	263 679	306 155	359 821	438 002	572 908	726 989	807 773	923 754
5112 Sales tax	0	0	0	0	0	0	0	0	0	0
5113 Other	0	0	0	0	0	0	0	0	0	0
5120 Taxes on specific goods and services	393 789	463 530	675 059	1 308 725	1 401 050	1 676 509	2 001 152	2 093 181	2 546 933	2 995 115

Table 4.16. Uganda / Ouganda *(cont.)*
Details of tax revenue / Recettes fiscales détaillées

Million UGX

	1997	2000	2005	2009	2010	2011	2012	2013	2014	2015
5121 Excises	104 264	132 953	187 615	256 213	275 929	316 626	472 853	610 214	700 426	834 589
Excise tax on beer	40 704	59 938	60 704	85 183	98 864	118 781	159 485	170 717	144 223	146 853
Excise tax on phone talk time	0	0	24 901	88 730	99 490	100 751	113 826	147 560	170 432	184 175
Excise tax on soft drinks	14 439	13 348	15 304	24 560	27 907	37 834	47 616	53 520	59 338	71 799
Excise tax on cigarettes	29 761	33 572	28 633	7 308	7 698	6 553	7 386	9 911	14 246	14 979
Excise tax on spirits/waragi	1 353	915	6 463	11 955	10 376	17 999	19 664	34 240	45 555	53 331
Excise on international calls	0	0	0	0	0	0	0	0	68 162	65 142
Excise tax on sugar	0	0	0	13 004	17 187	13 744	5 539	7 351	7 479	17 854
Excise tax on cement	1	1	1	8 296	8 228	11 719	10 898	13 179	15 729	17 773
Other excise taxes	18 007	25 180	51 610	83 287	84 179	101 543	140 312	173 737	175 262	262 684
Tax refunds due to diesel tax exemption	0	0	0	-66 110	-77 999	-92 297	-31 872	0	0	0
5122 Profits of fiscal monopolies	0	0	0	0	0	0	0	0	0	0
5123 Customs and import duties	288 233	330 339	485 911	1 050 307	1 123 130	1 347 159	1 522 321	1 475 564	1 832 368	2 133 482
Petroleum duty	197 456	197 202	309 024	632 319	716 234	821 181	920 898	794 836	984 245	1 197 749
Surcharge on used imports	0	0	0	32 867	38 621	47 760	50 268	61 213	72 889	95 895
Non-oil imports	2 233	5 301	3 653	25 050	21 651	30 798	45 091	20 780	27 702	0
Commission on imports	16 271	22 746	19 567	0	2	0	0	0	0	0
Other import duties	72 274	105 090	153 668	360 071	346 622	447 420	506 063	598 735	747 533	839 838
5124 Taxes on exports	0	0	1 165	1 137	122	7 929	586	1	3 126	13 186
5125 Taxes on investment goods	0	0	0	0	0	0	0	0	0	0
5126 Taxes on specific services	1 293	238	368	1 068	1 869	4 795	5 392	7 401	11 012	13 858
Casino and lottery tax	1 293	238	368	1 068	1 869	4 795	5 392	7 401	11 012	13 858
Bank charges	0	0	0	0	0	0	0	0	0	0
5127 Other taxes on internat. trade and transactions	0	0	0	0	0	0	0	0	0	0
5128 Other taxes	0	0	0	0	0	0	0	0	0	0
5130 Unallocable between 5110 and 5120	0	0	0	0	0	0	0	0	0	0
5200 Taxes on use of goods and perform activities	19 285	22 551	64 073	71 388	89 531	112 566	106 312	118 779	143 345	149 472
5210 Recurrent taxes	16 823	17 890	52 440	47 834	64 096	67 421	63 786	69 983	92 857	91 886
5211 Paid by households: motor vehicles	16 823	17 890	52 440	47 834	64 096	67 421	63 786	69 983	92 857	91 886
Fees and licences	16 823	17 890	52 440	47 834	64 096	67 421	63 786	69 983	92 857	91 886
Road user charges	0	0	0	0	0	0	0	0	0	0
5212 Paid by others: motor vehicles	0	0	0	0	0	0	0	0	0	0
5213 Paid in respect of other goods	0	0	0	0	0	0	0	0	0	0
5220 Non-recurrent taxes	2 462	4 660	11 633	23 554	25 434	45 144	42 525	48 796	50 488	57 586
5300 Unallocable between 5100 and 5200	0	0	0	0	0	0	0	0	0	0
6000 Other taxes	**-3 268**	**-28 081**	**-39 461**	**-14 849**	**28 119**	**39 513**	**-27 093**	**-136 975**	**-148 618**	**-128 049**
6100 Paid solely by business	0	0	0	0	0	0	0	0	0	0
6200 Other	-3 268	-28 081	-39 461	-14 849	28 119	39 513	-27 093	-136 975	-148 618	-128 049
Stamp duties and embossing fees	1 818	1 919	6 946	20 952	26 256	32 018	106 749	26 620	39 558	48 557
Coffee stabilisation tax	2 484	0	0	0	0	0	0	0	0	0
Government payments on behalf of private companies	0	0	0	0	0	0	0	15 059	0	0
Un-allocated revenue	0	0	0	0	29 457	58 767	2 772	2 046	0	0
Tax refunds	-7 570	-30 000	-46 407	-35 800	-27 594	-51 273	-136 614	-180 700	-188 175	-176 606

Note: Data are reported on a fiscal year basis beginning 1st July. For example, the data for 2015 represent July 2014 to June 2015.

The data are on a cash basis.

Figures exclude tax revenues collected by sub-national governments as the data are not available.

Heading 4000: Property tax is levied annually by local authorities. Revenue from property tax is not available.

Heading 5111: "VAT on imports" is the sum of VAT on imports in "the taxes on international trade" section and VAT on imports in the "government taxes" section of the Uganda Revenue Authority's budget document. "Other VAT revenues" combines revenues from spirits/waragi, bottled water, water, and other goods and services.

Heading 5121: The "other excises taxes" category combines excise revenues from bottled water, cosmetics and mobile money transfers (all three in the "Indirect Domestic Taxes: excises" section of the Uganda Revenue Authority's budget document) with revenue from the excise duty (in the "taxes on international trade" section) and the excise duty (in the "government taxes" section).

Heading 6200: Revenue in this category is negative as it includes tax refunds that could not be allocated to the appropriate tax category.

Revenue from driver permits are considered non-tax revenue under the OECD classification, as set out in the Interpretative Guide in Annex A. The national classification of Uganda classifies this revenue as tax revenue.

Source: Uganda Revenue Authority.

StatLink http://dx.doi.org/10.1787/888933570656

Chapter 5

Non-tax revenues, 1997-2015

Chapitre 5

Recettes non fiscales, 1997-2015

Chapter 5 / Chapitre 5

Non-tax revenue tables, 1997-2015

In all of the following tables a ("..") indicates not available or not applicable. The main series in this volume cover the years 1990 to 2015.

Figures referring to 1998-99, 2001-04 and 2006-08 in Table 5.1 and Tables 5.4 to 5.20 have been omitted because of lack of space. Complete series are, however, available on line at *http://dx.doi.org/10.1787/93add7a4-en*.

Tableaux des recettes non fiscales, 1997-2015

Dans tous les tableaux suivants le symbole (« .. ») signifie que l'information n'est pas disponible ou qu'elle n'est pas applicable. Les principales séries dans ce volume couvrent les années 1990 à 2015.

Les années 1998-99, 2001-04 et 2006-08 dans le tableau 5.1 et les tableaux 5.4 à 5.20 ont été omis en raison du manque d'espace. Les séries complètes sont cependant disponibles en ligne sur *http://dx.doi.org/10.1787/ef1bbbc4-fr*.

Table 5.1. Total non-tax revenue as % of GDP, 1997-2015
Tableau 5.1. Total des recettes non fiscales en % du PIB, 1997-2015

	1997	2000	2005	2009	2010	2011	2012	2013	2014	2015
Cabo Verde	16.1	7.6	9.2	8.8	9.7	5.6	6.0	6.2	5.3	7.4
Cameroon / Cameroun	5.3	8.0	6.9	4.6	4.8	6.2	5.0	4.9	4.2	4.3
Congo, Dem. Rep. / Congo, Rép. dém.[1]	..	..	..	..	9.9	3.9	5.7	3.6	5.3	4.9
Côte d'Ivoire	1.4	1.1	2.3	3.6	1.7	1.5	1.9	2.5	2.6	3.4
Ghana[1,2]	..	2.2	4.3	5.7	5.0	5.3	6.1	6.2	5.6	6.1
Kenya[1,3]	..	..	2.9	1.5	0.9	..	..	1.3	0.9	1.0
Mauritius / Maurice[4]	4.0	2.8	2.5	4.3	3.8	3.5	3.1	3.2	2.7	2.7
Morocco / Maroc	..	2.2	3.0	3.7	3.6	3.9	3.7	4.1	3.8	3.9
Niger	..	..	8.2	5.6	6.3	4.9	8.0	9.5	8.0	7.6
Rwanda	7.5	11.8	12.7	11.9	12.3	12.3	8.8	11.2	9.4	8.9
Senegal / Sénégal	2.4	2.7	2.3	3.6	3.2	2.9	3.8	3.8	5.2	4.6
South Africa / Afrique du Sud	0.3	0.5	0.5	0.4	0.6	0.7	0.7	0.7	0.6	0.6
Swaziland[5]	12.4	12.4	15.9	18.2	8.1	6.8	19.5	17.4	17.1	15.1
Togo[1]	..	2.1	2.5	5.9	7.2	6.2	4.3	5.3	4.2	4.1
Tunisia / Tunisie[1]	..	4.6	2.6	3.2	2.9	4.0	3.5	3.6	2.4	2.1
Uganda / Ouganda[1]	..	..	6.7	2.8	2.9	2.1	2.2	1.2	1.3	1.8

Note: The figures include sub-national government non-tax revenues for Mauritius, Morocco and Swaziland. Sub-national government tax revenues are not available in other countries.

1. Historical data are not available for the Democratic Republic of the Congo (prior to 2010), Ghana (prior to 2000), Kenya (in 2006 and prior to 2005), Niger (prior to 2005), Togo (prior to 2000), Tunisia (prior to 2000) and Uganda (prior to 2002).
2. The figures should be treated with caution. The data prior to 2010 exclude oil and mineral royalties that could not be distinguished from tax revenues.
3. The data are incomplete for 2011 and 2012 and a figure for total non-tax revenue was not derived for these years.
4. Estimated figures for 2015.
5. The figures exclude grants prior to 2012 as the data are not available.

Note : Les chiffres incluent les recettes non fiscales des collectivités infranationales pour le Maroc, Maurice et le Swaziland.

1. Les données historiques ne sont pas disponibles pour la République démocratique du Congo (avant 2010), le Ghana (avant 2000), le Kenya (en 2006 et avant 2005), le Niger (avant 2005), le Togo (avant 2000), la Tunisie (avant 2005) et en Ouganda (avant 2002).
2. Les chiffres doivent être interprétés avec prudence. Les données antérieures à 2010 excluent les redevances pétrolières et minérales qui ne peuvent être distinguées des recettes fiscales.
3. Les données sont incomplètes pour 2011 et 2012 et un chiffre des recettes non fiscales totales n'a pas été calculé pour ces années.
4. Les chiffres sont estimés pour 2015.
5. Les chiffres excluent les dons avant 2012 car les données ne sont pas disponibles.

StatLink http://dx.doi.org/10.1787/888933570675

Table 5.2. Non-tax revenue of main headings as percentage of GDP, 2015
Tableau 5.2. Recettes non fiscales sous les principales rubriques en % du PIB, 2015

	Grants / Dons	Property income / Revenus de la propriété	Sales of goods and services / Ventes de biens et de services	Fines, penalties and forfeits / Amendes, pénalités et confiscations	Miscellaneous and unidentified revenue / Recettes diverses et non identifiées[3]
Cabo Verde	2.5	0.6	2.9	0.3	1.1
Cameroon / Cameroun	0.1	2.8	1.1	0.2	0.1
Congo, Dem. Rep. / Congo, Rép. dém.	3.4	0.9	0.5	0.1	0.0
Côte d'Ivoire	1.5	1.5	0.2	0.0	0.3
Ghana	1.9	1.9	2.3	0.0	0.0
Kenya	0.3	0.3	0.2	0.0	0.2
Mauritius / Maurice[1]	0.5	1.1	1.0	0.1	0.1
Morocco / Maroc	0.0	0.9	1.6	0.3	1.1
Niger	5.5	1.0	0.9	0.2	0.2
Rwanda[2]	6.3	..	..	..	2.6
Senegal / Sénégal	2.9	1.1	0.0	0.3	0.3
South Africa / Afrique du Sud	0.0	0.4	0.1	0.0	0.0
Swaziland	0.2	0.8	0.1	0.1	13.9
Togo	2.3	1.0	0.3	0.0	0.5
Tunisia / Tunisie	0.3	1.0	0.0	0.4	0.2
Uganda / Ouganda[2]	1.4	..	0.0	..	0.3

Note: The figures include sub-national government non-tax revenues for Mauritius, Morocco and Swaziland. Sub-national government tax revenues are not available in other countries.

1. Estimated figures for 2015.
2. Data for property income, sales of goods and services and fines, penalties and forfeits are included in miscellaneous and unidentified revenue.
3. Including capital transfers not elsewhere classified and voluntary transfers other than grants.

Note : Les chiffres incluent les recettes non fiscales des collectivités infranationales pour le Maroc, Maurice et le Swaziland. Les recettes non fiscales des collectivités infranationales ne sont pas disponibles pour les autres pays.

1. Les chiffres sont estimés pour 2015.
2. Les données relatives aux revenus de propriété, les ventes de biens et de services, les amendes, les pénalités et les confiscations sont incluses dans la rubrique « recettes diverses et non identifiées ».
3. Y compris les transferts de capitaux non classés ailleurs et les transferts volontaires autres que les subventions.

StatLink http://dx.doi.org/10.1787/888933570694

Table 5.3. Non-tax revenue of main headings as percentage of total non-tax revenues, 2015
Tableau 5.3. Recettes non fiscales sous les principales rubriques en % du total des recettes non fiscales, 2015

	Grants / Dons	Property income / Revenus de la propriété	Sales of goods and services / Ventes de biens et de services	Fines, penalties and forfeits / Amendes, pénalités et confiscations	Miscellaneous and unidentified revenue / Recettes diverses et non identifiées[3]
Cabo Verde	33.3	8.6	39.1	3.5	15.4
Cameroon / Cameroun	2.5	64.6	26.1	3.7	3.1
Congo, Dem. Rep. / Congo, Rép. dém.	68.8	19.0	9.3	2.9	0.1
Côte d'Ivoire	43.1	43.7	5.4	0.0	7.8
Ghana	31.6	30.9	37.5	0.0	0.0
Kenya	26.3	29.0	20.5	2.6	21.6
Mauritius / Maurice[1]	17.2	39.9	35.7	2.7	4.4
Morocco / Maroc	0.0	23.2	41.1	7.8	27.9
Niger	71.9	12.5	11.2	2.1	2.4
Rwanda[2]	70.8	..	..	..	29.2
Senegal / Sénégal	62.4	23.0	0.0	7.6	7.0
South Africa / Afrique du Sud	6.3	75.0	11.3	5.0	2.4
Swaziland	1.6	5.2	1.0	0.4	91.8
Togo	56.0	25.0	7.5	0.5	10.9
Tunisia / Tunisie	16.7	49.3	1.6	21.6	10.8
Uganda / Ouganda[2]	82.4	..	1.2	..	16.4

Note: The figures include sub-national government non-tax revenues for Mauritius, Morocco and Swaziland. Sub-national government tax revenues are not available in other countries.

1. Estimated figures for 2015.
2. Data for property income, sales of goods and services and fines, penalties and forfeits are included in miscellaneous and unidentified revenue.
3. Including capital transfers not elsewhere classified and voluntary transfers other than grants.

Note : Les chiffres incluent les recettes non fiscales des collectivités infranationales pour le Maroc, Maurice et le Swaziland. Les recettes non fiscales des collectivités infranationales ne sont pas disponibles pour les autres pays.

1. Les chiffres sont estimés pour 2015.
2. Les données relatives aux revenus de propriété, les ventes de biens et de services, les amendes, les pénalités et les confiscations sont incluses dans la rubrique « recettes diverses et non identifiées ».
3. Y compris les transferts de capitaux non classés ailleurs et les transferts volontaires autres que les subventions.

StatLink http://dx.doi.org/10.1787/888933570713

Table 5.4. Total non-tax revenue in millions of US Dollars at market exchange rates
Tableau 5.4. Totale des recettes non fiscales en millions de dollars américains au taux de change du marché

	1997	2000	2005	2009	2010	2011	2012	2013	2014	2015
Cabo Verde	87	45	100	150	161	105	106	115	99	116
Cameroon / Cameroun	524	720	1 141	1 070	1 134	1 661	1 336	1 462	1 351	1 220
Congo, Dem. Rep. / Congo, Rép. dém.	..	..	..	..	2 046	953	1 562	1 167	1 890	1 884
Côte d'Ivoire	163	121	387	883	415	394	499	771	906	1 108
Ghana	..	178	744	1 453	1 612	2 112	2 559	2 943	2 170	2 293
Kenya	..	..	564	550	343	..	..	687	501	601
Mauritius / Maurice	169	128	161	395	372	393	353	381	338	313
Morocco / Maroc	..	873	1 889	3 430	3 323	3 949	3 607	4 407	4 153	3 939
Niger	..	..	276	302	363	317	557	728	662	548
Rwanda	135	203	327	640	712	799	647	853	754	736
Senegal / Sénégal	112	126	200	467	412	423	544	563	800	629
South Africa / Afrique du Sud	399	627	1 399	1 149	2 292	2 978	2 605	2 548	1 978	1 830
Swaziland	242	216	520	704	372	329	910	766	719	445
Togo	..	27	53	189	228	234	167	231	195	173
Tunisia / Tunisie	..	990	831	1 405	1 257	1 835	1 570	1 664	1 121	891
Uganda / Ouganda	..	..	603	498	553	425	503	313	367	471

Note: This table is derived by multiplying total non-tax revenue figures for each country (in millions of national currency) by the exchange rate figures shown in Table 3.18.

Note : Ce tableau est obtenu en multipliant les chiffres des recettes non fiscales en millions de monnaie nationale pour chaque pays par les taux de change du tableau 3.18.

StatLink http://dx.doi.org/10.1787/888933570732

Table 5.5. Cabo Verde

Details of non-tax revenue / Recettes non fiscales détaillées

Million CVE

	1997	2000	2005	2009	2010	2011	2012	2013	2014	2015
Total des recettes non fiscales	**8 119**	**5 372**	**8 902**	**11 946**	**13 396**	**8 298**	**9 074**	**9 574**	**8 211**	**11 528**
Dons	6 360	3 931	6 610	7 536	9 440	4 342	4 203	4 024	2 787	3 841
Transferts courants de gouvernements étrangers	6 360	0	0	0	0	0	0	254	228	364
Aide budgétaire	0	..	..	..	..	..	..	0	0	0
Aide alimentaire	949	..	..	..	..	..	..	0	0	0
Dons directs	4 606	..	..	..	..	..	..	253	228	347
Autre transfert courants	805	..	..	..	..	..	..	1	0	17
Transferts en capital de gouvernements étrangers	0	3 931	6 610	7 536	9 440	4 342	4 203	3 769	2 559	3 477
Aide budgétaire	..	0	551	2 180	3 085	1 711	573	1 199	1 041	1 282
Aide alimentaire	..	672	750	317	338	389	230	329	17	0
Dons directs	..	3 260	5 138	5 039	6 018	2 242	3 399	2 235	1 501	2 046
Autre dons en capital	..	0	171	0	0	0	0	6	0	150
Revenus de la propriété	367	364	95	905	316	339	384	476	209	994
Loyers et redevances	..	..	..	..	..	..	..	..	..	..
Intérêts et dividendes	..	..	..	..	..	..	..	..	..	..
Autres revenus de la propriété	..	..	..	..	..	..	..	..	..	..
Ventes de biens et de services	489	592	1 496	3 063	3 077	3 143	3 874	3 897	4 010	4 508
Prestations de service	201	448	1 445	3 005	3 003	3 043	3 796	3 734	3 823	4 348
Ventes de biens courants	288	144	51	59	74	100	78	163	187	160
Amendes, pénalités et confiscations	67	54	169	270	376	280	332	511	706	404
Recettes diverses et non identifiées	836	431	532	171	187	194	281	666	499	1 781
Autres transferts	257	413	150	58	41	85	195	32	128	39
Autres recettes diverses et non spécifiées	579	18	382	113	146	110	86	635	371	1 742
Total des recettes fiscales et non fiscales	15 445	16 346	27 874	37 303	39 434	37 625	36 426	37 451	35 070	41 572
Pour mémoire *: Prélèvement communautaire de la CEDEAO*[1]	0	67	156	219	245	290	262	266	258	254

Note: Année civile se terminant le 31 décembre.

Les données sont sur la base des encaissements.

Les chiffres n'incluent pas les données des recettes non fiscales collectées par les collectivités locales car elles ne sont pas disponibles.

La présente publication n'inclut pas le produit de la vente d'actifs non financiers rapporté dans les documents budgétaires du Cabo Verde. La classification nationale du Cabo Verde compte le produit de la vente d'actifs non financiers comme une recette non fiscale. Selon la classification de l'OCDE (voir le guide d'interprétation en Annexe B), le produit de la vente d'actifs n'est pas considéré comme une recette (fiscale ou non fiscale) car il ne représente pas une augmentation de la valeur nette résultant d'une transaction.

1. Le prélèvement communautaire de la CEDEAO (Communauté économique des États de l'Afrique de l'Ouest) n'est pas compris dans le total des recettes non fiscales ou fiscales et est présenté à titre de rubrique « Pour mémoire ». Le prélèvement communautaire de la CEDEAO est considéré comme une recette fiscale au Cabo Verde. Selon la classification de l'OCDE (voir le guide d'interprétation en Annexe A § 4), ce paiement n'est pas compris parmi les impôts.

Source: Ministère de Finance et du Plan du Cabo Verde.

StatLink http://dx.doi.org/10.1787/888933570751

Table 5.6. Cameroon / Cameroun
Details of non-tax revenue / Recettes non fiscales détaillées

Million XAF

	1997	2000	2005	2009	2010	2011	2012	2013	2014	2015
Total des recettes non fiscales	**283 502**	**527 053**	**600 552**	**503 912**	**560 690**	**782 963**	**681 934**	**722 010**	**666 820**	**721 082**
Dons	0	6 900	91 404	118 472	78 805	62 084	56 049	75 879	23 813	18 089
Revenus de la propriété	221 100	404 500	446 825	343 193	442 296	668 984	566 680	577 877	580 497	465 541
Loyers et redevances[1]	221 100	404 500	410 657	337 442	437 650	662 428	556 891	568 962	570 574	445 587
Redevance pétrolière	219 000	399 300	367 955	318 528	418 971	541 153	532 375	538 733	517 040	384 630
Droits de passage du pipeline	0	0	14 065	8 344	9 080	8 248	7 747	8 802	24 675	36 201
Autres loyers et redevances	2 100	5 200	28 637	10 570	9 599	113 027	16 769	21 428	28 860	24 756
Intérêts et dividendes	0	0	36 169	5 751	4 646	6 557	9 789	8 915	9 922	19 954
Autres revenus de la propriété	0	0	0	0	0	0	0	0	0	0
Ventes de biens et de services	30 400	33 500	40 263	37 810	37 732	41 027	47 664	62 682	52 990	188 402
Amendes, pénalités et confiscations	0	0	444	2 401	1 858	1 664	2 498	5 362	3 975	26 849
Recettes diverses et non identifiées[2]	32 002	82 153	21 616	2 037	0	9 204	9 043	211	5 546	22 201
Total des recettes fiscales et non fiscales	865 900	1 370 453	1 784 409	2 156 024	2 200 718	2 637 698	2 754 209	3 026 500	3 217 803	3 484 175

Note: Année civile se terminant le 31 décembre.

Les données sont sur la base des encaissements.

Les chiffres n'incluent pas les données des recettes non fiscales collectées par les collectivités locales car elles ne sont pas disponibles.

Les recettes non fiscales excluent les amendes de l'enregistrement, les pénalités sur impôts & taxes et les amendes douanières. Ces recettes sont désormais considérées comme des recettes non fiscales suite à un changement de la classification OCDE depuis la publication de la première édition. Il n'a pas été possible pour cette édition de séparer le versement des amendes et pénalités des recettes correspondant aux impôts auxquels ces amendes et pénalités se rattachent. La classification nationale du Cameroun les compte comme des recettes fiscales.

1. Cette rubrique inclut les taxes domaniales, la taxe à l'extraction des carrières et la redevance à la production des eaux comme le préconise la classification OCDE (voir le guide d'interprétation en Annexe B). La classification nationale du Cameroun les compte comme des recettes fiscales.
2. Y compris transferts de capitaux non compris ailleurs et transferts volontaires autres que les dons.

Source: Ministère des Finances du Cameroun.

StatLink http://dx.doi.org/10.1787/888933570770

Table 5.7. Congo, Dem. Rep./Congo, Rép. dém.
Details of non-tax revenue / Recettes non fiscales détaillées

Million CDF

	1997	2000	2005	2009	2010	2011	2012	2013	2014	2015
Total des recettes non fiscales	..	..	..	..	**1 853 773**	**875 991**	**1 435 833**	**1 073 387**	**1 748 052**	**1 745 912**
Dons	..	..	110 362	433 338	1 296 212	421 965	536 195	522 072	1 444 380	1 200 395
Revenus de la propriété	..	..	..	..	397 774	353 485	762 112	415 293	233 043	331 349
Loyers et redevances	..	..	..	..	358 125	253 394	638 268	345 027	176 059	293 035
Royalties des sociétés pétrolières	..	..	..	..	39 705	37 475	43 745	40 763	38 717	19 050
Redevance et royalty minières	..	..	..	..	65 476	0	90 355	110 014	891	138 601
Droits superficie annuels	..	..	..	..	25 340	25 294	21 639	20 788	1 466	20 102
Bonus de signature/renouvellement	..	..	..	..	4 566	631	3 294	521	23	624
Redevance annuelle sur l'exploitation et autres	..	..	..	..	50 599	26 005	44 297	33 755	6 382	38 632
Autorisation de concessions,extraction et autres	..	..	..	..	9 126	7 876	56 607	137	4 619	5 789
Permis ressources forestières et faune	..	..	..	..	3 541	5 156	1 549	1 487	350	387
Marge distribuable (recettes pétrolières)	..	..	..	..	84 491	125 412	124 474	132 450	123 433	52 694
Redevances superficiaires sur permis d'exploration et sur concession	..	..	..	..	10	3	2 435	13	0	8 791
Autres loyers	..	..	..	..	75 272	25 542	249 873	5 099	179	8 365
Intérêts et dividendes	..	..	..	..	39 301	99 704	123 073	69 526	56 880	37 159
Dividendes on shore (recettes pétrolières)	..	..	..	..	8 068	14 100	20 020	21 846	17 376	14 666
Participations off shore (recettes pétrolières)	..	..	..	..	25 347	50 190	37 339	39 726	36 372	15 806
Autres dividendes et participations	..	..	..	..	5 886	35 415	65 713	7 953	3 133	6 688
Autres revenus de la propriété	..	..	..	..	348	386	771	740	104	1 155
Ventes de biens et de services	..	..	..	..	123 659	71 485	88 202	94 908	22 492	161 726
Vente des imprimés[1]	..	158	7	431	1 106	3 118	1 292	1 312	1 881	690
Taxe de numérotation[2]	..	..	..	..	16 464	9 734	8 659	17 414	0	26 110
Taxe de régulation et taxe de modification des titres obtenus / télécommunications[2]	..	..	..	..	13 180	25 885	16 446	22 433	6	36 198
Passeport, visa et carte de travail	..	..	..	..	20 345	15 877	17 673	18 917	7 105	30 957
Taxes sur le gardiennage par la Police Nationale Congolaise[2]	..	..	..	..	4 247	1 149	3 058	3 346	1 814	11 337
Contrôle des produits d'origine toxique, soporifique et stupéfiante	..	..	..	..	647	711	5 034	1 582	2 456	7 328
Redevance sur la désinfection et le contrôle sanitaire des friperies	..	..	..	..	3 828	177	1 565	64	477	3 111
Agréments	..	..	..	..	1 359	182	334	278	96	1 045
Autres	..	..	..	..	62 483	14 653	34 142	29 562	8 658	44 951
Amendes, pénalités et confiscations	..	..	..	..	35 379	28 779	48 152	36 630	47 834	50 772
Amendes et pénalités (DGI)	..	418	2	8 704	15 455	14 738	25 696	30 848	42 138	15 160
Amendes et pénalités (DGDA)	..	2	40	657	1 561	6 941	3 429	1 424	1 615	4 093
Amendes et pénalités (DGRAD)	..	..	..	..	18 363	7 100	19 027	4 358	4 081	31 518
Recettes diverses et non identifiées	..	..	..	..	750	277	1 172	4 484	304	1 671
Total des recettes fiscales et non fiscales	..	..	..	..	3 519 475	2 977 834	4 165 630	4 401 716	5 340 459	5 611 148

Note: Année civile se terminant le 31 décembre.

Les données sont sur la base des encaissements.

Les chiffres n'incluent pas les données des recettes non fiscales collectées par les collectivités locales car elles ne sont pas disponibles.

Les données des dons sont issues de la base de données de la publication PEM 2017 (*Perspectives de l'économie mondiale 2017*) publiée par le FMI.

Les données autres que les dons sont disponibles à partir de 2010.

Pour la période 2010-15, 5 % en moyenne des recettes considérées comme non fiscales par la République Démocratique du Congo ont été classifiées comme recettes fiscales dans cette publication comme le préconise la classification OCDE (voir le guide d'interprétation en Annexe A). Ces recettes collectées par la DGRAD (Direction Générale des Recettes Administratives, Judiciaires, Domaniales et de Participations) sont entre autres les redevances sur produits spécifiques, les droits proportionnels sur les S.A.R.L, la taxe ad valorem sur les gains des parieurs, les autorisations d'exportation et d'importation, la taxe d'implémentation établissements dangereux/insalubres/incommodes et diverses autorisations.

1. Les recettes provenant de la vente des imprimés sont incluses dans les recettes non fiscales comme le préconise la classification OCDE (voir le guide d'interprétation en Annexe B). La classification nationale en République Démocratique du Congo classifie les recettes de la vente des imprimés comme des recettes fiscales.
2. Ces recettes – appelées taxes en République Démocratique du Congo – sont considérées comme des frais administratifs. Ces frais sont considérés comme étant proportionnels au coût d'une prestation de service rendue par une administration publique et sont donc classifiés comme des recettes non fiscales comme le préconise la classification OCDE (voir le guide d'interprétation en Annexe B).

Source: Ministère des Finances de la République Démocratique du Congo.

StatLink http://dx.doi.org/10.1787/888933570789

Table 5.8. Côte d'Ivoire

Details of non-tax revenue / Recettes non fiscales détaillées

Million XOF

	1997	2000	2005	2009	2010	2011	2012	2013	2014	2015
Total des recettes non fiscales	**95 048**	**86 004**	**203 671**	**415 830**	**205 074**	**185 612**	**254 640**	**380 736**	**447 046**	**654 836**
Dons	44 069	33 500	94 628	310 928	106 540	81 208	81 208	201 460	303 989	282 200
Revenus de la propriété	2 895	4 204	5 555	80 859	76 308	88 874	148 815	149 233	91 828	285 955
Loyers et redevances[1]	2 895	4 204	5 555	51 869	44 902	74 620	137 504	119 015	82 046	255 515
Revenus du domaine	0	0	0	186	283	172	396	941	1 363	2 111
Taxe d'exploitation pétrolière	0	0	0	32 945	27 275	60 966	87 080	60 764	39 595	30 851
Taxes domaniales[2]	2 895	4 204	5 555	7 911	7 696	7 852	22 309	37 396	31 737	37 224
Autres loyers et redevances	0	0	0	10 827	9 647	5 631	27 720	19 915	9 351	185 329
Intérêts et dividendes	0	0	0	28 969	27 981	13 678	11 230	29 973	9 693	30 440
Autres revenus de la propriété	0	0	0	21	3 426	576	80	245	89	0
Ventes de biens et de services[3]	0	0	13 200	18 945	21 700	15 177	24 306	28 098	31 556	35 414
Redevance RTI (Radiodiffusion Télévision Ivoirienne)	..	..	0	4 173	4 107	2 340	5 564	5 568	6 021	6 244
Taxe audiovisuelle	..	..	0	6	0	0	0	0	0	0
Autres ventes de biens et de services	..	..	13 200	14 766	17 592	12 837	18 742	22 529	25 535	29 170
Amendes, pénalités et confiscations	0	0	0	200	173	99	99	219	291	0
Recettes diverses et non identifiées[4]	48 084	48 300	90 288	4 898	353	253	213	1 727	19 382	51 267
Total des recettes fiscales et non fiscales	1 262 216	1 255 611	1 610 947	2 343 658	2 240 541	2 038 951	2 675 604	3 102 516	3 393 149	4 068 584

Note: Année civile se terminant le 31 décembre.

Les données sont sur la base des encaissements.

Les chiffres n'incluent pas les données des recettes non fiscales collectées par les collectivités locales car elles ne sont pas disponibles. Les recettes diverses et non identifiées comprennent les transferts de capitaux non compris ailleurs et transferts volontaires autres que les dons.

1. Les recettes des taxes domaniales, la taxe ad valorem et la taxe d'exploitation pétrolière étaient classées comme des recettes fiscales dans la rubrique 5128 (autres impôts sur les biens et services) dans la première édition des *Statistiques des recettes publiques en Afrique*. Ces recettes à part celles de la taxe ad-valorem sont considérées comme des recettes non fiscales selon la classification OCDE (voir le guide d'interprétation en Annexe B) et ont été classifiées comme telles dans cette édition. La classification nationale de la Côte d'Ivoire les compte comme des recettes fiscales.
2. Les recettes des taxes domaniales sont hors taxe ad-valorem pour la période 2012 à 2015, période pour laquelle il a été possible de distinguer ces recettes.
3. La taxe audiovisuelle et la redevance radiodiffusion télévision ivoirienne (RTI) étaient rapportés dans la rubrique 5126 (Impôts sur services déterminés) dans la première édition des *Statistiques des recettes publiques en Afrique*. Elles sont considérées comme des recettes non fiscales selon la classification OCDE (voir le guide d'interprétation en Annexe B) et ont été classifiées comme telles dans cette édition dans la rubrique « vente de biens et services ». La classification nationale de la Côte d'Ivoire les compte comme des recettes fiscales.
4. Les recettes diverses et non identifiées comprennent les transferts de capitaux non compris ailleurs et transferts volontaires autres que les dons.

Source: Ministère de l'Économie et des Finances.

StatLink http://dx.doi.org/10.1787/888933570808

Table 5.9. Ghana

Details of non-tax revenue / Recettes non fiscales détaillées

Million GHS

	1997	2000	2005	2009	2010	2011	2012	2013	2014	2015
Total non-tax revenue	**..**	**97**	**675**	**2 078**	**2 306**	**3 193**	**4 595**	**5 751**	**6 369**	**8 512**
Grants	..	57	510	1 207	1 080	1 231	1 160	739	814	2 689
Project grants	..	24	287	650	591	708	512	374	787	1 744
Programme grants	..	34	127	399	288	281	503	158	27	945
International debt relief	..	0	96	158	201	242	146	207	0	0
Property income	..	0	144	287	347	927	1 283	2 123	2 727	2 628
Rents and royalties	..	..	0	0	0	445	583	748	1 075	908
Mineral royalties (aside from oil)[1]	..	..	..	..	..	261	312	408	517	518
Oil revenues[1]	..	..	..	..	..	184	270	339	554	384
Lodgements to MDAs and MMDAs: surface rentals from oil/PHF interest[2]	..	..	..	..	..	0	1	2	4	6
Lodgements to MDAs and MMDAs: fees from granting of new stability agreements[2]	..	..	..	..	..	0	0	0	0	0
Revenue from oil companies (includes corporate tax)[1]	..	..	..	..	..	0	0	0	0	0
Interest and dividends	..	..	144	287	347	482	700	1 375	1 653	1 720
Lodgements to MDAs and MMDAs: dividend, interest and profits from oil companies[2]	..	..	0	0	0	482	700	875	1 435	995
Lodgements to MDAs and MMDAs: dividend, interest and profits aside from oil companies[2]	..	..	144	287	347	0	0	500	218	726
Other property income	..	..	0	0	0	0	0	0	0	0
Sales of goods and services	..	40	21	584	879	1 034	2 152	2 889	2 827	3 195
Retentions by MDAs and MMDAs[2]	..	0	0	409	685	722	1 791	2 516	2 497	2 531
Lodgements to MDAs and MMDAs: fees and charges[2]	..	40	21	175	194	312	362	372	330	663
Lodgements to MDAs and MMDAs: gas receipts[2]	..	0	0	0	0	0	0	0	0	2
Fines, penalties and forfeits	..	0	0	0	0	0	0	0	0	0
Miscellaneous and unidentified revenue	..	0	0	0	0	0	0	0	0	0
Total tax and non-tax revenue	..	539	2 793	6 867	8 379	11 878	15 726	18 448	23 371	29 355

Note: Year ending 31st December.

The data are on a cash basis.

Figures exclude non-tax revenues collected by sub-national governments as the data are not available.

1. Rents and royalties include oil and mineral royalties for the period 2010 to 2015. These are reported as taxes on income and property in Ghana's budget documents and are included within tax classifications in this publication for the years up to 2009 since they cannot be reported separately from other revenues.
2. Revenues for MDAs (Municipalities, Departments and Agencies) and MMDAs (Metropolitan, Municipal and District Assemblies) contain a mixture of revenues collected at the local level, and revenues collected at a federal level. These are reported as revenues to the central government.

Source: Ghana Statistical Service.

StatLink http://dx.doi.org/10.1787/888933570827

Table 5.10. Kenya
Details of non-tax revenue / Recettes non fiscales détaillées

Million KES

	1997	2000	2005	2009	2010	2011	2012	2013	2014	2015
Total non-tax revenue	..	..	**43 575**	**40 303**	**26 853**	..	..	**58 607**	**43 609**	**55 861**
Grants	..	..	29 810	19 669	14 060	..	..	26 155	27 397	14 664
Foreign governments-capital	..	..	14 905	19 669	0	..	..	5 459	7 355	2 644
Foreign governments-current	..	..	0	0	0	..	..	0	0	0
Foreign governments-cash through exchequer	..	..	5 564	0	3 108	..	..	2 566	514	1 383
Foreign governments-direct payments treated as Appropriations in Aid (AIA)	..	..	9 341	0	6 107	..	..	2 893	6 841	1 261
International organizations-capital	..	..	0	0	0	..	..	0	0	5 533
International organizations-current	..	..	0	0	0	..	..	4	0	3 843
International organizations-cash through exchequer	..	..	0	0	4 845	..	..	2 622	5 205	0
International organizations-direct payments-treated as Appropriations in Aid (AIA)	..	..	0	0	0	..	..	12 611	7 482	0
Property income	..	..	5 255	9 616	9 921	13 002	17 001	18 508	11 876	16 216
Rents and royalties	..	..	727	1 134	1 184	1 157	1 633	1 887	1 695	695
Rent of land	..	..	674	1 063	1 108	1 073	1 544	1 789	1 588	8
Kenya Airports Authority (KAA) concession fees	..	..	53	71	77	84	89	99	107	114
Base titanium royalty	..	..	0	0	0	0	0	0	0	338
Mining royalties	..	..	0	0	0	0	0	0	0	136
Royalties from soda ash	..	..	0	0	0	0	0	0	0	100
Interest and dividends	..	..	2 027	8 483	8 737	11 845	15 367	16 621	5 865	10 781
Profits and dividends	..	..	1 185	6 919	8 354	11 086	14 132	15 264	5 865	9 002
Interests	..	..	843	1 564	383	759	1 236	1 356	0	1 779
Other property income	..	..	2 500	0	0	0	0	0	4 317	4 740
Surplus funds from regulatory authority	..	..	2 500	0	0	0	0	0	4 317	4 740
Sales of goods and services	..	..	1 548	2 773	2 302	..	..	12 479	2 690	11 452
Work permits	..	..	0	0	0	..	..	4 278	900	4 098
Road transit toll	..	..	293	463	457	468	591	546	495	562
Immigration visas and other consular fees	..	..	0	0	0	..	..	2 751	606	2 822
Fees under traffic act	..	..	304	1 659	1 188	..	..	548	108	0
Land administration fees	..	..	55	0	0	..	..	64	148	1 826
Motor driver's licences	..	..	376	650	656	..	..	762	0	0
Passport fees	..	..	0	0	0	..	..	502	125	570
Rent of government buildings and housing	..	..	520	0	0	..	366	274	54	135
Other fees for administrative services	..	..	0	0	0	..	..	2 606	129	555
Hire of security service fees	..	..	0	0	0	..	..	9	18	372
Registration of organisations, professionals and agreements	..	..	0	0	0	..	..	70	46	296
Registration of births, deaths and marriages	..	..	0	0	0	..	..	71	62	215
Fines, penalties and forfeits	..	..	200	140	229	290	1 079	1 466	1 443	1 459
Miscellaneous and unidentified revenue	..	..	6 762	8 105	341	8 483	2 300	0	204	12 071
Contribution from government employees to social and welfare schemes within government	..	..	558	0	341	660	111	0	204	871
Miscellaneous and unidentified revenue	..	..	6 204	8 105	0	7 823	2 189	0	0	11 200
Total tax and non-tax revenue	..	..	317 659	520 666	560 991	..	..	858 449	1 006 894	1 125 255

Note: Data are reported on a fiscal year basis beginning 1st July. For example, the data for 2015 represent July 2014 to June 2015.

The data are on a cash basis.

Detailed non-tax revenue data are not readily available for 2001, 2002, 2003, 2004, 2006, 2011 and 2012.

Figures exclude non-tax revenues collected by sub-national governments as the data are not available.

The national classification of Kenya classifies revenues from the airport revenue, aviation revenue, petroleum development levy, FMV, road maintenance levy, sugar levy, petroleum regulatory levy, merchant superintendent shipping levy, railway development levy, revenue Stamps, KEBS and land rates as non-tax revenues. They are considered in this publication as tax revenues under the OECD classification, as set out in the Interpretative Guide in Annex A.

Source: Kenya Revenue Authority Statistical Service.

StatLink http://dx.doi.org/10.1787/888933570846

Table 5.11. Mauritius / Maurice

Details of non-tax revenue / Recettes non fiscales détaillées

Million MUR

	1997	2000	2005	2009	2010	2011	2012	2013	2014	2015
Total non-tax revenue	**3 286**	**3 293**	**4 590**	**11 914**	**11 458**	**11 275**	**10 620**	**11 688**	**10 355**	**10 962**
Grants	63	161	444	2 783	1 991	2 345	2 398	1 416	940	1 886
Grants from foreign governments	..	..	..	1	2	222	122	121	569	165
Grants from international organizations	..	..	..	2 782	1 989	2 122	2 276	1 295	371	1 721
Property income	2 577	2 370	2 395	6 627	5 020	4 328	4 846	5 315	5 233	4 376
Rents and royalties	0	0	0	962	1 284	1 167	1 068	1 219	1 087	755
Interest and dividends	0	0	0	1 344	979	1 018	1 074	1 827	1 404	854
Interest	..	..	..	415	392	376	589	408	462	362
Dividends	..	..	..	929	587	643	484	1 418	943	492
Other property income	2 577	2 370	2 395	4 320	2 756	2 142	2 705	2 269	2 742	2 767
Budgetary	1 954	1 692	1 235	2 406	1 549	1 127	1 167	1 066	1 437	1 398
Extra-budgetary[1]	43	58	136	504	349	341	325	272	211	196
Social security funds[1]	527	544	973	1 313	777	598	1 131	756	921	971
Regional government[1]	0	0	6	10	11	11	10	14	11	12
Local government[2]	54	76	45	87	71	64	73	161	162	190
Sales of goods and services	520	626	1 385	1 810	2 028	2 427	2 576	3 002	3 548	3 916
Work/occupational permits	0	0	47	66	95	112	125	163	206	194
Extra-budgetary fees, charges, and non-industrial sales[1]	185	177	397	571	543	621	689	689	1 078	1 066
Fees, charges, and non-industrial sales by social security funds[1]	22	20	40	0	51	145	216	234	267	340
Regional government sales of goods and services[1]	0	0	6	4	5	7	8	7	7	8
Local government sales of goods and services[2]	32	60	96	98	113	127	101	419	413	503
Other sales of goods and services	282	370	799	1 071	1 222	1 415	1 436	1 490	1 577	1 805
Fines, penalties and forfeits	44	65	152	219	272	306	282	313	332	298
Budgetary fines, penalties and forfeits	44	65	151	198	269	302	276	308	326	291
Extra-budgetary fines, penalties and forfeits[1]	0	0	0	19	0	0	1	1	2	2
Regional government fines, penalties and forfeits[1]	0	0	1	2	3	4	6	4	4	5
Miscellaneous and unidentified revenue	83	70	214	477	2 147	1 870	518	1 642	302	485
Budgetary miscellaneous and unidentified revenue	4	10	13	46	1 803	1 468	187	1 360	140	368
Extra-budgetary miscellaneous and unidentified revenue[3]	75	44	185	365	293	223	267	280	0	0
Miscellaneous and unidentified revenue for social security funds[3]	0	4	0	0	3	117	0	0	0	0
Regional government miscellaneous and unidentified revenue[3]	0	0	0	3	1	1	1	2	0	0
Local government miscellaneous and unidentified revenue[2]	4	13	16	63	47	61	64	0	162	117
Total tax and non-tax revenue	18 654	25 684	39 491	67 963	70 630	74 733	79 920	84 135	87 073	91 370

Note: Data are on a fiscal year basis beginning 1st July for years prior to 2010 (for example the data for 2009 represent July 2008 to June 2009) and are on a calendar year basis from 2010 onwards.

Mauritius went back to a July-June fiscal year in 2015 and figures are not available for all revenue categories for the 2015 calendar year, especially when it comes to non-budgetary figures and figures for other levels of government. Where data was missing, quarterly revenue figures at the aggregate level were used along with fiscal year revenue data to produce estimates for the calendar year 2015.

In some cases in 2015, linear interpolation was used to estimate missing values. These cases are indicated with footnotes.

The data are on a cash basis, except for revenue from grants, which is reported on an accrual basis.

1. Values for 2015 are estimated using linear trends.
2. Values for 2014 and 2015 are estimated using linear trends.
3. Missing values in years 2013-15 are set to zero.

Source: Mauritius Revenue Authority for central government budgetary non-tax revenue data from 2007 to 2015; Statistics Mauritius for extra budgetary, local and regional government non-tax revenues from 1990 to 2014; Statistics Mauritius for budgetary central government non-tax revenues up to 2006; Ministry of Finance budget estimates for detailed revenue figures for the period July 2005-June 2008 and for the figures used to estimate calendar year 2015 revenues.

StatLink http://dx.doi.org/10.1787/888933570865

Table 5.12. Morocco / Maroc

Details of non-tax revenue / Recettes non fiscales détaillées

Million MAR

	1997	2000	2005	2009	2010	2011	2012	2013	2014	2015
Total des recettes non fiscales	..	**9 278**	**16 746**	**27 634**	**27 970**	**31 945**	**31 121**	**37 039**	**34 913**	**38 463**
Dons	..	2	1 163	2	199	10	8	7	0	0
Revenus de la propriété	..	3 125	4 878	9 470	9 786	12 181	12 257	13 063	10 938	8 934
Loyers et redevances	..	1 507	2 892	3 813	3 868	5 279	4 577	5 361	5 387	5 193
Redevance gazoduc	..	298	1 369	1 695	1 442	2 152	2 146	2 328	2 438	1 765
Redevances et contribution pour licence de pêche en haute mer	..	94	38	399	330	635	3	177	538	520
Redevances pour l'occupation du domaine public	..	132	214	233	331	325	289	566	279	281
Autres redevances reçues par l'administration centrale	..	7	8	54	63	3	3	9	3	6
Loyers et redevances reçues par les collectivités locales	..	977	1 262	1 432	1 703	2 165	2 136	2 281	2 128	2 620
Intérêts et dividendes	..	1 618	1 986	5 657	5 918	6 902	7 680	7 702	5 551	3 742
Dividendes des monopoles	..	1 008	1 540	5 422	5 584	6 510	7 376	7 378	4 970	3 236
Intérêts sur placements et avances	..	419	199	20	96	158	74	73	323	195
Interêts et dividendes reçus par les collectivités locales	..	191	248	215	239	234	230	251	259	311
Autres revenus de la propriété	..	0	0	0	0	0	0	0	0	0
Ventes de biens et de services	..	4 573	7 315	11 352	10 286	11 745	11 796	14 244	14 417	15 799
Cartes d'identité, passeports et divers documents	..	453	511	483	567	555	515	490	220	288
Produits de certains établissements publics	..	1 544	3 038	4 949	2 990	3 684	3 855	5 411	4 551	5 462
Revenus des immeubles domaniaux (loyers, charges locatives ...)	..	137	172	226	250	184	287	239	217	265
Autres produits de l'administration centrale	..	175	824	663	646	1 494	649	801	864	966
Ventes de biens et de services par les collectivités locales	..	2 265	2 770	5 031	5 833	5 828	6 490	7 305	8 566	8 820
Amendes, pénalités et confiscations	..	398	851	2 495	2 802	2 262	2 364	2 526	2 690	2 994
Amendes et condamnations pécuniaires	..	17	42	30	21	23	32	46	56	61
Amendes transactionnelles	..	36	90	149	130	184	345	485	893	706
Autres (produits des confiscations, pénalités et amendes autres que fiscales)	..	6	10	1	1	1	1	1	1	0
Majorations et pénalités (DGI)[1]	..	339	709	2 315	2 650	2 055	1 986	1 994	1 740	2 226
Recettes diverses et non identifiées	..	1 180	2 539	4 315	4 898	5 748	4 696	7 200	6 868	10 736
Fonds de concours	..	147	968	3 191	3 597	3 624	2 246	4 441	2 564	3 453
Recettes en atténuation des dépenses de la dette	..	801	880	230	480	1 044	725	1 024	2 230	4 386
Reversements sur traitements et salaires	..	55	157	249	99	106	155	96	63	62
Créances sur le trésor prescrites	..	30	225	54	39	56	186	112	78	97
Autres (divers remboursements à l'État) reçues par l'administration centrale	..	7	29	6	6	133	198	281	396	254
Recettes diverses et non identifiées des collectivités locales	..	139	281	587	677	785	1 186	1 246	1 536	2 484
Total des recettes fiscales et non fiscales	..	106 504	153 332	229 344	244 956	265 606	281 143	289 529	284 335	294 642

Note: Année civile se terminant le 31 décembre.

Les données sont sur la base des encaissements.

1. Les recettes des majorations et pénalités relatives aux impôts sont désormais considérées comme des recettes non fiscales suite à un changement de la classification OCDE depuis la publication de la première édition. La classification nationale du Maroc les compte comme des recettes fiscales.

Source: Ministère de l'Économie et des Finances.

StatLink http://dx.doi.org/10.1787/888933570884

Table 5.13. Niger

Details of non-tax revenue / Recettes non fiscales détaillées

Million XOF

	1997	2000	2005	2009	2010	2011	2012	2013	2014	2015
Total des recettes non fiscales	**..**	**..**	**145 119**	**142 254**	**179 681**	**149 542**	**284 036**	**359 601**	**326 622**	**323 732**
Dons	..	59 312	134 100	110 908	130 144	113 497	216 542	304 855	222 124	232 611
Revenus de la propriété	..	4 797	6 009	24 693	28 439	28 884	53 806	35 534	43 114	40 364
Loyers et redevances	..	..	5 168	13 586	14 980	18 683	22 783	20 268	34 865	33 078
Bonus de signature	..	0	0	0	0	0	0	0	16 082	17 044
Redevance minière (RM)	..	4 519	4 732	11 660	14 381	16 832	21 334	18 526	13 195	11 323
Redevance superficaire pétrole	..	0	0	0	0	0	0	0	3 064	2 776
Publicité foncière	..	50	282	498	429	801	711	980	1 024	950
Redevance superficaire mine	..	0	0	0	0	0	0	0	396	449
Retenue pour logements	..	6	4	0	25	23	43	193	276	173
Concessions provisoires	..	1	73	544	86	550	289	299	212	164
Domaine mobilier	..	46	11	827	3	383	330	95	276	115
Permis de coupe de bois	..	65	18	34	42	62	54	125	277	52
Bornage de terrains	..	4	13	17	10	20	19	14	32	20
Concessions définitives	..	29	35	6	5	11	2	37	31	12
Intérêts et dividendes	..	..	653	10 950	13 166	9 973	30 828	15 018	7 990	6 997
Dividendes	..	..	653	7 716	12 081	9 630	28 814	9 663	2 994	2 990
Bénéfices pétroliers	..	..	0	0	0	0	1 671	5 190	4 857	3 577
Intérêts créditeurs	..	..	0	3 235	1 084	343	343	165	140	430
Autres revenus de la propriété	..	78	189	157	293	228	195	249	259	290
Droits d'occupation du domaine public	..	78	189	157	293	228	195	249	259	290
Ventes de biens et de services	..	..	270	2 008	286	487	317	3 474	38 844	36 378
Vente de licence de téléphonie cellulaire	..	..	0	0	0	0	0	0	34 000	34 000
Commission sur transferts banque centrale (BCEAO)	..	..	0	1 571	42	0	1	2 002	3 691	1 090
Vente passeports/visa interpol	..	..	0	0	0	0	0	670	288	469
Vaccination internationale	..	..	0	0	0	0	0	215	201	239
Emission cartes grises/transport	..	..	0	0	0	0	0	125	141	143
Recettes des régies forestières	..	30	111	171	159	175	202	280	263	127
Ventes imprimés DGI/DGD	..	..	0	0	0	0	0	70	90	104
Droit de chancellerie	..	..	4	3	3	4	6	12	4	76
Location d'immeubles	..	9	135	248	64	279	89	41	22	9
Autres ventes de biens et services	..	0	21	16	18	29	19	60	143	120
Amendes, pénalités et confiscations	..	..	1 700	2 240	3 816	3 221	3 304	6 040	6 653	6 744
Amendes et pénalités de la DGI	..	1 188	1 062	933	2 296	1 813	1 588	4 108	4 289	4 035
Amendes et frais de police	..	..	76	433	482	384	543	656	916	1 230
Amendes et confiscations	..	159	122	229	214	220	328	414	478	842
Amendes, frais et pénalités (gendarmerie et police)	..	..	403	614	769	749	786	807	861	595
Amendes et saisies forêts et chasse	..	1	27	23	45	43	42	47	84	26
Amendes et frais de justice	..	..	4	7	8	10	8	3	18	9
Amendes et saisies sur contrôle des prix-poids-mesure	..	..	6	1	1	1	9	5	7	8
Recettes diverses et non identifiées	..	248	3 040	2 405	16 996	3 454	10 068	9 698	15 888	7 635
Autres recettes diverses - Trésor National	..	0	0	1 000	16 461	2 899	9 737	9 241	15 155	4 921
Autres recettes diverses	..	248	250	364	421	555	324	457	732	779
Reversement UEMOA et produits divers de l'African Risk Capacity (ARC)	..	0	2 790	1 041	114	0	8	0	0	1 935
Total des recettes fiscales et non fiscales	..	..	335 337	499 703	553 142	568 952	795 030	1 001 009	989 793	1 044 271
Pour mémoire: [1]										
Prélèvement communautaire de la CEDEAO	..	448	1 479	2 650	5 302	5 109	5 044	3 893	4 433	4 893
Prélèvement communautaire UEMOA	..	866	0	0	0	0	0	0	0	0

Note: Année civile se terminant le 31 décembre.

Les données sont sur la base des encaissements.

Les chiffres n'incluent pas les données des recettes non fiscales collectées par les collectivités locales car elles ne sont pas disponibles.

Les données des dons sont issues de la base de données de la publication PEM 2017 (*Perspectives de l'économie mondiale 2017*) publiée par le FMI.

Les données pour la période 2000-04 doivent être interprétées avec prudence car les données non fiscales collectées par la Direction Générale du Trésor et de la Comptabilité Publique (DGTCP) ne sont pas disponibles pour cette période.

Selon la classification OCDE (voir le guide d'interprétation en Annexe B), le produit de la vente d'immeuble bâtis n'est pas considéré comme une recette (fiscale ou non fiscale) car il ne représente pas une augmentation de la valeur nette résultant d'une transaction. La classification du Niger compte ces recettes comme des recettes non fiscales.

1. Le prélèvement communautaire de la CEDEAO (Communauté économique des États de l'Afrique de l'Ouest) et le prélèvement communautaire de solidarité de l'UEMOA (Union Economique et Monétaire Ouest Africaine) ne sont pas compris dans le total des recettes fiscales ou des recettes non fiscales comme le préconise la classification OCDE (voir le guide d'interprétation en Annexe A) et est présenté ici à titre de rubrique « Pour mémoire ». La classification du Niger les compte comme des recettes.

Source: Institut National de la Statistique.

StatLink http://dx.doi.org/10.1787/888933570903

Table 5.14. Rwanda

Details of non-tax revenue / Recettes non fiscales détaillées

Million RWF

	1997	2000	2005	2009	2010	2011	2012	2013	2014	2015
Total non-tax revenue	**40 858**	**79 888**	**182 339**	**363 942**	**415 465**	**479 815**	**397 600**	**551 411**	**514 565**	**529 400**
Grants	37 731	76 710	164 477	347 397	397 352	443 150	345 510	459 200	421 821	374 600
Property income	..	..	..	..	..	..	..	..	..	..
Rents and royalties	..	..	..	..	..	..	..	..	..	..
Interest and dividends	..	..	..	..	..	..	..	..	..	..
Other property income	..	..	..	..	..	..	..	..	..	..
Sales of goods and services	..	..	..	..	..	..	..	..	..	..
Fines, penalties and forfeits	..	..	..	..	..	..	..	..	..	..
Miscellaneous and unidentified revenue[1]	3 127	3 178	17 863	16 545	18 113	36 665	52 090	92 211	92 745	154 800
Total tax and non-tax revenue	97 107	148 797	356 945	753 881	856 189	1 017 253	1 043 048	1 311 569	1 380 119	1 522 448

Note: Year ending 31st December.

The data are on a cash basis.

Figures exclude non-tax revenues collected by sub-national governments as the data are not available.

Figures exclude fines related to tax revenues as it is not possible to split these out from tax revenues. Revenues from fines related to taxes are now classified as non-tax revenues following a change in the OECD classification. Rwanda considers these revenues as tax revenues.

1. This category includes non-tax fines, administrative fees and revenue from public property and public assets for Rwanda. These data could not be disaggregated to allocate revenue to the relevant non-tax revenue categories.

Source: Rwanda Revenue Authority.

StatLink http://dx.doi.org/10.1787/888933570922

Table 5.15. Senegal / Sénégal

Details of non-tax revenue / Recettes non fiscales détaillées

Million XOF

	1997	2000	2005	2009	2010	2011	2012	2013	2014	2015
Total des recettes non fiscales	**65 600**	**89 100**	**105 100**	**220 100**	**203 550**	**199 500**	**277 800**	**277 835**	**394 700**	**371 943**
Dons	65 600	64 000	75 600	182 800	161 850	150 000	206 300	187 540	253 500	232 034
Revenus de la propriété	0	21 100	26 400	34 900	39 600	34 100	68 500	61 695	81 300	85 590
Loyers et redevances	..	..	14 500	6 500	20 300	15 800	38 000	18 320	25 200	35 790
Intérêts et dividendes	..	..	11 900	28 400	19 300	18 300	30 500	43 375	56 100	49 800
Autres revenus de la propriété	..	..	0	0	0	0	0	0	0	0
Ventes de biens et de services	0	0	0	0	0	0	0	0	0	0
Amendes, pénalités et confiscations	0	0	0	0	0	0	0	27 100	49 000	28 220
Recettes diverses et non identifiées[1]	0	4 000	3 100	2 400	2 100	15 400	3 000	1 500	10 900	26 100
Total des recettes fiscales et non fiscales	483 144	648 395	992 348	1 358 598	1 471 349	1 545 987	1 697 081	1 692 555	1 955 132	2 055 571

Note: Année civile se terminant le 31 décembre.

Les données sont sur la base des encaissements.

Les chiffres n'incluent pas les données des recettes non fiscales collectées par les collectivités locales car elles ne sont pas disponibles.

La nomenclature actuelle des recettes budgétaires du Sénégal ne considère pas les dons comme une recette non fiscale.

Les recettes non fiscales excluent les amendes et les pénalités sur impôts et taxes. Ces recettes sont désormais considérées comme des recettes non fiscales suite à un changement de la classification OCDE depuis la publication de la première édition. Il n'a pas été possible pour cette édition de séparer le versement des amendes et pénalités des recettes correspondant aux impôts auxquels ces amendes et pénalités se rattachent. La classification nationale du Sénégal les compte comme des recettes fiscales.

1. Y compris transferts de capitaux non compris ailleurs.

Source: Ministère de l'Économie, des Finances et du Plan.

StatLink http://dx.doi.org/10.1787/888933570941

Table 5.16. South Africa / Afrique du Sud
Details of non-tax revenue / Recettes non fiscales détaillées

Million ZAR

	1997	2000	2005	2009	2010	2011	2012	2013	2014	2015
Total non-tax revenue	**1 838**	**4 350**	**8 899**	**9 739**	**16 779**	**21 620**	**21 386**	**24 601**	**21 464**	**23 352**
Grants[1]	265	637	1 118	1 844	1 012	1 480	1 966	2 335	1 960	1 467
Property income	1 222	1 593	5 208	3 652	11 725	15 952	15 236	17 511	17 512	17 524
Rents and royalties	0	0	0	0	3 555	5 612	5 015	6 439	5 413	5 422
Interest and dividends	1 222	1 378	4 937	2 798	3 721	4 554	5 098	4 524	6 602	6 613
Other property income	0	215	271	854	4 449	5 787	5 123	6 548	5 497	5 489
Sales of goods and services	218	2 006	2 243	2 314	2 335	2 894	2 620	2 866	767	2 638
Fines, penalties and forfeits	134	114	280	1 698	1 457	934	993	1 466	1 162	1 174
Miscellaneous and unidentified revenue	0	0	50	232	251	360	572	423	63	549
Total tax and non-tax revenue	160 395	215 916	421 356	653 881	719 095	815 965	893 557	991 159	1 078 330	1 191 868
***Memo items:** SACU expenditure*[2]	..	..	14 107	27 859	17 862	21 719	42 108	41 979	51 661	45 927

Note: Data are reported on a fiscal year basis beginning 1st April. For example, the data for 2015 data represent April 2015 to March 2016.
The data are on a cash basis.
Figures exclude non-tax revenues collected by sub-national governments as the data are not available.

1. The grants data represent total grants and donations received mainly from foreign governments and multilateral institutions. Moreover, this flow does not go through the Government Revenue fund, it is earmarked for specific projects implemented across government (by line departments).
2. Memo items: the Southern African Customs Union (SACU) expenditure records the difference between South Africa contributions to the SACU pool and the South Africa revenue share from the SACU pool that includes the balance of the "surplus/deficit" for that fiscal year and allocations to the SACU secretariat.

Source: National Treasury of South Africa. Data for grants are from the financial statements of the Reconstruction and Development Fund Programme (RDP) Fund administered by the office of Accountant General.

StatLink http://dx.doi.org/10.1787/888933570960

Table 5.17. Swaziland

Details of non-tax revenue / Recettes non fiscales détaillées

Thousand SZL

	1997	2000	2005	2009	2010	2011	2012	2013	2014	2015
Total non-tax revenue	**1 138 958**	**1 542 213**	**3 278 532**	**5 610 762**	**2 667 738**	**2 404 788**	**7 605 811**	**7 440 846**	**7 967 640**	**7 564 170**
Grants[1]	..	..	..	..	..	..	98 800	133 300	98 200	121 300
Property income	90 245	91 367	66 746	281 916	552 683	114 978	173 326	173 067	264 390	394 451
Rents and royalties	12	3	1	1 343	3 461	3 536	3 675	4 289	13 811	24 731
Land concession rents, postal revenue	12	3	1	0	0	0	0	0	0	0
Rents attributed to social security funds	0	0	0	1 343	3 461	3 536	3 675	4 289	13 811	24 731
Interest and dividends	90 232	91 063	65 419	279 108	547 917	107 493	165 719	161 034	237 544	339 064
Local interest collected by central government	27 918	21 330	25 114	123 468	537 764	19 420	16 413	23 656	17	60 271
Central bank profit	4 264	0	0	145 136	0	73 614	119 941	110 124	213 608	245 276
External interest and interest on capital	53 845	68 954	12 839	525	273	2 383	5 458	5 245	11 393	90
Dividends	4 205	779	27 467	8 935	8 489	10 684	21 824	12 500	85	10 625
Interest and dividends collected by social security funds	0	0	0	1 044	1 392	1 392	2 083	9 509	12 442	22 802
Other property income	0	302	1 325	1 466	1 306	3 948	3 932	7 744	13 034	30 656
Quitrents	0	302	0	0	0	28	0	0	0	0
Local government property income	0	0	1 325	1 466	1 306	3 920	3 932	7 744	13 034	30 656
Sales of goods and services	39 024	40 422	62 935	116 039	115 002	96 613	81 647	75 637	70 862	73 003
Sundry fees	12 518	13 265	40 204	54 046	37 907	39 552	24 750	21 532	6 228	5 813
Passports, citizenship and resident permits	7 427	4 557	4 942	24 095	24 928	22 580	22 548	23 370	25 188	25 019
Rental of government real estate	2 488	2 583	6 061	7 307	7 004	8 416	8 385	9 829	10 217	11 424
Driver's licences, motor vehicle certification	616	931	3 415	4 735	7 644	7 987	5 965	6 586	7 845	11 404
Hospital and medical services	524	4 681	4 090	6 279	6 402	5 958	6 105	6 631	6 906	5 921
Hire of government plants and vehicles	27	0	87	12 760	20 671	407	2 758	323	230	185
Aviation fees	11 969	11 634	720	788	373	17	17	19	19	2
Sale of government furniture and vehicles	59	34	275	1 345	5 958	6 266	5 402	454	6 152	6 808
Sale of agricultural products and services	2 349	1 844	1 309	1 316	1 048	1 441	1 582	2 051	2 806	2 317
Public service transport fees	529	472	677	702	933	1 134	1 247	1 287	2 037	1 037
Sale of government publications	150	108	272	939	1 002	1 018	1 012	1 104	1 077	665
Prison industry sales	369	314	46	121	133	171	142	110	102	112
Local government sales of goods and services	0	0	838	1 607	999	1 667	1 734	2 343	2 056	2 298
Fines, penalties and forfeits[2]	2 554	3 722	11 080	20 466	27 724	27 646	55 453	30 075	32 009	33 241
Traffic fines	1 637	2 223	4 952	9 586	15 305	14 832	13 985	15 470	14 754	12 559
Judicial fines and other penalties	221	564	3 891	8 952	10 389	10 238	11 132	12 117	14 928	17 819
Interest and penalties on late tax payments	350	431	1 032	596	545	861	8 389	2 354	2 051	2 446
PAYE penalties	346	504	1 142	1 332	1 486	1 593	21 888	0	0	0
Fines, penalties and forfeits (local non-tax revenue)	0	0	62	0	0	122	60	135	276	418
Miscellaneous and unidentified revenue	1 007 136	1 406 701	3 137 772	5 192 342	1 972 329	2 165 552	7 196 586	7 028 766	7 502 179	6 942 175
SACU revenue	1 006 833	1 406 262	3 136 236	5 188 953	1 968 942	2 160 820	7 191 780	7 024 879	7 486 667	6 930 560
SACU penalties	303	439	1 125	1 811	1 717	2 538	3 298	50	14 126	8 506
Local non-tax revenue	0	0	411	1 578	1 670	2 194	1 508	3 838	1 386	3 108
Total tax and non-tax revenue	2 100 095	2 845 190	5 695 500	9 603 832	7 269 508	7 476 056	12 904 918	13 710 517	15 083 833	15 222 892

Note: Data are reported on a fiscal year basis beginning 1st April. For example, the data for 2015 data represent April 2015 to March 2016.

The data are on a cash basis.

Revenues from motor vehicle licences, the change of ownership fees and the registration of new motor vehicles are considered as tax revenue under the OECD classification as set out in the Interpretative Guide in Annex A and are classified under heading 5211 (Recurrent taxes paid by households: motor vehicles). The national classification of Swaziland classifies these revenues as non-tax revenues.

The revenues from business and sundry licences are considered as tax revenue under the OECD classification, as set out in the Interpretative Guide in Annex A and are classified under heading 5211 (Recurrent taxes paid on use of goods and perform activities other than on motor vehicles). The national classification of Swaziland classifies these revenues as non-tax revenues.

The revenues from the registrations of specific goods (e.g. firearms) are considered as tax revenue under the OECD classification, as set out in the Interpretative Guide in Annex A and are classified under heading 5220 (Non-recurrent taxes on use of goods and perform activities). The national classification of Swaziland classifies these revenues as non-tax revenues.

The revenues from the education loans' repayments do not represent an increase of net worth resulting from a transaction and therefore are not considered as revenues under the OECD classification, as set out in the Interpretative Guide in Annex B.

1. The data are not available up to 2011.
2. Revenue from PAYE Penalties, tax interests and penalties on taxes are considered as non-tax revenue under the OECD classification, as set out in the Interpretative Guide in Annex A. The national classification of Swaziland classifies it as tax revenues.

Source: Swaziland Revenue Authority.

StatLink http://dx.doi.org/10.1787/888933570979

Table 5.18. Togo

Details of non-tax revenue / Recettes non fiscales détaillées

Million XOF

	1997	2000	2005	2009	2010	2011	2012	2013	2014	2015
Total des recettes non fiscales	**..**	**18 964**	**27 699**	**88 844**	**112 863**	**110 141**	**85 082**	**114 019**	**96 255**	**102 156**
Dons	..	4 292	13 110	64 886	62 257	84 603	40 692	73 511	45 762	57 238
Dons projets	..	4 292	13 110	47 610	62 257	84 603	40 692	62 786	45 762	47 539
Dons programmes	..	0	0	17 276	0	0	0	10 725	0	9 699
Revenus de la propriété	..	10 040	11 942	22 005	50 073	24 118	41 827	30 852	29 585	25 555
Loyers et redevances	..	5 548	3 221	0	0	0	0	6 368	8 468	3 837
Redevances minières	..	0	0	..	..	..	..	3 181	7 367	1 270
Redevances de réhabilitation de l' Aéroport International Gnassingbé Eyadéma (AIGE)	..	5 548	3 221	..	..	..	..	35	1 101	2 240
Autres recettes domaniales	..	0	0	..	..	..	..	3 152	0	327
Intérêts et dividendes	..	4 492	8 722	22 005	50 073	24 118	41 827	24 484	21 117	21 718
Dividendes	..	2 416	2 696	8 090	6 745	4 451	18 088	16 453	13 172	16 179
Intérêts de placement	..	771	1 838	794	985	1 464	8 148	302	7 507	4 307
Produits divers (commissions, transferts BCEAO et intérêts)	..	0	0	0	0	0	0	0	190	201
Autres produits financiers	..	1 304	4 187	13 120	42 344	18 202	15 591	7 729	248	1 032
Autres revenus de la propriété	..	0	0	0	0	0	0	0	0	0
Ventes de biens et de services	..	1 365	851	1 291	140	1 011	2 045	6 450	17 690	7 692
Loyers d'immeuble	..	0	0	0	0	0	0	0	428	201
Redevances téléphoniques	..	0	0	0	0	0	0	2 000	11 949	2 000
Recettes de services	..	1 365	851	1 291	140	1 011	2 045	3 710	4 261	4 752
Recettes consulaires	..	0	0	0	0	0	0	740	1 052	739
Amendes, pénalités et confiscations	..	1 199	580	662	393	409	517	1 033	1 323	558
Amendes et pénalités (recettes fiscales)[1]	..	932	442	307	161	219	339	409	103	188
Amendes et penalités (recettes douanières)	..	267	138	355	232	190	178	624	1 219	369
Recettes diverses et non identifiées	..	2 069	1 216	0	0	0	0	2 174	1 895	11 114
Confiscations et ventes en douane[2]	..	0	0	..	..	..	..	0	385	954
Ordre de recettes (gestion antérieure)	..	0	0	..	..	..	..	166	0	6
Ordre de recettes (gestion courante)	..	0	0	..	..	..	..	0	85	95
Divers reversements	..	785	1 216	..	..	..	..	1 923	1 271	9 754
Autres recettes non fiscales	..	1 284	0	..	..	..	..	85	155	305
Total des recettes fiscales et non fiscales	..	118 981	187 594	317 272	359 143	401 144	412 262	523 262	558 245	625 853

Note: Année civile se terminant le 31 décembre.

Les données sont sur la base des encaissements.

Les chiffres n'incluent pas les données des recettes non fiscales collectées par les collectivités locales car elles ne sont pas disponibles.

La classification nationale du Togo compte le prélèvement pour apurement de la dette du secteur pétrolier (PADSP) comme une recette non fiscale. Cette recette est considérée comme une recette fiscale dans cette publication comme le préconise la classification OCDE (voir le guide d'interprétation en Annexe A).

1. Ces recettes sont classifiées comme des recettes non fiscales dans cette publication comme le préconise la classification OCDE (voir le guide d'interprétation en Annexe B). La classification nationale du Togo compte ces recettes comme des recettes fiscales.
2. Cette rubrique comprend les recettes provenant des confiscations et ventes en douane et les reversements du prélèvement communautaire de solidarité qui sont classifiées comme des recettes non fiscales dans cette publication comme le préconise la classification OCDE (voir le guide d'interprétation en Annexe B. La classification nationale du Togo compte ces recettes comme des recettes fiscales douanières.

Source: Office Togolais des Recettes.

StatLink http://dx.doi.org/10.1787/888933570998

Table 5.19. Tunisia / Tunisie
Details of non-tax revenue / Recettes non fiscales détaillées

Million TND

	1997	2000	2005	2009	2010	2011	2012	2013	2014	2015
Total des recettes non fiscales	..	**1 357**	**1 078**	**1 896**	**1 799**	**2 584**	**2 452**	**2 704**	**1 903**	**1 749**
Dons[1]	..	7	70	178	54	207	633	225	368	292
Revenus de la propriété	..	1 051	703	1 327	1 299	2 044	1 267	1 514	976	863
Loyers et redevances	..	369	295	445	435	419	394	372	357	350
Redevances pétrolières et du gaz	..	354	284	423	415	410	379	353	337	328
Loyers	..	16	11	21	19	10	15	18	20	22
Intérêts et dividendes	..	682	408	883	864	1 625	872	1 143	618	513
Intérêts	..	111	87	59	56	49	66	31	42	41
Transferts des entreprises publiques et bénéfices de la Banque Centrale	..	548	311	789	796	1 567	758	1 070	503	430
Remises sur crédit	..	6	3	2	3	2	2	2	3	3
Autres intérêts et dividendes non compris ailleurs	..	17	8	33	10	8	46	39	70	39
Autres revenus de la propriété	..	0	0	0	0	0	0	0	0	0
Ventes de biens et de services	..	43	38	33	40	20	54	26	24	28
Ventes de produits divers	..	42	37	31	38	19	53	25	23	26
Frais administratifs	..	1	1	2	2	1	1	2	2	2
Amendes, pénalités et confiscations	..	87	128	169	187	98	355	731	346	378
Recettes diverses et non identifiées[2]	..	170	139	190	220	214	143	208	189	189
Total des recettes fiscales et non fiscales	..	8 526	11 208	17 575	18 924	21 368	22 891	25 095	26 901	27 362

Note: Année civile se terminant le 31 décembre.

Les données sont sur la base des encaissements.

Les chiffres n'incluent pas les données des recettes non fiscales collectées par les collectivités locales car elles ne sont pas disponibles.

1. Les dons affectés pour les Fonds spéciaux du Trésor et les Fonds de concours sont compris dans les données des dons des gouvernements et institutions étrangers.
2. Les recettes diverses et non identifiées incluent entre autres des recettes accidentelles à divers titres et des recettes non fiscales des Fonds spéciaux du Trésor et des Fonds de concours.

Source: Ministère des Finances.

StatLink http://dx.doi.org/10.1787/888933571017

Table 5.20. Uganda / Ouganda
Details of non-tax revenue / Recettes non fiscales détaillées

Million UGX

	1997	2000	2005	2009	2010	2011	2012	2013	2014	2015
Total non-tax revenue	..	..	**1 082 897**	**937 168**	**1 164 997**	**999 894**	**1 263 208**	**796 027**	**952 847**	**1 365 111**
Grants[1]	420 235	769 480	1 065 538	893 045	1 106 737	932 381	1 184 237	692 855	828 229	1 125 097
Property income	..	..	..	..	..	..	..	..	..	..
Rents and royalties	..	..	..	..	..	..	..	..	..	..
Interest and dividends	..	..	..	..	..	..	..	..	..	..
Other property income	..	..	..	..	..	..	..	..	..	..
Sales of goods and services[2]	1 504	1 919	3 877	9 483	12 373	11 823	13 520	13 655	14 147	15 921
Fines, penalties and forfeits	..	..	..	..	..	..	..	..	..	..
Miscellaneous and unidentified revenue[3]	..	..	13 482	34 640	45 888	55 690	65 451	89 518	110 471	224 093
Total tax and non-tax revenue	..	..	3 017 901	4 740 219	5 494 607	6 250 044	7 566 554	8 016 565	9 017 895	11 062 995

Note: Data are reported on a fiscal year basis beginning 1st July. For example, the data for 2015 represent July 2014 to June 2015.

The data are on a cash basis.

Figures exclude non-tax revenues collected by sub-national governments as the data are not available.

1. Figures for grants are sourced from the WEO 2017 from the IMF (*World Economic Outlook 2017*).
2. Revenue from drivers permits are considered as non-tax revenue according the OECD classification described in the Interpretative Guide. The national classification of Uganda classifies it as tax revenues.
3. This category includes non-tax fines, administrative fees and revenue from public property and public assets. These data could not be disaggregated to allocate revenue to the relevant non-tax revenue categories.

Source: Uganda Revenue Authority.

StatLink http://dx.doi.org/10.1787/888933571036

Revenue Statistics in Africa 1990-2015/Statistiques des recettes publiques en Afrique 1990-2015

Annex A

The OECD Classification of Taxes and Interpretative Guide[1]

Table of contents

A.1. The OECD classification of taxes

1. 1000 *Taxes on income, profits and capital gains*
   - 1100 Taxes on income, profits and capital gains of individuals
     - 1110 On income and profits
     - 1120 On capital gains
   - 1200 Corporate taxes on income, profits and capital gains
     - 1210 On income and profits
     - 1220 On capital gains
   - 1300 Unallocable as between 1100 and 1200
2. 2000 *Social security contributions*
   - 2100 Employees
     - 2110 On a payroll basis
     - 2120 On an income tax basis
   - 2200 Employers
     - 2210 On a payroll basis
     - 2220 On an income tax basis
   - 2300 Self-employed or non-employed
     - 2310 On a payroll basis
     - 2320 On an income tax basis
   - 2400 Unallocable as between 2100, 2200 and 2300
     - 2410 On a payroll basis
     - 2420 On an income tax basis
3. 3000 *Taxes on payroll and workforce*
4. 4000 *Taxes on property*
   - 4100 Recurrent taxes on immovable property
     - 4110 Households
     - 4120 Other
   - 4200 Recurrent taxes on net wealth
     - 4210 Individual
     - 4220 Corporate
   - 4300 Estate, inheritance and gift taxes
     - 4310 Estate and inheritance taxes
     - 4320 Gift taxes
   - 4400 Taxes on financial and capital transactions
   - 4500 Other non-recurrent taxes on property
     - 4510 On net wealth
     - 4520 Other non-recurrent taxes
   - 4600 Other recurrent taxes on property

5. 5000 *Taxes on goods and services*

5100 Taxes on production, sale, transfer, leasing and delivery of goods and rendering of services

5110 General taxes

5111 Value added taxes

5112 Sales taxes

5113 Other general taxes on goods and services

5120 Taxes on specific goods and services

5121 Excises

5122 Profits of fiscal monopolies

5123 Customs and import duties

5124 Taxes on exports

5125 Taxes on investment goods

5126 Taxes on specific services

5127 Other taxes on international trade and transactions

5128 Other taxes on specific goods and services

5130 Unallocable as between 5110 and 5120

5200 Taxes on use of goods, or on permission to use goods or perform activities

5210 Recurrent taxes

5211 Paid by households in respect of motor vehicles

5212 Paid by others in respect of motor vehicles

5213 Other recurrent taxes

5220 Non-recurrent taxes

5300 Unallocable as between 5100 and 5200

6. 6000 *Other taxes*

6100 Paid solely by business

6200 Paid by other than business or unidentifiable

A.2. Coverage

General criteria

1. In the OECD classification the term "taxes" is confined to compulsory unrequited payments to general government. Taxes are unrequited in the sense that benefits provided by government to taxpayers are not normally in proportion to their payments.

2. The term "tax" does not include fines, penalties and compulsory loans paid to government. Borderline cases between tax and non-tax revenues in relation to certain fees and charges are discussed in §9–12.

3. General government consists of the central administration, agencies whose operations are under its effective control, state and local governments and their administrations, certain social security schemes and autonomous governmental entities, excluding public enterprises. This definition of government follows that of the 2008 *System of National Accounts* (SNA).[2] In that publication, the general government sector and its sub-sectors are defined in Chapter 4, section F, pages 80-84.

4. Compulsory payments to supra-national bodies and their agencies are no longer included as taxes as from 1998, with some exceptions. However, custom duties collected by EU member states on behalf of the European Union are still identified as memorandum items and included in overall tax revenue amounts in the country tables (Chapter 4)[1] of the country in which they are collected. (See §94). In countries where the church forms part of general government church taxes are included, provided they meet the criteria set out in §1 above. As the data refer to receipts of general government, levies paid to non-government bodies, welfare agencies or social insurance schemes outside general government, trade unions or trade associations, even where such levies are compulsory, are excluded. Compulsory payments to general government earmarked for such bodies are, however, included, provided that the government is not simply acting in an agency capacity.[3] Profits from fiscal monopolies are distinguished from those of other public enterprises and are treated as taxes because they reflect the exercise of the taxing power of the state by the use of monopoly powers (see §61–63), as are profits received by the government from the purchase and sale of foreign exchange at different rates (see §69).

5. Taxes paid by governments (e.g. social security contributions and payroll taxes paid by governments in their capacity as an employer, consumption taxes on their purchases or taxes on their property) are not excluded from the data provided. However, where it is possible to identify the amounts of revenue involved,[4] they are shown in Chapter 4.3 of this Report[1].

6. The relationship between this classification and that of the System of National Accounts (SNA) is set out in Sections A.9 and A.11 below. Because of the differences between the two classifications, the data shown in national accounts are sometimes calculated or classified differently from the practice set out in this guide. These and other differences are mentioned where appropriate (e.g. in §25 below) but it is not possible to refer to all of them. There may also be some differences between this classification and that employed domestically by certain national administrations (e.g. see §10 below), so that OECD and national statistics data may not always be consistent: any such differences, however, are likely to be very slight in terms of amounts of revenues involved.

Social security contributions

7. Compulsory social security contributions, as defined in §34 below, paid to general government, are treated here as tax revenues. Being compulsory payments to general government they clearly resemble taxes. They may, however, differ from other taxes in that the receipt of social security benefits depends, in most countries, upon appropriate contributions having been made, although the size of the benefits is not necessarily related to the amount of the contributions. Better comparability between countries is obtained by treating social security contributions as taxes, but they are listed under a separate heading so that they can be distinguished in any analysis.

8. Social security contributions which are either voluntary or not payable to general government (see §1) are not treated as taxes, though in some countries, as indicated in the country footnotes, there are difficulties in eliminating voluntary contributions and certain compulsory payments to the private sector. Imputed social security contributions are also not treated as taxes.

Fees, user charges and licence fees

9. Apart from vehicle licence fees, which are universally regarded as taxes, it is not easy to distinguish between those fees and user charges which are to be treated as taxes and those which are not, since, whilst a fee or charge is levied in connection with a specific service or activity, the strength of the link between the fee and the service provided may vary considerably, as may the relation between the amount of the fee and the cost of providing the service. Where the recipient of a service pays a fee clearly related to the cost of providing the service, the levy may be regarded as requited and under the definition of §1 would not be considered as a tax. In the following cases, however, a levy could be considered as "unrequited":

a. where the charge greatly exceeds the cost of providing the service;

b. where the payer of the levy is not the receiver of the benefit (e.g. a fee collected from slaughterhouses to finance a service which is provided to farmers);

c. where government is not providing a specific service in return for the levy which it receives even though a licence may be issued to the payer (e.g. where the government grants a hunting, fishing or shooting licence which is not accompanied by the right to use a specific area of government land);

d. where benefits are received only by those paying the levy but the benefits received by each individual are not necessarily in proportion to his payments (e.g. a milk marketing levy paid by dairy farmers and used to promote the consumption of milk).

10. In marginal cases, however, the application of the criteria set out in §1 can be particularly difficult. The solution adopted – given the desirability of international uniformity and the relatively small amounts of revenue usually involved – is to follow the predominant practice among tax administrations rather than to allow each country to adopt its own view as to whether such levies are regarded as taxes or as non-tax revenue.[5]

11. A list of the main fees and charges in question and their normal[6] treatment in this publication is as follows:

Non-tax revenues: court fees; driving licence fees; harbour fees; passport fees; radio and television licence fees where public authorities provide the service.

Taxes within heading 5200: permission to perform such activities as distributing films; hunting, fishing and shooting; providing entertainment or gambling facilities; selling alcohol or tobacco; permission to own dogs or to use or own motor vehicles or guns; severance taxes.

12. In practice it may not always be possible to isolate tax receipts from non-tax revenue receipts when they are recorded together. If it is estimated that the bulk of the receipts derive from non-tax revenues, the whole amount involved is treated as a non-tax revenue; otherwise, such government receipts are included and classified according to the rules provided in §27 below.

Royalties

13. Royalty payments for the right to extract oil and gas or to exploit other mineral resources are normally regarded as non-tax revenues since they are property income from government-owned land or resources.

Fines and penalties

14. In principle, fines and penalties charged on overdue taxes or penalties imposed for the attempted evasion of taxes should not be recorded as tax revenues. However it may not be possible to separate payments of fines or other penalties from the revenues from the taxes to which they relate. In this case the fines and penalties relating to a particular tax are recorded together with the revenues from that tax and fines and penalties paid with revenue from unidentifiable taxes are classified as other taxes in Category 6000. Fines not relating to tax offences (e.g. for parking offences), or not identifiable as relating to tax offences, are also not treated as tax revenues.

A.3. Basis of reporting

Accrual reporting

15. The data reported in this publication for recent years are predominantly recorded on an accrual basis, i.e. recorded at the time that the tax liability was created. Further information is provided in the footnotes to the country table in Chapter 4 of the Report[1].

16. However, data for earlier years are still predominantly recorded on a cash basis, i.e. at the time at which the payment was received by government. Thus, for example, taxes withheld by employers in one year but paid to the government in the following year and taxes due in one year but actually paid in the following year are both included in the receipts of the second year. Corrective transactions, such as refunds, repayments and drawbacks, are deducted from gross revenues of the period in which they are made.

17. Data on tax revenues are recorded without offsets for the administrative expenses connected with tax collection. Similarly, where the proceeds of tax are used to subsidise particular members of the community, the subsidy is not deducted from the yield of the tax, though the tax may be shown net of subsidies in the national records of some countries.

18. As regards fiscal monopolies (heading 5122), only the amount actually transferred to the government is included in government revenues. However, if any expenditures of fiscal monopolies are considered to be government expenditures (e.g. social expenditures undertaken by fiscal monopolies at the direction of the government) they are added back for the purpose of arriving at tax revenue figures (see §61 below).

The distinction between tax and expenditure provisions[7]

19. Because this publication is concerned only with the revenue side of government operations, no account being taken of the expenditure side, a distinction has to be made between tax and expenditure provisions. Normally there is no difficulty in making this distinction as expenditures are made outside the tax system and the tax accounts and under legislation separate from the tax legislation. In borderline cases, cash flow is used to distinguish between tax provisions and expenditure provisions. Insofar as a provision affects the flow of tax payments from the taxpayer to the government, it is regarded as a tax provision and is taken into account in the data shown in this publication. A provision which does not affect this flow is seen as an expenditure provision and is disregarded in the data recorded in this publication.

20. Tax allowances, exemptions and deductions against the tax base clearly affect the amount of tax paid to the government and are therefore considered as tax provisions. At the other extreme, those subsidies which cannot be offset against tax liability and which are clearly not connected with the assessment process, do not reduce tax revenues as recorded in this publication. Tax credits are amounts deductible from tax payable (as distinct from deductions from the tax base). Two types of tax credits are distinguished, those (referred to here as wastable tax credits) which are limited to the amount of the tax liability and therefore cannot give rise to a payment by the authorities to the taxpayer, and those (referred to as non-wastable tax credits) which are not so limited, so that the excess of the credit over the tax liability can be paid to the taxpayer.[8] A wastable tax credit, like a tax allowance, clearly affects the amount of tax paid to the government, and is therefore considered as a tax provision. The practice followed for non-wastable tax credits[9] is to distinguish between the "tax expenditure component",[10] which is that portion of the credit that is used to reduce or eliminate a taxpayer's liability, and the "transfer component", which is the portion that exceeds the taxpayer's liability and is paid to that taxpayer. Reported tax revenues should be reduced by the amount of the tax expenditure component but not by the amount of the transfer component. In addition, the amounts of the tax expenditure and transfer components should be reported as memorandum items in the country tables. Countries that are unable to distinguish between the tax expenditure and transfer components should indicate whether or not the tax revenues have been reduced by the total of these components, and provide any available estimates of the amounts of the two components. Further information is given in Chapter 2 of the Report[1], which illustrates the effect of alternative treatments of non-wastable tax credits on Tax to GDP.

Calendar and fiscal years

21. National authorities whose fiscal years do not correspond to the calendar year show data, where possible, on a calendar year basis to permit maximum comparability with the data of other countries. There remain a few countries where data refer to fiscal years. For these the GDP data used in the comparative tables also correspond to the fiscal years.

A.4. General classification criteria

The main classification criteria

22. The classification of receipts among the main headings (1000, 2000, 3000, 4000, 5000 and 6000) is generally governed by the base on which the tax is levied: 1000 income, profits and capital gains; 2000 and 3000 earnings, payroll or number of employees; 4000 property; 5000 goods and services; 6000 multiple bases, other bases or unidentifiable bases. Where a

tax is calculated on more than one base, the receipts are, where possible, split among the various headings (see §27 and §77). The headings 4000 and 5000 cover not only taxes where the tax base is the property, goods or services themselves but also certain related taxes. Thus, taxes on the transfer of property are included in 4400[11] and taxes on the use of goods or on permission to perform activities in 5200. In headings 4000 and 5000 a distinction is made in certain sub-headings between recurrent and non-recurrent taxes: recurrent taxes are defined as those levied at regular intervals (usually annually) and non-recurrent taxes are levied once and for all (see also §42 to §45, §48, §49 and §75 for particular applications of this distinction).

23. Earmarking of a tax for specific purposes does not affect the classification of tax receipts. However, as explained in §34 on the classification of social security contributions, the conferment of an entitlement to social benefits is crucial to the definition of the 2000 main heading.

24. The way that a tax is levied or collected (e.g. by use of stamps) does not affect classification.

Classification of taxpayers

25. In certain sub-headings distinctions are made between different categories of taxpayers. These distinctions vary from tax to tax:

a. *Between individuals and corporations in relation to income and net wealth taxes*

The basic distinction is that corporation income taxes, as distinct from individual income taxes, are levied on the corporation as an entity, not on the individuals who own it, and without regard to the personal circumstances of these individuals. The same distinction applies to net wealth taxes on corporations and those on individuals. Taxes paid on the profits of partnerships and the income of institutions, such as life insurance or pension funds, are classified according to the same rule. They are classified as corporate taxes (1200) if they are charged on the partnership or institution as an entity without regard to the personal circumstances of the owners. Otherwise, they are treated as individual taxes (1100). Usually, there is different legislation for the corporation taxes and for the individual taxes.[12] The distinction made here between individuals and corporations does not follow the sector classification between households, enterprises, and so on of the System of National Accounts for income and outlay accounts. The SNA classification requires certain unincorporated businesses[13] to be excluded from the household sector and included with non-financial enterprises and financial institutions. The tax on the profits of these businesses, however, cannot always be separated from the tax on the other income of their owners, or can be separated only on an arbitrary basis. No attempt at this separation is made here and the whole of the individual income tax is shown together without regard to the nature of the income chargeable.

b. *Between households and others in relation to taxes on immovable property*

Here the distinction is that adopted by the SNA for the production and consumption expenditure accounts. The distinction is between households as consumers (i.e. excluding non-incorporated business) on the one hand and producers on the other hand. However, taxes on dwellings occupied by households, whether paid by owner-occupiers, tenants or landlords, are classified under households. This follows the common distinction made between taxes on domestic property versus taxes on business property. Some countries are not, however, in a position to make this distinction.

c. *Between households and others in relation to motor vehicle licences*

Here the distinction is between households as consumers on the one hand and producers on the other, as in the production and consumption expenditure accounts of the SNA.

d. *Between business and others in relation to the residual taxes (6000)*

The distinction is the same as in c) above between producers on the one hand and households as consumers on the other hand. Taxes which are included under the heading 6000 because they involve more than one tax base or because the tax base does not fall within any of the previous categories but which are identifiable as levyable only on producers and not on households are included under "business". The rest of the taxes which are included under the heading 6000 are shown as "other" or non-identified.

Surcharges

26. Receipts from surcharges in respect of particular taxes are usually classified with the receipts from the relevant tax whether or not the surcharge is temporary. If, however, the surcharge has a characteristic which would render it classifiable in a different heading of the OECD list, receipts from the surcharge are classified under that heading separately from the relevant tax.

Unidentifiable tax receipts and residual sub-headings

27. A number of cases arise where taxes cannot be identified as belonging entirely to a heading or sub-heading of the OECD classification and the following practices are applied in such cases:

a. The heading is known, but it is not known how receipts should be allocated between sub-headings: receipts are classified in the appropriate residual sub-heading (1300, 2400, 4520, 4600, 5130, 5300 or 6200).

b. It is known that the bulk of receipts from a group of taxes (usually local taxes) is derived from taxes within a particular heading or sub-heading, but some of the taxes in the group whose amount cannot be precisely ascertained may be classifiable in other headings or sub-headings: receipts are shown in the heading or sub-heading under which most of the receipts fall.

c. Neither the heading nor sub-heading of a tax (usually local) can be identified: the tax is classified in 6200 unless it is known that it is a tax on business in which case it is classified in 6100.

A.5. Commentaries on items of the list

1000 — *Taxes on income, profits and capital gains*

28. This heading covers taxes levied on the net income or profits (i.e. gross income minus allowable tax reliefs) of individuals and enterprises. Also covered are taxes levied on the capital gains of individuals and enterprises, and gains from gambling.

29. Included in the heading are:

a. taxes levied predominantly on income or profits, though partially on other bases. Taxes on various bases which are not predominantly income or profits are classified according to the principles laid down in §27 and §77;

b. taxes on property, which are levied on a presumed or estimated income as part of an income tax (see also §42(a), (c) and (d));

c. compulsory payments to social security fund contributions that are levied on income but do not confer an entitlement to social benefits. When such contributions do confer an entitlement to social benefits, they are included in heading 2000 (see §34);

d. receipts from integrated scheduler income tax systems are classified as a whole in this heading, even though certain of the scheduler taxes may be based upon gross income and may not take into account the personal circumstances of the taxpayer.

30. The main subdivision of this heading is between levies on individuals (1100) and those on corporate enterprises (1200). Under each subdivision a distinction is made between taxes on income and profits (1110 and 1210), and taxes on capital gains (1120 and 1220). If certain receipts cannot be identified as appropriate to either 1100 or 1200, or if in practice this distinction cannot be made (e.g. because there are no reliable data on the recipients of payments from which withholding taxes are deducted) they are classified in 1300 as not-allocable.

Treatment of credits under imputation systems

31. Under imputation systems of corporate income tax, a company's shareholders are wholly or partly relieved of their liability to income tax on dividends paid by the company out of income or profits liable to corporate income tax. In countries with such systems,[14] part of the tax on the company's profits is available to provide relief against the shareholders' own tax liability. The relief to the shareholder takes the form of a tax credit, the amount of which may be less than, equal to, or more than the shareholders' overall tax liability. If the tax credit exceeds this tax liability the excess may be payable to the shareholder. As this type of tax credit is an integral part of the imputation system of corporate income tax, any payment to the shareholders is treated as a repayment of tax and not as expenditure (compare the treatment of other tax credits described in §20).

32. As the tax credit under imputation systems (even when exceeding tax liability) is to be regarded as a tax provision, the question arises whether it should be deducted from individual income tax receipts (1110) or corporate income tax receipts (1210). In this Report, the full amount of corporate income tax paid is shown under 1210 and no imputed tax is included under 1110. Thus, the full amount of the credit reduces the amount of 1110 whether the credit results in a reduction of personal income tax liability or whether an actual refund is made because the credit exceeds the income tax liability. (Where, however, such tax credits are deducted from corporation tax in respect of dividends paid to corporations the amounts are deducted from the receipts of 1210).

1120 and 1220 — *Taxes on capital gains*

33. These sub-headings comprise taxes imposed on capital gains, 1120 covering those levied on the gains of individuals and 1220 those levied on the gains of corporate enterprises, where receipts from such taxes can be separately identified. In many countries this is not the case and the receipts from such taxes are then classified with those from the income tax. Heading 1120 also includes taxes on gains from gambling.

2000 — *Social security contributions*

34. Classified here are all compulsory payments that confer an entitlement to receive a (contingent) future social benefit. Such payments are usually earmarked to finance social benefits and are often paid to institutions of general government that provide such benefits. However, such earmarking is not part of the definition of social security contributions and is not required for a tax to be classified here. However, conferment of an entitlement is

required for a tax to be classified under this heading. So, levies on income or payroll that are earmarked for social security funds but do not confer an entitlement to benefit are excluded from this heading and shown under personal income taxes (1100) or taxes on payroll and workforce (3000). Taxes on other bases, such as goods and services, which are earmarked for social security benefits are not shown here but are classified according to their respective bases because they generally confer no entitlement to social security benefits.

35. Contributions for the following types of social security benefits would, *inter alia*, be included: unemployment insurance benefits and supplements, accident, injury and sickness benefits, old-age, disability and survivors' pensions, family allowances, reimbursements for medical and hospital expenses or provision of hospital or medical services. Contributions may be levied on both employees and employers.

36. Contributions may be based on earnings or payroll ("on a payroll basis") or on net income after deductions and exemptions for personal circumstances ("on an income tax basis"), and the revenues from the two bases should be separately identified if possible. However, where contributions to a general social security scheme are on a payroll basis, but the contributions of particular groups (such as the self-employed) cannot be assessed on this basis and net income is used as a proxy for gross earnings, the receipts may still be classified as being on a payroll basis. In principle, this heading excludes voluntary contributions paid to social security schemes. When separately identifiable these are shown in the memorandum item on the financing of social security benefits. In practice, however, they cannot always be separately identified from compulsory contributions, in which case they are included in this heading.

37. Contributions to social insurance schemes which are not institutions of general government and to other types of insurance schemes, provident funds, pension funds, friendly societies or other saving schemes are not considered as social security contributions. Provident funds are arrangements under which the contributions of each employee and of the corresponding employer on his/her behalf are kept in a separate account earning interest and withdrawable under specific circumstances. Pension funds are separately organised schemes negotiated between employees and employers and carry provisions for different contributions and benefits, sometimes more directly tied to salary levels and length of service than under social security schemes. When contributions to these schemes are compulsory or quasi-compulsory (e.g. by virtue of agreement with professional and union organisations) they are shown in the memorandum item (refer to Chapter 4.2 of the Report)[1].

38. Contributions by government employees and by governments in respect of their employees, to social security schemes classified within general government are included in this heading. Contributions to separate schemes for government employees, which can be regarded as replacing general social security schemes, are also regarded as taxes.[15] Where, however, a separate scheme is not seen as replacing a general scheme and has been negotiated between the government, in its role as an employer, and its employees, it is not regarded as social security and contributions to it are not regarded as taxes, even though the scheme may have been established by legislation.

39. This heading excludes "imputed" contributions, which correspond to social benefits paid directly by employers to their employees or former employees or to their representatives (e.g. when employers are legally obliged to pay sickness benefits for a certain period).

40. Contributions are divided into those of employees (2100), employers (2200), and self-employed or non-employed (2300), and then further sub-divided according to the basis on which they are levied. Employees are defined for this purpose as all persons engaged in

activities of business units, government bodies, private non-profit institutions, or other paid employment, except the proprietors and their unpaid family members in the case of unincorporated businesses. Members of the armed forces are included, irrespective of the duration and type of their service, if they contribute to social security schemes. The contributions of employers are defined as their payments on account of their employees to social security schemes. Where employees or employers are required to continue the payment of social security contributions when the employee becomes unemployed these contributions, data permitting, are shown in 2100 and 2200 respectively. Accordingly, the sub-heading 2300 is confined to contributions paid by the self-employed and by those outside of the labour force (e.g. disabled or retired individuals).

3000 — *Taxes on payroll and workforce*

41. This heading covers taxes paid by employers, employees or the self-employed either as a proportion of payroll or as a fixed amount per person, and which do not confer entitlement to social benefits. Examples of taxes classified here are the United Kingdom national insurance surcharge (introduced in 1977), the Swedish payroll tax (1969–1979), and the Austrian Contribution to the Family Burden Equalisation Fund and Community Tax.

4000 — *Taxes on property*

42. This heading covers recurrent and non-recurrent taxes on the use, ownership or transfer of property. These include taxes on immovable property or net wealth, taxes on the change of ownership of property through inheritance or gift and taxes on financial and capital transactions. The following kinds of tax are excluded from this heading:

a. taxes on capital gains resulting from the sale of a property (1120 or 1220);
b. taxes on the use of goods or on permission to use goods or perform activities (5200); see §72;
c. taxes on immovable property levied on the basis of a presumed net income which take into account the personal circumstances of the taxpayer. They are classified as income taxes along with taxes on income and capital gains derived from property (1100);
d. taxes on the use of property for residence, where the tax is payable by either proprietor or tenant and the amount payable is a function of the user's personal circumstances (pay, dependants, and so on). They are classified as taxes on income (1100);
e. taxes on building in excess of permitted maximum density, taxes on the enlargement, construction or alteration of certain buildings beyond a permitted value and taxes on building construction. They are classified as taxes on permission to perform activities (5200);
f. taxes on the use of one's own property for special trading purposes like selling alcohol, tobacco, meat or for exploitation of land resources (e.g. United States severance taxes). They are classified as taxes on permission to perform activities (5200).

4100 — *Recurrent taxes on immovable property*

43. This sub-heading covers taxes levied regularly in respect of the use or ownership of immovable property.

- these taxes are levied on land and buildings;
- they can be in the form of a percentage of an assessed property value based on a national rental income, sales price, or capitalised yield; or in terms of other characteristics of real property, (for example size or location) from which a presumed rent or capital value can be derived.

- such taxes can be levied on proprietors, tenants, or both. They can also be paid by one level of government to another level of government in respect of property under the jurisdiction of the latter.
- debts are not taken into account in the assessment of these taxes, and they differ from taxes on net wealth in this respect.

44. Taxes on immovable property are further sub-divided into those paid by households (4110) and those paid by other entities (4120), according to the criteria set out in §25(*b*) above.

4200 — *Recurrent taxes on net wealth*

45. This sub-heading covers taxes levied regularly (in most cases annually) on net wealth, i.e. taxes on a wide range of movable and immovable property, net of debt. It is sub-divided into taxes paid by individuals (4210) and taxes paid by corporate enterprises (4220) according to the criteria set out in §25(*a*) above. If separate figures exist for receipts paid by institutions, the tax payments involved are added to those paid by corporations.

4300 — *Estate, inheritance and gift taxes*

46. This sub-heading is divided into taxes on estates and inheritances (4310) and taxes on gifts (4320).[16] Estate taxes are charged on the amount of the total estate whereas inheritance taxes are charged on the shares of the individual recipients; in addition the latter may take into account the relationship of the individual recipients to the deceased.

4400 — *Taxes on financial and capital transactions*

47. This sub-heading comprises, *inter alia*, taxes on the issue, transfer, purchase and sale of securities, taxes on cheques, and taxes levied on specific legal transactions such as validation of contracts and the sale of immovable property. The heading does not include:

a. taxes on the use of goods or property or permission to perform certain activities (5200);

b. fees paid to cover court charges, charges for birth, marriage or death certificates, which are normally regarded as non-tax revenues (see §9);

c. taxes on capital gains (1000);

d. recurrent taxes on immovable property (4100);

e. recurrent taxes on net wealth (4200);

f. once-and-for-all levies on property or wealth (4500).

4500 — *Other non-recurrent taxes on property*[16]

48. This sub-heading covers once-and-for-all, as distinct from recurrent, levies on property. It is divided into taxes on net wealth (4510) and other non-recurrent taxes on property (4520). Heading 4510 would include taxes levied to meet emergency expenditures, or for redistribution purposes. Heading 4520 would cover taxes levied to take account of increases in land value due to permission given to develop or provision of additional local facilities by general government, any taxes on the revaluation of capital and once-and-for-all taxes on particular items of property.

4600 — *Other recurrent taxes on property*

49. These rarely exist in OECD member countries, but the heading would include taxes on goods such as cattle, jewellery, windows, and other external signs of wealth.

5000 — *Taxes on goods and services*

50. All taxes and duties levied on the production, extraction, sale, transfer, leasing or delivery of goods, and the rendering of services (5100), or in respect of the use of goods or permission to use goods or to perform activities (5200) are included here. The heading thus covers:

a. multi-stage cumulative taxes;
b. general sales taxes — whether levied at manufacture/production, wholesale or retail level;
c. value-added taxes;
d. excises;
e. taxes levied on the import and export of goods;
f. taxes levied in respect of the use of goods and taxes on permission to use goods, or perform certain activities;
g. taxes on the extraction, processing or production of minerals and other products.

51. Borderline cases between this heading and heading 4000 (taxes on property) and 6100 (other taxes on business) are referred to in §42, §47 and §74. Residual sub-headings (5300) and (5130) cover tax receipts which cannot be allocated between 5100 and 5200 and between 5110 and 5120, respectively; see §27.

5100 — *Taxes on the production, sale, transfer, leasing and delivery of goods and rendering of services*

52. This sub-heading consists of all taxes, levied on transactions in goods and services on the basis of their intrinsic characteristics (e.g. value, weight of tobacco, strength of alcohol, and so on) as distinct from taxes imposed on the use of goods, or permission to use goods or perform activities, which fall under 5200.

5110 — *General taxes on goods and services*

53. This sub-heading includes all taxes, other than import and export duties (5123 and 5124), levied on the production, leasing, transfer, delivery or sales of a wide range of goods and/or the rendering of a wide range of services, irrespective of whether they are domestically produced or imported and irrespective of the stage of production or distribution at which they are levied. It thus covers value-added taxes, sales taxes and multi-stage cumulative taxes. Receipts from border adjustments in respect of such taxes when goods are imported are added to gross receipts for this category, and repayments of such taxes when goods are exported are deducted. These taxes are subdivided into 5111 value-added taxes, 5112 sales taxes, 5113 other general taxes on goods and services.

54. Borderline cases arise between this heading and taxes on specific goods (5120) when taxes are levied on a large number of goods, for example, the United Kingdom purchase tax (repealed in 1973) and the Japanese commodity tax (repealed in 1988). In conformity with national views, the former United Kingdom purchase tax is classified as a general tax (5112) and the former Japanese commodity tax as excises (5121).

5111 — *Value-added taxes*

55. All general consumption taxes charged on value-added are classified in this sub-heading, irrespective of the method of deduction and the stages at which the taxes are levied. In practice, all OECD countries with value-added taxes normally allow immediate deduction of taxes on purchases by all but the final consumer and impose tax at all stages. In some countries the heading may include certain taxes, such as those on financial and insurance

activities, either because receipts from them cannot be identified separately from those from the value-added tax, or because they are regarded as an integral part of the value-added tax, even though similar taxes in other countries might be classified elsewhere (e.g. 5126 as taxes on services or 4400 as taxes on financial and capital transactions).

5112 — *Sales taxes*

56. All general taxes levied at one stage only, whether at manufacturing or production, wholesale or retail stage are classified here.

5113 — *Other general taxes on goods and services*

57. This sub-heading covers multi-stage cumulative taxes (also known as "cascade taxes") where tax is levied each time a transaction takes place without deduction for tax paid on inputs, and also those general consumption taxes where elements of value-added, sales or cascade taxes are combined.

5120 — *Taxes on specific goods and services*

58. Excises, profits generated and transferred from fiscal monopolies, and customs and imports duties as well as taxes on exports, foreign exchange transactions, investment goods and betting stakes and special taxes on services, which do not form part of a general tax of 5110, are included in this category.

5121 — Excises

59. Excises are taxes levied on particular products, or on a limited range of products, which are not classifiable under 5110 (general taxes), 5123 (import duties) and 5124 (export duties). They may be imposed at any stage of production or distribution and are usually assessed by reference to the weight or strength or quantity of the product, but sometimes by reference to value. Thus, special taxes on, for example, sugar, beetroot, matches, chocolates, and taxes at varying rates on a certain range of goods, as well as those levied in most countries on tobacco goods, alcoholic drinks and hydrocarbon oils and other energy sources, are included in this sub-heading.

60. Excises are distinguished from:

a. 5110 (general taxes). This is discussed in §53-54;

b. 5123 (import duties). If a tax collected principally on imported goods also applies, or would apply, under the law by which the tax is imposed to comparable home-produced goods, the receipts there from would be classified as excises (5121). This principle applies even if there is no comparable home production or no possibility of it (see also §64);

c. 5126 (taxes on services). The problem here arises in respect of taxes on electricity, gas and energy. All of these are regarded as taxes on goods and are included under 5121.

5122 — *Profits of fiscal monopolies*

61. This sub-heading covers that part of the profits of fiscal monopolies which is transferred to general government or which is used to finance any expenditures considered to be government expenditures (see §18). Amounts are shown when they are transferred to general government or used to make expenditures considered to be government expenditures.

62. Fiscal monopolies reflect the exercise of the taxing power of government by the use of monopoly powers. Fiscal monopolies are non-financial public enterprises exercising a monopoly in most cases over the production or distribution of tobacco, alcoholic beverages, salt, matches, playing cards and petroleum or agricultural products (i.e. on the kind of products which are likely to be, alternatively or additionally, subject to the excises of 5121),

to raise the government revenues which in other countries are gathered through taxes on dealings in such commodities by private business units. The government monopoly may be at the production stage or, as in the case of government-owned and controlled liquor stores, at the distribution stage.

63. Fiscal monopolies are distinguished from public utilities such as rail transport, electricity, post offices, and other communications, which may enjoy a monopoly or quasi-monopoly position but where the primary purpose is normally to provide basic services rather than to raise revenue for government. Transfers from such other public enterprises to the government are considered as non-tax revenues. The traditional concept of fiscal monopoly is not generally extended to include state lotteries, the profits of which are usually accordingly regarded as non-tax revenues. However, they can be included as tax revenues if the prime reason for their operation is to raise revenues to finance government expenditure. Fiscal monopoly profits are distinguished from export and import monopoly profits (5127) transferred from marketing boards or other enterprises dealing with international trade.

5123 — *Customs and other import duties*

64. Taxes, stamp duties and surcharges restricted by law to imported products are included here. Also included are levies on imported agricultural products which are imposed in member countries of the European Union and amounts paid by certain of these countries under the Monetary Compensation Accounts (MCA) system.[17] Starting from 1998, customs duties collected by European Union member states on behalf of the European Union are no longer reported under this heading in the country tables (in Chapter 4 of the Report).[1] Excluded here are taxes collected on imports as part of a general tax on goods and services, or an excise applicable to both imported and domestically produced goods.

5124 — *Taxes on exports*

65. In the 1970s, export duties were levied in Australia, Canada and Portugal as a regular measure and they have been used in Finland for counter-cyclical purposes. Some member countries of the European Union pay, as part of the MCA system, a levy on exports (see note 16 to §64). Where these amounts are identifiable, they are shown in this heading. This heading does not include repayments of general consumption taxes or excises or customs duties on exported goods, which should be deducted from the gross receipts under 5110, 5121 or 5123, as appropriate.

5125 — *Taxes on investment goods*

66. This sub-heading covers taxes on investment goods, such as machinery. These taxes may be imposed for a number of years or temporarily for counter-cyclical purposes. Taxes on industrial inputs which are also levied on consumers [e.g. the Swedish energy tax which is classified under (5121)] are not included here.

5126 — *Taxes on specific services*

67. All taxes assessed on the payment for specific services, such as taxes on insurance premiums, banking services, gambling and betting stakes (e.g. from horse races, football pools, lottery tickets), transport, entertainment, restaurant and advertising charges, fall into this category. Taxes levied on the gross income of companies providing the service (e.g. gross insurance premiums or gambling stakes received by the company) are also classified under this heading. Tax revenues from bank levies and payments to deposit insurance and financial stability schemes are provisionally included here for the 2012 edition. The detailed classification is set out in paragraph 104.

68. Excluded from this sub-heading are:

1. taxes on services forming part of a general tax on goods and services (5110);
2. taxes on electricity, gas and energy (5121 as excises);
3. taxes on individual gains from gambling (1120 as taxes on capital gains of individuals and non-corporate enterprises) and lump-sum taxes on the transfer of private lotteries or on the permission to set up lotteries (5200);[18]
4. taxes on cheques and on the issue, transfer or redemption of securities (4400 as taxes on financial and capital transactions).

5127 — *Other taxes on international trade and transactions*

69. This sub-heading covers revenue received by the government from the purchase and sale of foreign exchange at different rates. When the government exercises monopoly powers to extract a margin between the purchase and sales price of foreign exchange, other than to cover administrative costs, the revenue derived constitutes a compulsory levy exacted in indeterminate proportions from both purchaser and seller of foreign exchange. It is the common equivalent of an import duty and export duty levied in a single exchange rate system or of a tax on the sale or purchase of foreign exchange. Like the profits of fiscal monopolies and import or export monopolies transferred to government, it represents the exercise of monopoly powers for tax purposes and is included in tax revenues.

70. The sub-heading covers also the profits of export or import monopolies, which do not however exist in OECD countries, taxes on purchase or sale of foreign exchange, and any other taxes levied specifically on international trade or transactions.

5128 — *Other taxes on specific goods and services*

71. This item includes taxes on the extraction of minerals, fossil fuels and other exhaustible resources from deposits owned privately or by another government together with any other unidentifiable receipts from taxes on specific goods and services. Taxes on the extraction of exhaustible resources are usually a fixed amount per unit of quality or weight, but can be a percentage of value. The taxes are recorded when the resources are extracted. Payments from the extraction of exhaustible resources from deposits owned by the government unit receiving the payment are classified as rent.

5200 — *Taxes on use of goods or on permission to use goods or perform activities*

72. This sub-heading covers taxes which are levied in respect of the use of goods as distinct from taxes on the goods themselves. Unlike the latter taxes – reported under 5100 –, they are not assessed on the value of the goods but usually as fixed amounts. Taxes on permission to use goods or to perform activities are also included here, as are pollution taxes not based upon the value of particular goods. It is sometimes difficult to distinguish between compulsory user charges and licence fees which are regarded as taxes and those which are excluded as non-tax revenues. The criteria which are employed are noted in §9–10.

73. Although the sub-heading refers to the "use" of goods, registration of ownership rather than use may be what generates liability to tax, so that the taxes of this heading may apply to the ownership of animals or goods rather than their use (e.g. race horses, dogs and motor vehicles) and may apply even to unusable goods (e.g. unusable motor vehicles or guns).

74. Borderline cases arise with:

a. taxes on the permission to perform business activities which are levied on a combined income, payroll or turnover base and, accordingly, are classified following the rules in §77;

b. taxes on the ownership or use of property of headings 4100, 4200 and 4600. The heading 4100 is confined to taxes on the ownership or tenancy of immovable property and – unlike the taxes of 5200 – they are related to the value of the property. The net wealth taxes and taxes on chattels of 4200 and 4600 respectively are confined to the ownership rather than the use of assets, apply to groups of assets rather than particular goods and again are related to the value of the assets,

5210 — *Recurrent taxes on use of goods and on permission to use goods or perform activities*

75. The principal characteristic of taxes classified here is that they are levied at regular intervals and that they are usually fixed amounts. The most important item in terms of revenue receipts is vehicle licence taxes. This sub-heading also covers taxes on permission to hunt, shoot, fish or to sell certain products and taxes on the ownership of dogs and on the performance of certain services, provided that they meet the criteria set out in §9–10. The sub-divisions of 5210 are user taxes on motor vehicles paid by households (5211) and those paid by others (5212).[19] Sub-heading 5213 covers dog licences and user charges for permission to perform activities such as selling meat or liquor when the levies are on a recurring basis. It also covers recurrent general licences for hunting, shooting and fishing where the right to carry out these activities is not granted as part of a normal commercial transaction (e.g. the granting of the licence is not accompanied by the right to use a specific area which is owned by government).

5220 — *Non-recurrent taxes on use of goods and on permission to use goods or perform activities*

76. This section covers non-recurrent taxes levied on the use of goods or on permission to use goods or perform activities and taxes levied each time goods are used. It includes taxes levied on the emission or discharge into the environment of noxious gases, liquids or other harmful substances.

- Payments for tradable emission permits issued by governments under cap and trade schemes should be recorded here at the time the emissions occur. No revenue should be recorded for permits that governments issue free of charge. The accrual basis of recording means that there can be a timing difference between the cash being received by government for the permits and the time the emission occurs. In the national accounts, this timing gives rise to a financial liability for government during the period.
- Payments made for the collection and disposal of waste or noxious substances by public authorities should be excluded as they constitute a sale of services to enterprises.

77. Other taxes falling under heading 5200 that are not levied recurrently are also included here. Thus, once-and-for-all payments for permission to sell liquor or tobacco or to set up betting shops are included provided they meet the criteria set out in §9–10.

6000 — *Other taxes*

78. Taxes levied on a base, or bases, other than those described under headings 1000, 3000, 4000 and 5000, or on bases of which none could be regarded as being predominantly the same as that of any one of these headings, are covered here. As regards taxes levied on a multiple base, if it is possible to estimate receipts related to each base (e.g. the Austrian and German "Gewerbesteuer") this is done and the separate amounts included under the appropriate headings. If the separate amounts cannot be estimated, but it is known that most of the receipts are derived from one base, the whole of the receipts are classified according to that base. If neither of these procedures can be followed, they are classified here. The sub-headings may also include receipts from taxes which governments are unable to identify or isolate (see §27). Included here also are fines and penalties paid for infringement of regulations relating to taxes but not identifiable as relating to a particular category of taxes (see §14).

A subdivision is made between taxes levied wholly or predominantly on business (6100) and those levied on others (6200).

A.6. Conciliation with National Accounts

79. This section of the tables provides a re-conciliation between the OECD calculation of total tax revenues and the total of all taxes and social contributions paid to general government as recorded in the country's National Accounts. Where the country is a member of the European Union (EU), the comparison is between the OECD calculation of total tax revenues and the sum of tax revenues and social contributions recorded in the combination of the general government and the institutions of the EU sectors of the National Accounts.

A.7. Memorandum item on the financing of social security benefits

80. In view of the varying relationship between taxation and social security contributions and the cases referred to in §34 to §40, a memorandum item collects together all payments earmarked for social security-type benefits, other than voluntary payments to the private sector. Data are presented as follows (refer Chapter 4.2 of the Report):[1]

a. Taxes of 2000 series.

b. Taxes earmarked for social security benefits.

c. Voluntary contributions to the government.

d. Compulsory contributions to the private sector.

Guidance on the breakdown of (a) to (d) above is provided in §34 to §40.

A.8. Memorandum item on identifiable taxes paid by government

81. Identifiable taxes actually paid by government are presented in a memorandum item classified by the main headings of the OECD classification of taxes. In the vast majority of countries, only social security contributions and payroll taxes paid by government can be identified. These are, however, usually the most important taxes paid by governments (refer to Chapter 4.3 of the Report).[1]

A.9. Relation of OECD classification of taxes to national accounting systems

82. A system of national accounts (SNA) seeks to provide a coherent framework for recording and presenting the main flows relating respectively to production, consumption, accumulation and external transactions of a given economic area, usually a country or a major region within a country. Government revenues are an important part of the transactions recorded in SNA. The final version of the 2008 SNA was jointly published by five international organisations: the United Nations, the International Monetary Fund, the European Union, the Organisation for Economic Co-operation and Development, and the World Bank in August 2009. The *System* is a comprehensive, consistent and flexible set of macroeconomic accounts. It is designed for use in countries with market economies, whatever their stage of economic development, and also in countries in transition to market economies. The important parts of the SNA's conceptual framework and its definitions of the various sectors of the economy have been reflected in the OECD's classification of taxes.

83. There are, however, some differences between the OECD classification of taxes and SNA concepts that are listed below. They arise because the aim of the former is to provide the maximum disaggregation of statistical data on what are generally regarded as taxes by tax administrations.

a. OECD includes compulsory social security contributions paid to general government in total tax revenues. Imputed and voluntary contributions plus those paid to private funds are not treated as taxes (§7 and §8 above);

b. there are different points of view on whether or not some levies and fees are classified as taxes (§9 and §10 above);

c. OECD excludes imputed taxes or subsidies resulting from the operation of official multiple exchange rates or from the central bank paying a rate of interest on required reserves that is different from other market rates;

d. there are differences in the treatment of non-wastable tax credits

84. As noted in §1 and §2, headings 1000 to 6000 of the OECD list of taxes cover all unrequited payments to general government, other than compulsory loans and fines. Such unrequited payments including fines, but excluding compulsory loans can be obtained from adding together the following figures in the 2008 SNA

- value-added type taxes (D.211);
- taxes and duties on imports, excluding VAT (D.212);
- export taxes (D.213);
- taxes on products, excluding VAT, import and export taxes (D.214);
- other taxes on production (D.29);
- taxes on income (D.51);
- other current taxes (D.59);
- social contributions (D.61), excluding voluntary contributions;
- capital taxes (D.91).

A.10. The OECD classification of taxes and the International Monetary Fund (GFS) system

85. The coverage and valuation of tax revenues in the GFS system and the 2008 SNA are very similar. Therefore, the differences between the OECD classification and that of the 2008 SNA (see §83 above) also apply to the GFS. In addition the International Monetary Fund subdivides the OECD 5000 heading into section IV (Domestic Taxes on Goods and Services) and section V (Taxes on International Trade and Transactions). This reflects the fact that while the latter usually yield insignificant amounts of revenue in OECD countries, this is not the case in many non-OECD countries.

A.11. Comparison of the OECD classification of taxes with other international classifications

86. The table below describes an item by item comparison of the OECD classification of taxes and the classifications used in the following:

i) System of National Accounts (2008 SNA);

ii) European System of Accounts (2010 ESA);

iii) IMF *Government Finance Statistics Manual* (GFSM2014).

87. These comparisons represent those that would be expected to apply in the majority of cases. However in practice some flexibility should be used in their application. This is because in particular cases, countries can adopt varying approaches to the classification of revenues in National Accounts.

	OECD Classification	2008 SNA	2010 ESA	GFSM2014
1000	Taxes on income, profits and capital gains			
	1100 Individuals			
	1110 Income and profits	D51-8.61a	D51A	1111
	1120 Capital gains	D51-8.61c, d	D51C, D	1111
	1200 Corporations			
	1210 Income and profits	D51-8.61b	D51B	1112
	1220 Capital gains	D51-8.61c	D51C	1112
	1300 Unallocable as between 1100 and 1200			1113
2000	Social security contributions			
	2100 Employees	D613-8.85	D613	1211
	2200 Employers	D611-8.83	D611	1212
	2300 Self-employed, non-employed	D613-8.85	D613	1213
	2400 Unallocable as between 2100, 2200 and 2300			1214
3000	Taxes on payroll and workforce	D29-7.97a	D29C	112
4000	Taxes on property			
	4100 Recurrent taxes on immovable property			
	4110 Households	D59-8.63a	D59A	1131
	4120 Other	D29-7.97b	D29A	1131
	4200 Recurrent net wealth taxes			
	4210 Individual	D59-8.63b	D59A	1132
	4220 Corporations	D59-8.63b	D59A	1132
	4300 Estate, inheritance and gift taxes			
	4310 Estate and inheritance taxes	D91-10.207b	D91A	1133
	4320 Gift taxes	D91-10.207b	D91A	1133
	4400 Taxes on financial and capital transactions	D59-7.96d; D29-7.97e	D214B, C	114114; 1161
	4500 Other non-recurrent taxes on property	D91-10.207a	D91B	1135
	4600 Other recurrent taxes on property	D59-8.63c	D59A	1136
5000	Taxes on goods and services			
	5100 Taxes on production, sale and transfer of goods and services			
	5110 General taxes on goods and services			
	5111 Value-added taxes	D211-7.89	D211; D29G	11411
	5112 Sales taxes	D2122-7.94a; D214-7.96a	D21224; D214I	11412
	5113 Other general taxes on goods and services	D214-7.96a	D214I	11413
	5120 Taxes on specific goods and services			
	5121 Excises	D2122-7.94b; D214-7.96b	D21223; D214A, B, D	1142
	5122 Profits of fiscal monopolies	D214-7.96e	D214J	1143
	5123 Customs and other import duties	D2121-7.93	D2121; D21221, 2	1151
	5124 On exports	D213-7.95a	D214K	1152-4
	5125 On investment goods			
	5126 On specific services	D2122-7.94c; D214-7.96c	D21225; D214E, F, G; D29F	1144; 1156
	5127 Other taxes on international trade and transactions	D2122-7.94d D29-7.95b D29-7.97g D59-8.64d	D21226; D29D; D59E	1153; 1155-6
	5128 Other taxes on specific goods and services			1146
	5130 Unallocable between 5110 and 5120			
	5200 Taxes on use of goods and on permission to use goods or perform activities			
	5210 Recurrent taxes on use of goods and on permission to use goods or perform activities			
	5211 Motor vehicle taxes households	D59-8.64c	D59D	11451
	5212 Motor vehicles taxes others	D29-7.97d	D214D; D29B	11451
	5213 Other recurrent taxes on use of goods and on permission to use goods or perform activities	D29-7.97c, d, f D59-8.64c	D29B, E, F; D59D	11452
	5220 Non-recurrent taxes on permission to use goods or perform activities			11452
	5300 Unallocable as between 5100 and 5200			
6000	Other taxes			
	6100 Payable solely by business			1161
	6200 Payable by other than business, or unidentifiable	D59-8.64a, b	D59B, C	1162

A.12. Attribution of tax revenues by sub-sectors of general government

88. The OECD classification requires a breakdown of tax revenues by sub-sectors of government. The definition of each sub-sector and the criteria to be used to attribute tax revenues between these sub-sectors are set out below. They follow the guidance of the 2008 SNA and GFSM 2014.

Sub-sectors of general government to be identified

a) Central government

89. The central government sub-sector includes all governmental departments, offices, establishments and other bodies which are agencies or instruments of the central authority whose competence extends over the whole territory, with the exception of the administration of social security funds. Central government therefore has the authority to impose taxes on all resident and non-resident units engaged in economic activities within the country.

b) State, provincial or regional government

90. This sub-sector consists of intermediate units of government exercising a competence at a level below that of central government. It includes all such units operating independently of central government in a part of a country's territory encompassing a number of smaller localities, with the exception of the administration of social security funds. In unitary countries, regional governments may be considered to have a separate existence where they have substantial autonomy to raise a significant proportion of their revenues from sources within their control and their officers are independent of external administrative control in the actual operation of the unit's activities.

91. At present, federal countries comprise the majority of cases where revenues attributed to intermediate units of government are identified separately. Spain is the only unitary country in this position. In the remaining unitary countries, regional revenues are included with those of local governments.

c) Local government

92. This sub-sector includes all other units of government exercising an independent competence in part of the territory of a country, with the exception of the administration of social security funds. It encompasses various urban and/or rural jurisdictions (e.g. local authorities, municipalities, cities, boroughs, districts).

d) Social security funds

93. Social security funds form a separate sub-sector of general government. The social security sub-sector is defined in the 2008 SNA by the following extracts from paragraphs 4.124 to 4.126 and 4.147:

"Social security schemes are social insurance schemes covering the community as a whole or large section of the community that are imposed and controlled by government units. The schemes cover a wide variety of programmes, providing benefits in cash or in kind for old age, invalidity or death, survivors, sickness and maternity, work injury, unemployment, family allowance, health care, etc. There is not necessarily a direct link between the amount of the contribution paid by an individual and the benefits he or she may receive." (Paragraph 4.124).

"When social security schemes are separately organised from the other activities of government units and hold their assets and liabilities separately from the latter and engage in financial transactions on their own account they qualify as institutional units that are described as social security funds." (Paragraph 4.125).

"The amounts raised, and paid out, in social security contributions and benefits may be deliberately varied in order to achieve objectives of government policy that have no direct connection with the concept of social security as a scheme to provide social benefits to members of the community. They may be raised or lowered in order to influence the level of aggregate demand in the economy, for example. Nevertheless, so long as they remain separately constituted funds, they must be treated as separate institutional units in the SNA. (Paragraph 4.126).

"The social security funds sub-sector (of general government) consists of the social security funds operating at all levels of government. Such funds are social insurance schemes covering the community as a whole or large section of the community that are imposed by government units." (Paragraph 4.147).

94. This definition of social security funds is followed in the OECD classification with the two following exceptions which are excluded

- Schemes imposed by government and operated by bodies outside the general government sector, as defined in §3 of this manual; and
- Schemes to which all contributions are voluntary.

Supra-national authorities

95. This sub-sector covers the revenue-raising operations of supra-national authorities within a country. In practice, the only relevant supra-national authority in the OECD area is that of the institutions of the European Union (EU). As from 1998, supra-national authorities are no longer included in the *Revenue Statistics*, to achieve consistency with the SNA definition of general government which excludes them. For example, income taxes and social security contributions collected by European Institutions and paid by European civil servants who are resident of EU member countries should not be included. However the specific levies paid by the member states of the EU continue to be included in total tax revenues and they are shown under this heading.

Criteria to be used for the attribution of tax revenues

96. When a government collects taxes and pays them over in whole or in part to other governments, it is necessary to determine whether the revenues should be considered to be those of the collecting government which it distributes to others as grants, or those of the beneficiary governments which the collecting government receives and passes on only as their agent. The criteria to be used in the attribution of revenues are set out in §97 to §100 which replicate paragraphs 3.70 to 3.73 from the 2008 SNA.

97. In general, a tax is attributed to the government unit that

a. exercises the authority to impose the tax (either as a principal or through the delegated authority of the principal),

b. has final discretion to set and vary the rate of the tax

98. Where an amount is collected by one government for and on behalf of another government, and the latter government has the authority to impose the tax, and set and vary its rate, then the former is acting as an agent for the latter and the tax is reassigned.

Any amount retained by the collecting government as a collection charge should be treated as a payment for a service. Any other amount retained by the collecting government, such as under a tax-sharing arrangement, should be treated as a current grant. If the collecting government was delegated the authority to set and vary the rate, then the amount collected should be treated as tax revenue of this government.

99. Where different governments jointly and equally set the rate of a tax and jointly and equally decide on the distribution of the proceeds, with no individual government having ultimate overriding authority, then the tax revenues are attributed to each government according to its respective share of the proceeds. If an arrangement allows one government unit to exercise ultimate overriding authority, then all of the tax revenue is attributed to that unit.

100. There may also be the circumstance where a tax is imposed under the constitutional or other authority of one government, but other governments individually set the tax rate in their jurisdictions. The proceeds of the tax generated in each respective government's jurisdiction are attributed as tax revenues of that government.

Levies paid by member states of the European Union

101. The levies paid by the member states of the EU take the form of specific levies which include

a. custom duties and levies on agricultural goods (5123),

b. gross monetary compensation accounts (5123 if relating to imports and 5124 if relating to exports); and

c. Steel, coal, sugar and milk levies (5128).

102. The custom duties collected by member states on behalf of the EU are recorded:

- on a gross of collection fee basis;
- using figures adjusted so that duties are shown on a "final destination" as opposed to a "country of first entry" basis where such adjustments can be made. These adjustments concern in particular duties collected at important (sea) ports. Although the EU duties are collected by the authorities of the country of first entry, when possible these duties should be excluded from the revenue of the collecting country and be included in the revenue of the country of final destination.

103. This is the specific EU levy that most clearly conforms to the attribution criterion described in §95 above. Consequently as from 1998, these amounts are footnoted as a memorandum item to the EU member state country tables (in Chapter 4)[1] and no longer shown under heading 5123. However the figures are included in the total tax revenue figures on the top line for all the relevant years shown in the tables.

A.13. Provisional classification of revenues from bank levies and payments to deposit insurance and financial stability schemes

104. The OECD have adopted the following interim approach to reporting revenue from bank levies plus deposit insurance and stability fees for the 2012 and subsequent editions of *OECD Revenue Statistics*. It is recommended that the amounts should be recorded under category 5126.

- Compulsory payments of stability fees, bank levies and deposit insurance should generally be treated as tax revenues where the payments are made to General Government and allocated to the governments' consolidated or general funds so that the Government is free to make immediate use of the money for the purposes that it chooses. This principle would apply regardless of whether the Government is promising to make payments to guarantee the banks' customer deposits in some future contingency.

- If the compulsory payments are made to general government and placed in funds that are earmarked to be entirely channelled back to the sector of the economy that comprises the companies that are subject to the payment, they would still generally be treated as tax revenues on the grounds that the funds would be available for the government and would reduce its budget deficit, the fee is unrequited for an individual entity and the amounts raised could be unrelated to any eventual pay out to depositors or expenditure on wider support for the financial sector.
- Payments to made to the smaller long-standing schemes for insuring "retail" deposits, where the payment levels are consistent with the costs of insurance should be classified as fee for service.
- Any payments which involve governments realising the assets of a failed institution or receiving a priority claim on its assets in liquidation in order to fund payments of compensation to customers for their lost deposits would be treated as a fee for a service as opposed to tax revenues.
- Compulsory payments that are made to funds operated outside the government sector and non-state institutions backed by the deposit takers and all payments to voluntary schemes should not be treated as tax revenues.

Notes

1. References in this OECD Interpretative Guide to Sections or Parts of "this Report" refer to OECD (2016), *Revenue Statistics 2016*, OECD Publishing, Paris.
2. All references to SNA are to the 2008 edition.
3. See section A.12 of this guide for a discussion of the concept of agency capacity.
4. It is usually possible to identify amounts of social security contributions and payroll taxes, but not other taxes paid by government.
5. If, however, a levy which is considered as non-tax revenue by most countries is regarded as a tax – or raises substantial revenue – in one or more countries, the amounts collected are footnoted at the end of the relevant country tables, even though the amounts are not included in total tax revenues.
6. Names, however, can frequently be misleading. For example, though a passport fee would normally be considered a non-tax revenue, if a supplementary levy on passports (as is the case in Portugal) were imposed in order to raise substantial amounts of revenue relative to the cost of providing the passport, the levy would be regarded as a tax under 5200.
7. A more detailed explanation of this distinction can be found in the special feature, "Current issues in reporting tax revenues", in the 2001 edition of the Revenue Statistics.
8. Sometimes the terms "non-refundable" and "refundable" are used, but it may be considered illogical to talk of 'refundable' when nothing has been paid.
9. A different treatment, however, is accorded to non-wastable tax credits under imputation systems of corporate income tax (§31–33).
10. This is not strictly a true tax expenditure in the formal sense. Such tax expenditures require identification of a benchmark tax system for each country or, preferably, a common international benchmark. In practice it has not been possible to reach agreement on a common international benchmark.
11. Unless based on the profit made on a sale, in which case they would be classified as capital gains taxes under 1120 or 1220.

12. In some countries the same legislation applies to both individual and corporate enterprises for particular taxes on income. However, the receipts from such taxes are usually allocable between individuals and enterprises and can therefore be shown in the appropriate sub-heading.

13. For example, "...sufficiently self-contained and independent that they behave in the same way as corporations....... (including) keeping a complete set of accounts" (2008 SNA, section 4.44).

14. In Canada – a country also referred to as having an imputation system – the (wastable) tax credit for the shareholder is in respect of domestic corporation tax deemed to have been paid whether or not a corporation tax liability has arisen. As there is no integral connection between the corporation tax liability and the credit given against income tax under such systems, these credits for dividends are treated, along with other tax credits, on the lines described in §20.

15. This may also apply where a scheme for government employees existed prior to the introduction of a general social security scheme.

16. In the 2008 SNA these are regarded as capital transfers and not as taxes (see section A.8).

17. This is the system by which the European Union adjusts for differences between the exchange rates used to determine prices under the Common Market Agricultural Policy and actual exchange rates. Payments under the system may relate to imports or exports and where these amounts are separately identifiable they are shown under the appropriate heading (5123 or 5124). In this Report, these amounts are shown gross (i.e. without deducting any subsidies paid out under the MCA system).

18. Transfers of profits of State lotteries are regarded as non-tax revenues (see also §63).

19. See §25(c) as regards this distinction.

Revenue Statistics in Africa 1990-2015/Statistiques des recettes publiques en Afrique 1990-2015

Annexe A

Classification des impôts de l'OCDE et Guide d'interprétation[1]

Table des matières

A.1. Classification des impôts de l'OCDE

1. 1000 *Impôts sur le revenu, les bénéfices et les gains en capital*

    1100 Impôts sur le revenu, les bénéfices et les gains en capital des personnes physiques

        1110 Sur le revenu et les bénéfices

        1120 Sur les gains en capital

    1200 Impôts sur le revenu, les bénéfices et les gains en capital des sociétés

        1210 Sur le revenu et les bénéfices

        1220 Sur les gains en capital

    1300 Non ventilables entres les rubriques 110 et 1200

2. 2000 *Cotisations de sécurité sociale*

    2100 A la charge des salariés

        2110 Sur la base du salaire

        2120 Sur la base de l'impôt sur le revenu

    2200 A la charge des employeurs

        2210 Sur la base du salaire

        2220 Sur la base de l'impôt sur le revenu

    2300 A la charge des travailleurs indépendants ou des personnes n'occupant pas d'emploi

        2310 Sur la base du salaire

        2320 Sur la base de l'impôt sur le revenu

    2400 Non ventilables entre les rubriques 2100, 2200 et 2300

        2410 Sur la base du salaire

        2420 Sur la base de l'impôt sur le revenu

3. 3000 *Impôts sur les salaires et la main-d'œuvre*

4. 4000 *Impôts sur le patrimoine*

    4100 Impôts périodiques sur la propriété immobilière

        4110 Ménages

        4120 Autres agents

    4200 Impôts périodiques sur l'actif net

        4210 Personnes physiques

        4220 Sociétés

    4300 Impôts sur les mutations par décès, les successions et les donations

        4310 Impôts sur les mutations par décès et les successions

        4320 Impôts sur les donations

    4400 Impôts sur les transactions mobilières et immobilières

    4500 Autres impôts non périodiques sur le patrimoine

        4510 Impôts sur l'actif net

        4520 Autres impôts non périodiques

    4600 Autres impôts périodiques sur le patrimoine

5. 5000 *Impôts sur les biens et services*

5100 Impôts sur la production, la vente, le transfert, la location et la livraison des biens et la prestation de services

5110 Impôts généraux

5111 Taxes sur la valeur ajoutée

5112 Impôts sur les ventes

5113 Autres impôts généraux sur les biens et services

5120 Impôts sur des biens et des services déterminés

5121 Accises

5122 Bénéfices des monopoles fiscaux

5123 Droits de douane et droits à l'importation

5124 Taxes à l'exportation

5125 Impôts sur les biens d'équipement

5126 Impôts sur des services déterminés

5127 Autres impôts sur les transactions et les échanges internationaux

5128 Autres impôts sur des biens et services déterminés

5130 Non ventilables entre les rubriques 5110 et 5120

5200 Impôts sur l'utilisation des biens ou l'autorisation d'utiliser des biens ou d'exercer des activités

5210 Impôts périodiques

5211 A la charge des ménages au titre de véhicules à moteur

5212 A la charge d'autres agents au titre de véhicules à moteur

5213 Autres impôts périodiques

5220 Impôts non périodiques

5300 Non ventilables entre les rubriques 5100 et 5200

6. 6000 *Autres impôts*

6100 A la charge exclusive des entreprises

6200 A la charge d'autre agents que les entreprises ou non identifiables

A.2. Champ couvert

Principes généraux

1. Dans la classification de l'OCDE, le terme « impôts » désigne uniquement les versements obligatoires effectués sans contrepartie au profit des administrations publiques. Les impôts n'ont pas de contrepartie en ce sens que, normalement, les prestations fournies par les administrations au contribuable ne sont pas proportionnelles à ses versements.

2. Le terme « impôts » ne couvre pas les amendes, les pénalités, ni les prêts obligatoires aux administrations. Les cas dans lesquels la délimitation entre recettes fiscales et non fiscales est délicate à tracer, pour certains droits et taxes d'utilisation, sont examinés dans les § 9 à § 12.

3. Les administrations publiques comprennent l'administration centrale et les organismes dont les opérations sont sous son contrôle effectif, les administrations régionales et locales et leurs services, les organismes de sécurité sociale et les entités publiques autonomes, à l'exception des entreprises publiques. Cette définition des administrations est calquée sur celle du *Système de comptabilité nationale* 2008 (SCN)[2]. Dans cette publication, les administrations publiques et leurs sous-secteurs sont décrits dans le chapitre 4, section F, pages 80-84.

4. Les paiements obligatoires à des organismes supranationaux et aux organismes qui en dépendent ne sont plus compris depuis 1998 parmi les impôts sauf quelques exceptions. En effet, les droits de douane collectés par les États membres de l'Union européenne pour le compte de celle-ci sont toujours présentés à titre de rubrique « Pour mémoire » et compris dans le total des recettes fiscales, au chapitre 4, tableaux par pays. (Voir § 94.) Dans les pays où les églises font partie des administrations publiques, les impôts sur les cultes sont inclus dans ces paiements, à condition qu'ils répondent aux critères énoncés au § 1 ci-dessus. Comme les données se réfèrent aux montants encaissés par les administrations publiques, les contributions versées à des organismes privés, aux organismes sociaux ou régimes de sécurité sociale extérieurs aux administrations publiques, aux syndicats ou aux associations professionnelles sont exclues, même si elles sont obligatoires. Sont toutefois inclus les versements obligatoires aux administrations publiques dont le montant est affecté à ces organismes, à condition que l'administration ne fasse pas simplement office d'agent collecteur[3]. On a distingué les bénéfices des monopoles fiscaux de ceux d'autres entreprises publiques et on les a considérés comme des impôts parce qu'ils reflètent l'exercice du pouvoir d'imposition de l'État par l'intermédiaire du monopole (voir § 61 à § 63), comme le sont les bénéfices de l'État provenant de l'achat et de la vente de monnaies étrangères à des taux différents (voir § 69).

5. Les impôts payés par les administrations elles-mêmes (tels que les cotisations de sécurité sociale et les impôts sur les salaires payés par les administrations en tant qu'employeurs (2200 et 3000), les impôts sur la consommation qu'elles acquittent à l'occasion de leurs achats ou les impôts sur leur patrimoine) sont inclus dans les données présentées. Toutefois, lorsqu'il est possible de les isoler, les montants provenant de ces impôts[4] sont indiqués dans le chapitre 4.3 de ce rapport[1].

6. Les rapports entre cette classification et celle du Système de comptabilité nationale (SCN) sont indiqués dans les sections A.9 et A.11. À cause des différences qui existent entre les deux classifications, les statistiques de la comptabilité nationale ne sont pas toujours établies ou classées suivant la pratique adoptée dans le présent guide. Ces différences et

d'autres encore sont mentionnées dans les cas appropriés (voir par exemple § 25), mais il est impossible de toutes les signaler. Il peut y avoir aussi certaines différences entre cette classification et celle utilisée par certaines administrations nationales (voir par exemple § 10), aussi les statistiques nationales et celles de l'OCDE ne peuvent pas toujours être compatibles ; ces différences, cependant, sont vraisemblablement très insignifiantes dans les montants des recettes en cause.

Cotisations de sécurité sociale

7. Les cotisations de sécurité sociale, définies au § 34, qui sont versées aux administrations publiques, font partie des recettes fiscales. Elles sont évidemment assimilables à des impôts puisqu'il s'agit de versements obligatoires à des administrations publiques. Mais elles peuvent différer toutefois des autres impôts du fait que le paiement des prestations de sécurité sociale dépend dans la plupart des pays du versement des cotisations appropriées, encore qu'il n'y ait pas forcément un lien entre l'importance des prestations et le montant des cotisations. La comparabilité entre les pays sera meilleure si on considère les cotisations de sécurité sociale comme des impôts ; elles figurent cependant sous une rubrique distincte de façon à permettre un traitement séparé pour n'importe quelle analyse.

8. Les cotisations de sécurité sociale qui sont volontaires ou qui ne sont pas versées à des administrations publiques (voir § 1) ne sont pas considérées comme des impôts, bien que dans certains pays (comme il est indiqué dans les notes correspondantes) il soit difficile d'éliminer les cotisations volontaires et certains versements obligatoires au secteur privé. Les cotisations de sécurité sociale imputées ne sont pas considérées comme des impôts.

Droits, taxes d'utilisation et droits de licence

9. Si l'on excepte les droits perçus sur les permis de circulation des véhicules à moteur, qui sont universellement considérés comme des impôts, il n'est pas facile de distinguer les droits et taxes d'utilisation qui doivent être traitées comme des impôts de celles qui ne doivent pas l'être. Si, en effet, un droit ou une taxe est perçu au titre d'un service ou d'une activité déterminée, le lien entre ce prélèvement et la prestation fournie peut être plus ou moins important, de même que la relation entre le montant du prélèvement et le coût de la prestation. Lorsque le bénéficiaire d'une prestation acquitte un droit dont le montant est clairement lié au coût de la prestation fournie, on peut considérer que le prélèvement comporte une contrepartie, et d'après la définition donnée au § 1, il ne sera pas traité comme un impôt. Toutefois, dans les cas suivants, les prélèvements seraient 'sans contrepartie':

a. lorsque le prélèvement est très supérieur au coût de la prestation fournie ;
b. lorsque le redevable de la contribution n'est pas le bénéficiaire de la prestation correspondante (par exemple, un droit perçu sur l'abattage du bétail pour financer un service qui est fourni aux agriculteurs) ;
c. lorsque l'État ne fournit pas un service déterminé en contrepartie du droit qu'il perçoit, même si un permis est délivré à celui qui acquitte le droit (par exemple, lorsque l'État délivre des permis de chasse, de pêche ou de port d'armes qui ne sont pas assortis du droit d'utiliser une parcelle déterminée de terres appartenant à l'État) ;
d. lorsque les bénéficiaires de la prestation sont les personnes qui ont acquitté le droit, mais que la prestation dont chacun bénéficie n'est pas nécessairement en rapport avec le montant de ses propres versements (par exemple, le droit de commercialisation du lait acquitté par les fermiers qui sert à promouvoir la consommation de lait.

10. Dans des cas limites, cependant, l'application des critères énoncés au § 1 peut être particulièrement difficile. La solution adoptée, dans un souci d'uniformité entre les pays et eu égard aux montants relativement faibles des recettes en cause, consiste à s'en tenir à la pratique prépondérante des administrations fiscales plutôt que de laisser chaque pays décider si ces prélèvements sont des impôts ou des recettes non fiscales[5].

11. On trouvera ci-après la liste des principaux droits et taxes en question et leur traitement normal[6] dans la présente publication :

Recettes non fiscales :	frais de justice ; droits de délivrance de permis de conduire ; droits portuaires ; redevances de passeport ; redevances de radio et de télévision lorsque le service est assuré par les pouvoirs publics.
Impôts du sous-groupe 5200 :	autorisation d'exercer certaines activités telles que : distribution de films ; chasse, pêche et utilisation d'armes à feu ; organisation de spectacles ou de jeux et paris ; vente de boissons alcoolisées ou de tabacs ; autorisation de posséder des chiens et d'utiliser ou posséder des véhicules à moteur ou des armes à feu ; droit de lotissement.

12. Dans la pratique, il se peut qu'il ne soit pas toujours possible d'isoler les recettes fiscales des recettes non fiscales quand elles sont enregistrées ensemble. Si l'on estime qu'il s'agit surtout de recettes non fiscales, l'ensemble sera traité comme tel ; dans le cas contraire, les recettes seront comptabilisées et classées conformément aux règles énoncées au § 27.

Redevances

13. Les redevances versées pour obtenir le droit d'extraire du pétrole et du gaz ou de mettre en valeur d'autres ressources minérales sont considérées normalement comme des recettes non fiscales, car il s'agit de revenus immobiliers procurés par des terres ou des ressources appartenant à l'État.

Amendes et pénalités

14. En principe, les amendes et pénalités portant sur les impôts impayés ou les pénalités appliquées en cas de tentative d'évasion fiscale ne doivent pas être enregistrées comme des recettes fiscales. Cependant, il se peut qu'il ne soit pas possible de séparer le versement des amendes et pénalités des recettes correspondant aux impôts auxquels ces amendes et pénalités se rattachent. Dans ce cas, les amendes et pénalités associés à un impôt particulier sont enregistrées avec les recettes correspondant à cet impôt alors que les amendes et pénalités liées à des recettes correspondant à des impôts non-identifiés sont classées comme autres impôts dans la catégorie 6000. Les amendes qui ne concernent pas des infractions fiscales (comme les infractions au stationnement), ou qui ne sont pas identifiables en tant que telles, ne sont pas non plus considérées comme des recettes fiscales.

A.3. Bases de comptabilisation

Droits constatés

15. Les données enregistrées dans cette publication pour les années récentes sont essentiellement indiquées en droits constatés, c'est-à-dire qu'elles sont enregistrées au moment du fait générateur de l'impôt. D'autres informations sont fournies dans les notes des tableaux par pays au chapitre 4 de ce rapport[1].

16. Toutefois, les données des années antérieures sont encore principalement comptabilisées sur la base des décaissements, c'est-à-dire au moment où l'administration reçoit le versement. Ainsi, les impôts retenus à la source par les employeurs au cours d'un exercice, mais versés à l'administration au cours de l'exercice suivant, et les impôts dus au titre d'une année mais effectivement versés l'année suivante, figurent les uns et les autres dans les recettes du second exercice. Les restitutions, remboursements et retraits résultant d'opérations rectificatives sont déduits des recettes brutes de la période au cours de laquelle ces opérations sont effectuées.

17. Les données relatives aux recettes fiscales sont comptabilisées, sans déduction compensatoire des dépenses administratives liées au recouvrement de l'impôt. De même, lorsque le produit d'un impôt sert à subventionner certains membres de la collectivité, la subvention n'est pas déduite du rendement de l'impôt, encore que certains pays fassent figurer dans leurs données l'impôt après déduction des subventions.

18. Pour les monopoles fiscaux (sous-groupe 5122), seul le montant effectivement transféré à l'État est inclus dans les recettes publiques. Toutefois, les dépenses des monopoles fiscaux qui sont considérées comme des dépenses publiques (par exemple, des dépenses de caractère social engagées par les monopoles fiscaux à l'instigation de l'État) sont ajoutées après coup pour calculer le montant des recettes fiscales (voir § 61).

La distinction entre dispositions fiscales et dépenses directes[7]

19. Étant donné que la présente publication ne vise que les recettes publiques en faisant abstraction des dépenses, il convient de distinguer entre les dispositions fiscales et les dépenses directes. Normalement, cette distinction ne soulève aucune difficulté, car les dépenses directes sont effectuées en dehors du système fiscal et des comptes fiscaux et en vertu de dispositions législatives distinctes. Dans les cas limites, on recourt, pour établir la distinction, au principe de la comptabilisation sur la base des paiements. Dans la mesure où une disposition affecte le montant des paiements du contribuable à l'État, elle est considérée comme une disposition fiscale dont il est tenu compte dans les données figurant dans cette publication. Une disposition qui n'affecte pas ce montant est considérée comme une dépense directe dont il n'est pas tenu compte dans les données reproduites dans cette publication.

20. Il est clair que les abattements fiscaux, exonérations et déductions de l'assiette de l'impôt modifient le montant de l'impôt acquitté à l'État ; il s'agit donc de dispositions fiscales. Inversement, les formes d'aides qui ne sont pas imputables sur l'impôt et n'ont donc aucun lien avec le processus d'imposition, ne réduisent pas les recettes publiques qui sont consignées dans ce volume. Les crédits d'impôt sont des montants déductibles de l'impôt à acquitter (par opposition aux déductions, qui sont opérées sur l'assiette de l'impôt). On distingue deux catégories de crédits d'impôt : ceux (que l'on qualifiera ici de « non récupérables ») qui sont limités au montant de l'impôt à acquitter et ne peuvent donc donner lieu à un versement de l'administration au contribuable, et ceux (qualifiés ici de « récupérables ») qui n'ont pas cette limite, de sorte que l'excédent du crédit sur l'impôt peut être versé au contribuable[8]. Le crédit d'impôt non récupérable, comme un abattement fiscal, affecte évidemment le montant de l'impôt acquitté à l'État ; aussi est-il considéré comme une disposition fiscale. La solution adoptée pour les crédits d'impôts récupérables[9] consiste à distinguer l'élément de « dépense fiscale »[10], qui est la part du crédit utilisée pour réduire ou supprimer l'impôt dû par le contribuable, et l'« élément de transfert », qui correspond à la part excédant l'impôt dû par le contribuable et qui lui est reversée. Les recettes fiscales rapportées doivent être diminuées du montant de l'élément de dépense,

mais non de l'élément de transfert. En outre, les montants de l'élément de dépense fiscale et de l'élément de transfert doivent être indiqués pour mémoire dans les tableaux par pays. Les pays qui ne sont pas en mesure de faire la distinction entre l'élément de dépense fiscale et l'élément de transfert doivent indiquer si leurs recettes fiscales ont été ou non diminuées du montant total de ces éléments, et fournir toutes les estimations dont ils disposent concernant les montants de ces deux éléments. Des informations complémentaires figurent dans le chapitre 2 de ce rapport[1], qui fait apparaître les effets des différents traitements possibles des crédits d'impôts récupérables sur les ratios impôt rapportant les impôts au PIB.

Année civile et année fiscale (exercice budgétaire)

21. Les autorités nationales dont l'exercice budgétaire ne correspond pas à l'année civile fournissent, autant que possible, leurs données sur la base de l'année civile afin de faciliter au maximum la comparaison avec les données des autres pays. Les données d'un petit nombre de pays se réfèrent à l'exercice budgétaire. Pour ceux-ci, les statistiques de PIB utilisées dans les tableaux comparatifs portent aussi sur les exercices budgétaires.

A.4. Principes généraux de classification

Les fondements essentiels de la classification

22. Les recettes sont classées par groupes principaux (1000, 2000, 3000, 4000, 5000, 6000) suivant l'assiette de l'impôt : 1000 revenus, bénéfices et gains en capital ; 2000 et 3000 salaires et nombre d'employés ; 4000 patrimoine ; 5000 biens et services ; 6000 assiettes diverses, autres ou non identifiables. Lorsqu'un impôt est calculé en fonction de plusieurs assiettes, les recettes sont, chaque fois que c'est possible, réparties entre les divers groupes (voir § 27 et § 77). Les groupes 4000 et 5000 ne comprennent pas seulement les impôts ayant pour assiette le patrimoine, les biens ou les services eux-mêmes, mais aussi certains impôts connexes. Ainsi, les impôts sur les mutations du patrimoine sont classés dans le groupe 4400[11] et les impôts sur l'utilisation des biens, ou l'autorisation d'exercer une activité, dans le groupe 5200. Dans les groupes 4000 et 5000, une distinction est faite dans certains sous-groupes entre impôts périodiques et impôts non périodiques : on entend par impôts périodiques ceux qui sont perçus à intervalles réguliers (ordinairement tous les ans) et par impôts non périodiques ceux qui ne sont perçus qu'une seule fois (voir aussi les § 42 à § 45, § 48, § 49, et § 75 pour une application particulière de cette distinction).

23. L'affectation spéciale de certaines recettes fiscales n'influe pas sur leur classification. Toutefois comme explicité au § 34 sur la classification des cotisations de sécurité sociale, l'octroi d'un droit aux prestations sociales est crucial dans la définition de la rubrique principale 2000.

24. La manière selon laquelle un impôt est perçu ou recouvré (par exemple, au moyen de timbres) n'affecte pas sa classification.

Classification des contribuables

25. Dans certains sous-groupes, des distinctions sont faites entre les différentes catégories de contribuables. Ces distinctions varient d'un impôt à l'autre :

a. *Ventilation des impôts sur le revenu et sur l'actif net entre personnes physiques et sociétés*

La distinction fondamentale entre les impôts sur le revenu des sociétés et les impôts sur le revenu des personnes physiques est que les premiers sont perçus sur la société en tant qu'entité et non sur les personnes physiques qui en sont propriétaires, donc sans tenir compte de la situation personnelle de celles-ci. La même distinction est applicable aux impôts sur l'actif net des sociétés et des personnes physiques. Les impôts perçus sur les bénéfices des sociétés de personnes et sur le revenu de certaines institutions comme les caisses d'assurance-vie ou de retraite, sont classés selon le même principe. Ils sont compris dans les impôts sur les sociétés (1200) lorsqu'ils sont perçus sur la société de personnes ou l'institution en tant qu'entité sans que la situation personnelle des propriétaires entre en ligne de compte ; dans les autres cas, ils sont considérés comme des impôts sur les personnes physiques (1100). Ordinairement, les impôts sur les sociétés et les impôts sur les personnes physiques sont régis par des dispositions législatives différentes[12]. La distinction qui est faite ici entre personnes physiques et sociétés ne reprend pas la classification par secteur (ménages, entreprises, etc.) adoptée dans les comptes de revenus et de dépenses du SCN. Cette dernière classification exclut du secteur des ménages certaines entreprises non constituées en sociétés[13] et les fait figurer parmi les entreprises non financières et les institutions financières. Toutefois, l'impôt sur les bénéfices de ces entreprises ne peut pas toujours être isolé de l'impôt sur les autres revenus des propriétaires de ces entreprises, ou ne peut l'être que d'une façon arbitraire. On n'a pas cherché ici à faire la distinction et l'impôt sur le revenu des personnes physiques figure globalement, quelle que soit la nature du revenu imposable.

b. *Ventilation des impôts sur les biens immobiliers entre ménages et autres agents*

En l'occurrence, la distinction est celle qui a été adoptée par le SCN dans les comptes de production et de consommation. On distingue, en effet, les ménages en tant que consommateurs d'une part (c'est-à-dire à l'exclusion des entreprises individuelles), et les producteurs d'autre part. Cependant, les impôts sur les logements occupés par les ménages, qu'ils soient à la charge des propriétaires qui les occupent, du locataire ou du propriétaire, sont classés comme étant à la charge des ménages. C'est la distinction faite habituellement entre les impôts sur les biens des personnes et les impôts sur les biens des entreprises. Toutefois, certains pays ne sont pas en mesure d'établir cette distinction.

c. *Ventilation des permis de circuler des véhicules à moteur entre taxes à la charge des ménages et à la charge d'autres agents*

On distingue ici les ménages en tant que consommateurs d'une part, et producteurs d'autre part, comme dans les comptes de production et de consommation du SCN.

d. *Ventilation des autres impôts (6000) entre les entreprises et les autres agents*

Il est fait la même distinction qu'au point (c) ci-dessus entre les producteurs, d'une part, et les ménages consommateurs d'autre part. Les impôts qui figurent dans le groupe 6000 parce qu'ils ne comportent pas une assiette unique ou parce que leur assiette ne relève d'aucune des catégories précédentes, mais qui ne sont manifestement perçus que sur les producteurs et non sur les ménages, sont classés comme étant « à la charge des entreprises ». Les autres impôts du groupe 6000 figurent sous la rubrique « à la charge d'autres agents » ou « non identifiés ».

Surtaxes

26. Les recettes des surtaxes relatives à des impôts particuliers sont classées ordinairement avec les recettes de l'impôt correspondant, que la surtaxe ait ou non un caractère temporaire. Toutefois, si l'une des caractéristiques de la surtaxe permet de la classer sous une rubrique différente de la classification de l'OCDE, les recettes de cette surtaxe sont classées sous cette rubrique et non pas avec les recettes de l'impôt correspondant.

Recettes fiscales non identifiables et sous-groupes résiduels

27. Il arrive parfois qu'on ne puisse déterminer si des impôts relèvent entièrement d'un groupe ou d'un sous-groupe de la classification de l'OCDE ; dans ces cas on applique les méthodes suivantes :

a. le groupe est connu, mais on ne sait pas comment répartir les recettes entre les sous-groupes ; les recettes sont alors classées dans le sous-groupe résiduel approprié (1300, 2400, 4520, 4600, 5130, 5300 ou 6200) ;

b. on sait que l'ensemble des recettes d'un groupe d'impôts (ordinairement des impôts locaux) provient d'impôts relevant d'un groupe ou sous-groupe particulier, mais certains impôts du groupe, dont le montant ne peut être déterminé avec précision, peuvent être classés dans d'autres groupes ou sous-groupes ; dans ce cas les recettes sont comptabilisées dans le groupe ou sous-groupe dont relève l'essentiel des recettes ;

c. il est impossible d'identifier le groupe ou le sous-groupe d'un impôt (ordinairement un impôt local) ; l'impôt est alors classé dans le groupe 6200, à moins qu'il ne s'agisse d'un impôt manifestement à la charge des entreprises, auquel cas il est classé dans le sous-groupe 6100.

A.5. Commentaires sur les postes de la liste

1000 — *Impôts sur le revenu, les bénéfices et les gains en capital*

28. Ce groupe couvre les impôts prélevés sur le revenu ou le bénéfice net (c'est-à-dire le revenu brut déduction faite des abattements autorisés) des personnes physiques et des entreprises. Sont aussi couverts les impôts prélevés sur les gains en capital des personnes physiques et des entreprises et sur les gains provenant de jeux.

29. Ce groupe comprend :

a. les impôts perçus principalement sur les revenus ou les bénéfices, bien qu'ils puissent l'être partiellement sur d'autres bases. Les impôts qui ont une autre assiette principale que le revenu ou les bénéfices sont classés selon les principes énoncés au § 27 et § 77 ;

b. les impôts sur la propriété immobilière, qui sont perçus sur la base d'un revenu présumé ou estimé faisant partie de l'assiette de l'impôt sur le revenu (voir aussi § 42 (a), (c) et (d)) ;

c. les versements obligatoires aux caisses de sécurité sociale qui sont prélevés sur les revenus mais ne donnent pas droit à des prestations sociales. Lorsque ces contributions donnent droit à des prestations sociales, elles figurent à la rubrique 2000 (voir § 34) ;

d. les recettes provenant d'impôts cédulaires sur le revenu intégrés dans le régime général qui sont globalement classés dans ce groupe, bien que certains de ces impôts soient sur le revenu brut et ne tiennent pas toujours compte de la situation personnelle du contribuable.

30. Les impôts figurant dans ce groupe sont subdivisés en deux grands sous-groupes, les impôts sur le revenu des personnes physiques (1100) et les impôts sur le revenu des sociétés (1200), une ventilation étant faite dans chacun d'eux entre les impôts sur le revenu et les bénéfices (1110 et 1210) et les impôts sur les gains en capital (1120 et 1220). Si certaines recettes ne peuvent être identifiées comme relevant soit du sous-groupe 1100, soit du

sous-groupe 1200, ou si cette distinction ne peut être faite dans la pratique (parce qu'il n'y a pas de données fiables sur les bénéficiaires des paiements sur lesquels la retenue à la source est faite), elles sont classées dans le sous-groupe 1300 (non ventilables).

Traitement des crédits d'impôt dans les systèmes d'imputation

31. Dans les régimes d'imputation de l'impôt sur les bénéfices des sociétés, les actionnaires bénéficient d'une compensation totale ou partielle d'imposition sur les dividendes que la société leur a versés et pour lesquels elle a acquitté l'impôt sur le revenu des sociétés. Dans les pays[14] qui appliquent un tel régime, une fraction de l'impôt sur les bénéfices des sociétés sert à alléger l'impôt dû par l'actionnaire. Cet allégement prend la forme d'un crédit d'impôt, dont le montant peut être inférieur, égal ou supérieur au montant total de l'impôt dont il est redevable. Si le crédit d'impôt dépasse ce montant, l'excédent peut être versé à l'actionnaire. Comme ce type de crédit d'impôt fait partie intégrante des systèmes d'imputation de l'impôt sur le revenu des sociétés, tout paiement à l'actionnaire est considéré comme un remboursement d'impôt et non comme une dépense (se référer au traitement des autres crédits d'impôt exposé au § 20).

32. Puisque, dans les systèmes d'imputation, le crédit d'impôt (même lorsqu'il dépasse l'impôt dû) est censé être une disposition fiscale, on peut se demander s'il doit être déduit des recettes de l'impôt sur le revenu des personnes physiques (1110) ou de celles de l'impôt sur les bénéfices de sociétés (1210). Dans ce rapport le montant intégral de l'impôt acquitté sur les bénéfices des sociétés figure sous le poste 1210 et aucun impôt imputé n'est inclus dans le poste 1110. Le montant total du crédit d'impôt réduit donc le montant des recettes du poste 1110, que ce crédit se traduise par une réduction de l'impôt dû sur le revenu des personnes physiques ou par un remboursement réel du fait que le crédit dépasse le montant de l'impôt. (Cependant, lorsque ces crédits sont déduits de l'impôt sur les sociétés au titre de dividendes versés à des sociétés, le montant est déduit des recettes du poste 1210).

1120 et 1220 — *Impôts sur les gains en capital*

33. Ces postes comprennent les impôts perçus sur les gains en capital, le sous-groupe 1120 comptabilisant les impôts prélevés sur les gains des personnes physiques et le sous-groupe 1220 ceux qui sont perçus sur les gains des entreprises constituées sous forme de sociétés, lorsque ces recettes peuvent être ventilées. Ce n'est pas le cas dans de nombreux pays et les recettes de ces impôts sont alors classées avec celles de l'impôt sur le revenu. Les impôts sur les gains provenant de jeux sont aussi classés sous le poste 1120.

2000 — *Cotisations de sécurité sociale*

34. Figurent dans ce groupe tous les versements obligatoires qui donnent le droit de bénéficier d'une prestation sociale future (éventuelle). Ces versements sont généralement affectés au financement de prestations sociales et souvent effectués au profit d'institutions ou d'administrations publiques qui fournissent de telles prestations. Cependant, cette affectation n'entre pas dans la définition des cotisations de sécurité sociale et n'est pas nécessaire pour qu'un impôt soit classé dans cette rubrique. Cependant, il faut qu'un impôt confère un droit pour être classé dans cette rubrique. Par conséquent, les prélèvements sur les revenus ou la masse salariale qui sont affectés aux caisses de sécurité sociale mais ne donnent aucun droit à des prestations sont exclus de cette rubrique et figurent à celle des impôts sur le revenu des personnes physiques (1100) ou des impôts sur les salaires et la main-d'œuvre (3000). Les impôts assis sur d'autres bases, telles que les biens et services, qui sont affectés à des prestations de sécurité sociale, ne sont pas indiqués ici, mais sont classés en fonction de leurs bases respectives parce qu'en général ils ne donnent pas droit à des prestations de sécurité sociale.

35. Seraient entre autres incluses les cotisations au titre des catégories suivantes de prestations de sécurité sociale : les allocations d'assurance-chômage et les compléments, les allocations pour accidents, blessures et maladie, les pensions de retraite, d'invalidité et de survivant, les allocations familiales, les remboursements de dépenses médicales et d'hospitalisation ou la fourniture de services médicaux ou hospitaliers. Les cotisations peuvent être collectées à la fois auprès des employés et des employeurs.

36. Les cotisations peuvent être assises sur les gains ou la masse salariale (« sur la base du salaire ») ou sur le revenu net après déductions et exemptions en fonction de la situation personnelle (« sur la base de l'impôt sur le revenu ») et les recettes correspondant à ces deux bases doivent être identifiées séparément si possible. Cependant, lorsque les cotisations à un régime général de sécurité sociale sont assises sur la masse salariale, mais que les cotisations de groupes particuliers (tels que les travailleurs indépendants) ne peuvent être évaluées sur cette base et que le revenu net est utilisé comme valeur rapprochée des gains bruts, les recettes peuvent encore être considérées comme assises sur la masse salariale. En principe, cette rubrique exclut les contributions volontaires à des régimes de sécurité sociale. Lorsqu'elles peuvent être identifiées séparément, elles figurent pour mémoire dans le tableau indiquant le financement des prestations de sécurité sociale. Toutefois, en pratique, elles ne peuvent pas toujours être distinguées des cotisations volontaires, et dans ce cas elles figurent à cette rubrique.

37. Les cotisations à des régimes d'assurance sociale qui ne relèvent pas des pouvoirs publics et à d'autres régimes d'assurance ou de prévoyance, aux caisses de retraite, sociétés de secours mutuel ou autres systèmes d'épargne, ne sont pas considérées comme des cotisations de sécurité sociale. Les caisses de prévoyance résultant d'arrangements aux termes desquels les cotisations de chaque salarié et celles que l'employeur verse en son nom sont comptabilisées séparément dans un compte productif d'intérêts d'où elles peuvent être retirées dans des conditions biens déterminées. Les caisses de retraite sont des régimes autonomes organisés par négociations entre salariés et employeurs, qui comportent diverses contributions et prestations, parfois liées plus directement au salaire et à la durée d'activité que dans les régimes de sécurité sociale. Lorsque les cotisations à ces régimes sont obligatoires ou quasi obligatoires (par exemple en vertu d'un accord entre organisations professionnelles et syndicales), elles sont comptabilisées dans le poste pour mémoire (voir le chapitre 4.2 du rapport)[1].

38. Les cotisations versées par les agents des administrations et par les administrations au titre de leurs agents à des régimes de sécurité sociale relevant des pouvoirs publics sont incluses dans ce groupe. Sont aussi assimilées à des impôts les cotisations à des régimes particuliers réservés aux agents des administrations qui sont censés remplacer un régime général de la sécurité sociale[15]. Par contre, lorsqu'un régime distinct n'est pas censé remplacer un régime général et résulte de négociations entre l'administration, agissant en qualité d'employeur, et ses agents, il n'est pas considéré comme un régime de sécurité sociale et les cotisations à ce titre ne sont pas assimilées à des impôts, même si le régime a été institué par des dispositions législatives.

39. Cette rubrique ne comprend pas les cotisations « imputées », qui correspondent aux prestations sociales versées directement par les employeurs à leurs salariés, ou anciens salariés, ou à leurs représentants (par exemple, lorsque des employeurs sont légalement tenus de verser des prestations maladies pendant une certaine période).

40. Le groupe comprend les cotisations à la charge des salariés (2100), à la charge des employeurs (2200), et à la charge des travailleurs indépendants ou des personnes n'occupant pas d'emploi (2300). À cet effet, on entend par salariés toutes les personnes qui exercent une activité dans des entreprises, des administrations, des institutions privées sans but lucratif, ou qui occupent d'autres emplois rémunérés, à l'exception des propriétaires et des membres de leur famille non rémunérés dans le cas d'entreprises individuelles. Sont également compris les membres des forces armées, quelle que soit la durée et la nature de leurs services, s'ils cotisent à un régime de sécurité sociale. Par cotisations à la charge des employeurs, on entend les versements qu'ils effectuent au régime de sécurité sociale pour le compte de leurs salariés. Si, en cas de chômage, les salariés ou employeurs sont tenus de continuer à effectuer ces versements, ces derniers doivent figurer respectivement dans les sous-groupes 2100 et 2200. En conséquence, le sous-groupe 2300 est réservé aux cotisations versées par les travailleurs indépendants et par ceux qui n'appartiennent pas à la population active (comme les handicapés ou les retraités).

3000 — *Impôts sur les salaires et la main-d'œuvre*

41. Ce groupe couvre les impôts acquittés par les employeurs, les salariés et les travailleurs indépendants, en pourcentage du salaire ou d'après un montant forfaitaire par personne, qui ne sont pas affectés aux dépenses de sécurité sociale. Parmi les impôts classés ici, on peut citer l'impôt complémentaire d'assurance nationale sans affectation (institué en 1977) au Royaume-Uni, l'impôt sur la masse salariale en Suède (1969–1979), la fraction du « Gewerbesteuer » autrichien et allemand qui reposait sur la masse salariale (1965–1978).

4000 — *Impôts sur le patrimoine*

42. Ce groupe couvre les impôts périodiques et non périodiques sur l'utilisation, la propriété ou la mutation des biens. Sont comptabilisés ici les impôts sur la propriété immobilière et sur l'actif net, les impôts sur les mutations par décès, les successions et les donations, et les impôts sur les transactions mobilières et immobilières. Sont exclus de ce groupe :

a. les impôts sur les gains en capital provenant de la vente d'un bien (1120 ou 1220) ;

b. les impôts sur l'utilisation des biens ou l'autorisation d'utiliser des biens ou d'exercer des activités (5200) [voir § 72] ;

c. les impôts immobiliers perçus sur la base d'un revenu net présumé qui tiennent compte de la situation personnelle du contribuable. Ces impôts sont classés dans le groupe 1100 en tant qu'impôts sur le revenu, avec les impôts sur le revenu et les gains en capital provenant des biens immobiliers ;

d. les impôts sur l'utilisation de biens immobiliers aux fins d'habitation qui sont à la charge du propriétaire ou du locataire et dont le montant est fonction de la situation personnelle de l'utilisateur (salaire, personnes à charge, etc.). Ils sont classés dans le groupe 1100 en tant qu'impôts sur le revenu ;

e. les impôts sur les constructions dépassant la densité autorisée, les impôts sur l'extension, la construction ou la modification de certains immeubles au-delà d'une valeur autorisée et les impôts sur la construction d'immeubles. Ces impôts sont classés dans le poste 5200 en tant qu'impôts sur l'autorisation d'exercer certaines activités ;

f. les impôts sur l'utilisation de biens immobiliers par le propriétaire à des fins commerciales particulières, comme la vente de boissons alcoolisées, de tabac, de viande, ou pour l'exploitation de sols ou terrains (par exemple aux États-Unis, les taxes de lotissement). Ils sont classés dans le poste 5200 en tant qu'impôts sur l'autorisation d'exercer certaines activités.

4100 — *Impôts périodiques sur la propriété immobilière*

43. Ce sous-groupe comprend les impôts prélevés régulièrement au titre de l'utilisation ou de la propriété de biens immobiliers.

- ces impôts sont prélevés sur les terrains et les bâtiments ;
- ces impôts sont calculés en pourcentage de la valeur du bien évalué d'après un revenu locatif fictif, le prix de vente ou le rendement capitalisé, ou en fonction d'autres caractéristiques du bien, comme sa dimension ou son emplacement, d'où l'on peut déduire une valeur locative présumée ou la valeur du capital.
- ces impôts sont à la charge du propriétaire, du locataire ou des deux. Ils peuvent également être payés par une administration à une autre administration au titre d'un bien relevant de la compétence de cette dernière.
- il n'est pas tenu compte des dettes pour la détermination de l'assiette de ces impôts, contrairement aux impôts sur l'actif net.

44. Les impôts sur la propriété immobilière sont en outre subdivisés en impôts acquittés par les ménages (4110) et impôts acquittés par d'autres agents (4120), suivant les critères exposés au § 25(*b*) ci-dessus.

4200 — *Impôts périodiques sur l'actif net*

45. Ce sous-groupe comprend les impôts prélevés régulièrement (dans la plupart des cas annuellement) sur l'actif net, c'est-à-dire les impôts perçus sur un large éventail de biens mobiliers et immobiliers, endettement déduit. Il est subdivisé en impôts acquittés par des personnes physiques (4210), et en impôts acquittés par des sociétés (4220) selon les critères exposés plus haut au § 25(*a*). Si les recettes provenant des institutions sont comptabilisées à part, elles doivent être ajoutées aux impôts des entreprises.

4300 — *Impôts sur les mutations par décès, les successions et les donations*

46. Ce sous-groupe comprend les impôts sur les mutations par décès et les successions (4310) et les impôts sur les donations (4320)[16]. Les impôts sur les mutations par décès sont calculés soit sur l'ensemble de la masse successorale, soit en fonction de la part de chacun des bénéficiaires (« part héréditaire ») ; en outre, ces derniers impôts peuvent tenir compte du degré de parenté entre chacun des bénéficiaires et le défunt.

4400 — *Impôts sur les transactions mobilières et immobilières*

47. Sont compris, entre autres, dans ce sous-groupe les impôts sur l'émission, le transfert, l'achat et la vente de valeurs mobilières, les impôts sur les chèques, ainsi que les droits perçus à l'occasion d'actes juridiques déterminés, comme la validation de contrats et la vente de biens immobiliers. Sont exclus :

a. les impôts sur l'utilisation de biens, mobiliers ou immobiliers, ou l'autorisation d'exercer certaines activités (5200) ;
b. les droits acquittés au titre de frais de justice, ou pour la délivrance de certificats de naissance, de mariage ou de décès, car ces droits sont considérés comme des recettes non fiscales (voir § 9) ;
c. les impôts sur les gains en capital (1000) ;
d. les impôts périodiques sur la propriété immobilière (4100) ;
e. les impôts périodiques sur l'actif net (4200) ;
f. les prélèvements sur le patrimoine ou sur l'actif net effectués une fois pour toutes (4500) ;

4500 — *Autres impôts non périodiques sur le patrimoine*[16]

48. Ce sous-groupe comprend les prélèvements sur le patrimoine effectués une fois pour toutes (par opposition aux prélèvements périodiques). Il est subdivisé en impôts sur l'actif net (4510) et en autres impôts non périodiques sur le patrimoine (4520). Le poste 4510 inclurait les impôts perçus pour couvrir des dépenses exceptionnelles ou à des fins de redistribution. Le poste 4520 comprendrait les impôts prélevés pour tenir compte d'une plus-value prise par les terrains du fait que les administrations publiques ont autorisé l'extension ou l'aménagement d'installations locales, ainsi que les impôts sur la réévaluation du capital ou les impôts perçus une seule fois sur certains biens déterminés.

4600 — *Autres impôts périodiques sur le patrimoine*

49. Ils sont rares dans des pays Membres de l'OCDE ; ce sous-groupe comprendrait les impôts sur des biens tels que le cheptel, les bijoux, les fenêtres et les signes extérieurs de richesse.

5000 — *Impôts sur les biens et services*

50. Ce poste couvre tous les impôts et droits perçus sur la production, l'extraction, la vente, le transfert, la location ou la livraison de biens et la prestation de services (5100), ou sur l'utilisation ou l'autorisation d'utiliser des biens ou d'exercer des activités (5200). Ce groupe comprend donc :

a. les taxes cumulatives en cascade ;

b. les taxes générales sur les ventes – perçues au stade de la production ou de la fabrication, du gros ou du détail ;

c. les taxes sur la valeur ajoutée ;

d. les accises ;

e. les taxes perçues à l'importation et à l'exportation de biens ;

f. les impôts perçus sur l'utilisation de biens et sur l'autorisation d'utiliser des biens ou d'exercer certaines activités ;

g. les impôts sur l'extraction, le traitement ou la production de minéraux et autres produits.

51. Les cas douteux de délimitation entre ce groupe et le groupe 4000 (impôts sur le patrimoine) et le sous-groupe 6100 (autres impôts à la charge des entreprises) sont examinés au § 42, § 47 et § 74. Des postes résiduels (5300 et 5130) ont été prévus pour comptabiliser les recettes fiscales qui ne peuvent être ventilées respectivement entre les postes 5100 et 5200 et entre les postes 5110 et 5120 (voir § 27).

5100 — *Impôts sur la production, la vente, le transfert, la location et la livraison de biens et la prestation de services*

52. Ce sous-groupe comprend tous les impôts perçus sur les transactions afférentes à des biens ou services, en fonction de leurs caractéristiques propres (comme la valeur, le poids du tabac, le degré d'alcool, etc.), à la différence des impôts perçus au titre de l'utilisation ou de l'autorisation d'utiliser des biens ou d'exercer des activités, qui entrent dans le sous-groupe 5200.

5110 — *Impôts généraux sur les biens et services*

53. Ce sous-groupe comprend tous les impôts, autres que les droits à l'importation et à l'exportation (5123 et 5124), perçus sur la production, la location, le transfert, la livraison ou la vente d'une gamme de biens ou la prestation d'une gamme de services, qu'ils soient

produits dans le pays ou importés, et quel que soit le stade de la production ou de la distribution aux quel ils sont perçus. Il couvre ainsi les taxes sur la valeur ajoutée, les taxes sur les ventes et les taxes de caractère cumulatif en cascade. On a ajouté aux recettes brutes de cette catégorie les recettes provenant de la compensation à la frontière de ces impôts lorsque les biens sont importés, et déduit les remboursements d'impôts effectués lorsque les marchandises sont exportées. Ces impôts sont ventilés en : taxes sur la valeur ajoutée (5111), impôts sur les ventes (5112), autres impôts généraux sur les biens et services (5113).

54. Certains cas se trouvent à la limite entre ce sous-groupe et celui des impôts sur des biens et services déterminés (5120) lorsque ces impôts sont perçus sur un grand nombre de biens, comme dans le cas de la « purchase tax » au Royaume-Uni (abrogée en 1973) et l'impôt japonais sur les biens marchands (abrogé en 1988). Conformément aux options nationales, la « purchase tax » britannique est classée impôt général (5112) et l'impôt japonais dans les accises (5121).

5111 — *Taxes sur la valeur ajoutée*

55. Sont classés dans ce sous-groupe tous les impôts généraux sur la consommation prélevés sur la valeur ajoutée, quels que soient le mode de déduction et les stades auxquels ils sont perçus. En pratique, tous les pays de l'OCDE où existe une taxe sur la valeur ajoutée autorisent normalement la déduction immédiate des taxes sur les achats par tous les redevables, à l'exception du consommateur final, et imposent la taxe à tous les stades. Dans certains pays, le poste peut inclure aussi certains impôts, comme les taxes sur les activités financières et les assurances, soit parce que les recettes correspondantes ne peuvent être dissociées de celles de la taxe sur la valeur ajoutée, soit parce qu'elles sont considérées comme faisant partie intégrante de la taxe sur la valeur ajoutée, même si les taxes similaires qui existent dans d'autres pays peuvent être classées autrement (par exemple, sous le poste 5126 comme impôts sur les services ou sous le poste 4400 comme impôts sur les transactions mobilières et immobilières).

5112 — *Impôts sur les ventes*

56. Sont classés ici tous les impôts perçus à un stade unique, que ce soit celui de la fabrication, de la production, du gros ou du détail.

5113 — *Autres impôts généraux sur les biens et services*

57. Ce sous-groupe comprend les impôts cumulatifs, connus également sous le nom d'impôt en cascade, qui sont perçus sans déduction de l'impôt sur les moyens de production chaque fois qu'une opération a lieu, ainsi que les impôts généraux sur la consommation lorsqu'il s'y ajoute des éléments qui les font assimiler à la taxe sur la valeur ajoutée, à la taxe sur les ventes ou à des taxes en cascade.

5120 — *Impôts sur des biens et des services déterminés*

58. Ce sous-groupe couvre les accises, les bénéfices engendrés et transférés par les monopoles fiscaux, et les droits de douane et à l'importation, ainsi que les taxes à l'exportation, les opérations de change, les biens d'équipement et les paris, et aussi les impôts spéciaux sur les services qui ne font pas partie d'un impôt général du sous-groupe 5110.

5121 — Accises

59. Les accises sont perçues sur des produits particuliers, ou sur une gamme limitée de produits, qui ne peuvent être classés sous le poste 5110 (impôts généraux), 5123 (droits à l'importation) ou 5124 (droits à l'exportation). Elles peuvent être perçues à un stade

quelconque de la production ou de la distribution et sont calculées ordinairement par référence au poids, au degré ou au volume du produit, mais parfois aussi à sa valeur. Cette subdivision couvre ainsi les impôts spéciaux, qui frappent notamment le sucre, la betterave, les allumettes, les chocolats, et les impôts auxquels sont soumis à des taux divers certains produits, comme ceux perçus dans la plupart des pays sur les tabacs, boissons alcoolisées, hydrocarbures et autres sources d'énergie.

60. Les accises sont à distinguer de :

a. 5110 (impôts généraux) ; ce cas est examiné aux § 53 et § 54 ;

b. 5123 (droits à l'importation) ; lorsqu'un impôt perçu principalement sur des biens importés s'applique, ou s'appliquerait, aussi légalement à un bien comparable produit dans le pays, les recettes procurées par cet impôt seront classées avec les accises (5121) ; ce principe s'applique même lorsqu'il n'y a pas de production locale, réelle ou potentielle, comparable (voir aussi § 64) ;

c. 5126 (impôts sur les services) ; le problème ici concerne les impôts sur l'électricité, le gaz et l'énergie ; ils sont tous considérés comme des impôts sur les biens et inclus dans le poste 5121.

5122 — *Bénéfices des monopoles fiscaux*

61. Ce sous-groupe couvre la fraction des bénéfices des monopoles fiscaux qui est transférée aux administrations publiques ou qui sert à financer des dépenses considérées comme dépenses publiques (voir § 18). Les montants sont comptabilisés lorsqu'ils sont transférés aux administrations publiques ou utilisés pour effectuer des dépenses considérées comme des dépenses publiques.

62. Les monopoles fiscaux reflètent l'exercice du pouvoir d'imposition de l'État par l'intermédiaire du monopole. Les monopoles fiscaux sont des entreprises publiques non financières, qui exercent dans la plupart des cas un monopole sur la production ou la distribution du tabac, des boissons alcoolisées, du sel, des allumettes, des cartes à jouer et des produits pétroliers ou agricoles (c'est-à-dire, sur le genre de produits qui peuvent être soumis, principalement ou accessoirement, aux accises du poste 5121), pour procurer des recettes publiques qui, dans d'autres pays, sont obtenues par le biais d'impôts frappant les transactions sur ces produits d'entreprises privées. Le monopole d'État peut être exercé au stade de la production, ou au stade de la distribution comme dans le cas des magasins de vente de boissons alcoolisées qui appartiennent à l'État et sont contrôlés par lui.

63. Les monopoles fiscaux sont différents des services publics, comme les chemins de fer, l'électricité, les postes et autres moyens de communication, qui peuvent avoir une position de monopole ou de quasi-monopole, mais dont l'objet principal est, normalement, de fournir des services essentiels et non pas de procurer des recettes à l'État. Les transferts à l'administration de ces autres entreprises publiques sont considérés comme des recettes non fiscales. La notion traditionnelle de monopole fiscal n'a généralement pas été élargie pour inclure les loteries nationales, dont les bénéfices sont habituellement considérés comme des recettes non fiscales. Cependant, ces bénéfices peuvent être considérés comme des recettes fiscales quand la raison principale de la mise en œuvre de ces loteries est l'augmentation des recettes pour financer les dépenses publiques. On distingue les bénéfices des monopoles fiscaux des bénéfices des monopoles d'exportation et d'importation (5127), qui sont transférés des offices de commercialisation ou d'autres entreprises s'occupant du commerce international.

5123 — *Droits de douane et autres droits à l'importation*

64. Figurent ici les taxes, droits de timbre et surtaxes qui, selon la loi sont perçus exclusivement sur des produits importés. Sont aussi inclus dans ce poste les droits perçus sur l'importation de denrées agricoles dans les pays Membres de l'Union Européenne et les montants acquittés par certains de ces pays en vertu du Système de Montants Compensatoires[17]. À partir de 1998 les droits de douane collectés par les États membres de l'Union européenne pour le compte de l'Union européenne ne sont plus reportés sous cette rubrique dans les tableaux par pays (chapitre 4 de ce rapport)[1]. Sont exclues ici les taxes perçues sur les importations au titre d'un impôt général sur les biens et les services ou d'une accise applicable aussi bien aux produits importés qu'aux produits fabriqués dans le pays.

5124 — *Taxes à l'exportation*

65. Pendant les années 70, les droits à l'exportation étaient perçus normalement en Australie, au Canada et au Portugal, et ils étaient utilisés en Finlande à des fins conjoncturelles. Certains pays Membres de l'Union Européenne acquittent, dans le cadre du système des montants compensatoires, une taxe sur les exportations (voir la note 17 du § 64). Lorsque ces montants sont identifiables, ils sont inclus dans ce poste. Ce dernier ne comprend pas les remboursements effectués au titre d'impôts généraux sur la consommation d'accises ou de droits de douane sur des biens exportés, qui doivent être déduits des recettes brutes comptabilisées, selon le cas, sous le poste 5110, 5121 ou 5123.

5125 — *Impôts sur les biens d'équipement*

66. Ce sous-groupe comprend les impôts perçus sur les biens d'équipement, comme les machines. Ils peuvent exister depuis un certain nombre d'années ou avoir un caractère temporaire et être prélevés à des fins conjoncturelles. Ne sont pas inclus les impôts sur les 'inputs' industriels qui frappent aussi les consommateurs (comme l'impôt suédois sur l'énergie qui est classé sous le poste 5121).

5126 — *Impôts sur des services déterminés*

67. Sous ce poste figurent tous les impôts calculés sur la rémunération de services spécifiques, comme les taxes sur les primes d'assurance, les taxes sur les services bancaires, sur les jeux et paris (par exemple : courses de chevaux, pronostics de football, billets de loterie nationale), les transports, les spectacles, les restaurants et la publicité. Les impôts prélevés sur le revenu brut des sociétés prestataires d'un service (exemple : primes d'assurance brutes, mises de jeux encaissées par les sociétés) sont classés sous ce poste. Les recettes fiscales provenant des prélèvements sur les banques et des contributions aux mécanismes de garantie des dépôts et de stabilité financière sont provisoirement classés ici pour l'édition 2012. La classification détaillée est présentée dans le paragraphe 104.

68. Ne figurent pas sous ce poste :

a. les impôts sur les services qui font partie d'un impôt général sur les biens et services et sont classés sous le poste 5110 ;

b. les taxes sur l'électricité, le gaz et l'énergie (classées sous le poste 5121 en tant qu'accises) ;

c. les taxes sur les gains personnels tirés de jeux et paris (qui sont classées sous le poste 1120, en tant qu'impôts sur les gains en capital des personnes physiques et entreprises individuelles) et les montants forfaitaires perçus sur le transfert de loteries privées ou sur l'autorisation de créer des loteries (5200)[18] ;

d. les impôts sur les chèques et sur l'émission, le transfert ou le remboursement de valeurs mobilières, (qui sont classés sous le poste 4400, en tant qu'impôts sur les transactions mobilières et immobilières).

5127 — *Autres impôts sur les transactions et les échanges internationaux*

69. Ce sous-groupe couvre les recettes perçues par l'État sur l'achat et la vente de monnaies étrangères à des taux différents. Lorsque l'État exerce le privilège exclusif dont il dispose pour s'assurer une marge entre le prix d'achat et le prix de vente de devises qui ne se réduit pas à la simple couverture des frais administratifs, ce bénéfice représente un prélèvement obligatoire imposé dans des proportions indéterminées à l'acheteur et au vendeur des monnaies étrangères. Il équivaut normalement au droit à l'importation et au droit à l'exportation perçus dans un système de taux de change unique, ou à une taxe sur la vente ou l'achat de monnaies étrangères. Comme les bénéfices des monopoles fiscaux et des monopoles d'importation ou d'exportation transférés à l'État, il représente l'exercice d'un monopole aux fins d'imposition et est inclus dans les recettes fiscales.

70. Ce sous-groupe comprend aussi les bénéfices des monopoles d'exportation ou d'importation, bien qu'il n'en existe pas dans les pays de l'OCDE, les impôts sur l'achat ou la vente de devises et tous les autres impôts perçus spécifiquement sur les opérations ou les échanges internationaux.

5128 — *Autres impôts sur des biens et services déterminés*

71. Cette rubrique comprend les impôts sur l'extraction de minéraux, combustibles fossiles et autres ressources non renouvelables provenant de gisements privés ou détenus par une autre administration, ainsi que toute autre recette non ventilable provenant des impôts sur des biens et services déterminés. Les impôts sur l'extraction de ressources non renouvelables correspondent généralement à un montant forfaitaire par unité de qualité ou de poids, mais peuvent être calculés ad valorem. Les impôts sont comptabilisés à la date d'extraction des ressources. Les versements tirés de l'extraction de ressources non renouvelables issues de gisements appartenant à l'administration publique qui perçoit ces versements sont classés en tant que loyers.

5200 — *Impôts sur l'utilisation des biens ou l'autorisation d'utiliser des biens ou d'exercer des activités*

72. Ce sous-groupe comprend les taxes prélevées en raison de l'utilisation de biens, indépendamment des impôts frappant les biens eux-mêmes. Contrairement à ceux-ci (5100), les impôts du sous-groupe 5200 ne sont pas calculés d'après la valeur des biens, mais ordinairement d'après un montant forfaitaire. Sont aussi couverts les impôts perçus au titre du droit d'utiliser des biens ou d'exercer des activités, comme les taxes sur la pollution qui ne reposent pas sur la valeur de biens déterminés. Il est parfois difficile de distinguer les taxes d'utilisation et droits de licence obligatoires, qui sont considérés comme des impôts, de ceux qui ne le sont pas parce qu'ils sont assimilés à des recettes non fiscales ; les critères appliqués sont ceux indiqués aux § 9 et § 10.

73. Bien que le sous-groupe se réfère à l'utilisation des biens, le fait générateur de l'impôt peut être aussi bien l'enregistrement de la propriété, de sorte que les impôts relevant de ce sous-groupe peuvent viser la possession d'animaux ou de biens plutôt que leur utilisation (par exemple, les chevaux de course, les chiens, les véhicules à moteur) et même s'appliquer à des biens inutilisables (comme les véhicules à moteur ou les fusils inutilisables).

74. Les cas limites concernent :

a. les impôts sur l'autorisation d'exercer des activités commerciales, qui sont classés selon les règles exposées au § 77 lorsqu'ils ont une assiette mixte associant le revenu, les salaires versés ou le chiffre d'affaires ;

b. les impôts sur la propriété ou l'utilisation de la propriété de biens visés par les postes 4100, 4200 et 4600. Le poste 4100 ne vise que les impôts sur la propriété ou la location de biens immobiliers et, contrairement aux impôts du sous-groupe 5200, ils sont fonction de la valeur du bien. Les impôts sur l'actif net et les impôts sur les biens meubles des sous-groupes 4200 et 4600 visent la propriété et non pas l'utilisation des biens, couvrent un groupe d'actifs et non pas de biens particuliers et sont aussi fonction de la valeur du bien.

5210 — *Impôts périodiques sur l'utilisation de biens ou sur l'autorisation d'utiliser des biens ou d'exercer certaines activités*

75. Ces impôts ont pour principale caractéristique d'être perçus à intervalles réguliers et de représenter ordinairement des montants forfaitaires. Le poste le plus important, du point de vue du volume des recettes, est constitué par les permis de circulation des véhicules. Ce sous-groupe inclut aussi les taxes perçues lors de la délivrance de permis de chasse, de tir ou de pêche, ou l'autorisation de vendre certains produits, ainsi que les taxes sur la possession de chiens et sur la prestation de certains services à condition qu'elles répondent aux critères définis aux § 9 et § 10. Les subdivisions du poste 5210 comprennent les taxes d'utilisation de véhicules à moteur à la charge des ménages (5211) et à la charge d'autres agents (5212)[19]. Le poste 5213 couvre les plaques de chiens et les taxes perçues pour l'autorisation d'exercer certaines activités, comme la vente de viande et d'alcool, lorsque les prélèvements ont un caractère périodique. Il couvre aussi les permis généraux de chasse, de port d'armes et de pêche, lorsque le droit d'exercer ces activités n'est pas accordé au titre d'une opération commerciale normale (par exemple, la délivrance du permis ne comporte pas le droit d'utiliser une parcelle déterminée de terrain appartenant à l'État).

5220 — *Impôts non périodiques sur l'utilisation de biens ou sur l'autorisation d'utiliser des biens ou d'exercer certaines activités*

76. Cette rubrique recouvre les taxes non périodiques perçues sur l'utilisation de biens ou sur l'autorisation d'utiliser des biens ou d'exercer certaines activités et celles qui sont prélevées chaque fois que des biens sont utilisés.

- Les impôts prélevés sur l'émission ou le rejet dans l'environnement de gaz toxiques, liquides nocifs ou autres substances dangereuses figurent ici. Les paiements au titre des permis d'émission négociables délivrés par les administrations publiques dans le cadre des dispositifs de plafonnement et d'échange doivent également être comptabilisés sous cette rubrique au moment où les émissions sont produites. Les permis délivrés gratuitement par les administrations ne donnent lieu à aucun enregistrement comptable de recettes.
- La comptabilisation en droits constatés implique un éventuel délai entre la date à laquelle l'administration perçoit le règlement des permis et la date à laquelle les émissions sont produites. Dans les comptes nationaux, ce délai se traduit pour l'administration par un engagement financier sur la période.

- Il convient d'exclure les paiements effectués au titre de la collecte et de l'élimination de déchets ou de substances nocives par les autorités publiques, étant donné qu'il s'agit là de vente de services aux entreprises.

77. D'autres impôts non périodiques qui relèvent du poste 5200 sont aussi classés dans cette rubrique. Ainsi figurent les paiements uniques effectués au titre de l'autorisation de vendre des boissons alcoolisées ou des tabacs ou d'ouvrir des guichets de « paris mutuels », à condition qu'ils répondent aux critères définis aux § 9 et § 10.

6000 — *Autres impôts*

78. Ce groupe couvre les impôts prélevés sur une ou plusieurs bases différentes de celles qui sont indiquées pour les groupes 1000, 3000, 4000 et 5000, ou sur des bases dont aucune ne pourrait être considérée comme étant essentiellement la même que l'une de celles afférentes à ces groupes. Quant aux impôts perçus sur plusieurs bases différentes, il convient si possible d'évaluer les recettes liées à chaque base de perception (par exemple, pour l'impôt allemand « Gewerbesteuer ») et d'inclure les montants séparés dans le groupe approprié. S'il est impossible d'évaluer les montants séparés, mais si l'on sait que la plus grande partie des recettes provient de l'impôt perçu sur une même base, la totalité des recettes sont classées en fonction de cette base. Si aucune de ces procédures ne peut être appliquée, les impôts sont classés dans le présent groupe. Les sous-groupes peuvent comprendre également les recettes provenant d'impôts que les administrations ne sont pas en mesure d'identifier ou d'isoler (voir § 27). Figurent aussi dans ce groupe les recettes provenant d'amendes et de pénalités acquittées pour infraction aux réglementations fiscales, mais qui ne peuvent être identifiées comme se rapportant à une catégorie particulière d'impôts (voir § 14). Ce poste est divisé en impôts exclusivement ou principalement à la charge des entreprises (6100) et en impôts à la charge d'autres contribuables (6200).

A.6. Conciliation avec les comptes nationaux

79. Cette section des tableaux permet de concilier les calculs des recettes fiscales totales de l'OCDE et l'ensemble des impôts et cotisations sociales versés aux administrations publiques qui sont enregistrés dans les comptes nationaux par pays. Lorsque le pays en question est membre de l'Union européenne (UE) la comparaison est effectuée entre les calculs des recettes fiscales totales des pays de l'OCDE et la somme des recettes fiscales et cotisations de sécurité sociale perçues par les administrations publiques et les institutions des secteurs de l'Union européenne des comptes nationaux.

A.7. Poste pour mémoire relatif au financement des prestations de sécurité sociale

80. Le rapport entre les impôts et les cotisations de sécurité sociale étant variable, et en raison des problèmes évoqués aux § 34 et § 40, on a réuni dans un poste pour mémoire l'ensemble des versements affectés à des prestations du type sécurité sociale, en dehors des versements volontaires au secteur privé. Les données sont présentées de la façon suivante (voir le chapitre 4.2 de ce rapport)[1].

a. impôts du groupe 2000 ;

b. impôts affectés aux prestations de sécurité sociale ;

c. cotisations volontaires à l'administration ;

d. cotisations obligatoires au secteur privé.

Les § 34 et § 40 ci-dessus contiennent des directives pour la ventilation entre ces quatre catégories

A.8. Poste pour mémoire relatif aux impôts identifiables payés par les administrations

81. Les impôts effectivement payés par les administrations elles-mêmes et que l'on peut identifier sont indiqués dans un poste pour mémoire et classés suivant les grandes rubriques de la classification des impôts de l'OCDE. Dans la très grande majorité des pays, seuls peuvent être identifiées en l'occurrence les cotisations de sécurité sociale et les impôts sur les salaires, mais il s'agit là en général des impôts les plus importants acquittés par les administrations (voir le chapitre 4.3 de ce rapport)[1].

A.9. Rapport de la classification des impôts de l'OCDE avec les systèmes nationaux de comptabilité nationale

82. Un système de comptabilité nationale (SCN) tend à fournir un cadre cohérent pour enregistrer et présenter les principaux flux relatifs à la production, à la consommation, à l'accumulation et aux transactions extérieures d'une zone économique donnée, d'ordinaire un pays ou une grande région d'un pays. Les recettes publiques sont une partie importante des transactions enregistrées dans le SCN. La version finale du SCN 2008 a été diffusée conjointement par cinq organisations internationales : les Nations Unies, le Fonds Monétaire International, l'Union européenne, l'Organisation de Coopération et de Développement Économiques et la Banque Mondiale, en août 2009. Le *Système* est un ensemble complet, cohérent et souple de comptes macro-économiques. Il est élaboré pour être utilisé dans les pays à économie de marché quel que soit leur niveau de développement économique ainsi que dans les pays en transition vers l'économie de marché. De larges extraits du cadre théorique ainsi que les définitions des divers secteurs de l'économie du SCN figurent dans la classification des impôts de l'OCDE.

83. Il existe cependant un certain nombre de différences entre la classification des impôts de l'OCDE et les concepts du SCN qui sont indiqués ci-dessous. Ils proviennent du fait que l'objectif de cette classification est de permettre une ventilation aussi large que possible des données statistiques pour ce que les administrations fiscales conviennent de considérer de manière générale comme des impôts.

a. l'OCDE inclut les cotisations obligatoires de sécurité sociale payées aux administrations publiques dans les recettes fiscales totales. Les cotisations sociales volontaires et imputées ainsi que celles versées aux caisses privées ne sont pas considérées comme des impôts (§ 7 et § 8 ci-dessus) ;

b. les avis diffèrent sur la question de savoir s'il y a lieu de classer certains prélèvements et redevances dans les impôts (§ 9 et § 10 ci-dessus) ;

c. l'OCDE exclut les impôts imputés ou les subventions résultant d'opérations de taux de change officiels multiples et ceux résultant du fait que la banque centrale paye un taux d'intérêt sur les réserves obligatoires différent des autres taux du marché ;

d. il existe des différences dans le traitement des crédits d'impôt récupérables.

84. Comme on l'a noté aux § 1 et § 2, les groupes 1000 à 6000 de la classification de l'OCDE comprennent tous les versements sans contrepartie aux administrations publiques, à l'exclusion des prêts obligatoires et des amendes. On peut obtenir le total de ces versements sans contrepartie, amendes incluses, mais prêts obligatoires exclus, en additionnant les postes suivants du SCN 2008 :

- impôts du type valeur ajoutée (D.211) ;
- droits et taxes sur les importations à l'exclusion de la TVA (D.212) ;
- droits sur les exportations (D.213) ;
- taxes sur les produits, à l'exclusion de la TVA, des droits sur les importations et les exportations (D.214) ;
- autres impôts sur la production (D.29) ;
- impôts sur le revenu (D.51) ;
- autres impôts périodiques (D.59) ;
- cotisations de sécurité sociale (D.61) à l'exclusion des cotisations volontaires ;
- impôts sur le capital (D.91).

A.10. La classification des impôts de l'OCDE et le système du Fonds monétaire international (GFS)

85. Le champ d'application et l'évaluation des recettes fiscales dans le système GFS et dans le système SCN 2008 sont très proches. Par conséquent, les différences entre la classification de l'OCDE et celle du SCN 2008 (voir § 83 ci-dessus) sont également valables pour le GFS. En outre, le Fonds monétaire international subdivise le groupe 5000 de la classification de l'OCDE en une section iv (Taxes intérieures sur les biens et services) et une section v (Taxes sur les transactions et les échanges internationaux). Cela tient à ce que le rendement de ces dernières taxes représente généralement des sommes infimes dans les pays de l'OCDE ce qui n'est pas le cas dans beaucoup de pays non membres.

A.11. Comparaison de la classification des impôts de l'OCDE et des autres classifications internationales des recettes publiques

86. Le tableau ci-dessous décrit point par point la comparaison entre la classification des impôts de l'OCDE et les classifications suivantes :

i) Système des comptes nationaux (SCN 2008) ;

ii) Système européen des comptes (SEC 2010) ;

iii) Manuel de statistiques des finances publiques du Fonds monétaire international (MSFP 2014).

87. Ces comparaisons correspondent à celles qui devraient s'appliquer dans la majorité des cas. Toutefois, en pratique il faut faire preuve d'une certaine souplesse dans leur application. En effet, dans certains cas, les pays peuvent adopter des méthodes diverses de classification des recettes dans les comptes nationaux.

	Classification OCDE	2008 SNA	2010 ESA	GFSM2014
1000	Impôts sur le revenu, les bénéfices et les gains en capital			
	1100 Personnes physiques			
	1110 Sur le revenu et les bénéfices	D51-8.61a	D51A	1111
	1120 Sur les gains en capital	D51-8.61c, d	D51C, D	1111
	1200 Sociétés			
	1210 Sur le revenu et les bénéfices	D51-8.61b	D51B	1112
	1220 Sur les gains en capital	D51-8.61c	D51C	1112
	1300 Non ventilables entre les rubriques 1100 et 1200			1113
2000	Cotisations de sécurité sociale			
	2100 Salariés	D613-8.85	D613	1211
	2200 Employeurs	D611-8.83	D611	1212
	2300 A la charge des travailleurs indépendants ou des personnes sans occupation	D613-8.85	D613	1213
	2400 Non ventilables entre les rubriques 2100, 2200 et 2300			1214
3000	Impôts sur les salaires et la main-d'œuvre	D29-7.97a	D29C	112
4000	Impôts sur le patrimoine			
	4100 Impôts périodiques sur la propriété immobilière			
	4110 Ménages	D59-8.63a	D59A	1131
	4120 Autres agents	D29-7.97b	D29A	1131
	4200 Impôts périodiques sur l'actif net			
	4210 Personnes physiques	D59-8.63b	D59A	1132
	4220 Sociétés	D59-8.63b	D59A	1132
	4300 Impôts sur les mutations par décès, les successions et les donations			
	4310 Impôts sur les mutations par décès et les successions	D91-10.207b	D91A	1133
	4320 Impôts sur les donations	D91-10.207b	D91A	1133
	4400 Impôts sur les transactions mobilières et immobilières	D59-7.96d; D29-7.97e	D214B, C	114114; 1161
	4500 Autres impôts non périodiques sur le patrimoine	D91-10.207a	D91B	1135
	4600 Autres impôts périodiques sur le patrimoine	D59-8.63c	D59A	1136
5000	Impôts sur les biens et services			
	5100 Impôts sur les biens et services			
	5110 Impôts généraux sur les biens et services			
	5111 Taxes sur la valeur ajoutée	D211-7.89	D211; D29G	11411
	5112 Impôts sur les ventes	D2122-7.94a; D214-7.96a	D21224; D214I	11412
	5113 Autres impôts généraux sur les biens et services	D214-7.96a	D214I	11413
	5120 Impôts sur des biens et services déterminés			
	5121 Accises	D2122-7.94b; D214-7.96b	D21223; D214A, B, D	1142
	5122 Bénéfices des monopoles fiscaux	D214-7.96e	D214J	1143
	5123 Droits de douane et autres droits à l'importation	D2121-7.93	D2121; D21221, 2	1151
	5124 Taxes à l'exportation	D213-7.95a	D214K	1152-4
	5125 Impôts sur les biens d'équipements			
	5126 Impôts sur les services déterminés	D2122-7.94c; D214-7.96c	D21225; D214E, F, G; D29F	1144; 1156
	5127 Autres impôts sur les transactions et les échanges internationaux	D2122-7.94d D29-7.95b D29-7.97g D59-8.64d	D21226; D29D; D59E	1153; 1155-6
	5128 Autres impôts sur des et services déterminés			1146
	5130 Non ventilable entre les rubriques 5110 et 5120			
	5200 Impôts sur l'utilisation des biens ou l'autorisation d'utiliser des biens ou d'exercer des activités			
	5210 Impôts périodiques sur l'utilisation des biens ou l'autorisation d'utiliser des biens ou d'exercer des activités			
	5211 A la charge des ménages au titre de véhicules à moteurs	D59-8.64c	D59D	11451
	5212 A la charge d'autres agents au titre de véhicules à moteurs	D29-7.97d	D214D; D29B	11451
	5213 Autres impôts périodiques sur l'utilisation des biens u l'autorisation d'utiliser des biens ou d'exercer des activités	D29-7.97c, d, f D59-8.64c	D29B, E, F; D59D	11452
	5220 Impôts non périodiques			11452
	5300 Non ventilable entre les rubriques 5100 et 5200			
6000	Autres impôts			
	6100 A la charge exclusive des entreprises			1161
	6200 A la charge d'autres agents que les entreprises ou non identifiables	D59-8.64a, b	D59B, C	1162

A.12. Répartition des recettes fiscales par sous-secteurs d'administration publique

88. La classification de l'OCDE appelle une ventilation des recettes fiscales par sous-secteurs d'administration. On trouvera ci-après la définition de chaque sous-secteur et les critères à utiliser pour répartir entre eux les recettes fiscales. Ces définitions et critères suivent les orientations qui figurent dans le SCN 2008 et le MSFP 2014.

Sous-secteurs des administrations publiques à identifier

a) Administration centrale

89. Le sous-secteur des administrations centrales groupe tous les ministères, bureaux, établissements et autres organismes qui sont des services ou des moyens d'action du pouvoir central et dont la compétence s'étend à la totalité du territoire, à l'exception de l'administration des caisses de sécurité sociale. L'administration centrale a donc le pouvoir de prélever des impôts sur toutes les unités résidentes et non résidentes exerçant des activités économiques à l'intérieur du pays.

b) Administration d'un État fédéré, d'une province ou d'une région

90. Ce sous-secteur comprend les unités administratives intermédiaires et inclut toutes les unités administratives dont la compétence s'exerce indépendamment de l'Administration centrale sur une partie du territoire englobant un certain nombre de petites localités, à l'exception des caisses de sécurité sociale. Dans les pays unitaires, les administrations régionales peuvent être considérées comme dotées d'une existence distincte lorsqu'elles disposent d'une autonomie substantielle pour percevoir une part importante de leurs recettes de sources placées sous leur contrôle et lorsque leurs agents ne sont pas soumis à un contrôle administratif externe dans l'exercice des activités de l'unité.

91. Actuellement, les pays à structure fédérale représentent la majorité des cas dans lesquels les recettes attribuées aux unités administratives intermédiaires sont identifiées séparément. L'Espagne est le seul pays à structure unitaire qui se trouve dans cette situation. Dans les autres pays unitaires, les recettes des administrations régionales sont incluses dans celles des administrations locales.

c) Collectivités locales

92. Ce sous-secteur comprend toutes les autres unités administratives exerçant une compétence indépendante sur une partie du territoire d'un pays, à l'exception des administrations des caisses de sécurité sociale. Il englobe les diverses circonscriptions urbaines et/ou rurales (par exemple les collectivités locales, les municipalités, les villes, les bourgs ou les districts).

d) Caisses de sécurité sociale

93. Les caisses de sécurité sociale constituent un sous-secteur distinct des administrations publiques. Le sous-secteur de la sécurité sociale est défini dans le SCN de 2008 par les extraits suivants des paragraphes 4.124 à 4.126 et 4.147 :

« Les systèmes de sécurité sociale sont des systèmes d'assurance sociale qui couvrent l'ensemble de la collectivité ou d'importants sous-ensembles de la collectivité : ces systèmes sont imposés et contrôlés par les administrations publiques. Ces systèmes couvrent une grande variété de programmes qui consistent à fournir des prestations, en espèces ou en nature, au titre des circonstances suivantes : vieillesse, invalidité ou décès, survie, maladie et maternité, accident du travail, chômage, allocations familiales, soins de santé etc. Il n'existe pas nécessairement de lien direct entre le montant de la cotisation versée par un particulier et les prestations qu'il est susceptible de recevoir » (paragraphe 4.124).

« Lorsque les systèmes de sécurité sociale ont une organisation distincte des autres activités des administrations publiques et détiennent des actifs et des engagements indépendamment de ces dernières et effectuent des opérations financières pour leur propre compte, ils peuvent être considérés comme des unités institutionnelles désignées sous le nom de caisses de sécurité sociale » (paragraphe 4.125).

« Il est possible de faire varier de façon discrétionnaire les montants prélevés et versés sous forme de cotisations de sécurité sociale et de prestations afin d'atteindre des objectifs de politique publique qui n'ont pas de lien direct avec la notion de sécurité sociale en tant que système visant à fournir des prestations à des membres de la collectivité. Ainsi, ces cotisations ou prestations peuvent être augmentées ou diminuées afin d'influer sur le niveau de la demande globale au sein de l'économie. Néanmoins, tant que ces caisses restent indépendantes, elles doivent être traitées comme des unités institutionnelles distinctes dans le SCN ». (paragraphe 4.126).

« Le sous-secteur des administrations de sécurité sociale comprend les administrations de sécurité sociale opérant à tous les niveaux des administrations publiques. Les administrations de sécurité sociale sont des systèmes couvrant l'ensemble de la collectivité ou d'importants sous-ensembles de la collectivité qui sont rendus obligatoires et contrôlés par des administrations publiques » (paragraphe 4.147).

94. Cette définition des administrations de sécurité sociale est suivie dans la classification de l'OCDE à l'exception des régimes suivants :

- Les régimes imposés par l'administration et exploités par des organismes extérieurs au secteur des administrations publiques, tel qu'il est défini au § 3 de ce manuel et
- Les régimes qui perçoivent des cotisations volontaires.

Autorités supranationales

95. Ce sous-secteur s'applique aux activités de collecte de recettes publiques des autorités supranationales sur le territoire d'un pays. En pratique, le seul cas d'autorité supranationale de la zone de l'OCDE est celui des institutions de l'Union européenne (UE). Depuis 1998, les autorités supranationales ne figurent plus dans les *Statistiques des recettes publiques* dans un souci de cohérence avec la définition du SCN des administrations publiques qui les exclut. Par exemple, les impôts sur le revenu et des contributions de sécurité sociale rassemblées par des Institutions européennes et payé par les fonctionnaires européens qui sont résidents de pays membres de l'Union européenne ne devraient pas être inclus. Toutefois, les prélèvements spécifiques versés par les États membres à l'Union européenne continuent à être inclus dans les recettes fiscales totales et ils sont indiqués sous cette rubrique.

Critères à utiliser pour l'attribution des recettes fiscales

96. Lorsqu'une administration collecte l'impôt et le reverse, en totalité ou en partie, à d'autres administrations, il est nécessaire de déterminer si ces recettes doivent être considérées comme étant celles de l'administration qui les perçoit et les répartit entre d'autres administrations ou celles des administrations bénéficiaires auxquelles l'administration qui les a perçues les a transférées en simple qualité d'agent. Les critères à utiliser dans

l'attribution des recettes sont indiqués aux paragraphes 97 à 100, qui reprennent les paragraphes 3.70 à 3.73 du SCN 2008.

97. En général, un impôt est attribué à l'Unité administrative qui

a. exerce le pouvoir de percevoir l'impôt (soit en tant que détenteur de ce pouvoir soit par délégation de l'autorité qui le détient),

b. dispose du pouvoir discrétionnaire final de fixer et de faire varier le taux de l'impôt.

98. Lorsqu'une somme est collectée par une administration au profit d'une autre administration et en son nom, et que cette dernière a le pouvoir de percevoir l'impôt et de fixer et de faire varier son taux, la première intervient comme agent pour le compte de la dernière et l'impôt est réaffecté. Toute somme retenue par l'administration collectrice au titre des frais de recouvrement doit être considérée comme la rémunération d'un service rendu. Toute autre somme conservée par l'administration collectrice, notamment dans le cadre d'un accord de partage d'impôt, doit être considérée comme une subvention courante. Si l'administration collectrice s'est vu déléguer le pouvoir de fixer et de faire varier le taux, le montant recouvré doit être considéré comme une recette fiscale de cette administration.

99. Lorsque des administrations différentes fixent conjointement et sur un pied d'égalité la répartition du produit de cet impôt, aucune administration ne disposant d'un pouvoir prépondérant en dernier ressort, les recettes fiscales sont attribuées à chaque administration en fonction de sa part respective du produit de l'impôt. Si un accord permet à une unité administrative d'exercer un pouvoir prépondérant en dernier ressort, la totalité des recettes fiscales est attribuée à cette unité.

100. Dans certains cas aussi, un impôt est perçu dans le cadre des compétences d'une administration qui résulte de la constitution ou d'autres dispositions mais d'autres administrations fixent individuellement le taux d'imposition sur leurs territoires. Le produit de l'impôt généré sur les territoires respectifs de chaque administration est attribué à l'administration en question comme constituant ses recettes fiscales.

Versements effectués par les États membres de l'Union européenne

101. Les versements effectués par les États membres de l'Union européenne prennent la forme de prélèvements spécifiques qui comprennent :

a. les droits de douane et les prélèvements agricoles (5123),

b. les montants compensatoires monétaires bruts (5123 si relatifs aux importations et 5124 si relatifs aux exportations), et

c. les prélèvements de la CECA, les cotisations sucre et les taxes de co-responsabilité sur le lait (5128).

102. Les droits de douane collectés par les États membres pour le compte de l'Union européenne sont comptabilisés :

- sur une base qui ne tient pas compte des droits d'encaissement,
- en utilisant des chiffres corrigés de manière à exprimer les droits sur la base de la « destination finale » et non du « pays de première entrée » lorsque de telles corrections sont possibles. Ces corrections concernent en particulier les droits prélevés dans des ports (maritimes) importants. Bien que les droits de l'UE soient prélevés par les autorités du pays de première entrée, ces droits doivent être dans la mesure du possible déduits des recettes du pays qui les recouvre et inclus dans les recettes du pays de destination finale.

103. Ces droits de l'UE sont le plus clairement conformes au critère d'attribution décrit au § 95 ci-dessus. En conséquence, à partir de 1998, ces montants sont mentionnés dans une note de bas de page à titre de rubrique « Pour mémoire » dans les tableaux des États membres de l'UE (chapitre 4 du rapport)[1] et ne figurent plus sous la rubrique 5123. Toutefois, ces montants sont inclus dans les grands totaux des recettes fiscales à la ligne supérieure pour toutes les années indiquées dans les tableaux.

A.13. Classification provisoire des recettes provenant des prélèvements sur les banques et des contributions aux mécanismes de garantie des dépôts et de stabilité financière

104. L'OCDE a provisoirement adopté, depuis l'édition 2012 de ses *Statistiques des recettes publiques*, le principe suivant concernant l'enregistrement comptable des recettes issues des prélèvements sur les banques ainsi que des redevances acquittées au titre de la garantie des dépôts et de la stabilité financière. Il est recommandé que les montants concernés soient comptabilisés à la rubrique 5126.

- Les redevances de stabilité, les prélèvements sur les banques et les contributions à la garantie des dépôts, qu'il est obligatoire d'acquitter, doivent généralement être traitées comme des recettes fiscales lorsque les versements sont effectués au profit de l'administration publique et affectés au budget consolidé ou général des administrations de sorte que les pouvoirs publics soient libres d'utiliser les fonds sans délai aux fins qu'ils jugent opportunes. Ce principe s'appliquerait indépendamment du fait que l'administration promette ou non d'effectuer des versements pour garantir les dépôts des clients des établissements bancaires si la situation l'exigeait à l'avenir.
- Si les paiements obligatoires sont effectués au profit de l'administration publique et imputés à des budgets dont les ressources doivent être entièrement réaffectées au secteur de l'économie qui englobe les entreprises assujetties à ces paiements, ceux-ci seront toujours traités, en règle générale, comme des recettes fiscales étant donné que les fonds seraient disponibles pour l'administration et réduiraient son déficit budgétaire, que la redevance est sans contrepartie pour les entités individuelles et que les montants collectés pourraient être dissociés de tout versement en faveur des déposants ou de toute dépense visant à soutenir plus largement le secteur financier.
- Les contributions aux mécanismes traditionnels de moindre envergure destinés à garantir les dépôts de détail, contributions dont le montant est aligné sur le coût de la garantie, doivent être classées en tant que redevances pour services rendus.
- Tout versement au titre de la réalisation par une administration des actifs d'un établissement en faillite ou du recouvrement par cette administration d'une créance prioritaire sur les actifs de l'établissement en cours de liquidation, effectué en vue de financer l'indemnisation des clients ayant perdu leurs dépôts, serait traité comme une redevance par opposition aux recettes fiscales.
- Les contributions obligatoires aux fonds administrés en-dehors du secteur public et aux organismes non étatiques bénéficiant du soutien des institutions collectrices de dépôts ainsi que toutes les contributions aux mécanismes volontaires ne doivent pas être traitées comme des recettes fiscales.

Notes

1. Les références dans cette annexe aux chapitres ou aux sections de « ce rapport » sont issues de OCDE (2016), *Statistiques des recettes publiques* 1965-2015, Éditions OCDE, Paris.
2. Toutes les références au SCN concernent l'édition de 2008.
3. Se reporter à la section A.12 de ce manuel pour l'examen de cette notion.
4. Il est en général possible d'identifier les montants des cotisations de sécurité sociale et les impôts sur les salaires, mais pas les autres impôts payés par les administrations.
5. En revanche si un ou plusieurs pays considèrent comme un impôt un droit que la plupart des pays font entrer dans les recettes non fiscales ou qui procure des recettes substantielles, les montants ainsi perçus figureront dans une note de renvoi à la fin des tableaux par pays correspondants, même s'ils ne sont pas inclus dans le total des recettes fiscales.
6. Les appellations peuvent cependant être souvent trompeuses. Ainsi, une redevance de passeport sera normalement considérée comme une recette non fiscale, alors qu'un prélèvement additionnel sur les passeports (comme c'est le cas au Portugal), qui a pour but de procurer un montant substantiel de recettes eu égard au coût de délivrance du passeport, sera considéré comme un impôt du sous-groupe 5200.
7. On trouvera des précisions sur cette distinction dans l'étude spéciale intitulée « L'information sur les recettes fiscales : problèmes actuels », de l'édition de 2001 des *Statistiques des recettes publiques*.
8. On utilise parfois les expressions « non remboursable » et « remboursable » mais il peut paraître illogique de parler de « remboursement » lorsque rien n'a été versé.
9. Toutefois, dans les systèmes d'imputation de l'impôt sur les sociétés, les crédits d'impôts récupérables sont traités différemment (§ 31-33).
10. Il ne s'agit pas d'une véritable dépense fiscale au sens strict. De telles dépenses fiscales supposent que l'on identifie un système fiscal de référence pour chaque pays ou, de préférence, une norme internationale commune. En pratique, il n'a pas été possible de parvenir à un accord sur une norme internationale commune.
11. Sauf s'ils sont calculés sur le bénéfice résultant de la vente, auquel cas ils seraient classés parmi les impôts sur les gains en capital dans le sous-groupe 1120 ou 1220.
12. Dans certains pays, la même législation est applicable aux personnes physiques et aux entreprises dans le cas d'impôts sur le revenu particuliers. Cependant, les recettes procurées par ces impôts peuvent, en général, être ventilées et figurent donc dans les deux sous-groupes appropriés.
13. Ainsi, « celles qui sont suffisamment autonomes et indépendantes pour que leur fonctionnement soit comparable à celui d'une société… (y compris) la tenue de comptes complets » (2008 SCN section 4.44).
14. Au Canada – pays généralement considéré comme appliquant un système d'imputation – le crédit d'impôt (non récupérable) offert à l'actionnaire concerne l'impôt national sur les sociétés censé avoir été acquitté, qu'un impôt sur les sociétés soit ou ne soit pas dû. Comme, dans ces systèmes, il n'y a aucun lien complet entre le montant de l'impôt sur le revenu, ces crédits pour les dividendes sont traités, comme les autres crédits d'impôt, selon les principes exposés au § 20.
15. Il peut en être ainsi lorsqu'un régime en faveur des administrations existait avant l'instauration d'un régime général de sécurité sociale.
16. Dans le SCN 2008, ils sont considérés comme des transferts en capital et non pas comme des impôts (voir section A8).
17. Système selon lequel l'Union Européenne ajuste les effets des différences entre les taux de change utilisés pour fixer les prix des produits agricoles dans le cadre de la politique agricole commune, et le taux de change réel. Les paiements effectués selon ce système portent sur les importations ou les exportations; lorsqu'ils sont identifiables, ces montants figurent dans la rubrique appropriée (5123 ou 5124). Dans ce guide, sont inclus les montants bruts, c'est-à-dire sans déduction d'aucune prime payée par le SMC.
18. Les transferts de bénéfices de loteries d'État sont considérés comme des recettes non fiscales (voir aussi § 63).
19. Voir à ce sujet le § 25(c).

Revenue Statistics in Africa 1990-2015/Statistiques des recettes publiques en Afrique 1990-2015

ANNEX B

Interpretative guide to non-tax revenue in Revenue Statistics in Africa

Table of contents

1. Coverage

The definition of non-tax revenues and the main subcategories identified in this publication generally correspond to the concepts laid out in the 2014 IMF Government Finance Statistics Manual (GSFM). Non-tax revenues refer to increases in government net worth resulting from transactions other than tax revenues. They exclude funds arising from the repayment of previous lending by governments or from borrowing, or proceeds derived from sales of fixed capital assets, stocks, land and intangible assets or private gifts.

Non-tax revenues are made up of the following elements:

2. Grants

The GSFM 2014 states "Grants are transfers receivable by government units from non-resident government units or international organisations without the receipt of any goods, services, or assets in return. Grants are normally receivable in cash, but may also take the form of the receipt of goods or services (in kind)". These transfers are un-refundable and unrequited. Grants encompass reparations and gifts given for particular projects or programmes. The term "grants" is not used to refer to transfers to or from non-governmental units and excludes inter-governmental transfers. The remission of funds collected by one government for another in an agency capacity should not be shown as receipt of a grant by the beneficiary government but as its direct receipt of revenue.

3. Property income

This category includes income to government arising from their ownership of property, enterprises, financial assets, or intangible assets when government units place them at the disposal of other units. Sales of nonfinancial assets such as the sales of lands are not recorded as revenue because disposal of such an asset does not increase the net worth. Similarly, repayments on loans and loan disbursements are not revenue. Property income may take the form of dividends, interest, land rents, royalties, or withdrawals from entrepreneurial income. The main components are:

- Interest and dividends: Interest is the revenue earned by the government unit from a financial asset by putting it at the disposal of another institutional unit. Dividends are the revenue earned by placing equity funds at the disposal of a corporation (resident or non-resident corporation). This category also consists of profits of state-owned enterprises except those classified as fiscal monopolies (see §62-§64 of the OECD Interpretative Guide to tax revenue in Annex A), export and import monopoly profits (see §70-§71 of the same document) or those providing public utilities such as rail transport, electricity, post offices and other communications. In this category are included revenue from public financial institutions such as the central banks' profits, profits transferred or distributed from the operation of monetary authority functions outside the central bank and the profits of state lotteries transferred to the government. Transfers from public utilities enterprises are recorded as non-tax revenue under "sales of goods and services" whereas profits for fiscal, export or import monopolies are classified as tax revenue.
- Rents or royalties: Rent is the revenue generated from natural resources, such as land, mining, or oil resources, when a government unit places these at the disposal of private or foreign entities. The rents received relate to a resource lease-giving agreement for the exploitation and extraction of a natural resource by the lessee in return for a payment. Payments for exploration rights are also treated as rent. Rents should not be confused

with other payments a government may receive related to the exploitation of subsoil and similar assets, such as severance taxes, business licenses, or other taxes (e.g. value added taxes, excises, taxes on exports, etc.). They should also not be taken to mean incomes from the rental of buildings and equipment, which are treated as sales of goods and services. Revenues from rents and royalties are in some cases difficult to establish and depend on the agreement between the government unit and the lessee. For example rents, royalties and taxes such as corporate income taxes and VAT are sometimes encompassed in a single payment to the general government. In such cases the revenue should be classified under the category to which the majority of revenue belongs (see §71 of Annex A for further explanation.)

- Other property income: This includes revenue earned by a government unit placing funds at a disposal of quasi-corporations.[1] Conceptually this source of revenue is equivalent to that of dividends from a corporation but by definition, quasi-corporations cannot distribute income in the form of dividends. This category of 'other property income' also includes retained or reinvested earnings, i.e. the percentage of distributable revenue not paid out as dividends, but retained by the corporation or quasi-corporation on foreign investment; property income from investment income disbursements and unidentified property income.

4. Sales of goods and services

Revenue under the category "sales of goods and services" is generally reported on a gross basis, without deduction of costs. Since these costs can represent a significant proportion of revenues, they cannot be regarded in total as funds available for governments to finance their general activities. This contrasts with tax revenues, where the collection costs are usually a small proportion of revenue. This difference implies that it may not be meaningful to sum tax and non-tax revenues as part of a calculation of generally available funds.

The proceeds of sales of nonfinancial assets such as the sale of buildings or lands are not classified as revenues since their disposal does not increase the net worth.

Sales of goods and services consist of:

- Sales by market establishments.[2]
- Administrative fees for services (i.e. fees for drivers' licences, passports, visas, court fees, harbour fees, fees for birth, marriage or death certificates, patent registrations, radio and television licenses when public authorities provide general broadcasting services).
- Administrative fees that are sales of services associated with a regulatory function of government (such as fees for the inspection of premises before delivering a business licence) and considered to be proportional to the cost of producing the service are included in this category. If the fee in return for the service provided by the government unit is disproportionate, then the fee will be classified as a tax. Specific examples of fees that are considered taxes include fees for permission to perform activities such as hunting, fishing and shooting; and fees for business registration where this is a legal requirement for the business to operate.
- Sales by nonmarket establishments such as fees at government hospitals, tuition fees at government schools and admission fees to museums and parks.
- Leasing of buildings and equipment.

5. Fines, penalties and forfeits

The GSFM 2014 states "Fines and penalties are compulsory transfers imposed by courts of law or bodies for violations of laws or administrative rules. Out-of-court agreements are also included (...). Forfeits are amounts deposited with a general government unit pending a legal or administrative proceeding, and that will be transferred to the unit upon resolution". For example traffic fines are included here. Fines and penalties charged on overdue taxes or penalties imposed for the evasion of taxes should be recorded in this category and not as taxes. However if it is not possible to separate the amounts paid in taxes and fines, the whole amount should be classified under the tax to which the fine relates (see §14 of Annex A for further explanation).

6. Other social contributions

This category includes the actual and imputed contributions to social insurance schemes operated by governments as employers on behalf of their employees that do not create a future defined liability. This category also includes the sum of the total voluntary contributions.[3] Excluded from this category are any contributions to funds in which the contributions of each participant and of his employer on his behalf are kept in a separate account earning interest and withdrawable under specified circumstances or any contributions to a pension fund autonomous to the general government. This category is not included in this publication.

7. Miscellaneous and unidentified revenue

This category consists of unidentified non-tax revenues or those that do not fit into any of the other categories listed above. It includes revenue such as gifts and transfers from individuals, private non-profit institutions, nongovernmental foundations, corporations, or sources other than governments and international organisations. Major non-recurrent payments receivable in compensation for extensive damages or serious injuries not covered by insurance policies are also included, such as payments of compensation for damages caused by major explosions; oil spillages; or payments receivable for damage to property other than payments from an insurance settlement.

Notes

1. Quasi-corporations are unincorporated enterprises that exercises some functions of corporations, but have not been granted separate legal personality by statute.
2. A market establishment is an establishment that charges economically significant prices.
3. The IMF includes these contributions as part of their total of social security contributions.

Revenue Statistics in Africa 1990-2015/Statistiques des recettes publiques en Afrique 1990-2015

ANNEXE B

Guide d'interprétation des recettes non fiscales dans les Statistiques des recettes publiques en Afrique

Table des matières

1. Champ couvert

La définition des recettes non fiscales et des principales sous-catégories décrites dans la présente publication coïncident en grande partie avec les notions retenues dans le Manuel des statistiques de finances publiques du FMI de 2014 (Manuel SFP 2014). Les recettes non fiscales désignent des augmentations de la valeur nette résultant d'une transaction et qui ne sont pas des recettes fiscales. Elles excluent les fonds relatifs au remboursement de prêts consentis antérieurement par les administrations ou liés à des emprunts, ainsi que le produit de la cession d'actifs immobilisés, d'éléments de stocks, de terrains, d'actifs immatériels et les dons à titre privé.

Les recettes non fiscales se composent des éléments suivants :

2. Dons

Selon le Manuel SFP 2014, les dons sont des transferts qu'une administration publique reçoit d'une autre administration publique étrangère ou d'une organisation internationale, sans recevoir de cette dernière un bien, un service ou un actif en contrepartie directe. Les dons sont habituellement reçus en espèces, mais peuvent aussi prendre la forme de biens ou de services (en nature). Ces transferts sont non remboursables et sans contrepartie. Les dons recouvrent les réparations et dons assignés à des projets ou programmes particuliers. Le terme de « dons » n'est pas employé pour désigner les transferts réalisés par des entités autres que des administrations publiques ou effectués en leur faveur et exclut les transferts entre administrations. Le versement de fonds collectés par une administration qui agit en qualité de mandataire ne devrait pas entrer dans la catégorie des dons perçus par l'administration bénéficiaire, mais bien s'ajouter aux recettes directement perçues par cette dernière.

3. Revenus de la propriété

Cette catégorie regroupe les recettes publiques découlant de la détention de biens fonciers, de parts de sociétés, d'actifs financiers ou d'actifs immatériels que certaines unités administratives ont mis à la disposition d'autres unités administratives. Les cessions d'actifs non financiers comme la vente de terrains ne sont pas enregistrés en tant que recettes parce que la cession de tels actifs n'a pas d'effet sur la valeur nette. De même, les remboursements de prêts et les prêts octroyés ne sont pas des recettes. Les revenus de la propriété peuvent prendre la forme de dividendes, d'intérêts, de revenus fonciers, de redevances, ou de prélèvements sur des revenus d'entreprises. Les principales composantes en sont les suivantes :

- Intérêts et dividendes : Les intérêts sont les revenus perçus par une unité administrative au titre d'un actif financier qu'elle met à la disposition d'une autre unité institutionnelle. Les dividendes sont les recettes perçues par une unité qui met des capitaux à la disposition d'une société (qu'elle soit ou non un résident du pays concerné). Cette catégorie recouvre également les bénéfices d'entreprises détenues par une administration, en excluant les monopoles fiscaux (voir paragraphes 62 à 64 du Guide d'interprétation de l'OCDE en Annexe A), les monopoles d'exportation et d'importation (voir paragraphes 70 et 71 du même document) ainsi que les entreprises qui fournissent des services publics comme les chemins de fer, l'électricité, les postes et autres moyens de communication. Sont regroupés dans cette catégorie les revenus provenant d'institutions financières publiques comme les bénéfices de la banque centrale, les bénéfices transférés ou distribués au titre de fonctions de l'autorité monétaire exercées en dehors de la banque centrale et les bénéfices liés aux loteries nationales qui sont transférés à l'administration. Les transferts émanant d'entreprises qui assurent des services publics sont comptabilisés dans la rubrique « ventes de biens et de services » alors que les bénéfices des monopoles fiscaux, d'exportation ou d'importation constituent des recettes fiscales.

- Loyers et redevances : Les loyers sont des revenus générés lorsqu'une unité administrative met à la disposition d'autres entités privées ou étrangères des ressources naturelles, comme des terrains ou des gisements de minéraux ou de pétrole. Les loyers perçus sont liés à des accords de concession relatifs à l'exploitation et à l'extraction d'une ressource naturelle par un concessionnaire en contrepartie d'un paiement. Les paiements en échange de droits de prospection doivent également être traités comme des loyers. Les loyers sont à distinguer des autres paiements qu'une administration publique peut recevoir pour l'exploitation d'actifs du sous-sol et d'autres actifs du même type, par exemple les paiements de taxes d'extraction, patentes ou autres impôts (taxes sur la valeur ajoutée, accises, taxes à l'exportation, etc.). Il ne faut pas non plus confondre loyers et revenus de la location de bâtiments et d'équipements, par exemple, qui sont classés dans les ventes de biens et de services. Les revenus liés aux loyers et redevances sont parfois difficiles à déterminer car ils dépendent de la nature de l'accord conclu entre l'unité administration et le concessionnaire. À titre d'exemple, un versement unique effectué en faveur des administrations publiques peut regrouper le paiement de loyers, de redevances et d'autres obligations fiscales comme l'impôt sur les bénéfices des sociétés ou la TVA. Dans un tel cas, le paiement est classé dans la catégorie qui correspond à la majeure partie du versement considéré (Voir paragraphe 71 en Annexe A pour plus de précisions).
- Autres revenus de la propriété : Cette catégorie inclus les recettes perçues par une unité administrative qui met des capitaux à la disposition de quasi-sociétés[1]. Cette source de recettes est en substance équivalente à des dividendes versés par une société mais, par définition, les quasi-sociétés ne distribuent pas de bénéfices sous forme de dividendes. Cette catégorie englobe de plus les bénéfices non distribués ou réinvestis, à savoir la fraction du bénéfice distribuable qui n'a pas été versée sous forme de dividendes, mais conservée par la société ou quasi-société sur des investissements étrangers ; les revenus de la propriété provenant de versements de revenus d'investissements et revenus de la propriété non identifiés.

4. Ventes de biens et de services

Les recettes qui entrent dans cette catégorie sont enregistrées en valeur brute, sans déduction de coûts. Dans la mesure où les coûts peuvent représenter une part importante des recettes, le montant total des ventes biens et de services ne peut pas être considéré comme un montant dont l'administration dispose dans son intégralité pour financer ses activités générales. C'est une différence notable avec les recettes fiscales, auxquelles sont associés des coûts de recouvrement qui ne représentent le plus souvent qu'une faible part des recettes. De ce fait, le montant obtenu par addition des recettes fiscales et non fiscales ne fournit pas forcément une bonne évaluation des fonds généralement disponibles.

Le produit généré par la cession d'actifs non financiers tels que des bâtiments ou des terrains n'est pas enregistré en tant que recettes étant donné que la cession de tels actifs n'a pas d'effet sur la valeur nette.

Les ventes de biens et de services se composent des éléments suivants :

- les ventes des établissements marchands[2].
- les droits administratifs pour services fournis (droits sur les permis de conduire, sur les passeports, sur les visas ; droits de procédure ; droits portuaires ; droits pour l'établissement d'actes de naissance, de mariage, de décès ; frais de dépôt de brevet ; licences de radio et télévision lorsque les autorités publiques fournissent des services généraux de radiodiffusion). Les droits administratifs qui sont des ventes de biens et de services associés à une fonction régulatrice des administrations publiques (comme les droits perçus au titre d'une inspection d'installations menée en vue de la délivrance d'un permis d'exploitation) sont inclus lorsqu'ils sont considérés comme étant proportionnels au coût de production du service en question. Lorsque les droits perçus en contrepartie d'un service fourni par l'administration sont disproportionnés par rapport aux coûts, ils sont considérés comme des impôts. Parmi les droits ainsi classés dans la catégorie des recettes fiscales figurent notamment les droits perçus pour l'octroi de permis d'exercer des activités telles que la chasse, la pêche et l'utilisation d'armes à feu ; et les droits d'enregistrement d'une société dès lors que les entreprises sont tenues par la loi de procéder à un tel enregistrement pour pouvoir exercer leur activité.
- les ventes par les établissements non marchands, comme les droits prélevés par les hôpitaux publics, les droits de scolarité des écoles publiques et les droits d'entrée aux musées et parcs.
- la location de bâtiments et d'équipements.

5. Amendes, pénalités et confiscations

Le Manuel des statistiques de finances publiques du FMI de 2014 définit les amendes et pénalités comme des transferts obligatoires imposés aux unités par des tribunaux ou des organismes pour infraction à la loi ou aux règlements administratifs. Les accords extra-judiciaires sont également inclus. Les confiscations sont les montants déposés auprès d'une unité d'administration publique pendant le déroulement d'une procédure judiciaire ou administrative puis transférés à cette unité au moment du règlement de celle-ci. À titre d'exemple, les amendes sanctionnant les contraventions au code de la route entrent dans cette catégorie. Les amendes et pénalités appliquées au titre d'arriérés d'impôts ou les pénalités pour fraude fiscale devraient également être comptabilisées ici et non comme des recettes fiscales. Toutefois, s'il est impossible de distinguer les montants qui correspondent respectivement à l'impôt et aux pénalités, la somme totale est rattachée aux recettes générées par l'impôt qui a motivé l'application des pénalités (Voir paragraphe 14 en Annexe A pour plus de précisions).

6. Autres cotisations sociales

Cette catégorie englobe les cotisations sociales effectives et imputées aux régimes d'assurance sociale gérés par des administrations publiques en qualité d'employeurs pour le compte de leurs employés qui ne génèrent pas de passif défini dans des périodes futures. Cette catégorie inclut également la somme des contributions volontaires totales[3]. Toutefois, sont exclues les cotisations à des fonds dans lesquels les cotisations de chaque salarié et celles que l'employeur verse en son nom sont comptabilisées séparément dans un compte productif d'intérêts d'où elles peuvent être retirées dans des conditions biens déterminées, ainsi que les cotisations à des fonds de pension autonomes vis-à-vis des administrations publiques. Cette catégorie n'est pas incluse aux fins de la présente publication.

7. Recettes diverses et non identifiées

Cette catégorie regroupe toutes les recettes non fiscales qui ne peuvent être identifiées ou qui n'entrent dans aucune des catégories décrites précédemment. Elle englobe des dons et transferts provenant de personnes physiques, d'institutions privées sans but lucratif, de fondations non gouvernementales, de sociétés ou de sources autres que les administrations publiques et les organisations internationales. Les paiements non récurrents d'un montant élevé reçus par les administrations publiques en compensation de dommages importants non couverts par des polices d'assurance sont également inclus, ainsi que des paiements d'indemnités en compensation de dommages causés par des explosions de grande ampleur, le déversement d'hydrocarbures, ou des paiements exigibles en cas de dommages matériels autres que les paiements au titre d'une indemnisation par une assurance.

Notes

1. Entreprises non constituées en sociétés qui exercent certaines de leurs activités comme des sociétés, mais qui n'ont pas été octroyées une personnalité juridique distincte par statut.
2. Un établissement marchand est une entité qui pratique des prix économiquement significatifs.
3. Le FMI comptabilise ces cotisations dans le total des cotisations de sécurité sociale.

OECD PUBLISHING, 2, rue André-Pascal, 75775 PARIS CEDEX 16
(23 2017 23 3 P) ISBN 978-92-64-28084-7 – 2017

www.ingramcontent.com/pod-product-compliance
Lightning Source LLC
Chambersburg PA
CBHW061203240926
51846CB00006B/1101